MW00784356

ENCYCLOPEDIA OF LANG

SECOND EDITION

Encyclopedia of Language and Education

VOLUME 1: LANGUAGE POLICY AND POLITICAL ISSUES IN EDUCATION

General Editor
Nancy H. Hornberger, *University of Pennsylvania, Philadelphia, USA*

The volume titles of this encyclopedia are listed at the end of this volume.

Encyclopedia of Language and Education

Volume 1

LANGUAGE POLICY AND POLITICAL ISSUES IN EDUCATION

Edited by

STEPHEN MAY

University of Auckland
School of Critical Studies in Education
New Zealand

and

NANCY H. HORNBERGER

University of Pennsylvania
Graduate School of Education
USA

 Springer

Volume Editors:
Stephen May
School of Critical Studies in Education
Faculty of Education
University of Auckland
Auckland 1150
New Zealand
s.may@auckland.ac.nz

Nancy H. Hornberger
University of Pennsylvania
Graduate School of Education
Philadelphia, PA 19104-6216
USA
nancyh@gse.upenn.edu

General Editor:
Nancy H. Hornberger
University of Pennsylvania
Graduate School of Education
Philadelphia, PA 19104-6216
USA
nancyh@gse.upenn.edu

Library of Congress Control Number: 2007925265

ISBN-13: 978-0-387-32875-1 (hard cover)
ISBN-13: 978-90-481-9460-5 (soft cover)

The electronic version will be available under ISBN 978-0-387-30424-3
The print and electronic bundle will be available under ISBN 978-0-387-35420-0

Printed on acid-free paper.

9 8 7 6 5 4 3 2 1 0

springer.com

TABLE OF CONTENTS

VOLUME 1: LANGUAGE POLICY AND POLITICAL ISSUES
IN EDUCATION

Section 2: Minorities and Education

Section 3: Theory, Pedagogy and Practice

Section 4: Focus on Selected Regions of the World

NANCY H. HORNBERGER

GENERAL EDITOR'S INTRODUCTION[1]

ENCYCLOPEDIA OF LANGUAGE AND EDUCATION

This is one of ten volumes of the *Encyclopedia of Language and Education* published by Springer. The Encyclopedia bears testimony to the dynamism and evolution of the language and education field, as it confronts the ever-burgeoning and irrepressible linguistic diversity and ongoing pressures and expectations placed on education around the world.

The publication of this work charts the deepening and broadening of the field of language and education since the 1997 publication of the first Encyclopedia. It also confirms the vision of David Corson, general editor of the first edition, who hailed the international and interdisciplinary significance and cohesion of the field. These trademark characteristics are evident in every volume and chapter of the present Encyclopedia.

In the selection of topics and contributors, the Encyclopedia seeks to reflect the depth of disciplinary knowledge, breadth of interdisciplinary perspective, and diversity of sociogeographic experience in our field. Language socialization and language ecology have been added to the original eight volume topics, reflecting these growing emphases in language education theory, research, and practice, alongside the enduring emphases on language policy, literacies, discourse, language acquisition, bilingual education, knowledge about language, language testing, and research methods. Throughout all the volumes, there is greater inclusion of scholarly contributions from non-English speaking and non-Western parts of the world, providing truly global coverage of the issues in the field. Furthermore, we have sought to integrate these voices more fully into the whole, rather than as special cases or international perspectives in separate sections.

This interdisciplinary and internationalizing impetus has been immeasurably enhanced by the advice and support of the editorial advisory board members, several of whom served as volume editors in the Encyclopedia's first edition (designated here with*), and all of whom I acknowledge here with gratitude: Neville Alexander (South Africa), Colin Baker (Wales), Marilda Cavalcanti (Brazil), Caroline Clapham* (Britain),

---

[1] This introduction is based on, and takes inspiration from, David Corson's general editor's Introduction to the First Edition (Kluwer, 1997).

S. May and N. H. Hornberger (eds), Encyclopedia of Language and Education,
2nd Edition, Volume 1: Language Policy and Political Issues in Education, ix–xi.
©2010 Springer Science+Business Media LLC.

Bronwyn Davies* (Australia), Viv Edwards* (Britain), Frederick Erickson (USA), Joseph Lo Bianco (Australia), Luis Enrique Lopez (Bolivia and Peru), Allan Luke (Singapore and Australia), Tove Skutnabb-Kangas (Denmark), Bernard Spolsky (Israel), G. Richard Tucker* (USA), Leo van Lier* (USA), Terrence G. Wiley (USA), Ruth Wodak* (Austria), and Ana Celia Zentella (USA).

In conceptualizing an encyclopedic approach to a field, there is always the challenge of the hierarchical structure of themes, topics, and subjects to be covered. In this *Encyclopedia of Language and Education*, the stated topics in each volume's table of contents are complemented by several cross-cutting thematic strands recurring across the volumes, including the classroom/pedagogic side of language and education; issues of identity in language and education; language ideology and education; computer technology and language education; and language rights in relation to education.

The volume editors' disciplinary and interdisciplinary academic interests and their international areas of expertise also reflect the depth and breadth of the language and education field. As principal volume editor for Volume 1, Stephen May brings academic interests in the sociology of language and language education policy, arising from his work in Britain, North America, and New Zealand. For Volume 2, Brian Street approaches language and education as social and cultural anthropologist and critical literacy theorist, drawing on his work in Iran, Britain, and around the world. For Volume 3, Marilyn Martin-Jones and Anne-Marie de Mejía bring combined perspectives as applied and educational linguists, working primarily in Britain and Latin America, respectively. For Volume 4, Nelleke Van Deusen-Scholl has academic interests in linguistics and sociolinguistics, and has worked primarily in the Netherlands and the USA. Jim Cummins, principal volume editor for Volume 5 of both the first and second editions of the Encyclopedia, has interests in the psychology of language, critical applied linguistics, and language policy, informed by his work in Canada, the USA, and internationally. For Volume 6, Jasone Cenoz has academic interests in applied linguistics and language acquisition, drawing from her work in the Basque Country, Spain, and Europe. Elana Shohamy, principal volume editor for Volume 7, approaches language and education as an applied linguist with interests in critical language policy, language testing and measurement, and her own work based primarily in Israel and the USA. For Volume 8, Patricia Duff has interests in applied linguistics and sociolinguistics, and has worked primarily in North America, East Asia, and Central Europe. Volume editors for Volume 9, Angela Creese and Peter Martin, draw on their academic interests in educational linguistics and linguistic ethnography, and their research in Britain and Southeast Asia. And for Volume 10, Kendall A. King has academic interests in sociolinguistics and educational linguistics, with work in Ecuador, Sweden, and the USA. Francis Hult, editorial assistant for the Encyclopedia, has academic interests in educational and applied linguistics and educational language policy, and has worked in Sweden and the USA. Finally, as general editor, I have interests in anthropological linguistics, educational linguistics, and language policy, with work in Latin America, the USA, and internationally. Beyond our specific academic interests, all of us editors, and the contributors to the Encyclopedia, share a commitment to the practice and theory of education, critically informed by research and strategically directed toward addressing unsound or unjust language education policies and practices wherever they are found.

Each of the ten volumes presents core information and is international in scope, as well as diverse in the populations it covers. Each volume addresses a single subject area and provides 23–30 state-of-the-art chapters of the literature on that subject. Together, the chapters aim to comprehensively cover the subject. The volumes, edited by international experts in their respective topics, were designed and developed in close collaboration with the general editor of the Encyclopedia, who is a co-editor of each volume as well as general editor of the whole work.

Each chapter is written by one or more experts on the topic, consists of about 4,000 words of text, and generally follows a similar structure. A list of references to key works supplements the authoritative information that the review contains. Many contributors survey early developments, major contributions, work in progress, problems and difficulties, and future directions. The aim of the chapters, and of the Encyclopedia as a whole, is to give readers access to the international literature and research on the broad diversity of topics that make up the field.

The Encyclopedia is a necessary reference set for every university and college library in the world that serves a faculty or school of education. The encyclopedia aims to speak to a prospective readership that is multinational, and to do so as unambiguously as possible. Because each book-size volume deals with a discrete and important subject in language and education, these state-of-the-art volumes also offer highly authoritative course textbooks in the areas suggested by their titles.

The scholars contributing to the Encyclopedia hail from all continents of our globe and from 41 countries; they represent a great diversity of linguistic, cultural, and disciplinary traditions. For all that, what is most impressive about the contributions gathered here is the unity of purpose and outlook they express with regard to the central role of language as both vehicle and mediator of educational processes and to the need for continued and deepening research into the limits and possibilities that implies.

Nancy H. Hornberger

STEPHEN MAY

INTRODUCTION TO VOLUME 1: LANGUAGE POLICY AND POLITICAL ISSUES IN EDUCATION

ADDRESSING THE POLITICS OF LANGUAGE

The late David Corson, the General Editor of the first edition of the *Encyclopedia of Language and Education*, was both an outstanding social theorist of language and a committed activist in the language policy and language education fields. His position was that an acute understanding of theory was a necessary prerequisite for action, not an alternative to it—particularly if one were ever to hope to change existing language conditions that disadvantage, most often, minority groups. Corson articulated this position consistently throughout his work (see May, 2002) and this might explain why the first volume of that first edition of the Encyclopedia, under Ruth Wodak's editorship, began with the question of the politics of language.

Under Nancy Hornberger's General Editorship of the second edition, this understanding and commitment remain intact, and the first volume of this current edition again begins with a focus upon the politics of language—highlighting and foregrounding the importance of the social and political contexts of language policy and language education. And yet, for some, this might still seem surprising. After all, for much of its history, linguistics as an academic discipline, particularly in its more trenchant structuralist forms, has been preoccupied with idealist, abstracted approaches to the study of language. But this is precisely the problem. Language has too often been examined in isolation from the social and political conditions in which it is used, resulting in a synchronic or 'presentist' approach to language (Bourdieu, 1982, 1991; May, 2005). As the French sociologist and social anthropologist, Pierre Bourdieu, comments ironically of this process:

> bracketing out the social ... allows language or any other symbolic object to be treated like an end in itself, [this] contributed considerably to the success of structural linguistics, for it endowed the 'pure' exercises that characterise a purely internal and formal analysis with the charm of a game devoid of consequences. (1991, p. 34.)

The legacy of this decontexualized approach to language analysis can be seen in the ahistorical, apolitical approach perspectives that have too often characterized academic discussions of language policy and language education. In the language policy (LP) arena, for example, this was most evident in the early stages of formal LP development, in the 1960s–1970s. During this period, LP was seen by its proponents as a non-political, non-ideological, pragmatic, even technicist, paradigm (see Tollefson, Language Planning in Education, Volume 1). Its apparently simple and straightforward aim was to solve the immediate language problems of newly emergent postcolonial states in Africa, Asia and the Middle East. While concern was often expressed for the ongoing maintenance of minority languages in these contexts, the principal emphasis of LP at this time was on the establishment and promotion of "unifying" national languages in postcolonial contexts, along the lines of those in Western, developed contexts.

What was not addressed by these early efforts at LP were the wider historical, social and political issues attendant upon these processes, and the particular ideologies underpinning them. As Luke, McHoul and Mey observe, while maintaining a 'veneer of scientific objectivity' (something of great concern to early language planners), LP 'tended to avoid directly addressing social and political matters within which language change, use and development, and indeed language planning itself, are embedded' (1990, pp. 26–27.).

To take just one example: this presentist approach to LP did not question or critique the specific historical processes that had led to the hierarchizing of majority and minority languages, along with their speakers, in the first place. As we shall see, these processes are deeply imbricated with the politics of modern nationalism, and its emphasis on the establishment of national languages and public linguistic homogeneity as central, even essential, tenets of both modernization and Westernization (see, for example, May, Language Education, Pluralism and Citizenship, Volume 1; Branson and Miller, National Sign Languages and Language Policies, Volume 1). Consequently, the normative ascendancy of national languages was simply assumed, even championed, by early advocates of LP, and all other languages were compared in relation to them. As Bourdieu again observes of this process:

> To speak of *the* language, without further specification, as linguists do, is tacitly to accept the *official* definition of the *official* language of a political unit. This language is the one which, within the territorial limits of that unit, imposes itself on the whole population as the only legitimate language . . . The official language is bound up with the state, both in its genesis and its social uses . . . this state language becomes the theoretical norm against which all linguistic practices are objectively measured. (Bourdieu, 1991, p. 45.; emphases in original)

As Jan Blommaert argues, this kind of approach to LP—or to sociolinguistics more generally—takes no account of human agency, political intervention, power and authority in the formation of particular (national) language ideologies. Nor, by definition, is it able to identify the establishment and maintenance of majority and minority languages as a specific 'form of practice, historically contingent and socially embedded' (1999, p. 7.). In contrast, all the contributions to this volume highlight the importance of adopting a wider sociohistorical, sociocultural, socioeconomic and sociopolitical analysis of LP and/or language education. In particular, the contributions explore ongoing questions surrounding the status, use, and power of various languages or language varieties, along with the contexts in which they are situated. These contexts include a wide variety of local, national and transnational ones and, at least for English, a global context as well, given its current ascendancy as the world language, or lingua mundi.

This focus on the wider social, economic and political contexts of language policy and language education is consonant with recent research on the ideological influences of language policy (Blommaert, 1999; May, 2001, 2005; Patrick and Freeland, 2004; Ricento, 2006; Schiffman, 1996; Schmid, 2001; Woolard, 1998). It is also consonant with more critical, postmodernist conceptions of language (Makoni and Pennycook, 2007; Pennycook, 2001). As such, the contributions in this volume incorporate and address the very latest developments in language policy and education.

Section 1 focuses directly on contextual factors. James Tollefson begins the section with a summary of key developments in language policy and planning. Stephen May addresses the highly relevant, and still-often controversial challenge faced by many modern nation-states—how to accommodate cultural and linguistic diversity without prejudicing social cohesion. David Block discusses key trends and challenges in the current globalization of language(s), particularly English. Joan Kelly Hall explores the multiple connections between language and culture, while Aneta Pavlenko and Ingrid Piller examine the intersections of language and gender, particularly in multilingual contexts. These latter two contributions, along with Ben Rampton, Roxy Harris, James Collins and Jan Blommaert's analysis of language and class, address directly questions of identity politics, as well as their material consequences. The material consequences of language policies, and language education, are also a principal concern of François Grin, who provides a timely analysis of language and economics. The final contribution in this section, by Bill Johnston and Cary Buzzelli, explores the moral dimensions of language education and some of the potential challenges and controversies therein.

A key concern that threads throughout this volume is given particular attention in Section 2. This section focuses on the importance of addressing, and where possible remedying, underlying, often highly discriminatory processes that stigmatize and undermine minority languages and their speakers—not only linguistically, but also culturally, socially, economically and politically. Tove Skutnabb-Kangas examines how linguistic human rights for minority language speakers might ameliorate existing contexts of linguistic disadvantage and/or discrimination, arguing strongly for their further development in both national and supranational contexts. Fernand de Varennes discusses this issue also but in relation to wider developments in international law, outlining the history of minority rights protection schemes and the possibilities that recent changes offer for the further development of minority language rights, particularly at the supranational level. Teresa McCarty explores how the world's indigenous peoples have established a highly effective international movement over the last 40 years or so, aimed specifically at redressing the long colonial histories of minoritization and disadvantage they have faced. This has included a particular focus on the revitalization of indigenous languages and cultures, and the crucial role that education has come to play in this. Jan Branson and Donald Miller conclude this section by discussing the language rights of deaf communities around the world, with a particular focus on their long struggle for the recognition of sign languages.

Section 3 focuses on key theoretical and related pedagogical developments in the language education field. Alastair Pennycook provides an overview of the critical turn in sociolinguistics and language education, discussing the ongoing development of the still nascent field of critical applied linguistics. Hilary Janks explores the impact of such developments on language pedagogy and practice, particularly via the emergence of critical literacy approaches to teaching and learning, which highlight and deconstruct notions of power. Mary Kalantzis and Bill Cope examine these developments from another direction— the emergence of an educational approach focused on the promotion of multiliteracies. Multiliteracies include those new literacies needed in a digital age and in relation to new forms of work in an increasingly globalized world. The remaining three chapters in this section explore the implications of these various developments in critical language theory and practice in relation to particular fields of education. Suresh Canagarajah examines, and at times problematizes, the arena of second language education, particularly in relation to the increasingly global reach of English. Terrence Wiley discusses the field of teacher education and how neophyte teachers might be better equipped to address positively these new literacy demands and the increasing cultural and linguistic diversity of our student populations. Noeline Wright extends this analysis into schools themselves, exploring what schools require in order to change their literacy practices along these lines.

Section 4 completes this volume by providing a wide range of contributions that focus on the language policies and language education
characteristics of particular regional or national contexts. While this
section is inevitably selective, there has been a deliberate attempt to
include more non-Western contexts—extending the range of contexts
discussed and providing at least the beginnings of a more representative overview of such contexts. Links are also made throughout this
section with the more general issues and concerns discussed in the previous sections. Robert Phillipson begins by analysing language policy
developments at the European supranational level. Naz Rassool discusses
language policy in Britain—including the often-overlooked areas of
Scotland, Wales and Ireland. Thomas Ricento and Wayne Wright provide
an overview of language debates in the USA, including the latest developments in the so-called English-Only movement. Enrique Hamel discusses
Mexico and Juan Carlos Godenzzi the region of the Andes, with both
authors highlighting the significance of indigenous language education
initiatives within their respective regions, as well as the ongoing legacy
of Spanish colonialism. Barbara Burnaby updates the language policy
context in Canada, while Joseph Lo Bianco discusses recent developments in Australian language policy, most notably, with respect to the
retrenchment of some of the key multicultural language policy initiatives
of the 1980s. Kathleen Heugh provides an overview of the latest language policy and language education developments in South Africa,
highlighting how the potential of the new, ostensibly multilingual, South
African Constitution is being undermined by an increasingly de facto
English-language education approach. Lachman Khubchandani examines the multiple challenges and opportunities for language policy and
language education in multilingual India, while Tariq Rahman focuses
on the similarly multilingual language context in Pakistan. Sachiyo
Fujita-Round and John C. Maher discuss language policy in Japan,
while Agnes Lam concludes this volume by examining the complexity
of language policy and language education in Greater China.

    All of the contributions to this volume acknowledge the centrality of
the politics of language in discussions of language policy and language
education. Such policies and educational practices are *always* situated
in relation to wider issues of power, access, opportunity, inequality
and, at times, discrimination and disadvantage. Returning to the quote
by Bourdieu at the beginning of this introduction: language policy and
language education are demonstrably not games 'devoid of consequences' which can be examined blithely by a synchronic or presentist approach. Rather, as these contributions hope to show, it is only
when a diachronic, critical view is taken that we can begin to understand just what is at stake—socially, politically, economically and

linguistically—for all those affected by language policy and language
education initiatives. As David Corson would have argued, such an
understanding is also the only effective basis we have for changing such
policies for the better.

Stephen May

REFERENCES

Blommaert, J. (ed.): 1999, *Language Ideological Debates*, Mouton de Gruyter, Berlin.
Bourdieu, P.: 1982, *Ce Que Parler Veut Dire: l'économie des échanges linguistiques*,
    Arthème Fayard, Paris.
Bourdieu, P.: 1991, *Language and Symbolic Power*, Polity Press, Cambridge.
Luke, A., McHoul, A., and Mey, J.: 1990, 'On the limits of language planning: Class,
    state and power', in R. Baldauf and A. Luke (eds.), *Language Planning and
    Education in Australia and the South Pacific*, Multilingual Matters, Clevedon,
    UK, 25–44.
Makoni, S. and Pennycook (eds.): 2007, *Disinventing and Reconstituting Languages*,
    Multilingual Matters, Clevedon, UK.
May, S.: 2001, *Language and Minority Rights: Ethnicity, Nationalism and the Politics
    of Language*, Longman, London, (Reprinted by Routledge, 2007).
May, S.: 2002, 'In tribute to David Corson', *Journal of Language, Identity and Edu-
    cation* 1, 1, 8–11.
May, S.: 2005, 'Language rights: Moving the debate forward', *Journal of Sociolin-
    guistics* 9 (3), 319–347.
Patrick, D. and Freeland, J. (eds.): 2004, *Language Rights and Language 'Survival':
    A Sociolinguistic Exploration*, St Jerome Publishing, Manchester, UK.
Pennycook, A.: 2001, *Critical Applied Linguistics: A Critical Introduction*, Lawrence
    Erlbaum Associates, Mahwah, NJ.
Ricento, T.: 2006, *An Introduction to Language Policy: Theory and Method*, Blackwell,
    New York.
Schiffman, H.: 1996, *Linguistic Culture and Language Policy*, Routledge, London.
Schmid, C.: 2001, *The Politics of Language: Conflict, Identity, and Cultural Pluralism
    in Comparative Perspective*, Oxford University Press, Oxford.
Woolard, K.: 1998, 'Introduction: Language ideology as a field of inquiry', in
    B. Schieffelin, K. Woolard and P. Kroskrity (eds.), *Language Ideologies: Practice
    and Theory*, Oxford University Press, New York, 3–47.

CONTRIBUTORS

VOLUME 1: LANGUAGE POLICY AND POLITICAL ISSUES IN EDUCATION

David Block
University of London, Institute of
Education, London, UK

Jan Blommaert
University of London, Institute of
Education, London, UK

Jan Branson
La Trobe University, National
Institute for Deaf Studies & Sign
Language Research, Melbourne,
Australia

Barbara Burnaby
Memorial University of Newfoundland,
Faculty of Education, St. John's,
Canada

Cary A. Buzzelli
Indiana University, School of Education,
Bloomington, USA

A. Suresh Canagarajah
Pennsylvania State University, Department
of Linguistics and Applied Language Study,
University Park, USA

James Collins
University at Albany/SUNY, Department of
Anthropology, Albany NY, USA

Bill Cope
University of Illinois at Urbana-Champaign,
College of Education, Champaign, USA

Sachiyo Fujita-Round
Obrin University, Tokyo, Japan

Juan Carlos Godenzzi
Université de Montréal, Département de
littératures et de langues modernes,
Montréal, Canada

François Grin
University of Geneva, School of
Translation and Interpretation,
Geneva, Switzerland

Joan Kelly Hall
Pennsylvania State University,
Department of Linguistics
and Applied Language Study,
University Park, USA

Rainer Enrique Hamel
Universidad Autónoma Metropolitana,
Mexico City

Roxy Harris
King's College London,
School of Social Science & Public
Policy, London, UK

Kathleen Heugh
Education, Science and Skills
Development, Human Sciences
Research Council, Cape Town,
South Africa

Hilary Janks
University of the Witwatersrand,
School of Literature and Language Studies,
Johannesburg, South Africa

Bill Johnston
Indiana University, Bloomington, USA

Mary Kalantzis
University of Illinois,
Urbana-Champaign, USA

Lachman Khubchandani
Centre for Communication Studies,
Indus Education Foundation,
Pune, India

Agnes S. L. Lam
The University of Hong Kong, English
Centre, Hong Kong

Joseph Lo Bianco
The University of Melbourne, Australia

John C. Maher
International Christian University,
Department of Communication and
Linguistics, Tokyo, Japan

Stephen May
University of Waikato,
School of Education, Hamilton,
New Zealand

Teresa L. McCarty
Arizona State University, College
of Education, Tempe, USA

Don Miller
La Trobe University, National Institute for
Deaf Studies & Sign Language Research,
Melbourne, Australia

Aneta Pavlenko
Temple University, College of Education,
Philadelphia, USA

Alastair Pennycook
University of Technology,
Sydney, Australia

Robert Phillipson
Copenhagen Business School,
Department of English, Frederiksberg,
Denmark

Ingrid Piller
Basel University, Switzerland

Tariq Rahman
Quaid-l-Azam University, Islamabad,
Pakistan

Ben Rampton
King's College London, School of
Social Science & Public Policy,
London, UK

Naz Rassool
University of Reading, Institute of
Education, Reading, UK

Thomas K. Ricento
University of Calgary, USA

Tove Skutnabb-Kangas
Roskilde University,
Department of Language and Culture,
Roskilde, Denmark

James W. Tollefson
International Christian University,
Tokyo, Japan

Fernand de Varennes
Murdoch University, School of Law,
Murdoch, Australia

Terrence G. Wiley
Arizona State University,
College of Education, Tempe, USA

Noeline Wright
University of Waikato, School of Education,
Hamilton, New Zealand

Wayne E. Wright
The University of Texas, College of
Education and Human Development,
San Antonio, USA

REVIEWERS

VOLUME 1: LANGUAGE POLICY AND POLITICAL ISSUES
IN EDUCATION

Julian Edge
David Gillborn
Hu GuangWei
Kristin Henrard
Nancy H. Hornberger
Francis M. Hult
Lachman Khubchandani
Gerda De Klerk
Luis Enrique Lopez
Diarmait Mac Giolla Chríost
Stephen May
Mary McGroarty
Rachel McKee
Robert Phillipson
Gerard A. Postiglio
Tariq Rahman
James Ryan
Selma Sonntag
Jane Sunderland
François Vaillancourt
Terrence Wiley
Ruth Wodak
Sue Wright

Section 1

Social and Policy Contexts

JAMES W. TOLLEFSON

LANGUAGE PLANNING IN EDUCATION

INTRODUCTION

Language planning refers to deliberate efforts to affect the structure, function, and acquisition of languages. In education, the most important language planning decisions are about the choice of medium of instruction (Tollefson and Tsui, 2004)—which variety or varieties should be used as the medium (or media) of instruction? In many settings, it is widely assumed that the obvious choice is a standard variety, normally with high prestige and spoken by powerful groups, including the upper-middle class. Particular varieties become standardized as a result of complex social processes in which powerful groups shape language attitudes, and linguistic norms are codified (e.g., in dictionaries and grammar books). When official bodies, such as ministries of education, undertake language planning, the result may be *language policies* in education, that is, statements of goals and means for achieving them that constitute guidelines or rules shaping language structure, language use, and language acquisition within educational institutions. This chapter summarizes research on the role of language policy and planning (LPP) within educational institutions.

EARLY DEVELOPMENTS

LPP emerged as a distinct field of research in the 1960s. The term *language planning* was initially used in Haugen's (1959) study of the development of standard Norwegian, and referred to both corpus planning and status planning. Corpus planning entails efforts to affect the structure of language varieties, and includes processes such as standardization, graphization, purification, and terminology development. Status planning involves efforts to affect the status of language varieties —which varieties should be used in government, the media, the courts, schools, and elsewhere? The initial period of development in the field of LPP took place through a series of influential publications in the 1960s and early 1970s (Fishman, 1968a, 1972, 1974; Fishman, Ferguson, and Das Gupta, 1968; Rubin and Jernudd, 1971).

Much of the earliest research in LPP focused attention on devising a conceptual framework for LPP and on a limited range of practical concerns, primarily involving corpus planning in newly emerging

S. May and N. H. Hornberger (eds), Encyclopedia of Language and Education,
2nd Edition, Volume 1: Language Policy and Political Issues in Education, 3–14.
©*2010 Springer Science+Business Media LLC.*

nation-states. Thus in its early years, LPP was closely linked with "modernization" and "development" programs in "developing" countries, and it was heavily influenced by modernization theory (Rostow, 1960). Although LPP in education was not a major focus of this initial research, it soon emerged as a central concern, because corpus-planning issues such as language standardization and script reform necessarily involve educational institutions. It was widely believed that LPP in education could play a significant role in the processes of political and sociocultural integration that were crucial for new states formed at the end of colonialism in Africa and Asia (see Fishman, 1968b). Thus, by the early 1970s, LPP research examined such central educational issues as the role of vernacular and standard varieties in schools, bilingualism, teacher training, and the education of linguistic minorities (Spolsky, 1972).

Early LPP in education shared three key assumptions with modernization and development theory. The first assumption was an optimistic belief that LPP in education would benefit ethnolinguistic minorities. The spread of Malay and Indonesian, for example, exemplified the important consequences of LPP in education for newly independent states. A second key assumption was that technical experts in LPP should play a central role in formulating and implementing efficient, rational plans and policies. This separation of LPP from the political process reflected a belief in the skills of LPP specialists and an emphasis on the technical aspects of corpus planning, as well as a failure to appreciate the fundamentally political nature of LPP generally. A third assumption of early LPP in education was that the nation-state should be the focus of research and practice. The main actors in LPP were believed to be government educational agencies at the national level, and thus a top-down perspective dominated early LPP research.

During the 1980s, a critique of early LPP in education focused on the impact of the local context on national policies and the limitations of a technical rather than political context for LPP, as well as the failure of many language plans and policies to achieve their stated goals. Critics argued that the early approach was flawed in several ways. First, it ignored the complexity of sociopolitical systems, in which cause–effect relationships between policies and outcomes are highly complex and social groups often have covert and competing goals (see also May, Language Education, Pluralism and Citizenship, Volume 1). Second, by focusing on national plans and policies, early research largely ignored the attitudes and practices of communities affected by LPP in education, particularly the processes by which local communities can challenge or transform national plans. Third, the optimistic belief in the value of LPP in education for integrating linguistic minorities into national political and economic systems could not be maintained in the light of research on contexts such as apartheid South Africa, where the white minority government promoted mother-tongue instruction and used codification and standardization as tools of apartheid while promoting Afrikaans as the dominant language (de Klerk, 2002; see also Probyn, Policy, Practice and Power: Language Ecologies of South African Classroom, Volume 9; Heugh, Language Policy and Education in Southern Africa, Volume 1). Similarly, in some states in sub-Saharan Africa, LPP in education helped to overcome the immediate problem of national integration (e.g., in Tanzania), but often the result was an educated elite in control of educational systems that largely ignored the educational needs of masses of the population with limited political power (Mazrui, 2002). Summarizing the impact of this critique, Blommaert (1996) stated that LPP "can no longer stand exclusively for practical issues of standardization, graphization, terminological elaboration, and so on. The link between language planning and sociopolitical developments is obviously of paramount importance" (p. 217).

RECENT CONTRIBUTIONS

The major achievement of early LPP research was an understanding of the relationship between language structure and language function on the one hand, and various forms of social organization (ethnic groups, nation-states) on the other. This early work in LPP was also linked with microsociolinguistics, particularly research on interaction in educational settings (e.g., Cazden, John, and Hymes, 1972) and the relationship between bilingualism and diglossia (Fishman, 1967). The later critique of LPP shifted attention to questions of ideology, power, and inequality. This research, based on a growing body of empirical studies in widely varying contexts, focused on three key areas in education: language and ideology; the role of nonstandard varieties in education; and monolingual versus bilingual approaches to education. (For an extended discussion of recent work in this area, see Ricento, 2006.)

Language and Ideology

The term "ideology" refers to implicit or unstated ("common sense") notions about the nature of language and communication that position individuals and groups within a social order (Woolard, 1992; see also Rubdy, Language Planning Ideologies, Communication Practices and their Consequences, Volume 3). Various ideologies of language have been examined, including linguistic assimilation, linguistic pluralism, and internationalization (see Reagan and Osborn, 2002). In LPP, *standard language ideology* (Lippi-Green, 1997) has received particular attention. Standard language ideology refers to a "bias toward an abstract, idealized homogenous spoken language, which is imposed and maintained by dominant bloc institutions and which names as its model the written language, but which is drawn primarily from the spoken language of the upper middle class" (Lippi-Green, 1997, p. 64). Educational institutions play a central role in imposing standard language ideology, by rewarding users of standard varieties and imposing sanctions against those who use other varieties (Tollefson, 1991). Critical analysis of standard-language ideology raises important empirical questions about the impact of nonstandard varieties in education (see also Williams, Discourses about English: Class, Codes and Identities in Britain, Volume 3).

Nonstandard Varieties in Education

Nonstandard varieties (also called "stigmatized" varieties) include regional dialects, social varieties used by poor or working-class groups, and pidgins and creoles. In many contexts, medium of instruction policies require standard varieties, whereas nonstandard varieties are blamed for the limited educational and employment opportunities of their users. Policies that exclude nonstandard varieties from the schools are often justified on pedagogical grounds, namely that they interfere with effective instruction in the standard variety. In a review of research on this claim, Siegel (1999) found clear evidence that the use of nonstandard varieties has a positive effect on the acquisition of the standard, as well as on students' participation, self-esteem, performance on standardized tests, and overall academic achievement. Indeed, there is little evidence that using nonstandard varieties as media of instruction interferes with learning of the standard (Corson, 1997, 2000). Despite these research findings, however, language policies in many educational contexts continue to preclude the use of nonstandard varieties, perhaps due to the continuing influence of standard language ideology (cf. Cummins, 1999).

Monolingual and Bilingual Approaches to Education

Emphasis on the use of standard varieties in schools implies a largely monolingual approach to LPP, in which students' home varieties are excluded from classes. Thus, an important empirical issue for evaluating language policies is a comparison of monolingual versus bilingual approaches in education (see also May, Bilingual/Immersion Education: What the Research Tells Us, Volume 5). Auerbach (1993) argues that there is virtually no research supporting the claim that exclusive use of the target (standard) language is the most efficient way to promote language- or subject-matter-learning. Moreover, research on English-only instruction exploring its impact on students' dropout rates, social isolation, progress in subject-matter instruction, and other variables, finds significant advantages for the use of students' vernaculars, along with the standard (see Snow, 1990; Watson-Gegeo and Gegeo, 1995). Despite these findings supporting bilingual policies in education, policy makers and practitioners in many contexts continue to favor monolingual approaches (see also Lo Bianco, Bilingual Education and Socio-political Issues, Volume 5; May, Bilingual/Immersion Education: What the Research Tells Us, Volume 5).

WORK IN PROGRESS

The revitalization of interest in LPP since 1990 is due in part to the collapse of the idealized vision of the linguistically and ethnically homogenous nation-state. Indeed, not only is the monolingual state largely impossible in an age of migration, but there is also a growing recognition that language issues are at the core of political and military conflict in a range of settings worldwide, including Spain, UK, Yugoslavia, India, Pakistan, Indonesia, Philippines, Mexico, Guatemala, Uganda, Nigeria, Iraq, Turkey, and elsewhere (see Blackledge, 2004; Chriost, 2003; May, 2001). Thus, much of the current research in LPP focuses on globalization and language loss, as well as language maintenance and revitalization. In addition, there is growing interest in language rights.

The impact of globalization on the unprecedented spread of English and on the rapid loss of languages worldwide has received serious attention in LPP (Nettle and Romaine, 2000; see also Block, Language Education and Globalization, Volume 1). A central question in this research is the role of planning bodies in the spread of English and in language loss (Philippson, 1992). In addition, programs of language maintenance and revitalization are the focus of research in many settings (Fishman, 2001). Work in the US Southwest is particularly important in this area, as scholars examine efforts to use Navajo as a medium of instruction (McCarty, 2002a). Similarly, policies supporting the Māori language in New Zealand offer an opportunity to discover factors that facilitate successful language revitalization (May, 2004).

Research on language revitalization is closely linked with efforts to develop a critical research methodology that places indigenous groups at the center of the research process, shaping fundamental questions such as: What research questions are legitimate? What research methodologies are acceptable? What forms of evidence are persuasive? What are the ethical responsibilities of scholars engaged in LPP research? Who should benefit from the research? This direction in research methodology is in part a response to criticisms of the research process. For example, Smith (1999, p. 1) points out that "from the vantage point of the colonized . . . the term 'research' is inextricably linked to European imperialism and colonialism. The word itself, 'research,' is probably one of the dirtiest words in the indigenous world's vocabulary." Thus, some LPP scholars are developing a "critical method" in which an examination of their relationship to "others" who are the focus of research is at the center of the research process (see Blommaert, 1996; Watson-Gegeo and Gegeo, 1995; see also McCarty, Language Education Planning and Policies by and for Indigenous Peoples, Volume 1; Spolsky, Investigating Language Education Policy, Volume 10).

Research on language rights in education has also expanded in recent years, fueled in part by the attention to human rights in international organizations such as the United Nations and European Union (see also Skutnabb-Kangas, Human Rights and Language Policy in Education, Volume 1). In some settings indigenous groups have been able to invoke a discourse of language rights to win support for community schools in which an indigenous language is the medium of instruction (see also Candelier, "Awakening to Languages" and Educational Language Policy, Volume 6). In New Zealand, for instance, the rapid spread of Māori in the schools has been shaped by a renewed discourse of social justice and the effort to confront the legacy of discrimination against the Māori (May, 2003a). Research on the symbolic politics of language suggests that a broad system of language rights may offer significant protections for linguistic minorities in some contexts (Tollefson, 2002; Wiley, 2002). The key question is under what conditions language rights may have such an impact (McCarty, 2002b; Pennycook, 2002; see also Skutnabb-Kangas, Language Rights and Bilingual Education, Volume 5). Perhaps research on new forms of citizenship emerging under globalization will help LPP scholars answer this important question (McGroarty, 2002).

PROBLEMS AND DIFFICULTIES

Despite its many advances, LPP continues to face several problems, among them: disillusionment with the language rights movement in education, an inadequate relationship between LPP and other social sciences, and lack of impact of research on policy and practice in many settings.

Disillusionment with the Language Rights Movement

Some LPP scholars argue that the main impact of the language rights movement in education is "marvelous human rights rhetoric" (Skutnabb-Kangas, 2002, p. 179; see also May, Language Education, Pluralism and Citizenship, Volume 1) that has not improved the lives of linguistic minorities. Indeed, "the sad conclusion is that so far, a HRs [human rights] approach to language planning and policy has not been effective in promoting educational equity for diverse student populations" (Skutnabb-Kangas, 2002, p. 179). Whereas some scholars have concluded that language rights provide an inadequate basis for LPP theory or for practical efforts to reduce the link between language and inequality (Brutt-Griffler, 2002), others argue that language rights should remain central to LPP (Skutnabb-Kangas, 2002). With the importance of language rights in LPP research and practice, this debate will continue (see May, 2003b, 2005).

Inadequate Relationship Between LPP and Other Social Sciences

Both Fishman (1992) and Williams (1992) have articulated the disappointing failure of LPP to be sufficiently influenced by (or to influence) other fields in the social sciences. The paucity of sociological research on language is particularly striking, given the belief among LPP scholars that language is central to many social processes. Nevertheless, some theoretical work in LPP has begun to forge links with other areas in the social sciences. Particularly important is research by Dua (1996) and May (2001, 2003) that connects LPP with political theory. Another connection is between LPP and the local legal framework for plans and policies (Wiley, 2002). For example, the body of law on "free speech" in the USA affects debates about state efforts to restrict languages *[Need for*
other than English and the use of stigmatized varieties in schools. *multidisciplinary*
Supporters of policies favoring multilingualism and language diversity *study]*
rely on constitutional protections of speech as a basis for promoting languages other than English in state institutions such as the schools. In the Philippines, ongoing policy debates about the bilingual education program make sense only when viewed within the long history of constitutional regulation of the role of English, Filipino, and other languages. Thus, LPP may increasingly consider local legal frameworks in analysis of plans and policies in education.

Lack of Impact of Research on Policy and Practice

LPP scholars have increasingly expressed frustration about their inability to influence the policy-making process. For example, Cummins *[← CB:*
(1999) points out that language-policy debates in the USA are charac- *"evidence-*
terized by a remarkable disregard for research and "blatant internal *free"*
contradictions" (p. 13; see also May, Bilingual/Immersion Education: *Cummins*
What the Research Tells Us, Volume 5). Examining the lack of rational *2014]*
analysis in public discussion of official-English laws in the USA, Donahue (2002) argues that incoherent and unsystematic debate provides opportunity for dominant groups with access to mass media to

manipulate public opinion. He concludes that the resulting "frustrating sense of anomic normlessness" and ideological confusion preserve "an extraordinary advantage for those in power" (p. 138 and p. 159). To some LPP scholars, this situation is a result of the continuing impact of standard language ideology (Lippi-Green, 1997). Others argue that a renewed effort to influence policy making is essential (Tollefson, 2004).

FUTURE DEVELOPMENTS

With the recent expansion in LPP research, new and unexpected directions are likely to emerge. Among these, work is likely to focus on LPP and inequality, LPP and identity, the impact of global institutions, and critical pedagogy for social change.

LPP and Inequality

Much of the research in LPP in the past decade has focused on the role of LPP in education in creating and sustaining inequality. This work is likely to continue, but perhaps with a change in focus. While recent research has amply documented the ways in which LPP in education is used by dominant groups to sustain their systems of privilege, additional work is needed to develop a better understanding of how common institutional practices contribute to inequality, largely without conscious discussion or critical awareness by participants in educational systems. Particularly promising in this regard is work by Pennycook (2002) and Moore (2002) on "governmentality," which refers to discourses, practices, and patterns of language use as techniques by which individuals and institutions shape public behavior and enact programs of government. This research, which shifts attention away from explicit policies adopted by the state, promises to link LPP in education with work in discourse analysis and various approaches to interaction analysis and microsociolinguistics.

LPP and Identity

Recent work on language and identity has focused in part on LPP in education. Particularly promising is the effort by some scholars to examine language and identity explicitly within educational institutions. Institutional patterns of language use and the multiple institutional roles played by language users have broad implications for understanding LPP and identity. On the theoretical level, innovative work on language, gender, and language learning should be tied explicitly to research on LPP (see Davis and Skilton-Sylvester, 2004; Norton, 2000; see also Pavlenko and Piller, Language Education and Gender, Volume 1).

The Impact of Global Institutions

While research on state educational institutions continues, equally important is study of the increasing role of multinational corporations and other global institutions that affect LPP in education (see also Block, Language Education and Globalization, Volume 1). Work by Alidou (2004), for instance, on the World Bank's influence on education in sub-Saharan Africa, offers a model for this research. How are some state education ministries constrained by policies of the World Bank and other global institutions? How are decisions of such global institutions implemented at the local level? How can local educators, students, and their families shape the policies that affect them? These are questions for research in this direction.

Critical Pedagogy and Social Change

With a growing number of LPP scholars openly advocating involvement in efforts for social change (Nettle and Romaine, 2000; Skutnabb-Kangas, 2000), a focus on critical pedagogy for social change is likely to continue. Particularly influential is seminal work on indigenous schooling in the Solomon Islands (Gegeo and Watson-Gegeo, 2002), in the Southwestern USA (McCarty, 2002a) and in New Zealand (May, 2004). Although some researchers fear that critical pedagogy has politicized scholarship, the crisis of language loss among indigenous people and pervasive economic, social, and political inequalities based on language will continue to motivate LPP scholars to participate in language maintenance and revitalization programs, as well as efforts to develop language policies that further social justice (see also McCarty, Language Education Planning and Policies by and for Indigenous Peoples, Volume 1 and Kaplan and Baldauf, An Ecological Perspective on Language Planning, Volume 9).

See Also: *Ann Williams: Discourses about English: Class, Codes and Identities in Britain (Volume 3); Rani Rubdy: Language Planning Ideologies, Communication Practices and their Consequences (Volume 3); Joseph Lo Bianco: Bilingual Education and Socio-political Issues (Volume 5); Tove Skutnabb-Kangas: Language Rights and Bilingual Education (Volume 5); Michel Candelier: "Awakening to Languages" and Educational Language Policy (Volume 6); Robert Kaplan and Richard Baldauf Jr.: An Ecological Perspective on Language Planning (Volume 9); Margie Probyn: Policy, Practice and Power: Language Ecologies of South African Classrooms (Volume 9); Bernard Spolsky: Investigating Language Education Policy (Volume 10); Stephen May: Language Education, Pluralism and Citizenship (Volume 1); Teresa*

L McCarty: Language Education Planning and Policies by and for Indigenous Peoples (Volume 1); Skutnabb-Kangas: Human Rights and Languge Policy in Education (Volume 1); Kathleen Heugh: Language Policy and Education in Southern Africa (Volume 1); David Block: Language Education and Globalization (Volume 1); Aneta Pavlenko and Ingrid Piller: Language Education and Gender (Volume 1); Stephen May: Bilingual/Immersion Education: What the Research Tells Us (Volume 5)

REFERENCES

Alidou, H.: 2004, 'Medium of instruction in post-colonial Africa', in J.W. Tollefson and A.B.M. Tsui (eds.), *Medium of Instruction Policies: Which Agenda? Whose Agenda?* Lawrence Erlbaum, Mahwah, NJ.

Auerbach, E.: 1993, 'Reexamining English-only in the ESOL classroom', *TESOL Quarterly* 27, 9–32.

Blackledge, A.: 2004, *Literacy, Power and Social Justice*, Trentham Books, Stoke on Trent.

Blommaert, J.: 1996, 'Language planning as a discourse on language and society: The linguistic ideology of a scholarly tradition', *Language Problems and Language Planning* 20, 199–222.

Brutt-Griffler, J.: 2002, 'Class, ethnicity and language rights', *Journal of Language, Identity, and Education* 1, 207–234.

Cazden, C., John, V.P., and Hymes, D. (eds.): 1972, *Functions of Language in the Classroom*, Teachers College Press, New York.

Chriost, D.M.G.: 2003, *Language, Identity and Conflict*, Routledge, London.

Corson, D.: 1997, Language policies for indigenous peoples, in R. Wodak and D. Corson (eds.), *Encyclopedia of Language and Education, Volume 1: Language Policy and Political Issues in Education*, Kluwer, Dordrecht, The Netherlands.

Corson, D.: 2000, *Language Diversity and Education*, Lawrence Erlbaum, Mahwah, NJ.

Cummins, J.: 1999, 'The ethics of doublethink: Language rights and the bilingual education debate', *TESOL Journal* 8(3), 13–17.

Davis, K.A. and Skilton-Sylvester, E.: 2004, 'Looking back, taking stock, moving forward: Investigating gender in TESOL', *TESOL Quarterly* 38, 381–404.

de Klerk, G.: 2002, 'Mother tongue education in South Africa: The weight of history', *International Journal of the Sociology of Language* 154, 29–46.

Donahue, T.S.: 2002, 'Language planning and the perils of ideological solipsism', in J.W. Tollefson (ed.), *Language Policies in Education*, Lawrence Erlbaum, Mahwah, NJ.

Dua, H.: 1996, 'The politics of language conflict: Implications for language planning and political theory', *Language Problems and Language Planning* 20, 1–17.

Fishman, J.A.: 1967, 'Bilingualism with and without diglossia: Diglossia with and without bilingualism', *Journal of Social Issues* 23, 29–38.

Fishman, J.A. (ed.): 1968a, *Readings in the Sociology of Language*, Mouton, The Hague.

Fishman, J.A.: 1968b, 'Nationality-nationalism and nation-nationism', in J.A. Fishman, C.A. Ferguson, and J. Das Gupta (eds.), *Language Problems of Developing Nations*, John Wiley, New York.

Fishman, J.A. (ed.): 1972, *Advances in the Sociology of Language (Volumes I–II)*, Mouton, The Hague.

Fishman, J.A. (ed.): 1974, *Advances in Language Planning*, Mouton, The Hague.

Fishman, J.A.: 1992. 'Forward: What can sociology contribute to the sociolinguistic enterprise?,' in G. Williams (ed.), *Sociolinguistics: A Sociological Critique*, Routledge, London.

Fishman, J.A. (ed.): 2001, *Can Threatened Languages Be Saved?*, Multilingual Matters, Clevedon.

Fishman, J.A., Ferguson, C.A., and Das Gupta, J. (eds.): 1968, *Language Problems of Developing Nations*, John Wiley, New York.

Gegeo, D.W. and Watson-Gegeo, K.A.: 2002, 'The critical villager: Transforming language and education in Solomon Islands', in J.W. Tollefson (ed.), *Language Policies in Education*, Lawrence Erlbaum, Mahwah, NJ.

Haugen, E.: 1959, 'Planning for a standard language in Norway', *Anthropological Linguistics* 1(3), 8–21.

Lippi-Green, R.: 1997, *English with an Accent: Language, Ideology, and Discrimination in the United States*, Routledge, London.

May, S.: 2001, *Language and Minority rights: Ethnicity, Nationalism, and the Politics of Language*, Longman, London (Reprinted by Routledge, 2007).

May, S.: 2003a, 'Misconceiving minority language rights: Implications for liberal political theory', in W. Kymlicka and A. Patten (eds.), *Language Rights and Political Theory*, Oxford University Press, Oxford.

May, S.: 2003b, 'Rearticulating the case for minority language rights', *Current Issues in Language Planning* 4(2), 95–125.

May, S.: 2004, 'Māori-medium education in Aotearoa/New Zealand', in J.W. Tollefson, and A.B.M. Tsui (eds.), *Medium of Instruction Policies: Which Agenda? Whose Agenda?*, Lawrence Erlbaum, Mahwah, NJ.

May, S.: 2005, 'Language rights: Moving the debate forward', *Journal of Sociolinguistics* 9, 319–347.

Mazrui, A.M.: 2002, 'The English language in African education: Dependency and decolonization', in J.W. Tollefson (ed.), *Language Policies in Education*, Lawrence Erlbaum, Mahwah, NJ.

McCarty, T.L.: 2002a, *A Place to be Navajo: Rough Rock and the Struggle for Self-Determination in Indigenous Schooling*, Lawrence Erlbaum, Mahwah, NJ.

McCarty, T.L.: 2002b, 'Between possibility and constraint: Indigenous language education, planning, and policy in the United States', in J.W. Tollefson (ed.), *Language Policies in Education*, Lawrence Erlbaum, Mahwah, NJ.

McGroarty, M.: 2002, 'Evolving influences on educational language policies', in J.W. Tollefson (ed.), *Language Policies in Education*, Lawrence Erlbaum, Mahwah, NJ.

Moore, H.: 2002, ' "Who will guard the guardians themselves?" National interest versus factional corruption in policymaking for ESL in Australia', in J.W. Tollefson (ed.), *Language Policies in Education*, Lawrence Erlbaum, Mahwah, NJ.

Nettle, D. and Romaine, S.: 2000, *Vanishing Voices: The Extinction of the World's Languages*, Oxford University Press, Oxford.

Norton, B.: 2000, *Identity and Language Learning: Gender, Ethnicity and Educational Change*, Longman, London.

Pennycook, A.: 2002, 'Language policy and docile bodies: Hong Kong and governmentality', in J.W. Tollefson (ed.), *Language Policies in Education*, Lawrence Erlbaum, Mahwah, NJ.

Phillipson, R.: 1992, *Linguistic Imperialism*, Oxford University Press, Oxford.

Reagan, T.G. and Osborn, T.A.: 2002, *The Foreign Language Educator in Society*, Lawrence Erlbaum, Mahwah, NJ.

Ricento, T.: 2006, *An Introduction to Language Policy*, Blackwell, Oxford.

Ricento, T. and Wiley, T.G. (eds.): 2004, 'The Forum', *Journal of Language, Identity, and Education* 3, 127–160.

Rostow, W.W.: 1960, *The Stages of Economic Growth*, Cambridge University Press, Cambridge.

Rubin, J. and Jernudd, B.H. (eds.): 1971, *Can Language Be Planned?*, University Press of Hawaii, Honolulu.

Siegel, J.: 1999, 'Stigmatized and standardized varieties in the classroom: Interference or separation?' *TESOL Quarterly* 33, 701–728.

Skutnabb-Kangas, T.: 2000, *Linguistic Genocide in Education—Or Worldwide Diversity and Human Rights?* Lawrence Erlbaum, Mahwah, NJ.

Skutnabb-Kangas, T.: 2002, 'Marvelous human rights rhetoric and grim realities: Language rights in education', *Journal of Language, Identity, and Education* 1, 179–205.

Smith, L.T.: 1999, *Decolonizing Methodologies: Research and Indigenous Peoples*, Zed, London.

Snow, C.: 1990, 'Rationales for native language instruction: Evidence from research', in A. Padilla, H.H. Fairchild, and C.M. Valadez (eds.), *Bilingual Education: Issues and Strategies*, Sage Publications, Newbury Park, CA.

Spolsky, B. (ed.): 1972, *The Language Education of Minority Children*, Newbury House, Rowley, MA.

Tollefson, J.W.: 1991, *Planning Language, Planning Inequality*, Longman, London.

Tollefson, J.W.: 2002, 'Language rights and the destruction of Yugoslavia', in J.W. Tollefson (ed.), *Language Policies in Education*, Lawrence Erlbaum, Mahwah, NJ.

Tollefson, J.W.: 2004, 'Theory and action in language policy and planning', *Journal of Language, Identity, and Education* 3, 150–155.

Tollefson, J.W. and Tsui, A.B.M. (eds.): 2004, *Medium of Instruction Policies: Which Agenda? Whose Agenda?* Lawrence Erlbaum, Mahwah, NJ.

Watson-Gegeo, K.A. and Gegeo, D.W.: 1995, 'Understanding language and power in the Solomon Islands: Methodological lessons for educational intervention', in J.W. Tollefson (ed.), *Power and Inequality in Language Education*, Cambridge University Press, Cambridge.

Wiley, T.G.: 2002, 'Accessing language rights in education: A brief history of the U.S. context', in J.W. Tollefson (ed.), *Language Policies in Education*, Lawrence Erlbaum, Mahwah, NJ.

Williams, G.: 1992, *Sociolinguistics: A Sociological Critique*, Routledge, London.

Woolard, K.A.: 1992, 'Language ideology: Issues and approaches', *Pragmatics* 2, 235–250.

STEPHEN MAY

LANGUAGE EDUCATION, PLURALISM
AND CITIZENSHIP

INTRODUCTION

Debates over citizenship in modern liberal democracies have often
focussed on the significance of language to both national identity and
state citizenship. These debates have addressed, in particular, two key
issues:

1. Whether speaking the state-mandated or national language—that
   is, the majority or dominant language of the state—is, or should
   be, a *requirement* of national citizenship and a demonstration of
   both political and social integration by its members (especially
   for those who speak other languages as a first language)
2. Whether this requirement should be at the *expense* of, or in *addition* to the maintenance of other languages—minority, or non-
   dominant languages, in effect—within the state. Or to put it another
   way, whether public monolingualism in the state-mandated language should be enforced upon an often-multilingual population
   or whether some degree of public as well as private multilingualism can be supported.

Needless to say, how these two issues are addressed has significant
implications for the development of language policy and the provision of language education in modern nation-states. In particular, they
require modern nation-states to address the balance between social
cohesion, a key concern of all such states, and the recognition (or lack
thereof) of cultural and linguistic *pluralism*. This chapter addresses this
important dialectic, although as we shall see, modern nation-states have
more often than not actually constructed these two positions in opposition to each other, rather than in tandem.

EARLY DEVELOPMENTS

The Pluralist Dilemma

The often-difficult balancing act between maintaining cohesion on the
one hand and recognising pluralism on the other within modern nation-
states has been termed by Brian Bullivant (1981) as 'the pluralist
dilemma'. The pluralist dilemma, for Bullivant, is 'the problem of

S. May and N. H. Hornberger (eds), Encyclopedia of Language and Education,
2nd Edition, Volume 1: Language Policy and Political Issues in Education, 15–29.
©*2010 Springer Science+Business Media LLC.*

reconciling the diverse political claims of constituent groups and individuals in a pluralist society *with the claims of the nation-state as a whole*' (1981, p. x; my emphasis); what he elsewhere describes as the competing aims of 'civism' and 'pluralism'. Other commentators have suggested similar distinctions (see, e.g. Dauenhauer, 1996; Edwards, 1994), while also emphasising, like Bullivant, the difficulties of reconciling social cohesion on the one hand with, on the other, a recognition and incorporation of ethnic, linguistic and cultural diversity within the nation-state.

In an earlier analysis, Schermerhorn has described these countervailing social and cultural forces as *centripetal* and *centrifugal* tendencies. As he observes:

> Centripetal tendencies refer both to cultural trends such as acceptance of common values, styles of life etc ... Conversely, centrifugal tendencies among subordinate groups are those that foster separation from the dominant group or from societal bonds in one way or another. Culturally this most frequently means retention and presentation of the group's distinctive tradition in spheres like *language*, religion, recreation etc. (1970, p. 81; my emphasis)

How then can the tensions arising from the pluralist dilemma best be resolved in the social and political arena? Drawing on political theory, two contrasting approaches have been adopted in response to this central question, which Gordon (1978, 1981) has described as 'liberal pluralism' and 'corporate pluralism'. Liberal pluralism is characterised by the absence, even prohibition, of any ethnic, religious, or national minority group possessing separate standing before the law or government. Its central tenets can be traced back to the French Revolution and Rousseau's conception of the modern polity as comprising three inseparable features: freedom (non-domination), the absence of differentiated roles, and a very tight common purpose. On this view, the margin for recognising difference within the modern nation-state is very small (Taylor, 1994; see also later).

In contrast, corporate pluralism—now more commonly known by the term 'multiculturalism'—involves the recognition of minority groups as legally constituted entities, on the basis of which, and depending on their size and influence, economic, social and political awards are allocated. Glazer (1975) and Walzer (1992) draw similar distinctions between an approach based on 'non-discrimination'—which involves, in Glazer's memorable phrase, the 'salutary neglect' of the state towards minority groups—and a 'corporatist' (Walzer) or 'group rights' (Glazer) model.

It is clear, however, that for most commentators the merits of liberal pluralism significantly outweigh those of a group-rights or multiculturalist approach. In effect, the answer to the pluralist dilemma has been consistently to favour civism over pluralism. This is certainly Bullivant, Glazer and Walzer's own conclusion (see also Edwards, 1985, 1994; Rawls, 1971; although for contrasting views, see the Major Contributions sections later). On this basis, the 'claims of the nation-state as a whole'—emphasising the apparently inextricable interconnections between social cohesion and national (including linguistic) homogeneity—have invariably won the day over more pluralist conceptions of the nation-state where ethnic, linguistic and cultural differences *between different groups* are accorded some degree of formal recognition. The resulting liberal consensus is well illustrated by Brian Bullivant:

> Certain common institutions essential for the well-being and smooth functioning of the nation-state as *a whole* must be maintained: common language, common political system, common economic market system and so on. Cultural pluralism can operate at the level of the *private*, rather than public, concerns such as use of ethnic [sic] language in the home... But, the idea that maintaining these aspects of ethnic life and encouraging the maintenance of ethnic groups almost in the sense of ethnic enclaves will assist their ability to cope with the political realities of the nation-state is manifestly absurd. (1981, p. 232; emphases in original)

Why is this apparent consensus so strongly in favour of cohesion at the expense of pluralism? In addressing this question, we have to turn to the origins of modern nation-states themselves, and the public role of language within them.

Nation-State Organisation and the Role of Language

Modern nation-state organisation is actually a relatively recent historical phenomenon, deriving from the rise of political nationalism in Europe from the middle of the last millennium onwards. In particular, the French Revolution of 1789 and its aftermath are often credited with establishing the archetypal modern nation-state—a form of political organisation not countenanced before, a polity represented and *unified* by a culturally and linguistically homogeneous civic realm (see Edwards, 1985; Fishman, 1989a, b; May, 2001; Wright, 2000 for further discussion). Previous forms of political organisation had not required this degree of linguistic uniformity. For example, empires were quite happy for the most part to leave unmolested the plethora of cultures and languages subsumed within them—as long as taxes were paid, all was well. But in the politics of European nationalism— which, of course, was also to spread subsequently throughout the world—the idea of a single, common 'national' language (sometimes, albeit rarely, a number of national languages) quickly became the leitmotif of modern social and political organisation.

How was this accomplished? Principally via the political machinery of these newly emergent European states, with mass education often playing a central role. As Gellner (1983) has outlined, the nationalist principle of 'one state, one culture, one language' saw the state, via its education system, increasingly identified with a specific language and culture—invariably, that of the majority ethnic group. The process of selecting and establishing a common national language as part of this wider process usually involved two key aspects: *legitimation* and *institutionalisation* (May, 2001; Nelde, Strubell and Williams, 1996). Legitimation is understood to mean here the formal recognition accorded to the language by the nation-state—usually, by the constitutional and/or legislative benediction of official status. Accordingly, 'la langue officielle a partie liée avec l'État' (Bourdieu, 1982, p. 27)—the legitimate (or standard) language becomes an arm of the state. Institutionalisation, perhaps the more important dimension, refers to the process by which the language comes to be accepted, or 'taken for granted' in a wide range of social, cultural and linguistic domains or contexts, both formal and informal. Both elements achieve a central requirement of the modern nation-state—that all its citizens adopt a common (usually singular) language and culture for use in the civic or public realm.

This establishment of chosen 'national' languages, however, usually also occurred alongside an often-punitive process of 'minoritising' or 'dialectalising' potentially competing language varieties within these same nation-states. These latter language varieties were, in effect, *positioned* by these newly formed states as languages of lesser political worth and value. Consequently, national languages came to be associated with modernity and progress, while their less fortunate counterparts were associated (conveniently) with tradition and obsolescence. More often than not, the latter were also specifically constructed as *obstacles* to the political project of nation-building—as threats to the 'unity' of the state. The inevitable consequence of this political imperative is the establishment of an ethnically exclusive and culturally and linguistically homogeneous nation-state—a realm from which minority languages and cultures are effectively banished. Indeed, this is the 'ideal' model to which most nation-states (and nationalist movements) still aspire—albeit in the face of a far more complex and contested multiethnic and multilinguistic reality (May, 2001; McGroarty, 2002, 2006). As Nancy Dorian summarises it: 'it is the concept of the nation-state coupled with its official standard language... that has in modern times posed the keenest threat to both the identities and the languages of small [minority] communities' (1988, p. 18). Florian Coulmas observes, even more succinctly, that 'the nation-state as it has evolved since the French Revolution is the natural enemy of minorities' (1998, p. 67).

The result of the pre-eminence of this organisational principle of cultural and linguistic homogeneity is that there are only a very few *formal* multilingual nation-states in the world today—India (see Khubchandani, Language Policy and Education in the Indian Subcontinent, Volume 1) and Switzerland being two notable examples. Where English is the dominant language, the prospects of formal multilingualism become even more remote, not least because of the additional position of English as the current world language or lingua mundi (see also Canagarajah, The Politics of English Language Teaching, Volume 1; Phillipson, Language Policy and Education in the European Union, Volume 1). In this respect, even nation-states such as Canada and Australia, who have adopted overtly multilingual policies in recent times, still continue to struggle to bring that multilingualism *effectively* into the public domain (see Burnaby, Language Policy and Education in Canada, Volume 1; Lo Bianco, Language Policy and Education in Australia, Volume 1).

Individual Versus Collective Rights

The ongoing influence of political nationalism, with its emphasis on cultural and linguistic homogeneity—most often via the promotion of public monolingualism—is one key reason why civism continues to be consistently favoured over pluralism in modern nation-states. Another reason is an emphasis in international and national law since the establishment of the United Nations after World War II on *individual* as opposed to *collective* rights (see Kymlicka, 1989, 1995; May, 2001: Chapter 5 for further discussion; see also de Varennes, International Law and Education in a Minority Language, Volume 1; Skutnabb-Kangas, Human Rights and Language Policy in Education, Volume 1). Such an approach, which may be described as orthodox liberalism, promotes individual rights as the *only* rights that can be attributable in democratic states. An orthodox view of liberalism thus addresses the person only as a political being, with rights and duties attached to their status as *citizens*. Such a position does not countenance private identity, including a person's communal membership (and/or the languages they speak), as something warranting similar recognition. These latter dimensions are excluded from the public realm because their inevitable diversity would lead to the complicated business of the state mediating between different conceptions of 'the good life' (Rawls, 1971). On this basis, personal *autonomy*—based on the political rights attributable to citizenship—always takes precedence over personal (and collective) *identity* and the widely differing ways of life that constitute the latter. In effect, personal and political participation in liberal democracies, as it has come to be constructed, ends up denying group difference and posits all persons as interchangeable from a moral and political point of view.

This position contrasts starkly with a *communitarian* view of rights, which posits that the strict separation of citizenship and identity in the modern polity understates, and at times disavows, the significance of wider communal (including linguistic) affiliations to the construction of individual identity. As Michael Sandel (1982) observes, there is no such thing as the 'unencumbered self'—we are all, to some extent, *situated* within wider communities which shape and influence who we are. Likewise, Charles Taylor argues that identity 'is who we are, "where we're coming from". As such, it is the background against which our tastes and desires and opinions and aspirations make sense' (1994, p. 33–34). Accordingly, individualistic conceptions of the good life may preclude shared community values that are central to one's identity. Conversely, as Habermas has put it, 'a correctly understood theory of [citizenship] rights requires a politics of recognition that protects the individual in the life contexts in which his or her identity is formed' (1994, p. 113). The languages one speaks would also thus be included in this communitarian view. However, communitarian critiques have themselves been widely criticised for privileging the collective over the individual and thus essentialising group identities. In effect, communitarians are charged with operating a model of group membership that is at odds with the complexities of identity in the modern world (for further discussion, see Coulombe, 1995; Donahue, 2002; May, 2001: Chapter 3).

Consequently, an ongoing emphasis on individual rights, and a related scepticism about collective rights, continues to make it difficult for minority language speakers in modern nation-states to argue for group-based language rights (such as the right to be educated in their first language). As the earlier quote from Bullivant indicates, following the principles of orthodox liberalism, the right to continue to speak a language other than the state language may *possibly* be allowed in the private domain, but not in public, since the latter is constructed as undermining personal and political autonomy, and fostering social and political fragmentation.

Closely allied with this position is a view that the ongoing promotion of ethnocultural and/or ethnolinguistic difference is problematic in and of itself. As Joshua Fishman summarises it:

> Unlike 'human rights' which strike Western and Westernized
> intellectuals as fostering wider participation in general societal

benefits and interactions, 'language rights' still are widely interpreted as 'regressive' since they would, most probably, prolong the existence of ethnolinguistic differences. The value of such differences and the right to value such differences have not yet generally been recognised by the modern Western sense of justice ... (1991, p. 72)

MAJOR CONTRIBUTIONS

Opponents of Pluralism

Given the dominance of the nation-state model of public monolingualism, allied with the ongoing ascendancy of orthodox liberalism's emphasis on individual rights, it is not surprising perhaps that opponents of multiculturalism or corporate pluralism are many and various. For the sake of brevity, I will focus here on the often-vituperative debates surrounding multiculturalism and bilingualism in the USA, particularly in relation to education, as broadly representative of this position.

One prominent example is Arthur Schlesinger's *The Disuniting of America* (1992). As his title suggests, Schlesinger, a noted liberal historian, has argued to much public acclaim against the 'disuniting' of America by the 'cult of ethnicity' which, in his view, 'reverses the historic theory of America as one people—the theory that has thus far managed to keep American society whole' (1992, p. 15–16). The result is a 'multiethnic dogma [which] abandons historic purposes, replacing assimilation by fragmentation, integration by separatism' (1992, p. 16–17). In the face of this assault, Schlesinger gloomily wonders: 'The national ideal had once been *e pluribus unum* [out of many, one]. Are we now to belittle *unum* and glorify *pluribus*? Will the centre hold? Or will the melting pot give way to the Tower of Babel?' (1992, p. 18).

The mention of the Tower of Babel is significant here, since Schlesinger directs particular opprobrium towards the bilingual movement in the USA, along with its strong links to various Latino communities there (for further discussion, see also Ricento and Wright, Language Policy and Education in the United States, Volume 1). In so doing, Schlesinger rejects out of hand the official recognition of minority languages. As he argues, '[b]ilingualism shuts doors. It nourishes self-ghettoisation, and ghettoisation nourishes racial antagonism ... using some language other than English *dooms* people to second class citizenship in American society' (1992, p. 108; my emphasis). In asserting this position, Schlesinger invokes the rhetoric of national cohesion: 'A common language is a *necessary* bond of national cohesion in so heterogeneous a nation as America... *institu-tionalised* bilingualism remains another source of the fragmentation of America, another threat to the dream of "one people" (1992, p. 109–110; my emphases).

These arguments have been closely echoed more recently by a number of other prominent US commentators. Samuel Huntingdon (2005) likewise rails against the apparent threat of Latinos (and Spanish) to a 'cohesive' (read: English-speaking) US public culture. While the political theorists Brian Barry (2000), Laitin and Reich (2003) and Pogge (2003) all pursue the line that continuing to promote Spanish in the USA, particularly via bilingual education, amounts to enforced ghettoisation, terminally restricting (in their view) the social mobility of its speakers. Laitin and Reich, for example, argue that the consequence of 'forcing' bilingual education on children would be the curtailing of 'their opportunities to learn the language of some broader societal culture' (2003, p. 92). And Pogge concludes that a public education *in* English, as opposed to a bilingual approach, is unquestionably in the 'best interests of the child' in relation both to developing 'fluency in English' and in 'enabling all students to participate fully in US society' (2003, p. 118; for a rejoinder, see May, 2003a).

The fact that these views contradict the well-attested research on the efficacy of bilingual education (see Skutnabb-Kangas, Human Rights and Language Policy in Education, Volume 1, and May, Bilingual/Immersion Education: What the Research Tells Us, Volume 5) highlights how linguistically ill-informed many commentators often are when discussing the role and influence of minority languages, and by extension minority language education, within modern nation-states. What is also strikingly apparent is a lack of any cognisance that linguistic inequality is often a daily experience for minority groups (cf. Sonntag and Poole, 1987), along with an implicit, and often explicit, assertion of the benefits, and inevitability, of linguistic modernisation—a process of modernisation, moreover, that is linked ineluctably with majority languages, and particularly English. Not surprisingly, minority languages come to be constructed in this view as irrelevant, quaint and/or antediluvian, by definition. Relatedly, there is an almost unquestioned legitimacy ascribed to majority languages—particularly national languages—in such discussions, and the similarly unquestioned acceptance of their dominant social and political position and function—their normative ascendancy—within modern nation-states. This ignores, or at best underemphasises, the specific sociohistorical and sociopolitical processes by which these majority languages have come to be created, and accepted as dominant and legitimate, in the first place (Bourdieu, 1982, 1991; May, 2005)—the result, in turn, of the political nationalism of the last three centuries, as discussed above.

Proponents of Pluralism

Despite the ascendancy of arguments for civism over pluralism in much academic and political commentary on nation-state organisation, there are still some dissenting voices advocating for a more inclusive, pluralist approach. One of the most prominent of these is the political theorist Will Kymlicka's advocacy of public multiculturalism (1995; see also Parekh 2000; Taylor 1994). Kymlicka's influential thesis involves arguing from within liberal political theory for the ongoing importance of individual rights while, at the same time, developing an understanding of the importance of wider cultural (and linguistic) membership to such rights. In this sense, he does not endorse the communitarian advocacy of collective rights. Rather, he argues for what he terms 'group-differentiated rights'. Crucially, these rights are not necessarily 'collective' in the sense that they privilege the group over the individual—they can in fact be accorded to individual members of a group, or to the group as a whole, or to a federal state/province within which the group forms a majority. For example, the group-differentiated right of Francophones in Canada to use French in federal courts is an *individual* right that may be exercised at any time. The right of Francophones to have their children educated in French-medium schools, outside of Québec, is an individual right also but one that is subject to the proviso in international law 'where numbers warrant' (see de Varennes, International Law and Education in a Minority Language, Volume 1; see also later). Alternatively, the right of the Québécois to preserve and promote their distinct culture in the province of Québec highlights how a minority group in a federal system may exercise group-differentiated rights in a territory where they form the majority. In short, there is no simple relationship between group-differentiated rights accorded on the basis of cultural membership and their subsequent application. As Kymlicka concludes, 'most such rights are not about the primacy of communities over individuals. Rather, they are based on the idea that justice between groups requires that the members of different groups be accorded different rights' (1995, p. 47).

A second argument that Kymlicka employs is to highlight that minority rights claims are principally concerned with wanting a measure of 'external protection' from larger groups. External protections relate to inter-group relations where a minority group seeks to protect its distinct identity (including a linguistic one) by limiting the impact of the decisions of the larger society. External protections are thus intended to ensure that individual members are able to maintain a distinctive way of life *if they so choose* and are not prevented from doing so by the decisions of members outside of their community (see Kymlicka, 1995, p.204. n.11). As Kymlicka argues: 'Granting special representation

rights, land claims, *or language rights* to a minority . . . can be seen as
putting the various groups on a more equal footing, by reducing the
extent to which the smaller group is vulnerable to the larger' (1995,
p. 36–37; my emphasis).

Given this, it is possible to argue that the maintenance of a minority
language constitutes a legitimate external protection (May, 2001; see
also later). After all, if majority group members within a nation-state
typically value their own cultural and linguistic habitus, it is clearly unfair
to prevent minorities from continuing to value theirs. As Kymlicka concludes, 'leaving one's culture, while possible, is best seen as renouncing
something to which one is reasonably entitled' (1995, p. 90).

Stephen May (2001, 2003a, b, 2005) has applied Kymlicka's more
general arguments about minority rights to argue specifically for the
extension of *ethnolinguistic democracy* in modern nation-states. May
argues that the preoccupation of modern nation-state organisation with
a single language and culture, and an allied public monolingualism, is
both unnecessarily unjust to and exclusive of minority language groups
(see also Skutnabb-Kangas, Human Rights and Language Policy in
Education, Volume 1). Contrary to the assertion by proponents of liberal pluralism such as Schlesinger, the public realm of nation-states is
not, nor has it ever been, a neutral or equal linguistic space. Rather,
as Fernand de Varennes argues, '[b]y imposing a language requirement,
the state shows a definite preference towards some individuals on the
basis of language' (1996, p. 86). As de Varennes proceeds to argue, this
is so for two reasons:

1. The state's chosen language becomes a condition for the full
   access to a number of services, resources and privileges, such
   as education or public employment. . . .
2. Those for whom the chosen state speech is not the primary
   language are thus treated differently from those for whom it is:
   the latter have the advantage or benefit of receiving the state's
   largesse in their primary tongue, whereas the former do not and
   find themselves in a more or less disadvantaged position. . . . a person faced with not being able to use his primary language [in the
   public domain] *assumes a heavier burden* (1996, pp. 86–87; my
   emphasis)

From this, May argues that speakers of the dominant language variety
are immediately placed at an advantage in both accessing and benefiting from the civic culture of the nation-state. A dominant language
group usually controls the crucial authority in the areas of administration, politics, education and the economy, and gives preference to those
with a command of that language. Meanwhile, other language groups
are invariably limited in their language use to specific domains, usually

solely private and/or low status, and are thus left with the choice of renouncing their social ambitions, assimilating, or resisting in order to gain greater access to the public realm.

In contrast, May argues, drawing on the work of Kloss (1977; see also Churchill, 1986), that minority groups be accorded not only 'tolerance-oriented' language rights (allowing individuals to continue speaking a language unmolested in the private or familial domain) but also, where appropriate, 'promotion-oriented' rights, which regulate the extent to which minority language rights are recognised within the *public* domain, or civic realm of the nation-state, including its key public institutions such as schools. Two particular contexts are outlined by May where such latter rights might be appropriate.

The first is for national minority groups—a term drawn from Kymlicka's work—who have always been associated historically with a particular territory, but who have been subject to colonisation, conquest, or confederation and, consequently, now have only minority status within a particular nation-state. These groups include, for example, the Welsh in Britain, Catalans and Basques in Spain, Bretons in France, Québécois in Canada, and some Latino groups (e.g. Puerto Ricans) in the USA, to name but a few. They also include indigenous peoples, who have increasingly been regarded in both international and national law as a separate category of peoples (see McCarty, Language Education Planning and Policies by and for Indigenous Peoples, Volume 1). Following Kymlicka, May argues that these groups can claim, *as of right*, at least some of the benefits that majority national languages currently enjoy—including publicly funded education in their languages.

A second possibility applies to ethnic minorities, who have migrated from their country of origin to a new host nation-state, or in the case of refugees have been the subject of forced relocation. Here, a promotion-oriented language right cannot be argued as of right, but can still be advanced on the basis of the widely accepted principle in international law of 'where numbers warrant'. That is, in order to avoid language discrimination, it is important that where there is a sufficient number of other language speakers, these speakers should be allowed to use that language as part of the exercise of their individual rights as citizens. Or to put it another way, they should have the *opportunity* to use their first language if they so choose—an opportunity which amounts, in effect, to Kymlicka's understanding of an 'external protection'.

By extension, May's argument questions and discards the requirement of a singular and/or replacement approach to the issue of other linguistic identities which, as we have seen, arises specifically from the nationalist principle of linguistic and cultural homogeneity.

Linguistic identities—and social and cultural identities more broadly—need not be constructed as irredeemably oppositional. Narrower identities do not necessarily need to be traded in for broader ones—one can clearly remain both Spanish-speaking and American, Catalan-speaking and Spanish, or Welsh-speaking and British. The same process applies to national and international language identities, where these differ (see May, 2001, 2003b for further discussion). Such a position more accurately reflects the communicative profiles of multilingual speakers, as well as according with postmodernist understandings of language and multiple linguistic identities (see Pennycook, Critical Applied Linguistics and Language Education, Volume 1).

PROBLEMS AND DIFFICULTIES AND FUTURE DIRECTIONS

As this chapter has made clear, the issue of granting minority languages some public recognition in modern nation-states continues to remain a highly controversial one, particularly with respect to education. Indeed, Addis has observed that the choice of language in public domains such as education is 'the most difficult question that a multicultural and multiethnic [and, one might add, multi*lingual*] society has to address' (1997, p. 138). However, an increasing number of scholars within both language policy and language education are beginning to address directly exactly this question. In so doing, they are also increasingly critiquing the limits of traditional nation-state organisation, along with its historical contingency, and the related exclusion of minority languages from the public domain that has resulted. Most notable here are contributions by Tollefson (1991, 1995, 2002, Language Planning in Education, Volume 1), Tollefson and Tsui (2004), McGroarty (2002, 2006) and Ricento (2000, 2006). These contributions also accord closely with important related research on the ideological influences of language policy (see, e.g. Blommaert, 1999; Schmid, 2001; Woolard, 1998).

All these contributions, along with the contributions of Kymlicka and May, discussed above, attempt to rethink nation-states in more linguistically plural and inclusive ways. The aim, in so doing, is to foster the prospect of more *representational* multinational and multilingual states by directly contesting the historical inequalities that have seen minority languages, and their speakers, relegated to the social and political margins. As James Tollefson has observed of these developments:

> the struggle to adopt minority languages within dominant institutions such as education, the law, and government, as well as the struggle over language rights, constitute efforts to legitimise the minority group itself and to alter its relationship

to the state. Thus while language planning reflects relation-ships of power, it can also be used to transform them. (1991: p. 202)

On this basis, changing the language preferences of the state and civil society, or at least broadening them, would clearly better reflect the diverse and legitimate linguistic interests of *all* those within them, even if such recognition may also present new organisational challenges for nation-states not used to the public accommodation of diversity (cf. McGroarty, 2002). Not only this, it could significantly improve the life chances of those minority language individuals and groups who are presently disadvantaged in their access to, and participation in public services, employment and education, as a result of restrictive, majoritarian language and language education policies.

And, finally, with traditional nation-state organisation increasingly under attack—both from above, via globalisation (cf. Block, Language Education and Globalization, Volume 1), and from below, via the increasing discontent and dissension of minority groups—rethinking the nation-state in more culturally and linguistically plural ways may provide it with a crucial further lease of life in a world where many think it has already passed its useful sell-by-date.

See Also: *James W. Tollefson: Language Planning in Education (Volume 1); Tove Skutnabb-Kangas: Human Rights and Language Policy in Education (Volume 1); Fernand de Varennes: International Law and Education in a Minority Language (Volume 1); Teresa L. McCarty: Language Education Planning and Policies by and for Indigenous Peoples (Volume 1)*

REFERENCES

Addis, A.: 1997, 'On human diversity and the limits of toleration', in I. Shapiro and W. Kymlicka (eds.), *Ethnicity and Group Rights (NOMOS XXXIX)* (Yearbook of the American Society for Political and Legal Philosophy), New York University Press, New York, 112–153.

Barry, B.: 2000, *Culture and Equality: An Egalitarian Critique of Multiculturalism*, Harvard University Press, Cambridge MA.

Blommaert, J. (ed.): 1999, *Language Ideological Debates*, Mouton de Gruyter, Berlin.

Bourdieu, P.: 1982, *Ce Que Parler Veut Dire: l'économie des échanges linguistiques*, Arthème Fayard, Paris.

Bourdieu, P.: 1991, *Language and Symbolic Power*, Polity Press, Cambridge.

Bullivant, B.: 1981, *The Pluralist Dilemma in Education: Six case studies*, Allen and Unwin, Sydney.

Churchill, S.: 1986, *The Education of Linguistic and Cultural Minorities in the OECD Countries*, Multilingual Matters, Clevedon, England.

Coulmas, F.: 1998, 'Language rights: Interests of states, language groups and the individual', *Language Sciences* 20, 63–72.

28   STEPHEN MAY

Coulombe, P.: 1995, *Language Rights in French Canada*, Peter Lang, New York.
Dauenhauer, B.: 1996, *Citizenship in a Fragile World*, Rowman and Littlefield, Lanham, MD.
de Varennes, F.: 1996, *Language, Minorities and Human Rights*, Kluwer Law International, The Hague.
Donahue, T.: 2002, Language planning and the perils of ideological solipism, in J. Tollefson (ed.), *Language Policies in Education: Critical issues*, Lawrence Erlbaum Associates, Mahwah, NJ, 137–162.
Dorian, N.: 1981, *Language Death*, University of Pennsylvania Press, Philadelphia, PA.
Dorian, N.: 1998, 'Western language ideologies and small-language prospects', in L. Grenoble and L. Whaley (eds.), *Endangered Languages: language loss and community response*, Cambridge University Press, Cambridge, pp. 3–21.
Edwards, J.: 1985, *Language, Society and Identity*, Basil Blackwell, Oxford.
Edwards, J.: 1994, *Multilingualism*, Routledge, London.
Fishman, J.: 1989a, 'Language and nationalism: Two integrative essays. Part 1. The nature of nationalism', in J. Fishman, *Language and Ethnicity in Minority Sociolinguistic Perspective*, Multilingual Matters, Clevedon, UK (original, 1972), 97–175.
Fishman, J.: 1989b, 'Language and nationalism: Two integrative essays. Part 2. The impact of nationalism on language planning', in J. Fishman, *Language and Ethnicity in Minority Sociolinguistic Perspective*, Multilingual Matters, Clevedon, UK (original, 1972), 269–367.
Fishman, J.: 1991, *Reversing Language Shift: Theoretical and Empirical Foundations of Assistance to Threatened Languages*, Multilingual Matters, Clevedon, UK.
Gellner, E.: 1983, *Nations and Nationalism: New Perspectives on the Past*, Basil Blackwell, Oxford.
Glazer, N.: 1975, *Affirmative Discrimination: Ethnic Inequality and Public Policy*, Basic Books, New York.
Gordon, M.: 1978, *Human Nature, Class and Ethnicity*, Oxford University Press, New York.
Gordon, M.: 1981, 'Models of pluralism: The new American dilemma', *Annals of the American Academy of Political and Social Science* 454, 178–188.
Habermas, J.: 1994, 'Struggles for recognition in the democratic constitutional state', in A. Gutmann (ed.), *Multiculturalism: Examining the Politics of Recognition*, Princeton University Press, 107–148, Princeton, NJ.
Huntingdon, S.: 2005, *Who Are We? America's great debate*, Free Press, New York.
Kloss, H.: 1977, *The American Bilingual Tradition*, Newbury House, Rowley, MA.
Kymlicka, W.: 1989, *Liberalism, Community and Culture*, Clarendon Press, Oxford.
Kymlicka, W.: 1995, *Multicultural Citizenship: A liberal theory of minority rights*, Clarendon Press, Oxford.
Laitin, D. and Reich, R.: 2003, 'A liberal democratic approach to language justice', in W. Kymlicka and A. Patten (eds.), *Language Rights and Political Theory*, Oxford University Press, Oxford, 80–104.
May, S.: 2001, *Language and Minority Rights: Ethnicity, Nationalism and the Politics of Language*, Longman, London and New York. (Reprinted by Routledge, 2007).
May, S.: 2003a, 'Misconceiving minority language rights: Implications for liberal political theory', in W. Kymlicka and A. Patten (eds.), *Language Rights and Political Theory*, Oxford University Press, Oxford, 123–152.
May, S.: 2003b, 'Rearticulating the case for minority language rights', *Current Issues in Language Planning* 4(2), 95–125.
May, S.: 2005, 'Language rights: Moving the debate forward', *Journal of Sociolinguistics* 9(3), 319–347.
McGroarty, M.: 2002, Evolving influences on education language policies, in J. Tollefson (ed.), *Language Policies in Education: Critical Issues*, Lawrence Erlbaum Associates, Mahwah, NJ, 17–36.

McGroarty, M.: 2006, 'Neoliberal collusion or strategic simultaneity? On multiple rationalse for language-in-education policies', *Language Policy* 5, 3–13.
Nelde, P., Strubell, M., and Williams, G.: 1996, *Euromosaic: The Production and Reproduction of the Minority Language Groups in the European Union*, Office for Official Publications of the European Communities, Luxembourg.
Parekh, B.: 2000, *Rethinking Multiculturalism: Cultural Diversity and Political Theory*, Macmillan, London.
Pogge, T.: 2003, 'Accommodation rights for Hispanics in the US', in W. Kymlicka and A. Patten (eds.), *Language Rights and Political Theory*, Oxford University Press, Oxford, 105–122.
Rawls, J.: 1971, *A Theory of Justice*, Oxford University Press, Oxford.
Ricento, T. (ed.): 2000, *Ideology, Politics and Language Policies: Focus on English*, John Benjamins, Amsterdam.
Ricento, T. (ed.): 2006, *An Introduction to Language Policy*, Blackwell, New York.
Schermerhorn, R.: 1970, *Comparative Ethnic Relations*, Random House, New York.
Schlesinger, A.: 1992, *The Disuniting of America: Reflections on a multicultural society*, W.W. Norton and Co, New York.
Schmid, C.: 2001, *The Politics of Language: Conflict, Identity, and Cultural Pluralism in Comparative Perspective*, Oxford University Press, Oxford.
Sonntag, S. and Poole, J.: 1987, 'Linguistic denial and linguistic self-denial: American ideologies of language', *Language Problems and Language Planning* 11, 46–65.
Taylor, C.: 1994, 'The politics of recognition', in A. Gutmann (ed.), *Multiculturalism: Examining the Politics of Recognition*, Princeton University Press, Princeton, NJ, 25–73.
Tollefson, J.: 1991, *Planning Language, Planning Inequality: Language Policy in the Community*, Longman, London.
Tollefson, J. (ed.): 1995, *Power and Inequality in Language Education*, Cambridge University Press, Cambridge.
Tollefson, J. (ed.): 2002, *Language Policies in Education: Critical issues*, Lawrence Erlbaum Associates, Mahwah, NJ.
Tollefson, J. and Tsui, A. (eds.): 2004, *Medium of Instruction Policies: Which agenda? Whose Agenda?*, Lawrence Erlbaum Associates, Mahwah, NJ.
Walzer, M.: 1992, *What it Means to be an American*, Marsilio, New York.
Woolard, K.: 1998, 'Introduction: Language ideology as a field of inquiry', in B. Schieffelin, K. Woolard, and P. Kroskrity (eds.), *Language Ideologies: Practice and Theory*, Oxford University Press, New York, 3–47.
Wright, S.: 2000, *Community and Communication: The Role of Language in Nation State Building and European Integration*, Multilingual Matters, Clevedon, UK.

DAVID BLOCK

LANGUAGE EDUCATION AND GLOBALIZATION

INTRODUCTION: GLOBALIZATION

In his oft-cited book on globalization and modernity, Anthony Giddens defines globalization as:

> the intensification of worldwide social relations which link distant localities in such a way that local happenings are shaped by events occurring many miles away and vice versa. (Giddens, 1990, p. 64)

A more elaborate definition, taken from Held, McGrew, Goldblatt and Perraton (1999, p. 15), is as follows:

> Globalization can be located on a continuum with the local, national and regional. At the one end of the continuum lie social and economic relations and networks which are organized on a local and/or national basis; at the other end lie social and economic relations and networks which crystallize on the wider scale of regional and global interactions. Globalization can be taken to refer to those spatio-temporal processes of change which underpin a transformation in the organization of human affairs by linking together and expanding human activity across regions and continents.

In these two definitions, globalization is framed as the ongoing process of the increasing and intensifying interconnectedness of communications, events, activities and relationships taking place at the local, national or international level. However, while globalization theorists tend to agree on the general parameters of globalization, there are differing views about when it actually started. Robertson (1995) and Held et al. (1999) acknowledge that globalization is perhaps a premodern phenomenon with beginnings in the fifteenth century. According to these authors, it was at this time that the nation-state in Europe was born, and with it the beginnings of international economics and politics. In addition, at this time, the Catholic Church began to spread worldwide and thus became the first global religion. Finally, the fifteenth century was when the European superpowers, such as Portugal, Spain and England, began to spread outwards and colonize the world.

However, other globalization theorists (e.g. Cox, 1996) take a more here-and-now position, situating the beginnings of globalization at the

S. May and N. H. Hornberger (eds), Encyclopedia of Language and Education, 2nd Edition, Volume 1: Language Policy and Political Issues in Education, 31–43.
©2010 Springer Science+Business Media LLC.

time of the first major fuel crisis of 1973, the decline of traditional modes of industrial production and the subsequent move towards a demand-led economy. It was at this time that the developed capitalist states began to abandon 'Fordism', the post-World War 2 economic model of rationalized mass production, stabilized work routines, organized labour, wage-driven demand for more products and the welfare state. In its place came what eventually was called the Washington Consensus, which was about the dismantling of Fordism, especially unionized labour and the welfare state.

In the globalization literature, there is also a question of whether globalization is the continued global spread of capitalism, albeit by more sophisticated and technologically advanced means, or if it is indeed something the likes of which humanity has never experienced. For the proponents of the former view (e.g. Smith, 1997; Wallerstein, 2004), we are still at a stage in history that is imminently modern, in which, for example, international capitalism, the nation-state and the national cultures are still very much intact. However, other theorists (e.g. Bauman, 1998) argue that modernity has been left behind and in its wake we live in world in which the nation-state is progressively more and more superfluous as regards its impact on people's lives, and culture is more an ongoing contested process than a solid social structure that withstands pressures from without.

Another issue arising in discussions of globalization is whether or not globalization is hegemonically Western, and above all an extension of American imperialism. For example, Latouche (1996) writes about the 'Westernization of the world' and the progressive 'worldwide standardization of lifestyles'. He and other authors (e.g. Ritzer, 1998) lament how Western ideology and culture, best exemplified in the USA, are becoming the norm around the world. Ritzer in particular argues convincingly that in recent years, there has been a convergence in all aspects of people's lives: how they dress, how they eat, their entertainment preferences, their work habits and so on.

However, other scholars would disagree with the view that globalization is merely US imperialism by other means. Writing in the early 1990s, Giddens acknowledges that '[t]he first phase of globalization was plainly governed, primarily, by the expansion of the West, and institutions which originated in the West' (Giddens, 1994, p. 96). However, he goes on to state:

> Although still dominated by Western power, globalization today can no longer be spoken of only as a matter of one-way imperialism ... now, increasingly, ... there is no obvious 'direction' to globalization at all, as its ramifications are ever-present . . . . (Giddens, 1994, p. 96)

To capture the great number of potential angles on globalization, some theorists have proposed frameworks that are meant to encapsulate the totality of the phenomenon.

For Held and his colleagues (Held et al., 1999), globalization can be examined from at least eight different angles: global politics and the nation-state; organized violence and military globalization; global trade and markets; global finance; multinational corporations and production networks; globalization and migration; cultural globalization; and globalization and the environment. Held et al.'s attempt to construct a comprehensive model has echoes of an earlier more modest framework developed by Arjun Appadurai (1990). For Appadurai, globalization is a 'complex, overlapping and disjunctive order' made up of five dimensions of cultural flows called 'scapes'. These scapes are listed, defined and exemplified in Table 1.

EARLY DEVELOPMENTS

The globalization themes discussed earlier are inextricably linked to questions of language, and more specifically to questions of language education. This was realised from the 1950s onwards by the authors of reports produced by international organisations such as UNESCO. For example, in an early publication about vernacular and national languages in these former European colonies, UNESCO (1963) addressed the tension between a desire to strengthen national identity in former

Table 1 Appadurai's (1990) scapes

Scape	Gloss	Examples
Ethnoscapes	Flows of people	Migrants, asylum seekers, exiles, tourists
Technoscapes	Flows of technology	Hardware components, technical know-how
Financescapes	Flows of money	National stock exchanges, commodity speculations
Mediascapes	Flows of information	Newspapers, magazines, satellite television channels, websites and the images and symbols they create and provide
Ideoscapes	Flows of ideas	Human rights, environmentalism, free trade movements, fear of terrorism

colonies and the continued technical, financial, mediatic and ideological power of former colonisers, in part via the continued predominance of languages such as English and French in education. The link between the global and the local has also been a constant in the work of African scholars such as Ali Mazrui. In his classic book, *The Political Sociology of the English Language*, Mazrui examines the predominance of English in the political, religious and educational spheres of post-colonial African societies, as well as the ambivalent feelings of individuals educated in English who then contest continued post-colonial imperialism (see also, the work of authors such as Chinua Achebe, 1975, and Ngũgĩ wa Thiong'o, 1993). Elsewhere, in collections such as Fishman, Cooper and Conrad (1977) and Kachru (1983), sociolinguists have explored in detail issues such as the spread of English across nation-state and cultural borders.

This is but a small sample of what might be considered early work on language education in globalization. These authors, and others not mentioned here for lack of space (see Pennycook, 1994, and Phillipson, 1992, for more thorough coverage), were focussing on some of the global phenomena identified in the introduction to this chapter, such as flows of people, money, technology and ideas; tensions between the global and the local; and questions of cultural imperialism. However, these discussions of global issues were not carried out according to the models of globalization outlined in the introduction for the simple reason that the latter were not common currency in the social sciences when most of this work was being carried out. For a more direct link between the discussion of globalization in the introduction and language education, one needs to examine research that is more recent. In the next section, I examine what I consider to be three key areas of inquiry.

WORK IN PROGRESS AND PROBLEMS AND DIFFICULTIES

The Commodification of Language

One could argue that disputes in different parts of the world over which of two or more languages are to dominate in different spheres of society have always been fundamentally about economics. Nevertheless, it has traditionally been national and cultural identity, and appeals to the authentic spirit and character of a people, to which language policy makers have appealed when supporting one language over another. This certainly has been the case for well-known minority language contexts around the world, such as French in Canada and Catalan in Spain. It has also been the case for nation-states around the world, which have identified nationhood with official national languages.

Examples include Bahasa in Indonesia and Swahili in Tanzania. However, with the rise of deregulated and hyper-competitive post-industrial economies and the global spread of the new work order—the conditions under which individuals work in these economies (Gee, Hull and Lankshear, 1996)—new ways of framing languages have arisen. Now languages not only are signs of authentic national identities, they are also seen as commodities, the possession of which is a valued skill in the job market.

Two consequences flow from this commodification of language. On the one hand, it changes the rationale for conserving and promoting a language: now it is not only about saving a nation or a people; it makes good economic sense. The second consequence flows from the first: as a commodity, a language comes to be seen 'as measurable skill, as opposed to a talent, or an inalienable characteristic of group members' (Heller, 2003, p. 474). In her research over the past decade, Monica Heller (2002, 2003) has explored the shift from 'an ideology of an authentic nation to an ideology of commodification' (Heller, 2002, p. 47), which has taken place in Canada with regard to French. Much of this shift is due to changes in the economy in Québec and Canada in general over the past 40 years. When Québécois nationalism began to gather strength in the 1960s, the majority of French speakers were gathered in agriculture, mining, fishing and manufacturing, where their French language skills were not valued and they were economically marginalized. However, since this time, the Canadian and Québec economies have evolved into globalized, post-industrial, services-based markets in which language is a key element and the command of more than one language or language variety is highly valued (see also Burnaby, Language Policy and Education in Canada, Volume 1).

In this pro-bilingual climate, Heller's research has focussed on both public and private sectors in which commodified bilingualism is flourishing. Thus, those working in education, health and welfare, as well as those working in the private sector (e.g. call centres, the tourist trade) must conform to the model of 'perfect' bilinguals in both French and English, that is, they are expected to have a command of what are considered standard varieties of both languages. The consequences for education are immense and, as Heller explains, they emerge in 'debates over when and if to introduce English teaching into French-language schools; over the relative importance of French versus other languages (Japanese or Spanish, for example) in language education in English-language schools; over the value of the vernacular versus standard French; over the very nature of standard French; and over how best to be bilingual; to name just a few of the debates current in Canadian society'(Heller, 2002, p. 62).

A large part of this commodification process is about framing language as a communication skill that can be taught, a topic that Deborah Cameron (2000, 2002) has researched in detail. Whereas in the past, it was assumed that human beings acquired the ability to communicate with one another through practice and experience, today the view is increasing that formal instruction provided by communication specialists is required. This communication skills revolution has taken place at three general levels. First, in an ever-increasing number of workplaces, communication skills training has become an integral part of staff development and, indeed, communication skills are seen as an essential qualification for many jobs. Second, outside the workplace, advice on the development and the enhancement of communication skills has become a basic element in the ever-growing self-help and self-improvement market. Third and finally, educational authorities in many parts of the world, no doubt with their eyes on what is happening in the job market, have made communication skills training a part of their national curricula.

The Spread of English as an International Language

The commodification process of languages is one thing; quite another is the choice of which language is to be adopted as a country's official language of education or which languages are to be taught as foreign languages in secondary schools. The one language that is the focus of debates at both levels in recent years is English. Indeed, the English language is for many people in the world today, the medium that makes possible what Giddens (op. cit.) refers to as 'the intensification of worldwide social relations'. It seems that there is no part of the world where there has not been at least some contact with English, although, paralleling globalization, the incidence and significance of English is unequal in different parts of the world. About such issues, there seems to be little disagreement.

By contrast, there is disagreement about whether or not the spread of English is a good thing, and in recent years the issues brought to the fore by scholars such as Mazrui (op. cit.) have resurfaced, but this time framed more deliberately within discourses of globalization. Thus, in recent years, Robert Phillipson (1992) has developed the concept of 'linguistic imperialism' to explain how the English language grows continually stronger around the world, at the expense of local languages. For Phillipson, there are economic and cultural powers in the world that prime English over other languages. For example, the business world, headed by English-speaking North America, has propagated the idea that English is the international language of business. In the cultural sphere, English language culture (e.g. Hollywood, pop music, fast food) is one thing that most inhabitants of the world have in common. Elsewhere, Tove Skutnabb-Kangas has introduced the terms 'linguicide' and 'linguistic genocide' (Skutnabb-Kangas, 2000; see also Skutnabb-Kangas, Human Rights and Language Policy in Education, Volume 1) to describe how English has effectively become a 'killer' of less powerful language around the world. The work of Phillipson, Skutnabb-Kangas and other scholars concerned about the spread of English and the death of smaller languages has led to general area of inquiry which May (2003, 2005) terms 'language rights'.

Over the past decade, the issue of English and minority language rights has generated much debate (e.g. Hall and Eggington, 2000; Tollefson, 1995, 2002; special issues of *Journal of Sociolinguistics* in 2003 and 2005), some of which has been quite confrontational. For example, Janina Brutt-Griffler (2002) takes issue with the concept of linguistic imperialism, in particular the suggestion that English was imposed on the colonized peoples of the British Empire. Brutt-Griffler (2002, p. 31) argues that 'the spread of English involved a contested terrain in which English was not unilaterally imposed on passive subjects, but wrested from an unwilling imperial authority as part of the struggle by them against colonialism'. Echoing Bisong's (1995) view of English as a valued language in Nigeria for its communication potential, she also argues that the protection of endangered languages, as proposed by Skutnabb-Kangas in her publications over the years, goes against the wishes of many parents in African and Asian countries, who would like their children to have the opportunity to learn English.

Brutt-Griffler's criticisms have spawned a series of rebuttals and counter rebuttals (see the special issues of the *Journal of Sociolinguistics*, 7/4, 2003 and the *Journal of Language Identity and Education*, 1/3, 2002, as well as the forum section of *JLIE*, 3/2, 2004). They also contrast with the views of other scholars who have framed the debate in different ways. Steering a course between those in favour of Phillipson and Skutnabb-Kangas's theses and those against, Marnie Holborow (1999) makes a clear distinction between what Pennycook (1994) calls 'discourses of colonialism' and what she sees as the material practices of colonialism. For Holborow, one cannot contest discourses, while one can engage with material reality. Adopting a Marxist stance, Holborow is far more attracted to the Phillpson and Sktunabb-Kangas view of the world, although here too she does have her criticisms. For example, she sees the broad contrast between the north and the south and the centre and periphery as over-simplistic, ignoring as it does the roles of ruling local elites, who are complicit in global capitalism. Similarly, she is wary of fostering local nationalism as a defence against imperialism: very often, it is conservative ruling local elites leading the defence of the local against imposition from without.

In addition to steering a course between and among different camps,
May (2003, 2005) notes how the framing of language rights strictly in
terms of economic prospects, as authors such as Brutt-Griffler (2002)
and John Edwards (1985) have done, ignores the way that people often
value their affective ties and affiliations to a particular language over
the relative 'usefulness' of that language in terms of gaining access to
key social and economic resources. Indeed, if abandonment of the minority language and the embracing of English were so obviously the
only rational way forward for ethnolinguistic minority groups in established nation-states, then Latinos in the USA would not continue using
Spanish; the Québécois, as citizens of Canada, would not have spent as
much time and money as they have over the past several decades on the
preservation and promotion of French; and the citizens of African countries would have abandoned local languages and vernaculars long ago.

Elsewhere, Pennycook (1994, 1998; Pennycook, Critical Applied
Linguistics and Language Education, Volume 1) and Canagarajah
(1999, 2005a; Canagarajah, The Politics of English Language Teaching,
Volume 1) take a post-modern view of the world informed by critical
theory, framing the spread of English as altogether too complicated to
be considered as oppressive and dehumanising as Phillipson and others
suggest. Both scholars allow for the capacity of L2 English users around
the world to resist (that is, to combat rationally and reflectively) linguistic imperialism (Canagarajah, 1999). This may be done by engaging
in what Pennycook (1994), following authors such as Achebe (1975),
terms 'writing back', the process by which users of English around the
world appropriate English and make it work for their various personal,
professional and political purposes. This appropriation may work at
the more literary and academic levels in the form of published articles
and books for national and international consumption. However, it
might also work at the local level, be it the nation-state, community or
even neighbourhood.

For example, in the context of post-colonial Tanzania, where Swahili
was promoted as the national language from the mid-1960s, Blommaert
(2005) notes that English remains an important and extended medium
of communication at all levels of society. However, rather than seeing
uses of English, such as in business signage, as evidence of 'an invasion of an imperialist or killer language' (p. 404), Blommaert finds it
more useful to situate them in a global hierarchy in which small business operators in Tanzania connect with their potential clientele, using
English to index their sophistication in taste (e.g. making reference to
European norms of consumption), their business knowledge (English
sounds business-like) or their connections to international business
(English is the international language). For Blommaert, over-simplified
essentialist associations of one language or one identity do not survive

the scrutiny of ethnographic research. Neither do de-essentialised approaches that in effect amount to rational choice theory, whereby individuals make interested choices about language affiliations based solely on factors such as economic gain or prestige (for further discussion and critique of this, see May, 2003, 2005). What is needed is an approach to English as an international phenomenon that escapes essentialism but recognises social structures, in particular the unequal access to all semiotic resources, including language, that reigns in the world today.

The Effects of Globalization on the Language Teaching Practices

As Pennycook (1994) and Phillipson (1992) note, inextricably intertwined with the spread of English as an international language is the spread of teaching methodologies that originate in countries like the USA and Britain. From the 1970s onwards, what is known as Communicative Language Teaching (CLT) has been at the forefront of debate about language teaching methodology in different parts of the world. From its beginnings in the Council of Europe (Van Ek, 1975), CLT has become the first truly global method. Thus, while it is not written into every national curriculum in the world today, it is a point of reference in discussions about language teaching around the world. In succinct form, CLT is an approach to language teaching which views language as being about communicative competence (Hymes, 1971), that is, the ability to use the linguistic system appropriately, and language learning as emergent from the use of the target language in interaction as opposed to an explicit focus on grammar (Richards and Rodgers, 2001). A key feature of CLT is the attempt to replicate, in the classroom, the experiences of regular users of the target language. Thus, there is an emphasis on classroom activities that mimic activities in the 'real' world (or in any case, what many language educators and materials writers imagine the world outside the classroom to be like). For its proponents, it represents a positive step forward in the history of language teaching, from more old-fashioned approaches to teaching, which are text-based (grammar translation) or based on generally discredited learning theories (e.g. Audiolingualism and behaviourist psychology).

In Appadurai's (op. cit.) terms, CLT is an example of a pedagogical *ideoscape*, a global flow of ideas about teaching. However, this flow has been neither one-way nor unproblematic, as more and more applied linguists have come to question the spread of CLT in recent years. In sections of their respective books dealing with language teaching methodology and social context, Holliday (1994), Pennycook (1994), and Phillipson (1992) discuss the gap between imported pedagogical principles and local teaching contexts. For example, Pennycook questions the assumption that learners of English must participate in information gap activities if they are to learn the target language in contexts such as Malaysia. This global exhortation to chat runs up against intercultural walls (Pennycook points out that silence is an integral part of communication in Malay), as well as intracultural walls (the different conversation roles according to gender which exist in some cultures). Following a similar line, Ellis (1996) writes specifically about CLT in East Asian countries such as China and Vietnam, making the point that the focus on process inherent in this approach to language teaching does not sit well in societies in which content is considered important. Kramsch and Sullivan (1996), referring to Vietnam as well, point out that the concept of group might better refer to the entire class as one unit, as opposed to collections of three or four students separated from their classmates.

Other authors have explored the extent to which teachers teach according to the basic tenets of CLT. Mitchell and Lee (2003) compared the teaching of French as a foreign language in a classroom in the UK with the teaching of EFL in a South Korean classroom. They found that in these two classrooms, CLT was not alive and well, as lessons were teacher-centred and there was not much in the way of pair- and group-speaking activities. Elsewhere, Sakui (2004) examined how 30 Japanese teachers defined and implemented CLT, the official methodology of the Japanese Ministry of Education since 1989. She found that while teachers were knowledgeable about pedagogical options, they tended to adopt something akin to grammar translation as their dominant methodology, because this was deemed to be the best way to prepare students for their university entrance exams, which were still grammar-based. Sakui documents a situation in which ministerial methodological dictates have changed while examination structures have not.

The resolution of conflicts arising when the global spread of method collides with local educational cultures has been discussed by many authors over the years (Bax, 2003; Canagarajah, 1999; Holliday, 1994; Kumaravadivelu, 1994; McKay, 2002). While the proposals of these authors vary considerably, they all involve a call for local teachers to work out their own solutions, appropriating what they deem suitable from without, while relying on home-grown strategies that have ecological validity. For example, Holliday (1994) discusses 'appropriate methodology' as a means of breaking away from pedagogical recommendations from without and moving towards approaches that start with the teacher's understanding of classroom activity, which in turn inform future classroom teaching. Starting with teachers' understandings in local context, of course, would mean moving away from the importation of teaching technology from abroad as part of the global network. Elsewhere, Kumaravadivelu (1994, 2003) discusses the 'post-method' condition, in which the adoption of a particular method has ceased to be regarded as the solution to all problems, and there is no longer a one-way flow of expertise from centre to periphery. As Canagarajah (2002) notes, this state of affairs opens up new opportunities for the knowledge and expertise of local teachers in periphery contexts to be recognized and valued.

FUTURE DIRECTIONS

The three areas of inquiry discussed earlier all show great potential and promise as regards research and debate in the future. Thus far, research into the commodification and skilling of language has focussed primarily on events in a few select locations. However, as applied linguists adopt a more global agenda, research begins to catch up with other instances of these phenomena around the world. There is a need, for example, for studies of the ways that languages around the world have been commodified. In addition, Cameron's (2000, 2002) research into communication skilling, originally based in the UK, should be extended to other parts of the world.

As regards the spread of English around the world, and concepts such as linguistic imperialism and linguicide, there is little doubt that Phillipson and Skutnabb-Kangas have initiated and helped to maintain on the applied linguistics agenda the issue of the spread of English and English language teaching around the world. And, with authors such as Brutt-Griffler questioning some of the foundational concepts and extensions of their arguments, English as a globalized language will no doubt continue to generate debate and research. However, following authors such as Blommaert, Canagarajah, May and Pennycook, this debate is becoming increasingly nuanced as relatively simple models and frameworks are replaced by even more complex ones.

Finally, the ongoing global–local tension emerging from the spread of CLT as something akin to a global language teaching methodology seems set to continue. Future research needs to be along the lines of the contributions to Canagarajah (2005b) and discussions such as Holliday (2005); while the former explores teacher-generated practices in a variety of local contexts, the latter looks at the difficulties facing native and non-native speakers of English as they reconcile global and local forces in the teaching of English as an international language.

See Also: Alastair Pennycook: Critical Applied Linguistics and Language Education (Volume 1); Tove Skutnabb-Kangas: Human Rights and Language Policy in Education (Volume 1); Suresh Canagarajah: The Politics of English Language Teaching (Volume 1); Joan Kelly

Hall: Language Education and Culture (Volume 1); Stephen May: Language Education, Pluralism and Citizenship (Volume 1); Mary Kalantzis and Bill Cope: Language Education and Multiliteracies (Volume 1)

REFERENCES

Achebe, C.: 1975, 'English and the African writer', in A. Mazrui (ed.), *The Political Sociology of the English Language*, Mouton, The Hague, 216–223.
Appadurai, A.: 1990, 'Disjuncture and difference in the global cultural economy', in M. Featherstone (ed.), *Global culture: Nationalism, Globalization and Modernity*, Sage, London,
Bauman, Z.: 1998, *Globalization: The Human Consequences*, Polity, Oxford.
Bax, S.: 2003, 'The end of CLT: a context approach to language teaching', *ELT Journal* 57(3), 278–287.
Bisong, J.: 1995 'Language choice and cultural imperialism', *English Language Teaching Journal* 49(2), 122–132.
Blommaert, J.: 2005, 'Situating language rights: English and Swahili in Tanzania revisited', *Journal of Sociolinguistics* 9(3), 390–417.
Brutt-Griffler, J.: 2002, *World English: A Study of its Development*, Multilingual Matters, Clevedon, UK.
Cameron, D.: 2000, *Good to talk? Living and Working in a Communication Culture*, Sage, London.
Cameron, D.: 2002, 'Globalization and the teaching of 'communication skills'', in D. Block and D. Cameron (eds.), *Globalization and Language Teaching*, Routledge, London, 67–82.
Canagarajah, S.: 1999, *Resisting Linguistic Imperialism in English Teaching*, Oxford University Press, Oxford.
Canagarajah, S.: 2002, 'Globalization, methods, and practice in periphery classrooms', in D. Block and D. Cameron (eds.), *Globalization and Language Teaching*, Routledge, London, 134–150.
Canagarajah, S.: 2005a, 'Dilemmas in planning English/vernacular relations in post-colonial communities', *Journal of Sociolinguistics* 9(3), 419–447.
Canagarajah, S.A. (ed.): 2005b, *Reclaiming the Local in Language Policy and Practice*, Lawrence Erlbaum, Mahwah, NJ.
Cox, R.: 1996, 'A perspective on globalization', in J.M. Mittelman (ed.), *Globalization: Critical Reflections*, Lynne Rienner, London,
Ellis, G.: 1996, 'How culturally appropriate is the communicative approach', *English Language Teaching Journal* 50(3), 213–218.
Fishman, J.A., Cooper, R.L., and Conrad, A.W. (eds.): 1977, *The Spread of English: The Sociology of English as an Additional Language*, Newbury House, Rowley, Mass.
Gee, J.P., Glynda, H., and Lankshear, C.: 1996, *The New Work Order: Behind the Language of the New Capitalism*, Westview Press, Boulder, CO.
Giddens, A.: 1990, *The Consequences of Modernity*, Polity Press, Cambridge.
Giddens, A.: 1994, 'Risk, trust, reflexivity', in U. Beck, A. Giddens, and S. Lash (eds.), *Reflexive Modernization: Politics, Tradition and Aesthetics in the Modern Social Order*, Stanford University Press, Stanford.
Hall, J.K. and Eggington, W.G. (eds.): 2000, *The Sociopolitics of English Language Teaching*, Multilingual Matters, Clevedon, UK.
Held, D., McGrew, A., Goldblatt, D., and Perraton, J.: 1999, *Global Transformations: Politics, Economics and Culture*, Polity, Cambridge.
Heller, M.: 2002, 'Globalization and the commodification of bilingualism in Canada', in D. Block and D. Cameron (eds.), *Globalization and Language Teaching*, Routledge, London, 47–63.

Heller, M.: 2003, 'Globalization the new economy, and the commodification of language and identity', *Journal of Sociolinguistics*, 7(4), 473–492.

Holliday, A.: 1994, *Appropriate Methodology and Social Context*, Cambridge University Press, Cambridge.

Holliday, A.: 2005, *The Struggle to Teach English as an International Language*, Oxford University Press, Oxford.

Holborow, M.: 1999, *The Politics of English*, Sage Publications, London.

Hymes, D.: 1971, *On Communicative Competence*, University of Pennsylvania Press, Philadelphia.

Kachru, B. (ed.): 1983, *The Other Tongue: English Across Cultures*, Pergamon, Oxford.

Kramsch, C. and Sullivan, P.: 1996, 'Appropriate pedagogy', *English Language Teaching Journal*, 50(3), 199–212.

Kumaravadivelu, B.: 1994, 'The postmethod condition: (E)merging strategies for second/foreign language teaching', *TESOL Quarterly*, 28(1), 27–48.

Kumaravadivelu, B.: 2003, *Beyond Methods*, Yale University Press, New Haven, CT.

Latouche, S.: 1996, *The Westernizing of the World*, Polity Press, Cambridge.

May, S.: 2003, 'Rearticulating the case for minority language rights', *Current Issues in Language Planning* 4(2), 95–125.

May, S.: 2005, 'Language rights: Moving the debate forward', *Journal of Sociolinguistics* 9(3), 319–347.

Mazrui, A.: 1975, *The Political Sociology of the English Language: An African Perspective*, Mouton, The Hague.

McKay, S.: 2002, *Teaching English as an International Language: Rethinking Goals and Approaches*, Oxford University Press, Oxford.

Mitchell, R. and Lee, J.H.-W.: 2003, 'Sameness and difference in classroom learning cultures: interpretations of communicative pedagogy in the UK and Korea', *Language Teaching Research* 7(1), 35–63.

Ngũgĩ, wa Thiong'o: 1993, *Moving the Centre: the struggle for cultural freedoms*, James Currey, London.

Pennycook, A.: 1994, *The Cultural Politics of English as an International Language*, Longman, London.

Pennycook, A.: 1998, *English and the Discourses of Colonialism*, Routledge, London.

Phillipson, R.: 1992, *Linguistic Imperialism*, Oxford University Press, Oxford.

Richards, J. and Rodgers, T.: 2001, *Approaches and Methods in Language Teaching: A Description and Analysis*, 2nd edition, Cambridge: Cambridge University Press.

Ritzer, G.: 1998, *The McDonaldization Thesis*, Sage, London.

Robertson, R.: 1995, 'Globalization: Time-Space and Homogeniety-Heterogenity', in M. Featherstone, S. Lash, and R. Robertson (eds.), *Global Modernities*, Sage Publications, London, 25–44.

Sakui, K.: 2004, 'Wearing two pairs of shoes: Language teaching in Japan', *English Language Teaching Journal* 58(2), 155–163.

Skutnabb-Kangas, T.: 2000, *Linguistic Genocide in Education—Or Worldwide Diversity and Human Rights?*, Lawrence Erlbaum, Mahwah, MJ.

Smith, P.: 1997, *Millennium Dreams*, Verso, London.

Tollefson, J. (ed.): 1995, *Power and Inequality in Language Education*, Cambridge University Press, Cambridge.

Tollefson, J. (ed.): 2002, *Language Policies in Education: Critical Issues*, Lawrence Erlbaum, Mahwah, MJ.

UNESCO: 1963, *The Use of Vernacular Languages in Education,* UNESCO, Paris.

Van Ek, J.: 1975, *The Threshold Level*, Council of Europe, Strasbourg.

Wallerstein, I.: 2004, *World Systems Analysis: An Introduction*, Durham University Press, Durham, NC.

JOAN KELLY HALL

LANGUAGE EDUCATION AND CULTURE

INTRODUCTION

No two concepts are more intimately linked than language and culture. In our interactions with others, we use language not only to refer to or represent our sociocultural worlds. It is also the central means by which we bring our cultural worlds into existence, maintain them, and shape them for our own purposes. Long recognized in fields such as linguistic anthropology and sociolinguistics, the interdependent nature of language and culture has been a key premise of a substantial body of research on linguistically and culturally diverse groups. Findings demonstrate in compelling ways the myriad linguistic resources that members of a wide range of sociocultural groups use to both reflect and create their social worlds.

Findings from this rather large body of research have led to new ways of understanding the connections between the linguistic and cultural diversity of learners in educational institutions and the nature of schooling. These new understandings have, in turn, led to the creation of several pedagogical innovations captured under the broadly conceived framework of culturally responsive pedagogy. A primary premise of this pedagogy holds that exemplary teaching builds on rather than ignores the rich reservoirs of knowledge, experiences, and beliefs that linguistically and culturally diverse learners bring to their schooling experiences from their homes and communities. Provided here is a review of some of the more prominent innovations founded on this premise and a brief discussion of possible pitfalls and future possibilities.

EARLY DEVELOPMENTS

Changing immigration patterns over the latter half of the twentieth century led to an increase in the linguistic and cultural diversity of communities in all corners of the world. Despite apparent good intentions of educational institutions in dealing with the upsurge in linguistic and cultural diversity of their learner populations, the efforts of teachers, administrators, and other institutional authorities were hampered by a widely held belief that linguistic and cultural *differences* reflected linguistic and cultural *deficiencies*. Consequently, differences in levels

S. May and N. H. Hornberger (eds), Encyclopedia of Language and Education, 2nd Edition, Volume 1: Language Policy and Political Issues in Education, 45–55.
©*2010 Springer Science+Business Media LLC.*

of academic achievement between mainstream, i.e. white, native English speaking, learners and nonmainstream learners were attributed to the latter's rearing in home and community settings considered to be linguistically and culturally deprived.

Early research in sociolinguistics and linguistic anthropology sought to counter this belief by detailing the richness of linguistically and culturally diverse learners' worlds outside schools. Studies from the 1960s and 1970s examining the dynamics of varieties of English found in the USA (e.g. Labov, 1972; Wolfram, 1974; Wolfram and Christian, 1976), for example, made apparent the structural soundness and functional importance of different dialects found in American society. Findings from these and other studies demonstrated rather conclusively that rather than a deficient version of some idealized standard, language varieties are systematized, legitimate tools by which members of different sociocultural groups and communities participate in and manage their social worlds.

Also influential in countering the deficit view of linguistically and culturally diverse learners is much ethnographic research from the field of linguistic anthropology. The studies by Shirley Brice Heath (1983) and Susan Phillips (1983) are arguably two of the more influential early investigations. Each study provides rich descriptions of the language practices and larger sociocultural beliefs and values found in communities of learners who are not considered standard or mainstream English speakers. Heath's study examined the practices of two rural US communities, Trackton, a black community, and Roadville, a white community, and one urban, middle-class community comprising both black and white families. Phillips investigated the home socialization practices of a native American community, the Warm Springs Indians. Both studies found that the home practices of these communities comprised a myriad of linguistic and cultural experiences, knowledge, skills and beliefs, which, although different from mainstream practices, were equally rich and of vital importance to these communities.

This early work paved the way for a great deal of subsequent research on language and literacy practices of many different communities and cultural groups around the world (Barton and Hamilton, 1998; Martin-Jones and Bhatt, 1998; Watahomigie and McCarty, 1997). In addition to enriching our understandings of the linguistic and cultural dynamics of these communities and groups, these findings have added greatly to our understandings of the significant connections between the home practices of linguistically and culturally diverse learners and the practices of mainstream schooling contexts. We know, for example, that the linguistic and cultural practices of sociocultural groups and communities who are not considered mainstream often differ from those practices found in schools. We also know that children who have been reared in nonmainstream practices often do not perform as well academically as those whose practices are more similar to those found in schools do. The differences in performances, however, are not because the home practices of the nonmainstream children are linguistically and culturally inferior. It has to do, instead, with compatibility. Children whose home activities reflect the linguistic and cultural practices of schools are likely to have more opportunities for success because they only need to link to and build on the practices into which they have been socialized at home. On the other hand, children whose home practices are linguistically and culturally differ- *Additive* ent are likely to have more difficulty because they must add new linguistic and cultural practices and create new links to those they already know.

MAJOR CONTRIBUTIONS

The findings from many studies illustrating the vitality and importance of linguistically and culturally diverse learners' worlds outside schools conducted throughout the last few decades of the twentieth century provided the foundation for the development of several innovative approaches to language education that can be subsumed under the broad framework of culturally responsive pedagogy. This pedagogy *Culturally responsive pedagogy* is based on a key premise that considers the different worlds that linguistically and culturally diverse learners bring with them to the classroom to be rich reservoirs of resources to draw on rather than sources of deprivation and thus obstacles to overcome. Thus, exemplary educational programs seek to build on rather than replace the languages and cultures that learners bring with them to school.

Several pedagogical innovations grounded in culturally responsive pedagogy deal with matters of curriculum. One innovation is often referred to as *language awareness* or *dialect education* curricula. *Lang. awareness* Drawing directly from the research on language variation, it proposes adding a curricular component designed specifically to raise learners' awareness of the variable nature of language and its link to their cultural identities. One way this is done is by involving learners in the study of the language varieties found in their local communities *Explicit* (Wolfram, Christian, and Adger, 1999). In addition to raising learners' awareness of the importance of their own language variety, such study helps learners to understand the social, political, and historical nature of languages considered standard and against which their own varieties are judged.

A second approach advocating curricular change is *funds of knowledge*, which calls for drawing on learners' diverse worlds outside the *Funds of knowledge* classroom to create linguistically and culturally meaningful curricula and instructional practices in the classroom. It was originally developed by Luis Moll and his colleagues (Moll, Amanti, Neff, and González, 1992) in their work with working-class Mexican-American communities in Arizona in the USA. The purpose of their work was to tap into these communities' funds of knowledge, a term coined to refer to the communities' significant sociocultural practices, bodies of knowledge, skills, and beliefs, and to use the funds to transform the curricula of these communities' schools. A defining feature of the approach is the active involvement of teachers in the ethnographic study of their students' worlds outside the school and in the use of their newfound understandings to redesign or transform their curricula and instructional activities. Most funds of knowledge projects have been conducted by teachers from public schools, primarily at the elementary level, in the USA (González et al., 1993).

Another, more broadly conceived approach calling for curricular changes that draw on learners' home practices is *multicultural education*, a term used by educational institutions primarily to refer to a range of programs and policies developed to address concerns of historically marginalized groups. Originating with the civil rights movement in the USA in the early 1960s, multicultural education was initially conceived to address the concerns of three groups in particular: those identified by race, class, and gender, but more recent articulations address concerns of linguistically and culturally diverse immigrant groups as well, and not just in the USA but around the world (Banks and Banks 1995; May 1999a). Considered one of the pioneers of multicultural education, James Banks (1981) called for a total transformation of schools, including their placement, disciplinary and other policies, and testing and assessment measures in addition to curricula and instructional practices and materials. Early attempts at reform were, for the most part, limited to making slight changes or additions to traditional school practices. These included integrating into the regular curriculum interpersonal activities and textual information about those groups marked as different that were meant primarily to enhance the group members' dispositions and attitudes about themselves.

More recently, education scholars such as Carl Grant and Christine Sleeter (2003), Sonia Nieto (2002), and Geneva Gay (2000) have made visible how longstanding schooling practices such as tracking (streaming) and standardized tests continue to constrain the educational advancement of nonmainstream learners. In response to this, they have called for more profound structural changes grounded in dual concerns with equal educational opportunity and social change. In noting the tendency for multicultural education practices to take accommodation to mainstream culture as its pedagogical goal, Stephen May (1999a, b) has also called for a more critical approach to multicultural education.

The changes he proposes seek to encourage and preserve "a reflexive critique of specific cultural practices that avoids the vacuity of cultural relativism... allows for criticism (both internal and external to the group), transformation, and change" (May, 1999b, p. 33).

A final, broadly conceived approach drawing on the basic premises of a culturally responsive pedagogy is *participatory pedagogy*. This approach has its roots in the work of Brazilian educator Paulo Freire (1972, 1973) who argued for a pedagogy that took into account rather than ignored the social, cultural, and political worlds of learners. In Freire's model, the teacher becomes a facilitator and the curriculum is organized around experiences, needs, and concerns that learners consider to be central to their lives. Also referred to as critical pedagogy (cf. Morgan, 1998; Pennycook, 2001), participatory pedagogy aims to create classroom environments that help learners first to understand more fully their local conditions and circumstances, and second, to take action toward changing their lives. One way this is done is by helping learners understand the myriad ways in which the contexts of their lives are publicly constructed and the means they have available for recreating their worlds in ways that are meaningful and appropriate for them.

The works of some of the more prominent participatory pedagogy scholars including, for example, Henry Giroux (1997), Ira Shor (1996), and Michael Apple (1996), are more theory-based in that they build on and extend Freire's philosophy in arguing against what they perceive to be deeply embedded inequities in the educational system and for major reform. The work of other critical pedagogues is more practice-based, in that it attempts to apply these ideas to specific learning contexts. The approaches advocated by Brian Morgan (1998), Elsa Auerbach (1992), and Bonnie Norton Peirce (1995), for example, are geared to community-based adult immigrant language programs, whereas that of Heath and Mangiola (1991) is aimed at school-aged children.

WORK IN PROGRESS

The move into the twenty-first century has brought with it myriad models and approaches to language education that are grounded in culturally responsive pedagogy. Although the basic premise of these approaches remains the same, there are some conceptual changes afoot in terms of how we understand language and culture that are having a significant impact on the design of educational programs. The acknowledgment of the intrinsic link between language and culture notwithstanding, it has been the case that most approaches associated with culturally responsive pedagogy have held on to, or, at the very least, have not questioned, a view of language as stable structural systems and of culture as fixed bodies of knowledge. Moreover, it has taken for granted the idea that the knowledge of both systems is shared equally by all members of a particular group and thus, homogeneous and stable across speakers and contexts.

*cB:
Need for
multicult.
habitus

This traditional view runs counter to contemporary understandings, which consider language to be fundamentally dynamic, provisional, grounded in and emergent from its locally situated uses in culturally framed and discursively patterned communicative activities, which, in turn, are tied to specific sociocultural communities of practice (Hall, Cheng, and Carlson, 2006; see also May, Language Education, Pluralism and Citizenship, Volume 1 and Pennycook, Critical Applied Linguistics and Language Education, Volume 1). The nature of culture is considered to be equally dynamic, comprising recurring constellations of dispositions and expectations that are continually recreated in the myriad intellectual and practical communicative activities constituting our daily lives. Culture is located then not in accumulated bodies of static knowledge, but in the daily interactions occurring between individuals in particular sociocultural contexts at particular moments of time. Through our participation in myriad, varied activities, we take on and negotiate multiple cultural identities. Cultural identity, then, is not seen as singular and unitary, but rather as multiple and malleable, a dynamic creation of the social, historical, and political contexts of our lived experiences.

*
Multiliteracies
New London
Grp.

One recently developed approach that fully incorporates contemporary perspectives on language and culture is the pedagogy of multiliteracies (New London Group, 1996; see also Kalantzis and Cope, Language Education and Multiliteracies, Volume 1). The approach was proposed by a group of ten scholars from the USA, England, and Australia in response to what they consider to be two important challenges to education. The first is the ever-increasing cultural and linguistic diversity of communities around the world. Such diversity, they argue, not only means "that there can be no standard." (p. 10). It also means "that the most important skill students need to learn is to negotiate regional, ethnic, or class-based dialects. . .hybrid cross-cultural discourses; the code switching often to be found within a text among different languages, dialects, or registers; different visual and iconic meanings; and variation in the gestural relationships among people, language, and material objects" (ibid.). The second challenge is the increasing creation and spread of multimodal means for communicating within and across these communities.

To meet these challenges, they call for a pedagogy whose goal is to develop in learners a critical understanding of how their communicative activities—oral, written, and multimodal—are historically and socially located and produced, along with skills for shaping available meaning-making resources into new patterns and activities with new meanings. To meet this goal, they propose that instruction be organized around four dimensions of learning opportunities. Situated practice / ⨉ immerses learners in practices that are important to their lives and provides opportunities for them to learn on their own, to figure out what they need to do to make sense in them. Overt instruction 2 helps learners to gain control over and develop a language for describing the resources and patterns by which meaning is made in their activities. The purpose of the third learning opportunity, critical framing, is to help learners understand more fully the historical, social, cultural, political, and ideological perspectives embodied in their activities. The New London Group argues that such reflective explorations will lead to learners' development of a broader perspective of the ways in which locally situated meanings both converge and diverge from the learners' own worldviews. They will also learn to recognize that meanings and rules for the use of communicative resources are arbitrary, tied to their contexts of use in complex, and sometimes contradictory, ways. Such awareness in turn can enable learners to make informed choices about their own participation. The final opportunity, transformed practice, provides learners with opportunities to use their new understandings, knowledge, and skills to try out different voices in familiar contexts, to invent new means and, where possible, create new practices and new goals for self-expression and connecting with others.

The approach proposed by the New London Group differs from earlier approaches grounded in culturally responsive pedagogy in at least two ways. First, it considers all members of educational institutions to be linguistically and culturally diverse and, in doing so, does away with the notion of one language standard and the act of cultural "othering" that has marked earlier approaches. Second, it considers the goal of learning to be not just mastery but also invention. The conditions for learning fostered in each of the four overlapping spheres of opportunities conceptualized by the New London Group not only promote learners' development of a complex range of understandings and perspectives, knowledge and skills, and values and motivations needed for full personal, social and cultural participation in their classroom communities as well as in their larger, social communities. It also fosters in learners the development of an ability to see from multiple perspectives, to be flexible in their thinking, to solve problems creatively and, ultimately, to develop new ways of becoming involved in their worlds. Cope and Kalantzis (2000) provide several case studies of attempts to put the ideas proposed by the New London Group into practice (see also http://multiliteracies.com/ for samples of current projects undertaken by groups of educators in Australia and Malaysia).

PROBLEMS, DIFFICULTIES, AND FUTURE
DIRECTIONS

The efforts described in this chapter have enjoyed success in transforming language programs and enhancing the academic performances of linguistically and culturally diverse learners in schooling contexts around the world. However, as the diversity of our communities continues to increase, educational institutions face two critical challenges. The first has to do with the issue of linguistic and cultural representation of learners' worlds outside schools. Much of the work cited earlier has indeed helped to raise our awareness of the richness of learners' linguistic and cultural worlds. However, even as understandings of the concepts of language and culture change, too often learners' worlds continue to be treated as stable and homogeneous, Moreover, possibilities for individual identity are often limited to membership in one group only, with boundaries between groups considered fixed and impermeable. So, for example, learners are identified as either Mexican, or African-American, or Caucasian, and are then held accountable for living in ways that reflect particular linguistic and cultural idealizations of these groups. Possibilities for hybridization, for living multiple, heterogeneous, malleable linguistic and cultural lives are too often treated as phenomena to be controlled or ignored rather than explored and celebrated (see also May, Language Education, Pluralism and Citizenship, Volume 1).

The second challenge comes from the larger political front. Despite the continued calls for social justice, scholars (Dyson, 2003; Gutierrez, Asato, Santos, and Gotanda 2002; May, 1999b) note that in many cases, current instantiations of culturally responsive pedagogy have become comfortable, neutral, stuck in liberal ideologies that offer few real solutions for effecting change to current structures. As these educational programs stagnate, public resistance to them has begun to grow louder and more insistent. Referred to as "backlash pedagogy" (Gutierrez, Asato, Santos, and Gotanda, 2002, p. 335), this counterattack places blame for the perceived educational crisis on "teachers, so-called 'liberal' pedagogies, and linguistically and culturally diverse and poor children" (ibid.). In educational institutions across the USA, for example, this resistance is reflected in the dismantling of educational programs that were created specifically to improve opportunities for learning for linguistically and culturally diverse groups, as well as in the continued reliance on structures and processes such as tracking students according to categories such as class, culture and language and diluting the curriculum for nonmainstream learners.

These challenges call for movement on at least two planes. On one, we must increase efforts in critically examining how school structures

and processes continue to subjugate those who are linguistically, culturally and in other ways different from the mainstream and constructing
a framework for reexamining both schools and society that are both
progressive and transformative. As we move forward in these efforts,
we must ensure that our discourses "affirm the critical but refuse the
cynical, and establish hope as central to a critical pedagogical and political practice" (Giroux, 2000, p. xv). We must also reach to extend the
conversation across national boundaries, to create as May (1999a, p. 6)
proposes "a cross-national dialectic" and include context-specific
efforts from settings that up until now have been largely unexplored territories (Makoni and Pennycook, 2005).

At another level, we need to increase efforts in formulating ways of
dealing with, indeed, making possible, the continual reinvention, of
learners' linguistic practices and cultural identities between and across
constructed and imagined boundaries, both within and outside our educational institutions (cf. Makoni and Pennycook, 2005). Shields,
Bishop and Mazawi (2005), Iddings, Haught, and Devlin (2004), Lin
and Luk (2004), and Locke and May (2004) are just a few telling examples from real classrooms around the world of possible directions for
these efforts.

Ultimately, calls for transformation will not—and, in fact—cannot
lead to the development of a panacea for addressing the myriad issues
and concerns with linguistic and cultural diversity, both reflected and
created in our educational institutions. As the sociohistorical conditions
of our learners' lives change, so do their needs and concerns, and their
linguistic and cultural resources for dealing with them. And so it may
be that as we move more fully into the twenty-first century, one mark
of effective educational programs will be their ability to remain provisional, always in the state-of-becoming, with their practices and policies tied to the specific historical, social, and political conditions that
arise from and in turn help shape the diversity of experiences in ours
and our learners' everyday lives.

See Also: *Mary Kalantzis and Bill Cope: Language Education and
Multiliteracies (Volume 1); Stephen May: Language Education, Plural-
ism and Citizenship (Volume 1); Alastair Pennycook: Critical Applied
Linguistics and Language Education (Volume 1)*

REFERENCES

Apple, M.: 1996, *Cultural Politics and Education*, Teachers College Press, New York.
Auerbach, E.: 1992, *Making Meaning, Making Change: Participatory Curriculum
    Development for Adult ESL Literacy*, Delta Systems, McHenry, IL.
Banks, J.: 1981, *Education in the 80s: Multiethnic education*, National Education
    Association, Washington, DC.

Banks, J.A. and Banks, C.A.M.: 1995, *Handbook of Research on Multicultural Education*, Macmillan, New York.
Barton, D. and Hamilton, M.: 1998, *Local Literacies: Reading and Writing in One Community*, Routledge, London.
Cope, B. and Kalantzis, M. (eds.): 2000, *Multiliteracies: Literacy Learning and the Design of Social Futures*, Routledge, London.
Dyson, A.H.: 2003, 'Popular literacies and the "all" children: Rethinking literacy development in contemporary childhoods', *Language Arts* 81(2): 100–109.
Freire, P.: 1972, *Pedagogy of the Oppressed*, Continuum, New York.
Freire, P.: 1973, *Pedagogy for Critical Consciousness*, Seabury Press, New York.
Gay, G.: 2000, *Culturally Responsive Teaching: Theory, Research, and Practice*, Teachers College Press, New York.
Giroux, H.: 1997, *Pedagogy and the Politics of Hope: Theory, Culture and Schooling*, Westview Press, Boulder, CO.
Giroux, H.: 2000, *Series Foreword. Critical Studies in Education and Culture: Critical Reflection and the Foreign Language Classroom*, Bergin & Garvey, Westport, CT, xv.
González, N., Moll, L., Floyd-Tenery, M., Rivera, A., Rendon, P., González, R., and Amanti, C.: 1993, *Teacher Research on Funds of Knowledge: Learning from Households*, Educational Practice Report 6. National Center for Research on Cultural Diversity and Second Language Learning.
Grant, C.A. and Sleeter, C.E.: 2003, *Making Choices for Multicultural Education: Five Approaches to Race, Class and Gender* (fourth edition), Wiley, New York.
Gutierrez, K., Asato, J., Santos, M., and Gotanda, N.: 2002, 'Backlash pedagogy: Language and culture and the politics of reform', *The Review of Education, Pedagogy and Cultural Studies* 24: 335–351.
Hall, J.K., Cheng, A., and Carlson, M.: 2006, 'Reconceptualizing multicompetence as a theory of language knowledge', *Applied Linguistics* 27: 220–240.
Heath, S.B.: 1983, *Ways with Words*, Cambridge University Press, Cambridge.
Heath, S.B. and Mangiola, L.: 1991, *Children of Promise: Literate Activity in Linguistically and Culturally Diverse Classrooms*, National Education Association, Washington, DC.
Iddings, C., Haught, J., and Devlin, R.: 2004, 'Multimodal re-representations of self and meaning for second language learners in English dominant classrooms', in J.K. Hall, G. Vitanova, and L. Marchenkova, (eds.), *Dialogue with Bakhtin on Second and Foreign Language Learning*, Lawrence Erlbaum, Mahwah, NJ.
Labov, W.: 1972, *Sociolinguistic Patterns*, University of Pennsylvania Press, Philadelphia, PA.
Lin, A. and Luk, C.: 2004, 'Local creativity in the face of global domination: Insights of Bakhtin for teaching English for dialogic communication', in J.K. Hall, G. Vitanova, and L. Marchenkova, (eds.), *Dialogue with Bakhtin on Second and Foreign Language Learning*, Lawrence Erlbaum, Mahwah, NJ.
Locke, T. and May, S.: 2004, 'Dis-lodging literature from English: Challenging linguistic hegemonies', *English Teaching: Practice and Critique* 3(1), 17–31.
Makoni, S. and Pennycook, A.: 2005, 'Disinventing and (re)constituting languages', *Critical Inquiry in Language Studies* 2(3): 137–156.
Martin-Jones, M. and Bhatt, A.: 1998, 'Literacies in the lives of young Gujerati speakers in Leicester', in A.Y. Durgunoglu and L. Verhoeven (eds.), *Literacy Development in a Multilingual Context*, Lawrence Erlbaum, Mahwah, NJ, 37–50.
May, S.: 1999a, 'Introduction: Toward critical multiculturalism', in S. May (ed.), *Critical Multiculturalism*, Falmer Press, London, 1–10.
May, S.: 1999b, 'Critical multiculturalism and cultural difference: Avoiding essentialism', in S. May (ed.), *Critical Multiculturalism*, Falmer Press, London, 11–41.

Moll, L.C., Amanti, C., Neff, D., and González, N.: 1992, 'Funds of knowledge for teaching: Using a qualitative approach to connect homes and classrooms', *Theory into Practice* 31(2), 132–141.

Morgan, B.: 1998, *The ESL Classroom: Teaching, Critical Practice, and Community Development*, University of Toronto Press, Toronto.

New London Group: 1996, 'Pedagogy of multiliteracies: Designing social futures', *Harvard Educational Review* 66(1), 66–92.

Nieto, S.: 2002, *Language, Culture and Teaching: Critical Perspectives for a New Century*, Lawrence Erlbaum, Mahwah, NJ.

Peirce, B.N.: 1995, 'Social identity, investment, and language learning', *TESOL Quarterly* 29(1), 9–31.

Pennycook, A.: 2001, *Critical Applied Linguistics: A Critical Introduction*, Lawrence Erlbaum Associates, Mahwah, NJ.

Phillips, S.: 1983, *The Invisible Culture: Communication in Classroom and Community in the Warm Springs Indian Reservation*, Longman, White Plains, NY.

Shields, C., Bishop, R., and Mazawi, A.: 2005, *Pathologizing Practices: The Impact of Deficit Thinking on Education*, Peter Lang, New York.

Shor, I.: 1996, *When Students Have Power: Negotiating Authority in a Critical Pedagogy*, University of Chicago Press, Chicago.

Watahomigie, L.J. and McCarty, T.L.: 1997, 'Literacy for what? Hualapai literacy and language maintenance', in N.H. Hornberger (ed.), *Indigenous Literacies in the Americas: Language Planning from the Bottom Up*, Mouton de Gruyter, New York, 95–113.

Wolfram, W.: 1974, *Sociolinguistic Aspects of Assimilation: Puerto Rican English in New York City*, Center for Applied Linguistics, Arlington, VA.

Wolfram, W., Christian, D., and Adger, C.: 1999, *Dialects in Schools and Communities*, Lawrence Erlbaum, Mahwah, NJ.

ANETA PAVLENKO AND INGRID PILLER

LANGUAGE EDUCATION AND GENDER

INTRODUCTION

In the past three decades, gender issues have received a wide coverage
in the education literature. Working at the intersections of gender, race,
and class, education scholars have tried to understand which students
are disadvantaged by particular contexts and what can be done to
address these inequities. Two areas remain largely invisible in the
larger field of research on gender in education, however. One relates
to the unique challenges faced by educators working in linguistically
and culturally diverse contexts, where learners bring with them distinct
and oftentimes conflicting gender ideologies and practices. Second, are
those working in foreign Language Classrooms, where students are
introduced to the 'imaginary worlds' of other languages whose gender
ideologies and practices may appear unfamiliar or perhaps even illegit-
imate. Consequently, the aim of this chapter is to survey research on
gender issues in the education of linguistically diverse speakers and
in foreign/second language education.

EARLY DEVELOPMENTS

Early research sparked by Lakoff's (1975) *Language and Woman's
Place* and Thorne and Henley's (1975) *Language and Sex: Difference
and Dominance* conceptualized the relationship between language
and gender through the notions of difference and dominance, and,
implicitly, the notion of deficit. In the deficit framework, women were
viewed as inferior language users and oftentimes as "the muted group"
who speaks a "powerless language." In the study of linguistic diversity,
this view translated into the *linguistic lag* hypothesis, the view of minority women as less bilingual than men, and thus lagging linguistically
behind them (Stevens, 1986). In the *dominance* framework, theorized
in Lakoff (1975) and Thorne and Henley (1975), "women-as-a-group"
were seen as linguistically oppressed and dominated by "men-as-a-
group." In the study of linguistic diversity, this view led to an argument that women lag behind because they are linguistically oppressed
by men (Burton, 1994).

S. May and N. H. Hornberger (eds), Encyclopedia of Language and Education,
2nd Edition, Volume 1: Language Policy and Political Issues in Education, 57–69.
©2010 Springer Science+Business Media LLC.

In the *differences* framework, introduced by Maltz and Borker (1982) and developed and popularized by Tannen (1990), "women-as-a-group" and "men-as-a-group" were seen as speakers of different "genderlects," developed through socialization in same-gender peer-groups. In the study of linguistic diversity, this approach explained instances of language shift spearheaded by women (Gal, 1978; McDonald, 1994) as rooted in women's preference for more prestigious languages and varieties. In the study of second/foreign language education, this approach led researchers to posit that females generally do better than males and to explain their achievement through more positive attitudes and better use of learning strategies (Oxford, 1994).

Crit. Beginning in the early 1990s, all three frameworks were criticized by feminist linguists for their essentialist assumptions about "men" and "women" as homogeneous categories, for lack of attention to the role of context and power relations, and for insensitivity to ethnic, racial, social, and cultural diversity that mediates gendered behaviors, performances, and outcomes in educational contexts (Cameron, 1992; Eckert and McConnell-Ginet, 1992).

MAJOR CONTRIBUTIONS AND WORK IN PROGRESS

The postmodern turn in educational and gender scholarship (see also Pennycook, Critical Applied Linguistics and Language Education, Volume 1) led to a reconceptualization of gender as a socially constructed and dynamic system of power relations and discursive practices, rather than an intrinsic property of particular individuals (Cameron, 1992, 2005; Eckert and McConnell-Ginet, 1992). This means that "women" and "men" are no longer seen as uniform natural categories where all members have common behavioral traits. Rather, these labels function as discursive categories imposed by society on individuals through a variety of gendering practices and accompanying ideologies about "normative" ways of being "men" and "women." It is these practices, and ways in which individuals adopt or resist them, that are at the center of current research. Gender categories in this inquiry intersect with those of age, race, class, sexuality, and (dis)ability to understand how particular groups of people are privileged or marginalized. They are also placed within the larger context of globalization to examine ways in which social, political, and economic changes affect gender ideologies, relationships, and practices (Cameron, 2005; see also Block, Language Education and Globalization, Volume 1).

Consequently, where possible, our discussion will not focus on "men" and "women" per se, but on particular groups of people, such as older immigrant women or working-class men in specific cultural and institutional contexts. We will review four major contributions of recent scholarship that have influenced the ongoing work in the field. These contributions have advanced our understanding of: (i) gendered access to linguistic resources; (ii) gendered agency in language learning; (iii) gendered interactions in the classroom; and (iv) gender in the foreign and second language curriculum.

Gendered Access to Linguistic Resources

Research conducted since the early 1990s has significantly enhanced our understanding of ways in which gendered practices mediate immigrants' access to educational and interactional opportunities. Studies conducted in North America demonstrate that immigrant women from traditionally patriarchal communities, and in particular older women and women with families, face a range of gatekeeping practices that restrict and at times even prevent their access to English as a Second Language (ESL) classes and to opportunities that would allow them to practice the language (Goldstein, 1995, 2001; Kouritzin, 2000; Norton, 2000; Norton Peirce, Harper and Burnaby, 1993; Tran, 1988; Warriner, 2004).

Gatekeeping practices in the majority community include the lack of daycare, inconvenient locations that make access to classes difficult for women who do not drive, and inconvenient times that make access impossible for women who work or for women who are afraid of being out of the house late at night. Access may also be complicated by economic factors that force women to prioritize immediate employment (Norton Peirce et al. 1993). Gatekeeping practices in some immigrant communities may prevent young women from being in the same classroom as men (Goldstein, 1995) and require that family care be offered exclusively by wives and mothers (Kouritzin, 2000). A study of workplace instruction by Norton Peirce et al. (1993) also revealed that some immigrant women were reluctant to attend ESL classes because their husbands did not want the wives to become more educated than they were. Lack of prior education, together with family responsibilities, was also shown to negatively affect older immigrant women's access to interactional opportunities outside the classroom (Norton, 2000; Tran, 1988).

Other studies in this area document successful attempts to respond to the needs of immigrant women and offer evening and weekend programs, externally funded daycare, and programs centered around these women's needs (Frye, 1999; Norton Peirce et al. 1993; Rivera, 1999). For instance, Rivera (1999) describes a program based in the United States, where all classes, those in Spanish and in English, aim at helping working-class immigrant Latina women acquire literacy skills, improve their basic education, increase English proficiency, and prepare for the high school equivalency exam. The curriculum and the pedagogy implemented in the program build on the strengths, survival skills, and linguistic and cultural resources of these women and question and challenge the social and economic forces that shape their lives.

Studies by Gordon (2004), Kouritzin (2000), Norton (2000), Pavlenko (2005), and Warriner (2004), also remind us that immigrant women in western countries are not helpless creatures who passively await help from the majority society—rather, they are adults who are able to use their linguistic and cultural resources creatively to deal with everyday challenges of living in a new language and to contest and negotiate their positioning in the labor force. The gendering of household responsibilities may become an advantage to these women as they benefit from linguistic opportunities offered by domestic language events, that is, interactions with social institutions connected to care for children and the home (e.g. childcare, schools, welfare offices, etc.) (Gordon, 2004; Norton, 2000). Greater access to educational and employment opportunities offered to immigrant women in western societies may eventually lead to their empowerment, whereas immigrant men who are not fluent in the majority language may actually experience a loss of power and authority (Gordon, 2004).

Gendered Agency in Language Learning

Recent research has also resulted in a more nuanced picture of ways in which gender ideologies and practices shape learners' desires, investments, and actions with regard to what languages they choose to learn and speak. Perhaps, the best-known finding in this field is that in some contexts girls and women may be more inclined to study foreign and second languages and that they may outperform boys or men in this area (Sunderland, 2000). Rather than a cause for celebration of feminine accomplishments, as it would have been earlier, this finding became an impetus for inquiry into the social and economic factors affecting investments and disinvestments of particular learners.

Studies conducted in Japan show that young Japanese women are more likely than their male peers to study English, train for English-related professions, and travel to English-speaking countries (Kobayashi, 2002; see also Fujita-Round and Maher, Language Education Policy in Japan, Volume 1). This trend is most commonly explained by the marginalized status of young women in mainstream Japanese society and their limited choice of employment opportunities; English offers the women an advantage in the marketplace (Kobayashi, 2002), it also becomes a means of empowerment and a lens that offers a critical perspective on their lives and society (McMahill, 2001). Piller and Takahashi (2006) show that this trend is exploited by the booming English language industry in Japan that aims to sell English language to young women as a way to change their lives, to enter a glamorous western world, to enjoy an emancipated lifestyle, and to form relationships with "chivalrous" western men.

Ideologies that link gender and language may also inspire resistance toward particular linguistic markers or practices. Studies of English-speaking women learning Japanese in Japan show that some women resist certain linguistic features associated with native-speaker competence (e.g., high pitch), because they associate these features with an undesirable gender performance of excessive, "silly" or "fake" femininity (Ohara, 2001; Siegal, 1996).

Overall, the studies to date suggest that it is not the essential nature of femininity or masculinity that shapes language learning trajectories of particular individuals, but rather the nature of gendered social and economic relations, as well as culture-specific ideologies of language and gender that mediate these relations and assign particular symbolic values to linguistic forms and discursive practices (cf., Rampton et al., Language, Class and Education, Volume 1).

Gendered Interactions in the Classroom

Recent research has also contributed toward a more nuanced view of ways in which gender shapes interactions in the classroom, asking which participants have the right to speak and to define meaning, and who remains invisible and why. Heller's (1999, 2001) ethnography of a French-language school in Toronto demonstrated that older immigrant girls had least access to the school's linguistic resources, in particular, English, whereas academically successful middle-class males were most likely to become bilingual in a way envisaged by school. Girls who are ethnically or racially distinct from the mainstream population are particularly likely to be rendered invisible or inaudible. Miller's (2003) study of immigrant students in an Australian school shows that blond white-skinned Bosnian girls were easily accepted by their teachers and peers and perceived as competent speakers of English, whereas Chinese girls who arrived in the school at about the same time were oftentimes excluded from social interactions and positioned as incompetent. What is at play here is not gender or race or culture per se, but assumptions made about members of a particular community. The role of assumptions is highlighted in Julé's (2004) study of a Canadian classroom, where a middle-class white Canadian teacher firmly believed that Punjabi culture was a disadvantage from which the students, in particular girls, had to be rescued. She also ignored Punjabi girls' contributions in her class, thus contributing to their silencing.

Yet immigrant girls are not necessarily the only disenfranchised group. Heller's (1999, 2001) study points to another population alienated by the French-language school in Toronto—working-class male speakers of vernacular Canadian French. Marginalized by the discourses of *francophonie internationale* that devalued their variety of French, these men often stopped speaking French at school altogether.

Studies conducted in kindergartens and elementary schools show that gender ideologies and practices shape access, interactions, and outcomes not only for the older learners, but also for the youngest ones (Hruska, 2004; Willett, 1995). Hruska's (2004) study, for example, shows how a discussion of soccer in a US classroom drew on gendered cultural knowledge and constrained opportunities for participation for girls from Latin America. McKay and Wong (1996) and Kanno (2003) also draw attention to the links between athletic prowess and the "normative" narrative of masculinity, and demonstrate that athletic Chinese and Japanese boys in their studies had an easier time gaining acceptance by the mainstream students and access to interactional opportunities than girls or nonathletic boys.

Together, these studies indicate that, rather than favoring undifferentiated "men" or "women," patterns of classroom interaction marginalize *specific* learners and/or groups of learners, such as immigrant and minority girls, working-class boys or nonathletic boys. Cultures of learning play an important role in this process as learners often hold beliefs about classroom behaviors and patterns of teacher–student interaction that do not fit well with majority classroom discursive practices and may be further alienating the learners. As a result, students whose voices are not being acknowledged in the classroom may lose their desire to learn the language, or even engage in passive resistance to classroom practices and curriculum demands.

Gender in the Curriculum

Recent scholarship has also made a major contribution toward ways in which issues regarding gender and sexuality can be broached in the classroom (Norton and Pavlenko, 2004). Boxer and Tyler (2004) propose scenarios as a way to discuss diverging views of what constitutes sexual harassment in International Teaching Assistant training. Nelson (2004) shows how one ESL teacher incorporated a discussion of gay and lesbian identities into the unit on modal auxiliary verbs. She argues that such discussions offer a relatively safe space in which students could explore their own and others' views of potentially ambiguous gender and sexual identities and acquire new interpretive skills.

Studies conducted in Japan illustrate practical ways in which critical reflection about language and gender can be incorporated in EFL curricula through examinations of gendered vocabulary and discursive practices in English and Japanese, and through discussions of sexuality, sexual harassment, domestic violence, and sexism in textbooks and the media (Cohen, 2004; McMahill, 2001; Saft and Ohara, 2004; Simon-Maeda, 2004; Toff, 2002). Toff (2002) uses lifewriting to help her female students to discuss and analyze topics that they might otherwise find too difficult or controversial. A reliance on personal narratives is also found in a grassroots feminist class described by McMahill (2001), where the teacher acts as a discussion facilitator, while Japanese women take charge of the learning process and class management, inviting or disinviting instructors and negotiating the class content with them. Both the teachers and the learners approach English as a tool that would allow Japanese women to resist their marginalization and give them an edge in the sexist job market. The class time is used to discuss feminist readings and analyze and critique gender ideologies and practices prevalent in the women's own lives. These analyses are often embedded in personal narratives, where individual experiences are used as a source of knowledge and authority.

Similar practices emerge in Frye's (1999) study that examines implementation of critical feminist pedagogy in a literacy class for immigrant low-income Latina women in the USA. Among the favorite forms of participation in this class were discussions and storytelling where the women could share experiences, give each other advice, and explore differences in age, race, social class, religious background, sexual orientation, national origin, educational background, and the use of Spanish. It is these explorations that engendered most meaningful— albeit heated and at times even angry—conversations, discussions, and activities where the participants learned to negotiate differences and to practice their own new voices. The comparison of their own stories to those of others allowed the women to see commonalities and disparities, to question the oppressive social and cultural forces which shaped their lives, and to perform new critical selves, constructing new possibilities and new visions for the future.

PROBLEMS AND DIFFICULTIES

Problems and difficulties in current research on gender in language education often stem from oversimplified assumptions about gender effects, inherited from earlier research. One research area plagued by such problems is the study of gender differences in the amount and quality of classroom interaction (Chavez, 2001; Julé, 2004; Losey, 1995; Shehadeh, 1999). These studies show that in some contexts teachers address boys more than girls, that boys and men may dominate classroom talk and mixed-gender interactions through interruptions and unsolicited responses, whereas girls and women profit more from same-gender group discussions, and that girls may be silenced by the classroom culture. These findings are undoubtedly important and informative, but they may also be misleading because they are based on problematic assumptions.

The first problematic assumption is the essential nature of men and women: boys and men are assumed to be dominant, whereas girls and women are seen as easily silenced. These assumptions may well hold true for certain contexts, but not without an explanation as to why particular men and women behave in particular ways in these contexts. Second, these studies commonly assume that a high amount of interaction is in itself a positive phenomenon that leads to higher achievement. In reality, it is quite possible that some students may speak up quite frequently but progress very little, if at all, whereas others, who contribute little to classroom discussions, for individual or cultural reasons, may succeed in accomplishing their own language learning goals. For instance, in a foreign language class studied by Sunderland (2004) boys received more attention from the teacher overall, but girls received more academically useful attention. These results suggest that studies of interactional patterns in foreign and second language classrooms should focus on the distribution of interactional opportunities beneficial for language learning, such as speaking practice or requests for clarification and feedback. Even more importantly, we should look beyond "donation" of equal classroom time, as this focus skirts "the structural problematic of who, in schools or universities, has the authority to speak, to critique, and to judge what is worthwhile (student) speech and critique" (Luke, 1992, p. 39).

Another area that often suffers from shortcomings is the study of textbook representations of gender. These studies show that language textbook stereotypes that place men in the public domain and women in the home had continued well into the 1980s, despite the appearance of nonsexist guidelines for educational materials. Since the 1990s, the situation has been steadily improving. Nevertheless, analyses of ESL and EFL texts published around the world (Sunderland, 1994) and of Greek, Russian, and Japanese textbooks published in the USA (Poulou, 1997; Rifkin, 1998; Shardakova and Pavlenko, 2004; Siegal and Okamoto 1996) reveal that many foreign and second language textbooks continue to reproduce gender biases. Siegal and Okamoto (1996) found that Japanese textbooks aimed at American students present highly stereotypical linguistic "norms" based on the hegemonic ideologies of class, language, and gender. Poulou (1997) demonstrated that Greek textbooks reproduce traditional gender roles through discursive roles assigned to men and women in dialogues.

Though important and informative, this line of inquiry is also overly narrow in that it does not document the uptake of materials by the students. Very few studies clarify the link between what is deemed to be gender biases or sexist representations, the role these representations play in the teaching process, and students' learning outcomes. Consequently, it is possible that biased representations may not affect the students at all. This lack of connection is documented in Pavlenko's (2005) historiographic study of gendered aspects of the Americanization movement in the early twentieth century. The study shows that Americanizers had distinct "hidden curricula" for men and women of different racial and ethnic origins: European-born men were offered instructional support for their citizenship exams, European-born women were offered "pots and pans" English and encouraged to remain at home, and Asian and Mexican immigrants were conceived of as a cheap labor force and were not encouraged to assimilate at all. Using oral histories, immigrant memoirs, and Americanization reports, the study showed that immigrant women mostly ignored Americanizers' messages. Even when they took the classes and used the texts in question, the women did not necessarily adopt the femininities imposed on them—rather, many were appropriating English to join the labor force.

Interesting questions with regard to the impact of perceived gender biases are raised in Durham's (1995) study of the controversy at Yale, where students filed a complaint stating that their textbook, *French in Action*, and the accompanying video were explicitly sexist and offensive. Durham argues that the students engaged in an ethnocentric reading of the text and—since their teachers did not attempt to counteract such a reading—lost an opportunity to access important dimensions of French culture. Their interpretation of depictions of the female body as sexist and of female silence as powerless was consistent with the principles of American academic feminism, but displayed a lack of knowledge and understanding of French discourses of feminism, sexuality, and gender. In other words, argues the researcher, they imposed their own culturally informed beliefs and stereotypes on what could be alternatively perceived as an ironic postmodernist feminist critique of Hollywood's sexual romance narrative and of conventional discourses of masculinity. These concerns are echoed in the work of Kramsch and von Hoene (1995, 2001) who argue that foreign language instruction in the USA promotes a biased and ethnocentric knowledge, or "single-voiced consciousness", and does not allow students to view themselves from the perspective of other cultures and thus acquire intercultural competence, or "multi-voiced consciousness."

FUTURE DIRECTIONS

To sum up, we have discussed four focal points where gender issues are central in language education: (i) access to linguistic resources; (ii) agency and (dis)investment into language learning; (iii) classroom interaction; (iv) textbooks and teaching practices. Throughout, we have

tried to highlight studies of educational contexts that respond to the
needs of marginalized learners, striving to (i) ensure equal access and
equal conditions for participation for all students, (ii) create curricula
that legitimize the students' daily realities and multilingual lives, and
(iii) approach language teaching from an intercultural and critical perspective which, on the one hand, engages students with cross-linguistic
and cross-cultural differences in gender ideologies, constructions and performances and, on the other, allows students to analyze how dominant
discourses of gender function to subordinate individuals.

Future research in this area should go beyond the issues of access,
interaction, and representation, and consider ways in which changes
in the global economy affect linguistic, educational, and labor markets
(Piller and Pavlenko, in press; see also Block, Language Education and
Globalization, Volume 1; Kalantzis and Cope, Language Education and
Multiliteracies, Volume 1). It also needs to pay close attention to
changes in gender ideologies and relationships in particular communities and to ways in which these changes affect learners' investments
into particular languages or resistance to them. Studies of foreign
and second language pedagogy should engage with the challenging
questions raised in the work of Durham (1995), Kramsch and von
Hoene (1995, 2001) and Pavlenko (2004), and particularly relevant
for North American contexts, often accused of linguistic imperialism:
What conceptions and discourses of gender do we aim at reflecting in
our texts and classes, the ones accepted in the target language communities or the ones that have currency in our own? And if we aim at
avoiding gender biases in our foreign language materials, are we
engaged in ethnocentric oversimplification, portraying the world on
our own terms and not providing our students with important linguistic
and cultural capital? On the other hand, if we are aiming at reflecting
gender discourses of other cultures—which may be quite different
from our own—what if in the process we offend or upset our students
who by now are fairly used to bland and noncontroversial teaching
materials? And what if, in our attempt to ensure the students' comfort,
we erase differences in cross-cultural understandings of gender—
will we simply end up teaching our students to speak English in a variety of languages?

*See Also: David Block: Language Education and Globalization
(Volume 1); Ben Rampton, et al.: Language, Class and Education
(Volume 1); Mary Kalantzis and Bill Cope: Language Education and
Multiliteracies (Volume 1); Alastair Pennycook: Critical Applied Lin-
guistics and Language Education (Volume 1)*

LANGUAGE EDUCATION AND GENDER 67

REFERENCES

Boxer, D. and Tyler, A.: 2004, 'Gender, sexual harassment, and the international teaching assistant', in B. Norton and A. Pavlenko (eds.), *Gender and English Language Learners*, TESOL Inc., Alexandria, VA, 29–42.

Burton, P.: 1994, 'Women and second-language use: An introduction', in P. Burton, K. Dyson, and Sh. Ardener (eds.), *Bilingual Women: Anthropological Approaches to Second-Language Use*, Berg, Oxford/Providence, 1–29.

Cameron, D.: 1992, *Feminism and Linguistic Theory* (second edition), McMillan, London.

Cameron, D.: 2005, 'Language, gender, and sexuality: Current issues and new directions', *Applied Linguistics* 26(4), 482–502.

Chavez, M.: 2001, *Gender in the Language Classroom*, McGraw Hill, Boston.

Cohen, T.: 2004, 'Critical feminist engagement in the EFL classroom: From supplement to staple', in B. Norton and A. Pavlenko (eds.), *Gender and English Language Learners*, TESOL Inc., Alexandria, VA, 155–169.

Durham, C.: 1995, 'At the crossroads of gender and culture: Where feminism and sexism intersect', *Modern Language Journal* 79(2), 153–165.

Eckert, P. and McConnell-Ginet, S.: 1992, 'Think practically and look locally: Language and gender as community-based practice', *Annual Review of Anthropology* 21, 461–490.

Frye, D.: 1999, 'Participatory education as a critical framework for immigrant women's ESL class', *TESOL Quarterly* 33(3), 501–513.

Gal, S.: 1978, 'Peasant men can't get wives: Language and sex roles in a bilingual community', *Language in Society* 7(1), 1–17.

Goldstein, T.: 1995, '"Nobody is talking bad": Creating community and claiming power on the production lines', in K. Hall and M. Bucholtz (eds.), *Gender Articulated: Language and the Socially Constructed Self*, Routledge, New York/London, 375–400.

Goldstein, T.: 2001, 'Researching women's language practices in multilingual practices', in A. Pavlenko, A. Blackledge, I. Piller, and M. Teutsch-Dwyer (eds.), *Multilingualism, Second Language Learning, and Gender*, Mouton de Gruyter, Berlin, 77–101.

Gordon, D.: 2004, '"I'm tired. You clean and cook." Shifting gender identities and second language socialization', *TESOL Quarterly* 38(3), 437–457.

Heller, M.: 1999, *Linguistic Minorities and Modernity: A Sociolinguistic Ethnography*, Longman, London/New York.

Heller, M.: 2001, 'Gender and public space in a bilingual school', in A. Pavlenko, A. Blackledge, I. Piller, and M. Teutsch-Dwyer (eds.), *Multilingualism, Second Language Learning, and Gender*, Mouton de Gruyter, Berlin, 257–282.

Hruska, B.: 2004, 'Constructing gender in an English dominant kindergarten: Implications for second language learners', *TESOL Quarterly* 38(3), 459–485.

Julé, A.: 2004, *Gender, Participation, and Silence in the Language Classroom: Sh-shushing the Girls*, Houndmills, Palgrave.

Kanno, Y.: 2003, *Negotiating Bilingual and Bicultural Identities: Japanese Returnees Betwixt Two Worlds*, Lawrence Erlbaum, Mahwah, NJ.

Kobayashi, Y.: 2002, 'The role of gender in foreign language learning attitudes: Japanese female students', attitudes toward English learning', *Gender and Education* 14(2), 181–197.

Kouritzin, S.: 2000, 'Immigrant mothers redefine access to ESL classes: Contradiction and ambivalence', *Journal of Multilingual and Multicultural Development* 21(1), 14–32.

Kramsch, C. and von Hoene, L.: 1995, 'The dialogic emergence of difference: Feminist explorations in foreign language learning and teaching', in D. Stanton and A. Stewart (eds.), *Feminisms in the Academy*, The University of Michigan Press, Ann Arbor, MI, 330–357.

Kramsch, C. and von Hoene, L.: 2001, 'Cross-cultural excursions: Foreign language study and feminist discourses of travel', in A. Pavlenko, A. Blackledge, I. Piller, and M. Teutsch-Dwyer (eds.), *Multilingualism, Second Language Learning, and Gender*, Mouton de Gruyter, Berlin, 283–306.

Lakoff, R.: 1975, *Language and Woman's Place*, Harper and Row, New York.

Losey, K.: 1995, 'Gender and ethnicity as factors in the development of verbal skills in bilingual Mexican American women', *TESOL Quarterly* 29(4), 635–661.

Luke, C.: 1992, 'Feminist politics in radical pedagogy', in C. Luke and J. Gore (eds.), *Feminisms and Critical Pedagogy*, Routledge, New York/London, 25–53.

Maltz, D. and Borker, R.: 1982, 'A cultural approach to male-female miscommunication', in J. Gumperz (ed.), *Language and Social Identity*, Cambridge University Press, Cambridge, 196–206.

McDonald, M.: 1994, 'Women and linguistic innovation in Brittany', in P. Burton, K. Dyson, and Sh. Ardener (eds.), *Bilingual Women: Anthropological Approaches to Second-Language Use*, Berg, Oxford/Providence, 85–110.

McKay, S. and Wong, S.: 1996, 'Multiple discourses, multiple identities: Investment and agency in second language learning among Chinese adolescent immigrant students', *Harvard Educational Review* 66(3), 577–608.

McMahill, Ch.: 2001, 'Self-expression, gender, and community: A Japanese feminist English class', in A. Pavlenko, A. Blackledge, I. Piller, and M. Teutsch-Dwyer (eds.), *Multilingualism, Second Language Learning, and Gender*, Mouton De Gruyter, Berlin, 307–344.

Miller, J.: 2003, *Audible Difference: ESL and Social Identity in Schools*, Multilingual Matters, Clevedon, UK.

Nelson, C.: 2004, 'Beyond straight grammar: Using lesbian/gay themes to explore cultural meanings', in B. Norton and A. Pavlenko (eds.), *Gender and English Language Learners*, TESOL Inc., Alexandria, VA, 15–28.

Norton, B.: 2000, *Identity and Language Learning: Gender, Ethnicity, and Educational Change*, Pearson Education, Harlow, UK.

Norton, B. and Pavlenko, A.: 2004, *Gender and English Language Learners*, TESOL Inc., Alexandria, VA.

Norton Peirce, B., Harper, H., and Burnaby, B.: 1993, 'Workplace ESL at Levi Strauss: 'Dropouts' speak out', *TESL Canada Journal* 10(2), 9–30.

Ohara, Y.: 2001, 'Finding one's voice in Japanese: A study of pitch levels of L2 users', in A. Pavlenko, A. Blackledge, I. Piller, and M. Teutsch-Dwyer (eds.), *Multilingualism, Second Language Learning, and Gender*, Mouton De Gruyter, Berlin, 231–254.

Oxford, R.: 1994, 'La différence continue ... Gender differences in second/foreign language learning styles and strategies', in J. Sunderland (ed.), *Exploring Gender:Questions and Implications for English Language Education*, Prentice Hall, London, 140–147.

Pavlenko, A.: 2004, 'Gender and sexuality in foreign and second language education: Critical and feminist approaches', in B. Norton and K. Toohey (eds.), *Critical Pedagogies and Language Learning*, Cambridge University Press, Cambridge, 53–71.

Pavlenko, A.: 2005, '"Ask each pupil about her methods of cleaning": Ideologies of language and gender in Americanization instruction (1900–1924)', *International Journal of Bilingual Education and Bilingualism* 8, 4, 275–297.

Piller, I. and Pavlenko, A.: in press, Globalization, gender, and multilingualism', in L. Volkmann and H. Decke-Cornill (eds.), *Gender Studies and Foreign Language Teaching*, Narr, Tübingen.

Piller, I. and Takahashi, K.: 2006, 'A passion for English: Desire and the language Market', in A. Pavlenko (ed.), *Bilingual Minds: Emotional Experience, Expression, and Representation*, Multilingual Matters, Clevedon, UK, 59–83.

Poulou, S.: 1997, 'Sexism in the discourse roles of textbook dialogues', *Language Learning Journal* 15, 68–73.

Rifkin, B.: 1998, 'Gender representation in foreign language textbooks: A case study of textbooks of Russian', *The Modern Language Journal* 82(2), 217–236.

Rivera, K.: 1999, 'Popular research and social transformation: A community-based approach to critical pedagogy', *TESOL Quarterly* 33(3), 485–500.

Saft, S. and Ohara, Y.: 2004, 'Promoting critical reflection about gender in EFL classes at a Japanese university', in B. Norton and A. Pavlenko (eds.), *Gender and English Language Learners*, TESOL Inc., Alexandria, VA, 143–154.

Shardakova, M. and Pavlenko, A.: 2004, 'Identity options in Russian textbooks', *Journal of Language, Identity, and Education* 3(1), 25–46.

Shehadeh, A.: 1999, 'Gender differences and equal opportunities in the ESL classroom', *ELT Journal* 53(4), 256–261.

Siegal, M.: 1996, 'The role of learner subjectivity in second language sociolinguistic competency: Western women learning Japanese', *Applied Linguistics* 17, 356–382.

Siegal, M. and Okamoto, Sh.: 1996, 'Imagined worlds: Language, gender, and sociocultural "norms" in Japanese language textbooks', in N. Warner, J. Ahlers, L. Bilmes, M. Oliver, S. Wertheim, and M. Chen (eds.), *Gender and Belief Systems. Proceedings of the Fourth Berkeley Women and Language Conference, April 9–12, 1996*, University of California, BWLG, Berkeley, CA, 667–678.

Simon-Maeda, A.: 2004, 'Transforming emerging feminist identities: A course on gender and language issues', in B. Norton and A. Pavlenko (eds.), *Gender and English Language Learners*, TESOL Inc., Alexandria, VA, 127–141.

Stevens, G.: 1986, 'Sex differences in language shift in the United States', *Sociology and Social Research* 71(1), 31–34.

Sunderland, J. (ed.): 1994, *Exploring Gender: Questions and Implications for English Language Education'*, Prentice Hall, New York/London.

Sunderland, J.: 2000, 'Issues of language and gender in second and foreign language Education', *Language Teaching* 33, 203–223.4,

Sunderland, J.: 2004, 'Classroom interaction, gender, and foreign language learning', in B. Norton and K. Toohey (eds.), *Critical Pedagogies and Language Learning*, Cambridge University Press, Cambridge, 222–241.

Tannen, D.: 1990, *You Just Don't Understand: Women and Men in Conversation*, Morrow, New York.

Thorne, B. and Henley, N.: 1975, *Language and Sex: Difference and Dominance*, Newbury House, Rowley, MA.

Toff, M.: 2002, 'A language of their own: Young Japanese women writing their life in English', *The Japan Association for Language Teachers* 26(6), 22–26.

Tran, T.: 1988, 'Sex differences in English language acculturation and learning strategies among Vietnamese adults aged 40 and over in the United States', *Sex Roles* 19(11–12), 747–758.

Warriner, D.: 2004, '"The days now is very hard for my family": The negotiation and construction of gendered work identities among newly arrived women refugees', *Journal of Language, Identity, and Education* 3(4), 279–294.

Willett, J.: 1995, 'Becoming first graders in an L2: An ethnographic study of L2 Socialization', *TESOL Quarterly* 29(3), 473–503.

BEN RAMPTON, ROXY HARRIS,
JAMES COLLINS AND JAN BLOMMAERT

LANGUAGE, CLASS AND EDUCATION

INTRODUCTION

The twentieth century saw some significant efforts to redistribute
wealth and income throughout most of the century, but over the last
25 years, material inequalities have persisted and in many ways
increased. Traditionally, 'class' has been a term used to define and analyse identities and relations between groups located at different levels
of the national socioeconomic hierarchy. In Britain, for example, class
'linked together and summarized... many aspects of any individual's
life' (Abercrombie and Warde, 2000, pp. 145–6): family background,
main source of income, cultural tastes and political associations. However, in spite of continued inequalities, the analytic utility and the cultural salience of social class have been drawn into question by a
number of shifts over the last 30 years: the socioeconomic changes
associated with globalisation, the decline of traditional collectivist politics, the emergence of gender, race and ethnicity as political issues
and the ascendance of the individual as consumer (Abercrombie and
Warde, 2000, p. 148).

Our contribution focuses on the connections between class stratification, education and language. We argue that class remains an important
concept in the analysis of stratification and its effects, and suggest that
it can be productively extended beyond the nation-state to issues of
language and inequality in colonial and post-colonial settings. We
begin with some comments on the definition of social class, clarifying
its relation to other axes of inequality (race, ethnicity, gender, generation, etc.). Then we provide a sketch of debates about language, education and class leading up to the 1980s, and point to similarities of the
dynamics in both 'First' and 'Third World' countries. After that, we
consider processes involved in the 'retreat' from class analysis over
the last 15–20 years.

DEFINING SOCIAL CLASS

The term 'class' points to a very broad principle of organization in capitalist societies, a principle of inequality ('stratification') structuring the
distribution of resources, both material and symbolic, a source of domination, conflict and suffering. As with other 'principles of organization'

S. May and N. H. Hornberger (eds), Encyclopedia of Language and Education,
2nd Edition, Volume 1: Language Policy and Political Issues in Education, 71–81.
©2010 Springer Science+Business Media LLC.

(e.g. race, gender), class is lived with varying degrees of awareness and expression. It may be mutely experienced or given full-throated articulation; it may be a key to self-understanding, group mobilization and society-wide struggles for power, or it may be denied and displaced—personally, socially and politically. As lived, class is always entangled with other forms of social being and social consciousness.

'Social being' and 'social consciousness'—terms introduced by Marx and Engels in *The German Ideology*—merit elaboration (cf. Thompson, 1978, p. 18). 'Social being' refers to material conditions, ordinary experience and everyday discourses, activities and practices—the 'primary realities' of practical activity. 'Social consciousness' refers to secondary or 'meta-level' representation developed by participants and analysts: ideologies, images and discourses *about* social groups. When focussing on the primary realities of social being/practical activity—the routine interaction of embodied individuals in real world tasks—singling out class as an influence distinct from gender, race and lots of other social categories is likely to be difficult. However, at the level of 'social consciousness'/ secondary representations, there are clear differences between discourses *about* class, ethnicity, gender and generation, etc.—they have different histories and direct attention to different social processes and arenas. Discourses about class, gender, race and ethnicity differ substantially in the kinds of solidarity and opposition they propose, and in the ways in which the inequalities they are associated with are described, challenged and defended. Therefore, while 'class' as a social category refers to lived relations surrounding social relations of production, exchange, distribution and consumption, 'race' and 'ethnicity' are used to explain a highly complex set of territorial relationships involving conquest, migration and the development of nation-states (Bradley, 1996, pp. 19–20). In fact the play between social being and social consciousness, between everyday experience and its secondary representation, is often a central issue in politics, with different interests promoting rival accounts of the processes, relations and identities shaping social life. The 'being'/'consciousness' distinction partly resembles the relationship between objective social structure on the one hand, and subjecthood and identity on the other, the former referring to patterns and processes of stratification, and the latter to claims, attributions and denials around 'groupness'. The implications of both distinctions are threefold: (i) they provide a rationale for including 'class' and 'race' in the same discussion, as different ways of construing inequality and domination in (objective) 'social being'; (ii) they mean that analysis is itself part of the ideological debate and (iii) they remind us that systematic inequalities in the distribution of hardship, pain and pleasure do not disappear just because people stop talking about them in the ways they used to.

EARLY DEVELOPMENTS: CLASS, LANGUAGE AND EDUCATION UNTIL THE 1980s

The Industrialized West: the UK and USA

Nineteenth and early twentieth centuries: The 'industrial revolution' of the nineteenth century shaped the modern working classes in much of Western Europe and North America. It coincided with the heyday of nationalism, the period of building and consolidating modern nation-states. And in the nationalist tool kit, schooling and the promulgation of standard languages were important elements, especially through schooled literacy. Standard or 'legitimate' languages were historically resources of metropolitan elites, of reforming middle classes, but in an ideological manoeuvre described by Marx, what was particular—the language of a literate middle class—was presented as universal, as 'the language of the nation'. In Britain and the USA, schooling, literacy and the teaching of Standard English were seen by many education activists and reformers as the means to self-improvement and social harmony—they would ameliorate social differences, replace 'seditious' with 'helpful' literacies, and in general serve as an equalising and unifying influence. However in actuality, the nineteenth- and twentieth-century provisioning of universal education and literacy was the product of struggle, a process of exclusion and hierarchisation much more than equalizing (Collins and Blot, 2003).

Rather late in Britain, universal public education was established in the 1870s, more than half a century after the upheavals of the industrial revolution and much class-based political conflict, and perhaps for this reason, the relation between standard and non-standard languages was always understood in class terms. In the USA in the 1820–1840s, the 'Common Schools' were one of the earliest systems of universal schooling, predating a good deal of the industrializing of the nation as well as the Civil War. However, for much of the nineteenth and twentieth centuries, they were not universal. Before the Civil War, southern states made educating African-American slaves a crime, and after the short-lived reconstruction, they established the infamous Jim Crow system of two-tiered education that lasted until the 1960s. Throughout much of this period, if they were formally educated, Native Americans were not part of the public school system, and with its working-class majorities formed through enslavement (African Americans), through expropriation and containment (Native Americans), through military appropriation (Mexican Americans) as well as the better known immigration, schooling was seen more as a project of ethnic and racial assimilation than of social class harmonizing (e.g. Nasaw, 1979). So typically in the USA, the relationship between standard and non-standard languages (and the educational problems attributed thereto) has been understood in race and ethnic terms.

1960s–1980s: In the decades after World War II, it was clear in Britain that public education had not eradicated class difference, and that non-standard speech had not disappeared. During the 1960s and 1970s, language took over from IQ as an explanation of social stratification and it was analysed by sociolinguists as a constitutive element contributing to class differentiation in education. In the USA, the failure of the school-based equalizing project was seen differently. There were references to 'disadvantaged' and 'low-income' children, but class was regularly obscured by the prominence of ethnicity and race during the era of Civil Rights mobilization (Collins, 1988). But whether seen as class or race/ethnicity-that-happened-to-be-working-class, there were two major approaches in research on language and inequality in education, one orienting more to 'social being' and the other more to 'social consciousness'.

The former emphasized the role that everyday discourse played in the cultural reproduction of class inequality. In one strand of this work, research focussed on the home and argued that traditional patterns of language use produced communicative dispositions, which influenced people's performance at school and opportunities in life. The home practices of subordinate groups were seen as leading to subordinate identities/positions in cycles of reproduction (Bernstein, 1971; Bourdieu and Passeron, 1977; Heath, 1983). In the other strand, research focussed on schools and argued that conventional classroom discourse was inhospitable to the speech styles of students from subordinated communities (Philips, 1972).

The second major approach stressed the part that language ideologies and attitudes to grammar and accent played in the production of subordinate identities. Sociolinguists and education researchers argued that teachers picked up on dialect features, that they held lower expectations for children with working-class accents, and that the lower achievement of these children was thus the outcome of sociolinguistically tuned 'self-fulfilling prophecies' (Edwards, 1976; Labov, 1972). On another tack, it was argued that the schools' standard language ideologies made working-class people think that their subordinate position was justified (Bourdieu and Passeron, 1977; Hymes, 1996, p. 84; Labov, 1972).

However particularly when class, rather than race or ethnicity, was in focus, neither of these two approaches attributed any political agency to the subordinate groups they studied. In the first perspective, the working class was the unknowing victim of either its own or the dominant culture, and in the second, it was the victim of class prejudice and standard language ideology. Neither approach recognized the skilful ways in which people blend dominant and subordinate varieties of language (Gumperz, 1982; Rampton, 1995), or focussed on the ways in which language use was integrated with both family life, morality, sense of person and institutional encounters (Lareau, 2003). This neglect of class agency was partly due to 'class' being treated as a structural category rather than a group identification (Ortner, 1991, pp. 168–169). Structural and statistical notions of class were ascendant in research, and informants were allocated to classes by analysts on the basis of fact-sheet variables like 'occupation' and 'level of education'. When studies used ethnographic methods, class was cast as an abstract and macroscopic process, at some remove from lived cultural experience— for the latter, researchers used other labels and focussed on local networks rather than societal groupings (Eckert, 2000; Ohmann, 1982).

Colonial and Post-Colonial Settings

In some respects, colonial settings resembled the industrialized west. Systems of education-and-language were/are stratified, class-specific linguistic resources were/are presented as the general idiom of nation and modernity, and education was/is meant to improve the lower orders, here seen in race and ethnic terms as 'natives' rather than 'lower classes'. However, there were also substantial differences. The hierarchies were more sharply drawn, education was more clearly exclusionary, and debates about inequality and difference referred to distinct languages rather than to differences within a language.

The colonial period: The class analysis of colonial societies came very late and remained the province of left wing movements. That does not mean that there were no class politics or class effects in colonial societies—these were racially organized societies with extremely deep class rifts.

Colonial education systems addressed 'the natives' ('Indians', 'Negroes', etc.) rather than 'the lower classes', and to the extent that emancipatory goals were formulated, colonial education sought to 'civilize the natives', rescuing them from ignorance (and sin), inserting them into the small emergent class of schooled workers and clerks needed to support the colonial administrative, industrial or religious complex. Education was not aimed at self-liberation or self-improvement, nor seen as a tool for making the colonial populations less dependent on the colonial apparatuses. It was a highly selective and exclusionary add-on to the colonial enterprise. There was little formal education beyond primary school levels, there was tight control by the colonial authorities, and this control intensified at higher levels of education (Mazrui, 1978). This created a strongly stratified sociolinguistic market, in which control over particular linguistic resources was an immediate result of access to higher levels of education—for example, English equalled elite identity. In this way, the colonial system established a class-sensitive linguistic pyramid, in which language pointed towards (non-)membership of particular strata in society and in which the strata became more prestigious the closer they came to the centres of colonial power (Blommaert, 1999).

The post-colonial context: After colonialism, the nationalist leaderships consisted of people who had been successful in colonial education, experiencing post-school education in the metropolitan languages and centres of the empire. However, their very real self-interest as a class was generally disguised by nationalist fervor immediately post-independence, and in this atmosphere, a massive expansion of educational access, rather than system change, was often treated as the top priority. In this way, the linguistic hierarchies of colonialism were reproduced and extended, and the retention of colonial languages as media of instruction and literacy was legitimated (i) in terms of national unity in ethnically divided societies, (ii) as the most efficient use of economic resources, (iii) in terms of available teacher resources and printed materials and (iv) as symbolising modernization and progress (Fardon and Furniss, 1994).

At the same time, these leaderships often maximized the opportunities for their own children to acquire prestige varieties of languages like English and French (through their use in the home, at pre-school, and in university education in the former colonial centres), and to become part of a global elite with mobile, well-paid employment. The rest of their populations have either become more or less marginal (depending on the overall wealth of their countries), or have accessed local varieties of the powerful global languages by migrating en-masse to the cities of the former colonial centres where they have joined the low-wage sectors of the economy, becoming members of the local working classes. There, the schooling of their children generates new versions of the old debates on language, class and education, though once again, the class element is normally misread or reconfigured as an ethnic minority problem, with the main emphasis on transition to European languages as the key to educational achievement.

Summary of Class, Language and Education until the 1980s

Language and class were conspicuous educational issues in countries like the UK and USA up until the mid/late 1980s, although racialized stratification in the USA and the distortions of colonialism and the post-colonial system often camouflaged class, replacing it with a preoccupation with inequalities of race/ethnicity. In the era of the new globalized economy, mass migration and population mobility, analysis without a sense of class has become both increasingly common and increasingly inadequate. We turn now to reasons for the retreat from class in official, popular and academic discourses.

CURRENT DEVELOPMENTS: THE DISCURSIVE ERASURE OF CLASS SINCE THE 1980s

Beginning in the 1980s, Thatcherism in the UK and Reaganism in the USA were successful conservative movements that attacked social democratic (class-oriented) policies and politics (public ownership of housing and transport, social welfare provisions, trade unions) and promoted private ownership, individual choice and ideologies of merit over concerns with equality. By arguing that social position is due to individual merit (or lack thereof), and not to advantages or disadvantages perpetrated by the institutional systems, these 'neo-liberal' movements discursively discredited the notion of class, while themselves being savvy orchestrations of ruling class power and working-class dissatisfaction. At the same time, the 'politics of redistribution' was being displaced by a 'politics of recognition' rooted in the feminist and anti-racist movements of the 1960s and 1970s (Fraser, 1995). These advanced the causes of women and ethnoracial minorities in numerous institutional and public arenas, but did not prioritize the challenge for state power. The politics of redistribution occupied the traditional terrain of class, combating economic inequalities and poverty, but the politics of recognition targeted cultural and legal evaluation structures, stigma and discrimination based on ethnicity, gender and sexuality.

These shifts seemed profound for the popular apprehension of injustice, and workplace exploitation (a basic issue in class politics) became much harder to articulate and oppose. In education in the USA and UK, reports and policies since the 1980s have stressed the importance of 'maintaining standards' and promoting general-purpose literacy skills, but have detached these from any analysis of class inequalities (e.g. the Kingman Report on language awareness in the UK, 1988, and the Reagan-commissioned 'A Nation At Risk', 1983 in the USA). More recently, the UK's 'New Literacy Strategy' and the USA's 'No Child Left Behind' programme share a belief that literacy skills in the standard language can be disseminated by formal pedagogy closely monitored by the national government, but they operate with a very narrow conception of literacy and standard language, and they largely ignore the economic resources necessary to begin the change they prescribe (Allington, 2002; Rothstein, 2004).

In research, class analysis has generally been less prominent in the USA than the UK, for reasons already identified (Bradley, 1996,

p. 75; Ortner, 1991, p. 64). In addition in the USA, anthropology has
been much more influential in the study of education than it has been
in the UK, where sociology has played a more important role: '[f]or
the (American) anthropologist the classroom is the site of cultural differences, often ethnic in origin, and the teacher an agent of cultural
imposition. For the (British) sociologist the frame of reference is a
class-based social structure, in which teachers and pupils alike are subject to the everyday disciplines of work' (Delamont and Atkinson,
1995, p. 34). However, during the late 1980s and 1990s in Britain, language and education research lost much of this traditional interest in
class. This was partly in line with growing social scientific interest
in human agency—in the 1960s and 1970s, research had over-
emphasized the structural and normative dimensions of class, neglect-
ing the agentive, performative, interactive aspects of class-as-lived
(Ohmann, 1982), and as a result, 'class' felt too deterministic a concept
for the 1990s. However, at the same time, sociolinguists interested in
education refocused on the new populations from the ex-colonies (see
earlier), and in doing so, they drew their inspiration from the ethnography of communication in North America, with its anthropological roots
and pre-occupation with ethnicity, rather than from the more class-
focussed, sociological ethnographies produced in Britain in the 1970s
and 1980s (e.g. Willis, 1977). In their socioeconomic positioning, the
ethnic minority students they studied might be working class, but
theoretical explications tended to dwell primarily on ethnicity and race.

FUTURE DIRECTIONS: THE CONTINUING
REALITIES OF STRATIFICATION

As is now widely recognized, metadiscourses about social groups and
categories form part of the dialectical processes through which specific
groups and categories are constituted, reproduced and/or contested.
Whether and how class is defined is a significant element in what class
is, and this adds to concern about the reification of class in the 1970s
and 1980s, about the retreat from class analysis in research in the
1990s, and about the failure to understand the connections between
class, gender and ethnicity. In our view, what used to be called 'class'
in rather totalizing ways can be usefully seen as the patterns of stratification that emerge in social systems in which a range of differences
come to mean inequality within schemes and hierarchies of value linked
to the hard economy. Class in this sense is a structuring principle, tied
in some way to modes of production and divisions of labor in a social
system, but with considerable room for interaction with other structuring principles. Thus, other widely used parameters—gender, race,

ethnicity, linguistic difference—may display the same processes of stratification as what was previously called 'class'.

The ascendancy of neo-liberal doctrine and governance since the 1980s may have undermined the dominance and legitimacy of discourses of class, but it has been accompanied by a widely acknowledged increase in socioeconomic inequality, both within nations and internationally (Rothstein, 2004). Exactly how we think about that inequality in language and education remains an open question, but to facilitate further reflection, we conclude by listing some of the continuing realities of stratification.

1. Immigrant minority populations often find themselves in run down areas and schools, and situations of relative poverty, and though the public discourse might focus on ethnicity and gender, factors traditionally associated with class still affect educational achievement in the UK (Gillborn and Mirza, 2000).

2. Survey studies of language variation may have suggested that regional difference between non-standard dialects may have diminished in the UK, and there is also evidence that British Received Pronunciation has lost quite a lot of its cultural status. However, no one suggests that style-shifting between standard and vernacular speech varieties has disappeared, and it is this that displays a class-habitus in Bourdieu's terms. Indeed, what evidence there is suggests that as the children and grandchildren of immigrants grow up using English, they acquire both class-marked features and a style-shifting capacity tuned to the sociolinguistic stratification traditionally linked to class hierarchy (Harris, 2003; Rampton, 2006, Part III).

3. There has been quite a lot of both UK and US work on the ways in which minority speech features are taken up by young whites (Creole, Panjabi, African-American Vernacular English, etc.), but the manner and extent to which this happens is extensively influenced by actual familiarity with the inheritors of these languages, which is itself extensively shaped by socioeconomic positioning (Cutler, 1999; Rampton, 1995).

4. Recent survey research on the stratifying dynamics of class and ethnicity in US education (Rothstein, 2004) demonstrates the cognitive and non-cognitive consequences of basic inequalities in resources such as income, housing, health care and nutrition, as well as linguistic habits and personality traits. This research is complemented by Lareau's (2003) long-term in-depth ethnographic work on class, race and language socialization, and this concludes that class is the most significant dimension in the 'unequal childhoods' of urban and suburban children.

See Also: *François Grin: The Economics of Language Education (Volume 1); Naz Rassool: Language Policy and Education in Britain (Volume 1)*

REFERENCES

Abercrombie, N. and Warde, A. 2000, with Deem, R., Penna, S., Soothill, K., Urry, J., Sayer, A. and Walby, S.: (third edition), *Contemporary British Society* Polity, Oxford.
Allington, R. (ed.): 2002, *Big Brother and the National Reading Curriculum*, Heinemann, Portsmouth, NH.
Bernstein, B.: 1971, *Class, Codes and Control Volume 1*, RKP, London.
Blommaert, J.: 1999, *State Ideology and Language in Tanzania*, Köppe, Cologne.
Bourdieu, P. and Passeron, J.-C.: 1977, *Reproduction in Education, Society and Culture* (second edition), Sage, London.
Bradley, H.: 1996, *Fractured Identities: Changing Patterns of Inequality*, Polity Press, Cambridge.
Collins, J.: 1988, 'Language and class in minority education', *Anthropology and Education Quarterly* 19(4), 299–326.
Collins, J. and Blot, R.: 2003, *Literacy and Literacies*, Cambridge University Press, Cambridge.
Cutler, C.: 1999, 'Yorkville crossing: White teens, hip hop and African American English', *Journal of Sociolinguistics* 3(4), 428–442.
Delamont, S. and Atkinson, P.: 1995, *Fighting Familiarity: Essays on Education and Ethnography*, Hampton Press, Cresskill, NJ.
Eckert, P.: 2000, *Linguistic Variation as Social Practice*, Blackwell, Oxford.
Edwards, A.: 1976, *Class, Culture, and Language*, Heinemann, London.
Fardon, R. and Furniss, G. (eds.): 1994, *African Languages, Development, and the State*, Routledge, London.
Fraser, N.: 1995, 'From redistribution to recognition: Dilemmas of justice in a 'post-socialist' age', *New Left Review* 212, 68–92.
Gillborn, D. and Mirza, H.: 2000, *Educational Inequality: Mapping Race, Class and Gender—A Synthesis of research evidence*, Office for Standards in Education, London.
Gumperz, J.: 1982, *Discourse Strategies*, Cambridge University Press, Cambridge.
Harris, R.: 2003, 'Language and new ethnicities: Multilingual youth and diaspora', *Working Papers in Urban Language and Literacies 22*, King's College London, London. http: //www.kcl.ac.uk/education/wpull.html
Heath, S.: 1983, *Ways with Words*, Cambridge University Press, Cambridge.
Hymes, D.: 1996, *Ethnography, Linguistics, Narrative Inequality*, Taylor & Francis, London.
Labov, W.: 1972, *Language in the Inner City*, University of Pennsylvania Press, Philadelphia.
Lareau, A.: 2003, *Unequal Childhoods: Class, Race, and Family Life*, University of California, Berkeley.
Mazrui, A.: 1978, *Political Values and the Educated Class in Africa*, University of California Press, Berkeley.
Nasaw, D.: 1979, *Schooled to Order*, Oxford University Press, New York.
Ohmann, R.: 1982, 'Some reflections on language and class', *College English* 47, 675–679.
Ortner, S.: 1991, 'Reading America: Preliminary notes on class and culture', in R. Fox (ed.), *Recapturing Anthropology*, School of American Research Press, Santa Fe, 164–189.

Philips, S.U.: 1972, 'Participant structures and communicative competence: Warm springs Indian children in community and classroom', in C. Cazden, D. Hymes, and V. John (eds.), *Functions of Language in the Classroom*, Teachers College Press, New York, 370–94.

Rampton, B.: 1995, *Crossing: Language and Ethnicity among Adolescents*, Longman, London.

Rampton, B.: 2006, *Language in Late Modernity: Interaction in an Urban School*, Cambridge University Press, Cambridge.

Rothstein, R.: 2004, *Class and Schools*, Teachers College Press, New York.

Thompson, E.P.: 1978, *The Poverty of Theory and Other Essays*, Merlin, London.

Willis, P.: 1977, *Learning to Labour*, Saxon House, Farnborough.

FRANÇOIS GRIN

THE ECONOMICS OF LANGUAGE EDUCATION

INTRODUCTION

Because the economics of language education, as a field of investigation, differs somewhat from most of the scholarly work on language and education presented in this volume, this entry does not offer a descriptive or historical account of research, but instead emphasises the presentation of analytical concepts along with their meaning, their function and the relationships between them.

The following section "Definitions and Scope" provides a general framework that explains the position of the economics of language education with respect to three closely related areas, namely education economics, language economics and policy evaluation, before introducing key concepts and analytical distinctions. The section on "Major Contributions" presents the application of human capital theory to foreign language (FL) skills, which makes up the bulk of the literature on the economics of language education. The section on "Problems and Difficulties" turns to important issues of resource distribution. The section on "Challenges" addresses a set of unsolved issues in the field. The last section, on "Future Directions" discusses likely developments in the light of policy needs.

We shall not examine the teaching of children's mother tongue when the latter also is the dominant or official language (e.g. the teaching of French to children of francophone families in France), because the corresponding economic issues are analytically very different from those that arise in the context of foreign language teaching, which is the focus of this entry.

DEFINITIONS AND SCOPE: ALLOCATION AND DISTRIBUTION OF RESOURCES IN LANGUAGE EDUCATION

The economics of language education is a specific area of inquiry that may be approached from different disciplinary perspectives. Starting out from mainstream economics, one would generally use the well-established conceptual and methodological apparatus of education economics as a stepping stone (Johnes and Johnes, 2004). This strategy, however, may confine the examination to a relatively narrow range of

S. May and N. H. Hornberger (eds), Encyclopedia of Language and Education,
2nd Edition, Volume 1: Language Policy and Political Issues in Education, 83–93.
©2010 *Springer Science+Business Media LLC.*

84 FRANÇOIS GRIN

issues, particularly applications of human capital theory to FL learning. However, FL education raises economic questions that go far beyond human capital investment, because it is also a key component of language policy. For this reason, this entry approaches the economics of FL education through the distinct (and less institutionally established) subfield of language economics (Grin, 1996).

Language economics studies the mutual relationships between linguistic and economic variables. What matters, however, is not their mere co-occurrence, but the fact that they actually influence each other. In this perspective, the use of various languages at work, for example, does not per se constitute a relevant research object unless it has an impact on the economic processes at hand. The focus of attention may be either an economic or a linguistic variable. For example, an economist of language may investigate whether a company can increase its profits (the dependent *economic* variable) by advertising its goods in the local language even on a very small market. Reciprocally, she may examine language maintenance among immigrants (the dependent *linguistic* variable) and assess whether the pattern observed reflects labour market participation. However, particularly since the mid 1990s, language economics has been paying increasing attention to language policy issues (Grin, 2003). Even if none of the variables involved in the selection, design and implementation of a given language policy explicitly refers to economic activity, choosing an appropriate policy requires weighing the advantages and drawbacks of the options considered. This represents a very direct application of economic analysis because it is, at heart, a theory of how choices are made, and this rationale also applies to the economics of language education. Therefore, the economics of language education largely coincides with an in-depth application of policy evaluation techniques to language education, in the broader context of language policy (on the links with language policy, see also Tollefson, Language Planning in Education, Volume 1).

The rationale of policy evaluation is straightforward and can be characterised, in the case of *ex ante* evaluation, by the following steps: define policy alternatives, identify their consequences, translate the latter into advantages and drawbacks, compute the 'net value' of each alternative by subtracting drawbacks from advantages expressed in terms of a comparable unit of measurement, and select the policy with the highest net value. Policy evaluation casts the net wide and should in principle take account of advantages (or 'benefits') and drawbacks (or 'costs') in the broadest sense. More specifically, proper policy evaluation is not interested in financial or material advantages and drawbacks only; non-material and symbolic values are just as relevant. This is why the distinction often made in other disciplines between 'instrumental' and 'intrinsic' values or motivations has little analytical relevance in economics, although it does make a difference at the empirical level, when these effects have to be evaluated (see Major Contributions).

The costs and benefits of each policy option can often be interpreted as inputs and outputs respectively. It is safe to assume that all other things being equal, social actors prefer efficient policies, that is, those that yield more output (benefit) per unit of input (cost). This generates a useful set of criteria for comparing options. In the field of education, however, it is essential to make a distinction between *internal* and *external* efficiency.

Internal efficiency refers to processes that occur *within* the educational sphere. In the particular case of FL education, the FL skills acquired normally play the role of the output, while the inputs comprise all the resources used to teach those skills, taking account of the way in which they are used (teacher and learner time, textbooks, pedagogical approach, etc.). Internal efficiency evaluations are not specific to education economics, and are carried out in various areas of educational research; there is, however, surprisingly little empirical work focusing on the internal efficiency of FL teaching.

External efficiency, by contrast, starts out from the assumption that education is not pursued for its own sake, but in order to secure benefits *outside* of the education system. External efficiency evaluation is crucial (and arguably more important than internal efficiency evaluation) because it addresses the questions 'what?' (i.e. 'what FLs should we teach?') and 'why'('for what reasons?'), whereas internal effectiveness evaluation focuses on the question 'how?' ('how best to teach FLs?'). For this reason, we shall now concentrate on external efficiency evaluation.

Some of these benefits may be *market related*, such as higher earnings, access to more desirable jobs, etc.; other benefits are of the *non-market* kind, such as direct access, thanks to language competence, to other cultures and the people carrying them. In usual practice, however, the external efficiency of FL skills is only assessed in terms of market value (more precisely, through earnings differentials; see section "Major Contributions"), because the necessary data can be collected relatively easily through surveys or, in a favourable statistical context like Canada, retrieved from the decennial census. By contrast, the data required to assess the existence and magnitude of non-market benefits are difficult to collect, and this has apparently never been done in large-scale surveys.

Whether of the market or of the non-market kind, the benefits and costs of education, and hence the more or less efficient relationship between them, may be evaluated at the *private* or *social* level. The private level reflects the conditions confronting the typical or average person, whereas the social level concerns benefits and costs for society as a whole. In mainstream education economics, defining social benefits and costs as the simple sum, across members of society, of individual benefits and costs, is usually an acceptable simplification. In the case of FL education, however, such a procedure is less satisfactory, because of one specific feature of language, namely, the fact that language learning gives rise to what is known, in economic theory, as 'externalities', which are best explained with a hypothetical example. As more people learn a given language (say, language L), the value of knowing this language is affected. It is commonly assumed that this effect can only be positive (De Swaan, 2002; van Parijs, 2004) because people who already speak L gain additional potential interlocutors. However, the effect can work both ways, because this amounts to an increase in the overall supply of L-language skills, which would lower their value on the labour market. Which of the two effects dominates under various conditions remains an unsolved issue, and the attending theoretical difficulties this raises have not been fully explored. Consequently, empirical results on the social value of FL education must be interpreted with caution, even within the better-known market values (see section "Problems and Difficulties").

Empirical work therefore yields estimates of the labour market value, to the average person and/or to society (under the limitations just pointed out), of competence in various FLs. The standard policy recommendation would be to prioritise the teaching of FLs that give rise to the highest returns, because these are taken as a good indicator of the usefulness of those skills. FL teaching can therefore be seen as an efficient allocation of resources by one generation that pays for it while the beneficiaries are from a younger generation.

However, policy evaluation is not confined to *allocative* efficiency. It also assesses competing scenarios in terms of their respective fairness. Since all policy choices make some people better off and other worse off, they have a *distributive* effect. One important criterion for choosing among scenarios, therefore, is whether these distributive effects are morally and socially acceptable, and if not, if those who 'win' from a policy can offer appropriate compensation, in money or otherwise, to the 'losers'. Such questions tie into discussions of social justice applied to language policy choices (van Parijs, 2002), and are discussed in the section "Problems and Difficulties".

Combining the four analytical distinctions just made, we can use a diagram to provide of bird's-eye view of the scope of the economics of language education (Figure 1).

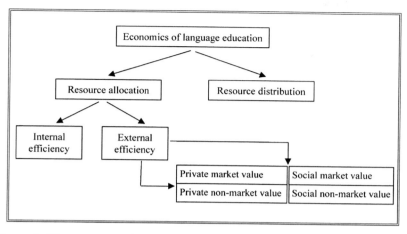

Figure 1 The structure of the economics of foreign language education

MAJOR CONTRIBUTIONS: RATES OF RETURN ON FOREIGN LANGUAGE SKILLS

The estimation of the market rates of return on FL skills makes up the main part of published work in the economics of language education even though, as we have just seen, this captures only one side of their value. These rates of return may be estimated at the level of the individual or of society. In either case, two main research orientations can be identified. Let us first discuss them in the case of private returns, which accrue to individuals.

The first orientation studies the value to immigrants of learning the dominant language of their new country of residence. In this case, 'FL' must be understood as a language other than the speaker's mother tongue or L1, although it is the main and/or official language of the country of residence. Most of the empirical work uses samples of immigrants to the USA, occasionally Australia, Canada, Israel, or Germany (see e.g. Chiswick, 1999, 2002; Chiswick and Miller, 1995). In general, their (unsurprising) finding is that competence in the country's dominant or official language yields statistically significant advantages to immigrants, although this gain is less pronounced in so-called language enclaves where immigrants are more concentrated (Bloom and Grenier, 1996).

The second line of research examines the rates of return on skills in a language which, apart from not being the actor's mother tongue, is also other than the main language in the actor's place of residence. This case is therefore closer to the standard notion of FL. A further distinction can be made between two types of cases. The first is that of the 'other' language(s) in multilingual countries with a de facto and/or officially enshrined territorial distribution of languages, for example English in Québec (Vaillancourt, 1996), French in German-speaking Switzerland (Grin, 1999), or Russian in Western Ukraine (Kastoukievitch, 2003). The second is that of truly foreign languages like English in Switzerland (Grin, 1999) or Luxembourg (Klein, 2004).

Across these various situations, results show that FL skills can be highly valuable and significantly add to a person's labour income, although major variations are observed depending on various elements of context and on the FL concerned. Of course, in any of the situations discussed in this section, it is essential to disentangle the effect of FL skills from that of other determinants of income, particularly when the latter are likely to be correlated with the presence of FL skills. The typical response to this challenge is to apply multivariate analysis to estimate language-augmented earnings equations (Psacharopoulos and Patrinos, 2004), usually with ordinary least squares. Applying this technique generally confirms the profitability of FL skills after even controlling for (at least) education and work experience. This nevertheless requires detailed and reliable individual (as opposed to grouped) data. Suitable databases are rare, which probably explains why this has only been done for relatively few countries. The information needed includes, at the very least, each person's labour income (often using after-tax earnings), education, gender, age and/or experience, L1 and, of course, FL skills. Depending on the degree of detail of the data base, it is sometimes possible to distinguish the impact of productive versus receptive and of oral versus written skills in the language concerned, and to differentiate between basic, advanced and native-like competence. It is also desirable to include additional information, in particular individual respondents' economic sector of activity, hierarchical position at work, and geographical location. Interested readers can find more practical detail on the procedure in Vaillancourt (1985) or Grin (1999).

The type of estimates described so far are, in fact, *net earnings differentials*, in the sense that they attempt to single out the effect of FL skills on earnings, *net* of the effect of other variables like education. They are often called 'rates of return' because FL skills can be seen, in line with human capital theory, as an investment made at a certain time and yielding a certain return in the form of higher earnings later in life. However, estimating rates of return in the strict sense requires taking account of the time lag between the investment and the reaping of the corresponding benefits. Though this is usually not done in the type of estimates presented so far, it is an essential part of the calculation of *social* rates of return, whose goal is to assess the value, for society as a whole, of teaching FLs through the education system.

Social benefits are generally assumed to be the sum of private benefits; there again, given the absence of data on non-market benefits, calculations are usually confined to market benefits in the form of earnings differentials. However, calculations will be based on pre-tax instead of after-tax earnings. Furthermore, earnings differentials accruing in the distant future are worth less than those that appear immediately, and they must therefore be discounted. FL teaching costs are then deducted from the sum, over a person's lifetime, of discounted pre-tax earnings differentials. This requires additional information on public expenditure on foreign language teaching. Typically, educational statistics do not offer subject-based expenditure accounting, which means that approximations of the expenditure specifically devoted to FL teaching must be derived from data on enrolments, time endowments for FLs, and per capita spending, for successive cycles in the education system. To our knowledge, social rates of return on FL skills have only been estimated for Switzerland, where they are shown to be positive for French (in German- and Italian-speaking Switzerland), German (in French- and Italian-speaking Switzerland) and English (across the country) (Grin, 1999).

The general policy implication of high rates of return (whether private or, if possible, social) on FL skills is that it is efficient to allocate resources to FL education.

PROBLEMS AND DIFFICULTIES: LANGUAGE EDUCATION AND LINGUISTIC JUSTICE

The estimation of rates of return responds to a concern for the efficient allocation of resources (even if it focuses on the market dimensions of value, largely ignoring, for lack of data, its non-market dimensions). Let us now turn to matters of resource distribution, which raise questions of social justice.

Any policy choice, including in language of education, will tend to make some groups better off and other groups worse off. Theorists have considered different criteria for deciding whether this redistribution of resources is just or not (Arnsperger and van Parijs, 2003). These effects can be considered socially acceptable if it improves the lot of those who were worst off, if those previously better off enjoyed unjust advantages, or if the policy gives rise to sufficient net gains in the aggregate for the winners to be *able* to offer compensation to the losers (whether such compensation is actually paid being a separate question). We shall not discuss this particular issue further here, but note that one crucial, and generally under-researched dimension of the problem is that of the *criteria* on the basis of which we should define groups between which policies redistribute resources. Most of the literature on equity or fairness concerns socioeconomic groups defined by income, education, indicators of social class, etc. (see also Rampton et al., Language, Class and Education, Volume 1). However, it is also possible to investigate resource redistribution between age groups, men and women, ethnic groups, families and single households, etc. In the case of FL education, peoples' L1 becomes a relevant dimension. This reflects the fact that the cost of FL learning is often borne unequally.

This point is best explained by using the example of international communication, although it could also be illustrated in terms of the respective position of speakers of minority languages who have to adopt a majority language. Consider the case of the 25-member European Union (EU). For a variety of reasons (Graddol, 2005; Phillipson, 2003; Phillipson, Language Policy and Education in the European Union, Volume 1), English is currently the most frequently used language between Europeans of different mother tongues. Consequently, non-native speakers of English devote considerable time and effort to learning the language, at a massive cost to the education systems of the countries of about 85% of Europe's residents. By contrast, the United Kingdom has decreased its effort in FL teaching. Current public effort on FL teaching in the UK can be estimated at between one third and one fourth of that of other EU member countries. The amounts thus saved can be invested in other forms of human capital development. In other words, the non English-speaking countries of the EU are subsidising the UK on this plane as well. Controversy is currently ongoing over the extent of these transfers, and the identification of the best solution to this problem, taking account of both efficiency and fairness; this debate, however, raises questions that go well beyond language education and plugs into wider issues of language policy and macro-level language dynamics (see also Block, Language Education and Globalization, Volume 1).

CHALLENGES

To a large extent, the controversies just mentioned hark back to empirical questions. This also applies to the issue of the actual magnitude of non-market returns to language skills, which have never been evaluated but could, in principle, be estimated by adapting instruments applied in the evaluation of environmental assets. A number of other questions in the economics of language education, however, raise theoretical challenges.

One of the most important is that of the long-term evolution of rates of return. As we have seen, rates of return are estimated at time t, but language education policy decisions made on their basis will affect learners who already are in the education system or who will enter it in the future. Suppose for example that high rates of return on competence in a certain FL, say language L, have been observed at time t, and that a policy decision is made to increase, from time $t + 1$, the endowment for L-language teaching across the education system. Therefore, those learners who actually receive more L-language training only arrive on the labour market some years later. There is no certainty that, at that time, L-language skills will still be as profitable. High rates of return are therefore a relevant, but not a sufficient guide for language education policy decisions.

In order to make reliable policy recommendations to education authorities, it would be necessary to have a robust predictive model of the evolution of the value of FL skills. This, in turn, requires a deeper understanding than the literature currently offers of several interconnected processes, particularly of the ways in which employees' FL skills are exploited by employers. It should be clear that ethnographic accounts (often found in the applied linguistics literature) of how various languages are used in the workplace are of limited usefulness, because what matters is whether FL skills, when appropriately used in specific jobs within a company, have an actual impact on *economic* processes of production and distribution, and can therefore contribute to increased profits, market shares, etc. Only if such impacts do exist will firms have an incentive to recruit people with particular FL skills, thereby driving up the demand for such skills and keeping up, by way of consequence, the rate of return on them. If not, the language learning that occurs in response to earnings differentials observed, at time t, in favour of persons who are fluent in language L, will soon erode these very differentials. The incentive to learn language L will therefore decline, and language spread will continue on a large scale only if other factors come into play—for example, the fact that the social relevance of the language keeps increasing along with the number of learners and users, thereby renewing the incentive for more actors to learn it.

This question is particularly intriguing in the case of English. The reasons for its rapid spread are only partly understood (Graddol, 2005). Circumstantial evidence suggests that a plausible scenario is one of long-term decline in the labour market value of competence in English, as such skills are acquired by more people and become banal (just like the ability to read and write, once the preserve of a numerically small group of literate individuals, has become a basic requirement for all). Competence in English, at least up to a certain level, is likely to keep spreading, but for reasons distinct from labour market value, such as social participation. Consequently, maintaining a competitive advantage in the labour market is likely to constitute an incentive for individuals to learn additional FLs, and competence in Chinese may become a significant asset for this reason (cf. Lam, Language Education Policy in Greater China, Volume 1).

FUTURE DIRECTIONS

The economic analysis of language addresses a wide range of questions of considerable social and political significance; many of them also tie into major language policy debates. This is likely to be reflected in research in coming years. We may therefore expect future work to emphasise policy issues and to address both the relative efficiency and the fairness of various forms of multilingual communication. In particular, should policies favour the emergence of one lingua franca (e.g. at the European level) or encourage a partnership between a few major languages? In the former case, is a natural language like English a suitable lingua franca despite the major equity problems that its spread generates, or should some alternative like Esperanto be actively promoted through internationally coordinated action? How extensive should social plurilingualism be, given that linguistic diversity carries benefits and costs (both of the market and non-market kind)? All these questions clearly indicate that language education needs to be investigated, also when using economic analysis, in relation to broader social and political issues. The research needed, however, is not necessarily located entirely at the macro level, and also requires micro-level investigation.

At the same time, there is also work to be done on processes within education systems. Economics may help in the measurement of the respective contribution of school and non-school channels of FL acquisition, or by providing instruments for the systematic comparison of the performance of various forms of FL instruction, such as CLIL, 'intercomprehension' within language groups, etc., in comparison with more traditional forms of instruction. Empirical results in those areas can help design efficient, yet differentiated FL education curricula appropriate for different language learning contexts.

In all cases, however, it is important to remember that the issues at hand are highly complex. It would undoubtedly be useful for them to receive more sustained attention from economists. At the same time, further research needs to be carried out with a strongly interdisciplinary ethos in order to yield policy-relevant results.

See Also: *David Block: Language Education and Globalization (Volume 1); Ben Rampton, et al.: Language, Class and Education (Volume 1); Robert Phillipson: Language Policy and Education in the European Union(Volume 1); James W. Tollefson: Language Planning in Education (Volume 1)*

REFERENCES

Arnsperger, C. and van Parijs, P.: 2003, Éthique économique et sociale, La Découverte, Paris.

Bloom, D. and Grenier, G.: 1996, 'Language, employment and earnings in the United States: Spanish-English differentials from 1970 to 1990', *International Journal of the Sociology of Language* 121, 45–68.

Chiswick, B.: 1999, 'Language skills and earnings among legalized alien', *Journal of Population Economics* 12, 63–91.

Chiswick, B.: 2002, 'Immigrant earnings: Language skills, linguistic concentrations and the business cycle', *Journal of Population Economics* 15, 31–57.

Chiswick, B. and Miller, P.: 1995, 'The endogeneity between language and earnings: International analyse', *Journal of Labor Economics* 13, 246–288.

De Swan, A.: 2002, *Words of the World. The Global Language System*, Polity Press, Cambridge, MA.

Graddol, D.: 2005, *English Next*, The British Council, London.

Grin, F. (ed.): 1996, 'Economic approaches to language and language planning', Theme issue of the *International Journal of the Sociology of Language*, 121.

Grin, F.: 1999, Compétences et récompenses. La valeur des langues en Suisse, Éditions Universitaires, Fribourg.

Grin, F.: 2003, 'Economics and language planning', *Current Issues in Language Planning* 4, 1–66.

Johnes, G. and Johnes, J. (eds.): 2004, *International Handbook on the Economics of Education*, Edward Elgar, London.

Kastoukievitch, N.: 2003, *Language Effects on Labor Market Outcomes in a Bilingual Economy: The Case of Ukraine*, Unpublished MA dissertation, University of Kyiv-Mohyla.

Klein, C.: 2004, La valorisation des compétences linguistiques: importance du sexe et/ou du statut professionnel?, Paper presented at the 11e Journées d'étude sur les données longitudinales, Dijon, May 27–28.

Phillipson, R.: 2003, *English-Only Europe?*, Routledge, London.

Psacharopoulos, G. and Patrinos, H.: 2004, 'Human capital and rates of return', in G. Johnes and J. Johnes (eds.), *International Handbook on the Economics of Education*, Edward Elgar, London.

Vaillancourt, F.: 1985, Économie et langue. Conseil de la langue française, Québec.

Vaillancourt, F.: 1996, 'Language and socioeconomic status in Quebec: measurement, findings, determinants, and policy costs', *International Journal of the Sociology of Language* 121, 69–92.

van Parijs, P.: 2001, *Linguistic Justice, Politics, Philosophy & Economics* 1, 59–74.

van Parijs, P.: 2004, *Europe's Linguistic Challenge, Archives Européennes de Sociologie*, XLV, 113–154.

BILL JOHNSTON AND CARY BUZZELLI

THE MORAL DIMENSIONS OF LANGUAGE EDUCATION

INTRODUCTION

Like other kinds of teaching, language education is fundamentally and, some would argue, primarily moral in nature. By "moral," we mean that it involves crucial yet difficult and ambiguous beliefs and decisions about what is right and good for learners and others. The moral dimensions of teaching inhere in certain key facts. First, all teaching aims to change people; there is an implicit assumption that this change is for the better. Second, there are limitations on the degree to which science, research, and objective facts about teaching and learning can guide teachers in the decisions they make; the great majority of teachers' work in actual classrooms has to be based on teachers' beliefs about what is right and good for their learners—that is to say, it is rooted in moral values. Third, like any relations between human beings, relations between a teacher and her students are moral in nature, revolving around key issues such as trust and respect. The innate power differential between teacher and students merely reinforces this basic fact. The moral landscape of the language classroom is rendered even more complex than in other contexts by the fact that the teaching of languages by definition takes place at the intersection between different national, cultural, and political boundaries, representing often radically different sets of values. Furthermore, the different cultures and value systems represented in classrooms, like the individuals taking part in language education, are not equally positioned in terms of cultural capital (see also Kelly Hall, Language Education and Culture, Volume 1) but, quite the opposite, are usually in unequal relations in ways frequently involving race, gender, sexual orientation, and other crucial differences.

EARLY DEVELOPMENTS: FINDINGS FROM GENERAL EDUCATION

As the preceding paragraph suggests, work on the moral dimensions of language teaching has largely been grounded in work on morality in general education. In this section, we review the principal contributions to this line of research.

S. May and N. H. Hornberger (eds), Encyclopedia of Language and Education,
2nd Edition, Volume 1: Language Policy and Political Issues in Education, 95–104.
©2010 Springer Science+Business Media LLC.

John Dewey, in his seminal book, *Moral Principles in Education* (1909), drew an important distinction between the *teaching of morality*—the explicit teaching of specific moral values, and the *morality of teaching*—the ways teaching is imbued with moral significance. Despite the importance of Dewey's early writings in this area, little attention was paid to the morality of teaching until the early 1980s.

The publication of Tom (1984) marked the beginning of a renewed interest in the moral aspects of teaching. Tom critiqued the long-held view of teaching as an applied science, according to which research in the social and behavioral sciences will yield principles and strategies teachers "apply" to the problems they encounter in their classrooms. Tom proposed the metaphor of teaching as a moral craft. For Tom, two aspects of teaching imbue it with moral meaning: the relationship between teacher and student is a moral relationship, and the curriculum, as selectively planned and taught, reflects a desired goal. Craft can be described as an activity involving the application of analytical knowledge, synthetic thinking, and technical skill to a specific situation. By combining the moral aspects of teaching with the notion of craft, teaching as a moral craft is the "reflective, diligent, and skillful approach toward the pursuit of desirable ends" (p. 128).

Noddings' (1984) ethic of caring has been very influential over the past 20 years. Central to Noddings' work is her fundamental premise about teaching: that the relationship between teacher and student is at the core of teaching; concern for students comes before concern for content, assessment, and other aspects of schooling. These aspects are not ignored, nor considered of minor importance; but they are understood first and foremost through their connection to students and their learning.

Palmer (1998) offers another view of teaching and teachers' lives, one that draws primarily on personal reflection with a strong spiritual dimension. His deep explorations of his own work as a teacher and that of other teachers are inspirational rather than academic in tone and intent. While not based upon empirical investigations, his writings have nevertheless greatly influenced a number of researchers.

The ways teachers engage students in activities, indeed, the ways teachers act in all ways in the classroom, was the focus of the Moral Life of Schools Project undertaken by Jackson, Boostrom, and Hansen (1993). Through their extensive observations of K-12 classrooms in the USA, the authors sought to uncover and understand how the moral is present in schools. From their observations, two sets of categories emerged. The first set included five types of activities through which teachers and schools overtly teach moral content or nurture moral behaviors: moral instruction as a formal part of the curriculum, moral instruction as woven into the set curriculum, the use of ritual and ceremonies, visual displays of moral messages, and spontaneously introduced moral commentary in the flow of classroom activities.

The second set of categories involves practices of teachers and schools that intentionally or unintentionally are of moral significance. This set of three categories include: the moral content of classroom practices and rules; the curricular substructure, a set of assumptions which allow teachers to teach and students to learn; and expressive morality—the moral significance of the many ways teachers act and speak in classrooms.

Hansen (2001) has continued to explore many of these themes. His central premise throughout is that teaching draws its moral significance from the very nature of its practice. Thus, rather than seeking moral meaning from sources outside of teaching, for example from philosophical discussions of virtue, teaching as a practice is itself imbued with moral significance.

For Fenstermacher (1992), the moral in teaching is present in the manner of the teacher. This position is based upon an Aristotelian view of how virtue is acquired by the young: teachers act as models and moral agents in the lives of their students. Teachers who act justly, honestly, and with compassion and tolerance, express these virtues through their teaching, thus instilling these traits and virtues in their students. Manner, then, is seen as separate from a teacher's method of teaching, the behaviors teachers use that promote children's learning.

Sockett (1993) offers a moral basis for teacher professionalism by describing its four dimensions: the professional community, professional expertise, professional accountability, and the professional ideal of service. Yet, Sockett acknowledges that discussions of teaching and teacher professionalism sorely lack any type of moral vocabulary and moral language. Thus, Sockett frames each of the dimensions of teacher professionalism in moral terms through which the descriptions and criteria for the quality of practice are guided by moral rather than technical language.

Another major study conducted by Noblit and Dempsey (1996) examined the ways schools and communities construct values and virtues that often guide their teaching practices and curricula. Through interviews with teachers, students, families, and community members, Noblit and Dempsey uncovered how the virtues and values deemed important by each group were a major moral influence on teachers and children.

More recently, Buzzelli and Johnston (2002) have examined the moral nature of classroom interaction through the lenses of language, power, and culture. The examination of teaching practices through these lenses uncovers the moral significance of various types of classroom discourse, of classroom rules, and of the ways that majority culture teachers can limit the participation of minority students in classroom learning activities. These findings have implications for how teachers' practices directly and indirectly influence the ways students are represented through curricular materials and subsequently how educational practices contribute to the identities that students construct of themselves and that are attributed to them by peers.

MAJOR CONTRIBUTIONS

Two articles in the mid-1990s can be said to have opened up inquiry into the moral dimensions of language education. Edge (1996), in a paper examining what he called the "cross-cultural paradoxes" of the profession of English teaching, identified three such paradoxes of values. These were first, the mismatch that is frequently found between the values of what Edge calls "TESOL culture" (p. 9) and the national educational cultures in which English teaching is conducted. Second, the fact that in any context, English teaching is unavoidably wrapped up with political issues of both "liberation and domination" (p. 17). Third, the paradox between "respect for the right to be different" (p. 21), a value Edge claims that the field of English teaching embraces, and the intolerance sometimes expressed by the students whose views teachers are supposed to respect.

Johnston, Juhász, Marken, and Ruiz (1998) in turn, took a much more "local" and small-scale approach, examining discourse from the classrooms of three ESL teachers at a university-based intensive English program (IEP) to reveal aspects of what they called the "moral agency" of the teacher: that is, the ways in which the teacher's actions and words convey usually implicit moral messages to her learners. Johnston et al. borrowed part of the theoretical framework of "categories of moral influence" proposed by Jackson et al. (1993) (see earlier), and looked at the three categories said to capture the "morality of teaching" in introducing implicit moral messages into teaching: classroom rules and regulations; the curricular substructure; and expressive morality. Johnston et al. (1998) identified examples of all three categories in the classroom data they studied. They argued further that in relatively culturally homogeneous classrooms, such as those studied by Jackson et al. (1993), there is likely to be a large degree of shared understanding between teacher and students about elements such as the curricular substructure. However, in multilingual and multicultural classrooms there may be profound disjunctures between the moral messages sent, usually unconsciously, by teachers and the way those messages are interpreted, also usually unconsciously, by different learners.

Subsequent research in the moral dimensions of language education has partially followed the lead of these two pieces and has concentrated around certain key topics. These include: the moral dimensions of classroom interaction; values and politics; professional ethics; and the role of religious beliefs in language teaching.

Various aspects of the moral dimensions of classroom interaction have been examined. Ewald (in press) looked at student perceptions of critical moral incidents in a US university Spanish classroom; she found the students highly sensitive to moral messages in the words and actions of their teachers. Johnson (2003) described clashes of values between a white American female mentor teacher and an African Muslim man in a practicum (teaching practice) placement in a US IEP. Buzzelli and Johnston (2002) looked at a range of classroom issues including, in particular, cultural aspects of minority children in mainstream classes.

As Edge's (1996) work indicates, moral values have always been at least implicitly present in the expanding literature on the politics of language teaching (Pennycook, 1994; Phillipson, 1992; see also Canagarajah, The Politics of English Language Teaching, Volume 1). Above all, as Edge pointed out, the central moral question that this literature raises for teachers is how to position themselves morally in relation to national and international political realities in which they are implicated, yet with which they may vehemently disagree.

Along with inquiry into morality, narrowly conceived, there have also been several investigations into ethical issues in language teaching, many of which cover similar ground to that found in research on morality. (It is worth pointing out that in philosophy no distinction is usually drawn between morals and ethics, though some authors, e.g., Buzzelli and Johnston (2002), suggest that it can be helpful to use *ethics* to refer to codes of conduct and to behavior, and *morality* to refer to personal beliefs.) Research has looked, amongst other things, at the ethics of testing (Hamp-Lyons, 1998; Shohamy, 2001), and at the centrality of ethical issues in the work of teachers (Hafernik, Messerschmitt, and Vandrick, 2002).

Finally, there have been the beginnings of attention to the vast area formed by the intersection between language teaching and religious beliefs, a domain in which moral values are particularly prominent and often highly contentious. This is an area of central concern in language education, in particular because of the strong connection between English teaching and mission work worldwide, an issue on which moral views are strongly divided in the field. The Christian viewpoint has been put forward by Smith and Carvill (2000) and Snow (2001). On the other hand, there have recently been severe critiques of evangelical involvement in English teaching around the world, amongst others by Pennycook and Coutand-Marin (2003) and Edge (2003). There are also the beginnings of empirical research on evangelical teachers by nonevangelicals (Varghese and Johnston, 2004).

The most extensive examination of the moral dimensions of language teaching to date is probably Johnston (2003). In his book, which focuses specifically on English language teaching while considering examples from different national settings, Johnston looks in particular at five major areas, some of which overlap with the areas outlined earlier: the moral dimensions of classroom discourse and classroom interaction; moral aspects of critical pedagogy and the political dimensions of language teaching; the morality of forms of assessment and evaluation; the moral underpinnings of language teacher identity, including religious identity; and the role of values in various aspects of teacher professional development.

Johnston's work is built around the notion of *moral dilemmas*: that is to say, points at which teachers are obliged to choose between two or more courses of action knowing that any possible choice will have both good and bad consequences, many of which are largely unpredictable. Johnston identifies a number of key moral dilemmas frequently encountered in the field of English language teaching, categorizing them into dilemmas of pedagogy, of teacher–student relations, and of beliefs and values (pp. 145–146). Johnston claims that moral ambiguity and polyvalence are permanent features of all teaching, including language teaching; but he argues that an awareness of the moral dimensions of teaching and of the moral consequences of alternative courses of action is crucial for effective decision-making in classrooms and schools.

In summary, it is clear that inquiry into the moral dimensions of language teaching has extended to numerous aspects of classroom teaching, schools, and educational systems, and has frequently overlapped with areas such as ethics, the politics of language teaching, social responsibility, teacher education and development, and religion. Many of these lines of inquiry continue to be expanded as the following section indicates.

WORK IN PROGRESS

A number of projects currently in progress expand on or otherwise develop many of the ideas and topics outlined earlier, and also introduce new fields of interest and new theoretical possibilities.

Research has continued to look at the ways in which moral issues are enacted in classrooms. Johnston, Ruiz, and Juhász (2002) conducted a follow-up study to Johnston, Juhász, Marken, and Ruiz (1998) in which they examined student perspectives on moral critical incidents in an adult ESL classroom. Student perspectives often differed from teacher and researcher perspectives and from each other; but all students perceived the classroom as a place of moral interaction. Zahler

(2003) looked at one nonnative English-speaking ESL teacher in a North American IEP, analyzing his relations with his students in terms of the solidarity-authority distinction.

A number of scholars have followed Johnston's (2003) lead in extending research on the moral dimensions of teaching into language teacher education. For example, Johnston and Buzzelli (in progress) describe a study of two teacher education programs, one of which is an MA program in TESOL and applied linguistics. The authors' goal is to explore real-life moral dilemmas of teaching and teacher education while seeking new theoretical and conceptual lenses with which to understand classroom and program events; they are particularly interested in the moral dimensions of community, ideology, and identity as these play out in the context of teacher education classrooms.

Wong and Canagarajah (in progress), both evangelical Christians, have undertaken to attempt a professional dialog concerning the significant presence of evangelicals in the field of English teaching. Their book contains chapters and responses by both evangelical and nonevangelical (often non-Christian) scholars, in an attempt to find common ground.

Lastly, research on the political dimensions of language teaching has moved beyond the relatively narrow confines of critical pedagogy to take in more varied perspectives. An example of this development is Edge's (2006) edited volume, which offers multiple perspectives on responses in the field of English teaching to US neo-imperialism, especially in the post-9/11 world.

PROBLEMS AND DIFFICULTIES

The problems and difficulties of research on the moral dimensions of language teaching are both evident and numerous.

First, there is the most obvious matter of how "morality" is understood and defined for research purposes. Conceptual work is still needed to clarify what is meant by basic terms such as "moral," "right," and "good." There is an ever-present temptation to drift toward everyday understandings of these terms, which can be dangerous and misleading.

Second, the location of morality and values at the intersection between the social and the individual makes it hard to attempt valid generalizations about moral dilemmas. Societal values (for example, individualism, collectivism, privacy, solidarity) can be identified, but it is hard to say to what extent particular individuals share them. Working at the intersection of cultures and languages compounds the difficulties of research.

Third, the aspects of morality that are of most interest are also those that are buried deepest and are least available for inspection. For this reason, speculation is often the only recourse for the researcher. For example, in the study by Johnston, Ruiz, and Juhász (2002) mentioned earlier, looking at student perspectives on critical moral incidents in an ESL classroom, the researchers interviewed the students extensively, yet even so, the interviews themselves still had to be analyzed and interpreted. As with much cultural and psychological behavior, motivations and perceptions are in most cases simply not available for easy introspective access for research purposes.

Fourth, there are considerable barriers to conducting effective research across cultural and linguistic borders. Linguistic and discourse limitations make it very difficult to find stable points of vantage from which to work conceptually and to analyze and evaluate data and evidence. Notions such as "morality" or "right," for instance, do not translate easily across languages.

Lastly, it is worth noting that in some areas of research, objectivity is hard to come by. A case in point is the topic of religious beliefs in language teaching, in particular that looking at the presence of evangelical Christians in English teaching. The professional discourse on this topic has been marked by extreme polarization, and it remains unclear whether it is even possible to find a common language in which to conduct a debate (Varghese and Johnston, 2004). This seems a reflection of the broader fact that questions of morality and values tend to "push people's buttons," and that this can happen even in academic circles and can seriously compromise possibilities for inquiry.

The net result of the problems and difficulties reviewed here is that all work on the moral dimensions of teaching must acknowledge its own limitations, and the field as a whole must move forward cautiously and tentatively. Findings must always be regarded as provisional and subject to change.

FUTURE DIRECTIONS

Research on the moral dimensions of language teaching is in its infancy, and numerous important future directions suggest themselves. First of all, a deeper understanding of the moral dimensions of language classroom discourse necessitates discourse-analytic research in a range of contexts and settings. Understandings of moral meanings differ widely across cultural and national boundaries, and it would be a grave mistake to imagine that the moral landscape, say, of North American classrooms can be used to understand that of classrooms in other countries—quite aside from the radical differences from setting to setting within each country.

Second, as pointed out earlier, values differ significantly from one culture to the next, and these differences have a profound impact on local educational cultures; inquiry into the moral landscapes of language classrooms in different national settings would do much to give this work a fuller international and comparative dimension.

Third, a crucial arena in which moral values and issues are played out is that of curriculum and coursebooks; the moral dimensions of published materials, and the moral consequences of choices about which vocabulary, what form of pronunciation, what grammar, and what pragmatics competencies to teach is an area that is ripe for inquiry (see e.g., Smith and Carvill, 2000, pp. 55–56). This matter also extends to the question of the representation of cultures, individuals, and their values in curricular materials (see Buzzelli and Johnston, 2002, pp. 97–105).

Fourth, the specifically moral aspects of the intersection between language teaching and power also require closer examination (see Janks, Teaching Language and Power, Volume 1); whether considering the work of expatriate teachers of English around the world, or the presentation of unfamiliar cultures and peoples in the foreign language classroom, the juncture of individual or communally held moral beliefs and political hegemonies represents a major yet under-investigated aspect of language teaching.

Fifth, and finally, there is still much more work to be done in the area of religious beliefs and their place in language teaching. The work on evangelical Christianity mentioned in the previous sections needs to be expanded to include other forms of Christianity and other religions; there is an ever more pressing need to look closely at the complex moral dilemmas that arise when teachers' personal religious beliefs directly affect classroom instruction and relations with students.

See Also: Joan Kelly Hall: Language Education and Culture (Volume 1); Suresh Canagarajah: The Politics of English Language Teaching (Volume 1); Hilary Janks: Teaching Language and Power (Volume 1)

REFERENCES

Buzzelli, C.A. and Johnston, B.: 2002, *The Moral Dimensions of Teaching: Language, Power, and Culture in Classroom Interaction*, RoutledgeFalmer, New York.
Dewey, J.: 1909/1975, *Moral Principles in Education*, Southern Illinois University Press, Carbondale, IL.
Edge, J.: 1996, 'Cross-cultural paradoxes in a profession of values', *TESOL Quarterly* 30, 9–30.
Edge, J.: 2003, 'Imperial troopers and servants of the lord: A vision of TESOL for the 21st century', *TESOL Quarterly* 37, 701–708.
Edge, J. (ed.): 2006, *(Re-)locating TESOL in an Age of Empire*, Palgrave, London.
Ewald, J.: in press, 'Students' stories of teachers' moral influence in SL classrooms: Exploring the curricular substructure', *Issues in Applied Linguistics*.

104   BILL JOHNSTON AND CARY BUZZELLI

Fenstermacher, G.: 1992, 'The concepts of method and manner in teaching', in F.K. Oser, A. Dick, and J.-L. Patry (eds.), *Effective and Responsible Teaching: The New Synthesis*, Jossey-Bass, San Francisco, 95–108.

Hafernik, J.J., Messerschmitt, D.S., and Vandrick, S.: 2002, *Ethical Issues for ESL Faculty: Social Justice in Practice*, Lawrence Erlbaum Associates, Mahwah, NJ.

Hamp-Lyons, L.: 1998, 'Ethical test preparation practice: The case of the TOEFL', *TESOL Quarterly* 32, 329–337.

Hansen, D.T.: 2001, *Exploring the Moral Heart of Teaching: Toward a Teacher's Creed*, Teachers College Press, New York.

Jackson, P.W., Boostrom, R.E., and Hansen, D.T.: 1993, *The Moral Life of Schools*, Jossey-Bass, San Francisco, CA.

Johnson, K.A.: 2003, '"Every experience is a moving force": Identity and growth through mentoring', *Teaching and Teacher Education* 19, 787–800.

Johnston, B.: 2003, *Values in English Language Teaching*, Lawrence Erlbaum Associates, Mahwah, NJ.

Johnston and Buzzeli (in progress): *Caring for the many: The moral complexities of schooling*, State University of New York Press, Albany, NY.

Johnston, B., Ruiz, B.R., and Juhász, A.: 2002, *The Moral Dimension of ESL Classroom Interaction: Multiple Perspectives on Critical Incidents*, paper presented at AILA (International Association for Applied Linguistics), Singapore, December.

Johnston, B., Juhász, A., Marken, J., and Ruiz, B.R.: 1998, 'The ESL teacher as moral agent', *Research in the Teaching of English* 32, 161–181.

Noblit, G.W. and Dempsey, V.O.: 1996, *The Social Construction of Virtue: The Moral Life of Schools*, State University of New York Press, Albany, NY.

Noddings, N.: 1984, *Caring: A Feminine Approach to Care in Schools*, Teachers College Press, New York.

Palmer, P.J.: 1998, *The Courage to Teach*, Jossey-Bass, San Francisco.

Pennycook, A.: 1994, *The Cultural Politics of English as an International Language*, Longman, London.

Pennycook, A. and Coutand-Marin, S.: 2003, 'Teaching English as a missionary language (TEML)', *Discourse: Studies in the Cultural Politics of Education* 24, 338–353.

Phillipson, R.: 1992, *Linguistic Imperialism*, Oxford University Press, Oxford.

Shohamy, E.G.: 2001, *The Power of Tests: A Critical Perspective on the Uses of Language Tests*, Longman, New York.

Smith, D.I. and Carvill, B.: 2000, *The Gift of the Stranger: Faith, Hospitality, and Foreign Language Learning*, William B. Eerdemans Publishing Company, Grand Rapids, MI.

Snow, D.B.: 2001, *English Teaching as Christian Mission: An Applied Theology*, Herald Press, Scottsdale, PA.

Tom, A.: 1984, *Teaching as a Moral Craft*, Longman, London.

Varghese, M. and Johnston, B.: 2004, *"Planting seeds": Dilemmas in Religious Beliefs and Language Teaching*, paper presented at the Annual Meeting of the American Association for Applied Linguistics, Portland, OR, April.

Wong, M.S. and Canagarajah, S.: in progress, *Christianity and English Language Teaching: Cultural, Political, Pedagogical, and Professional Tensions*.

Zahler, T.: 2003, *The Teacher-Student Relationship: Balancing Solidarity and Authority*, paper presented at the Third International Conference on Language Teacher Education, Minneapolis, MN.

Section 2

Minorities and Education

TOVE SKUTNABB-KANGAS

HUMAN RIGHTS AND LANGUAGE POLICY
IN EDUCATION

INTRODUCTION

The United Nation's 2004 Human Development Report (http://hdr.
undp.org/reports/global/2004/) links cultural liberty to language rights
and human development and argues that there is

> ... no more powerful means of 'encouraging' individuals to
> assimilate to a dominant culture than having the economic,
> social and political returns stacked against their mother
> tongue. Such assimilation is not freely chosen if the choice
> is between one's mother tongue and one's future. (p. 33)

The press release about the UN report (see web address provided
earlier) exemplifies the role of language as an exclusionary tool:

> Limitations on people's ability to use their native language—
> and limited facility in speaking the dominant or official
> national language—can exclude people from education,
> political life and access to justice. Sub-Saharan Africa has
> more than 2,500 languages, but the ability of many people
> to use their language in education and in dealing with the state
> is particularly limited. In more than 30 countries in the region,
> the official language is different from the one most commonly
> used. Only 13 percent of the children who receive primary
> education do so in their native language.

One might expect that the report would suggest a positive solution,
which not only respects human rights (HRs), but is also based on solid
research. Sadly, this is not the case. The report suggests that:

Multilingual countries often need a three-language formula
1. A national or official state language.
2. A lingua franca to facilitate communications among different
   groups (in some cases the official language serves this purpose).
3. Official recognition of the mother tongue or of indigenous languages *for those without full command of the official language
   or lingua franca* (ibid.; emphasis added).

The first two, enabling children through education to become fully
competent in one or two languages of wider communication, is what
a human rights-oriented educational language policy should include.
The third suggestion is clearly based on deficit theories and either/or

*S. May and N. H. Hornberger (eds), Encyclopedia of Language and Education,
2nd Edition, Volume 1: Language Policy and Political Issues in Education, 107–119.*
© *2010 Springer Science+Business Media LLC.*

thinking, characteristic of much of language policy today in indigenous and minority education (see also Kelly Hall, Language Education and Culture, Volume 1). Schools often see the mother tongues of minorities as necessary but negative temporary tools while the minority child is learning a dominant language. As soon as he or she is deemed in some way competent in the dominant language, the mother tongue can be left behind, and the child has no right to maintain it and develop it further in the educational system.

This can be seen as a serious HRs violation. It violates the right to education (see Magga, Nicolaisen, Trask, Dunbar and Skutnabb-Kangas, 2004; Tomaševski, 2001; and www.right-to-education.org/content/primers/_rte03.pdf). It may result in linguistic genocide, according to two of the United Nations' definitions of genocide (Skutnabb-Kangas, 2000; see also the section Work in Progress).

EARLY DEVELOPMENTS

There have been many language rights for dominant language speakers for millennia, without anybody calling them language rights. Additionally, several linguistic minorities have for centuries had some language rights, in some countries even legally formalised. Rights have been formulated pragmatically, and mostly by lawyers. The first bilateral agreements (between two countries), also old, were mostly about religious not linguistic minorities, but often the two coincided. The first multilateral agreement covering national minorities was the Final Act of the Congress of Vienna 1815 (Capotorti, 1979, p. 2). During the nineteenth century, several national constitutions and some multilateral instruments safeguarded some national linguistic minorities (see the historical overview in Skutnabb-Kangas and Phillipson, 1994). The Peace Treaties that concluded the First 'World' War and major multilateral and international conventions under the League of Nations improved the protection. After the Second World War, the individual rights formulated by the United Nations were supposed to protect minority persons as individuals and collective minority rights were seen as unnecessary. A better protection of linguistic minorities only started to develop after Francesco Capotorti, as a UN Special Rapporteur on the Rights of Minorities, published his 1979 report. The protection is still far from satisfactory (see also de Varennes, International Law and Education in a Minority Language, Volume 1).

It was only in the early 1990s that the area of linguistic human rights (LHRs) started crystallising as a multidisciplinary research area. Earlier, language rights and human rights were more separated from each other; both were the domain of lawyers, with few, if any, linguists involved. Both areas were driven by practical–political concerns and the research was mainly descriptive, not analytical. Even today, there is a fairly tight separation. Few lawyers know much about language (some exceptions are Fernand de Varennes, e.g. 1996, International Law and Education in a Minority Language, Volume 1; Dunbar, 2001; Fife, 2005) or education. Many of those sociolinguists, political scientists and educationists who are today writing about LHRs, know too little about international law (also here there are exceptions, e.g. May 2001, Language Education, Pluralism and Citizenship, Volume 1; Tollefson and Tsui 2003). This is a fast growing area where major concept clarification and multidisciplinary teamwork is urgently needed. It should be clear, though, that those language rights are LHRs, which are so basic for a dignified life that everybody has them because of being human; therefore, in principle no state (or individual) is allowed to violate them. The first multidisciplinary book about LHRs seems to be from the mid-1990s (Skutnabb-Kangas and Phillipson, 1994).

MAJOR CONTRIBUTIONS

The world's spoken languages are disappearing fast: pessimistic but realistic estimates fear that 90–95% of them may be extinct or very seriously endangered by the year 2100. Transmission of languages from the parent generation to children is *the* most vital factor for the maintenance of both oral and sign languages. When more children gain access to formal education, much of their more formal language learning, which occurred earlier in the community, takes place in schools. If an alien language is used in schools—i.e. if children do not have the right to learn and use their language in schools (and, of course, later in their working life)—the language is not going to survive. Thus educational LHRs, especially an unconditional right to mother tongue medium (MTM) education, are central for the maintenance of languages and for the prevention of linguistic and cultural genocide. 'Modernisation' has accelerated the death/murder of languages, which, without formal education, had survived for centuries or millennia. It is clear, though, that neither LHRs nor schools alone can in any way guarantee the maintenance and further development of languages—they are both necessary but not sufficient for this purpose. There are no miracle cures or panaceas.

Dominant and/or majority language speakers in many cases have most of those rights that can be seen as LHRs, also in education, and most of them seem to take their existence for granted. Indigenous peoples and minorities are the ones whose LHRs need strengthening. The Office of the United Nations High Commissioner for Human Rights website www.unhchr.ch is a good place to start finding out what educational LHRs exist today in international or regional HRs instruments. See http://www.ohchr.org/english/law/index.htm for texts of the HRs instruments themselves and http://www.unhchr.ch/tbs/doc.nsf for States parties to the treaties; Mercator Linguistic Rights and Legislation website is also useful: http://www.ciemen.org/mercator/Menu_nou/index. cfm?lg=gb.

Minorities have some HRs support for other aspects of using their languages in areas such as public administration, courts and the media (Frowein and co-worker's edited books about minority rights in European States 1993 and 1994 give excellent overviews of Europe). However, international and European binding Covenants, Conventions and Charters provide in fact very little support for LHRs in education, and language is accorded in them much poorer treatment than other central human characteristics such as 'race', gender and religion (see also de Varennes, International Law and Education in a Minority Language, Volume 1). Often language disappears completely in educational paragraphs. For instance, the (non-binding) Universal Declaration of Human Rights (1948) paragraph on education (26) does not refer to language at all. Similarly, the UN International Covenant on Economic, Social and Cultural Rights, having mentioned language on par with race, colour, sex, religion, etc. in its general Article (2.2), explicitly refers to 'racial, ethnic or religious groups' in its educational Article (13), but omits reference to language or linguistic groups.

When 'language' is present in Articles on education, especially MTM education, the formulations are more vague and/or contain many more opt-outs, modifications and claw-backs than other Articles; these create obligations and contain demanding formulations, where the states are firm duty-holders and '*shall*' do something positive in order to ensure the rights. Many books and articles on LHRs show this. For some key books on language rights, see: Skutnabb-Kangas and Phillipson, 1994; Kibbee, 1998; Guillorel/Koubi, 1999; Kontra, Phillipson, Skutnabb-Kangas and Várady, 1999; Phillipson, 2000; Skutnabb-Kangas, 2000; May, 2001.

We can see these patterns of vague formulations, modifications and alternatives even in the latest minority or language-specific international and regional instruments. In the Council of Europe's European Charter for Regional or Minority Languages (1998), a state can choose which paragraphs or subparagraphs it wishes to apply (a minimum of 35 is required). The education Article 8, includes a range of qualifications, including 'as far as possible', 'relevant', 'appropriate', 'where necessary', 'pupils who so wish in a number considered sufficient', 'if the number of users of a regional or minority language justifies it', as well as a number of alternatives, as in 'to allow, encourage or provide teaching in or of the regional or minority language at all the appropriate stages of education'. Similar formulations abound in the Council of Europe's Framework Convention for the Protection of National

Minorities (1998). The Article covering medium of education is so heavily qualified that the minority is completely at the mercy of the state:

> In areas inhabited by persons belonging to national minorities traditionally or in **substantial** numbers, **if there is sufficient demand**, the parties shall **endeavour** to ensure, **as far as possible** and **within the framework of their education systems**, that persons belonging to those minorities have **adequate** opportunities for being taught in the minority language **or** for receiving instruction in this language (emphases added for modifications).

The Framework Convention has been criticised by politicians and international lawyers, who are normally very careful in their comments. Law professor Patrick Thornberry's general assessment is:

> In case any of this [provisions in the Convention] should threaten the delicate sensibilities of States, the Explanatory Report makes it clear that they are under no obligation to conclude 'agreements'.... Despite the presumed good intentions, the provision represents a low point in drafting a minority right; there is just enough substance in the formulation to prevent it becoming completely vacuous. (Thornberry, 1997, pp. 356–357)

Of course the balance between binding formulations and sensitivity to local conditions is a difficult one. The Charter permits a reluctant state to meet the requirements in a minimalist way, which it can legitimate by claiming that a provision was not 'possible' or 'appropriate', or that numbers were not 'sufficient' or did not 'justify' a provision, or that it 'allowed' the minority to organise teaching of their language as a subject, at their own cost. Both the European Charter and the Framework Convention (for the latest news about both, see http://conventions. coe.int/Treaty/EN/v3News.asp; their treaty numbers are 148 and 157) have monitoring bodies which seem to be doing a good job in trying to stretch the states' willingness to follow more than minimalist requirements—but, again, when it comes to MTM education, these bodies seem to be somewhat ignorant about language-in-education issues (see Skutnabb-Kangas, 2004; Wilson, 2004). The (non-binding) UN Declaration on the Rights of Persons Belonging to National or Ethnic, Religious and Linguistic Minorities (http://www.unhchr.ch/ html/menu3/b/d_minori.htm) suffers from similar vague formulations.

A recent NGO attempt to promote language rights (a draft Universal Declaration of Linguistic Rights, handed over to UNESCO in Barcelona in June 1996; see http://www.linguistic-declaration.org/index-gb.htm; from the index one can go to the Declaration itself), also suffers from similar shortcomings, even if, for several beneficiaries ('language communities' and, to some extent, 'language groups'), it represents great progress in relation to the other instruments described. Still, indirectly, its education section forces all others except those defined as members of language communities (which roughly correspond to national territorially based minorities) to assimilate. Despite hard work by Catalans (who, together with the Basques, have been extremely active in getting LHRs on a global agenda), the draft Declaration is not going to be accepted by UNESCO member states in its present form.

WORK IN PROGRESS

New interpretations (Article 27, discussed subsequently) or enlargement of the scope (linguistic genocide) of older instruments, new instruments under negotiation (e.g. indigenous instruments, see McCarty, Language Education Planning and Policies by and for Indigenous Peoples, Volume 1; or LHRs for the Deaf, see Branson and Miller, National Sign Languages and Language Policies, Volume 1), and the development of non-binding Declarations or Recommendations (e.g. the Hague Recommendations) in a more binding direction may in time improve the situation.

Article 27 of the International Covenant on Civil and Political Rights (ICCPR) 1966, in force since 1976), still contains the most far-reaching binding protection for LHRs for minority languages (see also de Varennes, International Law and Education in a Minority Language, Volume 1). It declares:

> In those States in which ethnic, religious or linguistic minor-
> ities exist, persons belonging to such minorities shall not be
> denied the right, in community with the other members of
> their group, to enjoy their own culture, to profess and prac-
> tice their own religion, or to use their own language.

Earlier interpretations of this Article did not grant much support to LHRs. It was seen as only granting negative non-discrimination rights and did not place any obligations on states. The linguistic protection of national minorities rests, according to van der Stoel, on two HRs pillars:

> the right to non-discrimination in the enjoyment of human
> rights; and the right to the maintenance and development of
> identity through the freedom to practice or use those special
> and unique aspects of their minority life - typically culture,
> religion, and language. The first protection ... ensures that
> minorities receive all of the other protections without regard
> to their ethnic, national, or religious status; they thus enjoy a
> number of linguistic rights that all persons in the state enjoy,
> such as freedom of expression and the right in criminal

proceedings to be informed of the charge against them in a
language they understand, if necessary through an interpreter
provided free of charge. The second pillar, encompassing
affirmative obligations beyond non-discrimination.... It
includes a number of rights pertinent to minorities simply
by virtue of their minority status, such as the right to use
their language. This pillar is necessary because a pure non-
discrimination norm could have the effect of forcing people
belonging to minorities to adhere to a majority language,
effectively denying them their rights to identity. (OSCE—
Organisation for Security and Co-operation in Europe, High
Commissioner on National Minorities, 1999, p. 8–9)

In 1994, the United Nations Human Rights Committee (UNHRC) published a General Comment on UN ICCPR, Article 27 (4 April 1996,
UN Doc. CCPR/C/21/Rev.1/Add.5). The UNHRC interpreted Article
27 as protecting all individuals on the state's territory or under its
jurisdiction (i.e. also immigrants and refugees), irrespective of whether
they belong to the minorities specified in the article or not. It stated
that the existence of a minority does not depend on a decision by the
state, but requires to be established by objective criteria (important in
relation to countries which deny having linguistic minorities—e.g.
France, Greece, Turkey). It recognised the existence of a 'right', and
imposed positive obligations on the states. The revised Human Rights
Fact Sheet No. 15 on ICCPR from the Committee (2005) sustains this
interpretation.

When the United Nations did preparatory work for what became the
International Convention for the Prevention and Punishment of the
Crime of Genocide (E 793, 1948), linguistic genocide as a central
aspect of cultural genocide was discussed alongside physical genocide
as a serious crime against humanity (see Capotorti, 1979, p. 37).

When the UN General Assembly finally accepted the Convention,
Article III covering linguistic and cultural genocide was voted down
by 16 states (see Official Records of the General Assembly, Third Session, Part I, Sixth Committee, 83rd meeting). It is thus not included in
the final Convention of 1948. Denmark, USA and UK were among
those who opposed the prohibition of cultural genocide and UK wanted
the Convention to be limited in the strict sense to the physical extermi-
nation of human groups. The Soviet bloc countries, China, Pakistan
and Venezuela, among others, wanted to keep Article 3 in force.

The present Convention has five definitions of genocide. Two of
them fit most indigenous and minority education today

II(e), '*forcibly transferring children of the group to another group*';
II(b), '*causing serious bodily* or mental *harm to members of the
group*'; (emphasis added).

Assimilationist submersion education, where indigenous and minority children are forced to accept teaching through the medium of dominant languages (see also McCarty, Language Education Planning and Policies by and for Indigenous Peoples, Volume 1), can cause serious mental harm and often leads to the students using the dominant language with their own children later on—i.e. over a generation or two the children are linguistically, and often in other ways too, forcibly transferred to a dominant group. This happens to millions of speakers of threatened languages all over the world. There are no schools or classes teaching the children through the medium of the threatened indigenous or minority languages. The transfer to the majority language-speaking group is not voluntary; alternatives do not exist, and parents do not have enough reliable information about the long-term consequences of the various choices. Because of this, disappearance of languages cannot be labelled 'language suicide', even if it might at first seem like the speakers are themselves abandoning their languages.

Most children obviously want in their own interest to learn the official language of their country. This is also one of the important LHRs and implies the right to become a high-level bilingual. Most children also want to learn English if it is not one of the official languages. But learning new languages, including the dominant languages, should not happen subtractively, but rather additively, in addition to their own languages. Subtractive formal education, which teaches children (something of) a dominant language at the cost of their first language, is genocidal. This dominant language can be official (e.g. French in France) or semi-official (e.g. English in the USA); it can be the language of a numerical majority (as in France or the USA); often it is an old colonial language, spoken only by a small but powerful numerical minority (e.g. as in many African countries). A false educational philosophy claims that minority children learn the dominant language best if they have most of their education through the medium of it. Many studies have shown that the longer the mother tongue remains the main medium of education, the better the minority children learn the dominant language and other subjects (see, e.g. Thomas and Collier, at http://www.crede.ucsc.edu/research/llaa/1.1_final.html; May, Hill and Tiaikiwai (2004), at http://www.minedu.govt.nz/index.cfm?layout= document&documentid=9712&data=1, and other articles in Volumes 1 and 5).

Some lawyers claim that the deliberate intention required by the Convention is not there. If minority education has been and is organised against what considerable research evidence proposes, while the authorities (including churches) have (and have had for at least one and a half centuries) solid information about how it should be organised, the prohibition, the mental harm caused and the forcible transfer must be seen as deliberate and intentional acts on behalf of states (see Magga, Nicolaisen, Trask, Dunbar and Skutnabb-Kangas, 2004).

The (non-binding) Hague Recommendations Regarding the Education Rights of National Minorities (http://www.osce.org/documents/html/pdftohtml/2700_en.pdf.html) from OSCE's High Commissioner on National Minorities were worked out by a small group of experts on HRs and education. They represent an authoritative interpretation and concretisation of the minimum in present HRs standards. In the section, 'The spirit of international instruments', bilingualism is seen as a right and responsibility for persons belonging to national minorities (Article 1), and states are reminded not to interpret their obligations in a restrictive manner (Article 3). In the section on 'Minority education at primary and secondary levels', MTM education is recommended at all levels, including bilingual teachers in the dominant language as a second language (Articles 11–13). Teacher training is made a duty on the state (Article 14). Finally, the Explanatory Note states that 'submersion-type approaches whereby the curriculum is taught exclusively through the medium of the State language and minority children are entirely integrated into classes with children of the majority are not in line with international standards' (p. 5). UNESCO's 2003 Position paper 'Education in a Multilingual World' (http://unesdoc.unesco.org/images/0012/001297/129728e.pdf) follows the Hague Recommendations fairly closely.

PROBLEMS, DIFFICULTIES AND FUTURE DIRECTIONS

One problem has been that, even if minorities have been granted the right to found private schools with their own language as the main medium of education, the state has not had any obligation to participate in the costs. This was made clear in a landmark case in Belgium (the Belgian Linguistic Case, http://www.arts.uwaterloo.ca/MINELRES/coe/court/Belglin.htm). Few minorities can bear the full cost of primary education while contributing through their taxes to dominant-language-medium education. If the Human Rights Committee's reinterpretation of Article 27 starts having some effect (and new litigation would be needed to test this), the economic hurdles might be solved. After all, it hardly costs the state more to change the language in minority schools, as compared with using the dominant language (see also Grin, The Economics of Language Education, Volume 1). This is also pointed out in The Asmara Declaration on African Languages and Literatures, from a conference 17 January 2000 (http://www.outreach.psu.edu/C&I/AllOdds/declaration.html) when demanding MTM education.

The Draft United Nations Declaration on the Rights of Indigenous Peoples (contained in the 1994 Sub-Commission annual report, document E/CN.4/Sub.2/1994/56, annexed to resolution number 45; go to it through http://www.ohchr.org/english/issues/indigenous/declaration. htm) was, after a decade of careful work, handed over to the UN in 1994 and has been under negotiation ever since. The USA, Canada and Australia seem to be among the countries most prominent in delaying its acceptance. In an interview in PFII's Quarterly Newsletter *Message Stick 3:2*; (http://www.un.org/esa/socdev/unpfii/en/newsletter. html; choose Message Stick Vol. 4, number 2), PFII's (UN Permanent Forum on Indigenous Issues) first Chair, Professor Ole Henrik Magga sums up the connections between the concepts in the title of this entry: human rights, language, language policy and education. He sees LHRs in education as a necessary prerequisite for the maintenance of indigenous languages and traditional knowledge. See also Hamel, 1994, 1997; May, 1999; McCarty, 2005; Magga, Nicolaisen, Trask, Dunbar and Skutnabb-Kangas, 2004, for some assessments of the situation.

Without implementation, monitoring and proper complaint procedures, many of the possibilities in the new or emerging instruments are lost. The European Charter is supposed to be an inclusive, positive language rights instrument. Still, it excludes many more languages in Europe than it includes. It excludes explicitly immigrant languages and 'dialects' of languages. Covertly, it has also excluded all Sign languages, using completely false argumentation (see also Branson and Miller, National Sign Languages and Language Policies, Volume 1).

The often-appalling ignorance about basic language matters is a serious gap, and it should be the ethical responsibility of researchers to remedy it. False information or lack of information about both research results and details in HRs instruments that the various countries have signed and ratified are also more the rule than the exception when decisions are made about education. Important language status planning decisions are often based on false information, even in situations where the correct information is easily available and has in fact been offered to the decision makers. More transdisciplinary cooperation between HRs lawyers, sociolinguists and educationists is urgently needed (see the Introduction in Kontra, Phillipson, Skutnabb-Kangas and Várady, 1999; May, 1999, 2001). Often Western researchers also suffer from ethnocentricity, and lack of knowledge of the languages and cultures of others (see, e.g. Tuhiwai Smith, 1999; Kontra, 2000; Hountondji, 2002).

But lack of LHRs is not only an information problem. The political will of states to grant LHRs is the main problem. HRs, especially economic and social rights, are, according to HRs lawyer Katarina Tomaševski (1996, p. 104), to act as correctives to the free market.

She claims (ibid., p. 104) that the 'purpose of international human rights law is [. . .] to overrule the law of supply and demand and remove price-tags from people and from necessities for their survival'. These necessities for survival include not only basic food and housing (which would come under economic and social rights), but also basics for the sustenance of a dignified life, including basic civil, political and cultural rights—and LHRs are a part here of cultural rights. The message from both sociologists like Zygmunt Bauman and HRs lawyers like Katarina Tomaševski, and many others, is that unless there is a redistribution of resources for implementing HRs, progress will be limited. It is probably not even of any use to spread knowledge of HRs as a basis for self-directed human development, unless the resources for implementation follow, and that can only happen through a radical redistribution of the world's material resources.

Why have states not granted LHRs to indigenous peoples and most minorities? The general attitudes behind state policies leading towards diminishing numbers of languages see, falsely, monolingualism as something:

1. Normal and natural; however, most countries are multilingual
2. Desirable, more efficient and economical; however, if citizens do not understand the language they are governed in and if huge talent is wasted because children do not profit and are even harmed by formal education, this is inefficient and wasteful
3. Inevitable; modernisation leads to linguistic homogenisation and only romantics regret it; however, linguistic diversity and multilingualism enhance creativity (see May, Bilingual/Immersion Education: What the Research Tells Us, Volume 5) and are necessary in information societies where the main products are diverse ideas and diverse knowledges (see Kalantzis and Cope, Language Education and Multiliteracies, Volume 1).

In addition, states seem to see granting of LHRs as divisive. The rationale is that they result in minorities reproducing themselves as minorities. These minorities then supposedly follow the old nation-state thinking and want cultural autonomy, economic autonomy and, in the end, political autonomy: their own state. Thus MTM education for minorities is ultimately seen as leading to the disintegration of nation states. These erroneous beliefs are an important causal factor in linguistic genocide and lack of LHRs in education.

See Also: *Fernand de Varennes: International Law and Education in a Minority Language (Volume 1); Stephen May: Language Education, Pluralism and Citizenship (Volume 1); Teresa L. McCarty: Language Education Planning and Policies by and for Indigenous Peoples (Volume 1); Jan Branson and Don Miller: National Sign Languages* *and Language Policies (Volume 1); Joan Kelly Hall: Language Education and Culture (Volume 1); François Grin: The Economics of Language Education (Volume 1); Tove Skutnabb-Kangas: Language Rights and Bilingual Education (Volume 5); Stephen May: Bilingual/ Immersion Education: What the Research Tells Us (Volume 5)*

REFERENCES

Capotorti, F.: 1979, *Study of the Rights of Persons Belonging to Ethnic, Religious and Linguistic Minorities*, United Nations, New York.

Dunbar, R.: 2001, Minority Language Rights in International Law, *International and Comparative Law Quarterly* 50, 90–120.

Fife, J.: 2005, 'The legal framework for indigenous language rights in the United States', *Willamette Law Review* 41(2), 325–371.

Frowein, J.A., Hofmann, R., and Oeter, S. (hrsg.): 1993/1994, Das Minderheitenrecht europäischer Staaten. Teil 1. Teil 2. Beiträge zum ausländischen öffentligen Recht und Völkerrecht. Band 108/109, Springer-Verlag, Berlin.

Guillorel, H. and Koubi, G. (red): 1999, *Langues et droits. Langues du droit, droit des langues*, Bruxelles, Bruylant.

Hamel, R.E.: 1994, 'Indigenous education in Latin America: policies and legal frameworks', in T. Skutnabb-Kangas and R. Phillipson (eds.), 271–287.

Hamel, R.E. (ed.): 1997, *Linguistic human rights from a sociolinguistic perspective*, International Journal of the Sociology of Language 127.

Hountondji, P.J.: 2002, 'Knowledge appropriation in a post-colonial context', in C.A. Odora Hoppers (ed.), *Indigenous Knowledge and the Integration of Knowledge Systems. Towards a Philosophy of Articulation*, New Africa Books, Claremont, 23–38.

Human Rights Fact Sheet No. 15 (Rev. 1): 2005, Civil and Political Rights: The Human Rights Committee, United Nations, Geneva.

Kibbee, D.A. (ed.): 1998, *Language Legislation and Linguistic Rights*, John Benjamins, Amsterdam.

Kontra, M.: 2000, 'Prefatory note', *Multilingua* 19(1/2), 1–2.

Kontra, M., Phillipson, R., Skutnabb-Kangas, T., and Várady, T. (eds.): 1999, *Language: a Right and a Resource. Approaching Linguistic Human Rights*, Central European University Press, Budapest.

Magga, O.H., Nicolaisen, I., Trask, M., Dunbar, R., and Skutnabb-Kangas, T.: 2004, 'Indigenous children's education and indigenous languages', Expert Paper Written for the United Nations Permanent Forum on Indigenous Issues, United Nations, New York.

May, S. (ed.): 1999, *Indigenous Community-Based Education*, Multilingual Matters, Clevedon, UK.

May, S.: 2001, *Language and Minority Rights: Ethnicity, Nationalism, and the Politics of Language*, Longman, London. (Reprinted by Routledge, 2007)

May, S., Hill, R., and Tiaikiwai: 2004, *Bilingual/Immersion Education: Indicators of Good Practice*, Ministry of Education, Wellington, New Zealand.

McCarty, T. (ed.): 2005, *Language, Literacy, and Power in Schooling*, Lawrence Erlbaum, Mahwah, NJ.

OSCE High Commissioner on National Minorities: 1999, Report on the linguistic rights of persons belonging to national minorities in the OSCE area, The Hague.

Phillipson, R. (ed.): 2000, *Rights to Language: Equity, Power, and Education*, Lawrence Erlbaum, Mahwah, NJ.

Skutnabb-Kangas, T.: 2000, *Linguistic Genocide in Education—or Worldwide Diversity and Human Rights?*, Lawrence Erlbaum, Mahwah, NJ.

Skutnabb-Kangas, T.: 2004, 'The status of minority languages in the education process, in *Filling the Frame. Five years of monitoring the Framework Convention
for the Protection of National Minorities*, Proceedings of the Conference held in
Strasbourg, 30–31 October 2003, Council of Europe Publishing, Strasbourg,
234–254.

Skutnabb-Kangas, T. and Phillipson, R.: 1994, 'Linguistic human rights: past and
present', in T. Skutnabb-Kangas and R. Phillipson (eds.), 71–110.

Skutnabb-Kangas, T. and Phillipson, R. (eds.), in collaboration with M. Rannut: 1994,
Linguistic Human Rights. Overcoming Linguistic Discrimination, Mouton de
Gruyter, Berlin and New York.

Smith Tuhiwai, L.: 1999, *Decolonizing Methodologies: Research and Indigenous
Peoples*, University of Otago Press, Dunedin; Zed Books, New York.

Thornberry, P.: 1997, 'Minority rights', in Collected Courses of the Academy of
European Law (ed.), *Academy of European Law*, Volume VI, Book 2, Kluwer
Law International, The Netherlands, 307–390.

Thornberry, P.: 2002, *Indigenous Peoples and Human Rights*, Manchester University
Press, Manchester.

Tollefson, J.W. and Tsui, A.B.M. (eds.): 2003, *Medium of Instruction Policies. Which
Agenda? Whose Agenda?*, Lawrence Erlbaum, Mahwah, NJ.

Tomaševski, K.: 1996, 'International prospects for the future of the welfare state',
in *Reconceptualizing the Welfare State*, The Danish Centre for Human Rights,
Copenhagen, 100–117.

de Varennes, F.: 1996, *Language, Minorities and Human Rights*, Martinus Nijhoff,
The Hague.

Wilson, D.: 2004, Report: A critical evaluation of the first results of the monitoring
of the Framework Convention on the issue of minority rights in, to and through
education (1998–2003), in *Filling the Frame. Five years of monitoring the Framework Convention for the Protection of National Minorities*, Proceedings of
the Conference Held in Strasbourg, 30–31 October 2003, Council of Europe Publishing, Strasbourg, 163–233.

FERNAND DE VARENNES

INTERNATIONAL LAW AND EDUCATION IN A MINORITY LANGUAGE

INTRODUCTION

While many linguists and educationalists often refer to a "right to language" or to a "right to be educated in one's own language", and have
done some extremely detailed and well-researched work (Skutnabb-
Kangas and Phillipson, 1994, pp. 71–110), the purely legal point of view
at the international level has not been so accommodating. Only in the
last few years have international legal instruments—those which impose
legally binding rules rather than noble aspirations—recognised, strictly
speaking, such a right. An increasing variety of documents such as
the United Nations' Declaration on the Rights of Persons Belonging to
National or Ethnic, Religious and Linguistic Minorities (http://www.
unhchr.ch/html/menu3/b/d_minori.htm) and the 1996 The Hague Recommendations regarding the Education Rights of National Minorities
(http://www.minelres.lv/osce/hagrec.htm), prepared on behalf of the High
Commissioner on National Minorities of the Organization for Security
and Cooperation in Europe (OSCE), have more recently articulated such
a "right" more clearly, but caution must be used in their use since, from
a legal point of view, they are not binding in international law (see also
Skutnabb-Kangas, Human Rights and Language Policy in Education,
Volume 1).

It is nevertheless true that, at least from the point of view of the
Council of Europe, two separate treaties—the Framework Convention
for the Protection of National Minorities (http://www.coe.int/T/E/
human_rights/minorities/) and the European Charter for Regional or
Minority Languages (http://conventions.coe.int/Treaty/EN/Treaties/
Html/148.htm)—have more recently enshrined unambiguously a right
to be educated in one's language, though in both cases this right is cir-
cumscribed to particular situations and conditions and is not a right
available in all situations.

Additionally, developments in the application of the rights to education and non-discrimination in international law suggest that further
clarifications as to the impact of this law on education in a minority
language are emerging and will take some time before there is a fuller
understanding of the role international law plays in this area.

*S. May and N. H. Hornberger (eds), Encyclopedia of Language and Education,
2nd Edition, Volume 1: Language Policy and Political Issues in Education, 121–135.*
©*2010 Springer Science+Business Media LLC.*

EARLY DEVELOPMENTS

International law is mainly found in treaties and international cus-
tomary law and dealt traditionally with relations between states. There
have, however, been throughout history some bilateral treaties—
treaties between two states—or multilateral treaties—involving more
than two states—which provided for "rights" to individuals belonging
to certain ethnic or religious communities (de Varennes, 1996, chapter 2).

Not many of these early examples of bilateral treaties in international
law referred specifically to language. The more notable of these were
the 1516 Treaty of Perpetual Union between the King of France and
the Helvetic state, which contained a provision identifying those who
were to receive certain benefits as the "Swiss who speak no language
other than German", and the Final Act of the Congress of Vienna of
1815, which contained certain rights to ensure the preservation of the
Polish "nationality", thus resulting in Poznan Poles retaining the right
to use Polish for official purposes.

International law as reflected in bilateral treaties protecting communities also occasionally had linguistic ramifications. For example, in the
nineteenth century when the Muslim minority in Greece had largely
adopted the Turkish language, the 1881 Convention for the Settlement
of the Frontier between Greece and Turkey, guaranteeing the free exercise of the Islamic faith and the maintenance of Islamic courts and other
community "structures", also in practice resulted in the continued use
of the Turkish language as part of the Muslim religious and community
activities.

At the start of the twentieth century, there appeared the first treaties
which were explicit in providing for the right to have schools teaching
in a minority language. Thus the Vlach- and German-speaking minorities schools were protected under the Treaty of Peace between Bulgaria,
Greece, Montenegro, Romania and Serbia of 1913, as Turkish language
private schools were for Muslims living in Serbia under the 1914 Treaty
between Serbia and Turkey.

These early developments were however of an ad hoc nature and
only affected a very small number of countries. It was not until the
advent of the League of Nations at the end of the First World War that
there emerged a slightly more generalised, though still not universal,
system under which it could be said that there existed—in some situations—a right to be educated in a minority language.

There were a number of so-called "minorities treaties" adopted and
subsequently overseen by the League of Nations. Essentially, the provisions for minorities fell into three different types of instruments:
first, there were a series of treaties imposed upon the defeated states of
Austria, Hungary, Bulgaria and Turkey. The second involved new states

born of the remains of the Ottoman Empire, as well as states whose boundaries were altered under the self-determination principle put forward by American President Woodrow Wilson (namely Czechoslovakia, Greece, Poland, Romania and Yugoslavia). The final category included a number of special provisions relating to minorities in Åland, Danzig, the Memel Territory and Upper Silesia, as well as a series of five unilateral declarations made by Albania, Lithuania, Latvia, Estonia and Iraq upon their admission to the League of Nations. Most of these treaties contained provisions which guaranteed the right of minorities to establish and control their own institutions, including schools using their own language as medium of instruction.

> [Those states] have further agreed, in towns and districts where a considerable proportion of nationals of the country whose mother tongue is not the official language of the country is resident, to make provision for adequate facilities for ensuring that, in the primary schools ... instruction shall be given to the children of such nationals through the medium of their own language, it being understood that this provision does not prevent the teaching of the official language being made obligatory in those schools. (Capotorti, 1979, pp. 18–19)

At that stage, international law seemed to be moving towards accepting a "right of education" in a minority language, though this right could perhaps more accurately be described as including two distinct rights: in the case of private schools, minorities were seemingly to be entitled to create and operate their own schools and use their own language free from any restrictions or obstacles by state authorities, except of course for requirements relating to curriculum content. In addition, they had the right to education in their own language in "adequate facilities" provided by states, as in state schools, though only in town and districts where the minority was present "in considerable numbers".

That movement came to a rather abrupt end with the disappearance of the League of Nations and its eventual replacement after the Second World War by the United Nations. Following the war, a study by the United Nations Secretariat concluded that the engagements entered into by states after First World War under the minorities system had ceased to exist, except for the Åland Islands agreement. The tentative movement of the League of Nations and international law towards perhaps recognising some kind of eventual right to education in a minority language thus seemed to also come to an abrupt end.

The rhetoric was seen to shift after 1945 to one emphasising universal protection of individual rights and freedoms, an approach which at least at surface seemingly shied away from recognising any rights to specific communities or groups such as minorities. Thus, discussions leading up to the creation of the United Nations based on a "new covenant" and a "fresh approach" (McKean, 1983, p. 53) were focussed on the principle of individual rights exclusively, no reference being made to the previous minorities treaties.

Indeed, an initial draft outline of what was to become the Universal Declaration of Human Rights proposed that states with "substantial numbers of persons differing in race, language, or religion from the majority of the population, should give such persons the right to establish and maintain out of an equitable proportion of public funds, schools, cultural and religious institutions, and they should be entitled to use their own language before the courts and other authorities and organs of state and in the press and in public assembly" (McKean, 1983, p. 63). This was ultimately rejected, partly because it was seen as inconsistent with the new individualistic approach (see also Skutnabb-Kangas, Human Rights and Language Policy in Education, Volume 1).

Thus, most of the early legal developments after the Second World War rejected any reference to minorities having specific rights in relation to education in their own language. There was therefore a fundamental shift in the treatment of the rights of minorities pre- and post-1945: the approach after that date is generally seen as only involving the protection of the human rights and fundamental freedoms of all human beings, and not to favour any measures designed especially to protect minorities (Capotorti, 1979, p. 27).

MAJOR CONTRIBUTIONS

As international law is not stagnant, the apparent *tabula rasa* in relation to the rights of minorities in the immediate aftermath of the Second World War was soon to be displaced by the gradual appearance of a number of treaty provisions. These quickly started to acknowledge that there are rights which minorities can invoke in relation to educational rights and language preferences, though there is a noteworthy evolution which can be detected in the actual content of these rights.

Initially, a small number of bilateral peace treaties concluded after the war provided for minority schools to operate and use a minority language in their activities. For example, the 1946 Treaty of Peace with Italy, specifically guaranteed the right of the German-speaking minority in the province of Bolzano (Bozen) to "elementary and secondary teaching in the mother-tongue".

These localised steps in relation to the rights of minorities in the area of education would however only begin to extend to the global scene a decade later, first with the adoption of a treaty which provided a degree of protection for indigenous and tribal populations (which may in some states constitute minorities but are not necessarily so) and then with a truly international treaty dealing with discrimination in education. The International Labour Organisation Convention No. 107 of 1957 concerning Indigenous and Tribal Populations provides for protected indigenous populations the right to be taught in their mother tongue or, where this is not practicable, in the language most commonly used by the group to which they belong (see also McCarty, Language Education Planning and Policies by and for Indigenous Peoples, Volume 1).

The more significant treaty at the global level for minorities from a legal point of view would be, however, the UNESCO Convention against Discrimination in Education of 1960 which makes it clear, in Article 2(b), that it does not constitute discrimination to establish or maintain, for linguistic reasons, separate educational systems or institutions. The UNESCO Convention also provides in Article 5(1)(c) that it is essential to "recognise the right of members of national minorities to carry on their own educational activities, including the maintenance of schools and, depending on the educational policy of each state, the use or the teaching of their own language", provided that "this right is not exercised in a manner which prevents the members of these minorities from understanding the culture and language of the community as a whole and from participating in its activities, or which prejudices national sovereignty".

The wording of these early provisions almost half a century ago does not necessarily grant a right of minorities to be educated in their language. On the one hand, the treaty acknowledges the fundamental entitlement of minorities to have their "own", meaning private as opposed as to state-operated, educational activities. On the other hand, the UNESCO Convention does not appear to extend this right automatically in terms of the choice of the language of instruction to be used in these private minority schools, as this choice is not left to the parents but is dependent "on the educational policy of each state". Furthermore, even if a state's educational policy permits the use of a minority language in these schools, it must never prevent "the members of these minorities from understanding the culture and language of the community as a whole and from participating in its activities, or which prejudices national sovereignty". It is at the very best a timid, undemanding provision in terms of language requirements (Hastings, 1988, p. 21).

There is therefore some ambivalence in this treaty which impairs the usefulness of Article 5 as a basis for the right of minorities to receive education in their own language: first, Article 5 only deals with the creation of private schools and does not actually require that state authorities establish publicly funded schools for minorities. Second, the treaty does not guarantee that the language used in these schools actually be the language of the minority. It is permissive rather than mandatory in this regard, meaning that this will only eventuate if the state's educational policy permits the use of a minority language. While some would have thought that a minority should be entitled automatically to freely determine the language of instruction used in its own schools, this early treaty—while not rejecting outright such use—did not go so far as to actually require it of all states from a strict reading of Article 5.

Still, the general tone of the UNESCO Convention is far from antagonistic to minorities being educated in their own language, quite the contrary. Read as a whole, it could be said to actively encourage states to permit minorities to use their language in their own schools, even if not making it a strict legal obligation on states. In this sense, the UNESCO Convention can be seen as an early precursor to later legal developments in international law of the modern post-war period.

The main developments in the last 25 years in terms of international law need to be divided into two parts: those at the truly global level which have been more timid and restrained, and those at the regional level of the Council of Europe that have been very significant in giving a truly legal recognition and structure to an actual right for minorities to be educated in their own language (see also Phillipson, Language Policy and Education in the European Union, Volume 1; Skutnabb-Kangas, Human Rights and Language Policy in Education, Volume 1).

At the global level, the legal instruments dealing with education in minority (or indigenous) languages are limited to provisions such as Article 27 of the International Covenant on Civil and Political Rights (ICCPR) which provides that "[i]n those states in which...linguistic minorities exist, persons belonging to such minorities shall not be denied the right, in community with the other members of their group, to enjoy their own culture...or to use their own language" (silent on education but widely believed to at least protect private minority schools), and the International Labour Organisation's Convention (No. 169) Concerning Indigenous and Tribal Peoples in Independent Countries, in relation to indigenous and tribal peoples, which guarantees a right to education in indigenous languages, but only "where practicable" and an entitlement to measures to preserve and promote the development and practice of indigenous languages. Even more recently at the global level, the 1989 Convention on the Rights of the Child asserts in Article 29 that the education of the child shall be directed to the development of respect for the child's parents, his or her own cultural identity, language and values. Here again, however, the wording clearly does not require any use of a minority language as a medium of education, or even any suggestion that it should be taught: it only requires that states must direct education in a way that develops respect for his or her language, cultural identity and values.

Other documents at the global level often referred to as proving a more direct or general "right" to education in a minority language, such as the UN Declaration on the Rights of Persons Belonging to National or Ethnic, Religious and Linguistic Minorities and the draft UN Declaration on the Rights of Indigenous Peoples, are unfortunately not legally binding instruments (see also Skutnabb-Kangas, Human Rights and Language Policy in Education, Volume 1). While they are indicative of a growing trend towards acceptance in international law of the principle that a right to be educated in one's language should be guaranteed, the fact remains that there is not yet such a general, unambiguous and legally binding obligation. The limitations and vague wording of Article 27 of the ICCPR and Article 29 of the Convention on the Rights of the Child, the small number of ratifications of the Convention (No. 169) Concerning Indigenous and Tribal Peoples in Independent Countries, and subjecting the Article 5 right in the UNESCO Convention to a state's policy all suggest that there is still, in strictly legal terms at the global level, some difficulty in getting the broad international consensus to make this a legally binding norm.

Developments within the Council of Europe in the last 20 years have been dramatically different and offer a much more solid basis for education in minority languages from a strictly legal point of view. Two legally binding treaties have given definite form and structure to this right: Article 14 of the Framework Convention for the Protection of National Minorities and Article 8 of the European Charter for Regional or Minority Languages both indicate that "in appropriate circumstances" states must make available in schools the teaching of or in a minority language. Although both treaties have been criticised for the various ways states could circumvent the impact of their provisions (such as limiting the treaties' application to national minorities or traditional languages, the possibility for states to "opt out" from some clauses or even only nominate certain specific minorities as being protected) and the weakness of both treaties' enforcement mechanisms, it remains that in legal terms they are the clearest expression of a right to not only learn, but in some cases to also receive some part of their education in, their own language.

Some scholars have urged caution in relation to these "European" legal standards (de Varennes and Thornberry, 2005, pp. 426–428). The right as expressed in the two treaties of the Council of Europe is either restricted to undefined "national minorities" under the Framework Convention for the Protection of National Minorities, a category seemingly different from the more inclusive concept of minorities contained in United Nations treaties, or to "regional or minority languages" as defined in the European Charter for Regional or Minority Languages. Furthermore, even in the case of either a national minority language or a regional language, education in this language is not automatic: it is limited to situations where it is "justified", "reasonable", or where the number of students in part of a territory is "substantial" or "sufficient". It would seem that the extent of the right varies, and that tiny minorities would in practical terms not be entitled to such a right.

Thus, the exact degree of use of a minority language as medium of instruction required varies according to the particular context of each situation: the extent of demand for such instruction, the degree of use of medium of instruction, the state's ability to respond to these demands and so on.

A national minority or speakers of a regional language would have, under these European treaties, at minimum, the right to be taught their language in schools where practical and justified, even if their numbers are not sufficient for the use of their language as medium of instruction.

The most detailed treaty in this area, the European Charter for Regional or Minority Languages, indicates, for example, that the numbers must be "sufficient" for this purpose. This could suggest that the mere presence of one or a handful of pupils in a district would not automatically give rise to a right to be taught a minority language in a public school. However, in light of the many international and European instruments which generally refer to a state's obligation to protect and promote the language (and culture) of minorities, it would seem that what is "sufficient" should be interpreted in a generous and flexible way, and that the number of pupils required to be able to claim the right to be taught the minority language should be quite small if a State's resources make it reasonably practical to accommodate them.

There are, beyond these legal developments, numerous political and other pronouncements which together create an impressive foundation acknowledging the validity of providing education in a minority language. Among the more prominent are of course the UN Declaration on the Rights of Persons Belonging to National or Ethnic, Religious and Linguistic Minorities, the draft UN Declaration on the Rights of Indigenous Peoples, the Organisation on Security and Cooperation in Europe's Document of the Copenhagen Meeting of the Conference on the Human Dimension, The Hague Recommendations regarding the Education Rights of National Minorities, as well as a very large number of resolutions from bodies such as the European Parliament.

While this corpus may appear as eloquent recognition of the right to education in one's language, these are not, strictly speaking, legally binding instruments, and thus cannot alone form the basis for such a right in international law. Confusingly, some writers in this area tend to refer to these documents as evidence of an "implicit" right, not distinguishing the provisions which create clear legal obligations from those which may later form the basis of an emerging standard for "what the law ought to be" (*lege ferenda*) (Thornberry, 1991, chapter VII).

WORK IN PROGRESS

The relative youth of the Framework Convention for the Protection of National Minorities and the European Charter for Regional or Minority Languages and other instruments means that there are still a large number of uncertainties as to the exact parameters for the exercise of these rights, and indeed some degree of inconsistency can be noted in the way the monitoring bodies under their supervisory mechanisms interpret the obligations from these two treaties (Weller, 2005, chapter 14).

Much of the earlier work on education in a minority language supposed that there was in international law, somewhere and almost mystically somehow, an implicit "right to identity" which could be used to buttress claims to education in a minority language (Smith, 2003, pp. 130–132), even though no treaty actually spelled this out. Most treaties, with the exception of the two more recent Council of Europe treaties, in fact appear to subject any use of a minority language as medium of instruction, outside of private schools, to the whims of state authorities' educational policies rather than providing for such instruction as of right under specific conditions.

Interestingly, a perhaps more "traditionalist" stream adopted the completely opposite point of view, claiming on the contrary that there was absolutely no basis for a right to minority instruction, at least in public schools, either because such a right was not specifically spelt out in a treaty provision or the right to education itself (see the European Court of Human Rights comments in the Belgian Linguistics Case, available at http://cmiskp.echr.coe.int/tkp197/search.asp?skin=hudoc-en, where it stated that the right to education does not automatically or necessarily include the right to education in a particular language), or because once a state has determined an official language, no other language could be used officially in state institutions, including presumably state schools and education provided in these schools (some of the minority views of the UN Human Rights Committee in Diergaardt v. Namibia, available at http://www1.umn.edu/humanrts/undocs/session69/view760.htm).

The latter views must not be underestimated. Most lawyers, judges and legal scholars in the world were advised during their legal training, and probably still hold the opinion, that "[o]nce a State party has adopted any particular language or languages as official language or languages, it would be legitimate for the State party to prohibit the use of any other language for official purposes ..." (Diergaardt v. Namibia, dissident views, par. 5). In other words, there is no obligation for state authorities to use any minority language for any purpose whatsoever, including in public schools, if a State so decides.

A better understanding, somewhere in the middle, is now starting to take shape. In Europe, the presence of specific treaties that enshrine a right to be educated in a minority language, at least where there is a sufficient critical mass to make this practical, means that more and more work from a purely legal perspective is proceeding as to the implementation and a better understanding of these legal obligations (generally de Varennes, 2004; Martín Estébanez and Gál, 1999; Weller, 2005; Wilson, 2002).

At the global level, despite the lack of an international treaty clearly protecting an unambiguous right to education in a minority language, two new trends are appearing: first, the relatively rigid view that no international law is applicable in language matters once a state has chosen an official language is starting to make way for the recognition that rights such as non-discrimination may permit the use of other languages in addition to an official one. In other words, it may be unreasonable and unjustified in some circumstances—such as where a large number of people use a minority language—and therefore discriminatory not to provide for some use of this language by state authorities. This is, in effect, the reasoning which can be extrapolated in the majority position in Diergaardt v. Namibia, and a more considered reading of the Belgian Linguistics Case. It is only very recently starting to be taken up by jurists (de Varennes, 1996, chapter 4).

Additionally, and surprisingly, the right to education itself is being "revisited" by some courts in a way which directly contradicts the more traditional views. In Cyprus v. Turkey (Judgement of 10 May 2001, Grand Chamber, http://cmiskp.echr.coe.int/tkp197/search.asp?skin= hudoc-en) the linguistic policies of Northern Cyprus authorities in the area of public education were essentially described as so inadequate in view of the circumstances as to constitute a violation of Article 2, Protocol 1 which deals with the right to education.

The Court noted that children of Greek-Cypriot parents in northern Cyprus wishing to pursue a secondary education through the medium of the Greek language were obliged to transfer to schools in the south, though children could continue their education at a Turkish or English-language school in the north.

On the basis of the court's previous reasoning in the Belgian Linguistics Case, most of the more traditionalist lawyers and experts on the right to education had assumed that this would be the end of the matter, since once a state has an official language, it can choose not to use any other language for official purposes, including public education. The European Court, however, completely upset that logical edifice when it wrote the following:

277. The Court notes that children of Greek-Cypriot parents in northern Cyprus wishing to pursue a secondary education through the medium of the Greek language are obliged to transfer to schools in the south, this facility being unavailable in the "TRNC" ever since the decision of the Turkish-Cypriot authorities to abolish it. Admittedly, it is open to children, on reaching the age of 12, to continue their education at a Turkish or English-language school in the north. In the strict sense, accordingly, there is no denial of the right to education, which is the primary obligation devolving on a Contracting Party under the first sentence of Article 2 of Protocol No. 1 (see the Kjeldsen, Busk Madsen and Pedersen v. Denmark judgment of 7 December 1976, Series A No. 23, pp. 25–26, Section 52). Moreover, this provision does not specify the language in which education must be conducted in order that the right to education be respected (see the Belgian linguistic judgement, pp. 30–31).

278. However, in the Court's opinion, the option available to Greek-Cypriot parents to continue their children's education in the north is unrealistic in view of the fact that the children in question have already received their primary education in a Greek-Cypriot school there. The authorities must no doubt be aware that it is the wish of Greek-Cypriot parents that the schooling of their children be completed through the medium of the Greek language. Having assumed responsibility for the provision of Greek-language primary schooling, the failure of the "TRNC" authorities to make continuing provision for it at the secondary-school level must be considered in effect to be a denial of the substance of the right at issue. It cannot be maintained that the provision of secondary education in the south in keeping with the linguistic tradition of the enclaved Greek Cypriots suffices to fulfil the obligation laid down in Article 2 of Protocol No. 1, having regard to the impact of that option on family life . . . .

280. Having regard to the above considerations, the Court concludes that there has been a violation of Article 2 of Protocol No. 1 in respect of Greek Cypriots living in northern Cyprus in so far as no appropriate secondary-school facilities were available to them.

The logic used by the European Court is rather perplexing, to say the least. It admits on the one hand that Article 2 of Protocol No. 1 is devoid of a linguistic component, but then says there is a linguistic component for secondary education because authorities in Northern Cyprus provided Greek-language primary education, and therefore to stop offering it after primary school "negated" the right to education. Indeed, commentators have for the most part remained so unsure on how to interpret the European Court of Human Rights' seemingly contradictory approaches that most have referred to it without trying to explain it any further (de Varennes, 2004).

Perhaps the European Court intended to say, in line with its previous reasoning in the Belgian Linguistics Case, that in light of the circumstances, the restrictions on public education in the Greek language in Northern Cyprus were unreasonable and unjustified because they were so blatantly inappropriate, and therefore discriminatory.

It is probably in this way that the judgement should be properly understood: otherwise, if the main reason—the absence of Greek language secondary education—was in breach of the right to education under Article 2 of Protocol No. 1, it would mean that the authorities of Northern Cyprus could avoid this human rights violation by simply abolishing all education in Greek provided in primary public schools: this is unlikely to be the direction and spirit of tolerance and inclusion the European Court had in mind.

PROBLEMS AND DIFFICULTIES

Be that as it may, the above judgement of the European Court of Human Rights raises a new view of the right to education, since it rejects in effect the official language used by authorities in Northern Cyprus as the exclusive language of education at the secondary level, and imposes the use of another language for purposes of public education, contrary to legislation in place. The traditionalist view as expressed by the dissident views in Diergaardt v. Namibia thus finds itself also—albeit perhaps implicitly—rejected by the European Court of Human Rights.

Few legal experts have however fully considered, or even acknowledged, the potential ramifications of both of these results. One of the main problems still currently facing most jurists formed along the more traditional lines of international law is that it is not easy to accept that language rights exist, sometimes on the basis of the right to non-discrimination, and require the use of a minority language even if it is not permitted under a state's official language legislation (Stefanescu and Georgeault, 2005, p. 313). For most of them, any language right, including provision of a minority language in a public school, is a "special" or "positive" measure which can only exist if and when specific legislative "permission" is granted by state authorities.

At the other end of the spectrum, jurists who had assumed that the right to education in a minority language in international law naturally had to exist "somewhere" now have another provision which can solidify such claims. The problem here is that even if more reliance may be had on the right to education, in combination with non-discrimination or the right to family life, it is not an unqualified right to education in a minority language. As shown by the Belgian Linguistics Case and the European Court of Human Rights rather hesitant and contradictory position in Cyprus v. Turkey, the exact extent or parameters of a linguistic component for such a right in international law are far from crystal clear, and probably require many more cases before there is a much greater degree of certitude in this area from a legal point of view.

One of the problems with this is that, in the absence of a specific international treaty provision setting out the conditions where a right to education in a minority language in public schools is guaranteed, those two more extreme positions among jurists will probably be battling out this matter internationally for many years to come. It also means that for minorities in most parts of the world, any recourse to the limited remedies and mechanisms available at the international level will likely be fraught with uncertainties and risks.

From a legal point of view at the European level, however, results are likely to be better, at least in states which have ratified one or both of the Council of Europe treaties that impact on the issue of language and education. There are undoubtedly difficulties in terms of the weakness of both implementation mechanisms for these treaties and inconsistencies of interpretation of the rights under the European Charter for Regional or Minority Languages and the Framework Convention for the Protection of National Minorities by the Committees charged with the supervision of these legal obligations. At least from a legal perspective, however, there is a formally recognised right to education in a minority language, where practical, which can be built upon.

FUTURE DIRECTIONS

It was never intended in international law that the right to education include the right to education in one's own language (Lebel, 1974, pp. 231–232). While various UN and other documents would frequently laud the benefits of providing some degree of instruction in a minority language, these documents were either not treaties (UN Declaration on the Rights of Persons Belonging to National or Ethnic, Religious and Linguistic Minorities) and therefore not a source of international legal obligations, or they contained ambiguous provisions which in the end seemed to leave the matter of choice of language of education in public schools to the discretion and determination of state authorities (see also Skutnabb-Kangas, Human Rights and Language Policy in Education, Volume 1).

For legal traditionalists, this meant that while a state could be generous and provide for education in a minority language if state authorities decided to take "special positive measures", it was not a right which anyone could claim.

For jurists seeking to protect and promote minorities and their languages, there were attempts to construct arguments for an implicit, if somehow amorphous, right to identity, or culture, or some other bases in support of an international right to education in a minority language.

While the latter's methods and arguments cannot be said to have won the day, it would seem that for the most part the direction of international law may be reaching the same ultimate goals in the future.

At the level of the Council of Europe, the legal obligation is now entrenched in two treaties: state authorities in countries having ratified these treaties must provide for education in a minority language where it is practical to do so, though acquisition of the official language must also always be assured. Future clarification of these legal norms is however still needed and likely to focus on the circumstances where it can be said to be practical, or not, for this right to be applied.

At the global level, the absence of a clear legal provision in any international treaty for states to unambiguously having the obligation to provide education in a minority language would seem initially to hamper any further recognition of such a right. There are nevertheless two distinct trends that may have considerable impact in the future: first, the more recent development at the global level of various instruments such as the UN Declaration on the Rights of Persons Belonging to National or Ethnic, Religious and Linguistic Minorities which, while not creating directly any legal obligations, still indicate an acceptance of the validity of an eventual right to education in a minority language. Second, the even more recent re-assessment by legal scholars and adjudicative and monitoring bodies such as the European Court of Human Rights and UN Human Rights Committee of the right to education and non-discrimination may breathe new life into existing legal standards. While not necessarily a view shared by most jurists trained to consider an official language policy in education and other areas of state involvement as exclusive, it would seem that our understanding of international human rights standards such as non-discrimination and education in the area of language is beginning to change. This therefore may be another new frontier that could be increasingly examined and clarified in the years to come, and may well have some potential for minorities and some kind of right to education in their language, where this is reasonable and practical.

See Also: *Tove Skutnabb-Kangas: Human Rights and Language Policy in Education (Volume 1); Teresa L. McCarty: Language Education Planning and Policies by and for Indigenous Peoples (Volume 1);*

Robert Phillipson: *Language Policy and Education in the European Union (Volume 1)*

REFERENCES

Capotorti, F.: 1979, *Study of the Rights of Persons Belonging to Ethnic*, Religious and Linguistic Minorities, New York.
de Varennes, F.: 1996, *Language, Minorities and Human Rights*, Martinus Nijhoff, The Hague.
de Varennes, F.: 2001, *A Guide to the Rights of Minorities and Language*, COLPI, Budapest, Hungary. Available at http://www.osi.hu/colpi/files/COLPI4.pdf
de Varennes, F.: 2004, *The Right to Education and Minority Language*, eumap.org, http://www.eumap.org/journal/features/2004/minority_education/edminlang/
de Varennes, F. and Thornberry, P.: 2005, in Weller (ed.), *The Rights of Minorities*, Oxford Commentaries on International Law, Oxford, UK.
Hastings, W.K.: 1988, *The Right to an Education in Maori: The Case from International Law*, Victoria University Press, Wellington, New Zealand.
Lebel, M.: 1974, 'Le choix de la langue d'enseignement et le droit international', *Revue Juridique Thémis* 9(2), 221–248.
Martín Estébanez, M.A. and Gál, K.: 1999, *Implementing the Framework Convention for the Protection of National Minorities*, Report No. 3, European Centre on Minority Issues, Flensburg, Germany.
McKean, W.: 1983, *Equality and Discrimination under International Law*, Oxford, UK: Clarendon Press, Oxford, UK.
Skutnabb-Kangas, T. and Phillipson, R.: 1994, *Linguistic Human Rights: Overcoming Linguistic Discrimination*, Mouton de Gruyter, Berlon and New York.
Smith, R.: 2003, 'Mother tongue education and the law: A legal review of bilingualism with reference to Scottish Gaelic', *International Journal of Bilingual Education and Bilingualism* 6(2), 129–145.
Stefanescu, A. and Georgeault, P. (eds.): 2005, *Le français au Québec: Les nouveaux défis*, Conseil supérieur de la langue française, Fides, Montréal.
Thornberry, P.: 1991, *International Law and the Rights of Minorities*, Clare Press, Oxford, UK.
Thornberry, P. and Gibbons, D.: 1996/1997, 'Education and minority rights: A short survey of international standards', *International Journal on Minority and Group Rights*, special issue on the *Education Rights of National Minorities* 4(2), 115–152.
Weller, M. (ed.): 2005, *The Rights of Minorities*, Oxford Commentaries on International Law, Oxford, UK.
Wilson, D.: 2002, *Minority Rights in Education: Lessons for the European Union from Estonia, Latvia, Romania and the Former Yugoslav Republic of Macedonia*, Minority Rights Group, London, UK.

TERESA L. McCARTY

LANGUAGE EDUCATION PLANNING AND POLICIES BY AND FOR INDIGENOUS PEOPLES

INTRODUCTION

The world's 300 million Indigenous peoples reside in 70 countries and every continent on earth. Identified as Indigenous according to international convention because of their aboriginal occupation of lands before colonization or the establishment of state boundaries, and because they retain some or all of their traditional social, economic, cultural, and political institutions, Indigenous peoples have experienced a history of genocide, the armed invasion of their homelands, and concomitant economic, political, and social disenfranchisement (see the United Nations International Labour Organisation (ILO) Convention 169 Concerning Indigenous and Tribal Peoples, www.unhchr.ch/html/menu3/b/62.htm). Central to these assaults have been official and unofficial policies that simultaneously dispossessed Indigenous peoples of their languages and their lands. A primary tool for achieving both ends has been state-sponsored schooling.

Thus, Indigenous struggles for language rights have been waged in tandem with those for cultural survival and self-determination. In this chapter, I analyze these struggles and the research into them from a framework that views language planning and policy (LPP) not solely as official government action or texts, but as complex modes of human interaction, negotiation, and production, mediated by relations of power (see also May, Language Education, Pluralism and Citizenship, Volume 1; Tollefson, Language Planning in Education, Volume 1). This framework enables us to examine LPP as de facto and de jure—as covert and overt, bottom-up and top-down—and to illuminate cross-cutting themes of cultural conflict and negotiation, identity, language ideology and linguistic human rights (see also de Varennes, International Law and Education in a Minority Language, Volume 1; Skutnabb-Kangas, Human Rights and Language Policy in Education, Volume 1).

Indigenous peoples represent 4% of the world's population, but they speak 60% of the world's languages. The contexts in which Indigenous languages are spoken are as diverse as humankind itself, spanning language situations such as that of Quechua, spoken by 8–12 million people in 6 South American countries; to Aotearoa/New Zealand, where a single Indigenous language, Māori, shares co-official status

S. May and N. H. Hornberger (eds), Encyclopedia of Language and Education,
2nd Edition, Volume 1: Language Policy and Political Issues in Education, 137–150.
©*2010 Springer Science+Business Media LLC.*

with English and New Zealand Sign Language; to diasporic speech communities such as the Garifuna Nation, dispersed across 3 Central American countries, the Caribbean and the USA; to the extraordinary linguistic diversity of Papua New Guinea, where some 760 distinct languages, most spoken by less than 1,000 people, coexist in an area the size of the US state of California. With some exceptions—Guaraní in Paraguay, for example—the viability of Indigenous languages is severely compromised by legacies of language repression and the modern forces of globalization (see Block, Language Education and Globalization, Volume 1). Even languages with large numbers of speakers are increasingly being displaced by dominating world languages. Thus, for Indigenous peoples, language revival, revitalization, maintenance and reversal of language shift are key LPP goals. As will be shown in the sections that follow, there are many positive examples of this from around the world.

EARLY DEVELOPMENTS

Although published accounts of Indigenous language policies have focused on colonial and post-colonial developments, language policies have been operative in Indigenous communities since time immemorial. Kulick, for instance, notes that Papua New Guinea's remarkable linguistic diversity has its roots in widespread language attitudes that emphasized the boundary-marking dimensions of language, cultivating linguistic differences as a way of exaggerating communal identity (1992, p. 2). At the same time, many Papua New Guinean communities placed a high value on multilingualism, with the display of foreign speech varieties viewed as 'one important means of gaining prestige in traditional society' (Kulick, 1992, p. 3). In Native North America, multi-lingualism was always highly valued as a tool of trade and survival in one of the most culturally, linguistically and ecologically diverse regions of the world. And in pre-colonial Africa, according to Brock-Utne and Hopson (2005, p. 3), 'the different ethno-linguistic groups . . . did not have a language of instruction problem', as 'each group used its own language to educate its children'.

Eradicating these language practices has been a prominent goal of every colonial regime. '[Castilian] is a tool for conquest abroad', Antonio de Nebrija, author of the first modern grammar of a European language, told Queen Isabella of Spain in 1492; 'language has always been the consort of empire' (cited in Skutnabb-Kangas, 2000, p. 506). Nearly 400 years later, the same one-nation/one-language ideology (see May, Language Education, Pluralism and Citizenship, Volume 1) justified a fierce English-only policy in American Indian boarding schools: 'No unity of community . . . can be established among different peoples unless they are brought to speak the same language, and thus to become imbued with like ideas of duty', Commissioner of Indian Affairs J.W.C. Atkins wrote in his 1887 report (cited in McCarty, 2004, p. 71).

Linguicidal policies (Skutnabb-Kangas, 2000, p. 222) went hand-in-hand with physical genocide and territorial usurpation. When the British annexed Australia in 1770, 300,000–600,000 Aboriginal people—speakers of at least 250 languages—came under British rule. By the mid-1930s, only 60,000 Aboriginal people remained. Although there are now 300,000 Aboriginal people in Australia, all but 10% have been dispossessed of their heritage language; of the 90 languages still spoken, 70 are seriously threatened. Similarly, in Aotearoa/New Zealand, the Māori population at the time of European contact in 1769 was 100,000. Within a century, it had been decimated to 42,113, and by 1975, only 5% of Māori school children spoke Māori (May, 2004, 2005).

These human rights violations have only recently been confronted by states and international organizations (de Varennes, International Law and Education in a Minority Language, Volume 1; Skutnabb-Kangas, 2000, Human Rights and Language Policy in Education, Volume 1). In 1919, the International Labour Organisation (ILO) was created to defend the rights of ethnic minorities; this was the first international body to address Indigenous issues in a comprehensive manner. It was not until 1957, however, that the ILO adopted Convention No. 107, the first international instrument setting forth the rights of Indigenous peoples and the obligations of ratifying states. Thirty more years would pass before the United Nations established its Working Group on Indigenous Populations. In 1984, the Working Group began preparing the *Draft Declaration of the Rights of Indigenous Peoples,* calling for freedom from ethnocide and the 'right to revitalize, use, develop and transmit to future generations their histories, languages, oral traditions, philosophies, writing systems and literatures' (Article 14, cited in May and Aikman, 2003, p. 141). The *Draft Declaration* was conveyed to the UN in 1994. In July 2006—22 years after work on the *Draft Declaration* began—this policy was ratified by the UN Human Rights Commission, but it still awaits official UN approval.

In addition to the *Declaration*, perhaps the most hopeful international development has been a shift in discourse from populations to peoples, and the parallel creation, in 2000, of the UN Permanent Forum on Indigenous Issues (PFII). 'The most basic right is to be recognized as peoples', Ole Henrik Magga, first chairperson of the PFII writes; '[t]he principle of self-determination is based on the principle of peoplehood' (Magga, 1995, p. 1). Contemporary LPP activities in support of Indigenous languages and speakers all flow from these principles.

MAJOR CONTRIBUTIONS

The published literature on language policies by and for Indigenous peoples spans a continuum from actual policy documents, to historical-descriptive accounts, to ethnographic studies and recent work that engages the social justice dimensions of research and the perspectives of Indigenous scholars and practitioners. Heath's seminal (1972) treatise on language policy in Mexico was the first of its kind, providing a description of the cultural contexts for language planning from the time of the Aztec empire (see also Hamel, Indigenous Language Policy and Education in Mexico, Volume 1). Romaine (1991) employs a similar comprehensive, descriptive approach to the study of Australian languages (see especially Part I, on Aboriginal and Islander languages and Romaine's introduction). In a recent monograph series, Kaplan and Baldauf examine LPP by and for Indigenous peoples (among others) in polities less well represented in the literature (as one example, see Kaplan and Baldauf, 1999). In complementary counterpoint to these comprehensive treatments are ethnographic case studies such as Hornberger's (1988) research on Quechua bilingual education in southern Peru, King's (2001) research on Quichua language revitalization in two Ecuadorian communities and McCarty's (2002) longitudinal study of Navajo bilingual education and federal Indian policy at Rough Rock, Arizona.

Increasingly, Indigenous and non-Western scholars are leading the way in scholarship on Indigenous LPP. Notable examples include Coronel-Molina's contributions on Quechua (1999; see also, Hornberger and Coronel-Molina, 2004); Kamwangamalu's (2005) analysis of mother tongues and language planning in Africa; Rau's (2005) work on Māori literacy, assessment and corpus planning; López's (2006) study of Indigenous education in Latin America; Magga's (1994) examination of the Sámi Language Act; Mohanty's (2006) studies of language maintenance and education for Aboriginal children in India; Nicholas' (2005) study of Hopi language loss and revitalization and Warner's (1999a, 2001) analysis of the Hawaiian language revitalization movement.

In reviewing more than 30 years of literature on LPP by and for Indigenous peoples, we can see clearly the steady march of linguistic assimilation. The Navajo Reading Study at the University of New Mexico provides a case in point. From 1969 to 1979, Bernard Spolsky directed this study, surveying the language proficiencies of 6-year-old Navajo schoolchildren as a means of informing medium-of-instruction policies. 'Whereas in 1970 some 90 percent of the Navajo children ... had no preschool experience of English', Spolsky (2002, p. 140) reflects, 'by 1990 the situation had virtually reversed, with six-year-old Navajo children ... suspected to have little, if any knowledge of the language of their people'.

To the root causes of language shift outlined in this chapter's introduction, we can add the inexorable forces of globalization (see also Block, Language Education and Globalization, Volume 1). Writing about Quechua, Hornberger and Coronel-Molina describe the dilemma of many parents who 'believe that bilingual education would deny students access to social mobility' (2004, p. 14). In post-colonial Africa, Brock-Utne and Hopson (2005) outline the LPP challenge faced by Indigenous communities worldwide: How to resolve the tension between languages of wider communication as tools of empowerment and international access, and the desire to maintain local languages as central to Indigenous identities and cultural survival?

These issues dominate recent contributions to the field, as Indigenous peoples work to carve out and protect Indigenous-language-only domains. The task, as Hornberger and King (1996, pp. 299–319) point out, is not bringing the language 'back', but moving it forward into new domains. Hinton and Hale's (2001) *Green Book of Language Revitalization in Practice* provides concrete descriptions of how this is being done through Native-language immersion programmes, the cultivation of Indigenous literacies, media and technology and teacher preparation. Similarly, the chapters in Fishman (2001) outline both the challenges and the possibilities in reversing language shift (RLS) for Ainu, Māori, Navajo, Otomí, Oka, and Australian Indigenous languages. Hornberger's (1996) *Indigenous Literacies in the Americas* contains lessons in grass roots or bottom-up language planning in the Americas; her 2007 volume asks (and provides varied answers to) the question, *Can Schools Save Indigenous Languages?*, on four continents. To these works can be added the PFII's 'Indigenous Children's Education and Indigenous Languages' (Magga, Nicolaisen, Trask, Skutnabb-Kangas and Dunbar, 2005), and a burgeoning corpus of themed journals: Henze and Davis (1999) address authenticity and identity in Indigenous LPP in the Pacific Rim; May (1999) analyzes community-based Indigenous language education by and for Māori, Native Americans, Sámi, Quechua and Australian Aboriginal peoples; May and Aikman (2003) explore possibilities and constraints in Indigenous language education in the USA, Amazon Basin, Norway, central India, Western Australia, Aotearoa/New Zealand and Nicaragua; McCarty and Zepeda (1998) and McCarty, Watahomigie, and Yamamoto (1999) examine Indigenous language use, change and RLS efforts in the Americas and King and Hornberger (2004) and May (2005) address Quechua and Māori, respectively. These LPP themes also have been explored in the series growing out of the annual international Stabilizing Indigenous Languages Conference (for a span of conference activity, see Cantoni, 1996; McCarty and Zepeda, 2006).

This brief overview suggests the diversity and extent of recent LPP research and on-the-ground LPP efforts by and for Indigenous peoples. Yet this listing only scratches the surface; a recent Web search on the topic reveals nearly 5 million sources. Although it is impossible to do justice to all of this activity, we can consider more deeply a few selective examples that illustrate concrete victories as well as the challenges that lie ahead.

WORK IN PROGRESS

This section is organized around three commonly used rubrics for LPP: status planning, or decisions surrounding how and where the Indigenous language will be used, particularly with respect to education; acquisition planning, or activities related to who will use the language and for what purposes; and corpus planning, or the development of linguistic norms and forms (see also Tollefson, Language Planning in Education, Volume 1). For each rubric, I begin with a brief overview. I then focus on specific illustrations of each type of activity: the Native American Languages Act (NALA) (status planning), Māori and Hawaiian language immersion (acquisition planning) and Quechua/Quichua unification and literacy development (corpus planning).

Status Planning: How and Where Will the Indigenous Language Be Used?

At the individual level, status planning involves the minute-by-minute choices made by speakers every day. When a bilingual Navajo child hears a request in Navajo from a parent and responds in English, the child is simultaneously responding to wider policy discourses and negotiating the language policy of the home (McCarty, 2004, p. 72). At the societal level, status planning involves some type of official language and/or medium-of-instruction policy. Both types of decisions are implicated in efforts to revive, revitalize, and maintain Indigenous languages and to assert Indigenous linguistic human rights (Skutnabb-Kangas, 2000, Human Rights and Language Policy in Education, Volume 1).

Formal, societal-level policies exist for Indigenous languages around the world, although their effects on language use and vitality are not easy to gauge. Māori, for instance, has shared co-official status with English since 1987, although restoring natural intergenerational transmission remains a challenge. At the other end of the continuum is Guaraní, co-official (with Spanish) in Paraguay, and spoken by more citizens than Spanish. In post-apartheid South Africa, a National Language Planning Framework recognizes 11 official languages, including

Indigenous languages. Norway's Sámi Language Act grants Sámi co-equal status with Norwegian in core Sámi areas, and promises to 'safeguard and develop [Sámi] language, culture, and way of life' (Magga, 1994, p. 223). Tribal language policies in the USA make tribal languages official on reservations where such policies have been developed (Zepeda, 1990), but even in these settings, language revitalization and maintenance are ongoing concerns.

These language policies have resulted from long-term, bottom-up struggles to assert Indigenous language rights. NALA provides a case in point. First passed by the US Congress in 1990 and authorized for funding in 1992, NALA vows to 'preserve, protect, and promote the rights and freedom of Native Americans to use, practice, and develop Native American languages', including using Native American languages as media of instruction in school (Sec. 104[4], 104[5], cited in Cantoni, 1996, pp. 70–71; see also www.nabe.org/documents/policy_legislation/NAlanguagesActs.pdf). Reversing two centuries of US federal Indian policy, NALA grew out of early Indigenous bilingual education programmes and the grass roots networks that developed around them. In the wake of the US Civil Rights Movement, Native American bilingual education programmes proliferated. One offshoot was the American Indian Language Development Institute (AILDI), a summer programme to prepare Native teachers and bilingual/bicultural teaching materials. As Institute participants grew in number, programme leaders recognized the need for a national policy in support of local efforts. At the same time, the passage in Hawai'i of a bill granting co-official status (with English) to Hawaiian provided a model and the political muscle for a broader initiative. These interests united at the 1988 AILDI, where participants from Native nations throughout the USA drafted the resolution that would become NALA. Although funding for NALA has been meagre, it has supported some of the boldest language revitalization efforts to date, including Indigenous-language immersion, master-apprentice language-learning teams and a growing network of Indigenous language planners and advocates such as those represented by AILDI (see the discussion of AILDI in Hinton and Hale, 2001, pp. 371–383, and www.u.arizona.edu/~aildi).

Acquisition Planning: Who Will Use the Language and for What Purposes?

In any situation of language shift and revitalization, a key goal is producing a new generation of speakers. In Hornberger's (1996, p. 7) LPP framework, this is the cultivation dimension of acquisition planning. Hinton (in Hinton and Hale, 2001, pp. 1–18) describes three strategies for achieving this goal: (1) teaching the endangered language as a subject—less than optimal but often the only option available; (2) bilingual education and (3) full heritage-language immersion (a strong form of bilingual education; see May, Bilingual/Immersion Education: What the Research Tells Us, Volume 5, for further discussion), in which all or most instruction is carried out in the Indigenous language. 'There is no doubt that [Indigenous-language immersion] is the best way to jump-start ... a new generation of fluent speakers for an endangered language', Hinton writes (in Hinton and Hale, 2001, p. 8).

Two well-documented Indigenous-language immersion efforts are Māori and Hawaiian. In both cases, by the 1970s, use of the Indigenous language had declined to the point at which language users were primarily of the parent generation and older. In both cases, Indigenous-language immersion programmes were sparked by grass roots ethnic revival movements that led to recognition of the Indigenous language as co-official with English (see May's [2004] and Spolsky's [2003] discussion of this for Māori, and Warner's [2001] and Wilson's [1999, 2001] discussion for Hawaiian). Thus, by the time immersion pre-schools were established, formal policies were in place to support the cultivation of younger speakers.

Full-immersion Māori language nest pre-schools or Te Kōhanga Reo began in the spring of 1982. Later that year, Dr. Tamati Reedy, then director of the New Zealand Office of Māori Affairs, visited Hawai'i, where a Hawaiian Renaissance was under way. Reedy encouraged the Office of Hawaiian Affairs to fund Indigenous-language pre-schools similar to the Kōhanga Reo. In 1984, the first Hawaiian immersion pre-schools (called Aha Pūnana Leo and also meaning language nest) were established (May, 1999, 2004; Warner, 1999a; Wilson, 1999; Wilson and Kamanā, 2001).

The Māori and Hawaiian immersion pre-schools recreate environments in which the Indigenous language and culture 'are conveyed and developed in much the same way that they were in the home in earlier generations' (Wilson and Kamanā, 2001, p. 151). The pre-schools are parent-driven and share the goal of developing a high level of proficiency in the Indigenous language (May, 2004, 2005; Warner, 2001; Wilson and Kamanā, 2001). Both pre-school initiatives have followed a similar trajectory, as parents successfully fought for Indigenous-language tracks in mainstream K-12 schools, and for full Indigenous-language immersion elementary and secondary schools.

The Māori and Hawaiian immersion efforts have been highly successful in at least four ways. First, they have dramatically increased the availability of bilingual/immersion education in mainstream schools. Second, they have produced significant numbers of new child speakers. Third, they have demonstrated significant academic gains (May, Hill, and Tiakiwai, 2004; Rau, 2005; Wilson and Kamanā, 2001). Finally, these programmes stand as powerful exemplars of Indigenous self-determination and the exercise of Indigenous/minority language rights.

Corpus Planning: What Forms and Norms Will the Language Take?

Corpus planning includes standardization, unification, modernization and the development of practical writing systems, lexicons, grammars and literacy materials. These activities often are described as internal to the language, but they are far from completely so. As Wong points out, 'There is a constant struggle for the right to influence the language use norms of others, and in that struggle each entity . . . seeks to claim higher authority by promoting its version as superior' (1999, p. 96). The case of Quechua/Quichua illustrates these tensions and suggests that efforts to standardize may have counterproductive results.

Quechua (called Quichua in Ecuador) claims the largest number of speakers of any Indigenous language in the Americas. Despite its numbers and huge geographic spread, Quechua's future is by no means guaranteed. As Hornberger and Coronel-Molina (2004, pp. 9–67) note, in the Andean regions where Quechua is spoken (see also Godenzzi, Language Policy and Education in the Andes, Volume 1), Spanish continues to reign as the dominant, high-status and official language, while Indigenous languages are stigmatized and devalued.

In this context, recent corpus planning has confronted two competing goals. On the one hand is the perceived need for linguistic unification—the development of language forms and norms acceptable across diverse speech communities. On the other hand are concerns for authenticity and autonomy involving the valuing and promotion of local varieties and their users. (See Warner [1999a] and Wong [1999] for similar analyses of these conflicts for Hawaiian.)

Hornberger and King (1999) examine these tensions as reflected in the three-vowel versus five-vowel debate in Peru, and for the case of Quichua Unificado (Unified Quichua) in Ecuador (King, 2001). The crux of the three-vowel/five-vowel debate is the fact that Quechua has only three vowel phonemes, yet five vowel sounds are pronounced in speech. Further, five vowels have been used in written Quechua since Spanish colonial times. As Hornberger and King (1999) analyze the standoff between Peruvian linguists and bilingual education personnel (three-vowel advocates) and the Peruvian Academy of the Quechua Language (five-vowel proponents), two deeper issues surface: who has the right to make language planning decisions (the linguists and bilingual education practitioners are not fluent speakers of Quechua, whereas Academy members are) and what constitutes language purity (the five-vowel system reflects Spanish influence) (Hornberger and King, 1999, pp. 162–169).

In Ecuador, Quichua Unificado was created to encourage Quichua literacy and language revitalization (Hornberger and King, 1999, p. 171). The difficulty, as King (2001) illustrates for Saraguros in southern Ecuador, is that two varieties, Quichua Unificado and Quichua auténtico (authentic Quichua) have been pitted against each other. Educated, economically successful Saraguros tend to speak the Unified Quichua learned as a second language in school, whereas older, less-educated and more rural Saraguros speak the authentic variety as a first language in everyday affairs. Paradoxically, authentic Quichua is viewed by users of Unified Quichua as impure because it includes Spanish loan words.

These problems can paralyze language revitalization. A more fruitful strategy, Hornberger and King (1999) suggest, is a transformative, diglossic approach that brings each language variety into new domains for distinct and complementary purposes.

PROBLEMS AND DIFFICULTIES

We cannot leave this topic without noting that in many parts of the world, Indigenous LPP goals are overshadowed by ongoing genocide and ethnocide. Further, Indigenous struggles for land rights and economic justice continue to be waged in nation-states around the world, deflecting resources and attention from language issues. Where these human rights violations are not at issue, language repression continues as official government policy, even in allegedly democratic states. In Australia's Northern Territory, for instance, bilingual education programmes were terminated in 1998, putatively because of their 'poor standards of English literacy', although empirical evidence for this claim is questionable (Nicholls, 2005, p. 161). As Nicholls (2005) relates, following the phase-out of bilingual programmes, speakers of Yolngu Matha, one of the affected language groups, organized under the slogan of 'Don't Cut Off Our Tongues'. The same metaphor aptly describes the effects of increasingly ascendant English-only policies in the USA (see also May, Language Education, Pluralism and Citizenship, Volume 1; Ricento and Wright, Language Policy and Education in the United States, Volume 1). These policies flatly contradict NALA and threaten to end proven bilingual/heritage-language programmes for Indigenous and other language minorities (McCarty, 2004, pp. 85–87).

These struggles expose core issues of social justice that underlie LPP decisions and outcomes. Language is 'the "canary in the coal mine" with regard to the democratic atmosphere in general' Luykx (2004, p. 156) points out; 'rather than flog the canary back to life, we might turn our attention to the air quality in the mine'. Attending to that air quality reminds us that the real challenges in our work lie in dismantling the structures that impede parents from imparting mother tongues to their children. In this sense, language planning and medium-of-instruction policies are one part of a larger democratizing project to assess and redress the inequities that disable intergenerational language transmission.

FUTURE DIRECTIONS

Warner (1999a, p. 89) reminds us that LPP by and for Indigenous peoples is not about saving a disembodied entity called language, but rather about bringing about 'changes in society that would lead to true equality, authenticity in the empowerment of a people, ... and social justice for all'. As we contemplate a second United Nations Decade of Indigenous Peoples, future directions in this work are both global and local in scale. At the international level, we should expect recent initiatives by the PFII—in particular, the drive to approve the *Draft Declaration on the Rights of Indigenous Peoples*—to bear fruit. This will go a long way towards realizing Corson's (1997, p. 85) call, published in an earlier edition of this encyclopedia, for all nation-states to 'designate their aboriginal languages as official', and to undertake appropriate language planning and teaching activities.

Research in support of these recommendations would address the interface between the local and the global, bottom-up and top-down LPP processes. This involves "studying up"—critically analyzing the actions and responsibilities of dominant national and international agents in promoting linguistic and social justice—as well as examining the development and impacts of LPP processes at the local level. We should continue to probe the academic consequences of LPP decisions, exemplified by the investigation of May, Hill and Tiakiwai (2004) of good practices for Māori education. We also need a much fuller understanding of the language ideologies and practices of Indigenous youth caught up in the process of language shift, a topic currently under investigation in a large-scale study of American Indian language shift and retention (McCarty, Romero-Little, and Zepeda, 2006). The increasing contributions of Indigenous scholars and practitioners to this and related research are crucial.

Finally, it is essential that we widen our analytical lens to focus more fully on out-of-school LPP processes. Warner (1999b), for example, examines community outreach programmes to promote the intergenerational use of Hawaiian language and culture in sports and task-based activities in the home. Programmes and research such as this illustrate Magga's point that 'language use is the best language planning and development' (United Nations Secretariat for the U.N. PFII, 2005, p. 10). Future research and policy activism should heed this advice, thereby assisting Indigenous communities in cultivating a wide variety of domains in which their languages—and the social bonds they sustain—can grow and thrive.

See Also: Tove Skutnabb-Kangas: *Human Rights and Language Policy in Education (Volume 1); Fernand de Varennes: International Law and Education in a Minority Language (Volume 1); David Block: Language Education and Globalization (Volume 1); Stephen May: Language Education, Pluralism and Citizenship (Volume 1); James W. Tollefson: Language Planning in Education (Volume 1); Juan Carlos Godenzzi: Language Policy and Education in the Andes (Volume 1); Stephen May: Bilingual/Immersion Education: What the Research Tells Us (Volume 5); Teresa L. McCarty: Bilingual Education by and for American Indians, Alaska Natives and Native Hawaiian (Volume 5).*

REFERENCES

Brock-Utne, B. and Hopson, K.: 2005, *Languages of Instruction for African Emancipation: Focus on Postcolonial Contexts and Considerations*, Centre for Advanced Studies of African Society (CASAS), Cape Town, South Africa.

Cantoni, G. (ed.): 1996, *Stabilizing Indigenous Languages*, Northern Arizona University Center for Excellence in Education, Flagstaff.

Coronel-Molina, S.M.: 1999, 'Functonal domains of the Quechua language in Peru: Issues of status planning', *International Journal of Bilingual Education and Bilingualism* 2, 3, 166–180.

Corson, D.: 1997, 'Language policies for Indigenous peoples', *Encyclopedia of Language and Education, Volume 1: Language Policy and Political Issues in Education*, Kluwer, Netherlands, 77–87.

Fishman, J.A. (ed.): 2001, *Can Threatened Languages Be Saved? Reversing Language Shift, Revisited: A 21st Century Perspective*, Multilingual Matters, Clevedon, UK.

Hamel, R.E. (ed.): 1997, 'Linguistic Human Rights from a Sociolinguistic Perspective', theme issue, *International Journal of the Sociology of Language* 127 (entire).

Heath, S.B.: 1972, *Telling Tongues: Language Policy in Mexico—Colony to Nation*, Teachers College Press, NY.

Henze, R. and Davis, K.A. (guest eds.): 1999, 'Authenticity and Identity: Lessons from Indigenous Language Education', theme issue, *Anthropology and Education Quarterly* 30 (entire).

Hinton, L. and Hale, K.: 2001, *The Green Book of Language Revitalization in Practice*, Academic Press, San Diego, CA.

Hornberger, N.H.: 1988, *Bilingual Education and Language Maintenance: A Southern Peruvian Quechua Case*, Mouton de Gruyter, Berlin.

Hornberger, N.H. (ed.): 1996, *Indigenous Literacies in the Americas: Language Planning from the Bottom up*, Mouton de Gruyter, Berlin.

Hornberger, N.H. (ed.): 2007, *Can Schools Save Indigenous Languages? Policy and Practice on Four Continents*, Palgrave/Macmillan, Houndsmills, Basingstoke, UK.

Hornberger, N.H. and Coronel-Molina, S.M.: 2004, 'Quechua language shift, maintenance, and revitalization in the Andes: The case for language planning', *International Journal of the Sociology of Language* 167, 9–67.

Hornberger, N.H. and King, K.A.: 1996, 'Bringing the language forward: School-based initiatives for Quechua language revitalization in Ecuador and Bolivia', in

N.H. Hornberger (ed.), *Indigenous Literacies in the Americas: Language Planning from the Bottom Up*, Mouton de Gruyter, Berlin, 299–319.

Hornberger, N.H. and King, K.A.: 1999, 'Authenticy and unification in Quechua language planning', in S. May (ed.), *Indigenous Community-Based Education*, Multilingual Matters, Clevedon, UK, 160–180.

Kamwangamalu, N.M.: 2005, 'Mother tongues and language planning in Africa', *TESOL Quarterly* 39(4), 734–738.

Kaplan, R.B. and Baldauf, R.B., Jr.: 1999, *Language Planning in Malawi, Mozambique and the Philippines*, Multilingual Matters, Clevedon, UK.

King, K.A.: 2001, *Language Revitalization Processes and Prospects: Quichua in the Ecuadorian Andes*, Multilingual Matters, Clevedon, UK.

King, K.A. and Hornberger, N.H. (guest eds.): 2004, 'Quechua Sociolinguistics', theme issue, *International Journal of the Sociology of Language* 167 (entire).

Kulick, D.: 1992, *Language Shift and Cultural Reproduction: Socialization, Self, and Syncretism in a Papua New Guinean Village*, Cambridge University Press, Cambridge, UK.

López, L.E.: 2006, 'Cultural diversity, multilingualism, and Indigenous education in Latin America', in O. García, T. Skutnabb-Kangas and M.E. Torres-Guzmán (eds.), *Imagining Multilingual Schools: Languages in Education and Globalization*, Multilingual Matters, Clevedon, UK, 238–261.

Luykx, A.: 2004, 'The future of Quechua and the Quechua of the future: Language ideologies and language planning in Boliva', *International Journal of the Sociology of Language* 167, 147–158.

Magga, O.H.: 1994, 'The Sámi Language Act', in T. Skutnabb-Kangas and R. Phillipson (eds.), *Linguistic Human Rights*, Mouton de Gruyter, Berlin, 219–233.

Magga, O.H.: 1995, *Rights for Indigenous peoples*, presentation at the Fifth Annual Conference of the International Association for the Study of Common Property, May 24–28, Bodoe, Norway, available online at http://www.Indiana.edu/~iasep/abstracts/351.html, accessed October 7, 2005.

Magga, O.H., Nicolaisen, I., Trask, M., Skutnabb-Kangas, T., and Dunbar, R.: 2005, *Indigenous children's education and Indigenous languages*, expert paper written for the United Nations Permanent Forum on Indigenous Issues, United Nations, NY.

May, S. (ed.): 1999, *Indigenous Community-Based Education*, Multilingual Matters, Clevedon, UK.

May, S.: 2004, 'Māori-medium education in Aotearoa/New Zealand', in J.W. Tollefson and A.B.M. Tsui (eds.), *Medium of Instruction Policies: Which Agenda? Whose Agenda?*, Lawrence Erlbaum, Mahwah, NJ, 21–41.

May, S. (guest ed.): 2005, 'Bilingual/Immersion Education in Aotearoa/New Zealand', theme issue, *International Journal of Bilingual Education and Bilingualism* 8(5) (entire).

May, S. and Aikman, S.: 2003, 'Indigenous Education: New Possibilities, Ongoing Constraints', theme issue, *Comparative Education* 39(2) (entire).

May, S., Hill, R., and Tiakiwai, S.: 2004, *Bilingual/Immersion Education: Indicators of Good Practice: Final Report to the Ministry of Education*, Ministry of Education, NZ.

McCarty, T.L.: 2002, *A Place to be Navajo—Rough Rock and the Struggle for Self-Determination in Indigenous Schooling*, Lawrence Erlbaum, Mahwah, NJ.

McCarty, T.L.: 2004, 'Dangerous difference: A critical-historical analysis of language education policies in the United States', in J.W. Tollefson and A.B.M. Tsui (eds.), *Medium of Instruction Policies: Which Agenda? Whose Agenda?*, Lawrence Erlbaum, Mahwah, NJ, 71–93.

McCarty, T.L. and Zepeda, O. (guest eds.): 1998, 'Indigenous Language Use and Change in the Americas', theme issue, *International Journal of the Sociology of Language* 132 (entire).

McCarty, T.L. and Zepeda, O. (eds.): 2006, *One Voice, Many Voices: Recreating Indigenous Language Communities*, Arizona State University College of Education Center for Indian Education, Tempe.

McCarty, T.L., Romero-Little, M.E., and Zepeda, O.: 2006, 'Native American youth discourses on language shift and retention: Ideological cross-currents and their implications for language planning', *International Journal of Bilingual Education and Bilingualism* 9(5), 659–677.

McCarty, T.L., Watahomigie, L.J., and Yamamoto, A.Y. (guest eds.): 1999, 'Reversing Language Shift in Indigenous America: Collaborations and Views from the Field', theme issue, Practicing Anthropology 21, 1–47.

Mohanty, A.K.: 2006, 'Multilingualism of the unequals and predicaments of education in India: Mother tongue or other tongue?', in O. García, T. Skutnabb-Kangas, and M.E. Torres-Guzmán (eds.), *Imagining Multilingual Schools: Languages in Education and Glocalization*, Multilingual Matters, Clevedon, UK, 262–283.

Nicholas, S.: 2005, 'Negotiating for the Hopi way of life through literacy and schooling', in T.L. McCarty (ed.), *Language, Literacy, and Power in Schooling*, Lawrence Erlbaum, Mahwah, NJ, 29–46.

Nicholls, C.: 2005, 'Death by a thousand cuts: Indigenous language bilingual education programmes in the Northern Territory of Australia, 1972–1998', *International Journal of Bilingual Education and Bilingualism* 8, 160–177.

Rau, C.: 2005, 'Literacy acquisition, assessment and achievement of Year Two students in total immersion in Māori programmes', *International Journal of the Sociology of Language* 8(5), 404–432.

Romaine, S. (ed.): 1991, *Language in Australia*, Cambridge University Press, Cambridge, UK.

Skutnabb-Kangas, T.: 2000, *Linguistic Genocide in Education—Or Worldwide Diversity and Human Rights?*, Lawrence Erlbaum, Mahwah, NJ.

Spolsky, B.: 2002, 'Prospects for the survival of the Navajo language: A reconsideration', *Anthropology and Education Quarterly* 33, 139–162.

United Nations Secretariat for the U.N. Permanent Forum on Indigenous Issues: 2005, 'Interview with the first chairperson of the UNPFII, Mr. Ole Henrik Magga', *Message Stick* 3, 9–11.

Warner, S.L.N.: 1999a, '*Kuleana*: The right, responsibility, and authority of Indigenous peoples to speak and make decisions for themselves in language and culture revitalization', *Anthropology and Education Quarterly* 30(1), 68–93.

Warner, S.N.: 1999b, 'Hawaiian language regenesis: Planning for intergenerational use of Hawaiian beyond the school', in T. Huebner and K.A. Davis (eds.), *Sociopolitical Perspectives on Language Policy and Planning in the USA*, John Benjamins, Amsterdam/Philadelphia, 313–331.

Warner, S.L.N.: 2001, 'The movement to revitalize Hawaiian language and culture', in L. Hinton and K. Hale (eds.), *The Green Book of Language Revitalization in Practice*, Academic Press, San Diego, CA, 133–144.

Wilson, W.H.: 1999, 'The sociopolitical context of establishing Hawaiian-medium education', in S. May (ed.), *Indigenous Community-Based Education*, Multilingual Matters, Clevedon, UK, 95–108.

Wilson, W.H. and Kamanā, K.: 2001, '"*Mai loko mai o ka 'I'ini*: Proceeding from a dream," The 'Aha Pūnana Leo connection in Hawaiian language revitalization', in L. Hinton and K. Hale (eds.), *The Green Book of Language Revitalization in Practice*, Academic Press, San Diego, CA, 147–176.

Wong, L.: 1999, 'Authenticity and the revitalization of Hawaiian', *Anthropology and Education Quarterly* 30(1), 94–113.

Zepeda, O.: 1990, 'American Indian language policy', in K.L. Adams and D.T. Brink (eds.), *Perspectives on Official English: The Campaign for English as the Official Language of the USA*, Mouton de Gruyter, Berlin, 247–256.

JAN BRANSON AND DON MILLER

NATIONAL SIGN LANGUAGES AND LANGUAGE POLICIES

INTRODUCTION

On 27 June 1999, 4,000 people marched through London in support of British Sign Language (BSL), demanding its recognition as the language of the British Deaf community and asserting the right of Deaf children to be educated in a bilingual environment with BSL as the language of instruction (*Deaf History Journal*, 1999). While the British Deaf were marching, the Parliament of Thailand was in the process of formally recognizing Thai Sign Language as a fully fledged language, as the first language of Thai deaf people, and as the language through which Thai deaf people should be educated in a bilingual environment. By late March 2005, the British Deaf community were celebrating the fact that the government had recognized the existence of BSL[1] but were fervent about the need to continue agitating to have BSL legalized so that BSL users have the legal right to use it, "bringing years of language discrimination to an end," indeed for BSL to be recognized as "the UK's fourth indigenous language" (BDA News/ Press Releases for 16 May 2005, http://www.signcommunity.org.uk/ news). In June 2004, the New Zealand Sign Language Bill went before a Committee of the New Zealand Parliament. On 10 April 2006, Royal Assent was given to the Bill and NZSL became New Zealand's third official language, along with English and Maori (see http://www.odi. govt.nz). On 6 July 2005, the Austrian Parliament voted for the recognition of Austrian Sign Language, giving the language constitutional recognition.

In countries around the world, in the policy-making bodies of the EU and the UN, and in the World Federation of the Deaf (WFD), Deaf people and their hearing supporters have been agitating, with particular intensity over the past decade, for the formal, legal, and constitutional recognition of sign languages as the natural and first languages of Deaf people. It is a struggle that has challenged the firmly socialized prejudices of individuals and governments alike against the so-called "disabled," and has also eaten away at the very foundations of linguistics

---

[1] BSL was recognized as an official British language by the UK government on 18 March 2003, but it does not have any legal protection.

S. May and N. H. Hornberger (eds), Encyclopedia of Language and Education,
2nd Edition, Volume 1: Language Policy and Political Issues in Education, 151–165.
©*2010 Springer Science+Business Media LLC.*

and the philosophy of language. At its heart has been an ongoing confrontation with the shape and purpose of formal education.

Both the development of national sign languages and the development of formal government language policies associated with sign languages are relatively recent, products of the spread of nationalism and of national and international movements in the fields of human rights and education (cf. May, 2006, Language Education, Pluralism and Citizenship, Volume 1; Skutnabb-Kangas, 2006, Human Rights and Language Policy in Education, Volume 1). Do national sign languages exist, or are they constructed? This is an issue we will deal in the following sections.

Sign Language Policies

There have always been policies towards sign languages, policies which have overtly or covertly been influenced by wider attitudes towards language in general. These policies have often denied sign languages the status of languages and have in turn denied their users their full humanity. The impact of philosophers of language on these policies towards sign languages has often been profound, especially where speech has been assumed to be synonymous with language (see Wilbur, 1987).

Pre-Enlightenment policies towards sign languages were frequently linked to religious practice. Membership of a community was almost invariably membership of a religious community and that membership hinged on effective religious practice. Where speech was assumed to be central to this practice—for example, saying the creed or taking confession—and where signing was not regarded as the equivalent of speech, the Deaf were often denied full communal membership and thus denied their complete humanity. In the post-Enlightenment period, as detailed later, although the impact of religious groups on the use of sign language has remained important, the primary focus of these language policies has shifted to the sphere of education. Language policies in relation to education have both overtly and covertly impacted on the use of sign language not only in the education of the Deaf but in the wider community. Educational policies have operated at times to accept the use of sign languages and to accord them the status of languages, but have more often than not denigrated these languages either by banning their use altogether or by transforming them radically to serve as manually coded versions of the dominant spoken language (see also Skutnabb-Kangas, 2006, Human Rights and Language Policy in Education, Volume 1).

The key political issue in relation to policies on sign languages both in education and beyond, continues to be a battle, on the one hand, between signing and oralism (oralism referring to the position taken by those who believe that all deaf people should learn to speak, lip-read, and "hear" [through the use of aids such as hearing aids or cochlear implants] in the dominant language to the exclusion of sign language), and on the other between the use of sign language and the use of manually coded versions of the dominant spoken language. It must be added, however, that there are still sign languages which are not affected by these educationally based policies, since one country may have many indigenous sign languages used by communities which have not come under the impact of national or even regional language policies (see, e.g., Branson and Miller, 2004; Branson, Miller, and Marsaja, 1999).

Sign languages, like all fully fledged languages, are natural languages that develop through their use for communication within communal contexts. Signing communities might be residential localized communities or dispersed networks of people, and, since sign languages are unwritten languages, the boundaries of their sign languages are defined by the boundaries of their communal activity. The degree to which sign language users within a nation-state use a common sign language will depend on the effectiveness of national networks within the Deaf community, on the impact of national sign language-based education, and on the impact on Deaf communities of formal research into, and the associated standardization and teaching of, a national sign language.

The promotion and indeed the development of national sign languages, as distinct from more localized community sign languages, is associated with four basic movements: the development of national associations of Deaf people; the drive for the achievement of linguistic rights as an aspect of human rights; the development of formal language policies; and the drive for national education systems with sign language as the medium of instruction. This nationalism is manifested in the drive for the publication of national sign language dictionaries. As the WFD report on the status of sign languages reveals, no country has a dictionary for more than one sign language. Of the 43 countries surveyed, only six did not have sign language dictionaries, but all the rest had only one, a national sign language dictionary. The dictionaries themselves embody not only the symbolic representation of a language and thus its recognition, a vital ingredient in the move to achieve the bilingual education of deaf people with a natural sign language as the language of instruction, but also the standardization of language, the move towards linguistic purity that is a feature of literate languages (see Branson and Miller, 2002; Edwards, 1985, p. 27ff; *Sign Language Studies*, 2003). Assumptions about the unitary nature of national spoken and written languages are transferred to the way that sign languages are in turn conceptualized. National sign languages are not only formally standardized and developed through the publication of dictionaries and sign language teaching manuals but are also assumed to exist. An understanding of the concept of a national sign language and of the social, cultural, and linguistic dynamics involved in their development, therefore requires reference to literature on nationalism itself. Here the work of Benedict Anderson (1991) is particularly pertinent, with its focus on the forces that have created these "imagined communities." As Anderson points out, the nation assumes the status of a community, encompassing and transforming traditional communities, claiming the loyalties and orientations that were formerly afforded the village, the lineage, the clan, the tribe, the neighbour-hood (cf. May, 2006, Language Education, Pluralism and Citizenship, Volume 1). We examine the "problems and difficulties" of the drive for the recognition of "national" sign languages later.

Sign Languages and Educational Policies

As indicated earlier, since the Enlightenment, it has been educational policy which has exerted the greatest influence on policies towards sign languages. The development of national sign languages and the history of language policies associated with those languages is therefore an integral part of the history of the education of deaf people in the West and more recently beyond the West in Asia, Africa, and the Americas, particularly under the influence of Western educators. It is also through an examination of the use of sign languages in deaf education that the impact of dominant hearing communities and their languages on the use of "signing" is revealed, initially in the late nineteenth century through the overt banning of sign language use in school, associated with the denial of the linguistic status of sign languages, as well as later, from the 1960s, through the development and promotion of manually coded versions of national spoken and written languages in formal education. Manually coded versions of national spoken and written languages—such as Signed English, Signed Swedish, Signed French, Signed Thai, and Signed Indonesian—have been, and still often are, promoted as national sign languages, particularly by hearing professionals associated with the education of the deaf, who believe that the acquisition of literacy in the national (spoken and written) language occurs most effectively through the use of manually coded versions of that national (spoken and written) language.

These signed versions of dominant languages are neither fully fledged languages of communication nor natural languages, but rather manual codes based on written forms of language, using "frozen signs"—a single unchanging sign for each word or morpheme—and thus making little use of the dynamic and creative features of sign languages. While some signs in natural sign languages are "frozen signs," much of the lexicon is a productive lexicon—signs change and develop in response to the meaning being generated, using a range of conventions of transformation based on hand shapes, the use of space, orientation, the face, and body. These dynamic aspects of sign language lexicons contrast starkly with manually coded versions of sound-based languages.

In those non-Western countries which have developed Western-style educational systems, educational policy has also been the forum in which national policies towards sign languages have been developed. In these cases, policies have often been strongly influenced by Western experts, especially Western teachers of the deaf, who have taken a direct role in the development of national policies towards sign languages, frequently in the development of manually coded versions of the national spoken language, for example, Signed Thai and Signed Indonesian, which are then assumed to be the national sign language.

EARLY DEVELOPMENTS

Most early policies developed by default. While there is evidence of deaf people being taught through the medium of natural sign languages to read and write, first in Latin and later in the languages of everyday life, from well before the so-called Enlightenment, it is from the sixteenth century that educators emerge throughout Europe intent on teaching "the Deaf and Dumb" (privileged children of merchants and the nobility) not only to read and write but to speak. They paid little attention to existing sign languages but rather developed systems of finger spelling designed for the purposes of speech training. Finger spelling increasingly became associated with the manual representation of the dominant written language, rather than with the normal processes of borrowing between languages.

As the education of the Deaf moved beyond the very exclusive instruction of the nobility to the development of education for the poor deaf, the impact of national languages on the Deaf became more extreme. In the mid-eighteenth century, in 1755, the Abbé de l'Epée established a school for poor Deaf children in Paris (see Lane, 1988). While teaching the deaf children to speak was one of his educational aims, particularly in the beginning, he moved away from speech training as central to the education of the deaf towards the use of signing as a means for teaching the deaf pupils to read and write. But he did not use the two-handed alphabet in use among the Parisian Deaf communities and did not use existing sign languages with their distinctive syntax as the language of instruction. Rather he used the one-handed alphabet and developed a system of signed French. The die had been cast. While other educators in other times and places—Castberg in Denmark, Bébian in France later, and a string of British educators, for example, Charles Baker, Robert Kinniburgh, William Scott, and Drysdale (see Branson and Miller, 2002)—used natural sign languages to a greater

or lesser degree—often with a lot of finger spelling—and did not necessarily develop manually coded versions of the written language, hearing
educators constantly tampered with the signing traditions of their
pupils, subordinating and severely restricting their lexicon to the
demands of spoken and written languages, some insisting on the possibility of signing and speaking at the same time. The widespread use of
signing of various kinds throughout the eighteenth and nineteenth centuries gave way on an almost universal scale from the late nineteenth
century to the partial or complete banning of signing in schools and a
dedication to oralism—teaching deaf people to speak and lip-read the
dominant spoken language. In Milan in 1880, an international conference of teachers of the deaf consolidated processes that had been at
work for some time by voting overwhelmingly to ban the use of sign
language in the education of the deaf (see Branson and Miller, 2002;
Lane, 1988). Signing continued to be used in schools for some time,
not only in the USA but also in Britain and Australia, but what Milan
did mark very clearly was a change in the overall conceptualization of
the educational process as it applied to deaf people. The purpose of that
education was changing. By removing signing and deaf teachers from
the classroom and even the playground, teachers, therapists,
and associated experts sought to normalize deaf people, to destroy their
difference, and to destroy the cultural aspects of their deafness. As the
twentieth century progressed, sign languages were banned by an
increasing number of educational authorities. Their linguistic status
was denied. The climb back to linguistic and educational rights for the
Deaf was a hard one.

From the late 1960s, the use of signing, albeit often manually coded
versions of the dominant spoken language, emerged again in opposition to oralism. Today, the drive throughout much, but by no means
all, of the world, is for the use of natural sign languages in a bilingual
educational system (see in particular Ahlgren and Hylenstam, 1994
and also see the review by Small and Mason, American Sign Language
(ASL) Bilingual Bicultural Education, Volume 5). These bilingual policies are again linked to the transformation of national policies. Where
bilingual deaf education is promoted, the wider national recognition of
sign languages as viable communal languages tends to be found. In
Sweden, Denmark, Finland, Thailand, Venezuela, and Uruguay, for
example, bilingual education with sign languages as the primary mode
of instruction are national policy, supported in most cases by state-run
programs for the teaching of sign language to preschool children and
their families. Comprehensive international data on national policies
towards sign languages have yet to be collected and collated. A survey
by Gloria Pullen and Lesley Jones (1990) of policies towards Deaf

people in 11 European countries clearly showed that government policies towards Deaf people and their languages were, with the exception of the one Scandinavian country in the survey, Denmark, governed by their perception of Deaf people as disabled rather than as a linguistic minority. Skutnabb-Kangas has provided more up-to-date information for Europe, especially in her discussions of "Arguments to Exclude Sign Languages from the European Charter for Regional or Minority Languages" (see also Skutnabb-Kangas 2006, Human Rights and Language Policy in Education, Volume 1).

MAJOR CONTRIBUTIONS AND WORK IN PROGRESS

Most of the current research into, and commentary on, national sign languages and language policies is conducted under the auspices of international and national associations of the Deaf. Examples are discussed later. The best known work on the history of policies and practices relating to the use of sign language in the education of the Deaf in Western societies, with a particular focus on France and the USA, is Harlan Lane's *When the Mind Hears* (Lane, 1988), complemented by the valuable collection of historical documents in Lane and Philip (1984) and by Lane's treatment of the marginalization of the Deaf in the West in his *The Mask of Benevolence* (Lane, 1992). These works, however, misrepresent the history of the education of deaf people in Britain, characterizing it as "oralist" from the beginning of its history. In contrast to France and the USA, natural sign language was widely and effectively used in Britain, until the American educator Edward Miner Gallaudet and his Irish pupil, Francis Maginn succeeded in forcing natural sign languages from the schools in favour of the "combined method," the simultaneous use of speech and signing (see Branson and Miller, 2002). Comprehensive linguistic research into sign languages is relatively recent, and is associated with a small but very active international community of scholars, with research results published through a few specialized journals and in books based on international conferences (for a critique of sign language linguistics, see Branson and Miller, 2000). Much current writing on the relationship between language policies and educational policies, as they relate to the Deaf, is found in proceedings of national and international conferences of teachers of the deaf. International Congresses on Education of the Deaf are held every 5 years and although they have moved far beyond the complete intolerance of sign languages evident at their congress in Milan in 1880, they still include very few Deaf people. A large proportion of the papers reprinted in their proceedings are still devoted to papers advocating either pure oralism in deaf education or the use of manually coded versions of the national spoken and written language (e.g. see Taylor, 1988).

Linguistic research has played an important part in questioning the use of manually coded versions of spoken languages in Deaf education (see in particular Johnson, Liddle, and Erting, 1989), providing support to the demands of Deaf communities for the use of their natural sign languages. Examples of this process are well documented for Sweden in Bergman and Wallin (1990), particularly the interweaving of research and the Deaf community organizations in the development and promotion of Swedish Sign Language. Bilingual education for the deaf with a sign language as the prime medium of instruction is the focus for an increasing amount of research (see in particular Ahlgren and Hylenstam, 1994; Bouvet, 1990; Branson and Miller, 2002, p. 220ff.; Hansen, 1990; Heiling, 1995; Jokinen, 2000; Lewis, 1995; Mahshie, 1995; Skutnabb-Kangas, 2000). Specific discussion of the policies and practices relating to the use of sign languages in Canada, with reference also to the USA, is to be found in Corson and Lemay (1996). For a wide range of well informed papers dealing with the issue of the rights of minority language groups to education through their first language, see the articles in Phillipson (2000).

Sign Languages and Linguistic Rights

The WFD "Fact Sheet" on sign language (http://www.wfdeaf.org/documents.html) lists 32 countries in which sign language is formally recognized, constitutionally or in legislation or policy. To this list should be added (at least) Thailand (1999), the UK (2003), and Austria (2005). Today, as throughout much of their history, Deaf communities themselves are the prime movers in the establishment of linguistic rights for the Deaf, particularly in education, and are, in the process, the driving force for the recognition not only of sign languages but of national sign languages (see Jokinen, 2000). These principles and orientations are succinctly stated in the policies of the WFD, specifically their current statement on the "Educational Rights of Deaf Children" (http://www.wfdeaf.org/pdf/policy_child_ed.pdf).

The active pursuit of these linguistic human rights is to be seen not only in demands by associations of the Deaf for the formal recognition of sign languages but also in legal action, seeking compensation for the damage caused by the denial of access to education and other services through sign languages. Examples are to be seen in a number of Australian court cases brought on behalf of deaf children by Deaf Children Australia. Evidence of not only the national but international importance of these cases is seen in the following news item circulated in June 2005 by the European Union of the Deaf.

Court Decision Landmark for Deaf Education in Australia

The Federal Court of Australia has found that the Queensland government discriminated against a 12-year-old boy by not providing him with a sign language interpreter at school.

The boy who, according to Deaf Children Australia, has the academic skills of a 6-year-old was awarded $64,000 in compensation for future economic losses as a result of his inadequate education. The implications of this finding could prove to be a landmark decision for Deaf education in Australia as it establishes firmly deaf children's right to an Auslan (Australian Sign Language) interpreter in school.

As James Gray, counsel for the boy's family, asserts any educational authority that does not provide deaf children with an interpreter could be found to be in breach of commonwealth human rights legislation. State governments are not liable to pay compensation in such a situation, he added (*Source*: SIGNMatters, June 2005 http://www.eudnet.org/update/online/2005/jun05/worn_01.htm)[2].

PROBLEMS AND DIFFICULTIES

As indicated earlier, most of the dialogue dealing with the linguistic rights of Deaf people continues to be framed in terms of "national sign languages." From 24 January 2005 to 4 February 2005, the fifth session of an ad hoc committee of the United Nations, the Ad Hoc Committee on a Comprehensive and Integral International Convention on the Protection and Promotion of the Rights and Dignity of Persons with Disabilities, met in New York (http://www.un.org/esa/socdev/enable/rights/ahc5reporte.htm). Among other documents, they had before them a response from the WFD to proposals about the use of sign languages that had been tabled and reported at earlier sessions of the Ad Hoc Committee.[3] The focus of the WFD response was on article 13 of the Ad Hoc Committee's Draft Report. The chapeau of draft article 13 reads:

> States parties shall take all appropriate measures to ensure that persons with disabilities can exercise their right to freedom of expression and opinion, including the freedom to seek, receive and impart information and ideas on an equal basis with others and through sign languages, and Braille, and augmentative alternative communication and all other

---

[2] "SIGNMatters" is a newsletter of the British Deaf Association.
[3] See WFD web site (http://www.wfdeaf.org/) for their response and for other documents relating to sign languages.

accessible means, modes and formats of communication of
their choice ... (United Nations, 2005, p. 17).

The "means" of concern to WFD delegates was the means contained in
subparagraph (h), which, following a submission by Uganda, had read
"developing a national sign language." The WFD listed a range of
responses to this subparagraph, which requested the amendment of
the phrase "developing a national sign language" to read "recognizing"
or "promoting" a "national sign language," with the WFD proposing
the amending of the original to read "recognizing and promoting a
national sign language." In response to this proposal, the fifth session
of the United Nation's ad hoc committee reported that there was no
general agreement on how to word subparagraph (h) and therefore that
"Subparagraph(h), on which further discussions are required, reads:
'(h) [Developing/recognizing/promoting] a national sign language.'"
(United Nations, 2005, p. 19).

As indicated in our introduction, the majority of statements made
about the need to recognize and use sign languages are framed in terms
of "national" sign languages. The pressures for the *development* of
national sign languages are well illustrated by the example of the
Dictionary of Southern African Signs for Communication with the Deaf
(Penn, 1992). The signs illustrated there come from at least 12 cultural
regions, from 12 distinct communities with distinct natural sign languages, and yet, in one of the prefaces to the first volume, Timothy
Reagan (2006) states,

A beginning has now been made to record the beauty and
diversity of South African Sign Language .... Needed as
well are studies of the syntax of South African Sign Language in its many forms, ... This is a formidable challenge,
but it is one that the South African Deaf community is more
than capable of meeting (Penn, 1992, p. xi).

The slip from the recognition of the diversity and multilingual nature of
the South African Deaf, of the many Deaf communities in South
Africa, into a unitary orientation towards "South African Sign Language" and "the South African Deaf community," both in the singular,
is symptomatic of the approach taken by most governments, linguists,
and linguistic rights activists alike. Linguists in particular are involved
in the standardization of sign languages towards "national" variants—
British Sign Language, American Sign Language, South African Sign
Language, and so on—each with a dictionary (see Branson and Miller,
2000, 2002; *Sign Language Studies*, 2003).

The drive for the recognition of sign languages as "national" sign
languages thus poses a conundrum. The recognition of sign languages
involves:

1. the assertion by national Deaf associations of the existence of national sign languages;
2. the drive for formal recognition of these languages as national sign languages; and
3. the demand for and the development of education through these respective languages for all Deaf people nationally.

But the assertion and recognition of national sign languages can lead to the failure to recognize the existence of minority sign languages in precisely the same way as the assertion and promotion of national spoken and written languages lead to the oppression and suppression of minority spoken and written languages. And yet the recognition of the sign languages of the majority is an enormous and vital, even revolutionary, step forward for Deaf communities throughout the world, a conundrum posed by nationalism itself.

In 2003, the European Year of People with Disabilities, the European Union of the Deaf (EUD), in making a statement on sign languages to accompany its mission statement, titled its statement "Sign Languages of (sic) the Right to Use an Indigenous Sign Language." The statement began:

> This is a core tenet of EUD's working objectives and significant change has occurred over the past years. Successes include the European parliament's resolutions on the recognition of sign languages in 1988 and again in 1998 and the European Commission sponsored Sign Languages Project (1996–1997) carried out by EUD. These actions have acted as a catalyst for member associations to work with their national governments in securing practical, and in several cases, constitutional or legal recognition of their respective national sign language (http://www.eudeaf2003.org/en/chapter51.html).

Although the statement focused on recognition of "national sign languages," it went on to state that:

> EUD continues to strive for full and legal recognition of Sign language/s by the European Union, the Council of Europe and all EU national governments as a minority language, just like they have recognised certain spoken languages as minority and regional languages. There is no ground for excluding sign languages, especially not on linguistic grounds, since research has long since shown that sign languages ARE languages. The major barrier to tear down is the attitude of governments and legal advisers who do not believe that sign languages are real languages and do not realize or understand the importance of sign languages for Deaf people (ibid.).

The EUD statement thus begins to do something that few other statements on sign language rights do, to move away from the assumption
that "national sign languages" exist or are the important focus of linguistic rights, to refer to "indigenous sign languages" and to the recognition of "minority and regional languages." This change is also
reflected in the latest WFD statement on the "Educational Rights of
Deaf Children" referred to earlier, which states:

> To ensure that the educational rights of Deaf learners are ful-
> filled, WFD ... :
> • Reaffirms its position that all Deaf people, including Deaf
> children, have the right to full access to quality education
> through visual modes, including indigenous sign languages.

Reflecting this change, a recent statement by the Parliamentary Assembly of the Council of Europe states (in part):

> 9. ... the Assembly recommends that the Committee of
> Ministers devise a specific legal instrument on the rights of
> sign language users, and accordingly:
>
> . . .
>
> iii. consider drafting an additional protocol to the European
> Charter for Regional or Minority Languages incorporating
> sign languages into the charter, among the non-territorial
> minority languages.
>
> 10. The Assembly also recommends that the Committee of
> Ministers encourage member states:
>
> i. to give the sign languages used in their territory formal
> recognition; (http://www.eudeaf2003.org/en/counsildocument1.
> html).

The move away from referring simply to "national sign languages" is a
vital one. It should be noted that one of the few countries without a
"national" sign language is overtly multilingual Canada, where American
Sign Language (ASL) and Langue des Signes Quebecoise (LSQ) are
commonly used. On 11 February 2005, the Canadian Association of the
Deaf called for the official recognition of Inuit Sign Language (see
http://www.cad.ca/index2.php?lid=e&cid=9&pid=0 and http://www.
nunatsiaq.com/archives/50204/news/nunavut/50204_10.html).

FUTURE DIRECTIONS

The current statements on the linguistic human rights of Deaf people by
the WFD and the EUD, show that a solution to the conundrum posed
by a focus on "national sign languages" demands the integration of
research on sign languages with current research on minority language

rights (see Jokinen, 2000; Phillipson, 2000; Ricento, 2006[4]; Skutnabb-Kangas, 2000; Skutnabb-Kangas and Phillipson, 1994; and see the reviews by Phillipson, Language Policy and Education in the European Union, Volume 1; Skutnabb-Kangas, Human Rights and Language Policy in Education, Volume 1). Multilingual solutions involving national and local sign languages as well as literacy in the dominant national spoken language must be considered. Moves of this kind are under way in some countries, especially where they are asserting the need for the use of local sign languages in education rather than the use of imported Western sign languages such as American Sign Language, as has frequently been the case (see, e.g. de Carpentier, 1995). Models of bilingual education which assume that a national sign language does or can exist need to be complemented with multilingual models which recognize that sign languages are both natural and face-to-face languages and that it is local languages that must be used. Whether or not national sign languages will emerge is dependent on the networks of effective communication that can also be developed. Towards this end, the sociolinguistics of sign languages is moving towards the study of localized rather than national sign languages, studied within their distinct social and cultural contexts (Branson and Miller, 2004; Branson, Miller, and Marsaja, 1999; Johnson, 1994).

See Also: *Tove Skutnabb-Kangas: Human Rights and Language Policy in Education (Volume 1); Stephen May: Language Education, Pluralism and Citizenship (Volume 1); Thomas Ricento and Wayne Wright: Language Policy and Education in the United States (Volume 1); Anita Small and David Mason: American Sign Language (ASL) Bilingual Bicultural Education (Volume 5); Rebecca Freeman Field: Identity, Community and Power in Bilingual Education (Volume 5); Tove Skutnabb-Kangas: Language Rights and Bilingual Education (Volume 5); Tove Skutnabb-Kangas and Robert Phillipson: A Human Rights Perspective on Language Ecology (Volume 9)*

REFERENCES

Ahlgren, I.: 1990, 'Sign language in deaf education', in S. Prillwitz and T. Vollhaber (eds.), *Sign Language Research and Application: Proceedings of the International Congress, Hamburg, 1990*, Signum Press, Hamburg, 91–94.
Ahlgren, I. and Hylenstam, K. (eds.): 1994, *Bilingualism in Deaf Education*, Signum Press, Hamburg.

---

[4] See in particular the chapters by May (2006) on the impact of nationalism on minority rights; by Skutnabb-Kangas (2006) on language policies and linguistic human rights; by Reagan (2006) on language planning and sign languages; and by Phillipson (2006) on language policy and linguistic imperialism.

Anderson, B.: 1991, *Imagined Communities: Reflections on the Origin and Spread of Nationalism*, Verso, London.

Bergman, B. and Wallin, L.: 1990, 'Sign language research and the deaf community', in S. Prillwitz and T. Vollhaber (eds.), *Sign Language Research and Application: Proceedings of the International Congress, Hamburg, 1990*, Signum Press, Hamburg, 187–214.

Bouvet, D.: 1990, *The Path to Language: Bilingual Education for Deaf Children*, Multilingual Matters, Clevedon.

Branson, J. and Miller, D.: 2000, 'Maintaining, developing and sharing the knowledge and potential embedded in all our languages and cultures: On linguists as agents of epistemic violence', in R. Phillipson (ed.), *Rights to Language: Equity, Power and Education*, Lawrence Erlbaum Associates, London,

Branson, J. and Miller, D.: 2002, *Damned for Their Difference: The Cultural Construction of "the Disabled" and of the Deaf as "Disabled". A Sociological History*, Gallaudet University Press, Washington, DC.

Branson, J. and Miller, D.: 2004, 'The cultural construction of linguistic incompetence through schooling: Deaf education and the transformation of the linguistic environment in Bali, Indonesia', *Sign Language Studies* 5(1), 6–38.

Branson, J., Miller, D., and Marsaja, G.: 1999, 'Sign languages as a natural part of the linguistic mosaic: The impact of deaf people on discourse forms in North Bali, Indonesia', in *Sociolinguistics in Deaf Communities*, Gallaudet University Press, Washington, DC, 109–148.

Corson, D. and Lemay, S.: 1996, *Social Justice and Language Policy in Education: The Canadian Research*, OISE Press, Ontario.

de Carpentier, A.L.: 1995, *Deaf Education in Developing Countries*, Paper presented at the 18th International Congress on Education of the Deaf, Tel Aviv.

Deaf History Journal: 1999, 'BSL March: Its historical significance', *Deaf History Journal*, Vol. 3 No. 1, August, p. 2.

Edwards, J.: 1985, *Language, Society, and Identity*, Basil Blackwell, Oxford.

Hansen, B.: 1990, 'Trends in the progress towards bilingual education for deaf children in Denmark', in S. Prillwitz and T. Vollhaber (eds.), *Sign Language Research and Application: Proceedings of the International Congress, Hamburg, 1990*, Signum Press, Hamburg, 51–62.

Heiling, K.: 1995, *The Development of Deaf Children: Academic Achievement Levels and Social Processes*, Signum Press, Hamburg.

Johnson, R.E.: 1994, 'Sign language and the concept of deafness in a traditional Yucatec Mayan village', in C.J. Erting, R.C. Johnson, D.L. Smith, and D. Snider (eds.), *The Deaf Way*, Gallaudet University Press, Washington, DC, 102–109.

Johnson, R., Liddle, S., and Erting, C.: 1989, *Unlocking the Curriculum: Principles for Achieving Access in Deaf Education*, Gallaudet University Press, Washington, DC.

Jokinen, M.: 2000, 'The linguistic human rights of sign language users', in R. Phillipson (ed.), *Rights to Language: Equity, Power and Education*, Lawrence Erlbaum Associates, London.

Lane H. (ed) and F. Philip (Trans), 1984, *The Deaf Experience: Classics in Language and Education*, Harvard University Press, Cambridge, Massachusetts.

Lane, H.: 1988, *When the Mind Hears: A History of the Deaf*, Penguin Books, Harmondsworth.

Lane, H.: 1992, *The Mask of Benevolence: Disabling the Deaf Community*, Alfred A. Knopf, New York.

Lewis, W. (ed.): 1995, *Bilingual Teaching of Deaf Children in Denmark—Description of a Project 1982–1992*, Døveskolernes Materialecenter, Aalborg.

Mahshie, S.N.: 1995, *Educating Deaf Children Bilingually—With Insights and Applications from Sweden and Denmark*, Gallaudet University, Washington, DC.

May, S.: 2006, 'Language policy and minority rights', in T. Ricento (ed.), *Language Policy: Theory and Method*, Blackwell Publishing, Oxford.

Penn, C.: 1992, *Dictionary of Southern African Signs for Communicating with the Deaf*, Human Sciences Research Council, Cape Town.

Phillipson, R. (ed.): 2000, *Rights to Language: Equity, Power and Education*, Lawrence Erlbaum Associates, London.

Phillipson, R.: 2006, 'Language policy and linguistic imperialism', in T. Ricento (ed.), *Language Policy: Theory and Method*, Blackwell Publishing, Oxford.

Pullen, G. and Jones, L.: 1990, 'Social policy survey of deaf people in Europe', in J. Kyle (ed.), *Deafness and Sign Language into the 1990's: Ongoing Research Work in the Bristol Programme*, Deaf Studies Trust, Bristol.

Reagan, T.: 2006, 'Language policy and sign languages', in T. Ricento (ed.), *Language Policy: Theory and Method*, Blackwell Publishing, Oxford.

Ricento, T. (ed.): 2006, *Language Policy: Theory and Method*, Blackwell Publishing, Oxford.

Sign Language Studies: 2003, "Special issue on Dictionaries and Lexicography, Part II: The Development of National Sign Language Dictionaries", *Sign Language Studies*, 3:4 Gallaudet University Press, Washington, DC.

Skutnabb-Kangas, T.: 2000, *Linguistic Genocide in Education—or Worldwide Diversity and Human Rights?* Lawrence Erlbaum Associates, Mahwah, NJ and London.

Skutnabb-Kangas, T.: 2005, *Sign Languages—How the Deaf (and other Sign Language users) are Deprived of their Linguistic Rights*, http://www.terralingua.org/DeafHR.html

Skutnabb-Kangas, T.: 2006, 'Language policy and linguistic human rights', in T. Ricento (ed.), *Language Policy: Theory and Method*, Blackwell Publishing, Oxford.

Skutnabb-Kangas, T. and Phillipson, R. (eds.): 1994, *Linguistic Human Rights: Overcoming Linguistic Discrimination*, Mouton de Gruyter, Berlin.

Taylor, I.G. (ed.): 1988, *The Education of the Deaf: Current Perspectives*, Papers presented at the International Congress on Education of the Deaf 4–9 August, 1985, University of Manchester, Croom Helm, London.

United Nations 2005, Draft Report of the Ad Hoc Committee on a Comprehensive and Integral International Convention on the Protection and Promotion of the Rights and Dignity of Persons with Disabilities, http://www.un.org/esa/socdev/enable/rights/ahc5reporte.htm

Wilbur R.B.: 1987, *American Sign Language Lingustic and Applied Dimensions*, College-Hill Press, Boston.

Section 3

Theory, Pedagogy and Practice

ALASTAIR PENNYCOOK

CRITICAL APPLIED LINGUISTICS AND LANGUAGE EDUCATION

INTRODUCTION

Critical applied linguistics (CALx) is an emergent approach to language use and education that seeks to connect the local conditions of language to broader social formations, drawing connections between classrooms, conversations, textbooks, tests, or translations and issues of gender, class, sexuality, race, ethnicity, culture, identity, politics, ideology or discourse. In the following sections I provide an overview of this work as the intersection of different critically oriented domains, such as critical discourse analysis, critical literacy and critical pedagogy, before discussing various problems and difficulties faced by this work, including struggles over the meaning of the term *critical*, the need for work beyond only critique, and the question of its applicability to the majority (non-Western) world. Finally I discuss ways in which CALx opens up many new ways of thinking about applied linguistics, and thus presents to applied linguistics more broadly a fresh array of concerns about language, politics, identity, ethics and difference.

EARLY DEVELOPMENTS

Although the term CALx itself is relatively recent (see Pennycook, 2001), and related areas such as critical discourse analysis (CDA) only emerged in the 1980s, critical approaches to applied linguistics nevertheless draw on a critical tradition around language and pedagogy that has earlier origins. As Luke (2002) argues, critical language analysis can be seen as dating back to the work of Vološinov (1895–?), and more recently Foucault (1926–1984). Critical literacy and pedagogy have been greatly influenced by the work of Paulo Freire (1921–1997), while postcolonial critics such as Frantz Fanon (1925–1961) have been influential for the development of an understanding of language, identity, race and colonialism. CALx in its contemporary forms can best be understood as the intersection of various domains of applied linguistic work that operate under an explicit critical label, including critical discourse analysis, critical literacy, critical pedagogy, or critical language testing (CLT); as well as work that may have a less explicitly defined banner (critical approaches to translation, for

S. May and N. H. Hornberger (eds), Encyclopedia of Language and Education,
2nd Edition, Volume 1: Language Policy and Political Issues in Education, 169–181.
©*2010 Springer Science+Business Media LLC.*

example) or that defines its critical work more specifically, such as feminist or antiracist pedagogy. By and large, this work can be characterized as starting with the perspective that language is, as Joseph (2006) puts it, political from top to bottom. CALx therefore deals with applied linguistic concerns (broadly defined) from a perspective that is always mindful of the interrelationships among (adapting Janks, 2000) dominion (the contingent and contextual effects of power), disparity (inequitable access to material and cultural goods), difference (the construction of and engagement with diversity) and desire (the operations of ideology, agency and identity).

While some lament the development of CALx as being "dismissive totally of the attempt since the 1950s to develop a coherent applied linguistics" (Davies, 1999, p. 141.), others see it by contrast as a sign of disciplinary maturity: "the very existence of a transgressive critical applied linguistics which attacks the foundations and goals of applied linguistics is perhaps a sign that applied linguistics is a discipline which has come of age" (Elder, 2004, p. 430.). While CALx is concerned with far more immediate social and political concerns than disciplinary coherence, its development does seem to suggest that ALx may have outgrown its infancy. New journals now testify to the emergence of critical work around language and education: *The Journal of Language, Identity, and Education*, for example, includes in its scope "critical studies of literacy policies," "critical studies of school and community attitudes," "critical studies about bias in schooling practices" (Contributor information). The newly (2004) established *Critical Inquiry in Language Studies* publishes research on "issues of language, power, and community within educational, political, and sociocultural contexts ..." And the recent (2004), *Critical Discourse Studies* aims to "publish critical research that advances our understanding of how discourse figures in social processes, social structures and social change" (editorial page).

MAJOR CONTRIBUTIONS AND CURRENT WORK

CDA and critical literacy share a concern to understand texts and practices of reading and writing in relationship to questions of power, equity, diversity and change. Norman Fairclough, whose approach to CDA has received wide attention, explains that critical discourse analysis "aims to systematically explore often opaque relationships of causality and determination between (1) discursive practices, events and texts, and (2) wider social and cultural structures, relations and processes; to investigate how such practices, events and texts arise out of and are ideologically shaped by relations of power and struggles over power" (1995, p. 132.). More recently, Fairclough, Graham,

Lemke, and Wodak (2004) locate their approach to critical discourse studies within a broader field of critical social research and the growing awareness that major social issues such as the effects of global capitalism, issues of gender and sexuality, differential relations of power between languages, the need for critical citizenship, discrimination in terms of age or race, changing identities in relation to new transnational structures and changes to new communication media, are "to some significant degree, problems of discourse" (p. 2). They go on to suggest a threefold distinction among ideological critique, which focuses on the "effects of discourse on social structures of power," rhetorical critique, with its interest in "persuasion in individual texts or talk," and strategic critique, which looks at how "discourse figures within the strategies pursued by groups of social agents to change societies in particular directions" (p. 5).

Although critical literacy "does not stand for a unitary approach, it marks out a coalition of educational interests committed to engaging with the possibilities that the technologies of writing and other modes of inscription offer for social change, cultural diversity, economic equity, and political enfranchisement" (Luke and Freebody, 1997, p. 1). In some ways, critical literacy may be seen as a form of applied CDA—critical discourse analysis for the classroom—though it also has wider coverage in its focus on literacy in social contexts and practices of writing. Morgan and Ramanathan (2005) describe the contemporary educational task of critical literacy as "cultivating a citizenry that is able to negotiate and critically engage with the numerous texts, modalities, and technologies coming at learners" (p. 152). CDA and critical literacy also come together in the critical analysis of textbooks, showing, for example, how images of gender and race are reproduced in educational contexts (see Dendrinos, 1992; Van Dijk, 1993). CDA and critical literacy can also be seen as two approaches to critical language awareness, the aim of which is to "empower learners by providing them with a critical analytical framework to help them reflect on their own language experiences and practices and on the language practices of others in the institutions of which they are a part and in the wider society within which they live" (Clark and Ivanić, 1997, p. 217).

A further form of critical text analysis that has received less attention is a critical approach to translation, in part because translation itself is a minority focus of applied linguistics. Translation, argues Cronin (2003), nonetheless plays a crucial role within globalization, since one of its primary functions is "to replenish the intertextual resources of a culture" (p. 133). While the responsibility of the translator is conventionally thought of in terms of giving a fair and accurate representation of a source text, this focus on "textual scrupulousness" overlooks the importance of "an activist dimension to translation which involves an engagement with the cultural politics of society at national and international levels" (p. 134). This notion of activist translation links to Venuti's (1998) *translingualism*, which aims to disrupt the assimilationary and domesticating tendencies that eradicate difference through translation. Indeed, Venuti's (1997) approach to translation takes the position that to "shake the regime of English, a translator must be strategic both in selecting foreign texts and in developing discourses to translate them. Foreign texts can be chosen to redress patterns of unequal cultural exchange and to restore foreign literatures excluded by the standard dialect, by literary canons, or by ethnic stereotypes" (pp 10–11).

In addition, focusing on the global hegemony of English and the need to promote diversity, critical work in language policy and planning has opened up new perspectives on language and globalization (see also Block, Language Education and Globalization, Volume 1; Tollefson, Language Planning in Education, Volume 1). Work in language policy generally has been remarkable for its political quietism, only recently developing more critical theoretical frameworks (Ricento, 2006; Shohamy, 2005). Debates around the global spread of English and the destruction of the world's linguistic diversity have been at the forefront of this more overt critical agenda. Central here has been Phillipson's (1992) concept of (English) linguistic imperialism, an argument that English has been spread for the economic and political advantage of the core English-speaking nations. As Tollefson (2000) explains, Phillipson's work differs markedly from mainstream sociolinguistic work focusing on the global spread of English since he "focuses on the unequal distribution of benefits from the spread of English." Rather than viewing the spread of English in positive terms and focusing on descriptions of varieties of English, Phillipson's work "places English squarely in the center of the fundamental sociopolitical processes of imperialism, neo-colonialism, and global economic restructuring" (p. 13). These concerns have then been allied with allegations of "linguistic genocide" and the need for "linguistic human rights" to protect the global diversity of languages (Skutnabb-Kangas, 2000; see also Human Rights and Language Policy in Education, Volume 1). While these arguments have raised considerable debate, especially in relation to the need to understand how the global position of English is resisted and appropriated (Canagarajah, 1999; Pennycook, 2001), or how language rights can be understood in a more complex relation to ethnicity (May, 2001), the focus on the politics of language and globalization has become a key concern within CALx.

Sociolinguistics more generally has also been taken to task for lacking a critical dimension, Mey (1985) calling for a "critical sociolinguistics" that can "establish a connection between people's place in the societal hierarchy, and the linguistic and other kinds of oppression that they are subjected to at different levels" (p. 342). While sociolinguistics ought to have the tools to take questions of language and power seriously, it has been hampered by liberal social theory and sociologically deficient conceptions of class, gender and race (Williams, 1992). Some of the ways in which a critical sociolinguistics can operate can be seen in critical analyses of workplace settings which aim not just to describe inequitable practices but also to change them. Wodak's (1996) study of hospital encounters, for example, looks not only at the ways in which "doctors exercise power over their patients" (p. 170) but also at ways of intervening in this relationship. Studies of the literacy practices of young men in prison (Wilson, 2003), or of the discriminatory effects when Australian Aboriginal witnesses are silenced by the standard linguistic procedures of the courtroom (Eades, 2000) similarly seek both critical understanding and social restitution.

Critical approaches to language education—sometimes under the rubric of critical pedagogy—can be viewed, like critical literacy, as both a critical research enterprise and a domain of practice. Significant research in the first category, which, as *critical approaches to analysing learner language* (Ellis and Barkhuizen, 2005), has now been acknowledged as adding an important dimension to the often impervious domain of second language acquisition, includes work such as Canagarajah's (1999) critical ethnographies of 'periphery' students' and teachers' forms of resistance to English and English teaching methods: "It is important to understand the extent to which classroom resistance may play a significant role in larger transformations in the social sphere" (1999, p. 196.). Important here has been Norton's work on the ways in which gender, power and identity are interlinked in the process of language learning (2000; see also Pavlenko and Piller, Language Education and Gender, Volume 1). Kumaravadivelu (1999) offers a framework for *critical classroom discourse analysis*, which draws on critical ethnography as a research tool, and "seeks to play a reflective role, enabling practitioners to reflect on and cope with sociocultural and sociopolitical structures that directly or indirectly shape the character and content of classroom discourse" (p. 473). A critical turn in second language teacher education has suggested that the notion of *praxis*—the integration of critical reflection and action—can help transform the teaching practicum from a reproduction of prior practice into the teaching *praxicum* as an incessant problematizing of pedagogical thought and practice (Pennycook, 2004).

A focus on awareness of the inequitable conditions of language learning has produced approaches such as Darder's (1991) *critical biculturalism* or Walsh's (1991) *critical bilingualism*: "the ability to not just speak two languages, but to be conscious of the sociocultural, political, and ideological contexts in which the languages (and therefore the speakers) are positioned and function, and the multiple meanings that are fostered in each"(Walsh, 1991, p. 127.). Kubota's (2004) *critical multiculturalism* "critically examines how inequality and injustice are produced and perpetuated in relation to power and privilege" (p. 37). Based on a "a critical understanding of culture" (p. 38), such an approach is also both a research tool and a pedagogical approach, involving students "in critical inquiry into how taken-for-granted knowledge, such as history, geography, and lives of other people, is produced, legitimated, and contested in power struggles" (p. 40; see also May, 1999). Turning to forms of critical pedagogy in the second language classroom, Norton and Toohey (2004) explain that "Advocates of critical approaches to second language teaching are interested in relationships between language learning and social change" (p. 1). Morgan (1998) and many others (see Norton and Toohey, 2004; Pennycook, 1999) focus on how critical pedagogy in the classroom may address issues of power and inequality both within and outside the educational context, and how potential for change and resistance may be developed. Dealing with the very specific domain of academic English, Benesch's (2001) *critical English for academic purposes*, "assumes that current conditions should be interrogated in the interests of greater equity and democratic participation in and out of educational institutions" (p. 64).

In the related domain of language testing, Spolsky's (1995) history of the development of the TOEFL exam is clear from the outset that "testing has been exploited also as a method of control and power – as a way to select, to motivate, to punish." So-called objective tests, he points out, by virtue of their claims to scientific backing and impartiality, are "even more brutally effective in exercising this authority" (p. 1). These concerns have been pursued furthest by Shohamy (2001) in her notion of Critical Language Testing (CLT), which "implies the need to develop critical strategies to examine the uses and consequences of tests, to monitor their power, minimize their detrimental force, reveal the misuses, and empower the test takers" (p. 131). Shohamy's proposal for CLT clearly matches many of the principles that define other areas of CALx: language testing cannot be separated from social, cultural and political concerns; we need greater awareness and an ethical understanding of the effects and uses of tests; and a critical practice seeks transformative action. Doing applied linguistics critically, then, requires an understanding of the relationships between applied linguistic domains and the workings of power (dominion, disparity, difference, desire) as well as an ethical vision and tools for change.

PROBLEMS AND DIFFICULTIES

CALx faces four main problems: a rearguard action from the gatekeepers of disciplinary ALx; a tension between a normative political stance and the need for constant problematization; the need to move beyond critique to reconstitutive action; and the question of relevance to diverse contexts round the world. The emergence of these various critical projects has met with mixed responses. First, then, for some, CALx is little more than a critique of other orientations to applied linguistics; thus, Davies (1999) defines CALx as "a judgemental approach by some applied linguists to 'normal' applied linguistics on the grounds that it is not concerned with the transformation of society" (p. 145). As is clear from the previous discussion, however, CALx is far more than a mere critique of normative ALx. A more significant concern is that CALx's overt political stance on issues of inequality, racism, sexism or homophobia unacceptably "prejudges outcomes" (Davies, 2005, p. 32.). As Widdowson (2001) argues, by taking an a priori critical stance (rather than maintaining a critical distance—to use a different sense of the critical), CALx may impose its own views on the objects of inquiry, taking inappropriate and thus hypocritical stances on the social world because of the impossibility of choosing between different ethical and political concerns. A CALx standpoint, by contrast, while mindful precisely of the ethical dilemmas it opens up, suggests that such views overlook their own *locus of enunciation* (Mignolo, 2000): It is mainstream ALx that is hypocritical if it seeks to maintain a belief in critical distance while ignoring the very real social, political and ethical concerns that inevitably come to bear on any applied linguistic context.

This debate—contrasting a political with an apolitical ALx—unfortunately obscures the more important concern that CALx research does indeed need to be wary of its own political normativity. There is a tendency, second, for CALx research to operate with a normative, static politics based on various forms of neo-Marxian analyses of inequality and emancipation, and an equally static applied linguistic epistemology. To move forward, CALx needs a more reflexive politics, a form of *problematizing practice* (Pennycook, 2001). CALx is not only about relating micro-relations of applied linguistics to macro-relations of social and political power; nor is it only concerned with relating such questions to a priori critical analysis of inequality. A problematizing practice, by contrast, suggests a need to develop both a critical political stance and a critical epistemological stance, so that both inform each other, leaving neither the political nor the applied linguistic as static. From this point of view, then, CALx maintains a consistent focus on issues of dominion, disparity, difference and desire while at the same time maintaining a constant scepticism towards cherished concepts of applied linguistics, from language and ethnicity to identity and discourse.

Third, CALx needs to ensure that on the one hand it goes beyond a language only of critique, and that on the other hand its proposed interventions are not seen as purely partisan. As Luke (2004) warns, CDA needs to move beyond a mode of critique "towards a reconstructive agenda, one designed towards redress, reconciliation and the rebuilding of social structure, institutional lives and identities." (p. 151). While CDA locates itself as a project of consciousness raising (critical language awareness) or critical literacy, it is only when this becomes a more active project of critical writing—and thus goes beyond literacy as ideology critique—that it becomes a project aimed at active engagement rather than awareness. Critical pedagogy and other domains of CALx are similarly divided between domains that critique pedagogy, multiculturalism or English for Academic Purposes (EAP), and action-oriented domains that seek processes of change and engagement. There is always a challenge, therefore, to move beyond critique towards transformative and reconstitutive action. While this concern may be what Davies (2005) has in mind when he asserts that CALx "refrains from proposing interventions and explanations" (p. 32), paradoxically CALx has also been taken to task for proposing too many explanations and partisan interventions. Here CALx needs to ensure that the quality and reflexivity of its research, politics, epistemology and agendas for reform are more responsible than those in normative applied linguistics.

Finally, CALx is only useful insofar as it is applicable in diverse parts of the world. While applied linguistics generally has been challenged for its relevance to different contexts of global language use, CALx is equally open to such a challenge, in terms of both its critical and its applied linguistic epistemology. The concern here is that since much of the work that comes under the rubric of CALx is based on minority ('First'/'Western') world contexts and theories, CALx is simply not readily usable in the majority ('Third') world. As Makoni (2003) has argued, CALx does not have adequately contextualized strategies for engaging with local communities. Remaining aware of the diverse contexts in which it may hope to be applicable, CALx needs to be wary lest the very terms and concepts of any critical project at the same time inflict damage on the communities with which critical applied linguists wish to work (Makoni and Pennycook, 2007). The challenge here is to ensure that "the research agenda is formulated in collaboration and consultation with local communities" (Makoni, 2003, p. 135) in order not only to develop a relationship between this field of critical scholarship and local knowledge and practice but also to encourage the development of CALx as localized practice.

FUTURE DIRECTIONS

The emergence of a different, alternative, transgressive CALx has far wider implications than merely adding a political dimension to applied linguistics. It has become both a gateway through which new theories and ways of thinking about applied linguistics are entering and changing the discipline, as well as a developing domain that speaks to contemporary work in the social sciences. A newly emergent CALx that is going beyond the normative politics and epistemologies of emancipatory modernist critical approaches is responsive not only to shifts in mainstream linguistic and applied linguistic theory, but also to the linguistic, performative and somatic turns elsewhere in the social sciences. It is only recently, as Canagarajah (2004) points out, that we have come to "understand identities as multiple, conflictual, negotiated and evolving. We have traveled far from the traditional assumption in language studies that identities are static, unitary, discrete, and given" (p. 117).

To this discursive understanding of the subject has been added a conception of identities as *per*formed rather than *pre*formed. Drawing on Butler's (1990) insight that "gender proves to be performative – that is, constituting the identity it is purported to be" (p. 25), Cameron (1997) points out that whereas "sociolinguistics traditionally assumes that people talk the way they do because of who they (already) are," a performative approach to identity "suggests that people are who they are because of (among other things) the way they talk" (p. 49). A performative view of language, sexuality and education, for example, goes beyond a framing of identity in terms of lesbian and gay identification and instead embraces the broader category of Queer (Nelson, 1999; see also Pavlenko and Piller, Language Education and Gender, Volume 1), which as Cameron and Kulick (2003) explain "interrogates heterosexuality by dismissing its claims to naturalness, and examining, instead, how it is vigorously demanded and actively produced in specific sociocultural contexts and situated interactions" (p. 55). Once we take this performative turn in CALx, it becomes possible to explore the ways not only that identities are performed through language but also that languages are performed through acts of identity. Rather than assuming that languages preexist communicative activity, we can start to explore how languages are produced through communication (Makoni and Pennycook, 2007).

In response to a concern that these linguistic and performative turns may overemphasize discourse, text and semiotics at the expense of spatial, corporeal and institutional relations marked by conflictual relations of class, gender, sexuality, race and other forms of difference, a somatic turn (Shusterman, 2000) has reintroduced the body as a site of struggle. Language, as Bourdieu (1991, p. 86.) insists, "is a body technique, and specifically linguistic, especially phonetic, competence is a dimension of bodily hexis in which one's whole relation to the social world, and one's whole socially informed relation to the world, are expressed."

This emergent form of CALx, both responsive to and influential towards the linguistic, performative and somatic turns in the social sciences, rests therefore on principles of performativity, contextuality, and transgression (Pennycook, 2007): a performative understanding of language that opens up an understanding of the contingent nature of identity; a contextual engagement with the competing demands of dominion, disparity, difference and desire; and a transgressive approach to the boundaries of mainstream thought and politics, maintaining a constant scepticism towards cherished concepts and modes of thought. CALx is therefore far more than the addition of a critical/political dimension to applied linguistics; rather it opens up a whole new array of questions and concerns about language, politics, identity, ethics and difference.

See Also: *Tove Skutnabb-Kangas: Human Rights and Language Policy in Education (Volume 1); Aneta Pavlenko and Ingrid Piller: Language Education and Gender (Volume 1); David Block: Language Education and Globalization (Volume 1); Mary Kalantzis and Bill Cope: Language Education and Multiliteracies (Volume 1); Ben Rampton, et al.: Language, Class and Education (Volume 1); Teresa L. McCarty: Language Education Planning and Policies by and for Indigenous Peoples (Volume 1); Hilary Janks: Teaching Language and Power (Volume 1); Bill Johnston and Cary Buzzelli: The Moral Dimensions of Language Education (Volume 1); Suresh Canagarajah: The Politics of English Language Teaching (Volume 1); Peter Freebody: Critical Literacy Education: On Living with "Innocent Language" (Volume 2); Arlette Ingram Willis: Critical Race Theory (Volume 2); Gemma Moss: Gender and Literacy (Volume 2); Harvey J. Graff and John Duffy: Literacy Myths (Volume 2); Kwesi Kwaa Prah: Language, Literacy and Knowledge Production in Africa (Volume 2); Rebecca Rogers: Critical Discourse Analysis in Education (Volume 3); Harriet Bjerrum Nielsen and Bronwyn Davies: Discourse and the Construction of Gendered Identities in Education (Volume 3); Monica Heller: Language Choice and Symbolic Domination (Volume 3); Rani Rubdy: Language Planning Ideologies, Communication Practices and their Consequences (Volume 3); Judith Baxter: Post-structuralist Analysis of Classroom Discourse (Volume 3); Oleg Tarnopolsky: Nonnative Speaking Teachers of English as a Foreign Language (Volume 4); Rebecca Freeman Field: Identity, Community and Power in Bilingual Education (Volume 5); Tove Skutnabb-Kangas: Language Rights and Bilingual Education (Volume 5); Hilary Janks and Terry Locke: Discourse Awareness in Education: A Critical Perspective (Volume 6); Bonny Norton: Identity, Language Learning, and Critical Pedagogies (Volume 6); Kate Menken: High-Stakes Tests as de facto Language Education Policies (Volume 7); Tim McNamara:*

The Socio-political and Power Dimensions of Tests (Volume 7); Daryl Gordon: Gendered Second Language Socialization (Volume 8); Matthew C. Bronson and Karen Watson-Gegeo: The Critical Moment: Language Socialization and the (Re)visioning of First and Second Language Learning (Volume 8); Tove Skutnabb-Kangas and Robert Phillipson: A Human Rights Perspective on Language Ecology (Volume 9); Robert Kaplan and Richard Baldauf Jr.: An Ecological Perspective on Language Planning (Volume 9); Adrian Blackledge: Language Ecology and Language Ideology (Volume 9); Kelleen Toohey: Ethnography and Language Education (Volume 10); Bernard Spolsky: Investigating Language Education Policy (Volume 10)

REFERENCES

Benesch, S.: 2001, *Critical English for Academic Purposes: Theory, Politics, and Practice*, Lawrence Erlbaum, Mahwah, NJ.

Bourdieu, P.: 1991, *Language and Symbolic Power*, Polity Press, Oxford.

Butler, J.: 1990, *Gender Trouble: Feminism and the Subversion of Identity*, Routledge, London.

Cameron, D.: 1997, 'Performing gender identity: Young men's talk and the construction of heterosexual masculinity', in S. Johnson and U.H. Meinhof (eds.), *Language and Masculinity*, Blackwell, Oxford, 47–64.

Cameron, D. and Kulick, D.: 2003, *Language and Sexuality*, Cambridge University Press, Cambridge.

Canagarajah, S.: 1999, *Resisting Linguistic Imperialism in English Teaching*, Oxford University Press, Oxford.

Canagarajah, S.: 2004, 'Subversive identities, pedagogical safe houses, and critical learning', in B. Norton and K. Toohey (eds.), *Critical Pedagogies and Language Learning*, Cambridge University Press, Cambridge, 116–137.

Clark, R. and Ivanic, R.: 1997, *The Politics of Writing*, Routledge, London.

Cronin, M.: 2003, *Translation and Globalization*, Routledge, London.

Darder, A.: 1991, *Culture and Power in the Classroom: A Critical Foundation for Bicultural Education Westport*, Bergin and Garvey, CT.

Davies, A.: 1999, *An Introduction to Applied Linguistics: From Theory to Practice*, Edinburgh University Press, Edinburgh.

Davies, A.: 2005, *A Glossary of Applied Linguistics*, Edinburgh University Press, Edinburgh.

Dendrinos, B.: 1992, *The EFL Textbook and Ideology*, N.C. Grivas, Athens.

Eades, D.: 2000, 'I don't think it's an answer to the question: Silencing Aboriginal Witnesses in Court', *Language in Society* 29, 161–195.

Elder, C.: 2004, 'Introduction to Part II: Applied Linguistics (A-L)', in A. Davies and C. Elder (eds.), *Handbook of Applied Linguistics*, Blackwell, Oxford, 423–430.

Ellis, R. and Barkhuizen, G.: 2005, *Analysing Learner Language*, Oxford University Press, Oxford.

Fairclough, N.: 1995, *Critical Discourse Analysis*, Longman, London.

Fairclough, N., Graham, P., Lemke, J., and Wodak, R.: 2004, 'Introduction', *Critical Discourse Studies* 1(1), 1–7

Janks, H.: 2000, 'Domination, access, diversity and design: A synthesis for critical literacy education', *Educational Review* 52(2), 175–186.

Joseph, J.: 2006, *Language and Politics*, Edinburgh University Press, Edinburgh.

Kubota, R.: 2004, 'Critical multiculturalism and second language education', in B. Norton and K. Toohey (eds.), *Critical Pedagogies and Language Learning*, Cambridge University Press, Cambridge, 30–52.

Kumaravadivelu, B.: 1999, 'Critical classroom discourse analysis', *TESOL Quarterly* 33(3), 453–484.

Luke, A.: 2002, 'Beyond ideology critique: Critical discourse analysis', *Annual Review of Applied Linguistics* 22, 96–110.

Luke, A.: 2004, 'Notes on the future of critical discourse studies', *Critical Discourse Studies* 1(1), 149–152.

Luke, A. and Freebody, P. 1997, 'Critical literacy and the question of normativity: An introduction', in S. Muspratt, A. Luke, and P. Freebody (eds.), *Constructing Critical Literacies: Teaching and Learning Textual Practice* Allen & Unwin, St. Leonards, NSW, 1–18.

Makoni, S.: 2003, 'Review of A. Davies, An introduction to applied linguistics: From practice to theory; and A. Pennycook, Critical applied linguistics: A critical introduction', *Applied Linguistics* 24(1), 130–137.

Makoni, S. and Pennycook, A.: 2007, 'Disinventing and reconstituting languages', in S. Makoni and A. Pennycook (eds.), *Disinventing and Reconstituting Languages*, Multilingual Matters, Clevedon, 1–41.

May, S.: 1999, *Critical Multiculturalism: Rethinking Multicultural and Antiracist Education*, Routledge Falmer, London and New York.

May, S.: 2001, *Language and Minority Rights: Ethnicity, Nationalism and the Politics of Language*, Longman, Harlow (Reprinted by Routledge, 2007).

Mey, J.: 1985, *Whose Language? A Study in Linguistic Pragmatics*, John Benjamins, Amsterdam.

Mignolo, W.: 2000, *Local Histories/Global Designs: Coloniality, Subaltern Knowledges, and Border Thinking*, Princeton University Press, Princeton, NJ.

Morgan, B.: 1998, *The ESL Classroom: Teaching, Critical Practice and Community Development*, University of Toronto Press, Toronto.

Morgan, B. and Ramanathan, V.: 2005, 'Critical Literacies and Language Education: Global and Local Perspectives', *Annual Review of Applied Linguistics* 25, 151–169.

Nelson, C.: 1999, 'Sexual identities in ESL: Queer theory and classroom inquiry', *TESOL Quarterly* 33(3), 371–391.

Norton, B.: 2000, *Identity and Language Learning: Gender, Ethnicity and Educational Change*, Longman/Pearson, Harlow.

Norton, B. and Toohey, K.: 2004, 'Critical pedagogies and language learning: An introduction', in B. Norton and K. Toohey (eds.), *Critical Pedagogies and Language Learning*, Cambridge University Press, Cambridge, 1–17.

Pennycook, A. (ed.): 1999, 'Critical Approaches to TESOL', Special Issue of *TESOL Quarterly*, 33.

Pennycook, A.: 2001, *Critical Applied Linguistics: A Critical Introduction*, Lawrence Erlbaum, Mahwah, NJ.

Pennycook, A.: 2004, 'Critical moments in the TESOL praxicum', in B. Norton and K. Toohey (eds.), *Critical Pedagogies and Language Learning*, Cambridge University Press, Cambridge.

Pennycook, A.: 2007, *Global Englishes and Transcultural Flows*, Routledge, London.

Phillipson, R.: 1992, *Linguistic Imperialism*, Oxford University Press, Oxford.

Ricento, T.: 2006, 'Language policy: Theory and practice—an introduction', in T. Ricento (ed.), *An Introduction to Language Policy: Theory and Method*, Blackwell, Oxford, 10–23.

Shohamy, E.: 2001, *The Power of Tests: A Critical Perspective on the Uses of Language Tests*, Longman, London.

Shohamy E.: 2005, *Language Policy: Hidden Agendas and New Approaches*, Routledge, London.

Shusterman, R.: 2000, *Performing Live: Aesthetic Alternatives for the Ends of Art*, Cornell University Press, Ithaca, NY.
Spolsky, B.: 1995, *Measured Words*, Oxford University Press, Oxford.
Skutnabb-Kangas, T.: 2000, *Linguistic Genocide in Education—or Worldwide Diversity and Human Rights?*, Lawrence Erlbaum, Mahwah, NJ.
Tollefson, J.: 2000, 'Policy and ideology in the spread of English', in J.K. Hall and W. Eggington (eds.), *The Sociopolitics of English Language Teaching*, Multilingual Matters, Clevedon, 7–21.
Van Dijk, T.A.: 1993, *Elite Discourse and Racism*, Sage Publications, Newbury Park, CA.
Venuti, L.: 1997, *The Scandals of Translation: Towards an Ethics of Difference*. Routledge, London.
Walsh, C.: 1991, *Pedagogy and the Struggle for Voice: Issues of Language, Power, and Schooling for Puerto Ricans*, OISE Press, Toronto.
Widdowson, H.G.: 2001, 'Coming to terms with reality: Applied linguistics in perspective', in D. Graddol (ed.), *Applied Linguistics for the 21st Century*, AILA Review 14, 2–17.
Williams, G.: 1992, *Sociolinguistics: A Sociological Critique*, Routledge, London.
Wilson, A.: 2003, "Nike Trainers, My One True Love—Without You I am Nothing': Youth, identity and the language of trainers for young men in prison', in J. Androutsopoulos and A. Georgakopoulou (eds.), *Discourse Constructions of Youth Identities*, John Benjamins, Amsterdam, 173–196.
Wodak, R.: 1996, *Disorders of Discourse*, Longman, London.

HILARY JANKS

TEACHING LANGUAGE AND POWER

INTRODUCTION

The teaching of language and power is now a recognised approach to language education in primary and secondary schools, and in some countries, such as Australia and South Africa, is included in state curricula. Critical literacy is an umbrella term for language pedagogies that grew out of the discipline of linguistics (including critical linguistics, critical language awareness (CLA), genre theory, critical discourse analysis) and out of work in the field of adult literacy. This use of the word 'critical' signals a view of language as central to the workings of ideology—as a key means of mobilising meaning to sustain or contest relations of domination in society (see also Pennycook, Critical Applied Linguistics and Language Education, Volume 1). Critical literacy education seeks to enable students to ask and answer the questions—whose interests are served by the way in which language is used? Who benefits? Who is disadvantaged?—so that out of this understanding, possibilities for change can emerge. It is underpinned by a strong equity and social justice agenda.

The teaching of language and power depends on understanding that language is not a neutral tool for communication but is everywhere implicated in the ways in which we read and write the world, the ways in which knowledge is produced and legitimated, and the ways in which a human subject is constructed as a complex set of identities based on, amongst other things, race, class, gender, ability, age, nationality, sexual orientation.

Research on diversity, difference and othering, often from a feminist, post-colonial or gay and lesbian perspective, has included careful work on language and its power to construct and delimit the ways in which we think the other and ourselves. Although this work has played a formative role in the development of critical literacy, it is not the focus of this review (see Pavlenko and Piller, Language Education and Gender, Volume 1). Here the focus is on critical approaches to language and literacy education.

EARLY DEVELOPMENTS

When Dell Hymes argued in 1974 that in addition to acquiring linguistic competence children also had to acquire communicative competence,

S. May and N. H. Hornberger (eds), Encyclopedia of Language and Education,
2nd Edition, Volume 1: Language Policy and Political Issues in Education, 183–193.
©2010 Springer Science+Business Media LLC.

he brought about a fundamental change in language education. He established that language use is a fundamentally social activity and that communicative competence requires an ability to use language appropriately. Such competence includes knowing which language variety and register of a language is most suited to a social occasion; for multilingual children it requires knowing which language to use when, and the complicated social understanding necessary for codeswitching. His work made space for the social in language education.

At the same time, William Labov was doing important work on language varieties. His work demonstrated conclusively that the so-called non-standard varieties of English are fully systematic, rule-governed languages as capable of abstract logical reasoning as so-called standard varieties (Labov, 1972). What sets these varieties apart is their social status, not any inherent linguistic superiority or inferiority. Basil Bernstein's work, although widely misinterpreted at the time, drew attention to the cultural capital that was necessary for success in schools. Part of that cultural capital included having access to both the linguistic and communicative competences valued uncritically by the school.

The communicative approach was the pedagogic realisation of these theories in second language education. Here the emphasis was placed on effective communication and, for the first time, fluency and appropriateness were seen to be as important as accuracy, which had dominated earlier structural approaches to language teaching. Clark, Fairclough, Ivanic and Martin-Jones (1987) in a paper that gave birth to CLA provided the first challenge to approaches to language education that did not question existing social structures (see also Pennycook, Critical Applied Linguistics and Language Education, Volume 1). 'Appropriateness', the concept at the heart of the social in language education, came under their critical knife because what is appropriate is decided by social norms, which in contexts of power (institutions, prestigious job interviews, media) are inevitably the naturalised cultural practices of social élites. CLA developed by Norman Fairclough's research group at Lancaster University was one of the early forms of critical literacy in the UK. It was related to the pioneering work on critical linguistics, developed by Roger Fowler, Gunther Kress, Bob Hodge and Tony Trew (1979).

These developments would not have been possible without systemic functional linguistics (SFL), developed by Halliday (1985). SFL established the foundation for understanding language as a 'social semiotic' and for mapping the relationship between language, text and context. This grammar, which is 'a theory of meaning as choice' (Halliday, 1985, p. xiv), has provided the tools for critical discourse analysis, genre theory and multimodal analysis (see also Kalantzis and Cope, Language Education and Multiliteracies, Volume 1). It creates the opportunity to include the power-meaning potential when teaching linguistic structures.

So, for example, students learning grammar can simultaneously learn about the relationship between modality and authority, or about the connection between 'us' and 'them' pronouns and othering discourses, and they can learn to recognise who is a 'doer' and who is a 'done-to' when they are taught transitivity and voice. This critical approach to linguistic structures has also been effectively applied to the teaching of critical writing.

In the field of literacy, it was Paulo Freire's work that inspired the idea of critical literacy. His work in Brazil shows how in the process of learning to read both the word and the world critically, adult literacy learners regain their sense of themselves as agents who can act to transform the social situations in which they find themselves. Freire continues to be the main influence on critical literacy in North America, as can be seen in the work of Roger Simon, Carol Edelsky, Vivian Vasquez and Brian Morgan, for example. It was the work of linguists, such as Courtney Cazden, James Gee, Lisa Delpit, Nancy Hornberger, David Corson and Bonny Norton, on discourse analysis, language and diversity and language and identity that forged links between North American versions of critical literacy and developments elsewhere. Freire's work was extended by ethnographic research on literacy, which generated the New Literacy Studies (Gee, 1990; Street, 1984). Some of the classroom work it gave rise to focuses on situated literacy practices in contexts of power (e.g. Pahl and Rowsell, 2005; Stein, 2004). Under the editorship of Luke and Elkins, The *Journal for Adolescent and Adult Literacy* (1997 to 2002) made the range of critical approaches more available to teachers in North America.

Australia has been at the forefront of developing theorised classroom practice in the area of critical literacy. The theoretical contributions of Allan and Carmen Luke, Carolyn Baker and Peter Freebody, Bronwyn Mellor and Annette Patterson, Pam Gilbert, Bill Green, Barbara Comber, Barbara Kamler and the New Zealander Colin Lankshear laid the foundations for classroom practice. For example, Barbara Comber and her colleagues at the University of South Australia have for more than a decade theorised, supported and showcased the work of classroom teachers who have made a difference to the lives of marginal students. Their work offers some of the most nuanced descriptions of critical practice in the area of language and literacy education. Luke and his colleagues incorporated critical literacy into Queensland's *New Basics* curriculum. Patterson and Mellor, in Western Australia led the early development of classroom materials.

More recently, the changing communication landscape prompted theorists to re-think literacy in a digital age. Kress and van Leeuwen's (2001) work has focused attention on multimodal forms of communication which increasingly use forms of semeiosis (image, gesture, sound) other than language. Under the leadership of Cope and Kalantzis

(2000; see also Kalantzis and Cope, Language Education and Multi-literacies, Volume 1), the multiliteracies project has worked with the literacies needed for changes in both semeiosis and technology (computers, Internet, digital recorders). Education now has a responsibility to deliver access to print, screen, information and computer literacies, both productive and receptive, across the inequalities created by the digital divide.

MAJOR CONTRIBUTIONS TO THE TEACHING OF LANGUAGE AND POWER IN SCHOOLS

The purpose of this review is to consider the practical issues relating to the teaching of language, literacy and power. The major contributions to our understanding of practice are (i) accounts of critical literacy teaching in classroom-based research and (ii) classroom materials.

CLA edited by Fairclough (1992), was the first edited collection of CLA as practice and it raises and begins to answer some of the key questions on the teaching of language and power. How are students to be given access to the discourses of power in their educational institutions so that these are not simply reproduced unproblematically? How much language competence do students need before CLA can be taught in second or foreign language classes? What constitutes critical practice in relation to the place of students' own minority languages? What positions on students' access to the standardised variety are compatible with CLA? How does CLA impact on student subjectivities? Is awareness enough? When does CLA become emancipatory?

In these first accounts of CLA practice (Fairclough, 1992) there is little sense of disruption. Clark recognises that decisions 'to conform or not to conform' (p. 117) involve real risks, and Janks and Ivanič close the collection in the final paragraph with a reminder that 'people endanger themselves when they take on the prevailing power structures' (p. 330). But, the accounts themselves are seamless and there is no sense that CLA might impinge on students' and teachers' identity investments and rock the classroom boat.

However, other classroom-based research points to the disruptive potential of a critical pedagogy which disturbs students taken-for-granted discourses and threatens their sense of self. Ellsworth's (1989) critique of critical pedagogy, in which she raises important questions about critical pedagogy's claims to empower students, remains the seminal text. Several examples from South Africa offer accounts of conflict resulting from the teaching of language and power, particularly in heterogeneous classes. Watson's research on the production of a critical literacy comic (Watson, 1994) with students in a rural school highlights the difficulties that teachers confront when they invite students to generate materials out of their own ideologically constructed commonsense and the responsibilities and dilemmas a teacher faces in moving towards reconstructing students' belief systems. She shows that teaching can only be transformative in situations which allow different voices to enter and be heard, so that students come to understand the interested nature of all reading positions, including their own.

Readings and reading positions form the focus of secondary school critical literacy materials produced in Australia. The Chalkface Press workbooks introduce students to post-structuralist theory for textual deconstruction, focusing on literary texts, and they use innovative activities that teach an understanding of reading positions—how they are produced, regulated and challenged. The US edition of these workbooks by the National Council for Teachers of English in 2002 has further increased their influence. Two workbooks, *From the Margins* (Martino, 1997) and *Changing Places* (Kenworthy and Kenworthy, 1997), develop students' ability to read aboriginality, colonialism and gender from a post-colonial perspective. In the USA, the Rethinking Schools publications are specifically designed to teach students about equity and social justice. *Reading Writing and Rising Up* (Christenson, 2000) focuses specifically on the power of the written word. All these secondary school classroom materials establish a range of methods for developing students' understanding that discourse is implicated in the production of power and that texts are both constructed and interested. At their best, they require students to consider social effects and possible interventions. They focus on critical reading.

The work of Clark and Ivanič (1997), Ivanič (1998), Lillis (2001) and Kamler (2001) stands out for its focus on critical writing and the relationship between writing and subjectivity. Work still needs to be done to develop classroom-based approaches to critical writing.

Australia also pioneered critical literacy work in primary schools. Here the work of Peter Freebody, Allan Luke and Pam Gilbert has been important for its exploration of literacy practices in primary schools and the way these practices are inscribed on students' bodies to produce docile reading subjects. In addition, both Luke and Gilbert have drawn attention to the ideologies which inform the books children are given to read in primary schools. Luke studied early readers and Gilbert concentrated on gender bias. In South Australia, Barbara Comber and Jennifer O'Brien introduced the critical reading of everyday texts—cereal boxes, toy catalogues, mothers' day catalogues—into the early years of primary school. 'Critical literacies in the primary school' (Knobel and Healy, 1998) provides examples of critical literacy research in primary classrooms as does *Why wait? A way into teaching critical literacies in the early years* (Education Queensland, 2000). Vivian Vasquez' award-winning book *Negotiating Critical Literacies with Young Children* (2004) based on her lived critical literacy curriculum with a Grade 1/2 class in Canada, shows conclusively that there is no need to wait. Very young children are more than capable of problematising their world and of taking social action to transform the inequities that they discover.

Vasquez' book echoes intertextually with the edited collection *Negotiating Critical Literacies in Classrooms*, edited by Comber and Simpson (2001). Designed to include examples of theorised classroom practice from both the political north and the political south, this collection shows the different conditions of possibility for critical literacy at different historical moments in different contexts. For example, it was easy to defend critical literacy as a transformative political project in South Africa during apartheid. However, in the USA, where neo-conservatism and fear have produced 'homeland security' measures, language and power is not widely taught in schools. Instead, retrogressive literacy policies, which treat reading and writing as a set of skills rather than as social practices, continue to privilege middle class children in the US despite the 'no child left behind' rhetoric of the Bush administration.

Once Halliday moved to Australia, the University of Sydney became the centre for SFL. Using SFL, the genre theorists described the generic and linguistic features of six dominant factual genres—reports, recounts, procedures, explanations, expositions and discussions—to be able to teach them to students. Genre pedagogy was specifically designed to give marginalised students in Australia access to dominant forms of language and the Disadvantaged Schools Project developed both classroom materials and an explicit pedagogy. This strong position on access to dominant literacy is supported by Lisa Delpit who works with African American students in the USA. Primary English Teachers' Association (PETA) publications have made both Hallidayan grammar and genre theory widely accessible to teachers.

The genre theorists came into conflict with other critical literacy theorists in Australia. While genre theorists want to enable students to access and use the dominant genres, critical literacy theorists want students to deconstruct and reconstruct them. Serious attention to genre is not antithetical to the aims of critical literacy, provided that genres are not reified and taught as static conventions reduced, in some of the more rigid genre positions, to formulae operating according to fixed rules. What students need is an understanding of the historical and social determinants of these forms and an ability to adapt these forms as the conditions change, and to change these conditions.

How this translates into practice is not yet resolved. How *do* teachers work with the contradiction at the heart of educational access? If you provide extensive access to the dominant forms in a society (e.g. genres/knowledge/languages/varieties) you contribute to maintaining their dominance. If you deny students access, you perpetuate their marginalisation in a society that continues to recognise mastery of these genres as marks of distinction. A critical approach has to find a way of working inside this contradiction. Whole school ethnographic accounts by Stephen May (1994), Mary Kalantzis and associates (1991) and Rebecca Freeman (1998) have done so.

Wallace's (2003) work in the UK focuses on critical reading in second language education and shows how one can use marginality as a resource for criticality. Readers from the margins are frequently not the 'ideal readers' for whom texts are designed and they can learn to use their outsider insights as a resource for critical deconstruction. They can learn to harness their alternative world views as a means for resisting texts. Brian Morgan's (1998) account of his critical practice in his adult ESL classes demonstrates with Freirean panache how critical literacy enabled his immigrant students to read practices in their adopted society with a greater sense of agency. Norton's (2000) research, also with Canadian immigrants, had helped us to understand the relationship between language, identity and power in ESL. While this work is all with adults, it does provide direction for school-based critical ESL. Since 1994, Pennycook's work has provided a theoretical base for considering the politics of second and foreign language teaching. Although his work has focused on English, a powerful global language, it provides a way of thinking about language education in relation to the political economy of languages more broadly. In a challenge to the dominant applied linguistics paradigm in second language teaching and research, (Pennycook 2001; Critical Applied Linguistics and Language Education Volume 1) proposes a 'critical applied linguistics'.

Because of the current global power of English, bilingual and marginalised students tend to find critical literacy extremely engaging. Yet many ESL teachers delay engaging with issues of power in texts, arguing that the ability to decode is a prerequisite for deconstruction. Clearly, an understanding of textual positioning does require an understanding of the subtlety and nuances of words, but there are texts of different degrees of linguistic complexity and any text that is suitable for the level of learners to read is suitable for critical analysis at that level. The principles of critical literacy do not change.

The *CLA Series* (Janks, 1993) situates itself expressly across the first language/second language divide and is deliberately written in English that is accessible to students who speak African languages. This series is still the only set of classroom materials specifically designed to translate CLA into classroom practice. The apartheid context in which they were written gives a political edge to these workbooks, which make it clear that language is both a site and a stake in struggles for a more humane world.

The contributions to critical literacy referred to here have been limited to language education, but critical literacy has been applied across the school curriculum to the analysis of school history textbooks in Austria, to the exploration of the construction of gendered discourses in school geography, and to citizenship education. The Rethinking Schools project has produced resources for teaching geography, history, mathematics and social studies critically. One workbook focuses specifically on rethinking globalization.

FUTURE DIRECTIONS: PROBLEMS AND DIFFICULTIES

A central problem in early accounts of critical literacy was the assumption that critical 'awareness' leads to 'emancipation'. While many students report an ability to interrogate texts, to resist being constructed by othering discourses, to recognise and to refuse interpellation, this is too easy. Given that human subjects are multiply affiliated identities, we have no clear idea of what discursive emancipation might look like. A student who learns a feminist discourse at school might be severely punished for it in a traditional patriarchal home, particularly where sexist practices in the home are further underpinned by religious beliefs. Mellor and Patterson (1994) in fact argue that critical literacy is simply a new 'reading regime', requiring a new normativity. This needs to be weighed against Simon's (1992) 'pedagogy of possibility', which ties the critical endeavour to a political project with an ethical social justice agenda. These differing positions have very different outcomes in classrooms. For example, Mellor and Patterson would expect students to be able to produce an antiracist reading of a text whereas Simon would want to go further. He would want students to become transformed human subjects who reject racism.

The work of Vaquez and Comber provides a way forward. Their research highlights the possibilities for social action. Vasquez' 3 to 5-year old students were able to take action to transform unfair, discriminatory practices. Many of their interventions produced change: they challenged and changed school menus that did not include food for vegetarians; they successfully contested their exclusion from school events simply because they were young; they wrote and performed a play about the plight of the rain forests. The teachers that Comber writes about, Helen Grant and Marg Wells, are similarly successful in creating opportunities for their students to assume agency. Marg Wells began working with her students when they were in Grade 2/3. She developed a literacy and social power curriculum unit in which children were asked to identify aspects of their 'school, neighbourhood and world' that they were concerned about and to imagine how they might be changed for the better. Her children have since successfully campaigned for the planting of trees in their neighbourhood and they challenged and transformed the designs of urban renewal developers for a local park. Helen Grant has created opportunities for migrant children to use their diverse funds of knowledge in the videos that they produce.

Work in critical literacy is now trying to understand and imagine what pedagogies of 'reconstruction' and 'redesign' look like in schools and classrooms. Robert Hattam is working on an international project on 're-conciliation pedagogies'; Jim Martin is working with 'positive' as opposed to 'critical' discourse analysis; Comber, Thomson, Nixon and Janks' research, which focuses on projects that make a material difference to children's lives, is exploring the role played by literacy; Luke recently directed a major research project in Singapore to effect positive shifts in education in Asia (and by example, elsewhere). This influential new direction in the teaching of language and power signals a move from concerns with negative power and forces of resistance to a view that power can be harnessed by teachers and students for transformative projects of reconstruction.

Competing claims in the field of language and power have been counterproductive. One of the strengths of the multiliteracies project (see Kalantzis and Cope, Language Education and Multiliteracies, Volume 1) is that it created a space for thinking about links across the specialist interests brought by members of the New London Group: genre theory, discourse theory, language learning in multilingual and indigenous communities, social and citizenship education, feminist linguistics, cultural diversity in schools, language and learning for 'fast capitalist' workplaces. Janks (2000) in her synthesis model of critical literacy argues in relation to critical literacy that the different positions which foreground either domination, or diversity or access or design/ redesign are mutually interdependent, and that one without the other produces a problematic imbalance. Critical literacy has to take seriously the ways in which meaning systems are implicated in reproducing domination and it has to provide access to dominant languages, literacies and genres, while simultaneously using diversity as a productive resource for redesigning social futures and for changing the horizon of possibility (Simon, 1992). This includes both changing dominant discourses as well as changing which discourses are dominant. Genre theory without creativity runs the risk of reifying existing genres; deconstruction without reconstruction or design reduces human agency; diversity without access ghettoises students. Domination without difference and diversity loses the ruptures that produce contestation and change.

Finally, critical literacy has still to meet the criticism that it is fundamentally a rationalist activity that does not sufficiently address the nonrational investments that readers bring with them to texts and tasks. Norton's (1970) theory of 'investment' in relation to language acquisition and identity, Janks' work on identification (2002), Lillis' (2001) work on writing and desire and Kenway and Bullen's (2001) work on 'voluptuous pedagogies' are only a beginning. It is in the realm of discourse and the unconscious that the language/power conjunction produces subjects. Undoubtedly, this is why Foucault (1970, p. 110) maintains that 'discourse is the power which is to be seized'.

See Also: *Alastair Pennycook: Critical Applied Linguistics and Language Education (Volume 1); Mary Kalantzis and Bill Cope: Language Education and Multiliteracies (Volume 1)*

REFERENCES

Christenson, L.: 2000, *Reading, Writing and Rising Up: Teaching About Social Justice and the Power of the Written Word*, Rethinking Schools, Milwauke.
Clark, R. and Ivanič, I.: *The Politics of Writing*, Routledge, London.
Clark, R., Fairclough, N., Ivanic R., and Martin-Jones, M.: 1987, 'Critical Language Awareness', Centre for Language in Social Life, working paper series, Number 1, Lancaster University.
Comber, B. and O'Brien, J.: 1993, 'Critical literacy: Classroom explorations', *Critical Pedagogy Networker* 6 (1 and 2), June.
Comber, B. and Simpson, A. (eds.): 2001, *Negotiating Critical Literacy in Classrooms*, Lawrence Erlbaum and Associates, Mahwah, NJ.
Cope, B. and Kalantzis, M. (eds.): 2000, *Multiliteracies*, Routledge, London.
Education Queensland: 2000, *Why Wait: A Way in to Teaching Critical Literacies in the Early Years* (Teaching Units), Brisbane.
Ellsworth, E.: 1989, 'Why doesn't this feel empowering? Working through repressive myths of critical pedagogy', *Harvard Educational Review* 59(3), August 1989.
Fairclough, N. (ed.): 1992, *Critical Language Awareness*, Longman, London.
Foucault, M.: 1970, 'The order of discourse', in M. Shapiro (ed.) (1984), Inaugural Lecture at the College de France, *Language and Politics*, Basil Blackwell, Oxford.
Fowler, R., Kress, G., Hodge, B., and Trew, T.: 1979, *Language and Control*, Routledge and Kegan Paul, London.
Freeman, R.: 1998, *Bilingual Education and Social Change*, Multilingual Matters, Clevedon.
Gee, J.P.: 1990, *Sociolinguistics and Literacies: Ideology in Discourse*, Falmer Press, London.
Halliday, M.: 1985, *An Introduction to Functional Grammar*, Arnold, London.
Heath, S.: 1983, *Ways with Words*, Cambridge University Press, Cambridge.
Hymes, D.: 1974, 'On communicative competence', in C.J. Brumfit and and K. Johnson (1979) (eds.), *The Communicative Approach to Language Teaching*, Oxford University Press, Oxford.
Ivanič, R.: 1998, *Writing and Identity*, John Benjamins, Amsterdam.
Janks, H. (ed.): 1993, *Critical Language Awareness Series*, Hodder and Stoughton and Wits University Press, Johannesburg.

Janks, H.: 2000, 'Domination, access, diversity and design: A synthesis for critical literacy education', *Educational Review* 52(2), 175–186.

Janks, H.: 2002, 'Critical literacy: Beyond reason', *The Australian Educational Researcher* 29(1), 7–26.

Kalantzis, M., Cope, B., Noble, G., and Poynting, S.: 1991, *Cultures of Schooling: Pedagogies for Cultural Difference and Social Access*, Falmer Press, London.

Kamler, B.: 2001, *Relocating the Personal*, State University of New York, Albany.

Kenway, J. and Bullen, E.: 2001, *Consuming Children: Education-Entertainment-Advertising*, Open University Press, Buckingham.

Kenworthy, C. and Kenworthy, S.: 1997, *Changing Places: Aboriginality in Texts and Contexts*, Freemantle Press, Freemantle.

Knobel, M. and Healy, A. (eds.): 1998, *Critical Literacies in the Primary Classroom*, PETA, New South Wales.

Kress, G. and van Leeuwen, T.: 2001, *Multimodal Discourse*, Arnold, London.

Labov, W.: 1972, 'The logic of non-standard English', in Giglioli (ed.), *Language and Social Context*, Penguin, Harmondsworth.

Lillis, T.: 2001, *Student Writing: Access, Regulation and Desire*, Routledge, London.

Martino, W.: 1997, *From the Margins: Exploring Ethnicity, Gender and Aboriginality*, Freemantle Press, Freemantle.

May, S.: 1994, *Making Multicultural Education Work*, Multilingual Matters, Clevedon.

Mellor, B. and Patterson, A.: 1994, 'Producing readings: Freedom versus normativity', *English in Australia*, 109, 42–56.

Norton, B.: 2000, *Identity and Language Learning*, Longman, London.

Pahl, K. and Rowsell, J.: 2005, *Literacy and Education: Understanding the New Literacy Studies in the Classroom*, Paul Chapman, London.

Pennycook, A.: 2001, *Critical Applied Linguistics*, Lawrence Erlbaum and Associates, Mahwah, NJ.

Simon, R.: 1992, *Teaching Against the Grain: Texts for a Pedagogy of Possibility*, OISE Press, Toronto.

Stein, P.: 2004, 'Representation, rights and resources: Multimodal pedagogies in the language and literacy classroom', in B. Norton and and K. Toohey (eds.), *Critical Pedagogies and Language Learning*, Cambridge University Press, Cambridge,

Street, B.: 1984, *Literacy in Theory and Practice*, Cambridge University Press, Cambridge.

Vasquez, V.: 2004, *Negotiating Critical Literacies with Young Children*, Lawrence Erlbaum and Associates, Mahwah, NJ.

Wallace, C.: 2003, *Critical Reading in Language Education*, Palgrave Macmillan, London.

Watson, P.: 1994, *Heart to Heart*, The Storyteller Group, Johannesburg.

MARY KALANTZIS AND BILL COPE

LANGUAGE EDUCATION AND MULTILITERACIES

INTRODUCTION: INITIAL DEVELOPMENT OF THE 'MULTILITERACIES' CONCEPT

In September 1994, the Centre for Workplace Communication and Culture at James Cook University of North Queensland, Australia, initiated an international project to consider the future of literacy teaching: what would need to be taught in a rapidly changing near future, and how it would be taught. The Centre invited some of the world's leaders in the field of literacy pedagogy to come together for a week in the small town of New London, New Hampshire, USA, in order to consider the 'state of the art'.

As it turned out, there were multiple ironies in the very idea of New London. By the end of the twentieth century one billion people spoke that difficult little language, English, spoken four centuries before by only about a million or so people in the vicinity of London, old London. The story of the language, and the story of the last few centuries, including its many injustices, is the story of many new Londons. This issue—how the language meets with cultural and linguistic diversity—was one of our main concerns. Then there was the irony of the postcard serenity of this particular New London, the affluent, post-industrial village which sold little more than its idyllic eighteenth century postcard image. This, in a world where the fundamental mission of educators is to improve every child's educational opportunities—a world which, much of the time, is far from idyllic.

This seemed a strange place to be asking some of the hardest questions we now face as educators. What is appropriate education for women, for indigenous peoples, for immigrants who do not speak the national language (cf. May, Language Education, Pluralism and Citizenship, Volume 1), for speakers of non-standard dialects? What is appropriate for all in the context of the ever more critical factors of local diversity and global connectedness (cf. Block, Language Education and Globalization, Volume 1)? As educators attempt to address the difficult question of cultural and linguistic diversity, we hear shrill claims and counterclaims about the canon of great literature, grammar and 'back-to-basics'. These debates seemed a long way from the calm hills of a tourist's New Hampshire.

S. May and N. H. Hornberger (eds), Encyclopedia of Language and Education, 2nd Edition, Volume 1: Language Policy and Political Issues in Education, 195–211.
©2010 Springer Science+Business Media LLC.

Ten people met and talked for that week in New London. Courtney Cazden from the USA had spent a long and highly influential career working on classroom discourse (Cazden, 1988, 2001), language learning in multilingual contexts (Cazden, 1989) and on literacy pedagogy (Cazden, 1983). Bill Cope, from Australia, had written curricula addressing cultural diversity in schools (Kalantzis and Cope, 1989), and had researched literacy pedagogy (Cope and Kalantzis, 1993) and the changing cultures and discourses of workplaces (Cope and Kalantzis, 1997a). From Great Britain, Norman Fairclough was a theorist of language and social meaning, and was particularly interested in linguistic and discursive change as part of social and cultural change (Fairclough, 1989, 1992). James Gee, from the USA, was a leading researcher and theorist on language and mind (Gee, 1992, 1996), and on the language and learning demands of the latest 'fast capitalist' workplaces (Gee, Hull, and Lankshear, 1996). Mary Kalantzis, an Australian, had been involved in experimental social education and literacy curriculum projects (Cope and Kalantzis, 1993), and was particularly interested in multicultural and citizenship education (Kalantzis and Cope, 1999; Kalantzis, Cope, Noble, and Poynting, 1991; Kalantzis, Cope and Slade, 1989). Gunther Kress, from Great Britain, was best known for his work on language and learning, semiotics (Kress, 1990), visual literacy (Kress and van Leeuwen, 1996) and the multimodal literacies that are increasingly important to all communication, particularly the mass media. Allan Luke, from Australia, was a researcher and theorist of critical literacy who has brought sociological analysis to bear on the teaching of reading and writing (Luke, 1991, 1992a, 1993). Carmen Luke, also from Australia, had written extensively on feminist pedagogy (Luke, 1992b, 1994). Sarah Michaels, from the USA, has had extensive experience in developing and researching programs of classroom learning in urban settings (Michaels, 1986; Michaels, O'Conner, and Richards, 1993). Martin Nakata, an Australian, had researched and written on the issue of literacy in indigenous communities (Nakata, 1993).

Our purpose for meeting was to engage on the issue of what to do in literacy pedagogy on the basis of our different national and cultural experiences and on the basis of our different areas of expertise. The focus was the big picture, the changing word and the new demands being placed upon people as makers of meaning—in changing workplaces, as citizens in changing public spaces and in changing dimensions of our community lives, our lifeworlds.

We decided that the outcomes of the New London discussions could be encapsulated in a single word—'Multiliteracies'—a word we coined to describe two important arguments we might have with the emerging cultural, institutional and global order. The first was the growing significance of cultural and linguistic diversity (see also May, Language Education, Pluralism and Citizenship, Volume 1). The news on our television screens scream this message at us on a daily basis. And, in more constructive terms, we have to negotiate differences every day, in our local communities and in our increasingly globally interconnected working and community lives (see also Block, Language Education and Globalization, Volume 1). As a consequence, something paradoxical was happening to English. At the same time as it was becoming a lingua mundi, a world language, and a lingua franca, a common language of global commerce, media and politics, English was also breaking into multiple and increasingly differentiated 'Englishes', marked by accent, national origin, subcultural style and professional or technical communities. Increasingly, the key communicative challenge was to be able to cross linguistic boundaries, even within English. Gone were the days when learning a single, standard version of the language was sufficient. Migration, multiculturalism and global economic integration daily intensified this process of change. The globalisation of communications and labour markets made language diversity an ever more critical local issue.

The second major shift encompassed in the concept of Multiliteracies was the influence of new communications technologies. Meaning was increasingly being made in ways that were multimodal—in which written-linguistic modes of meaning are part and parcel of visual, audio and spatial patterns of meaning. The New London Group considered the multimodal ways in which meanings are made in places such as the (then very new) World Wide Web, or in video captioning, or in interactive multimedia, or in desktop publishing, or in the use of written texts in a shopping mall. To find our way around this emerging world of meaning required a new, multimodal literacy.

These two developments, the group concluded, had the potential to transform both the substance and pedagogy of literacy teaching in English, and in the other languages of the world. No longer did the old pedagogies of a formal, standard, written national language have the use they once had. Instead, the Multiliteracies argument suggested an open ended and flexible functional grammar which assists language learners to describe language differences (cultural, subcultural, regional/national, technical, context specific, etc.) and the multimodal channels of meaning now so important to communication.

The outcome of the New London meeting was a jointly authored paper—we decided to call ourselves the 'New London Group'—which was later published in the Spring 1996 edition of the Harvard Educational Review: 'A Pedagogy of Multiliteracies: Designing Social Futures' (New London Group, 1996) and subsequently, a book, *Multiliteracies: Literacy Learning and the Design of Social Futures* published in Australia by Macmillan and in the UK and North America by Routledge in 2000 (Cope and Kalantzis, 2000). As one measure of how far the idea has travelled in the subsequent decade, a Google search in 2007 returned 140,000 web pages that mentioned the word 'multiliteracies'.

MAJOR CONTRIBUTIONS: CHANGING SOCIETY AND CHANGING LITERACIES

The changing social worlds of work, citizenship and identities, require a new educational response. This was the core proposition underlying the Multiliteracies agenda from the start.

To take the world of work, the imagery of the old world of work is familiar—the factories with smokestacks piercing the horizon which we used to see as signs of progress. Behind the factory walls was the heavy plant which added up to the fixed assets of industrial capitalism. Geared for long-run mass production of manufactured things, human beings became mere appendages to the machine. Indeed, the logic of the production line minimised human skill requirements, as tasks were divided into smaller and smaller functions—screwing this particular bolt onto the manufactured object as it went past on the conveyor belt. This was the human degradation of the modern factory. It was also its genius, to arrange technology in such a way as to be able to manufacture items of unprecedented technological sophistication (such as Marconi's radio set, or Henry Ford's motor car), using an unskilled workforce (Cope and Kalantzis, 1997a).

Old education systems fitted very neatly into this world of work. The state determined the syllabus, the textbooks followed the syllabus, the teachers followed the textbooks, and the students followed the textbooks, hopefully, in order to pass the tests. Henry Ford knew what was best for his customers—'any colour you like, so long as it's black'—and the state knew what was best for children. And, in a way, teachers became a bit like production line workers, slaves to the syllabus, the textbooks and the examination system (cf. Wiley, Language Policy and Teacher Education, Volume 1). The curriculum was packed with information in the form of quite definite facts—'facts' about history, facts about science and language facts in the form of 'proper grammar' and correct spelling. Together, this was supposed to add up to useful-knowledge-for-life. Many of these facts have proven to be less durable than the curriculum of that time seemed to have been promising. Nevertheless, there was one important lesson which 'good' students took into the old workplace. From all the sitting up straight and listening to the teacher, from all the rigid classroom discipline, from all the knowledge imparted to them and uncritically ingested, they learnt to accept received authority and to do exactly as they were told (Kalantzis and Cope, 2001a).

The 'basics' of old learning were encapsulated in the 'three Rs'— reading, writing and arithmetic. The process was learning by rote and knowing the 'correct answers'. 'Discipline' was demonstrated in tests as the successful acquisition of received facts and the regurgitation of rigidly defined truths. This kind of education certainly produced people who had learnt things, but things which were too often narrow, decontextualised, abstract and fragmented into subject areas artificially created by the education system. More than anything, it produced compliant learners, people who would accept what was presented to them as correct, and who passively learnt off by heart knowledge which could not easily be applied in different and new contexts. They may have been superficially knowledgeable (Latin declensions, or the grammar of adverbial clauses, or the rivers of national geography, or the dates of European history), but they did not have knowledge of sufficient depth for a life of change and diversity. It was a knowledge that was appropriate for a time that imagined itself as ordered and controllable (Cope and Kalantzis, 1993).

If the predominant image of the old economy was the factory and the smokestack, the image of the so-called 'new economy' is the worker sitting in front of a computer screen. Information and communications technologies dominate this 'knowledge economy'. Actually, despite the hype, we do not just live on knowledge, as if the economy has suddenly abandoned making things for trading in information and symbols. We cannot live on symbols alone. But symbols are nevertheless everywhere. They are at the heart of new technologies, and especially the technologies of digital convergence—in the areas of communications, automated manufacturing, e-commerce and the media. Even in the manufacturing sector where people still energetically make things, they now make them using screen-based interfaces, and these are linguistically, visually and symbolically driven. The production line is still there, but now robots are screwing on the bolts. These technologies, moreover, are constantly shifting.

The new technologies are software rather than hardware intensive, as well as flexible and open to multiple uses. Software replacements are made far more frequently than was the case for plant replacement in the old economy. This means that technical knowledge has a shorter and shorter shelflife. Upskilling needs to occur continuously. Indeed, contrary to the old economy process of de-skilling, you need to be multiskilled, to be more flexible, more able to undertake a range of tasks, and able to shift from one task to another, as needs be. The key competitive advantage for an organisation, even the value of that organisation, is no longer grounded in the value of its fixed assets and plant, or at least not in that alone, but in the skills and knowledge of its workforce. Indeed, technology is now very much a relationship between tools and the knowledge of these tools in people's heads. Wealth increasingly has a human-skills rather than a fixed-capital basis.

Meanwhile, diversity is everywhere in the new economy organisation, and working with culture in fact means working with diversity. Instead of Henry Ford's assertion in which individual customer needs are irrelevant because customers are all the same, organisations now want to be close to customers, to find out what they really want, and to service their needs in a way which works for them. Taking customer service seriously inevitably means discovering that people are different, according to various combinations of age, ethnic background, geographical location, sexual orientation, interest, fashion, fad or fetish. 'Serving niche markets', this is called, and systems of 'mass customisation' are created at the point where 'high tech' meets 'soft touch'—such as the e-commerce systems or hotel registration procedures which build up the profile of a customer, and their precise needs and interests.

Then, there is the diversity within the organisation. Teams work with high levels of interpersonal contact, and work best, not when the members are forced to share the same values, but when differences—of interest, association, network, knowledge, experience, lifestyle and languages spoken—are respected and used as a source of creativity, or as a link into the myriad of niches in the world in which the organisation has to operate. This world of diversity exists both at the local level of increasingly multicultural societies, and at the global level where distant and different markets, products and organisations become, in a practical sense, closer and closer (Cope and Kalantzis, 1997a).

We are in the midst of a technology revolution, moreover, which not only changes the way we work but also the way we participate as citizens. From the old world of broadcasting to the new world of 'narrowcasting', consider what has happened to one of the media, television. Instead of the pressures to conformity, pressures to shape your person in the image of the mass media when everybody watched the old 'national networks', we now have hundreds of channels on cable or satellite television. These channels cater, not to the 'general public', but to ever-more finely defined communities: the services in different languages, the particular sporting interests, the genres of movie. Added to this, we are now watching on-demand TV streamed through the internet.

In fact, to take the internet of today, the millions of sites reflect any interest or style you want to name, nurturing a myriad of ever-more finely differentiated communities. Then there is the phenomenon of 'pointcasting' or syndication feeds, where the user customises the information feed they want—requesting information to be streamed to them only about a particular sporting team, a particular business sector, a particular country of origin. As a part of this process, the viewer becomes a user; transmission is replaced by user-selectivity; and instead of being passive receptors of mass culture we become active creators of information and sensibilities which precisely suit the nuances of who we are and the image in which we want to fashion ourselves.

In fact, digital convergence turns the whole media relationship around the other way—the digital image of a baby which can be broadcast to the world through the internet, or the digital movie which you can edit on your computer, burn on a CD or broadcast from your home page or YouTube. There is simply more scope to be yourself in this technology environment, and to be yourself in a way which is different. The technology convergence comes with cultural divergence, and who knows which is the greater influence in the development of the other? The only thing which is clear is that technology is one of the keys to these new kinds of self expression and community building. It is part of a process of creating new persons—persons of self-made identity instead of received identity, and diverse identities rather than a singular national identity. In this context, senses of belonging will arise from a common commitment to openness and inclusivity.

So what do all these changes in technology, work and community mean for education? The essence of old basics was encapsulated simply in the subject areas of the 'three Rs': reading, writing and arithmetic. Actually, the very idea of the basics indicated something about the nature of knowledge: it was a kind of shopping list of things-to-be-known—through drilling the 'times tables', memorising spelling lists, learning the parts of speech and correct grammar. This is not to say that multiplication or understanding the processes of written communication no longer have educational worth—they do, but in a different pedagogical form. The problem was with the former orientation to knowledge: first, the assumption that this kind of knowledge was a sufficient foundation; second, that knowledge involved clearly right and wrong answers (and if you were in any doubt about this, the test results would set you straight); and third, that knowledge was about being told by authority and that it was best to accept the correctness of authority passively. If the underlying lesson of the old basics was about the nature of knowledge, then it is a lesson which is less appropriate in a world which puts a premium on creativity, problem solving and the active contribution of every person in a workplace or community setting.

The fancier contemporary words for these old 'basics' are literacy and numeracy. And of course, mathematics, reading and writing are today as important as ever, perhaps even more important. However, literacy and numeracy can either stand as substitute words for the old basics, or they can mean something new, something appropriate to the new learning. When they are merely substitute words for the old basics, they are mostly no more than statements of nostalgic regret for a world which is disappearing, or else they reflect our incapacity as adults to imagine anything different from, or better than, our own experiences as children at school. 'Let's get back to the basics' people say, and the operative words are 'get back'.

When we use the term 'new basics' we are indicating a very different approach to knowledge. Mathematics is not a set of correct answers but a method of reasoning, a way of figuring out a certain kind of system and structure in the world. Nor is literacy a matter of correct usage (the word and sentence-bound rules of spelling and grammar). Rather, it is a way of communicating. Indeed, the new communications environment is one in which the old rules of literacy need to be supplemented. Although spelling remains important, it is now something for spell-checking programs, and email messages do not have to be grammatical in a formal sense (although they have new and quirky conventions which we have to learn-as-we-go—abbreviations, friendly informalities and cryptic 'in' expressions). And many texts involve complex relationships between visuals, space and text: the tens of thousands of words in a supermarket; the written text around the screen on the news, sports or business programs on the television; the text of an ATM; websites built on visual icons and active hypertext links; the subtle relationships of images and text in glossy magazines. Texts are now designed in a highly visual sense, and meaning is carried as much visually as it is by words and sentences (Kalantzis and Cope, 2001a, 2004, 2005).

This means that the old basics which attempt for whatever reason to teach adverbial clauses of time or the cases around the verb 'to be', need to be supplemented by learning about the visual design of texts (such as fonts and point sizes—concepts which only typesetters knew in the past). It also means that the old discipline division between language and art is not as relevant as it once was.

Nor is literacy any longer only about learning so called 'proper usage'. Rather, it is also about the myriad of different uses in different contexts: this particular email (personal, to a friend), as against that (applying for a job); this particular kind of desktop publishing presentation (a newsletter for your sports group), as against that (a page of advertising); and different uses of English as a global language (in different English speaking countries, by non-native speakers, by different subcultural groups). The capabilities of literacy involve not only knowledge of grammatical conventions but also effective communication in diverse settings, and using tools of text design which may include word processing, desktop publishing and image manipulation.

More than new contents like these, however, the new basics are also about new kinds of learning. Literacy, for instance, is not only about rules and their correct application. It is about being faced with an unfamiliar kind of text and being able to search for clues about its meaning without immediately feeling alienated and excluded from it. It is also about understanding how this text works in order to participate in its meanings (its own particular 'rules'), and about working out the particular context and purposes of the text (for herein you will find more clues to its meaning to the communicator and to you). Finally, literacy is about actively communicating in an unfamiliar context and learning from your successes and mistakes.

Education always creates 'kinds of persons'. The old basics were about that: people who learnt rules and obeyed them; people who would take answers to the world rather than regard the world as many problems-to-be-solved; and people who carried 'correct' things in their heads rather than flexible and collaborative learners. The new basics are clearly things which set out to shape new 'kinds of persons', persons better adapted to the kind of world we live in now and the world of the near future.

WORK IN PROGRESS: THE MEANING-MAKING PROCESS

The 'Multiliteracies' idea addresses some of the major dimensions of the change in our contemporary communications environment. Once, literacy could be understood as the business of putting words in sentences on pages, and doing this correctly according to the standard usage. Now literacies, in the plural, are inevitably multiple, in two major ways. The first is the many kinds of English literacy at work in many different cultural, social or professional contexts. As much as English is becoming a global language, these differences are becoming ever more significant to our communications environment. The second is the nature of new communications technologies. Meaning is made in ways that are increasingly multimodal—in which written-linguistic modes of meaning interface with visual, audio, gestural and spatial patterns of meaning.

The starting point for the Multiliteracies framework is the notion that knowledge and meaning are historically and socially located and produced, that they are 'designed' artefacts. But more than artefacts, Design is a dynamic process, a process of subjective self-interest and transformation, consisting of (i) The Designed (the available meaning-making resources, and patterns and conventions of meaning in a particular cultural context); (ii) Designing (the process of shaping emergent meaning which involves re-presentation and recontextuali-sation—this never involves a simple repetition of The Designed because every moment of meaning involves the transformation of the Available Designs of meaning); and (iii) The Redesigned (the outcome of designing, something through which the meaning-maker has remade themselves and created a new meaning-making resource—it is in this sense that we are truly designers of our social futures) (Cope and Kalantzis, 2000).

Two key aspects of the notion of Design distinguish it from the approach to the question of teaching language conventions taken by many earlier traditions of literacy pedagogy: variability and agency. Traditional grammar teaching, for example, taught to a single social-linguistic end: the official, standard or high forms of the national language (cf. Tollefson, Language Planning in Education, Volume 1). The issue of language variability was barely part of the teaching process. And always closely linked to this issue of variability is the issue of agency or subjectivity. The language experiences students brought to learning traditional grammars, for instance, were irrelevant; the aim was to induct students into the standard written form through a pedagogy of transmission. School was about the reproduction of received cultural and linguistic forms.

The Design notion takes the opposite tack on both of these fronts: the starting point is language variation—the different accents, registers and dialects that serve different ends in different social contexts and for different social groups. And the key issue of language use is agency and subjectivity—the way in which every act of language draws on disparate language resources and remakes the world into a form that it has never quite taken before. The reality of language is not simply the reproduction of regularised patterns and conventions. It is also a matter of intertextuality, hybridity and language as the basis of cultural change. In this sense, language is both an already Designed resource and the ground of Designs for social futures.

What, then, is the scope of the Designs of meaning? One of the key ideas informing the notion of Multiliteracies is the increasing complexity and interrelationship of different modes of meaning, in which language is often inseparably related to other modes of meaning. We have identified a number of major areas in which functional 'grammars'—metalanguages which describe and explain patterns of meaning—are required: Linguistic Design, Visual Design, Audio Design, Gestural Design, Spatial Design and Multimodal Design, in which meanings are made in the relation of different modes of meaning. Particularly with the rise of new information and communications technologies, these different modes of meaning are increasingly interrelated—in email, in desktop publishing, in video and in multimedia and hypermedia. This means that literacy teaching has to move well beyond its old, disciplinary boundaries.

As the basis for interpreting and creating meaning in this environment, we might usefully ask the following five questions.

1. *Representational*—What do the meanings refer to?
2. *Social*—How do the meanings connect the persons they involve?
3. *Organisational*—How do the meanings hang together?
4. *Contextual*—How do the meanings fit into the larger world of meaning?
5. *Ideological*—Whose interests are the meanings skewed to serve?

The answers to these questions form the basis for a functional grammar, for naming the 'what' of the particular representation of a particular meaning in relation to its 'why'.

Such questions are not the basis for rules of correct usage that students might learn. Rather, they are concepts that might be used in an educationally useable contrastive linguistics. They are tools which students can use to assess the reasons why particular Design choices are made in particular cultural and situational contexts. They are, in other words, a heuristic by means of which students can describe and account for Design variations in the world of meaning. The aim is to give students a sense of how patterns of meaning are the product of different contexts—particularly, in the changing contexts created by new communications technologies and the diverse and intercultural contexts in which language is used.

PROBLEMS AND DIFFICULTIES: TEACHING AND LEARNING

So how does the Multiliteracies view of the changing communications environment and its conception of the process of meaning translate into the pragmatics of pedagogy? The Multiliteracies framework proposes that teaching and learning should be approached from four angles, from the perspective of four orientations. There is nothing terribly surprising in each of these four angles; each is well represented in the history of educational theory and in teachers' contemporary pedagogical practices. However, all four need to be part of the learning process, though not necessarily in any particular fixed sequence or as neatly separate bits.

Teaching and learning about the Design of meaning, should include a mix of: Situated Practice, Overt Instruction, Critical Framing and Transformed Practice.

Situated Practice involves immersion in experience and the utilisation of Available Designs, including those from the students' lifeworlds and simulations of the relationships to be found in workplaces and public spaces. For example, this could involve immersion in Designs of meaning that make 'intuitive' sense, common sense, or at least something more than half sense. In a learning situation this might involve either working with Designs derived from students' own lifeworld experiences, or throwing students in at the deep end with less familiar Designs that will make perhaps only half sense at first, but providing lots of contextual clues. Successful teaching and learning using this pedagogical angle would culminate in a communication problem solved, albeit perhaps intuitively, or with an expert's help, or with scaffolded assistance.

Overt Instruction involves systematic, analytical, and conscious understanding. In the case of Multiliteracies, this requires the introduction of explicit metalanguages which describe and interpret the Design elements of different modes of meaning. For example, this involves developing a language that describes the patterns in Available Designs of meaning, how we do Designing and how meaning becomes Redesigned. 'How much does new text express voice and experience?' we might ask. Evidence of successful teaching and learning from the angle of Overt Instruction might be when students have a way to describe the processes and patterns of Design in a meaningful way.

Critical Framing means interpreting the social and cultural context of particular Designs of meaning. This involves the students standing back from the meanings they are studying and viewing them critically in relation to their context. For example, how does a Design fit in with local meanings and more global meanings? What is the purpose of the Design? What's it doing? To whom? For whom? By whom? Why? To what effect? What is the immediate social context (localised and particular structures, functions, connections, systems, relationships, effects)? What is the larger social context (culture, history, society, politics, values)? Evidence of successful teaching and learning from this pedagogical angle would be when students show that they know what the Design is for—what it does and why it does it.

Transformed Practice entails transfer in meaning-making practice, which puts a transformed meaning to work in other contexts or cultural sites. For example, this might involve applying a given Design in a different context, or making a new Design. It might involve taking a meaning out of context and adapting it in such a way that it works somewhere else. This will inevitably involve students adding something of themselves to the meaning. It will also involve intertextuality (the connections, influences, recreation of other texts and cross-references of history, culture and experience) and hybridity (a Design has voice, but where does the ring of familiarity come from?). Successful teaching and learning from this particular angle will involve either good reproduction (if that's the game) or some measure of the extent and value of creativity in the transformation and the aptness of the transformation or transfer to another context (does it work)?

These four aspects of pedagogy do not form a rigid learning sequence. Rather, they are four essential elements in a full and effective pedagogy. The Multiliteracies framework aims to supplement—not critique or negate—the various existing teaching practices. In fact, each of the aspects of the pedagogy represents a tradition in pedagogy in general. So, Situated Practice sits in the tradition of many of the various progressivisms, from Dewey to whole language and process writing. Overt Instruction sits in the tradition of many teacher-centred transmission pedagogies, from traditional grammar to direct instruction. Critical Framing is in the more recent tradition of critical literacy. Transformed Practice is somewhat harder to place, but its antecedents are various strategies for transfer of learning from one context to another, turning theory into practice, and so on.

The Multiliteracies case is that all four aspects are necessary to good teaching, albeit not in a rigid or sequential way. And when all four aspects are put together, each is at least softened, and at best transformed by the others. Situated Practice when linked to Overt Instruction is no longer simply situated—in the mindless, populist, commonsense, atheoretical, introspective, liberal-individualist way that many progressivisms are. Overt Instruction when linked to Situated Practice becomes more like teacher scaffolding than teacher-centred transmission pedagogy. Critical Framing when linked to the others becomes more grounded, and less airy-ideological. Yet, the four aspects of the pedagogy do dialogue with the main traditions in teaching, problematic as each of these may be.

The four aspects represent, in one sense, pedagogical universals. The paradox of these universals, however, is their departure point is from the inevitably heterogeneous lifeworlds of Situated Practice. And, to load paradox on paradox, the other three pedagogical angles involve three forms of departure from the Situated, but without ever leaving the Situated behind. The Situated is the realm of the lifeworld, of original 'uneducated' experience, of pragmatic everyday life. Each of the other three pedagogical angles, in its own way, expands the horizons of the lifeworld. Overt Instruction makes implicit patterns of meaning explicit; Critical Framing interrogates contexts and purposes; Transformed Practice takes meanings and subjectivity into new and less familiar domains.

Starting with the cultural phenomena of the lifeworld and always returning to those cultural phenomena, the other three angles add perspectives of depth and breadth. To take the depth dimension, we need to go beyond our reading of the phenomena of culture and differences and measure these phenomena against the deep structures of everyday life and meaning (which are harder to see when you are immersed in them) and the moral facts of our species being. This involves suspension of belief or 'bracketing': critical thinking, systems thinking, reflexivity, holistic thinking, working through interrelations between apparently separate phenomena, and figuring out paradox and contradiction.

And, on a breadth dimension, we need to undertake the process of crosscultural comparison; how does this particular lifeworld, our lifeworld (or, to be more precise, each of the layers of the multiplicity of overlapping lifeworld sources which constitutes our daily experience), measure up against alternative ways of being human, of doing culture? Nor is this crosscultural breadth simply the view of a disinterested observer, in the manner of a kind of anthropological curiosity. In an era of increasing local diversity and global interconnectedness, this breadth must be the stuff of practice, of learning by constantly crossing cultural boundaries, of shunting between one lifeworld context and another. Both depth and breadth dimensions are processes for 'denaturalising' the lifeworld, of making the everyday strange in order to cast new light on it and so as to have a more informed basis upon which to design both imminent meanings and our larger social futures.

FUTURE DIRECTIONS: APPLICATIONS OF THE MULTILITERACIES CONCEPT

In the decade since the first publication of the original Multiliteracies manifesto in the Harvard Educational Review, considerable work has been done internationally, including in South Africa (Newfield and Stein, 2000), Malaysia (Kalantzis and Pandian, 2001; Pandian, 1999), and in Greece (particularly in the work of Intzidis and Karantzola). This work has also been represented in a number of overview publications and anthologies (Cope and Kalantzis, 1997b; Kalantzis and Cope, 2000, 2001b; Kalantzis, Varnava-Skoura, and Cope, 2002). There have also been many applications of the multiliteracies notion beyond the original New London Group and the expanded group of international collaborators, including several books (Healy, 2000; Newman, 2002; Unsworth, 2001) and numerous academic articles.

The annual Learning Conference (www.LearningConference.com), continues to be a focal point for discussions of Multiliteracies and for presenting the ongoing work of various members of the New London Group. In recent years, the Learning Conference has been held in Malaysia (Penang, 1999), Australia (Melbourne, 2000), Greece

(Spetses, 2001), China (Beijing, 2002), the United Kingdom (London University, 2003), Cuba (Institute of Pedagogical Sciences, 2004), Spain (University of Granada, 2005) and Jamaica (Montego Bay Teachers' College, 2006). The conference now attracts approximately 800 people annually. The conference papers are published in the *International Journal of Learning* (www.Learning-Journal.com).

Recent work extending and developing the Multiliteracies notions have included Kress's work on images and multimodality (Kress and van Leeuwen, 1996) and contemporary media (Kress, 2003), James Paul Gee's work on video games (Gee, 2003, 2005), Kalantzis and Cope's work on pedagogy (Kalantzis and Cope, 2004, 2005) and a growing literature applying the Multiliteracies concept to the world of digital information and communications technologies (Chandler-Olcott and Mahar, 2003; Cope and Kalantzis, 2003; 2004).

See Also: *David Block: Language Education and Globalization (Volume 1); Stephen May: Language Education, Pluralism and Citizenship (Volume 1); James W. Tollefson: Language Planning in Education (Volume 1); Joan Kelly Hall: Language Education and Culture (Volume 1); Hilary Janks: Teaching Language and Power (Volume 1); Alastair Pennycook: Critical Applied Linguistics and Language Education (Volume 1)*

REFERENCES

Cazden, C.B.: 1983, *Whole Language Plus*, Teachers College Press, New York.

Cazden, C.B.: 1988, *Classroom Discourse: The Language of Teaching and Learning*, Heinemann, Portsmouth, NH.

Cazden, C.: 1989, 'Richmond Road: A multilingual/multicultural primary school in Auckland, New Zealand', *Language and Education* 3, 143–166.

Cazden, C.: 2001, *Classroom Discourse: The Language of Teaching and Learning*, Heinemann, Portsmouth, NH.

Chandler-Olcott, K. and Mahar, D.: 2003, 'Tech-Saviness meets multiliteracies: Exploring adolescent girls' technology-mediated literacy practices', *Reading Research Quarterly*, 38, 356–385.

Cope, B. and Kalantzis, M. (eds.): 1993, *The Powers of Literacy: Genre Approaches to Teaching Writing*, Falmer Press (UK edition) and University of Pennsylvania Press (US edition), London and Pittsburgh.

Cope, B. and Kalantzis, M.: 1997a, *Productive Diversity: A New Approach to Work and Management*, Pluto Press, Sydney.

Cope, B. and Kalantzis, M.: 1997b, ' "Multiliteracies," education and the new communications environment', *Discourse: Studies in the Cultural Politics of Education* 18, 469–478.

Cope, B. and Kalantzis, M. (eds.): 2000, *Multiliteracies: Literacy Learning and the Design of Social Futures*, Routledge, London.

Cope, B. and Kalantzis, M.: 2003, 'Digital meaning and the case for a pedagogy of multiliteracies', in Ambigapathy Pandian, Gitu Chakravarthy, and Peter Kell (eds.), *New Literacies, New Practices, New Times*, Universiti Putra Malaysia Press, Serdang, Malaysia, 26–52.

Cope, B. and Kalantzis, M.: 2004, 'Text-made text', *E-Learning* 1, 198–282.

Fairclough, N.: 1989, *Language and Power*, Longmans, London.

Fairclough, N.: 1992, *Discourse and Social Change*, Polity Press, Cambridge.

Gee, J.P.: 1992, *The Social Mind: Language, Ideology, and Social Practice*, Bergin & Garvey, New York.

Gee, J.P.: 1996, *Social Linguistics and Literacies: Ideology in Discourses*, Taylor and Francis, London.

Gee, J.P.: 2003, *What Video Games Have to Teach Us about Learning and Literacy*, Palgrave Macmillan, New York.

Gee, J.P.: 2005, *Why Video Games are Good for Your Soul: Pleasure and Learning*, Common Ground, Melbourne.

Gee, J.P., Hull, G., and Lankshear, C.: 1996, *The New Work Order*, Westview, Boulder, CO.

Healy, A.: 2000, *Teaching Reading and Writing in a Multiliteracies Context: Classroom Practice*, Post Pressed, Flaxton, Qld.

Kalantzis, M. and Cope, B.: 1989, *Social Literacy: An Overview*, Common Ground, Sydney.

Kalantzis, M. and Cope, B.: 1999, 'Multicultural education: Transforming the mainstream', in S. May (ed.), *Critical Multiculturalism: Rethinking Multicultural and Anti-Racist Education*, Falmer/Taylor and Francis, London, 245–276.

Kalantzis, M. and Cope, B.: 2000, 'Multiliteracies: Rethinking what we mean by literacy and what we teach as literacy in the context of global cultural diversity and new communications technologies', in A.-F. Christidis (ed.), *'Strong' and 'Weak' Languages in the European Union: Aspects of Linguistic Hegemonism*, Centre for the Greek Language, Thessaloniki, 667–679 (English); 80–96 (Greek).

Kalantzis, M. and Cope, B.: 2001a, *New Learning: A Charter for Australian Education*, Australian Council of Deans of Education, Canberra, 160.

Kalantzis, M. and Cope, B. (eds.): 2001b, *Transformations in Language and Learning: Perspectives on Multiliteracies*, Common Ground, Melbourne.

Kalantzis, M. and Pandian, A. (eds.): 2001, *Literacy Matters: Issues for New Times*, Universiti Sains Malaysia, Penang.

Kalantzis, M. and Pandian, A.: 2004, 'Designs for learning', *E-Learning* 1, 38–92.

Kalantzis, M. and Pandian, A.: 2005, *Learning by Design*, Victorian Schools Innovation Commission, Melbourne.

Kalantzis, M., Cope, B., and Slade, D.: 1989, *Minority Languages and Dominant Culture: Issues of Education, Assessment and Social Equity*, Falmer Press, London.

Kalantzis, M., Varnava-Skoura, G., and Cope, B. (eds.): 2002, *Learning for the Future*, Common Ground, Melbourne.

Kalantzis, M., Cope, B., Noble, G., and Poynting, S.: 1991, *Cultures of Schooling: Pedagogies for Cultural Difference and Social Access*, Falmer Press, London.

Kress, G.: 1990, *Linguistic Process and Sociocultural Change*, Oxford University Press, Oxford, England.

Kress, G.: 2003, *Literacy in the New Media Age*, Routledge, London.

Kress, G. and van Leeuwen, T.: 1996, *Reading Images: The Grammar of Visual Design*, Routledge, London.

Luke, A.: 1991, 'The secular word: Catholic reconstructions of Dick and Jane', in M.W. Apple and L.K. Christian-Smith (eds.), *The Politics of the Textbook*, Routledge, New York, 166–191.

Luke, A.: 1992a, 'The body literate: Discourse and inscription in early literacy training', *Linguistics and Education* 4, 107–129.

Luke, A.: 1993, 'Genres of power? Literacy education and the production of capital', in R. Hasan and G. Williams (eds.), *Literacy in Society*, Longman, London, 24.

Luke, C.: 1992b, 'The politicised 'I' and depoliticised 'We': The politics of theory in postmodern feminisms', *Social Semiotics* 2, 1–21.

Luke, C.: 1994, 'Feminist pedagogy and critical media literacy', *Journal of Communication Inquiry* 18, 30–47.

Michaels, S.: 1986, 'Narrative presentations: An oral preparation for literacy with first graders', in J. Cook-Gumperz (ed.), *The Social Construction of Literacy*, Cambridge University Press, New York.

Michaels, S., O'Conner, M.C., and Richards, J.: 1993, Literacy as reasoning within multiple discourse: Implications for restructuring learning. 1993 Restructuring Learning: 1990 Summer Institute Papers and Recommendation, Council of Chief State School Officers, Washington, DC, 107–21.

Nakata, M.: 1993, 'An islander's story of a struggle for "better" education', *Ngoonjook: A Journal of Australian Indigenous Issues* 52–66.

New London Group.: 1996, 'A pedagogy of multiliteracies: Designing social futures', Harvard Educational Review 66, 60–92.

Newfield, D. and Stein, P.: 2000, 'The multiliteracies project: South African teachers respond', in B. Cope and M. Kalantzis (ed.), *Multiliteracies: Literacy Learning and the Design of Social Futures*, Routledge, London, 292–310.

Newman, M.: 2002, *The Designs of Academic Literacy: A Multiliteracies Examination of Academic Achievement*, Begin and Garvey, New York.

Pandian, A. (ed.): 1999, *Global Literacy: Vision, Revisions and Vistas in Education*, Universiti Putra Malaysia Press, Serdang, Malaysia.

Unsworth, L.: 2001, *Teaching Multiliteracies Across The Curriculum*, Open University Press, London.

SURESH CANAGARAJAH

THE POLITICS OF ENGLISH LANGUAGE TEACHING[1]

INTRODUCTION

Because of its close association with structuralist and, later, Chomskyan linguistics, English language teaching (ELT) remained apolitical for a long time, treating language learning as the psycholinguistic mastery of value-free grammar for instrumental purposes. The uses of ELT in the process of colonization, the purposes of Cold War cultural hegemony, and the needs of economic globalization could be identified as other historical motivations for the delay in addressing the politics of ELT (see Canagarajah, 2005). It is only fairly recently, in the early 1990s, that issues of power have received sustained attention (see also Janks, Teaching Language and Power, Volume 1). Though it was initially treated as another optional school or method under the label critical pedagogy (hereafter CP), a power-sensitive orientation has quickly pervaded all areas of ELT. Although many teachers still find it uncomfortable to directly address the politics of ELT, a social and ideological sensitivity colors everything we do in the profession in unacknowledged and subtle ways. No sensible professional can practice ELT today without being alert to the heterogeneity of English varieties, the conflicting claims of community and identity, the values behind methods and materials, and unequal classroom relationships and roles.

EARLY DEVELOPMENTS

The early developments of a political orientation were understandably structuralist and Marxist. Phillipson's (1992) *Linguistic Imperialism*

---

[1] Due to limited space, this chapter focuses only on the conceptual debates and theoretical considerations relating to English language teaching. For how these considerations are negotiated in diverse classrooms at the everyday level, see ethnographies such as Canagarajah, 1999; Lin and Martin, 2005, Heller and Martin-Jones, 2001. A comprehensive geographical coverage of scholarship and pedagogy is not attempted here. The works reviewed derive mostly from ESL situations in North America and the postcolonial contexts. For a consideration of issues relating to EFL in Europe, see Phillipson, Language Policy and Education in the European Union (Volume 1). There is of course an under-representation of research and pedagogical practices in periphery communities in mainstream journals. Makoni et al. (2005) highlight this problem and also introduce some themes important for such communities.

S. May and N. H. Hornberger (eds), Encyclopedia of Language and Education,
2nd Edition, Volume 1: Language Policy and Political Issues in Education, 213–227.
©*2010 Springer Science+Business Media LLC.*

critiqued the intentions of British Council and other Anglo-American institutions sponsoring ELT worldwide. Showing how the dominant pedagogical assumptions based on monolingualist norms and the methods and materials influenced by Anglo-American interests affected the educational autonomy and socioeconomic development of other communities, Phillipson hoped for a time when the rise of global languages would challenge the dominance of English. Other scholars critiqued the hidden curriculum of ELT in American second language teaching contexts (Auerbach, 1993; Benesch, 1993; Pennycook, 1989). Though Freirean approaches were beginning to inspire a consideration of micro-level instructional relationships, offering the possibility of student empowerment, the early scholarship was still on broad issues of curriculum. It would take a different theoretical lens to address the manifestation of power in more local and personal contexts of language and education.

The next wave of scholarship, informed by the Frankfurt school of critical theory and poststructuralist orientations, opened ELT to issues of consciousness, discourse, and agency (see Canagarajah, 1993b; Peirce, 1995; Pennycook, 1994). The possibility of appropriating English in terms of local interests, and the resultant pluralization of English, shifted the discussion to resistance from within the field of ELT. We did not have to wait for challenges to English from outside—as Phillipson anticipated. The hybridity of English language and postcolonial identity provided a useful construct to complicate the interests of western homogeneity in ELT (see Canagarajah, 1999; Pennycook, 1996). However, the discussion was still couched in terms of national or ethnic considerations (i.e. Sri Lankan Tamils in the case of Canagarajah; East Asians in the case of Pennycook). The world systems perspective of Wallerstein informed the discussion as scholars addressed ELT in terms of a hegemonic English-speaking center and a resistant periphery (see also Block, Language Education and Globalization, Volume 1). It would take another wave of theoretical movements to critique the smug multiculturalist discourses fashionable in the West and address power in terms of other variables such as gender, race, and sexual orientation. In adopting constructivist and postmodern perspectives, later scholarship situates teachers and learners in multiple variables and discourses to consider the complex negotiations needed to engage with power in ELT.

Though the beginnings were late, it is remarkable that within a short period the political orientation has become very complex, keeping itself open to critique, rethinking, and paradigm shifts, constituting a vibrant movement in the profession. The CP orientation still maintains a healthy pluralism and openness to new pedagogical questions and research methods.

MAJOR CONTRIBUTIONS

We can consider the contributions of a political orientation to ELT according to several exemplary areas of critical learning and teaching. While we already have a string of labels with the adjective "critical" attached to it—such as critical contrastive rhetoric (Kubota, 1999), critical classroom discourse analysis (Kumaravadivelu, 1999), critical writing (Canagarajah, 1993a), critical applied linguistics (Pennycook, 2001; Critical Applied Linguistics and Language Education, Volume 1), and critical EAP (Benesch, 2001)—we do not have to stop there. A critical orientation has infiltrated many other pedagogical domains, even if no labels may have been coined yet. Here is a sampling of the contributions of CP.

Learning Processes and Teaching Methods

In recent pedagogical discourse, a process-oriented, student-centered, task-based approach has been treated as the most effective for teaching/learning. The ELT research and professional circles have treated this as "the optimum interactional parameters within which classroom language learning can take place" (Holliday, 1994, p. 54). Myron Tuman (1988) describes how the change toward process-oriented approaches of writing in the American academy is unconditionally treated as a more progressive pedagogical development. From this perspective, pedagogical cultures in many non-Western communities are denigrated. Not only are they essentialized as product-oriented, teacher-dominated, and passive, they are also considered pedagogically dysfunctional for those reasons. Therefore, teachers have attempted to impose the process-oriented pedagogy on other communities, assuming that it is more democratic and empowering (see Pennington, 1995). CP has complicated this pedagogical ideal with new realizations:

1. The social and psychological complexity of product-oriented learning is evident when we situate it in context. Students who are older (Leki, 1991) or those learning for academic/instrumental reasons (Chen, Warden, Chang, 2005) may thrive from a product-oriented approach. Even in the case of the much disparaged memorization techniques of Chinese students, one has to consider the fresh uses to which others' words are put (Pennycook, 1996).
2. Product-oriented learning may have oppositional significance. Students sometimes resist the cultural and ideological baggage that accompanies communicative English by resisting active use of the language or just acquiring enough to pass their examinations (Canagarajah, 1993b; Muchiri et al., 1995; Resnick, 1993). Teachers are now more sensitive to the ways in which students might negotiate

the dominant materials and methods to suit their values and interests.
3. The search for the best method is actually a myth (Prabhu, 1990). The periodic popularization of new methods is driven by marketing and power considerations of research centers, publishing houses, and scholarly communities (Canagarajah, 2002; Pennycook, 1989). What is now called the postmethod realization insists that practitioners in the professional periphery should develop teaching strategies that are more relevant to their pedagogical contexts, rather than depending on the center for methods that are considered authoritative. Such an approach is pedagogically empowering.

Literacy Practices

CP has also politicized literacy in English. Literacy was traditionally perceived as the impersonal decoding or encoding of detached texts (in the product-oriented tradition) or the dynamic cognitive strategies that construct personal meaning in the text (in the process-oriented tradition). The pedagogy failed to interrogate the content and genre conventions that shape textual meaning. CP helped inquire how literacy can serve to empower the student and the community. Presently, there are more critical studies relating to macro-textual domains than those on the use of grammar or vocabulary (but see Morgan, 1998). Though we have a well-established critical tradition on orientating to sentence-level rules from the time of critical linguistics (Fowler and Kress, 1979) and stretching to more recent forms of critical discourse analysis (Fairclough, 1995), there are few teachers who use these approaches in the classroom. At the discourse level, CP has corrected the English as an Academic Purposes (EAP) orientation that while academic conventions may be value-ridden and favor dominant ideologies, these are the conventions that students of all languages have to master in order to succeed in the educational setting. Benesch (1993) has taken this pragmatism to task. She has shown that leaving the underlying values and interests of a genre unquestioned is itself an ideological position and is by no means neutral. CP has argued for the need to teach students the ways in which these conventions serve to exclude membership in the academic community. It has shown the ways in which the typical academic posture of detachment and objectivity exclude other ways of knowing that are more empathic and personal, including writings that are more involved and narrative, from women and other minority communities (see Canagarajah, 2002). Benefiting from perspectives of feminism, poststructuralism, and postcolonialism on voice and hybridity, many practitioners have worked toward enabling ESL writers to negotiate the established conventions in their favor to develop multivocal texts (Belcher and Connor, 2001; Casanave and Vandrick, 2003). CP has also exposed how cultural descriptions of L2 writing suppress the complexity, historical dynamism, and even conflicts *within* cultures and subcultures (Kubota, 1999). In fact, with English enjoying hegemonic status globally, it is naive to treat students from other cultures as employing an uncontaminated "native" discourse. CP has argued for the need to make students critique their own discourses as well as that of English in order to practice a critical writing that negotiates cultures (see Canagarajah, 2002; Ramanathan, 2004).

Orientations to Second Language Acquisition

Traditionally, we have worked with constructs like *integrative* and *instrumental* motivation (see Gardener and Lambert, 1972) or (more recently, as a corrective to them) *intrinsic* and *extrinsic* motivation (Brown, 1991) to understand effective language learning. The first construct in each pair has emerged as accounting for success. That is, learning a language to join the target speech community (integrative motivation) rather than obtaining practical rewards (instrumental motivation), or learning a language for self-accomplishment and personal interests (intrinsic motivation) rather than under institutional compulsions (extrinsic motivation) are the valued forms of motivation. However, both sets fail to take account of issues of power in attaining one's objectives (see also Janks, Teaching Language and Power, Volume 1). These constructs give the impression that just having the right motivation will help succeed in language learning. There are serious socioeconomic constraints that shape one's motivations and the ability to attain one's objectives. Furthermore, motivations can be contradictory, multiple, and changing. The strategies one adopts to negotiate the available resources in relation to one's motivation will shape the mastery of the language.

Taking such realities of power and material conditions into account, Bonny Norton Peirce (1995) has come up with the construct *investment*–which is influenced by Bourdieu's economic metaphors for language learning and usage. Norton Peirce demonstrates how the investment of some of her adult immigrant students in learning English to achieve important symbolic and economic capital for their own and their family's survival helps them develop counter-discourses and oppositional identities to transcend silence and marginalization in the new language. One's social positioning and the alternate identities desired in the new community considerably influence the approaches and consequences in language learning. Influenced by these perspectives, we

now have a burgeoning tradition of research on the ways identity is negotiated by students for acquiring English in relation to their social interests
and positioning (see Blackledge and Pavlenko, 2004; Hawkins, 2005;
Lin et al., 2002).

Another socially grounded orientation to the process of language
acquisition is that of joining a community. The model of *legitimate
peripheral participation* has opened some interesting avenues in this
regard. According to Lave and Wenger (1991), any learning involves
practice in the discourses/activities of the dominant community, to
the point where the novice develops the proficiency to be accepted as
a full member. For this to occur, novices should enjoy access to the discourses of the community and the possibility of protected and nurturing
modes of participation. Many scholars have used this perspective to
understand how students develop communities in the classroom to
scaffold their language learning (Hawkins, 2005; Toohey, 1998). However, agency is sometimes exaggerated and the power of the community is simplified to the point where ESL students are vested with the
ability to join any community they want at their own sweet will (see
Zamel, 1997). But Paul Prior (1998) reminds us that ESL students
cannot leave their history and values at the door step as they enter into
a new community. In what he terms a *sociohistoric approach*, he notes
that it is the way students employ their cultural and linguistic resources
to inform the new discourse that empowers them. It is in this way that
they make a contribution to the activity of the new community,
enabling it to revise its discourses and democratize its assumptions.
Therefore ESL students have to assume that joining a community
involves conflict and struggle. Recent studies explore the critical
negotiation involved in becoming members of new language or discourse communities (see Canagarajah, 2003; Kramsch and Lam, 1999;
Toohey, 1998).

With studies of this nature, we have come a long way from the dominant psycholinguistic models treating learners as a bundle of nervous
reflexes. A political orientation treats learners as complex social beings
who must negotiate competing subject positions in conflicting discourse
communities to shape their practices of language learning. Also critical
researchers/teachers orientate to identities as multiple, conflictual, negotiated, and evolving, shifting from the traditional assumption of learner
identities as static, unitary, discrete, and given (see Canagarajah, 2004).

Classroom Discourse

Classroom discourse has implications for ELT as it serves as an input
and reinforcement for language acquisition. In any pedagogy, it is
important to consider how classroom interactions and discourse are

structured. The two dominant traditions of this orientation—i.e. inter-actional analysis which quantifies turns, length, and direction of utterances in teacher/student interaction in an ethnomethodological fashion and the Labovian and Hymsian discourse analytical traditions which describe speech events in relation to broader social and cultural contexts—fall short of addressing issues of power. Critical practitioners have developed interpretive frameworks to consider how the typical speech events and interactions in the classroom enforce unequal relations between the teacher and the student, limit the production of new and critical knowledge, and might work against the social interests relevant to the students (Kumaravadivelu, 1999). Others have identified spaces in the classroom that students and sometimes teachers might use to practice discourses oppositional to the policies in the classroom and the school. Especially in the context of English Only in both US and postcolonial classrooms, multilingual teachers and students might use instructional off-sites to introduce other languages. Labeled variously as classroom underlife (Canagarajah, 2004), safe houses (Pratt, 1991), or institutional interstices (Heller and Martin-Jones, 1996), these sites may find manifestation in deviations from the lesson, passing of notes between students, and unauthorized conversations and topics behind the back of the teacher. In most cases, these sites are constructed in locations outside the surveillance of authority figures. These sites are testament to the agency of the disempowered. However controlled or homogeneous the learning environment, students form spaces where they can develop values and interests that matter to them.

Target Language

The research on classroom underlife shows the desire for students to bring other codes into learning. However, ELT has traditionally insisted not only on an English-only classroom but also treated standard British English or General American English as the target to be achieved universally. In the context of legitimized varieties of World Englishes in postcolonial communities (see Kachru, 1986), there are now new questions to be asked: i.e. Whose norms? How proficient? Despite Kachru's arguments in favor of institutionalized varieties of local Englishes in second language contexts, instruction is still based on the traditional Anglo-American standards. However, globalization and the Internet have served to convince people of the need to be multi-dialectal, if not multilingual. We are now beginning to see research on the ways in which students are developing competence in other varieties of English outside the classroom by their own devices (see Harris et al., 2002; Ibrahim, 1999). We are also beginning to see how students bring in other varieties of English into the classroom to negotiate dominant varieties or appropriate English in their favor (Canagarajah, 1993b; Gebhard, 2005; Martin, 2005).

Discussions of target language should go further to include the place of the first languages ESL students speak. Gone are the days when we treated the L1 as interfering with and even hindering L2 acquisition. We know from recent research that skills and language awareness developed in L1 can transfer positively to L2 (Cummins, 1991), that a validation of the student's L1 can reduce the inhibitions against English and develop positive affect to enhance acquisition (Auerbach, 1993), and that a multilingual self can be formed of diverse languages without being dysfunctional for the students (Kramsch and Lam, 1999). (See also Skutnabb-Kangas, Human Rights and Language Policy in Education, Volume 1.) Skutnabb-Kangas considers it a violation of "linguistic human rights" to teach English in isolation from the first languages of the students. She argues that an ELT pedagogy based on English-only can lead to the gradual devaluation of L1 and subtractive bilingualism among students (cf. May, Bilingual/Immersion Education: What the Research Tells Us, Volume 5). This unequal relationship of languages can lead to the vernacular declining in currency and English continuing its global hegemony.

In this context, it is important to consider how ELT can foster skills of linguistic negotiation that enable students to move across languages. Teaching English without reference to their first language may handicap students for life in the postmodern multilingual world. Multilingual speakers may use their proficiency in languages for critical English expression. Even teachers who may not have a proficiency in the languages spoken by the students can adopt certain pedagogical strategies to help negotiate codes. These pedagogies have been developed by classroom ethnographers from the surreptitious uses of L1 they detect in the language classroom (see Canagarajah, 2004; Lucas and Katz, 1994). Pairing an English-proficient student with someone less proficient for interaction in their own language, grouping students speaking the same language for collaborative tasks, writing journals in the L1, and translating material in both languages are ways in which L1 can be accommodated in the ESL classroom to assist in critical English expression.

WORK IN PROGRESS

Although the work discussed earlier treats identity largely in terms of unitary constructs, such as nationality, race, or ethnicity, recent studies have started exploring how diverse subject positions interact in the learning experience. Gender is an important area of emerging research and pedagogy—as one can note from recent special topic issues in the *TESOL Quarterly* (in Autumn 2004) and the *Journal of Language,*

Identity, and Education (in December 2004). Though late to arrive in the field of ELT, research on gender has fashioned a complex framework integrating scholarship in other fields (see also Pavlenko and Piller, Language Education and Gender, Volume 1). Researchers attempt to move gender beyond deficit, difference, dominance, and dual-culture perspectives (see Langman, 2004) to treat gender as negotiated and constructed. In doing so, they move away from treating gender as an essentialized or overdetermined construct. Crucial to this shift is the way gender interacts with aspects like immigrant or "non-native" status in ELT (see JLIE articles). In some cases, while women's chances of learning a second language are curtailed by their lack of opportunities outside the home, in other cases their immigrant status enables them to suspend home cultural expectations and negotiate new competencies and identities effectively. There is, however, a felt need to analyze the constructivist orientation in the light of structural constraints. Lin et al. (2004) examine how gender interacts with diverse institutional hierarchies in ELT (e.g., teacher-trainers vs. teachers). Yet, Langman (2004) is correct to say that current research is tilted toward adult learners and immigrant women in United States, ignoring other identities, and limiting the ability to form generalizations about gender politics in ELT.

Race too is gaining importance in ELT. Researchers are adopting a constructivist orientation and exploring the way race interacts with other constructs like non-nativeness or gender (see the special topic issue of *TESOL Quarterly* in September 2006). The way race complicates native speaker status has been well studied so far. Ironically, speakers of English as a dominant language with non-white traits are stereotyped as non-natives by teachers and students, though they might have been born in the West. Within non-native speakers, on the other hand, those with 'white' traits have better prospects of "passing" as native speakers and developing confidence in their use of English, compared to those from non-white backgrounds (see also Pavlenko and Piller, Language Education and Gender, Volume 1). Black scholars have also articulated how their status is marginalized, though they are "native" to English (Romney, 2004). The recent publication of an ESL textbook that features Black English, and narratives and images from the Black community, attempts to pluralize ELT (see Romney, 2004).

Research is also underway outside the classroom, in sites such as the Internet and popular culture, to consider the prospects for language learning. Though the Internet has been presented as helping diversify English and providing authority to non-native speakers as it features the global English speech community (Murray 2000; Warschauer, 2000), others see discourses, conventions, and images that are biased

(Selfe and Selfe, 1994). We need more studies that consider how technology is used by learners to negotiate the power inequalities and achieve communicative proficiency (see also Kalantzis and Cope, Language Education and Multiliteracies, Volume 1). Similarly, music and popular culture that form the postmodern "transcultural flows" (Appadurai, 1996) are being studied for how they help learners gain new identities and resources for English acquisition. Consider the multidialectal facility students display and the more desirable identities they take up in the hip-hop culture (Ibrahim, 1999; Pennycook, 2003).

As we turn to constructivist research on the ways English provides new, often empowering, identities to English language learners, there is a need to align this with structural and material considerations. It is true that ELT shifted from the earlier political perspective that focused on structural and geopolitical factors to consider the fluid construction of identities at microlevel sites. There was a concomitant ideological shift from overdetermined analyses to volitionist perspectives on empowerment. Scholars now see the need to conduct a more nuanced reading of the interface between the macro and micro, mind and matter, classroom and society as they interact in language learning (see Gebhard, 2005; Hawkins, 2005).

PROBLEMS AND FUTURE DIRECTIONS

The politics of ELT must be always sensitive to the changes in social conditions. Power is not a zero-sum game. Power is negotiated, shifting, and constantly reconstituted. As students and teachers address power in ELT contexts, power finds newer and subtler manifestations in the field. There might arise a need to abandon earlier analytical frameworks and construct more relevant ones (see also Janks, Teaching Language and Power, Volume 1).

The tension between two broad historical movements is upon us, raising new questions about the place of ELT in all communities. Although non-Western communities were busy working on the decolonization project, the carpet has been pulled from under their feet by another movement, globalization (see Block, Language Education and Globalization, Volume 1). It is as if one historical process subsumed another before the first project was complete. There are significant differences in the project of both movements: decolonization entails resisting English in favor of building an autonomous nation-state; globalization has made the borders of the nation-state porous and reinserted the importance of English language for all communities (see Canagarajah, 2006). Apart from the pressures the nation-state is facing from outside, it is also facing pressures from within (as the claims of diverse social groups and ethnic communities within the nation have become more assertive).

Postmodern conditions have also created certain significant changes in discourse, calling for a different orientation to ELT planning. People are not prepared to think of their identities in essentialist terms (as belonging exclusively to one language or culture), their cultures as monolithic (closed against contact with other communities), and their knowledge forms as pure (uniformly local or centralized). It is fair to ask whether these fuzzy constructs, defined in more fluid and hybrid terms, can be used anymore as reliable frameworks for policy statements. On the other hand, increasing multilingualism, cultural pluralism, and the vernacularization of English bring into question the dichotomous ways in which language policies have been formulated: i.e. English or mother tongue? Individual rights or group rights? Mobility or preservation? (For recent debates, see Modiano, 2004). While we respond to these changes with suitable modification in the ways we articulate language rights, we mustn't simplify the significance of power differences between languages and communities, the continued importance of identities and groups in policy making, and the need for protecting minority interests.

In the midst of all this, scholars of the emerging school of Lingua Franca English find that there are new communicative norms developing as English is used for international communication by multilingual speakers (see, e.g., Seidlhofer, 2004). Studying how non-native speakers in the expanding and outer circle interact in English, researchers find that they do not defer to native speaker norms, as used in the inner circle. The scholars have started identifying a lingua franca core that seems to facilitate communication among speakers of different varieties. Would English as an international language benefit from the teaching of this lingua franca core, rather than the grammar of a specific dominant variety? Furthermore, as there is a need to shuttle between communities in the postmodern world, we have to teach students to negotiate diverse varieties of English in their everyday life. Since teaching one variety at a time is impractical, we have to consider a paradigm shift (for work along these lines, see Holliday, 2005). We have to move away from the traditionally valued "target language" to developing proficiency in a repertoire of Englishes needed in the postmodern world; from our traditional focus on joining a community to shuttling between communities; from the focus on rules of the grammatical system to strategies of negotiation; from an obsession with correctness to negotiating appropriate usage for diverse contexts. Proposals have ranged from teaching language awareness to developing sociolinguistic sensitivity or developing pragmatic strategies for negotiating codes (see McKay, 2005; Seidlhofer, 2004). Still, we have to be careful not to nurture the view that Lingua Franca English is a neutral language that all communities can use without inhibitions. Modiano summarizes the pedagogical dilemma raised by the new status of English in the following way: "Retaining our indigenous cultures and language (s) while reaping the benefits of large-scale integration via a language of wider communication is the challenge many of us will no doubt have to come to terms with in the years to come" (Modiano, 2004, p. 225; see also Phillipson, Language Policy and Education in the European Union Volume 1).

CONCLUSION

The political orientation has left an indelible mark in the field of ELT. It has challenged the dominant discourses of objectivity, pragmatism, and efficiency that characterized the field for a long time. Now we are sensitive to the fact that ELT is an interested activity. We have adopted an ecological orientation that situates language learning clearly in the social context (Phillipson and Skutnabb-Kangas, 1996). Knowledge in the field is now more multilateral, and open to experiences and views from the instructional and geopolitical peripheries. Even research and reporting are influenced by a political perspective (see Canagarajah, 1996). Researchers are now open to questions of ethics, subjectivity, and power as they break away from the positivistic tradition and bring in more diverse methodologies. Similarly, ELT journals are breaking away from the traditional IMRD (i.e., Introduction, Method, Results, Discussion) structure to represent knowledge through narratives, reflection, dialogue, drama, and other genres. Such developments assure us that teachers and researchers will continue to ask questions that relate to issues of power and difference, shaping a more democratic disciplinary discourse.

See Also: Alastair Pennycook: *Critical Applied Linguistics and Language Education (Volume 1); Hilary Janks: Teaching Language and Power (Volume 1); Aneta Pavlenko and Ingrid Piller: Language Education and Gender (Volume 1); David Block: Language Education and Globalization (Volume 1); Stephen May: Bilingual/Immersion Education: What the Research Tells Us (Volume 5); Mary Kalantzis and Bill Cope: Language Education and Multiliteracies (Volume 1); Tove Skutnabb-Kangas: Human Rights and Language Policy in Education (Volume 1); Robert Phillipson: Language Policy and Education in the European Union (Volume 1)*

REFERENCES

Appadurai, A.: 1996, *Modernity at Large: Cultural Dimensions of Globalization*, University of Minnesota Press, Minneapolis.
Auerbach, E.R.: 1993, 'Reexamining English only in the ESL classroom', *TESOL Quarterly* 27(1), 9–32.

Belcher, D. and Connor, U.: (eds.): 2001, *Reflections on Multiliterate Lives*, Multilingual Matters, Clevedon.

Benesch, S.: 1993, 'ESL, ideology and politics of pragmatism', *TESOL Quarterly* 27(2), 705–717.

Benesch, S.: 2001, *Critical English for Academic Purposes*, Lawrence Erlbaum, Mahwah, NJ.

Blackledge, A. and Aneta, P. (eds.): 2004, *Negotiation of Identities in Multilingual Contexts*, Multilingual Matters, Clevedon.

Brown, D.H.: 1991, 'TESOL at twenty-five: What are the issues?', *TESOL Quarterly* 25(2), 245–260.

Canagarajah, A.S.: 1993a, 'Up the garden path: Second language writing approaches, local knowledge, and pluralism', *TESOL Quarterly* 27(2), 301–306.

Canagarajah, A.S.: 1993b, 'Critical ethnography of a Sri Lankan classroom: Ambiguities in opposition to reproduction through ESOL', *TESOL Quarterly* 27(4), 601–626.

Canagarajah, A.S.: 1996, 'From critical research practice to critical research reporting', *TESOL Quarterly* 29(2), 320–330.

Canagarajah, A.S.: 1999, *Resisting Linguistic Imperialism in English Teaching*, Oxford University Press, Oxford.

Canagarajah, A.S.: 2002, *Critical Academic Writing and Multilingual Students*, University of Michigan Press, Ann Arbor, MI.

Canagarajah, A.S.: 2003, 'A somewhat legitimate, and very peripheral participation', in P.C. Christine and V. Stephanie, (eds.), *Writing for Scholarly Publication: Behind the Scenes in Language Education*, Lawrence Erlbaum Associates, Mahwah, NJ, 197–210.

Canagarajah, A.S.: 2004, 'Subversive identities, pedagogical safe houses, and critical learning', in B. Norton and K. Toohey (eds.), *Critical Pedagogies and Language Learning*, Cambridge University Press, Cambridge, 116–137.

Canagarajah, A.S.: 2005, 'Critical pedagogy in L2 learning and teaching', in E. Hinkel (ed.), *Handbook of Research in Second Language Teaching and Research*, Lawrence Erlbaum, London; Mahwah, NJ, 931–949.

Canagarajah, A.S.: 2006, 'Globalization of English and changing pedagogical priorities: The postmodern turn', in B. Beaven (ed.), *IATEFL 2005 Cardiff Conference Selections*, IATEFL, Canterbury, UK.

Casanave, C.P. and Stephanie, V. (eds.): 2003, *Writing for Scholarly Publication: Behind the Scenes in Language Education*, Lawrence Erlbaum Associates, Mahwah, NJ.

Chen, J.F., Warden, C.A., and Chang, H.-T.: 2005, 'Motivators that do not motivate: The case of Chinese EFL learners and the influence of culture on motivation', *TESOL Quarterly* 39/4, 609–633.

Cummins, J.: 1991, 'Interdependence of first- and second-language proficiency in bilingual children', in E. Bialystok (ed.), *Language Processing in Bilingual Children*, Cambridge University Press, Cambridge, 70–89.

Fairclough, N.: 1995, *Critical Discourse Analysis: The Critical Study of Language*, Longman, London.

Fowler, R. and Gunther K.: 1979, 'Critical linguistics', in R. Fowler, B. Hodge, G. Kress, and A. Trew (eds.), *Language and Control*, Routledge, London: 185–213.

Gardner, R.C and William, E.L.: 1972, *Attitudes and Motivation in Second Language Learning*, Newbury House, Rowley, MA.

Gebhard, M.: 2005, 'School reform, hybrid discourses, and second language literacies', *TESOL Quarterly* 39, 187–210.

Harris, R., Constance L., and Ben R.: 2002, 'Globalization, diaspora and language education in England', in D. Cameron and D. Block, *Globalization and Language Teaching*, Routledge, London, 29–46.

Hawkins, M.: 2005, 'Becoming a Student: Identity Work and Academic Literacies in Early Schooling', *TESOL Quarterly* 38/1, 59–82.

Heller, M. and Marilyn M.-J. (eds.): 2001, *Voices of Authority: Education and Linguistic Difference*. (Contemporary Studies in Linguistics and Education Volume 1) Ablex, Westport, CT and London.

Holliday, A.: 1994, *Appropriate Methodology and Social Context*, Cambridge University Press, Cambridge.

Holliday, A.: 2005, *The Struggle to Teach English as an International Language*, Oxford University Press, Oxford.

Ibrahim, A.M.: 1999, 'Becoming Black: Rap and Hip-Hop, race, gender, identity, and the politics of ESL learning', *TESOL Quarterly* 33(3), 349–370.

Kachru, B.B.: 1986, *The Alchemy of English: The Spread, Functions and Models of Non-native Englishes*, Pergamon, Oxford.

Kramsch, C. and Lam, W.S. Eva.: 1999, 'Textual identities: The importance of being non-native', in B. George, (ed.), *Non-native Educators in English Language Teaching*, Lawrence Erlbaum Associates, Mahwah, NJ, 57–72.

Kubota, R.: 1999, 'An investigation of L1-L2 transfer in writing among Japanese University students: Implications for contrastive rhetoric', *Journal of Second Language Writing* 7(1), 69–100.

Kumaravadivelu, B.: 1999, 'Critical classroom discourse analysis', *TESOL Quarterly* 33(3), 453–484.

Langman, J.: 2004, 'Reconstructing gender in a new voice', *JLIE* 3, 235–244.

Lave, J. and Etienne W.: 1991, *Situated Learning: Legitimate Peripheral Participation*, Cambridge University Press, Cambridge.

Leki, I.: 1991, 'The preferences of ESL students for error correction in college-level writing classes', *Foreign Language Annals* 24, 203–218.

Lin, A., Wendy, W., Akamatsu, N., and Riazi, M.: 2002, 'Appropriating English, expanding identities, and re-visioning the field: From TESOL to Teaching English for Glocalized Communication (TEGCOM)', *Journal of Language, Identity, and Education* 1(4), 295–316.

Lin, A., Grant, R., Kubota, R., Motha, S., Sachs, G., Vandrick, S., and Wong, S.: 2004, 'Women faculty of color in TESOL: Theorizing our lived experiences', *TESOL Quarterly* 38, 487–503.

Lin, A. and Peter M. (eds.): 2005, *Decolonisation, Globalisation: Language-in-Education Policy and Practice*, Multilingual Matters, Clevedon.

Lucas, T. and Anne K.: 1994, 'Reframing the debate: The roles of native languages in English-only programs for language minority students', *TESOL Quarterly* 28 (4), 537–562.

Makoni, S., Pakir, A., de Souza, L., Omoniyi, T., Kamwangamalu, N., Karmani, S., and Canagarajah, S.: 2005, 'Toward a more inclusive applied linguistics and English language teaching: A symposium', *TESOL Quarterly* 39(4), 716–752.

Martin, P.: 2005, 'Talking knowledge into being in an upriver primary school in Brunei, in A.S. Canagarajah (ed.), *Negotiating the Global and Local in Language Policies and Practices*, Erlbaum, Mahwah, NJ,

Martin-Jones, M. and Monica H.: 1996, 'Introduction to the special issues on education in multilingual settings: Discourse, identities, and power: Part 1: Constructing legitimacy', *Linguistics and Education* 8, 3–16.

McKay, S.: 2005. 'Teaching the pragmatics of English as an International Language', *Guidelines* 27(1), 3–9.

Morgan, B.: 1998, *The ESL Classroom*, University of Toronto Press, Toronto.

Modiano, M.: 2004, 'Monoculturalization and language dissemination', *Journal of Language, Identity, and Education* 3(3), 215–227.

Muchiri, M.N., Nshindi, G.M., Myers, G., and Ndoloi, D.B.: 1995, 'Importing composition: Teaching and researching academic writing beyond North America', *College Composition and Communication* 46(2), 175–198.

Murray, D.: 2000, 'Protean communication: The language of computer-mediated communication', *TESOL Quarterly* 34/3, 397–422.

Peirce, B.N.: 1995, 'Social identity, investment, and language learning', *TESOL Quarterly* 29(1), 9–32.

Pennington, M.: 1995, 'The teacher change cycle', *TESOL Quarterly* 29, 705–732.

Pennycook, A.: 1989, 'The concept of "method", interested knowledge, and the politics of language teaching', *TESOL Quarterly* 23(4), 589–618.

Pennycook, A.: 1994, *The Cultural Politics of English as an International Language*, Longman, London.

Pennycook, A.: 1996, 'Borrowing others' words: Text, ownership, memory, and plagiarism', *TESOL Quarterly* 30, 201–230.

Pennycook, A.: 2001, *Critical Applied Linguistics*, Lawrence Erlbaum, Mahwah, NJ.

Pennycook, A.: 2003, 'Global Englishes, Rip Slyme, and performativity', *Journal of Sociolinguistics* 7(4), 513–533.

Phillipson, R.: 1992, *Linguistic Imperialism*, Oxford University Press, Oxford, UK.

Phillipson, R. and Skutnabb-Kangas, T.: 1996, 'English Only worldwide, or language ecology', *TESOL Quarterly* 30(3), 429–452.

Pratt, M.L.: 1991, *Arts of the Contact Zone. Profession 91*, MLA, New York, 33–40.

Prabhu, N.S.: 1990, 'There is no best method–Why?', *TESOL Quarterly* 24(2), 161–176.

Prior, P.: 1998, *Writing/Disciplinarity: A Sociohistoric Account of Literate Activity in the Academy*, Lawrence Erlbaum, Mahwah, NJ.

Ramanathan, V.: 2004, *The English-vernacular Divide: Postcolonial Language Politics and Practice*, Multilingual Matters, Clevedon, UK.

Resnik, M.C.: 1993, 'ESL and language planning in Puerto Rico', *TESOL Quarterly* 27(2), 259–273.

Romney, M.: 2004, 'My experience writing and publishing Afro-centric ESOL materials', paper presented in TESOL convention, Long Beach, CA, 2nd April.

Seidlhofer, B.: 2004, Research perspectives on teaching English as a lingua franca', *Annual Review of Applied Linguistics* 24, 209–239.

Selfe, C. and Richard J.S.: 1994, 'The politics of the interface: Power and its exercise in electronic contact zones', *College Composition and Communication* 45(4), 480–504.

Skutnabb-Kangas, T.: 2002, 'Marvelous human rights rhetoric and grim realities: Language rights in education', *Journal of Language, Identity, and Education*, 1(3), 179–206.

Toohey, K.: 1998, '"Breaking them up, taking them away": ESL students in Grade 1', *TESOL Quarterly* 32(1), 61–84.

Tuman, M.C.: 1988, 'Class, codes, and composition: Basil Bernstein and the critique of pedagogy', *College Composition and Communication* 39(1), 42–51.

Warschauer, M.: 2000, 'The changing global economy and the future of English teaching', *TESOL Quarterly* 34(3), 511–536.

Zamel, V.: 1997, 'Toward a model of transculturation', *TESOL Quarterly* 31(2), 341–351.

TERRENCE G. WILEY

LANGUAGE POLICY AND TEACHER EDUCATION

EARLY DEVELOPMENTS

Language policy in education as an instrument for the promotion of hegemony has been utilized by nation-states over the course of the past five centuries. The scholar Antonio de Nebrija, through the promotion of his Castilian Grammar, was among the first to advocate for overt instruction in a standardized language as a means of advancing the interests of the state (Illich, 1979; Mignolo, 2003). François I of France, shortly thereafter likewise saw the importance of language policy in the interest of national hegemony (Christ, 1997). With the rise of common public schooling during the nineteenth century in a number of Western European countries, as well as in the USA, language policy has been at the core of teacher education, even though teachers have rarely received explicit subject matter preparation in language policy as a subject area. Similarly, with the onset of the 1868 Meiji period, language policy became a major focus of mass education in Japan (Carroll, 2001; Weinberg, 1997). Teachers had to keep pace with reforms in the writing system and the unification of spoken and written language, as well as the incorporation of new concepts into the Japanese language from abroad (Coulmas, 1990; cf. Fujita-Round and Maher, Language Education Policy in Japan, Volume 1). The use of vernacular and script reforms became a focus of Chinese educators throughout much of the twentieth century, as the spread of standard Mandarin continues to be a focus of educational policy currently into the twenty-first century (Peterson, 1997; see also Lam, Language Education Policy in Greater China, Volume 1). Long in the domain of missionary educators and colonial powers in Africa, educational language policies and the need for professional preparation of teachers of Africa's multilingual populations are ongoing needs in its postcolonial states (see also Heugh, Language Policy and Education in Southern Africa, Volume 1). Similarly, teacher education for indigenous language minorities in rural Central and South America represents a major need if educational opportunities are to expand to indigenous populations (see also Godenzzi, Language Policy and Education in the Andes, Volume 1; Hamel, Bilingual Education for Indigenous Communities in Mexico, Volume 5).

S. May and N. H. Hornberger (eds), Encyclopedia of Language and Education,
2nd Edition, Volume 1: Language Policy and Political Issues in Education, 229–241.
©2010 Springer Science+Business Media LLC.

PROBLEMS AND DIFFICULTIES

Although language policy may be a topic in teacher preparation courses, like other areas of applied linguistics, it is rarely a required area for in-depth study. Teacher preparation curricula place strong emphases on language and literacy education in which policies are prescribed or mandated. With specific reference to language minority student populations, teachers are asked to implement policies that either promote, accommodate, or restrict languages. In dealing with language policy in teacher education, it is necessary to distinguish among language policies that are intended to (1) promote literacy and education in national and/or official languages, (2) accommodate or promote mother tongues and community languages, and/or (3) promote foreign languages and/or languages of wider communication.

The United Nations holds that education is a basic human right without which the rights of citizenship and civic participation cannot be fully enjoyed (Daudet and Sigh, 2001). The promotion of national and common languages is often the primary focus of public or state-supported schooling, given that it allows access to social, economic, and political participation necessary to benefit from the rights of citizenship. The right to an education in one's mother tongue, heritage, or community language(s), was endorsed by the United Nations in a 1953 UNESCO resolution, which called for children to have the right to attain literacy in their mother tongue. The reality is that many nation-states have not seriously engaged this matter (Skutnabb-Kangas, 2000, 2002, Human Rights and Language Policy in Education, Volume 1; Wiley, 2002).

The language of the school may be mutually intelligible with the language of the home and community, but often it is not. Thus, a major consideration in teacher education is the extent to which language differences between the child's and the school's language is acknowledged and reflected in instructional and educational policies and instruction. Unfortunately, in many states, educational policy approaches are based on deficit views of language minority status (Churchill, 1986; May, 2001, Chapter 5).

Given that there are around 6,000 languages in the world as well as many social and regional varieties of languages, many children enter schools in which there are differences between their language variety and that used by the school. When instruction is provided in the language of home and community, there typically are fewer "language problems." Children acquire spoken languages naturally based on their interaction with their parents and local speech communities. However, because there are far fewer standardized languages of literacy than spoken ones, and given that few languages have achieved the status of school languages, promoting literacy may be a problem, particularly if teachers have not been prepared to recognize and accommodate differences between the language of the home and school. Many educators tend to be influenced more by the political climate and common discourse related to citizenship and language diversity than they are informed by theory and research (McGoarty, 2002; see also May, Bilingual/Immersion Education: What the Research Tells Us, Volume 5). Moreover, because many teacher educators view language varieties of the community or home as deficient, they do not believe that children should even have a right to instruction in their own language (Smitherman, 2005).

Although, the 1953 UNESCO resolution is supported by constructivist theory and research on the need for students to identify positively with their home and community languages, support for linguistic human rights in education has been mixed. In some countries, there has been gradual recognition of the rights of national minorities to promote their languages based on historical claims (May, 2001). In many countries, however, policy makers have rejected the use of minority languages for other groups, or have lacked the resources or will to promote instruction through them. Similarly, minority languages and "nonstandard" varieties of language have often been rejected, even when they are only to be used to accommodate schooling for language minorities (Ramírez, Wiley, de Klerk, Lee, and Wright, 2005).

Teacher education in many countries involves setting professional standards which may include accreditation of professional programs, licensing via examinations, or certification based on set coursework. Teachers may receive initial or preservice instruction, apprentice preparation, such as student teaching, and ongoing or in-service professional development. Countries such as France, Japan, and Mexico have centralized departments of education whereas the USA uses a federal model, in which states have responsibility for teacher licensing. US states began assuming this responsibility during the late nineteenth century (Darling-Hammond, 2001). Across the various states, however, programs are not uniform.

In some countries, teacher preparation may consist of only the most rudimentary levels of higher education, if even that. Teachers of rural language minority populations in Guatemala, for example, may receive only 1 year of teacher preparation. In 2000, in China, gaps in public education were filled by over 50,000 nonstate educational institutions, with much variation in quality of instruction and teacher preparation (Zhou and Ross, 2004). Despite officially stated requirements for teacher preparation, in some developing nations rural teachers may be only several years ahead of their students, and may be struggling along with their students to attain proficiency in the dominant and/or national language (cf. Heugh, Language Policy and Education in Southern

Africa, Volume 1). In certain countries, teachers may be required to receive four or five years or preparation, whereas in other countries they may receive graduate degrees either before or after their certification. Despite these differences internationally, there have been many similarities regarding teacher preparation and expectations for teacher performance with respect to language instruction.

How professional knowledge is conceptualized and presented in practitioner journals is a major concern in teacher education (Darling-Hammond, 2006). Despite their struggles for professional status, in many countries teachers have been viewed as instruments of the state, whose role is to implement national/state policies, rather than to critique or question such policies. In countries where market forces have strong influence, teachers have been viewed more as technicians of instruction, wherein preparation is viewed as a form of apprenticeship. They often lack control over the selection and adoption of materials and may not be able to control or influence instructional policies that would be more equitable for linguistically diverse populations. As Darling-Hammond argues, "Whereas professions typically assume responsibility for defining, transmitting, and enforcing standards of practice, teachers have historically had little or no control over most of the mechanisms that determine professional standards" (2001, p. 260).

Where professional goals and standards were addressed in second and/or foreign language teacher preparation, traditionally they focused on the relationship between language and a "target" culture. Mainstream and second language teachers were taught to teach to an idealized "native-like" competence, foster the ability to speak, and write like a "native speaker," develop insider cultural knowledge of rules of appropriateness so that students could pass, or nearly pass, as a native speaker in accent and articulation; and help students try to blend or assimilate into the target language community. In such preparation programs, there has been little consideration for the maintenance or loss of the learner's first language(s).

Beginning in the late 1990s, US teachers in the English-only states of California, Arizona, and Massachusetts were restricted in the range of program and instructional options they could employ for language minority students (see also Ricento and Wright, Language Policy and Education in the United States, Volume 1). The content of teacher preparation programs was constrained and specified approaches to basic literacy education, such as phonics, were prescribed. In cases such as these, political prescription has overridden professional judgment in teacher preparation. Thus, from the perspective of promoting equitable educational language policies, despite these obstacles, teacher preparation programs need to inform teachers about ways in which they may become conflicted by, and complicit in, promoting policies that disadvantage or discriminate against language minority children (see also Janks, Teaching Language and Power, Volume 1).

Some detrimental educational language policies are officially prescribed, but many more are likely to be implicit. Rather than being derived from formal policies of the school, they result more from institutional practices and teachers' folk theories about the importance of language learning and language in learning. Haas (1992) has examined how institutional practices involving language can contribute to institutional racism, which involves systematic practices that have the effect of advantaging some and disadvantaging others, even if such practices were not intended to do so. In his analysis of the state of Hawaii, Haas found a number of language-related school practices that adversely affected language minorities. Historically, oral language tests during the first half of the twentieth century in Hawaii were used to track or segregate "nonstandard" language speakers into separate schools from those with "standard" accents. Language performance also correlated with the ethnic and racial backgrounds of the children. Haas noted that this practice was abolished only after many children of color acquired "mainland sounding accents" (p. 191).

Other examples of biased schooling practices noted by Haas included insufficient use of language minority languages to communicate with parents; unequal grade distributions by race/ethnicity/language background; under-identification of students in need of language assistance; under-serving students needing language assistance; inappropriate staff composition to provide language assistance to language minority students; and discriminatory requirements for language certification among teachers (see pp. 191–214 for elaboration). To this list, other practices can be added: disallowing language minorities equal access to core academic curricula because of their proficiency in the dominant language, holding unequal expectations for the success of language minority children based on their language backgrounds, and failing to provide language minority communities with choice of the language of instruction (Wiley, 1996).

Language assessment policy is another area that needs attention in teacher preparation. Among the more enduring educational practices which needs scrutiny, is the use of language tests as one of the primary means of sorting children into special instructional tracks based on their proficiency, as measured by language texts, in the language of instruction (Hakuta, 1986). Valadez, MacSwan, and Martínez (2002) found misassessment and misclassification to be a major problem among some 6,800 students who allegedly lacked proficiency in both their purported first language and the language of instruction. On a linguistic assessment of 23 grammatical variables, drawn from natural speech samples rather than school-based assessment measures, the students

234 TERRENCE G. WILEY

who were held to be "low achievers," because of their alleged low
levels of language proficiency, were found not to "differ linguistically
in any interesting way from other children" (p. 246).

MAJOR CONTRIBUTIONS: THEORETICAL AND PROFESSIONAL PERSPECTIVES

Concurrent with the rise of state licensing in the USA, curriculum
reformers began placing emphasis on formal language education. Pre-
scriptive notions of standard language were emphasized for college
admission. Teachers increasingly were seen as the guardians of
"proper" language (Wright, 1980). In classrooms they were admon-
ished to use a formal register for questioning, and their students were
expected to answer in a formal recitation register. Children and speakers of nonstandard varieties of language quickly learned that "their oral
performance was inadequate even if they did not understand why"
(Wiley, 2005, p. 151). The expectation for standard language became
a school-based language policy in which use of a standard register,
modeled after formal writing, was expected for both oral and written
communication.

As Christ (1997) has correctly noted: "Hardly any research has been
conducted thus far on language policy in teacher education" (p. 224).
Some of the reasons for this relate to the relatively negligible impact
that applied linguistics has had on mainstream teacher education and
to the perception of teaching as a profession and teacher knowledge
more broadly. The applied linguistic knowledge base for second language, foreign language, and bilingual instruction is more developed,
teachers may be required to do some foundational work in theory and
methodology and some relevant materials are noteworthy (e.g., August
and Hakuta, 1998; Baker, 2001; Baetens-Beardsmore, 1993). Moreover, Corson's (1999) discussion of language policies in schools provides an excellent foundation for considering the range of policies
that might be more explicitly addressed in teacher education.

In recent decades in Europe, advances in foreign language theory
and instructional methodology drew from work done on the teaching
of English as a foreign/second language. During the 1990s, teacher preparation efforts such as the LINGUA project, sought to move beyond
that dependency by using learner-centered approaches in in-service
training for secondary teachers of German, Spanish, Modern Greek,
as well as English (Gewerh, 1998). Other recent work (e.g., Hawkins,
2004) has focused on teaching language as socially situated and variable rather than as merely "the sum of all its grammatical parts" (p. 4).
A greater emphasis is placed on the need for teachers to understand the
politics of discourses.

Professional organizations have been able to exert some influence on the direction of teacher preparation and ongoing professional development. Associations such as the National Council for Accreditation of Teacher Education (NCATE) in the USA, and the International Reading Association (IRA), exercise considerable influence on setting standards for teacher preparation. In recent years, these organizations have become more attuned to issues of cultural and linguistic diversity, at least within the context of the ideology of accountability, which has manifested itself in the educational standards movement (Wiley, 2005).

Given the push for higher educational standards for all students, this question may be asked: To what extent do educational standards adequately take into consideration and reflect the language needs of all students? Advocates of educational standards contend that standards provide an explicit foundation for measuring student progress against national expectations as well as for cross-national educational comparisons. Student demographics, resources, and materials, however, vary greatly between countries and within them. Language minority students can be disadvantaged by educational standards, particularly when their home and community languages are ignored or held in low regard by teachers. Therefore, in order for educational standards to be equitable, teachers must have an understanding of the specific linguistic and cultural resources all students bring with them to school (Wiley, 2005).

In the USA, the IRA and the National Council on the Teaching of English (NCTE) have created standards for the English language arts, which have become influential guides for teachers, most of whom will teach some language minority students, even if they are not ESL specialists. In a positive sense, these help to underscore the need for equitable treatment for language minority students who are increasingly a major portion of the student population. In theory, the standards can be adapted creatively to special populations. From the perspective of equity, IRA/NCTE notes that to ensure "equal educational opportunities and meet high expectations for performance" (IRA/NCTE, p. 9), students must have access to school resources, adequately trained and knowledgeable teachers, and safe, well-equipped schools (IRA/NCTE, p. 9).

For teachers of language minority students, IRA/NCTE standards underscore the importance of helping students develop "an understanding of and respect for diversity in language use, patterns, and dialects across cultures, ethnic groups, geographic regions, and social roles" (p. 9). The importance of home language is noted: "Students whose first language is not English make use of their first language to develop competency in the English language arts and to develop understanding of content across curriculum" (p. 9). These are important acknowledgments; however, there is a risk that a standard such as these may become empty slogans unless teachers are provided with appropriate training to work with linguistically diverse students. This is necessary because language use at home can be very different from expectations for language use in the school (cf. Heath, 1983). In a related effort, the international association of Teachers of English to Speakers of Other Languages (TESOL) has likewise taken steps to promote its own ESL Standards for Pre-K-12 Students (1997).

According to TESOL, its standards were drawn from research on first and second language acquisition. Its principles for language teaching are based on the assumptions that (1) language is functional; (2) language is not monolithic but varies in many ways by skill area and social and regional variety; (3) learning language involves cultural learning; (4) language acquisition is a long-term process; (5) language acquisition occurs through meaningful use and interaction; (6) language processes develop independently; (7) native language proficiency contributes to second language acquisition; and (8) bilingualism is an individual and social asset (TESOL, 1997, see pp. 6–8).

TESOL put forth broad goals for instruction whereby students would learn to use language for social and academic purposes in culturally appropriate ways. In particular, TESOL's standards call for teachers to emphasize appropriate use of language variety, register, and genre according to audience, purpose, and setting; use nonverbal communication appropriately according to audience, purpose, and setting; and use appropriate learning strategies to extend students' social and socio-cultural competence. This emphasis implies a target cultural and linguistic standard against which language performance could be assessed. Given that English is an international language of wider communication with competing standards and multiple cultural contexts for "appropriate" language use, contextualizing standards would appear to be problematic (cf. McKay, 2002). Which standards, or more directly, "whose" standards based on notions of cultural, class, or national norms for behavior should prevail? This is not a trivial question when considering how language policies should relate to teacher preparation. Are teachers to be the gatekeepers of rules of appropriateness, be referees, or consultants? Thus, considering the role of standards as a guide to language policy in teacher education, there is room for caution.

The history of curriculum accountability movements suggests that the push for standards often results in overly prescribed curricula, which can result in implicit biases for language minority students (Wiley and Wright, 2004). Thus, care is needed to clarify why standards are being selected and 'whose standards' they reflect. As Tumposky (1984) has noted, the "equation of the knowledge of a language with the mastery of isolated, discrete items would seem to have been disproven by the acknowledged failure of certain methods ... which focused almost exclusively on the minutiae of language's building blocks" (p. 303). Thus, to a degree, this perspective suggests limits to overly prespecified language planning in teacher education. John Dewey (1963) noted long ago that the challenge for the teacher is to achieve through conscious planning what nature does naturally. No matter how much the language curriculum is overtly planned by teachers, curriculum designers, and textbook writers, it is still experienced differently by the learners. Students interpret, reconstruct, and even resist those plans (cf. Canagarajah, 1999). To facilitate student learning, instructional standards, or plans must be sensitive to how those plans are understood and reconstructed by the students (for a more elaborated discussion of the standards for language minority instruction, see Wiley, 2005, Chapter 9).

Unfortunately, analyses of the content of mainstream language arts texts books indicate that many teacher preparation materials treat these topics generically and without enough depth to adequately prepare teachers (Berdan and Wiley, 1992). By acknowledging language diversity, the IRA/NCTE and TESOL standards represent an advance over previous organizational guidelines, but more is needed to provide in-depth guidance for teachers about policies and practices that would enhance the education of language minority learners. Some recent efforts, however, are more clearly directed at helping novice and in-service teachers develop language awareness in instruction (see Trappes-Lomax and Gerguson, 2002).

FUTURE DIRECTIONS

Around the world, the demand for English, and increasingly Spanish, Mandarin, Arabic, and other global/regional languages of wider communication presents challenges. First, these and other major languages are needed for access to the kinds of knowledge mediated through schools, which is necessary for social, economic, and political participation. Unless specific educational policies are put in place to promote and maintain minority languages, they may not have the resources or vitality to thrive or even survive. Second, as the demand for global and regional languages increases, so does the need for adequately prepared teachers of these languages, as well as teachers who must use these languages to teach.

As English and other major languages spread, they are used for many purposes by many types of learners, and these languages are changed by them. The globalization of English, in particular, is forcing changes in conceptions of the role of teachers and of language goals and policies in teacher preparation. Corson (2001) has suggested three things that could be done at the school and local levels: (1) creating

238   TERRENCE G. WILEY

better patterns of communication regarding language goals; (2) negotiating policies between the school and local communities; and (3) promoting "critical language awareness" within the school "through a
language curriculum that promotes social awareness of discourse ...
variety, and consciousness of practice for change" (p. 34; cf. May, 1994).

Increasingly, we can expect that languages will be learned for specific purposes including trade, business, and international communication, as well as to enhance personal knowledge and educational
opportunities. The need to communicate with others in global contexts
will require that language teachers better understand the need for languages to function as bridges in multilingual contexts, that some learners may resist implicit cultural discourses, and that languages will
be indigenized and code-mixed for local or regional communicative
purposes without following the conventions of the so-called target cultures (see Canagarajah, 1999; McKay, 2002; Sridhar, 1996). Thus, successful program models for promoting foreign language fall into three
broad categories: (1) those that are designed to meet specific learner
needs, (2) those that promote general communication strategies, and
(3) those that are needed for educational enhancement.

Given the negative legacy of discriminatory language policies in
education for language minorities, some focus on the history of educational language policies to the detriment of language minority students
should be a part of teacher preparation. Beyond that, there is a need for
teachers to become familiar with positive examples of culturally and
linguistically responsive schooling (see for example, May, 1994).

Some teacher training in the ethnography of communication and on
expectations for language usage is needed when languages are being
taught for purposes of wider communication. With the expansion of
economic interdependence and globalization, it is reasonable to assume
that language teachers, within local contexts, will increasingly need a
variety of methods and approaches to meet learner needs (cf. Block,
Language Education and Globalization, Volume 1). There will be
increasing demand for instruction in foreign or additional languages
of wider communication, both for academic and specific purposes, as
well as for wider communication. As this occurs, teachers of English
and other global/regional languages should not be surprised by the
appropriation of these languages by learners who are not native speakers. Moreover, in the expanding circles of global and regional languages of wider communication, there will likely be an increased
need to prepare bilingual teachers. Already, the majority of the world's
teachers of English, for example, are "nonnative" speakers. Given
the variety of learner needs and local contexts for learning and using
English and wider and regional languages of communication, there
is a variety of appropriate methods that range from Communicative

Language Teaching, focused on target inner circle discourse practices, to more locally congruent cultural expectations.

Increasingly, however, in the global age, English is being used as a medium of instruction in schools, as well as for the purpose of acquiring and conveying information in local contexts. Thus, the relationship between language and culture may increasingly be one where there will be a need for scrutiny and negotiation of instructional language policies, especially when the goal of instruction is communication rather than assimilation.

ACKNOWLEDGEMENT

The discussion on standards is based on Wiley (2005), with permission from the Center for Applied Linguistics, CAL. See Chapter 9, "The Standards Movement: Considerations for Language Minority Students" for an elaborated discussion.

See Also: *David Block: Language Education and Globalization (Volume 1); Tove Skutnabb-Kangas: Human Rights and Language Policy in Education (Volume 1); Thomas Ricento and Wayne Wright: Language Policy and Education in the United States (Volume 1); Noeline Wright: School Language Policies (Volume 1); Stephen May: Bilingual/Immersion Education: What the Research Tells Us (Volume 5)*

REFERENCES

August, D. and Hakuta, K.: 1998, *Educating Language-Minority Children*, National Academy Press, Washington, DC.
Baetens-Beardsmore, H. (ed.): 1993, *European Models of Bilingual Education*, Multilingual Matters, Clevedon, UK.
Baker, C.: 2001, *Foundations of Bilingual Education and Bilingualism* (third edition), Multilingual Matters, Clevedon, UK.
Barns, D.: 1976, *From Communication to Curriculum*, Penguin, London.
Berdan, R. and Wiley, T.G.: March 1992, *The Mainstreaming of ESL: Challenges for TESL Teacher Preparation*, Paper presented on Annual Teachers of English to Speakers of Other Languages (TESOL) International Conference in Vancouver, British Columbia.
Block, D. and Cameron, D.: 2002, *Globalization and Language Teaching*, Routledge, London.
Canagarajah, A.S.: 1999, *Resisting Linguistic Imperialism in English Teaching*, Oxford University Press, Oxford.
Carroll, T.: 2001, *Language Planning and Language Change in Japan*, Curzon, Richmond.
Christ, H.: 1997, 'Language policy in teacher education', in D. Corson (ed.), *Encyclopedia of Language and Education*, Vol. 1, Kluwer, Dordrecht, 219–227.
Churchill, S.: 1986, *The Education of Linguistic and Cultural Minorities in the OECD Countries*, Multilingual Matters, Clevedon, UK.

Corson, D.: 1999, *Language Polices in Schools. A Resource for Teachers and Administrators*, Lawrence Erlbaum Associates, Mahwah, NJ.

Corson, D.: 2001, *Language, Power and Social Justice in Education*, Lawrence Erlbaum Associates, Mahwah, NJ.

Coulmas, F.: 1990, 'Language in Meji Japan', in B. Weinstien (ed.), *Language Policy and Political Development*, Ablex, Norwood, NJ.

Darling-Hammond, L.: 2001, 'Standard setting in teaching', in Virginia Richardson (ed.), *Handbook of Research on Teaching* (fourth edition), American Educational Research Association (AERA), Washington, DC, 751–776.

Daudet, Y. and Sigh, K.: 2001, *The Right to Education: An Analysis of UNESCO's Standard Setting Instruments*, United Nations Educational, Scientific and Cultural Organization, Paris.

Dewey, J.: 1963, *Experience and Education*, MacMillan, New York (originally published 1938).

Gewerh, W. (ed.): 1998, *Aspects of Modern Langauge Teaching*, Routledge, London.

Haas, M.: 1992, *Institutional Racism: The Case of Hawai'i*, Praeger, Westport, CN.

Hakuta, K.: 1986, *Mirror of Language: The Debate over Bilingualism*, Basic Books, New York.

Hawkins, M.R. (ed.): 2004, *Language Learning and Teacher Education: A Sociocultural Approach*, Multilingual Matters, Clevedon.

Heath, S.B.: 1983, *Ways with Words: Language, Life, and Work in Communities and Classrooms*, Cambridge University Press, Cambridge.

Illich, I.: 1979, 'Vernacular values and education', *Teacher's College Record* 81(1), 31–75.

International Reading Association & National Council of Teachers of English: 1996, *Standards for the English Language Arts*, Author, Newark, DE; Urbana, IL.

May, S.: 1994, *Making Multicultural Education Work*, Multilingual Matters, Clevedon.

May, S.: 2001, *Language and Minority Rights: Ethnicity, Nationalism and the Politics of Language*, Longman, London (Reprinted by Routledge, 2007).

McKay, S.: 2002, *Teaching English as an International Language*, Oxford University Press, Oxford.

McGroarty, M.: 2002, 'Evolving influences on educational language policies', in J.W. Tollefson (ed.), *Language Policies in Education: Critical Issues*, Lawrence Erlbaum Associates, Mahwah, NJ, 17–38.

Mignolo, W.D.: 2003, *The Darker Side of the Renaissance: Literacy, Territoriality, & Colonization* (second edition), University of Michigan Press, Ann Arbor.

Peterson, G.: 1997, *The Power of Words. Literacy and Revolution in South China, 1945–95*, University of British Columbia Press, Vancouver, BC.

Ramírez, J.D., Wiley, T.G., de Klerk, G., Lee, E., and Wright, W. (eds.): 2005, *Ebonics in the Urban Education Debate* (second edition), Multilingual Matters, Clevedon, UK.

Skutnabb-Kangas, T.: 2000, *Linguistic Genocide in Education or Worldwide Diversity and Human Rights?* Lawrence Erlbaum Associates, Mahwah, NJ.

Skutnabb-Kangas, T.: 2002, 'Marvelous rights rhetoric and grim realities', *Journal of Language, Identity, and Education* 1(3), 179–205.

Smitherman, G.: 2005, 'Black language and the education of Black children', in J.D. Ramírez, T.G. Wiley, G. de Klerk, E. Lee, and W. Wright (eds.), *Ebonics in the Urban Education Debate* (second edition), Multilingual Matters, Clevedon, UK, 49–61.

Sridhar, K.K.: 1996, 'Societal multilingualism', in S.L. McKay and N. Hornberger (eds.), *Sociolinguistics and Language Teaching*, Cambridge University Press, Cambridge, 47–71.

Teachers of English to Speakers of other Languages (TESOL): 1997, *ESL Standards for Pre-K-12 Students*, Author, Arlington, VA.

Trappes-Lomax, H. and Gerguson, G.: 2002, *Language Teacher Education*, John Benjamins, Amsterdam.

Tumposky, N.R.: 1984, 'Behavioral objectives, the cult of efficiency, and foreign language learning. Are they compatible', *TESOL Quarterly* 18(2), 295–307.

Valadez, C., MacSwan, J., and Martínez, C.: 2002, 'Toward a new view of low achieving bilinguals: A study of linguistic competence in designated "semilinguals,"' *Bilingual Review* 25(3), 238–248.

Weinberg, M.: 1997, *Asian-American Education*, Lawrence Erlbaum Associates, Mahwah, NJ.

Wiley, T.G.: 1996, 'Language planning and language policy', in S. McKay and N. Hornberger (eds.), *Sociolinguistics and Language Teaching*, Cambridge University Press, Cambridge, 103–147.

Wiley, T.G.: 2002, 'Accessing language rights in education: A brief history of the U.S. context', in J. Tollefson (ed.), *Language Policies in Education: Critical Readings*, Lawrence Erlbaum Associates, Mahwah, NJ, 39–64.

Wiley, T.G.: 2005, *Literacy and Language Diversity in the United States*, Center for Applied Linguistics, Washington, DC.

Wiley, T.G. and Wright, W.: 2004, 'Against the undertow: Language-minority education and politics in the age of accountability', *Educational Policy* 18(1), 142–168.

Wright, E.: 1980, 'School English and public policy', *College English* 42(4), 327–342.

Zhou, M. and Ross, H.A.: 2004, 'Introduction: The context of theory and practice', in M. Zhou and S.H.A. Hongkai (eds.), *Language Policy in the Peoples Republic of China: Theory and Practice since 1949*, Kluwer Academic Publishers, Boston, xx.

SCHOOL LANGUAGE POLICIES

INTRODUCTION

This chapter considers developments in school language policies in the last decade. Such policies are often developed at a national level using mechanisms such as those discussed by Sue Wright (2004). However, these same policies may not always find their way to implementation at the school level. Stephen May (1997) defined a school language policy as "a policy document aimed at addressing the particular language needs of a school" (p. 229). Such a document should therefore centralize language in learning and address the relevant diverse language needs of its student population, especially if, as May argues, it is developed in consultation with the wider school community. How that consultation should or might take place, or what constitutes the wider school community, is not explained. Once complete however, the policy should identify "areas within school organisation, curriculum, pedagogy and assessment where specific language needs exist" and indicate directions and methods for dealing with specific issues, "within a discretionary and flexible framework" that also includes mechanisms for review and monitoring (May, 1997, p. 299).

Corson (1999), who was influential in initiating this school-based language policy research, endorsed this view of the role and purpose of a language policy. He argued that a language policy provides schools with a specific direction in dealing with the issues, challenges, and possibilities that diversity and disparate learning needs pose. His work (see also Corson, 1990, 1993) explored the role of language policies in schools, and how they might serve the needs of diverse students. Such policies, he noted, were often accompanied by professional development to influence teachers' practices and beliefs.

School language policies can also be centrally and politically driven. Coady and O'Laoire (2002) document this as they explain the mechanisms of the resurgence of Gaelic in the Republic of Ireland, where it became "a subject taught to bolster the government's aim of fostering an Irish-speaking identity on behalf of the nation" (p. 143).

S. May and N. H. Hornberger (eds), Encyclopedia of Language and Education,
2nd Edition, Volume 1: Language Policy and Political Issues in Education, 243–252.
©2010 Springer Science+Business Media LLC.

Language Policies and Literacy

The aspirations described earlier for school language policies can now be viewed in relation to the extent of their success in being a mechanism for dealing with disparity, diversity, literacy, and learning, particularly in Western contexts, the main focus of this chapter. Midway through the United Nations Decade of Literacy (2003–2012), it is pertinent to briefly examine links between language policies in specific countries and literacy actions at the school level. As May noted a decade ago, the prevalence of language policies at the school level in addressing these was not particularly widespread.

As Ager (2001) has observed, the world has, in the last decade, experienced some major upheavals: Yugoslavia is now a number of separate nations, the two Germanys have reunited and the European Union legislates for member countries on a number of practices normally the preserve of individual nations, such as currency and food standards. This is reflected in other international federations and treaties, which increasingly standardize economic and social practices stemming from corporate and political influences, highlighting the role of language and languages in standardization processes. Phillipson's chapter (Language Policy and Education in the European Union) in this volume is indicative of the issues involved (see also Block, Language Education and Globalization, Volume 1).

And while some countries persist in creating or adapting political language policies that privilege some languages or language practices over others, other practices aim to support diverse languages, such as the European Union's Charter for Regional or Minority Languages, one ramification of which, is the mandating in Britain at least, of a literacy hour in primary schools.

Concurrently, in countries like New Zealand, which has witnessed sustained revival in an indigenous language, there has been a review of literacy and languages provision in schools. In New Zealand's case, precipitating factors include the growth of Maori medium schools and the graduation of fluent Maori speakers from total immersion primary (elementary) schools to secondary schools, coupled with a rise in the number of foreign-fee-paying students and new migrants in schools. New Zealand's experience supports Hornberger's (2002) assertion that until the 1980s, language planning tended to be governed by the belief that linguistic diversity was a problem. Now, however, a conceptual shift in the country appears to recognize that it is an asset. Other factors relate to Progress in International Reading Literacy Study (PIRLS) and Programme for International Student Assessment (PISA) research findings (New Zealand Ministry of Education, 2001, 2003), which continue to be used to illustrate and inform government policy direction.

This chapter considers the last decade and reviews the extent to which the ideals of national language policies have been implemented in schools in ways in which Corson (1999) advocated, or moved on from May's (1997) description of the mismatch between national level and school level policies.

EARLY DEVELOPMENTS

May's (1997) review of the genesis and international spread of school language policies does not need reinventing, but it is useful to restate some of its key ideas, and subsequent additions. As described, the major tenets of language across the curriculum (LAC) were that:

1. Language plays a central role in all learning.
2. Students must be actively engaged in meaning-making processes. Concomitantly, teachers must facilitate active student-centered learning rather than adopting didactic and transmissionist approaches to teaching.
3. Active student learning involves the four principal modes of language: listening, talking, reading, and writing.
4. Students should be encouraged to use their own language in these various modes as the principal tool for interpreting and mastering curriculum content (May, 1997, p. 230).

Wright (2004) noted that language policy and planning operated on three key levels of planning: status (as in political and governmental levels, identified by Ager (1996, p. 54) as "constituent policies"); corpus (as in the institutional level, such as schools or universities, and as outlined by Fishman, 2000, implicated in corpus agendas); and acquisition (i.e., both learning a language and the processes and management of programs that facilitate this). This builds on Cooper's (1989) three levels explored in relation to language policy and social change. Wright suggested that a focus on the role of language is "an integral part of nation building" (p. 9), and that language planning is an "organizing principle and mobilizing force" (p. 13). This implies that the development of language policy and planning at the status level at least, has had a long political history, longer than the history of school language policies as intimated by May (1997), whose focus necessarily centered on the corpus level, where national expectations for implementation concentrated on schools. A recent addition is the international focus on literacy, and the way in which countries interpret and politicize this aspect of learning in schools.

In New Zealand for instance, the four principal modes of language (reading, writing, speaking, and listening) were transformed into eight in the late 1970s—listening, speaking, reading, writing, moving, shaping, watching, and viewing—partly as a result of the international influence of the 1966 Dartmouth conference, and to accommodate the development and influence of visual media. Later, these were adapted for the national curriculum document, *English in the New Zealand Curriculum* (Ministry of Education, 1994). This change recognized the existence of more visual texts, such as film and the Internet (see also Kalantzis and Cope, Language Education and Multiliteracies, Volume 1). This curriculum, now a decade old, has undergone further review, simplification, and paring—indicating something of the rapidity of change in coping with political, social, economic, and technological imperatives.

Alongside this, the 1994 curriculum reoriented primary school teachers' views of what had traditionally been labeled "reading" and "language" as "English." With a current national (and, it would seem, international) focus on literacy, there is a tendency for primary (elementary) teachers to call these same lessons "literacy," thus again affecting perceptions about what constitutes this kind of learning. However, "literacy" as a concept and focus has not been widely debated in New Zealand (as is also often the case elsewhere), nor has its meaning been explored; instead, its meaning seems to be taken for granted—that it is a synonym for both reading/language and English in primary schools. In New Zealand secondary schools, which have been exploring literacy as a focus for learning across the curriculum, subject specialists have been encouraged to reexamine their pedagogical practices and engage in more cross-curricular conversations about literacy and learning: a relatively new situation for such teachers, but one which Corson (1999) considered was imperative for more cohesive thinking about language.

Interestingly, very few of the schools heavily involved in this literacy professional development have developed language and literacy policies to support this endeavor. Instead, schools generally create systemic mechanisms to embed it, such as individual staff appraisal goals, or as mandated elements in departmental plans and programs. An overarching attempt to examine literacy and its implications in the wider school has not generally taken place, particularly in relation to language's role in learning and thinking. Long term, the effects of this omission are unknown, and may affect aspects of accommodating diversity, since it is literacy *in English* that is emphasized: the default position. New Zealand's case demonstrates ways in which political changes and policy developments can become reflected in the practices of schools, without recourse to the language policy debates advocated by Corson and May.

Another example is Spain, which has been examining the implications of multiple language learning in education as a response to some European Union membership ramifications. It has wrestled with ways of acknowledging and fostering multilingualism through policy directions (Madrid-Fernandez, 2005). This examination includes: how to improve language learning from primary to tertiary levels; what that means for staff expertise and resources; and the role of technology in implementing this language policy at the school level. Spain's attempts to develop processes for implementation suggest some of the complex struggles between "a spreading lingua franca and global networks" and a likely "growing desire to conserve community and traditional ways of meaning through attention on what happens at the school level" (Wright, 2004, p. 246).

Conversely, in countries where nationalism or "national state ideology" (Wright, 2004, p. 247) has become more prominent, language policy and planning can impose exclusionary practices on schools, effectively suppressing language diversity (see also May, Language Education, Pluralism and Citizenship, Volume 1). Some educational policy decisions in the USA suggest this possibility, especially in relation to both schools' abilities to provide first language support and maintenance (Meyer, 2004; Skutnabb-Kangas, 2002; see also Ricento and Wright, Language Policy and Education in the United States, Volume 1), and what counts in literacy and language (Gerstl-Pepin and Woodside-Jiron, 2005). Freeman (2004) engages with some of these issues in accounting for efforts to establish school language policies in some of Philadelphia's bilingual schools.

MAJOR CONTRIBUTIONS

A major contributor to the whole area of school language policies and language planning has been David Corson (1990, 1993, 1999). As May indicated, Corson extended "the conception of language to include not only the four conventional language modes, but also the additional activities of moving, watching, shaping, and viewing" (1997, p. 232), which can be directly related to educational developments in places like New Zealand from the 1970s to 1990s.

May also contended that Corson extended the original LAC focus to "include second language, bilingual, foreign language and wider social justice issues" (1997, p. 232). This extension, May argued, is "crucial" for it begins to acknowledge the greater multiethnic nature of many schools worldwide. In countries where addressing cultural differences in educational settings is important, this broader application of language planning and policies is significant, providing school-based educators with researched evidence to draw on.

Recent works on exploring multiculturalism and ethnic diversity (May, Modood, and Squires, 2004) in relation to wider political, social, and educational imperatives complement both Corson's (1999) work and Ager's (2001) examination of motivation in language planning and policy in international contexts. These broader understandings of the potential of language diversity to affect positions and hierarchies of identity and power highlight possible roles for language policy and planning in any country. The encompassing of linguistic difference in the design of language policies at national as well as local school levels can have wide ramifications on both students' achievement and the fabric of the society they live in. Ignoring these may indeed encourage continued subjection of language to the international power of others (see Skutnabb-Kangas's views on these issues in Human Rights and Language Policy in Education, Volume 1). Goldstein's (2003) work identified complexities inherent in teachers' work as they attempt to enact the intentions of diverse school language policies in North American contexts. This work may be even more difficult in the current educational climate of No Child Left Behind (Abedi, 2004). Wright (2004), in examining similar ideas at the political nation-state level, drew similar conclusions to Goldstein, whereas Marley's (2004) review of the political and national changes in language policy in Morocco, where they moved from a monolingual approach to a bilingual one, demonstrate some possible positive effects on attitudes at the local school level.

PROBLEMS AND DIFFICULTIES

At the school level, the desired outcomes for language policy development tend to remain somewhat idealistic. Sergiovanni, Burlingame, Coombs, and Thurston (1999) suggest that political demands, constraints, and choices can impinge on desirable educational goals and policy provisions, recognizing the influence of status planning requirements as Fishman (2000) intimates. Escamilla (1994) cited some of the difficulties with school language policies having the desired effect. Her study investigated the relationship between policy and practice in a Californian elementary school that promoted bilingualism. She found that the perception and reality were somewhat different. English was, in practice, the privileged language, even though the school's policy espoused an equal footing with Spanish. Perhaps this exemplifies Suarez's (2002) assertion that, "linguistic hegemony exerts and legitimates power by presenting the dominant language as an instrument, or tool to be used by those who acquire it in whatever way they choose" (p. 514). This highlights May's (1997; see also 1994) cautions regarding the efficacy and prevalence of school language policies, and is illustrative of New Zealand's focus on literacy in English as the default.

Perhaps these cautions illustrate the distance between the desire and detail; that schools seem unable to "walk the talk" for a range of reasons, not the least of which include some constraints imposed by external policy makers, coupled with the complex nature of teachers' work. Other constraints include: staff changes—including leadership, competing priorities, difficulties in coordinating, and sustaining consistent language-oriented professional development (PD) for staff, and restricted opportunities for cross-curricular internal debate about the key elements of school language policy issues. Although language-oriented PD may be relatively easy to initiate in elementary (primary) schools, the same cannot be said for secondary schools, where subject silos still exist, alongside a heavy emphasis on content at the expense of language processes that support and sustain access to learning. National secondary literacy projects (such as in New Zealand), which explore the relationship between language and learning in secondary schools, highlight these problems (see Wright, Smyth, May, Whitehead, and Smyth, 2005). May (1997) alluded to these issues when he noted that, "the *process* of implementing LAC within the school is crucial to gaining and maintaining teacher support. A school language policy needs to be both carefully thought through and carefully managed if *all* staff are to be convinced of its merits" (p. 234).

May's (1997) further observations about the necessity for school leaders to be involved along with sufficient time and other resourcing (such as designated personnel) to effect change, coupled with staff development, is borne out in the New Zealand experience, a researched 3-year-pilot study implementing literacy across the curriculum in secondary schools. The pilot clearly illustrated the importance of those factors. The researchers noted two additions—the value of a theorized approach and the value of a school developing and sustaining a literacy community of practice involving teachers in ongoing high-quality professional talk about language, literacy, and thinking. Both are likely to produce successful and positive changes in attitudes and teachers' practices in this regard (Wright et al., 2005). Another factor not addressed in May's (1997) synthesis was the importance of external agents to both precipitate awareness about and provide support and guidance in addressing literacy and language pedagogy and policy issues. Developing school language policies destined to have a robust shelf life, is thus a complex and long-term undertaking.

FUTURE DIRECTIONS

The model developing in New Zealand to support a concerted focus in secondary schools on literacy, language, and learning is useful to compare with May's (1997, p. 235) list of requirements for schools wanting to implement language policies successfully. Schools, he asserted, need to be "more democratic." In other words, aspects of teacher buy-in, decision-making processes, and collaborative pedagogy are implicated in any efforts to design and implement a language policy. Second, he indicated that "critically reflective" practices are vital so that teachers' attitudes, values, and beliefs about language and learning are challenged. Third, a "whole-school" orientation is required, although this may take some time to effect.

The New Zealand research (Wright et al., 2005) suggests that focusing pedagogical change on language and literacy has a better chance of long-term success if it is begun with a group of volunteers willing to alter their beliefs, attitudes, and practices regarding language and learning across the curriculum. This initial awareness-raising and trial period may take as long as 3 years to achieve. From there, wider buy-in and engagement is possible, especially if a nurtured literacy and language community of practice is fostered. A community of practice is, therefore, an umbrella under which these elements can combine to develop capacity and critical mass. This research, conducted nationally, may provide some insights for other jurisdictions to consider.

Mitchell and Sackney (2001) identified key capacities that should be nurtured if successful learning communities are a desirable cultural element in a school. They noted that if the personal, interpersonal, and organizational are acknowledged and developed, then there is a good chance that a language policy can be positively implemented. The personal aspect relates to a teacher's sense of agency and self-critique. Should teachers not engage in this, then any concerted professional development is likely to be ineffective. As Corson (1999) observed, ". . . changing teacher attitudes seems best achieved by changing teacher behavior first" (p. 91). The interpersonal factor is also important. Relationships with professional peers can have profound effects on the quality and rate of pedagogical and attitudinal change, as Reeves, Turner, Morris, and Forde (2005, p. 253) have indicated. They noted that for school leaders to change, "there was a complex dynamic involved . . . where the conceptual development of individuals was closely related to their experience of enacting new behaviours in the social setting of the workplace. . . . Change and development on their part was closely bound to the capacity and willingness to change on the part of others." And significantly, they observed that, "for established practitioners, changing practice transformatively involves both desisting from some of their habitual behaviours and enacting new ones, thus, to some extent, reinventing themselves within the same work setting" (2005, p. 255).

Finally, if May's (1997, p. 238) hope that developments in critical pedagogy and the centralizing of language will support the "successful incorporation of school language policies" is ever to come to fruition, a clear understanding of school change processes, plus the roles leaders and teachers play in this, is imperative.

See Also: *David Block: Language Education and Globalization (Volume 1); Robert Phillipson: Language Policy and Education in the European Union (Volume 1); Mary Kalantzis and Bill Cope: Language Education and Multiliteracies (Volume 1); Stephen May: Language Education, Pluralism and Citizenship (Volume 1); Terrence Wiley: Language Policy and Teacher Education (Volume 1)*

REFERENCES

Abedi, J.: 2004, 'The No Child Left Behind act and English language learners: Assessment and accountability issues', *Educational Researcher* 33(1), 4–15.

Ager, D.: 2001, *Motivation in Language Planning and Language Policy*, Multilingual Matters, Clevedon, UK.

Coady, M. and O'Laoire, M.: 2002, 'Mismatches in language policy and practice in education: The case of Gaelscoileanna in the Republic of Ireland', *Language Policy* 1, 143–158.

Cooper, R.L.: 1989, *Language Planning and Social Change*, Cambridge University Press, Cambridge, NY.

Corson, D.: 1990, *Language Policy across the Curriculum*, Multilingual Matters, Clevedon, England.

Corson, D.: 1993, *Language, Minority Education and Gender*, Multilingual Matters, Clevedon, England.

Corson, D.: 1999, *Language Policy in School: A Resource for Teachers and Administrators*, Lawrence Erlbaum Associates, Mahwah, NJ.

Escamilla, K.: 1994, 'The sociolinguistic environment of a Bilingual school: A case study introduction', *Bilingual Research Journal* 18(1–2), 21–47.

Fishman, J.A.: 2000, 'The status agenda in corpus planning', in E.L. Richard and S. Elana (eds.), *Language Policy and Pedagogy: Essays in Honor of A. Ronald Walton*, John Benjamins Publishing, Amsterdam, The Netherlands, 43–52.

Freeman, R.D.: 2004, *Building on Community Bilingualism*, Multilingual Matters, Philadephia.

Gerstl-Pepin, C.I. and Woodside-Jiron, H.: 2005, 'Tensions between the "science" of reading and a "love of learning": One high-poverty school's struggle with NCLB', *Equity and Excellence in Education* 38, 232–241.

Goldstein, T.: 2003, *Teaching and Learning in a Multilingual School: Choices, Risks, and Dilemmas*, Lawrence Erlbaum Associates, Mahwah, NJ.

Hornberger, N.H.: 2002, 'Multilingual language policies and the continua of biliteracy: An ecological approach', *Language Policy* 1, 27–51.

Kleifgen, J.A.: 2003, 'Afterword: Theories, policies, practices', *Current Issues in Comparative Education* 5, 2, 4 pages. Available at: http://www.tc.columbia.edu/cice/vol5nr2/al152.htm (Accessed date: 23/5/05).

Madrid-Fernandez, D.: 2005, *Bilingual and Plurilingual Education in the European and Andalusian Context*, Plenary address to the 12th International Conference on Learning, Granada, Spain, 11–14 July.

Marley, D.: 2004, 'Language attitudes in Morocco following recent changes in language policy', *Language Policy* 3, 25–46.

May, S.: 1994, 'School-based language policy reform: A New Zealand example', in A. Blackledge (ed.), *Teaching Bilingual Children*, Trentham Press, London, 19–41.

May, S.: 1997. 'School language policies', *Encyclopedia of Language and Education. Volume 1: Language Policy and Political Issues in Education*, 229–240.

May, S., Modood, T., and Squires, J. (eds.): 2004, *Ethnicity, Nationalism and Minority Rights*, Cambridge University Press, Cambridge, NY.

Meyer, L.: 2004, 'No Child left Behind fails to pass fairness test', *Albuquerque Journal*. Available at: http://ourworld.compuserve.com/homepages/JWCRAWFORD/AJ2.htm (Accessed date: 21/7/05).

Ministry of Education: 1994, *English in the New Zealand Curriculum,* Learning Media, Wellington, New Zealand.

Ministry of Education: 2001, *Progress in International Reading Literacy Study—PIRLS-01*. Available at: http://www.minedu.govt.nz/index.cfm?layout=document &documentid=4349&data=1 (Accessed date: 11/8/05).

Ministry of Education: 2003, *Programme for International Student Assessment*. Available at: http://www.minedu.govt.nz/index.cfm?layout=search_results&criteria= PISA (Accessed date: 11/8/05).

Mitchell, C. and Sackney, L.: 2001, *Profound Improvement: Building Capacity for a Learning Community*, Swets & Zeitlinger, Lisse, The Netherlands.

Reeves, J., Turner, E., Morris, B., and Forde, C.: 2005, 'Changing their minds: The social dynamics of school leaders' learning', *Cambridge Journal of Education* 35(2), 253–274.

Sergiovanni, T., Burlingame, M., Coombs, F., and Thurston, P.: 1999, 'Public values and school policy: The roots of conflict', in T. Sergiovanni, M. Burlingame, F. Coombs, and P. Thurston (eds.), *Educational Governance and Administration* (fourth edition), Allyn & Bacon, Boston, 1–19.

Skutnabb-Kangas, T.: 2002, *Language Policies and Education: The Role of Education in Destroying or Supporting the World's Linguistic Diversity*, Address to World Congress on Language Policies, Barcelona, Spain, April 16–20. Available at: http://www.linguapax.org/congres/plenaries/skutnabb.html (Accessed date: 21/7/05).

Suarez, D.: 2002, 'The paradox of linguistic hegemony and the maintenance of Spanish', *Journal of Multilingual and Multicultural Development* 23(6), 512–530.

Wright, S.: 2004, *Language Policy and Language Planning: From Nationalism to Globalisation*, Palgrave MacMillan, Houndsmills, Basingstoke, Hampshire, UK.

Wright, N., Smyth, J., May, S., Whitehead, D., and Smyth, S.: 2005, *Secondary Schools' Literacy Initiative Research Evaluation*. Report on 2004 Case Study Schools. Wilf Malcolm Institute of Educational Research, Hamilton, New Zealand.

Section 4

Focus on Selected Regions of the World

ROBERT PHILLIPSON

LANGUAGE POLICY AND EDUCATION IN THE EUROPEAN UNION

INTRODUCTION

Language policy is acquiring increasing importance in an age of intensive political and cultural change in Europe. Among the key educational language policy issues in contemporary Europe are ensuring the continued vitality of national languages, rights for minority languages, diversification in foreign language learning, and the formation of a European Higher Education Area (the Bologna process). English, due to its role in globalisation and European integration processes, impacts on each of these four issues in each European state. The role of the European Union (EU) is a second cross-cutting factor, because of its declared commitment to maintaining linguistic diversity and to promoting multilingualism in education. On the other hand, it is arguable that the dominance of English in many forms of international activity, the erosion of national borders by changes in communication technology, and the hierarchy of languages that exists de facto in EU institutions and EU-funded activities (such as student mobility) may be serving to strengthen English at the expense of other languages.

EARLY DEVELOPMENTS

The EU began life as an economic community in 1958 with six member states: Belgium, France, the Federal Republic of Germany, Italy, Luxemburg, and the Netherlands. Small enlargements occurred over the following four decades, bringing the total in the mid-1990s to 15 member states. Eleven languages had equal rights as the official and working languages of EU institutions. A major enlargement in 2004 brought in ten additional states (post-communist eastern European states, Cyprus and Malta). Nine languages were added to the world's largest translation and interpretation services. The EU is an immensely complex business: interpretation is provided for an average of 50 meetings each working day, and over 70% of national legislation entails enacting measures that have already been agreed on at the supranational level. European integration significantly affects economic, political, social and cultural life. Whether the present EU is a United States of Europe in the making is unclear. The rejection of the draft EU

S. May and N. H. Hornberger (eds), Encyclopedia of Language and Education, 2nd Edition, Volume 1: Language Policy and Political Issues in Education, 255–265.
©2010 Springer Science+Business Media LLC.

Constitution in 2005 confirmed the gap between citizens with a strong national identity and the European project of political leaders and a remote unaccountable bureaucracy. The EU has been decisively influenced by a trans-Atlantic corporate neoliberal agenda (Monbiot, 2000), which the constitution would have consolidated. It also covered 'fundamental rights' as a potential counter-balance to the workings of the market, but the provisions on cultural and linguistic rights are weak.

'Europe' is a fuzzy concept. Depending on context, Europe may be a toponym (territory, geography), an econonym (a common market with a common currency, one that some member states have not yet adhered to), a politonym (an amalgam of independent states in a complex new unit with some traits of a federation), or an ethnonym (cultures with shared cultural traits that stress a common Christian past, which some see as excluding Islamic Turkey as a member). Linguistically, Europe is diverse: many languages in the Romance and Germanic families of language derive from Indo-European sources, others are Finno-Ugric, Basque is neither, and many languages currently in use in Europe, often in substantial numbers, are of more recent diverse immigrant or refugee origins.

Europe is emphatically not synonymous with the EU, though this distinction is frequently blurred. The Council of Europe has twice as many member states as the EU, among them Norway, Russia, Switzerland, and Turkey, which are not members of the EU. It has played a key role in promoting human rights, and political and cultural collaboration. It has also coordinated a significant number of measures to strengthen foreign language learning, including, notably, the Common European Framework of Reference for Languages (Council of Europe, 2001; Trim, 2002). It is taking on a more proactive role in language policy formation (www.coe.int).

Many European languages have been consolidated as a dominant state language over the past two centuries. Domestic functions have been carried out in the key 'national' language, Danish, Estonian, French, Greek, etc. Promotion of a single national language occurred both in states with an ideology of ethnolinguistically uniform origins (with Germany as the archetype) and those with a republican statist model (typically France). Local minority languages were suppressed, but have gained increasing support in recent decades in several countries (Catalan, Welsh, Sámi, etc). Foreign languages were learned for external communication purposes and familiarity with the cultural heritage associated with 'great' powers. Since 1945, and more intensively in recent years, there has been a gradual shift towards English becoming by far the most widely learned foreign language on the continent of Europe, taking over space, both in western and eastern Europe, occupied earlier by other foreign languages, French, German and Russian in particular.

While it used to be primarily elites and those professionally concerned with trade or travel who learned foreign languages, these are now part of the curriculum for all. The advance of English in a range of key societal domains, commerce, finance, research and higher education, the media, and popular culture means that English in the modern world no longer fits into the traditional mould of a foreign language (which are referred to as 'modern' or 'living' languages in some countries). There are obvious instrumental reasons for learning the language. European citizens are massively exposed to Hollywood products (whereas in the USA the market share of films of foreign origin is 1%): '70–80% of all TV fiction shown on European TV is American ... American movies, American TV and the American lifestyle for the populations of the world and Europe at large have become the lingua franca of globalization, the closest we get to a visual world culture' (Bondebjerg, 2003, pp. 79, 81). These US products are transmitted with the original soundtrack in the Nordic countries and the Netherlands, which strengthens the learning of English, and are generally dubbed elsewhere.

MAJOR CONTRIBUTIONS

Foreign language education is embedded in national education systems and their distinct traditions (making generalisation perilous). There has been a progressive shift to more communicatively oriented foreign language learning, and starting ever younger, though the traditional focus on literature often remains at the upper secondary and university levels. Many European university language departments are less concerned with teacher education than with general academic development, literature being supplemented by an increasing focus on the cultures of English-speaking countries, particularly the USA and the UK. The diversity of approaches to foreign language teacher training is captured and summarised in a survey commissioned by the EU (Grenfell, Kelly and Jones, 2003). It sums up relevant theory and key variables, and highlights foreign language teacher competences and the reflective practitioner, bringing in examples from different countries ad hoc. It also presents 15 case studies that demonstrate innovative good practice, exemplified by various types of bilingual education, including the limited type, Content and Language Integrated Learning (see www. euroclic.net), which is currently regarded as more likely to achieve success than traditional methods. This study of language teacher training is not an isolated project, but rather a symptom of the way the EU is coordinating interaction between representatives of member states with an agenda of reform. Thus the 'Education and training 2010' programme (http://www.europa.eu.int/comm/education/policies/2010) is elaborating 'Common European principles for teacher competences and qualifications', with language learning as 1 of 12 'key objectives and areas of cooperation'.

Even in this professional field, where the goal is multilingual competence, English is much the most widely used language at European conferences and publications from them, although English and French are the working languages of the Council of Europe. In some regional European forums, multilingual competence is assumed (e.g. Danish, Norwegian and Swedish, with or without English), in others, receptive competence in a second language, such as German. German is the EU language with by far the largest number of native speakers, and has functioned as a lingua franca in many central and eastern European countries, a role which English is progressively taking over. The French government invests heavily in the promotion of French throughout Europe, and has been instrumental in persuading its EU partners to articulate discourses and policies that proclaim the value of linguistic diversity and language learning. However its efforts tend to be more aimed at preventing further erosion of the status of French as an international language than at ensuring linguistic human rights and equality for speakers of all languages (Phillipson, 2003, pp. 45–46 and pp. 133–134).

Teacher qualifications are of decisive importance, and there is evidence from most parts of Europe that many teachers of foreign languages are under-qualified. This in part explains differing degrees of success in foreign language learning, and why figures on the number of learners (data are collected by the EU educational information service www.eurydice.org) are not revealing on outcomes. Even if most European schoolchildren are now exposed to English in school, most of their elders have not been (for analysis of EU Eurobarometer self-report data on capacity to communicate in a foreign language, see Phillipson, 2003, pp. 8–9). It is therefore wishful thinking to suggest that English is a universal lingua franca in continental Europe.

WORK IN PROGRESS

Schoolchildren in the demographically small European countries have often been taught two foreign languages in school. This policy has been recommended since the 1980s by the Council of Europe, and became EU policy in the 1990s. One factor influencing this policy has been the fear that English represents a threat to the languages and cultures of EU member states, hence the goal of learners developing competence and familiarity with two foreign languages and their cultures. The EU Commission document *Promoting language learning and linguistic diversity: An Action Plan 2004–2006*, of July 2003 is designed to curb an excessive focus on English in continental education systems and the wider society. It states: 'learning one lingua franca alone is not enough ... English alone is not enough ... In non-anglophone countries recent trends to provide teaching in English may have unforeseen consequences on the vitality of the national language' (pp. 4 and 8). The policy statement advocates life-long foreign language learning, including two foreign languages in the primary school. It strives to bring language policy higher up on national agendas, and to raise awareness of linguistic diversity. It endorses the notion of an inclusive 'language-friendly environment', and states that this openness should include minority languages, those of both local regions and recent immigrants.

These laudable goals are a far cry from the reality, but representatives of member states are requested to attend meetings in Brussels and to describe implementation of the Action Plan and obstacles to it. Such activity is reported on the EU website (http://europa.eu.int/ comm/education), invariably in English, less often in French, and virtually never in any of the other 18 EU official languages. Two major proposals by the Commission in 2005, a New Framework Strategy for Multilingualism, and a 'common European language indicator'— that is Europe-wide language testing—are aimed at inducing member states to adjust their language policies along the lines of the Action Plan. The policy statements, and comparable ones from the Council of Europe, may or may not influence national policy formation, but the very existence of international pressure of this kind can serve to force states to address language policy issues that they would prefer to ignore.

Both the EU and the Council of Europe are involved in policies to accord rights to regional minority languages (Council of Europe, 2004). Minority language policies differ widely in each EU member state, and are well documented (Williams, 2005). There are three EU-funded centres with a specialist role: Mercator Media at the University of Wales Aberystwyth (UK) researches the media, defined broadly to include the press, book-publishing, archives and libraries as well as broadcast media and the new media; Mercator Legislation at the CIEMEN foundation, Barcelona (Spain) is concerned with language legislation and language in public administration, whereas Mercator Education at the Fryske Akademy, Ljouwert (Netherlands) studies education at all levels.

One pressure that cannot be ignored is the expanding role of English in higher education, especially in northern Europe (Ammon, 2001; Phillipson, 2002, 2006; Wilson, 2002; Wilkinson, 2004). This is one dimension of the 'Bologna process', the formation of a European Higher Education Area, which has been underway since 1999, and to which the governments of 45 European states are committed. There are bi-annual meetings at which national and university policies are coordinated. The EU has largely set the agenda for the Bologna process, which entails implementing a uniform undergraduate and graduate degree structure, internal and external quality control, student exchanges, double degrees, joint study programmes, etc. While the initial Bologna text stressed university autonomy, and respect for the languages and cultures of Europe, the most recent policy statement, from Bergen in 2005 (www.bologna-bergen2005.no), appears to conflate internationalisation and 'English-medium higher education', and does not refer to multilingualism or language policy.

It is no surprise that the only countries which are 'observers' in the Bologna process, and take part in the conferences, are the USA and Australia, since higher education for them is big business. According to a British Council study in 2004, the UK economy benefits by £11 billion per annum directly, and a further £12 billion indirectly, from 'international' education. The British goal is 8% annual growth across the sector, and to double the present number of 35,000 research graduates contributing to the UK's knowledge economy by 2020 (www.britishcouncil.org/mediacentre/apr04/vision_2020_press_notice. doc). In addition, over 500,000 attend language learning courses each year. A primary goal of the Bologna process is to make higher education in Europe as attractive to students worldwide as in the USA and Commonwealth countries. There is thus a commercial rationale behind English-medium higher education, as well as cultural and political dimensions. (Related but rather different issues are whether the expansion of the intake of foreign students, mostly from Asia, and primarily China, in 'English-speaking' countries has created institutional dependence on them for financial reasons, and whether the testing and teaching of such students has been appropriate.)

The quality of education is a key parameter if, say, Finnish or German institutions teach through the medium of English to attract foreign students. Research in Norway indicates that the reading skills in English of Norwegians entering higher education, when measured by the British-Australian IELTS tests, are not adequate for academic course books in English (Hellekjaer, 2004). The picture is probably similar in the other Nordic countries, where virtually all higher education degrees require reading proficiency in English. The Norwegian government is acting to strengthen both English teaching and the learning of a second foreign language through a comprehensive Strategy Plan for 2005–2009.

A related issue is whether continental European academics are qualified to teach as well through the medium of English as through the mother tongue. A few definitely are, but the trend since the early 1990s to expect many academics to do so, without professional support, has not been studied. Academics and researchers in virtually all fields are also expected to publish in English, either exclusively or in the local language, depending on disciplinary pressures and the discourse communities that scholars contribute to. University administrators in the Scandinavian countries are being encouraged to address the language policy implications of English being used more, and to formulate explicit policies for multilingual universities. The Swedish and Danish governments have set a target of 'parallel competence' in English and Swedish/Danish. Finland has invested considerable resources in research and higher education, and seems to have established an impressive infrastructure for strengthening multilingualism, see, for instance, the language policy of the University of Jyväskylä (www.jyu.fi/strategia/JU_language policy.pdf). This document is in English. It stresses the need for all educators to be aware of their responsibilities for the way language is used, the duty of a Finnish university to strengthen Finnish, as well as English and other languages. Mention is also made of Swedish, the mother tongue of 5.8% of the population, a language that most higher education subjects can be studied in at other Finnish universities. The University of Jyväskylä also offers a 5-year teacher training MA through the medium of Finnish Sign language. Doctoral theses are written in a variety of languages (for figures for the country as a whole, see the article on Finland in Ammon, 2001).

In southern and eastern Europe, English is much less firmly entrenched. In some countries the decision was made to teach a foreign language, mostly English, in the primary school, but with inadequate attention to teacher qualifications. In France, the Ministry of Education has implemented measures to ensure the learning of two foreign languages, and to monitor a diversification of the languages learned, so as to promote plurilingualism (a term the Council of Europe uses for personal competence in more than language, by comparison with societal multilingualism). There is also lively public debate about whether there is an excessive focus on English.

PROBLEMS AND DIFFICULTIES

Developments in language education at national and subnational levels are influenced by wider processes of globalisation and Europeanisation, such as the adoption of English as a corporate language in many of the larger businesses based in continental Europe and the way hierarchies of language are perceived as operating in international collaboration. This holds both for official contacts in EU institutions and for the informal channels of the internet, leisure interests, and travel. What is unclear in continental Europe is whether the learning and use of English remains an additive process, one that increases the repertoire of language competence of individuals and the society, or whether English threatens the viability of other languages through processes of domain loss and linguistic hierarchisation. In theory there ought to be no problem, because of the strong position of national languages such as German, Italian and Polish, and because of the declared policies of the EU. Article 22 of The Charter of Fundamental Rights of the EU, which represents principles that all member states are committed to, states: 'The Union shall respect cultural, religious and linguistic diversity' (also in the rejected draft Constitution, Articles I-3 and II-82). In reality there are fundamental paradoxes.

The first is that although the EU is essentially a Franco-German project, since France and Germany were founding member states and have continued to occupy the political high ground in shaping the integration of Europe, the use of English is expanding, and the French and German languages are on the defensive both at home and abroad. English is increasingly the dominant language both in EU affairs and in some societal domains in continental European countries.

The second paradox is that EU rhetoric proclaims support for multilingualism and cultural and linguistic diversity in official texts, and the equality of all official and working languages in the EU, but in practice there is laissez faire in the linguistic marketplace (Phillipson, 2003). At the policy-making supranational level of EU institutions (the European Parliament, Commission and Council), there is paralysis on broader language policy issues, apart from some support for regional minority languages, channelled through the European Bureau for Lesser Used Languages. The proportion of the European budget (representing only 1% of national budgets) allocated to cultural concerns is modest, as compared with agriculture, infrastructure and regional development. The rhetoric of diversity and linguistic equality is pitted against the unfree market and the forces that strengthen English. Young people are hugely exposed to US cultural products, but have little familiarity with the cultures of their partner states.

In the management of the internal affairs of EU institutions (European Parliament, Commission, Council of Ministers), there is equality between the 20 EU languages in some respects: all legislation is promulgated in parallel in all languages, and at the most important meetings, interpretation is provided between all languages. On the other hand, in day-to-day affairs, French and English dominate, and English is increasingly the language in which documents are drafted and discussed. Some governments are keen to save money by not insisting on the use of their languages, which has led interpreters for Danish and Swedish to fear that these languages will disappear as languages spoken in EU institutions within a decade. Many users of the EU language services see languages as serving purely instrumental purposes, whereas there is no doubt that the French (earlier) and British (now) regard use of their language as the default language as giving them a political competitive advantage. The language services are subjected to internal reviews of quality and efficiency, but there has never been an in-depth survey of how equality between speakers of different languages might be ensured in a variety of types of communication. This is a crucial issue of access and legitimacy in dealings between a European institution and citizens in each member state. It becomes more important as more languages are added (with Irish an official language and Spanish regional languages accorded restricted rights in 2005), and when pragmatic, economic considerations weigh more heavily than ensuring transparency and living up to a democratic ideal of equality irrespective of mother tongue. Within the EU, the language issue has been described as 'explosive' (French Members of the European Parliament) and as 'the most emotional topic in the EU' (German head of mission in Brussels), but work has begun to promote coordination between the European Federation of National Institutions for Language, www.eurfedling.org. When there is this much uncertainty at the level of decision-makers, it is not surprising that laissez-faire policies serve to strengthen the position of English.

FUTURE DIRECTIONS

A third paradox is that foreign languages have traditionally been learned in conjunction with cultural familiarisation, and although English is in countless ways a feature of British and US culture and globalisation processes, it is increasingly used by non-natives for purposes that have nothing to do with Anglophonic cultural norms. This has led to research into 'English as a Lingua Franca' in order to chart how this type of communication departs from native speaker norms (Seidlhofer, 2004). This might at some point have pedagogical implications, but analysis of 'lingua franca' English is still exploratory. The term 'lingua franca' is also deceptive if it refers to asymmetrical interaction between first and second language users of English. To a large extent foreign language learning is being expected, like much of education, to produce a European 'Knowledge society' serving economic needs, but there is some critical foreign language pedagogy (Guilherme, 2002). Dendrinos and Mitsikopoulou (2004) argue persuasively for a paradigm shift in foreign language education, with a different target than native speaker competence: contemporary realities necessitate a 'multilingual ethos of communication', reflecting and constituting a world that gives voice to different discourses, one that acknowledges that discourses, not least on language policy and foreign language education, are neither ideologically nor politically neutral.

See Also: *Suresh Canagarajah: The Politics of English Language Teaching (Volume 1); Noeline Wright: School Language Policies (Volume 1); David Block: Language Education and Globalization (Volume 1); Hilary Janks: Teaching Language and Power (Volume 1); François Grin: The Economics of Language Education (Volume 1); Do Coyle: CLIL—A Pedagogical Approach from the European Perspective (Volume 4); Peter Broeder and Waldemar Martyniuk: Language Education in Europe: The Common European Framework of Reference (Volume 4)*

REFERENCES

Ammon, U. (ed.): 2001, *The Dominance of English as a Language of Science. Effects on Other Languages and Language Communities*, Mouton de Gruyter, Berlin.

Bondebjerg, I.: 2003, *Culture, media and globalisation*, in *Humanities—essential research for Europe*, Danish Research Council for the Humanities, Copenhagen, 71–88.

Council of Europe: 2001, *Common European Framework of Reference for Languages: Learning, Teaching, Assessment*, Cambridge University Press, Cambridge.

Council of Europe: 2004, *Filling the Frame. Five Years of Monitoring the Framework Convention for the Protection of National Minorities*, Strasbourg.

Dendrinos, B. and Mitsikopoulou, B. (eds.): 2004, *Policies of linguistic pluralism and the teaching of languages in Europe*, Metaixmio, and the National and Kapodistrian University of Athens, Athens.

Grenfell, M., Kelly, M., and Jones, D.: 2003, *The European Language Teacher. Recent Trends and Future Developments in Teacher Education*, Peter Lang, Bern.

Guilherme, M.: 2002, *Critical Citizens for an Intercultural World. Foreign Language Education as Cultural Politics*, Multilingual Matters, Clevedon.

Hellekjaer, G.O.: 2004, 'Unprepared for English medium instruction: A critical look at beginner students', in R. Wilkinson (ed.), *Integrating Content and Language: Meeting the Challenge of A Multilingual Higher Education*, Maastricht University, the Netherlands, 147–161.

Monbiot, G.: 2000, *Captive State. The Corporate Takeover of Britain*, Macmillan, London.

Phillipson, R.: 2002, 'Review of Ammon 2001', *Journal of Language, Identity, and Education* 1(2), 163–169.

Phillipson, R.: 2003, *English-Only Europe? Challenging Language Policy*, Routledge, London.

Phillipson, R.: 2006, 'English, a cuckoo in the European higher education nest of languages?', *European Journal of English Studies* 10(1), 13–32.

Seidlhofer, B.: 2004, 'Research perspectives on teaching English as a lingua franca', *Annual Review of Applied Linguistics* 24, 209–239.

Trim, J.: 2002, 'Foreign language policies in Europe, with special reference to the roles of the Council of Europe and the European Union', in S.J. Baker (ed.), *Language Policy: Lessons from Global Models*, Monterey Institute of International Studies, Monterey, CA.

Williams, G.: 2005, *Sustaining Linguistic Diversity in Europe. Evidence from the Euromosaic Project*, Palgrave Macmillan, Basingstoke.

Wilkinson, R.: 2004, *Integrating Content and Language, Meeting the Challenge of a Multilingual Higher Education*, Maastricht University Press, Maastricht.

Wilson, D.: 2002, *The Englishisation of Academe: A Finnish Perspective*, University of Jyväskylä Language Centre, Jyväskylä.

NAZ RASSOOL

LANGUAGE POLICY AND EDUCATION IN BRITAIN

INTRODUCTION

The importance of being able to communicate effectively has been seen traditionally as a necessary outcome of the educational process. Much of this relates to the fact that literacy, language and communication represent a potent form of cultural capital, which can be exchanged within the labour market. Language in education plays a significant role in individual development whilst, at the same time, also providing a vehicle for *economic and social development* (cf. Grin, The Economics of Language Education, Volume 1). As the medium through which teaching and learning takes place, language plays an important role also in the transmission of culture through the literary canons and knowledge base sanctioned by educational policy. As such, it has potent *hegemonic cultural value*. In having the potential to provide the linguistic skills and knowledge that underpin democratic society it also has significant *cultural power* (cf. Hall, Language Education and Culture, Volume 1).

Language-in-education policy is integral to social policy and thus it is constituted in power relations. Hierarchies of languages generally reflect sociocultural, economic and political stratification within society. Languages that are excluded from or feature in a limited way in formal education, lack social status and have limited exchange value within the labour market (cf. Rampton, Harris, Collins and Blommaert, Language, Class and Education, Volume 1). Taking account of these complexities this chapter provides an historical overview of key issues related to language and education in Britain. The main argument presented is that cultural and linguistic landscapes are not static; they evolve as societies undergo political, economic and demographic changes. Therefore, whilst the chapter seeks to highlight the inherently multilingual basis of British society involving *autochthonous* language groups, it also documents language in education struggles and debates centred on *immigrant groups* as these have evolved over the past five decades. In addition, it also highlights the influence that changes taking place within the global cultural economy have had on language-in-education policy within the UK.

S. May and N. H. Hornberger (eds), Encyclopedia of Language and Education,
2nd Edition, Volume 1: Language Policy and Political Issues in Education, 267–284.
©*2010 Springer Science+Business Media LLC.*

NAZ RASSOOL

EARLY DEVELOPMENTS

Britain has been a multicultural and multilingual society throughout
its history with various social groups including the Irish, Picts, Welsh
and English farmers living here since before the Norman Conquest
(Lewis, 1980). Although bilingualism has been an everyday experience
for different social groups living in Britain throughout the centuries,
bilingual education followed a long process of struggle against English
language domination, and assimilation into English culture. Historically, education has provided a primary arena in which the dominance
of English has been hegemonized. Equally, language historically has
represented a primary arena of struggle for control over meaning as
well as cultural resources.

Wales

In the struggle for an English-dominated British nationhood, Celtic culture became commonly represented as inferior, and the speakers of the
Celtic languages as 'wild' and 'savage'. Despite this, the Welsh language has remained a living language and has featured as an important
identity variable in the history of nationalist struggle in Wales. Bilingual education was introduced into Welsh schools through the Church
during the 1700s when a clergyman, Griffith Jones, set up circulating
schools in which parents and children in the community were taught
to read and write in Welsh. This was aimed at enabling more people to
read the Bible. The British state's initial response to bilingual education in Wales was negative; it was regarded as being detrimental to
the moral progress of the people. As late as 1847, the Report of the
Church Commissioners on Schools in Wales 'viciously attacked
the Welsh language on the grounds that it isolated 'the masses' from the
'upper portions of society', denied its speakers access to the top of
the social scale and kept them 'under the hatches' (Alladina and
Edwards, 1993, p. 3). Children caught speaking Welsh in school were
forced to wear the notorious wooden halter called a 'Welsh not' as
punishment (ibid.).

The first positive state support came from Sir James Shuttleworth
who, as Secretary of State for Education in 1849 indicated that the
government would enable several members of the community who
were fluent speakers, and could read and write in Welsh, to become
inspectors in schools. The implicit understanding was that Welsh represented the medium of education. A major development came with
the appointment in 1907 of Owen Morgan Edwards, as the first Chief
Inspector of Schools for Wales within the newly established Welsh Education Department. Edwards played a key role in securing Welsh

language education in schools throughout Wales. His struggles were continued later by his son Ifan ab Owen Edwards, who founded the Aberystwyth Welsh School (*Ysgol Gymraeg Aberystwyth*) in 1939. This was the first Welsh primary school; the first Welsh language secondary school (*Ysgol Glan Clwyd*) was established in Rhyl in 1955.

Irish

Irish Gaelic represented the most widely spoken language throughout the entire island (including what is now Northern Ireland), at least until the mid-nineteenth century when the state-funded primary education system was introduced. At this time, the use of the Irish language in schools was prohibited and English was taught by the Order of the British Government. As was the case with Welsh, Irish was associated with 'backwardness' as against English which was seen as representing the language of progress and modernization. The association of English with better life chances contributed to the fact that parents also discouraged their children from using Irish. Incorporated through this into the hegemony of English, they were complicit in committing what Bourdieu (1999) refers to as 'symbolic violence'. That is to say, in choosing English over their own languages in education they colluded in their own cultural subordination (cf. May, 2001, Chapter 4). Large-scale emigration, as a result of the potato famine during the 1845–1850 period, contributed further to the long-term decline of the Irish language.

The late-nineteenth century saw the beginnings of a language revival mainly amongst the Irish Unionists, reinforced later by the linguist and clergyman William Neilson. The Gaelic League (*Conradh na Gaeilge*) was founded in 1893 by Douglas Hyde and Eionn MacNeill. Irish language as a key cultural identity variable was central to the growing radicalism of Irish politics at the time (O'Reilly, 1997). Although there are arguments that this largely represented the cultural project of the elite, this particular nationalist revival with its emphasis on de-anglicization had a major impact on Irish social life. It played a significant role in placing Irish in a central position within the national school system.

The newly independent Irish national state adopted Irish as the *national language* in the Constitution in 1937 with English as the *language of administration*. Thus the high status of English within society, as well as its exchange value within the labour market, was retained. The compulsory introduction of Irish in schools, and the fact that it was often badly taught, was ultimately counter-productive since it alienated many school children. Irish again went into long-term decline, and it has remained a minority language.

In Northern Ireland the Irish language has always had political con-
notations and has been associated mostly with Irish Republicanism,
although, as is discussed later, current debates prevail within Unionist
circles about the need to reclaim Irish as a national language (Pritchard,
2004). Although the Parliament of Northern Ireland prohibited the use
of Irish in public life, including schools until the early 1990s, Irish
medium schools (*gaelscoileanna*) have existed in Belfast and Derry
since at least the 1970s (see also later).

Another important minority language central to contemporary
debates about education and nationhood includes Ulster-Scots (*Ullans*),
which is associated mainly with the Protestant community of Northern
Ireland. Most Ulster-Scots speakers reside 'along the Antrim coast
line and in areas congruent with what the Ulster Defence Association
call the "retainable homeland", the territory that they define as theirs'
(Nic Craith, 2000, p. 399). Much controversy surrounds the status of
Ulster-Scots as a distinct language; whether it is a separate language
from Scots, or a dialect of Scots (Mac Poilin, 1999); moreover, whether
it can be distinguished from Ulster-English dialect, or whether it is
essentially a rural Ballymena accent (Coulter, 2004; see further discussion later).

Scotland

Gaelic first arrived in what is now known as Scotland at the end of the
Roman Empire, with the Irish colonists who established their Kingdom
of *Dàl Riada* in south-west Scotland—'the coastland of Gael'
(O Maolalaigh and MacAonghuis, 1996) by merging with the Pictish
Kingdom of *Fortui*. Scots-Gaelic, traditionally, has been associated
with the people of the Highlands and Hebrides, the *Gaidhealtachd,*
or Gaelic-speaking community. Many Scots-Gaelic speakers were displaced during the eighteenth and nineteenth centuries, some moving
to places such as Nova Scotia and Cape Breton Island. There are
small bilingual communities using Gaelic and local dialects as everyday languages, particularly in the Western Isles (*Na h-Eileanan an Iar*),
parts of the Highlands (*a' Ghaidhealtachd*), cities such as Glasgow
(*Glaschu*), Edinburgh (*Dùn Eideann*) and Inverness (*Inbhir Nis*)
(Robertson and Taylor, 1993). Since at least the nineteenth century, there
have been organizations involved in promoting Gaelic, notably, the educational pressure group *An Comunn Gaidhealach*, established in 1891,
which became the first language-loyalty movement.

The place of Gaelic in Scotland has been ambiguous. That is to say,
although it is widely represented as a key identity variable in the ideological construction of the Scottish nation, it, nevertheless, has had
to struggle to obtain official status (Oliver, 2005). For example, the

Statutes of Iona in 1609 placed emphasis on the diffusion of English (Campbell, 1950). The status of Gaelic is closely linked with the development of education in Scotland; schooling provided by the *Society in Scotland for Propagating Christian Knowledge*, started in 1709, played a major role in the diffusion of English through education. In 1710 the school master on St Kilda was instructed to 'be diligent not only to teach them to read English but also to write and lay it on such as profite by you to do all they can for the edification of others and teach them their duty to their superiors' (cited in Withers, 2000). Although the Education Act of 1872 made education compulsory for all Scottish children, it also marked the period when the use of Gaelic in education was, unofficially, but actively discouraged in schools (Shevlinn, [http://simplyscottish.com]). This was achieved in part by the appointment of English-speaking, and English teachers as well as the punishment of children caught speaking Gaelic by having to wear the 'stick on a cord' device, the *maide-crochaide*. This practice prevailed until the 1930s (Shevlinn, [http://www.simplyscottish.com]).

More recent transmigration has also impacted on the linguistic landscape of the UK, with its implications for educational policy and provision.

Language Diversity: Social Class and Immigrant Groups

Deficit Theory. Major debates about language in education in the UK occurred during the 1960s and 1970s when the notion of 'communicative competence' (Hymes, 1972) in education first came to prominence in academic debate. Much of this debate centred initially on the educational underachievement of working class children, and later, children from immigrant groups living, largely, in inner-city areas (cf. Rampton, Harris, Collins and Blommaert, Language, Class and Education, Volume 1). The debate revolved around the argument that social stratification between different socioeconomic groups was reflected in the hierarchies attached to different patterns of language use, and that this had an impact on the relative ability of children to succeed in school (Carby, 1982). Much of this debate was influenced by a strong form of the Sapir-Whorf hypothesis, supporting the theory that language use determines the ways in which people perceive, interpret and experience the world. In other words, thinking is determined by language, and that people speaking different languages perceive and interpret the world differently. Basil Bernstein (1971), a key contributor to the educational debate on language and social class in the UK, advanced the theory that different class groups had access to different language interaction patterns, or codes. Though not intended as such, his unfortunate use of the terms 'elaborated' and 'restricted' codes to describe middle class and working class language interactions respectively led to a deficit construction of the latter. On this view, middle class people spoke an 'elaborated code', which comprised a wide vocabulary, had the ability to use complex sentences, was not context-bound, was analytical and could express logical and abstract thought. Middle-class language was associated with the formal written word and therefore was imbued with power. Working class people, on the other hand, used a 'restricted code' that was context-tied, relied on descriptive concepts, and because it represented the language of close-knit groups was not deemed capable of expressing logical and abstract thought. Social and educational barriers between different classes in society were ascribed to language barriers; working class children, because of their language 'deficit', were disadvantaged in education. Consequently, this deficit construction, (mis)using Bernstein's notion of codes, had a major impact on language education and research at the time.

The general argument in education revolved around the idea that the ability to switch linguistic codes controlled speakers' ability to switch roles; therefore, if working class speech could be 'remedied', learners would be able to have equal access to the curriculum and subsequently have better life chances. This gave rise to welfare intervention programmes in schools centred on remediating cultural and linguistic 'deprivation' to alleviate working class underachievement. Working class children were to be socialized through language into the values and belief system of the dominant culture to enable them to have equal life chances with their middle class peers. The deficit theory applied to education was critiqued as adopting a sociopathological approach of 'blaming-the-victim', without addressing the structural determinants of inequality in a class-stratified society, how these affect power and knowledge in society, and influence working class expectations and aspirations.

The debate stimulated major research projects such as the Schools Council Communication Project, which centred on the relationship between talk and learning in the classroom, and the different experiences of talk between home and school (Tough, 1976). Ethnographic research during this period focused on the ways in which family discourse and literacy practices in the homes of different ethnic groups and social classes influenced children's progress in school (Cummins, 1979, Edwards, 1976, Skutnabb-Kangas and Toukomaa, 1976). These studies showed that early socialization into the literacy and discourse practices that prevailed in classrooms increased children's potential to achieve in school. Middle-class children therefore have an advantage within the formal contexts of the school and classroom.

Difference Theory. By the mid-1970s the *different-but-equal debate* informed by earlier anthropological and linguistic research (Labov, 1973), expounded the view that all languages, although different, are equal with regard to their ability to communicate and convey meaning. In other words, all languages are structured, rule-governed and have the capacity for abstract thought. Educational research conducted at this time rejected notions of cultural deprivation or deficit and placed emphasis on the validity and expressiveness of working class and 'black' languages and cultures. The argument was presented that schools needed to respect different cultures as being equal, and value their contributions to classroom learning culture. Being able to use non-standard English in classrooms would allow working class children to regain their self-confidence and sense of worth in their background. Thus their relative failure would be overcome, whilst also contributing to the cultural enrichment of classrooms; together this would facilitate equality of opportunity. Applied to immigrant language groups this framework supported multicultural education centred on the celebration of ethnic and religious differences.

The problem with this perspective was that it did not take account of the fact that whilst all languages may be equal in terms of the ability to communicate, they do not all have the same social, economic, cultural, symbolic and political power. Thus, it failed to take account also of the speakers of the languages and their relative power and status within society. It also did not acknowledge the predominance of Standard English (SE) as the language of teaching and learning which would impact on equality of access to knowledge in the curriculum. Moreover, it did not offer an analysis of power and class conflict reflected in language conflicts, for example, the use of slang and Black English Vernacular (BEV) (currently this would also include Rapping) as forms of cultural resistance.

Multicultural Language Debate

Social discourse centred on language in education as this relates to immigrant children first gained prominence within the aftermath of mass immigration policies in the 1950s when, during a period of economic boom, workers were recruited from former colonies, and particularly, the Caribbean to work in the service industries (see Modood and May, 2001). Other significant migrations included those from Southern Europe, Cyprus, the Indian sub-continent as well as the Hong Kong Chinese working predominantly in the catering industry (Linguistic Minorities Project, 1985). This was followed during the late 1960s by the arrival of large groups of second and even third generation 'Asians' from East Africa. Among these were refugees who had been expelled by the Ugandan regime at the time, as well as Vietnamese Chinese refugees (Plowden Report, 1967; Linguistic Minorities Project, 1985). The languages of immigrant children, notably the dialects spoken by Afro-Caribbean pupils (then generally referred to as 'West Indians') and the lack of fluency in English amongst those from the Indian subcontinent became widely regarded as a major challenge presented to teachers. Concerns about underachievement amongst children of Afro-Caribbean origin were based largely on notions of 'communication failure' in classrooms (NFER, 1966). 'West Indian' Creole was regarded as the cause of problems of listening, interpreting, reading and writing. As was the case with working class native British children during the 1960s, language deficits, associated with cognitive, cultural and social deficits became key signifiers of immigrant children's imputed ability, or inability, to succeed in school and later in society (Carby, 1982). Such representations of the intrinsic inferiority of minority languages provided a pedagogical rationale for the imperative to learn Standard English with an emphasis on oral language (Ministry of Education, 1963). As a result of the assimilationist ideology that prevailed at the time, new arrivals were accommodated in language reception centres where pupils would be 'inducted' into the language and culture of the host society for a period of at least a term. Second language teaching within this context largely followed the pedagogic principles of English as a Foreign Language (EFL).

In many local education authorities (LEAs), cultural and linguistic differences were catered for within the framework of multicultural education. Language provision for children from ethnic minority groups took place mainly in withdrawal classes, which denied pupils access to the mainstream curriculum for a significant part of the school day. Immigrant languages became rooted in the celebration of language diversity and the need to value minority cultures without recourse to the social experience of the speakers of these languages.

MAJOR CONTRIBUTIONS

Welsh

Until very recently, provision for Welsh education depended on the linguistic character of the region, since there are areas in Wales that are predominantly English speaking. Parents had the right to choose the language in which their children would be educated. A transitional model of bilingualism prevailed in Welsh-speaking areas, with English introduced later. Five types of bilingual education schools were introduced, including the designated bilingual school, the 'natural' bilingual school, the bilingual school with linguistic streaming, bilingually mixed schools and Welsh schools. The number of teaching hours per week for Welsh varied amongst different boroughs (Lewis, 1980). Welsh was not a prerequisite for university or college entrance, although bilingual programmes and teaching in Welsh did exist at this level. Until the 1980s, the main concerns revolved around teaching approaches and textbook availability.

The introduction of the National Curriculum in England and Wales in 1988 represented a landmark development in the teaching of Welsh in schools (see May, 2000). Since then, all students between the ages of 5–16 are required to learn Welsh either as a first or second language and also expand their knowledge of Welsh culture. The latter is referred to as the *Cwricwlwm Cymreig* (UK Report to the European Charter for Regional or Minority Languages, 2004). The Welsh Language Act (1993) established the Welsh Language Board, which has responsibility for promoting the Welsh language in culture and society including business and the administration of justice in Wales. Public organizations are required to develop a Welsh language scheme to facilitate the adoption of Welsh within public institutions. Section 32 of the Government of Wales Act (1998) stipulates that the National Assembly has the freedom to take the necessary steps to support the Welsh language.

Irish and Ulster-Scots

In Northern Ireland, the Education Order (1989) provides for the teaching of Irish as a modern language in the curriculum. The North/South Language Body (*An Foras Teanga*) came into being the following year (1999) and comprises two separate agencies, namely, the Irish Language Agency (*Foras na Gaelge*) and the Ulster-Scots Agency (*Tha Boord o Ulstèr Scotch*). The Good Friday Agreement signed on 10 April 1998 resulted in a move towards a unified approach with Ireland in supporting linguistic diversity (UK Report to the European Charter for Regional or Minority Languages, 2004).

Scots-Gaelic

As a result of pressure from groups such as *An Comunn Gaidhealach*, politicians, churchmen and Highland societies, Gaelic received statutory support in the Scotland Education Bill of 1918, supporting its teaching at all levels of education. This was reinforced by the Education Act of 1945 supporting bilingual education. Nevertheless, Scots-Gaelic has been in decline for a number of years. According to the 2001 Census there are 58,552 Scottish Gaelic speakers (about 1% of the population of Scotland)—a decline from 65,978 Scottish Gaelic speakers in the 1991 census and 79,000 in the 1981 census.

Two Gaelic-medium primary schools were established in 1985 in Inverness and Glasgow; this has now increased to 60 schools with approximately 2000 students. However, at secondary school there are fewer numbers of both Gaelic-medium schools and students. A Further and Higher Education College was established in 1972 and degree-level courses have been available at the university of the Highlands since 1998 (MacKinnon, 1993). Whilst students can be educated across the different phases through the medium of Gaelic, this seldom happens.

Support for regional languages in the UK has been given new impetus by the European Charter for Regional or Minority Languages (1992). Whilst this is undoubtedly a very positive development as this relates to *autochtonous* languages, the situation regarding educational support for languages of *immigrant groups* in the UK remains unresolved.

Immigrant Language Communities

Concerns about the issue of 'mother tongue' education regarding migrant workers in Northern Europe had been raised formally first within the context of UNESCO and the Council of Europe during the 1970s. These concerns related mainly to the need to facilitate the re-integration of the children of migrant workers into their culture of origin once their work permits have expired. This culminated in the introduction of the EC Council Directive on the education of children of migrant workers (77/486/EEC) which required member states to teach the languages of migrant groups living within their boundaries, for part of the school day. The Directive met with considerable ambivalence within the UK where concerns were expressed initially about costs, the difficulty in providing adequate numbers of 'mother tongue' teachers, as well as the fact that the situation regarding Britain's immigrant groups was different to those of other member countries such as Germany and Sweden who had, predominantly, migrant workers. In schools, provision for the teaching of English as a Second Language (ESL) pupils was allowed under Section 11 of the 1986 Local Government Act.

Projects funded by the Department of Education and Science (DES) included: (a) the Rosen and Burgess study (1979–1980) *Languages and Dialects of London School Children.* The study identified 55 languages and 24 overseas-based dialects spoken in London, drew on earlier integrationist definitions, and stressed the 'vitality' and 'strength' of the languages and dialects of London's immigrant population groups. The report highlighted the significance of dialect culture and advocated bilingualism to be advanced within the framework of multicultural education; (b) *Linguistic Minorities Project (LMP)* 1979–1980: The LMP Project aimed to assess the range of diversity of the languages spoken in Britain, patterns of bilingualism, as well as the educational implications of societal bilingualism. It was hoped that the data collected would inform educational assessment and policy formulation in different parts of the country. The LMP conducted several surveys: The Adult Learning Survey (ALUS); Schools Language Survey (SLS); Mother Tongue Teaching Directory (MTTD) in collaboration with the National Council for Mother Tongue Teaching and the Secondary Pupils Survey (SPS). (c) The Bradford *Mother Tongue and Teaching Project (MOTET)* (1978–1981): The sample study focused on the implementation, monitoring and evaluation of a bilingual teaching programme in the children's first year at school (d) The *EEC/Bedfordshire Pilot Project* (1976–1980) focused similarly on a bilingual teaching programme but was abandoned by Bedfordshire LEA when the EC funding grant ran out (Tosi, 1983).

The Swann Committee's report *Education for All* (1985) was published in the aftermath of racialized urban unrest throughout Britain. The Swann Report located its views on the education of black immigrant pupils within the ideological framework of cultural pluralism, which underlines the importance of the need to socialize ethnic minority groups into the belief system of mainstream culture, whilst simultaneously maintaining links with their culture of origin. However, although the Swann Report provided a useful overview of the language debate during the previous two decades, it was unclear on the issues of language diversity and bilingual education and opposed separate educational provision for 'mother tongue' teaching (Modood and May, 2001).

By the late 1980s, in a discourse structured mainly within the framework of neo-conservative 'think tanks' such as the Centre for Policy Studies, the Hillgate Group and the Salisbury Review, the New Right attack on education centred on the issues of multicultural/antiracist education and bilingual education. These, it was argued, challenged the national cultural and linguistic heritage and also contributed to 'falling standards' in schools (see Honeyford, 1984; Scruton, 1985). In spite of the marginalizing discourse taking place within the New Right ideological framework, in-class support as opposed to withdrawal classes for second language learners was incorporated into Section 11 funding within the framework of Home Office Circular 78/90. Under the new Educational Support Grant (ESG) system, projects requiring schools to engage in teacher partnership were now funded for a period of 3/5 years. Bids for ESGs also had to be detailed in terms of specific needs addressed, objectives, quantified targets, time scale, monitoring of results and consultation with community groups (Circular 78/90). This resulted in good examples of practice with a more coherent and coordinated approach within LEAs—and which was centrally monitored through funding requirements.

By November 1993, an overall restructuring of Section 11 funding arrangements took place. The Home Office transferred 55% of Section 11 funds to a new funding scheme, the Single Regeneration Budget (SRB) to be co-ordinated by the Department of the Environment and administered within nine local regions. The SRB involved the amalgamation of 20 separate budgets, from five different departments. LEAs falling within the ambit of identified Urban Priority Areas (UPAs) now had to apply for the funding of ethnic minority projects to the SRB.

WORK IN PROGRESS

Linguistic Diversity and Regional Languages

The European Union has provided an important context within which debates about linguistic diversity can take place (see Phillipson, Language Policy and Education in the European Union, Volume 1). One of the most significant developments in this regard has been the EU Charter for Regional or Minority Languages (1992) introduced under the auspices of the Council of Europe (see de Varennes, International Law and Education in a Minority Language, Volume 1). The Charter requires systems to be put into place within member countries to support minority languages (see later). Moreover, the importance of English as a global language in international business and public administration has meant that issues related to linguistic pluralism have become signally important within countries in Europe. It is argued that the EU Charter for Regional or Minority Languages represent a response to pressures from member states to support the development of their languages (O'Reilly, 2001). The Charter requires member states to make educational and institutional provision for regional or minority languages 'traditionally used within a given territory of a State by nationals of that State who form a group numerically smaller than the rest of the State's population; and different from the official language(s) of that State' (Council of Europe, 1992). Thus, focusing on languages having both a territorial and historical base within these societies, it excludes the languages of recent immigrants. Underlying this is the aim to support the principles of democracy and cultural diversity 'within the framework of national sovereignty and territorial integrity' (Council of Europe, 1992, p. 1). As is discussed earlier, this has had a major impact on support and provision for Irish, Ulster-Scots, Scots-Gaelic and Welsh at all levels of the education system through the establishment of Language Boards. With regard to Northern Ireland, the latter was established following the Belfast Agreement of 1998 (Good Friday Agreement). This Agreement stated that:

All participants recognize the importance of respect, under-standing and tolerance in relation to linguistic diversity, including in Northern Ireland, the Irish language, Ulster-Scots and the languages of the various ethnic communities, all of which are part of the cultural wealth of the island of Ireland. [http://www.ullans.com]

The drive for children to be educated in Irish has gained momentum and is reflected in the growth of Irish language immersion schools and the establishment of All-Irish Medium Primary Schools (*Gaelscoileanna*). Most children attending these schools are from the middle classes. Irish language education is a developing issue; at the moment Irish is still a minority language with low levels of fluency.

In Northern Ireland, the Irish language speaking community is rela-tively small. The 1991 Census data indicate 'functional Irish-speakers of the order of 40,000 to 45,000, with some 13,000 to 15,000 possess-ing fluency in the full range of language skills' (Mac Giolla Chriost, 2000, p. 3). Moreover, this group is dispersed in different locations throughout the region. Irish gained support and acknowledgement in the Belfast Agreement of 1998, and involved a 'statuary obligation on the Department of Education to encourage and facilitate Irish medi-um education in line with current provision for integrated education' (Crowley, 2005, p. 201).

There is an emergent debate about the significance of Ulster-Scots in developing a cohesive nationhood in Ireland, including Northern Ireland (McCoy, 1997). The Belfast Peace Agreement (1998) sup-ported the development of Ulster-Scots and in 2000 the British Govern-ment signed the European Charter for Lesser Used Languages, and in doing so formally recognized Ulster-Scots as a variety of Scots (Crowley, 2005).

The Welsh Language Act of 1993 for the first time placed English and Welsh on an equal basis in public life in Wales. Section 5 of this Act requires every organization that receives public funding to provide a language scheme, including a system put in place to support its implementation.

In Scotland, the *Gaelic Language (Scotland) Act 2005* recognized Gaelic Scots formally as an official language of Scotland having equal status to English. The Act established the Scottish Language Board (*Bòrd na Gaidhlig*) which is responsible for the creation of a national plan for the development of Gaelic. The Act provides guidance on Gaelic education. By 2004, there were 1,972 pupils in Gaelic medium primary schools, 284 in Gaelic medium secondary and 2,513 secondary learners; in the pre-school phase there were 1,236 pupils in Gaelic medium pre-school education (Kidner, 2004).

Immigrant Languages

In 1998, the Ethnic Minority Achievement Grant (EMAG) replaced Section 11 funding. EMAG is allocated to LEAs on a formula basis as part of the wider Standards Fund. The grant is aimed at raising the standards of school-based achievement of ethnic minority pupils, especially those whose first language is not English. The emphasis is on providing support for teaching English as an Additional Language (EAL; see Canagarajah, The Politics of English Language Teaching, Volume 1). Accordingly, many LEAs are allocating a major percentage of this money to supporting the cost of employing teachers and bilingual classroom attendants to teach EAL in schools. Despite good practice, including bilingual support in some LEAs (see Tikly et al. in DfES, 2002), the general emphasis on raising standards in education effectively means that an ESL approach to facilitate access to the National Curriculum would be a priority for schools under pressure to achieve their set educational attainment targets. Thus, the grant ultimately sustains a monolingual educational policy. The work by Bourne (2001) highlights pedagogical issues related to the use of bilingual assistants in the support of curriculum learning.

PROBLEMS AND DIFFICULTIES

Except for Wales where bilingual education throughout education is well-established, language diversity in education in the UK represents an evolving situation. In the case of Irish and Ulster-Scots, language in education remains a highly political issue in relation to contesting power interests amongst different political fractions, on the one hand, and the move towards political devolution within the national terrain, on the other. Further tensions prevail with regard to the potential use of these regional languages within the formal institutions of the European Union, as well as the ascendancy of English as an international lingua franca. The major problem in Scotland is a shortage of Gaelic medium and Gaelic subject teachers; this has implications for teacher education course provision.

Issues related to educational provision for the languages of immigrant groups, particularly those from ex-colonial countries, remain unresolved. Much of this relates to the implicit threat that these languages pose to the hegemony of British 'nationhood'. British citizenship now requires fluency in English language. Whilst for some immigrant groups the struggle for language maintenance programmes has continued, for others, language shift has taken place with support from parents keen for their children to integrate into British society. Recent research has shown that second generation 'immigrant' pupils have developed complex language repertoires and have the ability to switch amongst different languages and dialects depending on the context of interaction (Rassool, 2004). It signifies a need to have a more nuanced approach to issues related to minority language rights—a need to move away from a rigid rights-based framework to one that takes account of the role of agency in shaping identities, multiple identities, as well as the discursive nature of power within the global cultural economy and its organic relationship with language. For further discussion on the development of critical debate and discourse on multicultural/multilingual education in relation to the role of agency in the shaping of identities, as well as issues related to power and contestation see the work of May (2000, 2001), Modood and May (2001) and Rassool (2000).

FUTURE DIRECTIONS

Language plays a major role in the interactive, technologically driven global cultural economy (see also Block, Language Education and Globalization; Kalantzis and Cope, Language Education and Multiliteracies, Volume 1). Within this context, language barriers represent barriers to progress. The complex linguistic demands of the global cultural economy stimulate the need for educational support for the development of flexible language users as an important aspect of human resource development. With regard to language choice, the emphasis now shifts to communicative and linguistic competence. That is to say, there is an acknowledgement that different languages, registers and discourse strategies are choices that language users will need to be able to make—and in which they would need to have a considerable degree of competence. Within this interactive terrain effective communicative competence does not only involve choice of language suited to the context of use, it also includes knowledge of different discourse styles and cultural conventions.

Differential linguistic markets at local, regional, national and international levels suggest a balanced approach towards maintaining local and regional languages as media of instruction alongside the creation of opportunities to develop international lingua franca within both formal educational and community contexts. This includes not only informal arenas of instruction but also the identification of the normal contexts in which people use different languages for different purposes. In the UK, this has implications for bilingualism in relation to Welsh, Gaelic-Scots, Irish and Ulster-Scots—and English, and within the broader framework of the European Union, also the acquisition of Modern European Languages. Moreover, within the context of the interactive global cultural economy it would also suggest that learning languages of major trade and business partners would represent an important strategic policy choice. Whilst bilingual education programmes do not exist in mainstream schools for immigrant groups, some of the major languages such as Bengali, Urdu, Cantonese and Punjabi have been integrated into the Modern Languages Curriculum within some inner-city schools. In the UK, as is the case elsewhere in the contemporary world, there is growing awareness that linguistic and communicative competence represent an important economic, cultural and political resource to enable the country to participate effectively within the global cultural economy. Nevertheless, these meanings do not yet feature in language in education policy (see also the Nuffield Languages Inquiry, 2000).

See Also: David Block: Language Education and Globalization *(Volume 1); Suresh Canagarajah: The Politics of English Language Teaching (Volume 1); Fernand de Varennes: International Law and Education in a Minority Language (Volume 1); François Grin: The Economics of Language Education (Volume 1); Joan Kelly Hall: Language Education and Culture (Volume 1); Ben Rampton, et al.: Language, Class and Education (Volume 1); Robert Phillipson: Language Policy and Education in the European Union (Volume 1); Mary Kalantzis and Bill Cope: Language Education and Multiliteracies (Volume 1)*

REFERENCES

Alladina, S. and Edwards, V. (eds.): 1993, *Multilingualism in the British Isles: The Older Mother Tongues and Europe*, Longman, London and New York.
Bernstein, B.: 1971, 'Elaborated and restricted codes: Their social origins and some consequences, *American Anthropologist* New Series, Part 2 (The Ethnography of Communication), 66(6), 55–69.
Bourdieu, P.: 1999, *Language and Symbolic Power*, Polity Press in association with Blackwell Publishers Ltd., Cambridge.
Bourne, J.: 2001, 'Doing 'what comes naturally': How the discourses and routines of teachers' practice constrain opportunities for bilingual support in UK primary schools', *Language and Education* 15(4), 250–268.
Campbell, J.L.: 1950, *Gaelic in Scottish Education Life: Present, Past and Future*, The Saltire Society, Edinburgh.
Carby, H.: 1982, 'Schooling in Babylon', Contemporary Cultural Studies (CCCS) (ed.), *The Empire Strikes Back: Race and Racism in Britain in 70s Britain*, CCCS with Hutchinson University Library, Birmingham.
Coulter, J.: 2004, 'Reclaiming Irish', *The Blanket, A Journal of Protest and Dissent* 27 December [http://lark.phoblacht.net/phprint.php accessed on 30.08.2005]
Crowley, T.: 2005, *Wars of Words: The Politics of Language in Ireland 1537–2004*, Oxford University Press, Oxford.

Cummins, J.: 1979, 'Linguistic interdependence and the educational development of children', *Review of Educational Research* 49, 222–251.

Department of Education and Science: 1967, *Children and their Primary Schools, A Report of the Central Advisory Council for Education (England), Volume 1: Report*, (Plowden Report), HMSO, Birmingham.

Department for Education and Science: 1988, *The Education Reform Act*, HMSO, London.

Department for Education and Skills (DfES): 2002, *Ethnic Minority Achievement Grant: Analysis of LEA Action Plans*. L. Tikly, A. Osler, J. Hill, and K. Vincent with P. Andrews, Jeremy Jeffreys, T. Ibrahim, C. Panel, and M. Smith, The Graduate School of Education, University of Bristol and The Centre for Citizenship Studies in Education, University of Leicester. Research Report RR371. (Department for Education and Skills (DfES), http://dfes.gov.uk/readwriteplus/EMAG2)

Department of Education and Science: 1985, *Education for All: Report of the Committee of Inquiry into the Education of Ethnic Minority Groups*, Chairman Lord Swann, Home Office, London.

Edwards, V.: 1976, *The West Indian Language Issue in British Schools: Challenges and Responses*, Routledge and Kegan Paul, London.

European Charter for Regional or Minority Languages ETS No. 148, 5.XI.1992, Council of Europe, Strasbourg.

Honeyford, R.: 1984, 'Education and race: An alternative view', *Salisbury Review* 2(2), 30–32.

Hymes, D.: 1972, 'On communicative competence', in J. Pride and J. Holmes (eds.), *Sociolinguistics*, Penguin, Harmondsworth,

Kidner, C.: 2004, *Gaelic Education,* SPICe briefing, 04/82, The Scottish Parliament, 12 November 2004.

Labov, W.: 1973, 'The logic of nonstandard English', Nell Keddie (ed.), *Tinker, Tailor . . . The Myth of Cultural Deprivation*, Penguin, Harmondsworth, 21–66.

Lewis, E.G.: 1980, *Bilingualism and Bilingual Education*, Pergamon Press, Oxford.

Linguistic Minorities Project: 1985, *The Other Languages of England*, Routledge and Kegan Paul, London.

Mac Giolla Chrìost, D.: 2000, *Planning Issues for Irish Language Policy: 'A Foras Teanga' and 'Fiontair Teanga'*, CAIN Project, University of Ulster. [http://www.CAIN@ulst.ac.uk]

Mac Poilin, A.: 1999, 'Language, identity and politics in Ireland', *Ulster Folk Life*, Volume 45, Ulster Folk and Transport Museum, [http://www.bbc.co.uk/northernireland/learning/history/stateapart/agreement/culture/support, accessed 30.04.06]

McCoy, G.: 1997, 'Protestant learners of Irish in Northern Ireland, Aodán Mac Póilin (ed.), *The Irish Language in Northern Ireland*, Ultach Trust, Belfast, 131–170.

MacKinnon, K.: 1993, *Gaelic: A Past and Future Prospect*, Hyperion Books, London.

May, S.: 2000, 'Uncommon languages: The challenges and possibilities of minority language rights', *Journal of Multilingual and Multicultural Development* 21(5), 366–385.

May, S.: 2001, *Language and Minority Rights: Ethnicity, Nationalism and the Politics of Language*, Longman, London. (Reprinted by Routledge, 2007)

Ministry of Education: 1963, *English for Immigrants,* Ministry of Education Pamphlet No. 43, HMSO, London.

Modood, T. and May, S.: 2001, 'Multiculturalism and education in Britain: An internally contested debate', *International Journal of Educational Research* 35, 305–317.

National Foundation for Educational Research (NFER): 1966, *Coloured Immigrant Children: A Survey of Research, Studies and Literature on Their Educational Problems and Potential in Britain*, NFER, Slough.

Nic Craith, M.: 2000, 'Contested identities and the quest for legitimacy', *Journal of Multilingual and Multicultural Development* 21(5), 399–413.

Te Nuffield Foundation: 2000, *Languages: The Next Generation* (the final report and recommendations of the Nuffield Languages Inquiry), The Nuffield Languages Inquiry, The Nuffield Foundation.

O Maolalaigh, R. and Mac Aonghuis, I.: 1996, *Scottish in Three Months*, Hugo Language Books, New York.

O'Reilly, C. (ed.): 1997, 'Nationalists and the Irish language in Northern Ireland: Competing perspectives', in Aodán Mac Póilin (ed.), *The Irish Language in Northern Ireland*, Ultach Trust, Belfast, 95–130.

O'Reilly, C. (ed.): 2001, *Language, Ethnicity and the State: Minority Languages in the European Union*, Volume 1, Palgrave Macmillan, London.

Pritchard, R.: 2004, 'Protestants and the Irish language: Historical heritage and current attitudes in Northern Ireland, *Journal of Multilingual and Multicultural Development* 25(1), 62–81.

Rassool, N.: 2004, 'Sustaining linguistic diversity within the global cultural economy: Issues of language rights and linguistic possibilities', *Comparative Education, Special Issue: Postcolonialism and Comparative Education* 40(2), 199–214.

Rassool, N.: 2000, 'Contested and contesting identities: Conceptualizing linguistic minority rights within the global cultural economy', *Journal of Multilingual and Multicultural Development* 21(5), 386–398.

Robertson, B. and Taylor, I.: 1993, *Teach Yourself Gaelic*, NTC Publishing Group, Lincolnwood IL.

Rosen, H. and Burgess, T.: 1980, *Languages and Dialects of London School Children*, Wardlock, London.

Scruton, R.: 1985, *Education and Indoctrination*, Centre for Policy Studies, London.

Shevlinn, A., *Gaelic Education after 1872* [http://simplyscottish.com] accessed 10.09.2006).

Skutnabb-Kangas, T. and Toukoumaa, P.: 1976, 'Teaching migrant children's mother tongue and learning the language of the host country in the context of the sociocultural situation of the migrant family', Report written for UNESCO. Research Report 15. Tampere: Department of Sociology and Social Psychology, University of Tampere.

The European Charter for Regional or Minority Languages. Initial Periodical Report from the United Kingdom, May 2004. [www.doeni.gov.uk/uploads/European Charter.pdf.]

Tosi, A.: 1983, *Immigration and Bilingual Education: A Case Study of Movement of Population, Language Change and Education Within the EEC (Bedfordshire Project)*, Pergamon Press, Oxford.

Tough, J.: 1976, *'Listening to Children Talking: A Guide to the Appraisal of Children's use of Language'*, Wardlock Educational Associates, London.

Withers, C.W.J.: 1984, *Gaelic in Scotland 1698 to 198*, John Donald, Edinburgh.

Withers, C.W.J.: 2000, 'Gaelic and Scottish education', in H. Holmes (ed.), *Scottish Life and Society—Education: A Compendium of Scottish Ethnology*, Tuckwell Press, Edinburgh, 397–414.

THOMAS RICENTO AND WAYNE WRIGHT

LANGUAGE POLICY AND EDUCATION IN THE UNITED STATES

INTRODUCTION

The purpose of this review is to provide a balanced description of the important aspects of language policy in the USA as they relate, either directly or indirectly, to educational practices in the USA. Language policies derive from official enactments of governing bodies or authorities, such as legislation, executive directives, judicial orders or decrees, or policy statements; voter-approved initiatives; and nonofficial institutional or individual practices or customs. Policies may also evolve as a consequence of actions governments do *not* take, for example, by not providing support for the teaching or learning of a particular language, or language variety, or by designating and promoting an official language and ignoring other languages, or by failing to provide adequate resources to ensure that all groups have equal opportunities to acquire the official language in educational settings. Policies may also evolve from grassroots movements and become formalized through laws, practices, or some combination of both. In this review, theoretical perspectives on language policy and education will be addressed only briefly (for background information, see Wiley, 2005).

EARLY DEVELOPMENTS

The focus of much of the earliest work in language policy in the USA was on the status of English versus non-English languages from the colonial period through the mid-nineteenth century (Kloss, 1977/1998). Conklin and Lourie (1983) described the history of languages in North America, beginning with the arrival of the first Europeans in the sixteenth century; Heath and Mandabach (1983) describe the British legacy of tolerance toward the use of non-English languages, coupled with an aversion to rigid standardization of English prevalent in the USA until the mid-nineteenth century. However, tolerance was limited to speakers of European languages. Native American languages and cultures were stigmatized, and government policy, beginning in 1802, was to separate Indians from their cultures (Leibowitz, 1971; see also McCarty, Language Education Planning and Policies by and for Indigenous Peoples, Volume 1). Colonies, such as Virginia and

S. May and N. H. Hornberger (eds), Encyclopedia of Language and Education, 2nd Edition, Volume 1: Language Policy and Political Issues in Education, 285–300.
©2010 Springer Science+Business Media LLC.

South Carolina (and later, many states) passed "compulsory ignorance laws" which made it a crime to teach slaves, and sometimes free-blacks, to read or write (Crawford, 1992). Beginning in the 1850s, the development of a common public school system, coupled with a nativist movement beginning in the 1880s, led to the imposition of English as the sole language of instruction in public and most parochial schools by the 1920s (Heath, 1981). Before 1889, only three states had laws prescribing English as the language of instruction in private schools, whereas by 1923, 34 states required English (Leibowitz, 1971, p. 7). In Hawaii (1920) and California (1921), a series of laws were passed aimed at abolishing Japanese language at schools; by 1923, 22 states had laws prohibiting the teaching of foreign languages in primary schools. In *Meyer v. Nebraska* (1923), the US Supreme Court found a 1919 Nebraska statute that forbade teaching in any language other than English to be unconstitutional, and in 1927, the Court upheld a ruling by the Ninth Circuit Court of Appeals (1926), which had found laws prohibiting the teaching of non-English languages in 22 states to be unconstitutional (Tamura, 1993). Moreover in 1927, the US Supreme Court ruled in *Farrington v. Tokushige* that Hawaii's efforts to abolish private Japanese (Korean and Chinese) language schools were unconstitutional, and thus upheld the right of language minority communities to organize after-school and weekend heritage language programs.

The period 1930–1965 was relatively uneventful with regard to federal intervention in language policy issues, with several notable exceptions, such as the continued intrusion of US influence in language-in-education policy in Puerto Rico (Resnick, 1993), and restrictive policies toward the use of Japanese and German in public domains from the 1930s through World War II. In a more positive vein, oppressive boarding school policies for Native Americans were relaxed and the linkage of language minority status with segregation in political access was significant, anticipating major policy shifts culminating in federal legislation in the 1960s supporting bilingual education and voting ballots, which was expanded in the 1970s. However, despite these important policy initiatives that supported the learning and use of languages other than English in education and civic life, federal and state governments have been generally reluctant to address the educational needs of language minority students and other historically marginalized groups unless compelled to do so in reaction to political pressure brought by such groups.

MAJOR CONTRIBUTIONS

Beginning in the 1960s, the federal US government took an active role in accommodating and, in some cases, promoting non-English languages in education. The federal role increased in two ways—increased expenditures for students identified as lacking proficiency in English under the Elementary and Secondary Education Act (ESEA), and an increased role in the enforcement of civil rights laws in education (Macias, 1982). The first major federal involvement in the area of status planning was the Bilingual Education Act (BEA) of 1968 (Title VII of the ESEA) which authorized the use of non-English languages in the education of low-income language minority students who had been segregated in inferior schools, or had been placed in English-only (submersion) classes (Lyons, 1992, p. 365). However, the BEA came to an end following the passage of the No Child Left Behind Act (NCLB), which reauthorized the ESEA in 2002. All references to "bilingual education" were stripped from the law. Nevertheless, under Title III "language instruction for limited English proficient and immigrant Students," federal funds for "language instruction education programs" which "may make instructional use of both English and a child's native language" are available, and state education agencies may use these funds to support bilingual education programs if they choose (Wright, 2005a, b). In addition, Title I of NCLB calls for accommodations for "limited English proficient" (LEP)[1] students on state academic tests, including, "to the extent practicable," testing students in their native language for up to the first 5 years of enrollment. Other federally supported programs which deal with language and education include the Native American Language Act of 1990, which endorses the preservation of indigenous languages, and requires government agencies to ensure that their activities promote this, and the National Literacy Act of 1991, which authorized literacy programs and established the National Institute for Literacy.

Title VI of the 1964 Civil Rights Act and the Equal Educational Opportunities Act of 1974 have provided the statutory bases, whereas the equal protection clause of the Fourteenth Amendment of the US Constitution has provided the constitutional rationale for expanding educational opportunities for language minority students in a number of important court cases (see Fernandez, 1987). Among the most significant of these was the *Lau v. Nichols* (1974) decision, in which the US Supreme Court, relying on sections 601 and 602 of Title VI of the 1964 Civil Rights Act, found that the San Francisco School District had failed to provide a meaningful educational opportunity to Chinese ancestry students due to their lack of basic English skills. The Court did not specify an appropriate remedy; however, soon after the ruling the Office for Civil Rights of the Department of Education wrote

---

[1] The term preferred by scholars and researchers is ELL (English Language Learner); we use LEP only because it is the acronym used in NCLB.

guidelines (the Lau Remedies), which instructed school districts how to identify and evaluate limited and non-English-speaking children, identified instructional "treatments" to use (including bilingual education), and established exit criteria and professional teacher standards. At the time the Lau Remedies were in force, strong political opposition to one remedy, so-called maintenance bilingual education programs, led to increased federal support for transitional bilingual education programs, in which students are exited to English-only classrooms after 3 years in bilingual classrooms, as well as for alternative English-only instructional models. Currently, federal education policy under NCLB does not specify any instructional approach; it simply requires that states offer "language instruction education programs," which ensure that "LEP" students attain and develop English language proficiency, and meet challenging state academic content and achievement standards (Wright, 2005a).

Before 1978, children of Native American backgrounds were not eligible for admission to federally funded bilingual programs because English was reported as their dominant language. However, linguists and educators concluded that the variety of English used ("Indian English" code) creates difficulties in the English-only classroom (see also McCarty, Language Education Planning and Policies by and for Indigenous Peoples, Volume 1). By 1986–1987, only about 11% of BEA grants were designated for Indian children (about $10 million). In 1992, the Indian Nations at Risk Task Force reported to the Secretary of Education on its goals for the year 2000 for American Indian and Alaska Native students. They recommended that: (1) all schools serving Native students provide opportunities for students to maintain and develop their tribal languages; (2) all Native children have early childhood education, providing the needed "language, social, physical, spiritual, and cultural foundations" for school and later success; (3) state governments develop curricula that are "culturally and linguistically appropriate," and implement the provisions of the Native American Language Act of 1990 in the public schools (Waggoner, 1992a, p. 3). Title VII of NCLB (2002) focuses on support for "local educational agencies in their efforts to reform elementary school and secondary school programs that serve Indian students to ensure that such programs (1) are based on challenging State academic content and student academic achievement standards that are used for all students; and (2) are designed to assist Indian students in meeting those standards." There is no language in Title VII about opportunities for students to develop and maintain their tribal languages. Despite the relatively modest federal support for Native American languages over the past 15 years, a number of tribes adopted official language policies in the 1980s, including the Navajo, Red Lake Band of Chippewa, Northern Ute, Arapahoe, Pasqua Yaqui, and Tohono O'odlam (Papago) (Crawford,

1989, p. 246; see also McCarty, 2002; McCarty, Language Education Planning and Policies by and for Indigenous Peoples, Volume 1). However, tribal leaders and Native American educators have expressed grave concerns over NCLB, claiming its mandates are making it extremely difficult for reservation schools to focus on Native American language and cultural revitalization programs (Senate Democratic Native American Leadership Forum, 2005).

Policy for English as a second language education has been subsumed under a variety of federal and state programs, including: NCLB, the Head Start Program, the National Literacy Act of 1991, the Immigration Reform and Control Act (IRCA) of 1986, the Adult Education Act (AEA) and the Carl D. Perkins Vocational and Applied Technology Education Act (Perkins Act). According to the 2000 Census, nearly 47 million people (5+ years of age) speak a language other than English at home, and of these 7.2% reported that they had no proficiency in English; of the total US population, 4.9% report speaking English "not well" or "not at all" (Wiley, 2005, p. 16). Data from other surveys, such as the National Adult Literacy Survey, confirm that the number of adults requiring ESL services is somewhere between 12 and 14 million (Chisman, Wrigley, and Ewen, 1993). Despite the demonstrated need for English language programs for adults, there has been little coordination among the various federal, state, or private funding sources, and no overarching policy approach to meet this population's educational needs (Wrigley and Ewen, 1995). Prior to NCLB, limited federal funds to support specialized bilingual and ESL programs were available to schools through competitive grants. In the 1990–1991 school year, only about 15% of roughly 3 million eligible children were enrolled in BEA programs. Under NCLB, funding for LEP students has increased and funds are technically available to all schools with LEP students. Nevertheless, these funds are now more thinly spread (Crawford, 2002), meaning less money per eligible student.

According to the results of a survey of public schools in the USA conducted by the American Council on the Teaching of Foreign Languages, nearly 7 million students were enrolled in foreign language courses in grades 7–12 in Fall (Autumn) 2000—an increase of about 1 million students since 1994. Among high school students (grades 9–12), slightly more than 6 million students (43.8% of all public high school enrollees) were studying a foreign language in 2000, the highest enrollment rate since 1928, and an increase of ~2% over 1994 (Draper and Hicks, 2002, p. 1). Among elementary schools (based on data from 19 states), 5% of students in grades K-6 were enrolled in nonexploratory foreign language courses in 2000; this represents a decrease from 6.4% (24 states reporting) in 1994 (Draper and Hicks, 2002, p. 1). Spanish continues to attract the greatest number of students, accounting for 68.8% of all language enrollments, 7th–12th grade; French accounts for 18.3% (a decrease of 1.3%) and German for 4.8% (a decrease of less than 1%) of foreign language enrollments. Japanese and Italian are increasing in popularity, representing 8% and 1.2% of total foreign language enrollments in 2002, respectively. Data on foreign language enrollments in postsecondary institutions for Fall 2002 have been compiled by the Modern Language Association (Welles, 2003). The data are based on the results of a questionnaire sent to the registrars of 2,781 institutions, with 99.6% of the institutions responding. The 12 most studied languages, followed by total number of enrollments and percentage of total foreign language enrollments, are: Spanish (746,267) (53.4%); French (201,979) (14.5%); German (91,100) (6.5%); Italian (63,899) (4.6%); Japanese (52,238) (3.7%); Chinese (34,153) (2.4%); Latin (29,841) (2.1%); Russian (23,921) (1.7%); Ancient Greek (20,367) (1.5%); Hebrew (Biblical and Modern) (22,802) (1.6%); Portuguese (8,385) (0.6%); and Arabic (10,584) (0.8%). Enrollments in each of these languages have increased since 1998, with the largest increases observed for Arabic (92.3%), Biblical Hebrew (55.9%), Italian (29.6%), and Modern Hebrew (28%). Although study of a number of languages has grown in the past decade, increases in the number of students attending college (university), along with fluctuations in enrollments among various languages, have resulted in fairly steady registrations in modern foreign languages per 100 college students since 1977, ranging from 7.3–8.6.

According to Census 2000 data, among the nearly 47 million people in the USA aged 5+ years who speak a language other than English at home—an increase from 32 million in 1980—over 28 million (60%) speak Spanish (Wiley, 2005, pp. 10–11). Chinese is now the third most commonly spoken language in the USA, after English and Spanish, with slightly over 2 million speakers (replacing French in 1980). Languages with over 1 million speakers include French, German, Tagalog, Vietnamese, and Italian, whereas Korean, Russian, Polish, Arabic, Portuguese, and "Asian Indian Languages" (Gujarati, Hindi, and Urdu) were reported as having over half a million speakers (Wiley, 2005, pp. 11–12).

WORK IN PROGRESS

Issues which have received attention in the literature in recent years include the education of speakers of minority (non-English) languages and nonstandard varieties of English, education for the deaf, literacy, preparation of teachers for an increasingly diverse range of students, problems with NCLB's mandates for testing LEP students, and anti-bilingual education state ballot initiatives.

Despite significant within-group gains in educational achievement, many language minority (LM) students perform less well academically than their majority peers (see Genesee, 1994). Although the population of LM students is greatest in selected states (California, Texas, New York, Florida, Illinois, New Jersey, Arizona, and Pennsylvania), LM students reside in all 50 US states, and many states are experiencing unprecedented growth among their LM student populations (e.g., Alabama, Georgia, South Carolina, North Carolina, Tennessee, Kentucky, Idaho, and many others). Current federal law (NCLB) requires that LM students be identified and appropriate instructional programs be implemented to ensure LEP students learn English and meet state academic standards. Furthermore, the law mandates the full inclusion of LEP students in state high-stakes testing programs, and individual schools are held accountable for ensuring that LEP students meet the same "adequate yearly progress" goals as all other students (Abedi, 2003). Despite NCLB's call for accommodations, the vast majority of LEP students are tested in English with little to no accommodations. Amidst rising concerns about the validity of scores for students not yet proficient in the language of the test, schools nonetheless face threats of sanctions and eventual state or private takeover if too many LEP (or other) students fail the test each year (Abedi, 2004). In addition, each state is required to have a statewide English language proficiency test, and school districts are held accountable for ensuring that a growing percentage of students make progress in learning English each year. Given the pressure to raise test scores, the lack of tests in students' native languages, the lack of encouragement and financial support for bilingual programs, and the heavy emphasis on English, many view NCLB as an implicit (or covert) language policy encouraging English-only instruction (Crawford, 2004; Wiley and Wright, 2004; Wright, 2005b).

Given that the education system in the USA has generally been decentralized, NCLB's mandates are unprecedented. Nonetheless, with the absence of clearly defined instructional approaches in the federal law, US states are given flexibility to define what constitutes effective instruction for LEP students (Freeman, 2004), and thus can withhold federal funds from schools which do not meet state criteria (Wright, 2005a). This has been particularly problematic in three states that have passed anti-bilingual education voter initiatives: California (Proposition 227), Arizona (Proposition 203), and Massachusetts (Question 2). Together, these states are home to 36% of the nation's LEP student population. Despite federal allowances for native language instruction, the law in these states mandates that LEP students be placed in structured English immersion (SEI) classrooms, and makes it very difficult for schools to provide bilingual education as an option (de Jong, Gort, and Cobb, 2005; Wiley, Castro, and de Klerk, 2005; Wright, 2005c).

The lack of a coherent (explicit) national language policy reflects, in part, broader social divisions about the role of education, and especially language(s), in society (see Arias and Casanova, 1993). For example, pluralists favor maintaining immigrant and indigenous non-English languages and argue that all students—majority and minority—benefit cognitively, as well as socially, by educational programs that develop two languages; assimilationists, on the other hand, believe maintenance of non-English languages is a private matter, and that the most important measure of success for bilingual programs is how fast children acquire English, not the long-term academic achievement of students. Ramirez et al. (1991) and Thomas and Collier (2002) provide the best evidence to date that late-exit (maintenance or developmental) bilingual education programs are superior to most early-exit or so-called English immersion (submersion) programs in terms of students' long-term academic achievement in English-mediated instruction (see also May, Bilingual/Immersion Education: What the Research Tells Us, Volume 5). However, explaining underlying causes of student success (and failure) is extremely complex, and cannot be undertaken without reference to issues of language and identity, and socioeconomic status, among many other variables. For example, members of some LM groups are able to acculturate to the mainstream (English-speaking) society very rapidly, regardless of whether their non-English native language is included in the curriculum, and without losing their cultural (even linguistic) identity; on the other hand, members of other groups, with different histories in the USA, often including segregated and inferior public schooling, have come to believe that full socioeconomic access to the dominant (English-speaking) culture is not a viable option, and as a result are more at risk of school failure, regardless of the curriculum they are exposed to in school. Groups also vary in group adhesion, often displaying wide intragroup variation in members' attitudes toward language maintenance and cultural assimilation (Paulston, 1994, p. 16).

The publication of *A Nation at Risk* in 1984 rekindled a national debate on the "literacy crisis." The 1992 National Adult Literacy Survey (NALS), a comprehensive survey of English literacy in the USA, found, among other things, that 40–44 million adults (21–23% of the adult population) performed at the lowest levels in tasks involving prose literacy. The fact that 21% of the respondents were immigrants still acquiring English who were unfamiliar with US culture complicates the findings. Moreover, the findings do not indicate how well respondents, both native English and nonnative English speakers, are able to cope with literacy challenges on a daily basis. Recent reports have attempted to correct some of the errors in the original findings. Matthews (2001) claims that only 5% of those surveyed should be considered illiterate because they failed to answer any questions (cited in Wiley, 2005, p. 85). In addition, based on the analysis of test items, concerns about the validity of the survey have been raised (Berliner, 1996; Matthews, 2001). Nonetheless, these reports and concerns about American competitiveness in the global economy have led, in recent years, to the creation of programs for workplace and family literacy. In school settings, policy and curricula have tended to focus on the acquisition of literacy in Standard English, with little attention paid, until recently, to the acquisition and maintenance of non-English literacies, or to the effects of Standard English policies on speakers of so-called nonstandard varieties of English, such as African American Language (AAL) (Ramirez, Wiley, de Klerk, Lee, and Wright, 2005).

In recent years, a movement has emerged within the Deaf community in the USA to promote the teaching of American Sign Language, rather than English, as the first language of deaf persons, preferably in bilingual (ASL/English)–bicultural programs. This recommendation is based on research which shows that the acquisition of English literacy by deaf students instructed in sign systems, such as Manually Coded English (MCE), is less successful than it is for students who have had access to ASL during their formative language acquiring years (see also Branson and Miller, National Sign Languages and Language Policies, Volume 1). Critics, who oppose removing deaf children from their hearing parents to learn ASL and become acculturated into the deaf community, argue that this will result in permanent separation and rejection of English. Proponents of ASL as a first language view this as a language rights issue, since policies promoting oralism and restricting the use of sign language, usually developed by hearing persons, have historically oppressed the deaf community and limited their social and economic advancement (see Reagan, 2006).

An important policy issue, given the increasing diversity of the school age and adult population in the USA, concerns the preparation of teachers. State credentialing authorities have, in recent years, modified requirements for teacher certification to include courses in second language acquisition, culture, and methods and materials appropriate for linguistically and culturally diverse populations (see also Wiley, Language Policy and Teacher Education, Volume 1). Professional teacher organizations have lobbied state and federal agencies for greater funding and recognition of the specialized training required for teaching in multilingual and multicultural classrooms and schools. Many states now offer a certificate or endorsement in Bilingual Education (in various non-English languages), ESL and/or SEI. Publications integrating theory and practice in the education of LM students include Echevarria, Vogt, and Short (2003); Freeman (2004); Garcia and Baker (1995); Genesee (1994); Milk, Mercado, and Sapiens (1992); and Peregoy and Boyle (2004).

PROBLEMS AND DIFFICULTIES

The role of the US federal government in expanding educational opportunities for minorities, including language minorities, has been challenged in recent years on a number of fronts. Since the inception of
the BEA to its demise in 2002, opposition to Bilingual Education led
to changes each time the bill was reauthorized, typically resulting in
greater focus on transitioning students to English as quickly as possible, and designating greater percentages of funds for English-only
approaches (Ricento, 1996; Wright, 2005b). Nonetheless, in the final
reauthorization of the BEA (1994), the benefits of bilingualism were
recognized, and funds were allowed for maintenance of bilingual and
dual-language programs. In contrast, under NCLB, the term "bilingual
education" no longer appears in the federal law, and funds no longer
target specific bilingual or other program models.

The biggest attacks on bilingual education, however, have occurred
at the state level. A wealthy software engineer from California seeking
political name recognition sponsored and funded anti-bilingual education ballot initiatives in four states: California (Proposition 227),
Arizona (Proposition 203), Massachusetts (Question 2), and Colorado
(Amendment 31) (Crawford, 2004). Although the initiative was
soundly defeated in Colorado, the measure was approved by wide margins in the other three states. Under the deceptively simple and misleading title of "English for the Children," the initiative's sponsor
placed educational language policy-making in the hands of uninformed
voters, many of whom likely based their votes on their discomfort with
growing immigrant populations (primarily Hispanic) in their states
(Wiley and Wright, 2004). These state initiatives have made it difficult to secure new or continued support for bilingual education from
legislators at the federal level (Wiley and Wright, 2004).

Groups that oppose bilingual education, such as US English, also
tend to oppose other types of federal accommodations to non-English
speakers, such as bilingual ballots and the publication of government
documents, forms and brochures in non-English languages (although
a study by the US General Accounting Office found that 99.4% of
the documents produced by the federal government are in English,
excluding documents from the State and Defense departments). Such
provisions and programs are often cited by opponents as examples of
"ethnic-based" entitlements (see, e.g. Imhoff, 1990). These groups also
strongly advocate the establishment of English as the official language
of the USA, or of governmental entities at all levels. This movement
began in the early 1980s under the leadership of the late US Senator
S.I. Hayakawa, who introduced a constitutional amendment (S.J. Res.
72) in 1981 declaring English the official language of the USA.

Although the bill was never reported out of committee, by 2000, 27 states had adopted laws or amended their constitutions declaring English the official state language (US English, 2005). On August 1, 1996, the US House of Representatives, under Republican leadership, passed for the first time in US history a bill declaring English the official language of the US government (H.R. 123, The English Language Empowerment Act). Provisions of the bill include repeal of federal bilingual ballots and a prohibition against federal employees communicating in writing in non-English languages, although they may communicate orally in languages other than English. The Senate failed to act on a similar bill in the 104th Congress, thereby preventing the 104th Congress from enacting an official English law. The issue has frequently returned in subsequent sessions of Congress, including a proposal in 2006 amidst major debates over immigration, to declare English as the "national and unifying language," but to date none of the proposed bills has passed.

Although, research in second language acquisition has provided clear evidence of the benefits of late-exit bilingual education programs (Ramirez et al., 1991; Thomas and Collier, 2002), of the effectiveness of second language immersion programs for monolingual English speakers (Lambert and Tucker, 1972), of the transferability of conceptual knowledge learned in one language to another language (Cummins, 1979), and of the social and affective benefits of programs and curricula which value the culture and language of the so-called nonmainstream students (Baker, 1993), these findings have been distorted and politicized by opponents (cf. May, Bilingual/Immersion Education: What the Research Tells Us, Volume 5). Professional education organizations, such as Teachers of English to Speakers of Other Languages (TESOL), the National Association for Bilingual Education (NABE), the Modern Language Association (MLA), and the National Council of Teachers of English (NCTE), among many others, have offered their expertise on language education matters to policy makers at the state and federal level in the USA. However, the issues surrounding language in education policy—the use of non-English languages as the medium of instruction, the teaching of foreign languages from kindergarten through college, the maintenance of non-English languages through education, the valuing of non-English—as well as English—literacy among immigrant populations, the development of bilingual–bicultural language programs for the Deaf—have histories which extend back to the mid-nineteenth century. For example, the effects of the Americanization campaign (roughly 1914–1924) (McClymer, 1982), which saw severe restriction of non-English languages in public and private domains at the same time the teaching of English to adults through civics classes was promoted by the states and the federal government, continue to influence and shape attitudes, and hence policy, with regard to the learning and teaching of languages (Ricento, 2003, 2005).

LIKELY FUTURE DIRECTIONS IN RESEARCH AND PRACTICE

Research in language policy and planning is subsumed under three general headings: processes, agents, and goals. Under processes, researchers investigate the mechanisms by which and through which language policies are developed, implemented, and evaluated. Examples of possible research topics in the coming decade include the implementation of federal language policies at the state and local level; the role played by grassroots organizations in articulating policy and influencing legislative processes; the evaluation of policies by different constituencies; the implementation and evaluation of specific program types in specific educational settings; the interplay of the various components which collectively, and individually, determine language policies. Agents refer to the public and private individuals and collectivities which promote various policies. Examples of areas likely to be researched include: who controls language policy agendas, and by what means; what are the sources of authority for those agents who argue for particular policies; what are the characteristics of various interest groups that promote particular policies; what role do the media play in promoting particular policy views? Goals refer to sociopolitical and/or economic objectives sought by particular language policies. Examples of research topics in this area include: assessing the differences between stated and unstated goals; investigation of language in education policies from sociohistorical perspectives; articulation of alternative societal goals and the development of specific policies to achieve those goals; comparative analysis of language policy goals among polities. A good sampling of new directions in language policy research is found in Hornberger and Ricento (1996) (see also Ricento, 2006).

Regarding changes in practice, as federal involvement in the policy arena has decreased in recent years (at least in certain areas), the states are likely to play a greater role in policy development and implementation. Second, despite significant opposition to specialized language programs for LM and mainstream students, a number of states and localities have created innovative programs involving two-way bilingual programs in languages as diverse as Mandarin and Portuguese (even in states with anti-bilingual education initiatives). A growing number of states have increased foreign language requirements in elementary and secondary schools. Professional language and education organizations have, in many cases, been successful in influencing the legislative process at the state and federal levels. As more research in language policy becomes available to US decision-makers, and as more trained scholars enter the field, the impact on language policy development, implementation and evaluation could be significant.

See Also: Joan Kelly Hall: Language Education and Culture (Volume 1); Ben Rampton, et al.: Language, Class and Education (Volume 1); James W. Tollefson: Language Planning in Education (Volume 1); Stephen May: Language Education, Pluralism and Citizenship (Volume 1); Teresa L. McCarty: Language Education Planning and Policies by and for Indigenous Peoples (Volume 1); David Bloome: Literacies in the Classroom (Volume 2); Olga Kagan and Kathleen Dillon: Issues in Heritage Language Learning in the United States (Volume 4); Joseph Lo Bianco: Bilingual Education and Socio-political Issues (Volume 5); Stephen May: Bilingual/Immersion Education: What the Research Tells Us (Volume 5); Teresa L. McCarty: Bilingual Education by and for American Indians, Alaska Natives and Native Hawaiians (Volume 5); Tove Skutnabb-Kangas: Language Rights and Bilingual Education (Volume 5); Jan Branson and Don Miller: National Sign Languages and Language Policies (Volume 1); Terrence Wiley: Language Policy and Teacher Education (Volume 1)

REFERENCES

Abedi, J.: 2003, 'Standardized achievement tests and English language learners: Psychometric issues', *Educational Assessment* 8(3), 231–258.

Abedi, J.: 2004, 'The No Child Left Behind Act and English language learners: Assessment and accountability issues', *Educational Researcher* 33(1), 4–14.

Arias, M.B. and Casanova, U. (eds.): 1993, *Bilingual Education: Politics, Practice, Research*, University of Chicago Press, Chicago.

Baker, C.: 1993, *Foundations of Bilingual Education and Bilingualism*, Multilingual Matters, Clevedon.

Berliner, D.: 1996, 'Nowadays, even the illiterates read and write', *Research in the Teaching of English* 30(3), 334–351.

Chisman, F.P., Wrigley, H.S., and Ewen, D.T.: 1993, *ESL and the American Dream*, Southport Institute for Policy Analysis, Washington, DC.

Conklin, N.F. and Lourie, M.A.: 1983, *Host of Tongues: Language Communities in the United States*, The Free Press, New York.

Crawford, J.: 1989, *Bilingual Education: History, Politics, Theory and Practice*, Crane Publishing Co., Trenton, NJ.

Crawford, J.: 1992, *Hold Your Tongue: Bilingualism and the Politics of "English Only"*, Addison-Wesley, Reading, MA.

Crawford, J.: 2002, *Obituary: The Bilingual Education Act, 1968–2002*, Language Policy Research Unit, Education Policy Studies Laboratory, Arizona State University, Tempe, AZ. Available: www.asu.edu/educ/epsl/LPRU/features/article2.htm

Crawford, J.: 2004, *Educating English Learners: Language Diversity in the Classroom* (fifth edition), Bilingual Education Services Inc., Los Angeles.

Cummins, J.: 1979, 'Linguistic interdependence and the educational development of bilingual children', *Review of Educational Research* 49, 222–251.

de Jong, E., Gort, M., and Cobb, C.D.: 2005, 'Bilingual education within the context of English-only policies: Three districts' response to question 2 in Massachusetts', *Educational Policy* 19(4), 595–620.

Draper, J.B. and Hicks, J.H.: 2004, *Foreign Language Enrollments in Public Secondary Schools, Fall, 2002: Summary Report*, American Council on the Teaching of Foreign Languages, Alexandria, VA. Available: http://www.actfl.org/i4a/pages/index.cfm?pageid=3389

Echevarria, J., Vogt, M.E., and Short, D.J.: 2003, *Making Content Comprehensible for English Language Learners: The SIOP Model* (second edition), Allyn & Bacon, Boston.

Fernandez, R.R.: 1987, 'Legislation, regulation, and litigation: The origins and evolution of public policy on bilingual education in the United States', in W.A. Van Horne (ed.), *Ethnicity and Language*, The University of Wisconsin System, Institute on Race and Ethnicity, Milwaukee, 90–123.

Freeman, R.: 2004, *Building on Community Bilingualism: Promoting Multiculturalism Through Schooling*, Caslon Publishing, Philadelphia.

Garcia, E.E. (ed.): 2000, *Bilingual Research Journal, Special Issue, Implementation of California's Proposition 227: 1998–2000 Vol. 24 (1–2)*, National Association for Bilingual Education, Washington, DC.

Garcia, O. and Baker, C. (eds.): 1995, *Policy and Practice in Bilingual Education: Extending the Foundations*, Multilingual Matters, Clevedon.

Genesee, F.: 1994, *Educating Second Language Children*, Cambridge University Press, Cambridge.

Heath, S.B.: 1981, 'English in our language heritage', in C.A. Ferguson and S.B. Heath (eds.), *Language in the USA*, Cambridge University Press, Cambridge, 6–20.

Heath, S.B. and Mandabach, F.: 1983, 'Language status decisions and the law in the United States', in J. Cobarrubias and J.A. Fishman (eds.), *Progress in Language Planning: International Perspectives*, Mouton, Berlin, 87–105.

Hornberger, N.H. and Ricento, T.K. (eds.): 1996, 'Language planning and policy and the ELT profession, special topic issue', *TESOL Quarterly* 30(3), 397–651.

Imhoff, G.: 1990, 'The position of US English on Bilingual education', in C.B. Cazden and C.E. Snow (eds.), *The Annals of the American Academy of Political and Social Science*, Sage Newbury Park, CA, 48–61.

Kloss, H.: 1998/1988, *The American Bilingual Tradition*, Center for Applied Linguistics and Delta Systems, Washington, DC and McHenry, IL.

Lambert, W.E. and Tucker, R.: 1972, *Bilingual Education of Children. The St. Lambert Experiment*, Newbury House, Rowley, MA.

Leibowitz, A.H.: 1971, 'Educational policy and political acceptance: The imposition of English as the language of instruction in American schools', Eric No. ED 047 321.

Lyons, J.J.: 1990, 'The past and future directions of federal Bilingual-Education policy', in C.B. Cazden and C.E. Snow (eds.), *The Annals of the American Academy of Political and Social Science*, Sage Newbury Park, CA, 66–80.

Lyons, J.J.: 1992, 'Secretary Bennett versus equal educational opportunity', in J. Crawford (ed.), *Language Loyalties: A Source Book on the Official English Controversy*, University of Chicago Press, Chicago, 363–366.

Macias, R.: 1982, 'US language-in-Education policy: Issues in the schooling of language minorities', in R.B. Kaplan (ed.), *Annual Review of Applied Linguistics*, Newbury House, Rowley, MA, 144–160.

Matthews, J.: 2001, 'Landmark illiteracy analysis is flawed statistics faulty, study director says', *The Arizona Republic*, A16.

McCarty, T.: 2002, *A Place to be Navajo: Rough Rock and the Struggle for Self-Determination in Indigenous Schooling*, Lawrence Erlbaum, Mahwah, NJ.

McClymer, J.F.: 1982, 'The Americanization movement and the education of the foreign-born adult, 1914–1925', in B.J. Weiss (ed.), *American Education and the European Immigrant: 1840–1940*, University of Illinois Press, Urbana, 96–116.

Milk, R., Mercado, C., and Sapiens, A.: 1992, 'Re-Thinking the education of teachers of language minority children: Developing reflective teachers for changing schools', *Occasional Papers in Bilingual Education*, National Clearinghouse for Bilingual Education, Washington, DC, 6, Summer 1992.

Paulston, C.B.: 1994, *Linguistic Minorities in Multilingual Settings: Implications for Language Policies*, John Benjamins, Amsterdam.

Peregoy, S.F. and Boyle, O.F.: 2004, *Reading, Writing, and Learning in ESL* (fourth edition), Allyn & Bacon, Boston.

Ramirez, J.D., Wiley, T.G., de Klerk, G., Lee, E., and Wright, W.E.: 2005, *Ebonics in the Urban Education Debate* Multilingual (second edition), Matters, Clevedon, England.

Ramirez, J.D., Yuen, D.D., Ramley, D.R., and Pasta, D.: 1991, *Final Report: Longitudinal Study of Structured Immersion Strategy, Early-Exit, and Late-Exit Transitional Bilingual Education Programs for Language-Minority Children*, Aguirre International, San Mateo, CA.

Reagan, T.: 2006, 'Language policy and sign languages', in T. Ricento (ed.), *An Introduction to Language Policy: Theory and Method*, Blackwell, London, 329–345.

Resnick, M.C.: 1993, 'ESL and language planning in Puerto Rican education', *TESOL Quarterly* 27(2), 259–273.

Ricento, T.: 1996, 'Language policy in the United States', in M. Herriman and B. Burnaby (eds.), *Language Policies in English-Dominant Countries*, Multilingual Matters, Clevedon, 122–158.

Ricento, T.: 1998, 'National language policy in the United States', in T. Ricento and B. Burnaby (eds.), *Language and Politics in the United States and Canada: Myths and Realities*, Lawrence Erlbaum, Mahwah, NJ, 85–112.

Ricento, T.: 2003, 'The discursive construction of Americanism', *Discourse & Society* 14(5), 611–637.

Ricento, T.: 2005, 'Problems with the 'language-as-resource' discourse in the promotion of heritage languages in the USA', *Journal of Sociolinguistics* 9(3), 348–368.

Ricento, T. (ed.): 2006, *An introduction to Language Policy: Theory and Method*, Blackwell, London.

Senate Democratic Native American Leadership Forum: 2005, Recommendations for Congress on Indian Country, United States Senate, Washington, DC.

Tamura, E.H.: 1993, 'The English-only effort, the Anti-Japanese campaign, and language acquisition in the education of Japanese Americans in Hawaii', *History of Education Quarterly* 33(1), 37–58.

Thomas, W.P. and Collier, V.P.: 2002, *A National Study of School Effectiveness for Language Minority Students' Long Term Academic Achievement*, Center for Research on Education, Diversity, and Excellence, Santa Cruz, CA.

US English: 2005, *States with Official English Laws.* Available: http://www.us-english.org/inc/official/states.asp

Waggoner, D.: 1992a, 'Indian nations task force calls for maintenance of languages and cultures', in D. Waggoner (ed.), *Numbers and Needs: Ethnic and Linguistic Minorities in the United States*, Washington DC, 3(5), 2.

Waggoner, D.: 1992b, 'Four in five home speakers of Non-English languages in the US speak one of eight languages', in D. Waggoner (ed.), *Numbers and Needs: Ethnic and Linguistic Minorities in the United States*, Washington, DC, 2(5), 1.

Wiley, T.G.: 1996, 'Language planning and language policy', in S.L. McKay and N.H. Hornberger (eds.), *Sociolinguistics and Language Teaching*, Cambridge University Press, Cambridge, 103–147.

Wiley, T.G.: 2005, *Literacy and Language Diversity in the United States* (second edition), Center for Applied Linguistics and Delta Systems, Washington, DC and McHenry, IL.

Wiley, T.G. and Wright, W.E.: 2004, 'Against the undertow: The politics of language instruction in the United States', *Educational Policy* 18(1), 142–168.

Wiley, T.G., Castro, M.C., and de Klerk, G.: 2005, 'Editors' introduction: The condition of language-minority education in the State of Arizona', *Bilingual Research Journal* 29(1), 5–23.

Wright, W.E.: 2005a, 'English language learners left behind in Arizona: The nullification of accommodations in the intersection of federal and state policies', *Bilingual Research Journal* 29(1), 1–30.

Wright, W.E.: 2005b, *Evolution of Federal Policy and Implications of No Child Left Behind for Language Minority Students*, Language Policy Research Unit, Education Policy Studies Laboratory, Arizona State University, Tempe, AZ. Available: http://www.asu.edu/educ/epsl/EPRU/documents/EPSL-0501-101-LPRU.pdf

Wright, W.E.: 2005c, The political spectacle of Arizona's Proposition 203. *Educational Policy* 19(4), 1–40.

Wrigley, H.S. and Ewen, D.T.: 1995, *A National Language Policy for ESL*, Center for Applied Linguistics, National Clearinghouse for ESL Literacy Education, Washington, DC.

RAINER ENRIQUE HAMEL

INDIGENOUS LANGUAGE POLICY AND EDUCATION IN MEXICO

INTRODUCTION

The policies which nation-states, and their societal majorities, apply to their ethnic and linguistic minorities have become a touchstone to evaluate the quality of democracy, pluricultural commitment and the construction of modern states in almost any part of the world. Therefore, educational and language policies for the minorities can no longer be dismissed as marginal components of state policy that may be dealt with outside the domains of mainstream power relations and the state. Mexico is a paradigmatic case in point. At least in America it represents the probably most-centralized, all-embracing and vertical case of nation-state building. It did not, however, achieve its historical goals of creating a homogeneous nation (cf. May, Language Education, Pluralism and Citizenship, Volume 1) and fully assimilating the indigenous peoples in the 500 years since the beginning of Spanish colonization. On the contrary, the Mexican indigenous population is the largest in the continent, although language shift advances in many language groups. During the twentieth century the indigenous population, measured as speakers of the 62 surviving languages by the Mexican national census, has grown steadily in absolute numbers, but declined as a percentage of the total population from 2.2 million in 1930 (=16%) to 7.2 million (=7.2%) in 2000 (INEGI, 2000).

To understand the apparent paradox in Mexico between present overt policies that support diversity and indigenous language maintenance on the one hand, and covert pressure for assimilation on the other, we have to revise historical and present-day ideological orientations in language policy. In the following section, I briefly outline the history of language policy for indigenous peoples from colonial times to the present day in Mexico. Next, I consider the central problems of general language and culture orientations and the use of the languages in indigenous education. I then refer to recent changes in legislation and discuss to what extent a linguistic rights perspective developed over time. In this chapter, the focus is on general language policy and linguistic rights issues, which relate to indigenous education in Mexico. I deal with concrete programmes of bilingual education and their outcomes

S. May and N. H. Hornberger (eds), Encyclopedia of Language and Education,
2nd Edition, Volume 1: Language Policy and Political Issues in Education, 301–313.
©*2010 Springer Science+Business Media LLC.*

in the corresponding chapter on 'Bilingual Education for Indigenous Communities in Mexico' in Volume 5.

EARLY DEVELOPMENTS: LANGUAGE POLICY FROM COLONIZATION TO THE TWENTY-FIRST CENTURY

Education and language as instruments of state building and control have played a major role ever since complex states emerged on Mexican territory. The Aztecs developed their own educational system, an Academy of Science and a selective language policy to govern their vast empire (Heath, 1972). Throughout nearly three centuries of Colonial Empire (1519–1810) the Spanish Vice Kingdom attempted to build a hierarchical society modelled on Spain with the King, the Church and the Spanish language at the top. After independence in 1810, the new Mexican-born bourgeoisie pursued the construction of a unified, homogeneous nation-state as the main overall objective of state policy (cf. May, Language Education, Pluralism and Citizenship, Volume 1) up until the present (Cifuentes, 1999, 2002; del Valle and Gabriel-Stheeman, 2002; Hidalgo, 1994).

In which language(s) should public administration, exploitation and the saving of souls be accomplished? Two basic strategies of language policy for indigenous peoples established continuity between the two regimes (Hamel, 1994; the classical work is Heath, 1972; see also Nahmad Sitton, 1982). The first and generally dominant strategy considered the assimilation, that is dissolution, of indigenous peoples in Mexico and the suppression of their languages to be a prerequisite for building the new polity (see also McCarty, Language Education Planning and Policies by and for Indigenous Peoples, Volume 1). A second position favoured the preservation of indigenous languages and cultures in this process, without giving up the ultimate aim of uniting nation and state. The first strategy imposed direct Hispanicization (castellanización) through submersion programmes: the national language was considered to be the only target and medium of instruction. Transitional programmes reflecting the second strategy applied diverse bilingual methods where the indigenous languages played a subordinate, instrumental role as the languages of instruction and initial alphabetization. The complex process of implementing political, spiritual and cultural domination developed full of contradictions and advanced at different speeds in different phases of history (Hamel, 2006).

The century from independence in 1810 to the Mexican Revolution (1910–1920) meant a time of devastating destruction of indigenous organization and communities, a severe reduction of its population and the period when Spanish became the majority language in the country (83% by 1895, Cifuentes, 2002). Different from most other

Latin American countries, however, the turn into the twentieth century saw a national bourgeoisie that explicitly constructed a new national identity based on the Mestizo as the new prototypical citizen, the symbiosis of the two high cultures, the European and the Aztec-Mayan that Mexico inherited. The new national ideology was significantly reinforced after the Mexican Revolution. It allowed Mexico to create distance and at the same time weave multiple alliances along a triple cultural and linguistic borderline to foster its own nationalism:

1. Mexico encompassed the mystical indigenous identity founded in the high pre-Colombian indigenous civilizations, which distinguished the new nation from Spain, the USA and most other Latin American countries;
2. As part of the New World, Mexico forged a unity of American countries and contrasted them to Europe, especially to Spain;
3. At the same time, as inheritor of the Spanish colonial tradition, Mexico established bonds of solidarity with the other Spanish speaking countries and built a barrier against US cultural and linguistic hegemony.

Throughout the twentieth century, a paradoxical process developed: on the one hand, indigenous language loss accelerated dramatically, as in many other parts of the world; on the other, a contradictory state discourse emerged to preserve the indigenous languages. At first, homogenizing policies prevailed. The Mexican Revolution consolidated the Mestizo ideology as the racial, ideological and linguistic basis of the post-revolutionary society. Assimilationist education using direct methods of Spanish teaching dominated in indigenous areas (Garza Cuarón, 1997). The establishment of the new Federal Ministry of Education in 1921, an institution that by 1990 would employ some 1.5 million teachers and bureaucrats, propelled an education that aimed to 'overcome the evolutionary distance which separates the Indians from the present era, transforming their mentality, orientations and customs, to incorporate them into civilized modern life ...'. (SEP, 1927, p. 35; all translations are mine)

By the mid-1930s, Franz Boas' cultural relativism hypothesis gained ground through his teaching and research on Indian languages and cultures in Mexico. It helped to counterbalance evolutionary theories of the previous period with their linguistic and cultural hierarchies. The concept of *Indigenismo* emerged, which, similar to *Orientalism* in the British and French tradition, could be sketched as 'the whole set of ideas about Indians in the heads of non-Indians' (Villoro, 1950). Given the failure of assimilationist policies and Spanish-only programmes of education, a new recognition of the role of vernacular languages emerged. New pilot projects of mother tongue education were launched, among which was the well-known *Proyecto Tarasco* in central Mexico (Aguirre Beltrán, 1983; Barrera-Vázquez, 1953; see Hamel, Bilingual Education for Indigenous Communities in Mexico, Volume 5).

MAJOR CONTRIBUTIONS: LANGUAGE POLICY AND INDIGENOUS EDUCATION

In 1978, the Federal Ministry of Education in Mexico concentrated previously scattered programmes for K to grade 6 indigenous primary education in a new subsystem, the General Department of Indigenous Education (DGEI). The indigenous schools had to follow the same federal syllabus and to use the compulsory textbooks as the Spanish primary schools in the country. The main difference between the latter and the indigenous schools consisted in the important fact that all teachers in the bilingual programmes were indigenous and spoke a native language as their mother tongue. Since many, if not most, pupils entered primary school with little or no knowledge of Spanish, the teachers used the vernacular language as a means of communication and instruction as long as necessary, together with the primers in Spanish. Teachers improvised their work and used both languages in a non-systematic way. Literacy and most relevant content matters were in fact developed in Spanish. This de facto curriculum could be framed as a mixture of a submersion and a non-systematic transitional bilingual syllabus (Hamel, 1994).

In the 1980s, the official programme was labelled 'bilingual and bicultural'. Given very poor achievement and ongoing language shift among indigenous students, the department designed a new approach based on L1 medium instruction and the teaching of Spanish as L2 (see May, Bilingual/Immersion Education: What the Research Tells Us, Volume 5). However, these programmes were never put to work beyond pilot projects, given political opposition in many communities, within the bureaucracy and the teachers' trade union. The most significant activity of the department consisted in the development of primers in the 40 most widely spoken indigenous languages of the country. Again, implementation lagged behind, and these teaching materials were rarely used in the classrooms.

A decade later, the label 'bicultural' was substituted by a new one, 'intercultural'. The argument, which was imported from South America without any debate or development of its own in Mexico, maintained that the term 'bicultural' implied a dichotomous worldview that separated cultures inappropriately. The new intercultural bilingual perspective in turn would propel the recognition, knowledge and integration of both cultures in a pluralistic enrichment perspective (for a critique, see Muñoz Cruz, 2002). Both languages should now be the medium and object of instruction (DGEI, 1999). In 2001, a newly elected conservative government created a new Coordination in Intercultural Bilingual Education (CGEIB) within the Federal Ministry of Education, which developed a great number of projects, studies and proposals. The main thrust was put on the development of an intercultural orientation of knowledge and respect of indigenous cultures in mainstream education. Implementation, again, did not occur with the same intensity and speed. By the end of the administration in 2006, practically none of the proposals or even the new debates had reached the classrooms.

Contrary to what many authors (e.g. Modiano, 1988) had argued about indigenous education in Mexico in the past, systematic alphabetization in vernacular languages is not a real, general practice in public Indian education, although official policy established since the 1980s asserts that indigenous education should be carried out through the medium of L1. At present, a range of pedagogical practices are in use in the indigenous educational system in Mexico. The most widespread practical model propels transition to Spanish:

1. Indigenous schools have to apply the general primary school curriculum designed for monolingual Spanish speaking pupils; indigenous teachers and schools are expected to make minor adjustments to fit the needs and conditions of their pupils.
2. The national compulsory primers and textbooks are used as the main pedagogical tool; they are designed to teach the subject matter and literacy in Spanish as L1; in no way are they appropriate to learn Spanish as L2. The existing official materials in indigenous languages are rarely used alongside the Spanish textbooks.
3. Although most pupils have little knowledge of Spanish at entrance level, there is no specific place in the curriculum for Indian language and culture. Moreover, no systematic teaching of Spanish as L2 is provided.
4. The indigenous language serves a subordinate function as a language of instruction, and only as long as necessary. Depending on the general language distribution patterns and levels of proficiency in Spanish, instruction in L1 may cease by grade 4 or 5.
5. No culture and language domain separation is practiced or envisaged. Thus, the dominant culture in its material, social, linguistic and cognitive dimensions invades the domains of the indigenous culture and contributes to general culture and language shift among indigenous students.

Generally speaking, low levels of proficiency and achievement obtain for indigenous students in Mexico, as elsewhere (Bertely Busquets, 1998; Citarella, 1990; see also McCarty, Language Education Planning and Policies by and for Indigenous Peoples, Volume 1). A systematic mismatch can also be observed between the sociocultural, linguistic and educational needs of the indigenous student population on the one hand, and the curriculum, materials and language use at school on the other. From the point of view of both the individual and the community, these modalities of schooling tend to reproduce subordination, very often accompanied by traumatic effects for the psychological and cultural development of the pupils. As a matter of fact, the inappropriateness of the school system as such severely violates the indigenous students' educational and linguistic rights (Hamel, 1997).

Three important innovations characterize present-day linguistic dynamics in Mexico that have important consequences for indigenous education: First, the process of democratization over the past 20 years and the expansion of indigenous movements and demands, particularly since the Zapatista upsurge in 1994, have broken down the previous hegemony of multicultural and assimilationist positions within an authoritarian state. Second, Mexico's indigenous peoples are leaving behind their status as a relatively passive population, as targets of governmental programmes to combat poverty and educational backwardness. They have increasingly placed themselves as actors on the political and educational scenes. Third, the 'Indian question' could no longer be considered a marginal problem for the state that could be kept confined to indigenous rural areas. On the contrary, the most prominent claims put forward by the indigenous movement concern fundamental questions of constitutional law, of collective rights and the very essence of a pluralistic nation-state (see also May, Language Education, Pluralism and Citizenship, Volume 1).

WORK IN PROGRESS: LANGUAGE POLICY AND LINGUISTIC RIGHTS

In contrast to indigenist and language *policies,* legislation on languages has been much less explicit in Mexican history. Linguistic rights, usually conceptualized as linguistic human rights, have only become a concern since the late 1980s. They have to be considered in the intersection of language policies and general indigenous policies. In Mexico, linguistic human rights (LHR) have always been discussed in the larger context of indigenous rights (see also McCarty, Language Education Planning and Policies by and for Indigenous Peoples, Volume 1; Skutnabb-Kangas, Human Rights and Language Policy in Education, Volume 1).

Let us consider the development of the corresponding Mexican legislation for indigenous education and languages over the period since the early 1990s, until the general Amendment on Indigenous Rights in 2001 and the 2003 General Law on the Linguistic Rights of Indigenous Peoples. As we shall see, legislation moved from a fairly weak tolerance orientation to a more specific and overt promotion orientation regarding the role of indigenous language (Hidalgo, 2006; Nahmad Sitton, 2001; Pellicer, 1998; cf. May, Language Education, Pluralism and Citizenship, Volume 1). Experiences in many parts of the world show that laws and other legal dispositions need to contain very clear and specific definitions to protect minority rights effectively. Otherwise they can be easily perverted or simply not be applied, given the prevailing asymmetric power relations (see Skutnabb-Kangas, Human Rights and Language Policy in Education, Volume 1).

Nowhere in the colonial, republican, or post-revolutionary constitutions did the Mexican constitution recognize the existence of Indian peoples until 1991, when an amendment to Article 4 of the Constitution was passed in Congress:

> The Mexican nation has a pluricultural composition which is based originally on its Indian peoples. The law will protect and promote the development of their languages, cultures, usages, customs, resources, and specific forms of social organization....

This amendment was severely criticized as too limited to indigenous *cultural* rights in isolation, without granting at the same time their economic, social, political and territorial rights. After the outbreak of the indigenous Zapatista Army's (EZLN) rebellion in southeast Mexico in 1994, followed by extended peace negotiations with the government (Díaz-Polanco, 1997), a proposal for the constitutional recognition of indigenous cultural rights was finally sent to Congress in 2001. However, the amendment of Article 2 that was passed contained considerable changes in relation to the peace agreements; it left unsatisfied the Mexican indigenous movement far beyond the Zapatista Army and most partisan sectors of civil society. The legal text centres on the autonomic competence to regulate their internal social, political, economic and cultural life. Language and education are dealt with in passing. The indigenous peoples are granted the right to:

> A. IV Preserve and enrich their languages, knowledge and all the elements that constitute their culture and identity.

The state in turn will

> B. II Grant and increment the levels of education, favouring bilingual and intercultural education, literacy, completion of basic education, vocational training, secondary and tertiary education. Establish a system of grants for indigenous students at all levels. ... Stimulate the respect and knowledge of the diverse cultures that exist in the nation.

On the whole, indigenous peoples in Mexico are granted the right to preserve and enrich their ancestral knowledge, languages and cultures. Within the state programmes, bilingual intercultural education is mentioned but not made obligatory; it ranges among a series of other non-indigenous types of education with an assimilationist perspective.

In 2003, the Mexican Congress approved a new General Law of the Linguistic Rights for the Indigenous Peoples. It contains four chapters, including general provisions, the rights of the speakers of indigenous languages, the obligations and competencies of public institutions in this matter, and the foundation of a National Institute of Indigenous Languages, which started activities in 2005. The most significant dispositions and definitions are the following:
The object of the law is

> ... to regulate the recognition and protection of the indige-
> nous peoples' and communities' individual and collective
> linguistic rights, as well as the promotion of the use and
> development of the indigenous languages. (Article 1)

The indigenous languages (IL), along with Spanish, are defined as

> ... national languages due to their historical origin, and
> have the same validity en their territories, locations and the
> contexts where they are spoken. (Article 4)

The IL are declared valid to carry out any public business and to access public services in them (Article 7), and the speakers are granted the right to communicate in them in private and public spheres (Article 9). Furthermore, the state grants the indigenous peoples and communities the right to access the state jurisdiction in their languages, that their customs and culture be taken into account (Article 10), and that, if necessary, they will be provided with a translator.

In Article 11, access to bilingual and intercultural education is granted, and in secondary and tertiary (university) education, interculturalism, multilingualism and the respect for diversity and linguistic rights will be promoted.

PROBLEMS AND DIFFICULTIES

In their political fight, the Zapatistas developed strategies that integrated specific claims (territory, resources, justice, education and language) into the overarching target of local and regional autonomy as the specific modality to exercise the right of self-determination as indigenous peoples and nations. From this perspective, language related policies and legal regulations are most likely to succeed if they are incorporated into an attempt to create the necessary conditions, including resources for language maintenance and bilingual education.

Three issues that integrate language policy, linguistic rights and curriculum should be discussed. They relate to the legal basis of the indigenous languages, to the intercultural and bilingual (IB) curriculum, and the control over indigenous education. All these topics will have to be confronted with current implementation and its future perspectives.

As we can see, legislation of linguistic rights and indigenous education in Mexico went through significant changes in the time span of little more than a decade, from a first reference to the existence of indigenous people in the 1991 revision of the constitution to a specific body of linguistic rights and the creation of a National Institute of Indigenous Languages in 2005. The status of indigenous languages has no doubt improved. Although their definition as 'national languages' assigns no specific legal status to them, as would have been the status as 'official languages', the law established the speakers' right to use indigenous languages in public institutions and the obligation of the state to create the conditions for their successful use. In spite of significant improvement, the legal foundations of indigenous language status and, above all, of bilingual education still lack more specific definitions to protect and promote indigenous languages and enrichment bilingual education efficiently. Since intercultural bilingual education is nowhere defined in the law, the indigenous children's right to receive education, including the acquisition of literacy and other content matters in their mother tongue, remains unprotected (cf. Skutnabb-Kangas, Human Rights and Language Policy in Education, Volume 1). Such L1 instruction is considered a fundamental component of any enrichment bilingual curriculum for subordinated minority children.

The next question refers to the nature of the curriculum and control over indigenous education in Mexico. During recent years, a number of local innovations and creative initiatives have emerged to find new ways to develop alternative models of indigenous education, although their margins are narrow (Bertely Busquets, 1998; Bertely Busquets and González Apodaca, 2003). The most radical alternative experiments occur in the areas under Zapatista control.

In general terms, however, submersion and transitional programmes based on multicultural, assimilationist perspectives still prevail in Mexico. From the perspective of recent debates about autonomy and intercultural education, the question arises as to what extent the government is prepared to grant relative autonomy to the system of indigenous education in terms of alternative curricula and indigenous control over administration. Since the end of the 1980s, we observe an increasing disposition to grant the teaching of literacy and other content matters in the native languages where appropriate and wanted; but *content* as such has to be kept more or less homogeneous and must follow the national compulsory curriculum for Spanish-speaking children.

In other words, different from previous periods, bilingualism is now
accepted and even encouraged to a certain extent; yet pluriculturalism,
i.e. real diversity based on an enrichment perspective, is not. Nowhere
within the public school system are the school communities entitled to
propose and put into practice a syllabus that diverges significantly from
the official curriculum.

In spite of its vagueness in key issues (i.e. mother tongue education)
and a narrow margin for structural change, the new legal framework in
Mexico has moved from prohibition to tolerance and to an albeit weak
promotion of indigenous languages and cultures. It opens up new
spaces and opportunities for new experiences and innovations. Unfortunately, resistance against changes remains strong within mainstream
society and the indigenous communities themselves. Five hundred
years of domination has left profound traces in the subordinated peoples' culture, organization and worldview. Most indigenous schoolteach-
ers have settled for some kind of transitional bilingual programme. They
themselves have interiorized a diglossic ideology, which leaves no
room for their languages as the vehicle for the development
of academic skills such as literacy or, in a broader context, for the
development of their communities. As in many other contexts of
ethnolinguistic minorities in the world, resistance to mother tongue
education stems not so much from legal or curriculum constraints,
but is due to interiorized barriers and social pressure from inside and
outside the indigenous communities themselves. In principle, the legal
framework would allow for much greater indigenous language use and
related enrichment bilingual education programmes than that currently
practiced by the system and its indigenous actors. Given this contradictory situation, the growing numbers of successful initiatives
that show alternative ways of education (Podestá Siri and Martínez
Buenabad, 2003; see examples in Hamel, Bilingual Education for
Indigenous Communities in Mexico, Volume 5) can play a significant
role in the attempt to bring about more fundamental changes on a
broader basis.

FUTURE DIRECTIONS

The future perspectives of indigenous bilingual and intercultural education in Mexico are difficult to foresee. Neo-liberal economics and
North American integration through the NAFTA Trade Agreement
have to a large extent eroded the agricultural subsistence in Mexico
as the territorial base for indigenous survival. 3.4 million of peasants,
many of them indigenous, were forced to migrate to other areas of
Mexico or to the USA during the past administration. Although many
migrants maintain close connections with their home communities,

the territorial base, the density of the ancestral habitat and other fundamental components for cultural and linguistic reproduction are at risk. Given ongoing asymmetric conflict relations between Spanish (and English in the USA) and the indigenous languages (IL), the rapid reduction of monolingual IL speakers, and the severe weakening of intergenerational mother tongue transmission may all serve as indicators that rising bilingualism may only be transitional in the ongoing process of language shift.

Maintenance perspectives will rely on the growing number of indigenous organizations and grassroots initiatives, on a more profound acceptance of pluriculturalism by the dominant society, and significant changes in the economic model to re-establish social and economic sustainability in the indigenous territories.

In terms of research and academically guided development and implementation, individual ethnographic case studies abound (see an overview in Bertely Busquets, 2003). More research based on scientific approaches that permit national and international comparison is needed, however (cf. May, Bilingual/Immersion Education: What the Research Tells Us, Volume 5). In the last resort, changes will depend on the political forces and movements within both subordinated and mainstream society that are able and willing to incorporate major innovations in the construction of a new pluricultural and plurilingual Mexican nation-state.

See Also: *Teresa L. McCarty: Language Education Planning and Policies by and for Indigenous Peoples (Volume 1); Tove Skutnabb-Kangas: Human Rights and Language Policy in Education (Volume 1); Juan Carlos Godenzzi: Language Policy and Education in the Andes (Volume 1); Inge Sichra: Language Diversity and Indigenous Literacy in the Andes (Volume 2); Judy Kalman: Literacies in Latin America (Volume 2); Stephen May: Bilingual/Immersion Education: What the Research Tells Us (Volume 5); Rainer Enrique Hamel: Bilingual Education for Indigenous Communities in Mexico (Volume 5); Anne-Marie de Mejia: Enrichment Bilingual Education in South America (Volume 5); Luis Enrique López and Inge Sichra: Intercultural Bilingual Education Among Indigenous Peoples in Latin America (Volume 5); Stephen May: Language Policy and Political Issues in Education (Volume 1)*

REFERENCES

Aguirre Beltrán, G.: 1983, *Lenguas vernáculas. Su uso y desuso en la enseñanza: la experiencia de México*, CIESAS, México.

Barrera-Vázquez, A.: 1953, 'The Trascan project in Mexico', in UNESCO (ed.), *The Use of Vernacular Languages in Education*, UNESCO, Paris.

312 RAINER ENRIQUE HAMEL

Bertely Busquets, M.: 1998, 'Educación indígena del siglo XX en México', in P. Latapí Sarre (ed.), *Un siglo de educación en México*, Volume 2, Fondo de la Cultura Económica, México.

Bertely Busquets, M. and González Apodaca, E.: 2003, 'Etnicidad en la escuela', in M. Bertely Busquets (ed.), *Educación, derecho sociales y equidad*, SEP, México.

Cifuentes, B.: 1999, *Letras sobre voces. Multilingüismo a través de la historia*, INI and CIESAS, México.

Cifuentes, B.: 2002, *Lenguas para un pasado, huellas de una nación: Los estudios sobre lenguas indígenas de México en el siglo XIX*, INAH and Plaza y Valdés, México.

Citarella, L.: 1990, 'México', in F. Chiodi (ed.), *La educación indígena en América Latina*, Volume 1, PEBI and Abya Yala, Quito.

Del Valle, J. and Gabriel-Stheeman (eds.): 2002, *The Battle Over Spanish Between 1800 and 2000: Language Ideologies and Hispanic Intellectuals*, Routledge, London and New York.

DGEI (Dirección General de Educación Indígena): 1999, *Lineamientos generales para la Educación Intercultural Bilingüe para niñas y niños indígenas*, SEP, México.

Díaz-Polanco, H.: 1997, *La rebelión zapatista y la autonomía*, Siglo XXI, México.

Garza Cuarón (ed.): 1997, *Políticas lingüísticas en México*, La Jornada Ediciones and UNAM, México.

Hamel, R.E.: 1994, 'Indigenous education in Latin America: Policies and legal frameworks', in T. Skutnabb-Kangas and R. Phillipson (eds.), *Linguistic Human Rights: Overcoming Linguistic Discrimination*, Mouton de Gruyter, Berlin and New York.

Hamel, R.E.: 1997, 'Language conflict and language shift: A sociolinguistic framework for linguistic human rights', *International Journal of the Sociology of Language* 127, 105–134.

Hamel, R.E.: 2006, 'The development of language empires', in U. Ammon, N. Dittmar, Norbert, K.J. Mattheier, and P. Trudgill (eds.), *Sociolinguistics – Soziolinguistik. An International Handbook of the Science of Language and Society*, Volume 3, de Gruyter, Berlin and New York.

Heath, S.B.: 1972, *Telling Tongues. Language Policy in Mexico: From Colony to Nation*, Teacher's College Press, New York and London.

Hidalgo, M.: 1994, 'Bilingual education, nationalism and ethnicity in Mexico: From theory to practice', *Language Problems and Language Planning* 18(3), 184–207.

Hidalgo, M. (ed.): 2006, *Mexican indigenous languages at the dawn of the twenty-first century*, de Gruyter, Berlin and New York.

INEGI (Instituto Nacional de Estadística, Geografía e Informática): 2000, *Censo Nacional de Población 2000*, INEGI, México.

Modiano, N.: 1988, 'Public bilingual education in Mexico', in C.B. Paulston, (ed.), *International Handbook of Bilingualism and Bilingual Education*, Greenwood Press, New York.

Muñoz Cruz, H. (ed.): 2002, *Rumbo a la interculturalidad*, UAM-I, México.

Nahmad Sitton, S.: 1982, 'Indoamérica y educación: ¿etnocidio o etnodesarrollo?', in A.P. Scanlon and J. Lezama Morfin (eds.), *México pluricultural: De la castellanización a la educación indígena bilingüe bicultural*, SEP and Porrúa, México.

Nahmad Sitton, S.: 2001, 'Autonomía indígena y la soberanía nacional: El caso de la ley indígena de Oaxaca', in L. de León Pasquel (ed.), *Costumbres, leyes y movimiento indio en Oaxaca y Chiapas*, CIESAS and Porrúa, México.

Pellicer, Dora: 1998, 'El derecho al bilingüismo: De la Ley de Instrucción Rudimentaria al diálogo de San Andrés Sacam Ch'en', *Dimensión Antropológica* 3, 8, 91–110.

Podestá Siri, R. and Martínez Buenabad, E.: 2003, 'Sociolingüística educativa', in M. Bertely Busquets (ed.), *Educación, derecho sociales y equidad*, SEP, México.

SEP (Secretaría de Educación Pública): 1927, Internado nacional para indios, SEP, México.

Villoro, L.: 1950, *Los grandes momentos del indigenismo en México*, El Colegio de México, México.

JUAN CARLOS GODENZZI

LANGUAGE POLICY AND EDUCATION IN THE ANDES

INTRODUCTION

Language policy in the Andes appears as a set of dissimilar and rivalling constituents. There are some explicit constitutional provisions and legal dispositions declaring the protection of national language diversity and linguistic rights. However, in reality, there is a strong implicit imposition of Spanish as the sole national language of administration, subordinating and weakening indigenous languages (cf. Hamel, Indigenous Language Policy and Education in Mexico, Volume 1). Facing this contradictory situation is an emerging critical awareness as well as remonstrative efforts that demand the empowerment of indigenous languages and the effective exercise of linguistic rights.

Taking into consideration the interactions of those competing elements, this chapter examines recent developments in language policy, language planning, and education in Ecuador, Peru, and Bolivia, since these countries host the largest percentage of indigenous language speakers in the Andean region. It is believed that 34% of Ecuadorians, 37% of Peruvians, and 62% of Bolivians belong to indigenous communities speaking different languages. Besides Spanish, the languages most spoken are Quechua (more than 10 million speakers) and Aymara (2.5 million speakers). There are other vulnerable languages spoken by minorities, particularly in the Amazon area: 15 languages in the jungle region of Ecuador, 40 in Peru, and 34 in Bolivia.

EARLY DEVELOPMENTS

The Andean region, marked by colonialism and asymmetrical relations of power, is a site where European and Indigenous cultures meet and struggle, influencing each other in different ways. In this context, language policy and the entire political spectrum in the Andes have been suffused with social domination and assimilationism (Mannheim, 1991, p. 78).

Under Spanish colonial rule, language policies could not count on immediate or even short-term hispanization—except in a few areas along the coast. Therefore, they were oriented toward Quechua, raising its potential as a vehicle of communication. A process thus started in

S. May and N. H. Hornberger (eds), Encyclopedia of Language and Education,
2nd Edition, Volume 1: Language Policy and Political Issues in Education, 315–329.
©2010 Springer Science+Business Media LLC.

the Andes, characterized by the following trends: (i) hegemony of Spanish, associated with groups in power; (ii) spread of Quechua, and on a smaller scale Aymara, through widespread, impoverished areas along the Andes Mountains; and (iii) weakening or extinction of numerous languages that formerly showed signs of vitality (Torero, 2002). Although during this period Quechua enjoyed a relative prestige and was used as a literary language, during the post-independence republican period a hard-line linguistic assimilation took place. Gradually, Spanish expanded at the expense of the indigenous languages, becoming the language of the majority in Ecuador, Peru, and Bolivia. However, owing primarily to heavy migration from rural areas to cities, this Spanish is strongly marked by Quechua and Aymara linguistic features. Even if Spanish has subjugated the Andean indigenous languages, these languages are transforming Spanish. Consequently, linguistic conflict is being unleashed not only between languages, but also between the Andean and non-Andean varieties of Spanish.

Throughout the twentieth century, diverse efforts to standardize indigenous languages were made. The first officialization of a Quechua alphabet in Peru dates to 1946. In 1954, the Third Inter-American Indigenist Congress, held in La Paz, proposed an alphabet based on the International Phonetic Alphabet. During General Velasco's Peruvian government (1968–1975), Quechua was recognized as an official language, and an alphabet was produced for Quechua and Aymara. This alphabet, based on phonologic criteria and typographic simplicity, served to write dictionaries and grammars in six major varieties of Quechua. Later, in 1983, this alphabet was revised with the intention of negotiating a greater pan-Andean orthographic unity. The principal change consisted in ceasing to use the five vowels borrowed from Spanish. Instead, three vowels (a,i,u,) corresponding to the three vocalic and structurally functional phonemes in Quechua and Aymara were adopted. This change unleashed the "war of the vowels." The Academia Mayor de la Lengua Quechua, headquartered in Cuzco, along with other allied institutions, such as the Summer Institute of Linguistics (SIL), did not accept the measure in spite of it being the result of a joint negotiation (Itier, 1992). Since then, and for nearly 20 years, this impassioned quarrelling between linguists and members of the Quechua academy in Cuzco has diverted attention and energy that should have been directed toward an effective revitalization of indigenous languages. Amid these conflicts, in 1985, the revised alphabet of 1983—including punctuation and orthographic rules— acquired official status and, ever since, has been used in Intercultural Bilingual Education (IBE), both in Peru and Bolivia. Furthermore, its use goes beyond the academic sphere, having become present in the fields of communication media and literary production. Regarding the Amazonian indigenous languages with larger number of speakers, general agreements on alphabet and writing norms have been achieved and have included the active participation of indigenous leaders.

In the education domain, one must signal that the introduction of schooling in Andean communities in Ecuador, Peru, and Bolivia has been a slow and painful process (Fell, 1996, p. 191). Indigenous movements, while struggling to defend their lands, demanded their right to education. Andean communities succeeded in their fight to obtain schools, but more often than not, these schools were not what they expected, since they turned out to be spaces where the devaluation of indigenous languages and local knowledge took place. The first initiative of an education that took into consideration the students' language appeared as individual and isolated projects, at the beginning of the twentieth century. That is the case of Manuel Z. Camacho, founder in 1902 of the Private School for Indigenous People; of Daniel Espezúa Velasco, Alfonso Torres Luna, and María Asunción Galindo, in the Aymara area of the Peruvian South Andes; of Elizardo Pérez, founder in 1931 of the Warisata School in Bolivia; of Dolores Cacuango, in the Cayambe region in Ecuador, who promoted schools in which indigenous teachers would teach their courses in Quechua (Albó and Anaya, 2004; Fell, 1996).

The first official indigenous educational activities in Peru took place in 1945, when the Peasant School Nuclei program was started, developed in association with Bolivia. One of the program's characteristics was the recognition of Quechua and Aymara as languages of alphabetization. Even though the nuclei were widely known and accepted, indigenous language alphabetization did not receive enough support, and was soon abandoned. In 1987, the Bureau of Bilingual Education was created. Unfortunately, this Bureau was dismantled a few years later. Several experimental projects emerged, primarily with funding from international cooperation agencies. Some of the most interesting and successful were the Quinua, Ayacucho, Spanish–Quechua Bilingual Project; the Peruvian Amazonia Bilingual Teachers Training Program in Iquitos (Trapnell, 1996); and the Puno Experimental Bilingual Education Project (PEEB). This last program, started in 1977, was focused on implementing bilingual education with Quechua and Aymara children, and then evaluating the experience to validate the program for its general use by the Ministry of Education. In 1996, the National Office for Bilingual Intercultural Education (UNEBI in its Spanish acronym) was created, and in 2001, it was transformed into the National Bureau of Bilingual Intercultural Education (DINEBI).

In Bolivia, the 1952 National Revolution brought the first official intent of educational democratization. In 1983, the "Elizardo Pérez" National Alphabetization and Popular Education Service (SENALEP in its Spanish acronym) was initiated. The aim of this program was to support adult bilingual education and coordinate efforts with those of the Workers' Confederation and with the Rural Teachers' Confederation. After reaching a basic consensus on normalization and officialization of the Quechua and Aymara alphabets in 1985, the state program "Rural Bilingual Intercultural Education: Plan and Politics" was launched. In the period between the end of the 1980s and 1994, the Ministry of Education (in collaboration with UNICEF) and indigenous organizations developed the Bilingual Intercultural Education Project (PEIB) as a pilot program. This project, designed to cover the first 5 years of basic education, was successful. It had important repercussions, its curricular proposals serving as precursors to a state policy of IBE as part of the Educational Reform initiated in 1996 (Albó and Anaya, 2004, pp. 41–55; Luykx, 1999; Muñoz, 1997; also Hornberger and López, 1998, for a comparative treatment of Peru and Bolivia).

In Ecuador, there were several individually run projects, such as Shuar Centers' Federation, Runacunapac Foundation, and Zumbahua Bilingual Schools. Political and ideological awareness on the part of indigenous peoples allowed them to bring pressure for an education articulated with their cultures (King and Haboud, 2002). In 1984, the PEIB started, oriented toward basic schooling within the framework of an agreement between the Ministry of Education and Culture and the German Technical Cooperation Agency (GTZ). The Education Law was enacted in 1985, recommending the generalization of IBE projects in the country. That same year, and due to the requests of the Ecuadorian Indigenous Nationalities Confederation (CONAIE in its Spanish acronym), the National Bureau of Intercultural Bilingual Education (DINEIB) was created. By 1990, 1,200 schools had joined the DINEIB and were managed by both the Ministry and the CONAIE (Fell, 1996).

MAJOR CONTRIBUTIONS

Indigenous Organizations as Protagonists

Indigenous organizations have actively participated in gaining cultural and linguistic recognition and in consolidating alternative ways of teaching and agency (see also McCarty, Language Education Planning and Policies by and for Indigenous Peoples, Volume 1). In some cases, they demanded with increasing impetus the right to their territories, to their own development, and to a self-managed bilingual and intercultural education. A particularly notable role was played by the Shuar Federation and CONAIE in Ecuador, the Guarani People's Assembly in Bolivia, and the Association for the Development of the Peruvian Jungle (*Asociacion Interétnica de la Selva Peruana*, AIDESEP) in

Peru. This enhanced indigenous peoples' protagonism takes place in the context of major international concern about indigenous issues, represented by the ILO 169 Agreement, among other international statements (López and Küper, 2002). The role of the media should not be overlooked, especially that of the Internet, in the sharing of experiences and in the articulation of programs that defend indigenous peoples' interests.

New National Legal Provisions

Legal provisions have been modified, opening up positive trends toward linguistic diversity and its educational impact (Moya, 1999). In Bolivia, the 1994 constitutional reform recognized the multiethnic and pluricultural character of the nation. The 1994 *Educational Reform Law* institutionalized intercultural education for the entire education system and IBE for all students who speak an indigenous language. The *Popular Participation Law* and the *Decentralization Law* complement the educational reform law and strive for administrative decentralization. In Ecuador, the 1992 Constitution established Spanish as the official language, and adds "Quechua and other aboriginal languages are an integral part of national culture" (art. 1). Regarding education, it declares "... in areas where indigenous populations are predominant, the main language to be used in education will be Quechua or the language of the respective culture; Spanish will be used as intercultural relations language" (art. 27). Also, in 1992, Ecuador's *Education Law* was reformed, granting DINEIB technical, administrative, and financial autonomy to develop IBE.

In Peru, the 1993 Constitution establishes that every person has the right to an ethnic and cultural identity. It also asserts that the state recognizes and protects the nation's ethnic and cultural plurality, as well as "promotes Bilingual Intercultural Education in accordance with the characteristics of each area, preserving the diverse cultural and linguistic expressions in the country" (art. 17). The 1993 Constitution also declares Spanish as an official language, along with Quechua, Aymara, and other aboriginal languages in the areas in which they are predominant (art. 48). To a similar end, the 2003 Aboriginal Languages Protection and Dissemination Law (*Ley de Preservación y Difusión de las Lenguas Aborígenes*) declares as official languages, in the areas in which they are predominant, Quechua, Aymara, and the aboriginal languages accounted for in the map of "Linguistic and Cultural Patrimony of Peru, Linguistic Families and Peruvian Languages." The law places the Ministry of Education in charge of updating the said map. Likewise, it affirms that the denominations and the toponymy of indigenous languages will be promoted and preserved. The 2002

Bilingual Intercultural Education Law (*Ley para la Educación Bilingüe Intercultural*) entrusts the Ministry of Education with incorporating, by appointment or contract, indigenous teaching staff into educational institutions (art. 4). The law also obliges the ministry to promote the elaboration and employment of course outlines and curricular content that reflect the nation's ethnic and cultural diversity (art. 5). Likewise, it asserts that the state will make a priority of promoting indigenous peoples' access to state and privately owned social communication media, to ensure the development and the preservation of the nation's cultural diversity (art. 7). The 2003 General Law of Education (*Ley General de Educación*) establishes that Bilingual Intercultural Education should be offered in the entire education system. This would guarantee the pupils the use of their mother tongue for learning, the teaching of Spanish as a second language, as well as the subsequent learning of foreign languages (art. 20).

Advances in Language Planning Research

Statistical and cartographic work in the Andes has proven to be of crucial importance to political decision-making and linguistic planning. Two contributions stand out in this field: *The Linguistic Atlas of Peru* (Chirinos, 2001) and the guide and maps of plurilingual Bolivia (Albó, 1995). In addition to the wealth of data presented, these two studies offer interpretations of Andean sociolinguistic situations and yield orientations for planners and educators. Regarding research in Andean sociolinguistics, Cerrón-Palomino (2003) examines Spanish in contact with Quechua and Aymara, analyzing borrowing and transference phenomena. Sichra (2003) analyzes Cochabamba Quechua variants, and cases of code-switching between Quechua and Spanish. A series of papers on Quechua sociolinguistics was published in a special issue of the *International Journal of the Sociology of Language* (King and Hornberger, 2004). Howard's (2007) research offers empirical data proving that linguistic contact effects (code-mixing, code-switching) have a permanent presence in everyday interactions. In general, new data from recent research indicate that the multilingual subject makes diversified and flexible use of his/her linguistic repertoire to represent, identify, and relate himself/herself with those in his/her surroundings.

Concerning the research on *bilingual language acquisition*, Sanchez's work (2003) focuses on the issue of interference and convergence in the functional features associated with the direct object system among Quechua–Spanish bilingual children. It provides a formal account of the linguistic mechanisms that operate in cases of syntactic cross-linguistic influence. It further postulates that this interference plays a role in the creation of syntactic changes, and suggests that convergence "delineates the conditions under which a fusion of functional features takes place in the bilingual mind" (p. 1). Attention is drawn to the following phenomena found among the results: (i) in bilingual Quechua: SVO word order (instead of the canonical SOV word order), dropping of the accusative marker –*ta*, emergence of an indefinite determiner; (ii) in bilingual Spanish: gender-neutral specification of clitics and the emergence of null objects as continuing topics; (iii) in Quechua–Spanish bilinguals: clitics and determiners that are affected by functional convergence. The originality of this study rests on its contribution to the debate on bilingual language acquisition and on syntactic acquisition in children. It is also distinctive for the data it acquired in the Andean region where Spanish is in contact with Amerindian languages.

Other studies deal with IBE programs: Muñoz (1997) and Albó and Anaya (2004) show the evolution of a Bolivian project that developed into state policy; King (2004) on Ecuador, focused on the IBE Saraguro local development; López (2002) confirms, on observing the Peruvian context, initial IBE changes in rural bilingual schools. From a broader perspective, in López's (1998) review, indigenous children participating in those programs exhibit better linguistic competencies in their first language (Hornberger, 2003). They also show better performance in other subjects, better affective balance, and a more active participation in the learning process. In the *ethnographic research* field, there are important conclusions in Aikman's (2003) research on the San José Arakmbut community in south-eastern Peru. Aikman shows the contrast between an intercultural education, which takes place within the school under authoritarian pedagogy and an intercultural education as conceived and demanded by the Arakmbut. The epistemological conceptions of the school and of the community are differentiated: the first (official) model fragments knowledge and strives for progress, whereas the second (Arakmbut) integrates knowledge and strives for balance between the visible and the spiritual worlds. This study illuminates local knowledge, practices, and processes that challenge theoretical developments and question policies for educational change.

IBE Programs of National Scope

The introduction of indigenous languages in schools, as well as the developments of bilingual education projects, have ceased to be isolated initiatives or pilot projects supported, in general, through foreign funding. They have turned into programs that, in varying degrees, are now part of national education systems. The most daring program in the region is that of Bolivia. The chosen perspective is that of maintenance bilingual education (Albó and Anaya, 2004, p. 76). Some of the

Bolivian achievements were realized in a little more than 8 years. Following these reforms, the First Peoples' Educational Boards (CEPO in its Spanish acronym) were formed, which created the conditions for IBE expansion and massive IBE coverage: between 1996 and 2001, IBE reached 2,375 schools and 115,000 indigenous children (Albó and Anaya, 2004, p. 87).

In Ecuador, the IBE program is administratively and financially autonomous. It is carried out from within and with the participation of indigenous peoples through the Bilingual Intercultural Education System Model—MOSEIB. This model, developed by 1993 by the National Bureau for Bilingual Intercultural Education (DINEIB), in coordination with their indigenous organizations, is oriented toward the satisfaction of indigenous peoples' educational needs. Its purpose is to foster the use of indigenous languages as a means of oral and written communication in all areas of knowledge, as well as teaching Spanish as a second language. It should be mentioned that this program is highly significant in the region since it treats IBE as a right of indigenous peoples to organize and manage their children's education (King and Haboud, 2002).

In Peru, the program is run by DINEBI. Two official documents orient their actions. The first, *Bilingual Intercultural Education Policy Outline* (Ministerio de Educación, 2004a), states that its aim is to attain additive bilingualism (for further discussion of additive bilingualism, see May, Bilingual/Immersion Education: What the Research Tells Us, Volume 5), taking into consideration differentiated sociolinguistic contexts. The second document, *National Bilingual Intercultural Education Plan* (Ministerio de Educación, 2004b), indicates that the general objective of IBE is: "to contribute to the achievement of educational quality and equity while offering an education which considers diversity as a resource capable of generating educational proposals and experiences, at all levels and modalities of the system." Some of the program's achievements as of 2004 include: reaching around 127,000 indigenous children; training over 6,300 bilingual teachers; preparing and publishing textbooks in indigenous languages in communications and mathematics; and preparing materials and a handbook in support of teaching Spanish as a second language.

WORK IN PROGRESS

The political empowerment of indigenous languages is a work in progress. Let us consider some recent symbolic shifts. Quechua is the first language of Hilaria Supa and Maria Sumire, who are from rural Cuzco. Recently they were elected to Peru's Congress. These women have engaged in speaking to the legislature in Quechua, a move that is meant to bring visibility to Andean culture and to gain public space for a secularly discriminated language. This symbolic gesture, which irritated most members of the Congress and forced them to hire translators, is symptomatic of changes in the political and cultural arena (*El Comercio*, Peru, August 9, 2006; *The Economist*, August 17, 2006). Also, Google recently launched a Quechua version of its search engine, and Microsoft, in agreement with the Peruvian Ministry of Education, translated its Windows and Office software into Quechua. The formal introduction of this material took place in a high school in Pisac, a village near Cuzco and the former Inca capital, where the students already had begun to use these programs in their mother tongue (*El Comercio*, Peru, June 17, 2006; *The Economist*, August 17, 2006). Bolivia has followed this example and further included the Aymara language. In the same vein, some canonical works, such as *Le petit prince* or *Don Quijote*, have been translated into Quechua. The Quechua edition of *Don Quijote*, translated by Demetrio Tupac Yupanqui, is the first translation of this work into an Amerindian language. During the book's presentation at the *Casa de América de Madrid*, it was emphasized that the first chair of Quechua was created in Peru in 1570, 2 years before a chair of Dutch and 4 years before a chair of English. All these political gestures are contributing slowly to changing the prejudices, opinions, and racist opinions about indigenous languages.

A law that modifies the penal code on discrimination was recently passed in Peru (August 9, 2006). The purpose of this law is to counteract racism and exclusion for linguistic reasons. The modification explicitly includes a penalty of up to 3 years in prison for those who discriminate "for reasons of race, religion, sex, genetic factors, age, disability, language, ethnic, cultural and indumentary identity, political opinion, or of any character or economic condition, with the purpose of depriving or impairing the recognition, enjoyment or exercise of the rights of the person" (art. 1). In Bolivia, the recently elected president, Evo Morales, has announced that all Bolivian civil servants will have 2 years to learn an indigenous language to keep their jobs. In this way the state will become an inclusive entity and also a representative of those who have been secularly excluded. Likewise, the Bolivian state has decided to give indigenous people access to careers in the military, access that previously had been prohibited.

Another work in progress is the formulation of a new constitution in Bolivia, in view of a possible state restructuring and national refoundation, based on the principles of equality and nondiscrimination. This has stimulated the elaboration of a *Linguistic Rights and Politics Law* project, currently in review. This legal project aims to declare all existing languages in Bolivia as the "Intangible Historic and Cultural Oral Patrimony" of the Bolivian state. Its objective is to recognize, protect, promote, and regulate the individual and collective linguistic rights of all Bolivians. Similarly, in Ecuador, initiatives have emerged to incorporate the linguistic rights of indigenous peoples and nationalities into the legal order of the Ecuadorian state. A proposal has been elaborated, with the participation of UNESCO, called the "Operative plan of the rights of the nationalities and indigenous peoples of Ecuador." This plan aims to create the Institute of Ancestral Languages, which will promote scientific research on languages as well as the design of policies directed toward promoting the use of indigenous languages in radio-diffusion, the press, publications, cinema, theatre and performances, and sound and image production (http://www.ildis.org.ec/old/planddhh/plan02te.htm).

Another issue being discussed is the relationship between *gender, ethnicity, and education*. Research papers edited by Sichra (2004) serve as an introduction to this debate, and to the study of the symbolic construction of gender in historic and social contexts (see also Pavlenko and Piller, Language Education and Gender, Volume 1). This type of research contributes to the understanding of the double marginalization suffered by many people in the region who are both women and indigenous. The subjects of *orality and writing* have also been under discussion recently. The book edited by López and Jung (1998) includes sociolinguistic studies on reading and writing within Amerindian cultures. Zavala's (2002) research focuses on the presence and effects of writing in an Andean community. Some of the contributions gathered in Zavala, Niño-Murcia, and Ames (2004) deal with literacy in Quechua-speaking Andean areas, and of their connections to education. The multiple use of literacy in a communal and familiar setting is seldom accounted for by the school, which usually focuses on the decontextualized development of literate abilities.

One of the instruments devised to facilitate debate on language policy and education issues is the organization of Latin American IBE congresses. Six of these meetings have already taken place: Ciudad de Guatemala, 1995; Santa Cruz de la Sierra, Bolivia, 1996; Quito, Ecuador, 1998; Asunción, Paraguay, 2000; Lima, Peru, 2002, Santiago de Chile, 2004; and finally, Cochabamba, Bolivia, 2006 (http://viieib.proeibandes.org/conclusiones.html). A recently published document offers a review and summary of these events (Programa de Educación Bilingüe Intercultural, 2004). The Lima conference proceedings are already available (Zariquiey, 2003). The importance of these congresses lies in the participation of officers from the Ministry of Education, along with indigenous leaders, academics, experts, and others responsible for IBE policy design. They met with the purpose of producing and exchanging knowledge that will transform teaching practices while also having a wider impact on the construction of multilingual and intercultural societies.

PROBLEMS AND DIFFICULTIES

Ethnic, cultural, and linguistic differences often naturalize profound social inequalities. There is still strong resistance to and prejudice against the public use of indigenous languages (see also May, Language Education, Pluralism and Citizenship, Volume 1, and McCarty, Language Education Planning and Policies by and for Indigenous Peoples, Volume 1). Usually efforts to revitalize languages are neither accompanied by an effective recognition of the human and collective rights of indigenous peoples, nor do they tend to bring about concrete reforms that make way for social equality. Indigenous communities of the Amazon basin, for instance, are denouncing oil companies for the pollution of river water, which is causing serious physical and mental health problems, including cancer and genetic deformities. There is much work to be done to create the economic and political conditions that favor the development of a social bilingualism in the Andes.

Some legal provisions for native languages exist, but they are usually not implemented (cf., Skutnabb-Kangas, Human Rights and Language Policy in Education, Volume 1). According to an established custom that dates back to the colonial era, laws are accepted, but not adhered to. To break with this tradition is an Andean political challenge.

In addition, existing research on language variation, language contact, and sociolinguistic processes is insufficient. Further research is needed as a condition for coherent and adequate language planning.

Regarding the use of languages in education, an indigenous first language tends to be used as an instrument of learning, but its development is seldom reinforced and almost no discussion about the language itself takes place (López, 2002, pp. 159–164). It is not used to cultivate other dimensions of the culture it belongs to (Albó and Anaya, 2004, pp. 161–168). Another problem relates to materials written in some indigenous languages that have not developed alphabetic writing or whose alphabet has not been consolidated in a common written norm. Linguistically based selections turn out to be arbitrary or strange for prospective readers.

Even though it is true that IBE in the Andean region has been achieving official recognition within educational systems, its social legitimation is still an ongoing task. Another unresolved problem, affecting all programs, is the teaching of Spanish as a second language. As reports of López (2003) and Albó and Anaya (2004, pp. 171–181) indicate, official Latin American schools cannot speak of any major success in this task. Other problems are posed by budget cuts, by conflicts between pedagogical advisors and teachers, and by filling teaching positions with personnel untrained in IBE strategies.

FUTURE DIRECTIONS

The implicit imposition of Spanish as the state's only language in the Andes has been questioned and challenged during the past decades. The recent top-down constitutional provisions and laws have opened new spaces of negotiation between the indigenous organizations and different state sectors. These advances could be directed toward a more pluralistic, interactive, and creative language policy, which would help build responses in accordance with global and local contexts. A key issue in this process is the provision for popular participation, such as the Bolivian First Peoples' Educational Councils. From the time of their inception, these councils have been able to defend IBE's perspective when the Government had doubts about its importance (Albó and Anaya, 2004, p. 259). A process of decentralization, delegation, and devolution of power to all agents of cultural policy and educational activity is of utmost importance. Only then can a linguistic plan be generated.

It is crucial to acknowledge socio-educative and linguistic circumstances before making decisions on language policy and education. It is still necessary to promote new studies about the linguistic reality in the Andes, about the situation of rural and urban bilingualism and language contact, and about the effectiveness of indigenous language-in-education implementation.

From a Latin American perspective, intercultural proposals aim at changing the conditions and modalities in which exchanges take place. That is, they are directed toward a profound social and state transformation. As an ethical-political category, emerging from indigenous peoples' demands and projects, *interculturality* can be defined as an interlocutive modality of interactions and exchanges—between individuals and/or collective instances—consisting in negotiating, arriving at agreements, and making decisions to create basic material and symbolic conditions for the existence of pluralist societies and inclusive states. Real dialogue could take place horizontally; and, mutually enriching experiences could take the place of exclusion and violence. Interculturality is the proposed axis of educational systems in the Andean region, and in many Latin American countries (Godenzzi, 1996; Hornberger, 2000). The challenge is to make this concept operative in a creative way so that it will not remain as an empty rhetorical declaration (García, 2004, 2005). Rather it should transform social interactions and pedagogical practices. A theoretical–methodological instrument was elaborated by Walsh (2001), but needs to be adapted to the particular situation of each specific context. To accomplish this project, specialists need to continue doing research on indigenous categorizations (Valenzuela, 2000), on ways of transmitting knowledge and on the learning processes of indigenous peoples (Stobart and Howard, 2002; see also McCarty, Language Education Planning and Policies by and for Indigenous Peoples, Volume 1). The aim is to make intercultural inclusion not only social but also epistemic.

In the IBE domain, some actions have to be reinforced: to generate a bottom up form of IBE (López, 2002, p. 169); to consolidate the passage of IBE from project to state policy; to develop interculturality for all; and to decentralize educational systems (Albó and Anaya, 2004, p. 264; López and Küper, 2002, pp. 63–68).

In sum, a future language policy agenda in the Andes will include the effective officialization and revitalization of indigenous languages (Hornberger and King, 2002), the development of a new public idea about language and its diversity, the task of sensitizing public opinion to overcome racial and linguistic discrimination, and political and economic measures aiming toward social, ethnic, and cultural equity. The fulfillment of these points in the agenda will enhance participation in a plural society in which everyone recognizes the right to cultural creation and democratic coexistence. Therefore, a very well understood and implemented language policy could become an important tool for building the foundation upon which to rethink and renew Andean public life.

See Also: Tove Skutnabb-Kangas: Human Rights and Language Policy in Education (Volume 1); Teresa L. McCarty: Language Education Planning and Policies by and for Indigenous Peoples (Volume 1); Stephen May: Language Education, Pluralism and Citizenship (Volume 1); Inge Sichra: Language Diversity and Indigenous Literacy in the Andes (Volume 2); Virginia Zavala: Teacher Training in Bilingual Education in Peru (Volume 4); Luis Enrique López and Inge Sichra: Intercultural Bilingual Education Among Indigenous Peoples in Latin America (Volume 5); Tove Skutnabb-Kangas: Language Rights and Bilingual Education (Volume 5); Nancy H. Hornberger: Continua of Biliteracy (Volume 9); Rainer Enrique Hamel: Indigenous Language Policy and Education in Mexico (Volume 1); Rainer Enrique Hamel: Bilingual Education for Indigenous Communities in Mexico (Volume 5)

REFERENCES

Aikman, S.: 2003, *La educación indígena en Sudamérica. Interculturalidad y bilingüismo en Madre de Dios, Perú*, Instituto de Estudios Peruanos, Lima. (Versión original: Aikman, Sh.: 1999, *Intercultural Education and Literacy*, John Benjamins Publishing Company, Amsterdam/Philadelphia.)
Albó, X.: 1995, *Bolivia plurilingüe. Guía para planificadores y educadores*, UNICEF and CIPCA, La Paz.

Albó, X. and Anaya, A.: 2004, *Niños alegres, libres, expresivos. La audacia de la educación intercultural bilingüe en Bolivia*, UNICEF, CIPCA Cuadernos de Investigación 58, La Paz, Bolivia.

Cerrón-Palomino, R.: 2003, *Castellano andino. Aspectos sociolingüísticos, pedagógicos y gramaticales*, Pontificia Universidad Católica del Perú, Cooperación Técnica Alemana GTZ, Lima.

Chirinos, A.: 2001, *Atlas lingüístico del Perú*, Centro de Estudios Regionales Andinos Bartolomé de Las Casas, Cusco/Ministerio de Educación, Lima.

Fell, E-M.: 1996, 'Problematique de l'éducation bilingue dans les pays andins', in *Hommage des hispanistes français à Henry Bonneville*, Société des Hispanistes Français de l'Enseignement Supérieur, Poitiers 191–204.

García, M.: 2004, 'Rethinking Bilingual Education in Peru: Intercultural Politics, State Policy and Indigenous Rights', *International Journal of Bilingual Education and Bilingualism* 7(5), 348–367.

García, M.: 2005, *Making Indigenous Citizens. Identities, Education, and Multicultural Development in Peru*, Stanford University Press, Stanford, California.

Godenzzi, J. (ed.): 1996, *Educación e Interculturalidad en los Andes y la Amazonía*, Centro de Estudios Regionales Andinos Bartolomé de Las Casas, Cuzco.

Hornberger, N.: 2000, 'Bilingual education policy and practice in the Andes: Ideological paradox and intercultural possibility', *Anthropology and Education Quarterly* 31(2), 173–201.

Hornberger, N.: 2003, 'La enseñanza de y en quechua en el PEEB', in I. Jung and L.E. López (eds.), *Abriendo la escuela. Lingüística aplicada a la enseñanza de lenguas*, Ediciones Morata, Madrid/PROEIB, Cochabamba/InWEnt, Bonn, 160–181.

Hornberger, N. and King, K.: 2002, 'Reversing Quechua Language Shift in South America', in J.A. Fishman (ed.), *Can Threatened Languages Be Saved? Reversing Language Shift, Revisited: A 21st Century Perspective*, Multilingual Matters, Clevedon, 166–194.

Hornberger, N. and López, L.: 1998, 'Policy, possibility and paradox: Indigenous multilingualism and education in Peru and Bolivia', in J. Cenoz and F. Genesee (eds.), *Beyond Bilingualism: Multilingualism and Multilingual Education*, Multilingual Matters, Clevedon, England, 206–242.

Howard, R.: 2007, *Por los linderos de la lengua. Ideologías lingüísticas en los Andes*, Pontificia Universidad Católica del Perú/Instituto Francés de Estudios Andinos/ Instituto de Estudios Peruanos, Lima.

Itier, C.: 1992, 'Cuzqueñistas y foráneos: Las resistencias a la normalización de la escritura del quechua', in J.C. Godenzzi (ed.), *El Quechua en debate. Ideología, normalización y enseñanza*, Centro de Estudios Regionales Andinos Bartolomé de Las Casas, Cuzco, 85–93.

King, K.: 2004, 'Language Policy and Local Planning in South America: New Directions for Enrichment Bilingual Education in the Andes', *International Journal of Bilingual Education and Bilingualism* 7(5), 334–347.

King, K. and Haboud, M.: 2002, 'Language Planning and Policy in Ecuador', *Current Issues in Language Planning* 3(4), 359–424.

King, K. and Hornberger, N.: 2004, 'Introduction: Why a Special Issue on Quechua?', *International Journal of the Sociology of Language* (special issue on Quechua sociolinguistics edited by K. King and N. Hornberger) 167, 1–8.

López, L.: 1998, 'La eficacia y validez de lo obvio: lecciones aprendidas desde la evaluación de procesos educativos bilingües', *Revista Iberoamericana de Educación* 17, 51–89.

López, L.: 2002, *A ver, a ver... ¿Quién quiere salir a la pizarra? ¿Jumasti? ¿Jupasti? Cambios iniciales en la escuela rural bilingüe peruana*, Programa Especial de Mejoramiento de la Calidad de la Educación Peruana, Ministerio de Educación del Perú, Lima.

López, L.: 2003, '¿Dónde estamos con la enseñanza del castellano como segunda lengua en América Latina?', in I. Jung and L.E. López (eds.), *Abriendo la escuela. Lingüística aplicada a la enseñanza de lenguas*, Ediciones Morata, Madrid/ PROEIB, Cochabamba/InWEnt, Bonn, 39–71.

López, L. and Jung, I.: 1998, *Sobre las huellas de la voz. Sociolingüística de la oralidad y la escritura*, Ediciones Morata, Madrid.

López, L. and Küper, W.: 2002, *La educación intercultural bilingüe en América Latina: Balance y perspectivas*, GTZ (Informe educativo 94), Eschborn, Alemania.

Luykx, A.: 1999, *The Citizen Factory. Schooling and Cultural Practice in Bolivia, State*, University of New York, New York.

Mannheim, B.: 1991, *The Language of the Inka since the European Invasion*, University of Texas Press, Austin.

Ministerio de Educación: 2004a, *Lineamientos de política de la Educación Bilingüe Intercultural*, Dirección Nacional de Educación Bilingüe Intercultural, Lima.

Ministerio de Educación: 2004b, *Plan Nacional de Educación Bilingüe Intercultural*, Dirección Nacional de Educación Bilingüe Intercultural, Lima.

Moya, R.: 1999, 'Reformas educativas e interculturalidad en América Latina', *Revista Iberoamericana de Educación* 17, 105–187.

Muñoz, H.: 1997, *De proyecto a política de estado. La educación intercultural bilingüe en Bolivia, 1993*, Universidad Pedagógica Nacional, Oaxaca, México/PROEIB Andes, Cochabamba, Bolivia/UNICEF, La Paz, Bolivia.

Programa de Educación Intercultural Bilingüe: 2004, *Memorias de los Congresos latinoamericanos de Educación Intercultural Bilingüe*, Programa de Educación Intercultural Bilingüe, Ministerio de Educación del Gobierno de Chile, Santiago de Chile/PROEIB Andes, Cochabamba.

Sánchez, L.: 2003, *Quechua-Spanish Bilingualism. Interference and convergence in functional categories*, John Benjamins Publishing Company, Amsterdam/Philadelphia.

Sichra, I.: 2003, *La vitalidad del quechua: lengua y sociedad en dos provincias de Cochabamba*, Plural Editores, La Paz, Bolivia.

Sichra, I. (ed.): 2004, *Género, etnicidad y educación en América Latina*, Ediciones Morata, Madrid/InWent, Bonn/PROEIB Andes and Tantanakuy, Cochabamba.

Stobart, H. and Howard, R. (eds.): 2002, *Knowledge and learning in the Andes. Ethnographic perspectives*, University Press, Liverpool.

Torero, A.: 2002, *Idiomas de los Andes. Lingüística e historia*, Instituto Francés de Estudios Andinos y Editorial Horizonte, Lima.

Trapnell, L.: 1996, *Brought together: Informal and formal education in an indigenous programme in the Amazon Basin*, Internacional Jubilee Conference in Guovdageaidnu, Sami Education Council, Norway.

Valenzuela, P.: 2000, 'Major Categories in Shipibo Ethnobiological Taxonomy', *Anthropological Linguistics*, 42(1), 1–36.

Walsh, C.: 2001, *La interculturalidad en la Educación*, Dirección Nacional de Educación Bilingüe Intercultural, Lima.

Zariquiey, R. (ed.): 2003, *Realidad multilingüe y desafío intercultural. Ciudadanía, política y educación*, Actas del V Congreso Latinoamericano de Educación Intercultural Bilingüe, Ministerio de Educación del Perú, Pontificia Universidad Católica del Perú and Cooperación Técnica Alemana GTZ, Lima.

Zavala, V.: 2002, *Desencuentros con la escritura. Escuela y comunidad en los Andes peruanos*, Red para el Desarrollo de las Ciencias Sociales en el Perú, Lima.

Zavala, V., Mercedes Niño-Murcia, M., and Ames (eds.): Patricia 2004, *Escritura y sociedad: Nuevas perspectivas teóricas y etnográficas*, Red para el Desarrollo de las Ciencias Sociales en el Perú, Lima.

BARBARA BURNABY

LANGUAGE POLICY AND EDUCATION IN CANADA

INTRODUCTION

This sketch of Canadian language legislation and policies touches on background information, French and English as official languages, official and minority language policies for immigrants, and policies on Aboriginal languages.

Canada, a large country with a relatively small population (30 million), has a parliamentary democracy. Created legally in 1867, it now has ten provinces and three territories. Inter alia, the federal government has jurisdiction over Aboriginal matters and the territories, the provinces over education; responsibility for immigration is shared.

In about 1500 A.D., Aboriginal people lived across what is now Canada, speaking about 450 languages and dialects from 11 language families. Immigration, starting with colonization by Britain and France, has since increased the population and changed its ethnic or racial mixture. Although immigration from northern and western Europe predominated earlier, the proportion of immigrants from other continents has increased, particularly since the 1960s. In 2001, 59% of the population reported English as mother tongue, 23% French, less than 1% Aboriginal languages, and 17% other languages (Statistics Canada, 97F0007XCB2001001).

French and English as Official Languages

Struggles first between France and Britain, then Francophones and Anglophones dominate Canada's recorded history. In the 19th century, Canadian legal rights for the 'English' and 'French' populations focussed on religion rather than language (Neatby in Commissioner of Official Languages, 1992, pp. v–ix). Legislation specifically on language was rare. However, in the early 20th century, increased secularism, industrialization, national attention on Canada's role in the British Empire, and massive immigration encouraged a movement to 'Anglo-conformity', especially through legislated use of English as the language in schools in most provinces. Francophones in Québec were isolated in a French-language, church-run school system and in the social and political use of French in some areas of Québec. Only superficially did the Canadian federal government recognize the constitutionally equal status

S. May and N. H. Hornberger (eds), Encyclopedia of Language and Education,
2nd Edition, Volume 1: Language Policy and Political Issues in Education, 331–341.
©2010 Springer Science+Business Media LLC.

of French with English in parliament, in federal courts and in the legislature and courts of Québec.

After 1945, industrialization, immigration, and a low birth rate among Francophones threatened the critical mass of French, even in Québec (Neatby in Commissioner of Official Languages, 1992, p. vii). Most non-French immigrants to Québec chose English as their second language, English being the dominant language of large business in Québec, centred in Montreal. Being ethnically Québécois and unilingually Francophone was a severe economic disadvantage up to the early 1960s (Wardhaugh, 1983, pp. 74–80). In the 1960s, Francophones in Québec, through the 'Quiet Revolution' movement, acted to gain more control. In 1963, the Québec government created a ministry of education, replacing the parochial education system.

Such pressures moved the federal government to take the constitutionally equal status of the French language seriously. It established the Royal Commission on Bilingualism and Biculturalism (1963–1971), which made an elaborate study of political, cultural and economic use of all languages in Canada except the Aboriginal languages. The impact of its research began in 1964 with language training for public servants, leading, in 1973, to measures to make English and French equitably the languages of work in the federal civil service (Beaty, 1989, p. 186; Commissioner of Official Languages, 1992, pp. 14–17).

From 1967, some provinces, anticipating the commission's impact, changed their education acts towards more use of French as language of instruction (Commissioner of Official Languages, 1992, pp. 14–15). In a Montreal suburb, a group of Anglophone parents in 1965 persuaded a school board to teach their children through the medium of French so that the children would learn it as a second language faster and more effectively (Lambert and Tucker, 1972). This launched the now popular 'French immersion' programmes across the country. In virtually every part of the country, various versions of these programmes are now a significant part of Canadian public education (see Lapkin, 1998; May, Bilingual/Immersion Education: What the Research Tells Us, Volume 5).

The main outcome of the Royal Commission's Report was the *Official Languages Act* of 1969, making English and French Canada's official languages. In addition to declaring that English and French are to have 'equality of status and equal rights and privileges' for all the purposes of the Parliament and Government of Canada, the Act specifically imposes duties on all federal institutions to provide their services in either English or French: in the National Capital Region and in such 'bilingual districts' as might be subsequently designated, at their head offices, and in any other locations where there was 'significant demand' for such services. The Act also created the position of

Commissioner of Official Languages to oversee its implementation and generally act as official languages ombudsman (Beaty, 1989, pp. 185–186).

Beaty summarizes the main programmes supporting the *Official Languages Act* as encouraging 'a more general climate of respect and support for Canada's official languages in other jurisdictions and in Canadian society as a whole' by:

1. supporting minority groups [English in Québec and French elsewhere] in their attempts to achieve provincial recognition of their legal rights and their special linguistic needs
2. fostering and helping to finance minority language education...
3. giving similar financial encouragement to the effective learning of English and French as a second language country-wide and
4. supporting the efforts of national, private and voluntary organizations to develop their own capacity to do business in both official languages (Beaty, 1989, pp. 190–191).

However, implementation of various provisions early on involved controversy, for example, the choice of language to be used in air traffic control.

In 1970–1971, the federal government began its Official Languages in Education (OLE) Program. Education being a provincial responsibility, the federal government could not legislate on it directly but could encourage compliance by offering funding. Following the Royal Commission's recommendation that the federal government support the provinces in providing English education for Anglophones in Québec and French education for Francophones in the other provinces, and in improving second official language instruction, the OLE has made transfer payments to provinces, monitored by the Commissioner of Official Languages. Although the enrolment in English schooling in Québec and French schooling elsewhere has not changed substantially since 1971, numbers of children in second official language programmes have, especially French immersion programmes (Canadian Education Association, 1992, p. 3; Canadian Parents for French, 2004).

The province of New Brunswick declared itself bilingual in 1969, and most provinces legislated more status for French in the next few years. A series of actions in Québec, especially relating to parents' rights to have their children educated in languages other than French, provoked controversy. Separatism became a driving force in the province, but the Québec government in 1980 (and in 1995) lost a referendum for a mandate to negotiate 'sovereignty association' (Québec nationalism within the Canadian state) with the federal government (Commissioner of Official Languages, 1992, pp. 9–22; Labrie, 1992, pp. 30–32). In this climate, the nation made a number of efforts in the 1970s to prevent a total rift with Québec.

In 1980, the federal government 'patriated' the constitution, providing a major opportunity for constitutional changes. Canada's constitution was an act of the British Parliament; patriation meant enacting some form of it through the Canadian Parliament. The 1982 *Constitution Act* left the major structure, such as the responsibilities of the federal and provincial governments, the same. It added an amending formula, as well as the *Canadian Charter of Rights and Freedoms*, which included central developments on language since the early 1960s, such as the official language status of English and French for the governments of Canada and New Brunswick. Citizens can now challenge all legislation and policies in court against the *Charter* provisions.

Crucially, Québec did not agree to the *Constitution Act* because of concerns about its amending formula. Despite attempts at resolution, federal relationships remain uneasy, with the inclusion of Québec in the constitution unresolved. As for language in education, the *Act* precipitated many legal actions to align mother-tongue education provisions for Francophone children in English Canada and Anglophone children in Québec with the *Charter* (Foucher, 1985; Martel, 1991). The Commissioner of Official Languages noted recently that only half the students from Francophone minority communities, who are entitled to attend Francophone schools do so (Commissioner of Official Languages, 2003, p. 10). Official second language programmes for Anglophones and Francophones have been relatively uncontroversial. Nevertheless, for example, an ongoing source of tension in Québec has been rulings about the role of English and French on commercial signage.

The evolution of English and French as official languages and languages of education, work, commerce and so forth during the past 40 years provides no perfect model for language relations, especially since it has not yet satisfied either party. However, it has set a certain standard for some other language minorities in the country. The intense negotiations between Québec and the rest of Canada still dominate discussion at the national and provincial levels.

Language Issues for Speakers of Non-Official Languages

Reading official statements, one would scarcely believe that Canadians speak languages other than English and French. Federal statements carefully refer to speakers of non-official languages as other *cultural* groups. However, given the important role of immigration in Canada, to say nothing of the special position of the Aboriginal peoples, non-official languages are very much in evidence. This section discusses language issues for speakers of non-official languages other than

Aboriginal ones. It refers to 'immigrants' even though non-official language issues often continue well into the second and third generations after immigration.

Official Language Training for those Who Speak Neither Official Language

Canadian federal legislation covers official languages for those who speak an official language already; no federal legislation even suggests that speakers of neither English nor French have the *right* to support in learning one of those languages. However, some programmes address language for residents of Canada who do not speak either official language. Federal policy on OLE for Anglophones or Francophones refers almost entirely to children's education, but official language training for non-official language groups mainly targets adults, largely because the federal government strongly links immigration to the labour force.

The *Official Languages Act* (1969) makes no provisions for the learning of official languages by residents of Canada who do not speak either language (well). However, in 1971, the federal government declared itself by policy multicultural. Clearly aimed at calming backlash among non-English and French groups over the declaration of official languages, the multiculturalism policy pledged to promote respect and support for all of Canada's languages and cultures. The original policy stated that 'the government will continue to assist immigrants to acquire at least one of Canada's official languages in order to become full participants in Canadian society' (Saouab, 1993, p. 4). The policy passed through various stages, none including direct support for official language training for immigrants, and evolved into the present *Multiculturalism Act* (1988), which mainly fosters non-English and French cultures, antiracism and affirmative action in support of visible minorities.

Since about 1970, the *Immigration Act* has increasingly made knowing one official language an advantage in admissibility for certain classes of immigrants, but only some applicants are assessed this way. To become a Canadian citizen applicants must demonstrate a 'reasonable' knowledge (undefined) of either official language. From the early 1970s to the late 1980s, the federal department responsible for the *Citizenship Act* made agreements with most provinces for partial funding of provincial language and citizenship training for adults.

However, the federal government emphasized more the economic impact of immigration. The federal agency responsible for employment included language training for immigrants 'bound for the labour force' under its large programme of employment (re)training from the late 1960s to about 1990. The provinces' community colleges did the training (to accommodate education as a provincial responsibility) but federal officials chose the students. This programme provided about 24 weeks of full-time training with a training allowance. Controversy surrounded this programme, especially concerning decisions on who was destined for the labour force. Meanwhile, since the 1960s, provinces, local authorities, and non-governmental organizations (NGOs) have provided a wide variety of language training to immigrants.

Since 1991, the employment-related federal programme has been replaced by one serving immigrants who do not yet have Canadian citizenship, regardless of their labour market intentions. This includes individual assessment against nation-wide language standards, counselling and recommendations on local programmes. Canadian Language Benchmarks and Standards linguistiques canadiens, assessments of English and French language ability, including task-based level descriptors, provide the standards for assessment and curriculum (Centre for Canadian Language Benchmarks, 2005). Private and public institutions bid annually for contracts to provide training, either generic or targeted (e.g. for immigrants with low levels of education). Childminding and transportation may be provided, but no training allowances. Criticisms of this programme include that: newcomers who have obtained Canadian citizenship are not eligible; federal authorities have left provinces and NGOs with the main language training burden; and the 1-year contract bids stress the bidding agencies (Burnaby, 1992, 1996).

ESL for schoolchildren is simpler than adult programmes only in being delivered almost exclusively by school boards. In areas where there is little immigration (e.g. the Atlantic provinces), immigrant children may be unevenly served, if at all; however, in high-immigration regions, they usually get at least minimal attention, such as special classes, withdrawal from regular classes for part of the day or sensitization of regular teachers to their needs (Ashworth, 1992, pp. 36–40). There are no bilingual programmes to help orient children to Canadian schooling. Some part-time classes for immigrant women have been funded as 'parents and preschoolers' programmes so that the children get some language training too. A series of articles in *The Globe and Mail* (September, 2004) by Andrew Duffy indicated increasing stress points for non-English speaking students in English Canadian schools as well as some extraordinary programmes to address their needs (Duffy, 2004).

Teaching of Non-Official Languages as Ancestral Languages

Clearly Canada greatly values its official languages. But what of the value of other languages that immigrants bring to Canada? In the era of greatest Anglophone power, the system viewed languages other than

English with suspicion, and encouraged immigrants, especially children, to forget their mother tongues. From the nineteenth century, some immigrant communities organized and funded non-official language classes for their children. Until the early twentieth century, when provincial education acts were changed to prevent them, there were some publicly supported bilingual schools. Some religious groups struggled long into this century against compulsory English schooling (Ashworth, 1992, p. 40). Some immigrant groups have continued to fund private multilingual schools or classes in non-official languages.

The *Official Languages Act* of 1969 provoked a climate of linguistic uncertainty for non-official languages; the 1971 policy of multiculturalism hinted at some recognition of them. In 1977, under that policy, the federal government created the Cultural Enrichment Program. It included support for the teaching of non-official languages, primarily to children of communities where the target language was a 'heritage language' (the mother tongue or ancestral language of the children). Extensive and vitriolic resistance to the establishment of heritage language classes at public expense developed (Cummins and Danesi, 1990, Chapter 3; d'Anglejan and De Koninck, 1992, pp. 100–101; Fleras and Elliott, 1992, pp. 155–159). Since 1977, some programmes have been associated with the schools and at least partially publicly funded, and new ones have been created in the schools, but most remain non-academically recognized add-ons (Ashworth, 1992; Canadian Education Association, 1991; d'Anglejan and De Koninck, 1992; Toohey, 1992). Although the multiculturalism policy and *Act* encouraged learning of official languages, heritage language programmes were never associated with *fiscal* support for official language training programmes (i.e. linked to issues of children at risk concerning the learning of English or French).

Language Policies for Aboriginal Peoples

Official policy has largely considered Aboriginal peoples and their languages as outside the debates outlined earlier. Since Confederation in 1867, Aboriginal people—'Indians' in the *British North America Act* of 1867 and 'Eskimos' by a court ruling in 1939—were constitutionally the federal government's responsibility for all services. The Royal Commission on Bilingualism and Biculturalism excluded them on the grounds that their issues were more properly dealt with elsewhere. They have not been included, largely by their own choice, in subsequent definitions of cultural minorities. Administrations kept them isolated from the rest of the population. Such separate treatment left open opportunities for special policies suited to their unique needs; unfortunately, most of these opportunities have been wasted in racist and assimilative ways (National Indian Brotherhood, 1972; Royal Commission on Aboriginal Peoples, 1996).

Comparison of the proportions of mother-tongue speakers of Aboriginal languages among the Aboriginal population from the censuses of 1951 to 2001 dramatically illustrates a decline of Aboriginal languages. In 1951, 87.4% of the Aboriginal population had an Aboriginal language as a mother tongue whereas in 1981 it was 29.3% (Burnaby and Beaujot, 1986, p. 36) and in 2001, it was 21% (Statistics Canada, 97F0011XCB2001048). Clearly, Aboriginal languages in Canada are at great risk (some much more than others).

Although Aboriginal languages were sometimes used in Aboriginal education in the nineteenth and early twentieth centuries, more often draconian Aboriginal education policies forced Aboriginal children to speak English or French in school, even to the extent of severe physical punishment for speaking an Aboriginal language (cf. McCarty, Language Education Planning and Policies by and for Indigenous Peoples, Volume 1). Until about the 1950s, schooling for Aboriginal children was mostly contracted to Christian groups; a later policy moved to integrate all Aboriginal children into provincial schools or, in remote areas, to establish federally run schools. Today, those federal schools are nominally run by local Aboriginal authorities. Since the 1960s, Aboriginal languages have increasingly been taught in Aboriginal and provincial schools as subjects of instruction (Assembly of First Nations, 1990; Kirkness and Bowman, 1992). In addition, Aboriginal languages have been introduced recently as medium of instruction up to the third grade in some schools in the territories and Québec, where the children begin school speaking only or mainly their Aboriginal language. Aboriginal language immersion programmes have begun in several southern communities, where the children start school speaking only or mainly an official language. Nine Aboriginal languages have been made official languages in the Northwest Territories, together with English and French, and the new (1999) territory of Nunavut, having declared Inuktitut, Inuinaqtun, French and English as its official languages, is actively developing policies for extensive use of these languages in many domains (Government of Nunavut, 2005). A recent Task Force on Aboriginal Languages and Cultures (2005) has surveyed a variety of aspects of language use among Aboriginal peoples and strongly recommended measures to support Aboriginal language development, including the use of Aboriginal language immersion programmes.

Despite improvements in Aboriginal language programming in schools, Churchill's (1986) findings that policies for indigenous groups cluster at the lower levels of his scale of policy development—in that most programmes are for the youngest children, only for a few years, inadequately funded, and seen to be transitional to fluency in an official language—still stands. Language issues contribute to a continuing gap between Aboriginal children and all other Canadian children in terms of school success. The Office of the Auditor General of Canada (2004) stated: 'We remain concerned that a significant education gap exists between First Nations people living on reserves and the Canadian population as a whole and that the time estimated to close this gap has increased slightly, from about 27 to 28 years' (Section 5.2). Although there are many more Aboriginal languages and culture programmes in the early twenty-first century, current survey data (Burnaby, 2002) give the same impression that Clarke and MacKenzie (1980) found in their study of Aboriginal language programmes—namely, that Aboriginal language programmes give only lip service to pluralism and are actually assimilationist in intent. A significant recent development is the creation of an extensive Aboriginal language and culture curriculum, adopted by Manitoba, Saskatchewan, Alberta, British Columbia and the three territories (Western Canadian Protocol, 2000).

CONCLUSIONS

Canada's largest minority, Francophones, have challenged Canadian Anglo-dominance to the point of constitutional crisis. Smaller linguistic groups unfavourably compare the resources supporting official language services for English and French speakers with those available to them even to learn a first official language, much less enhance their own languages. Aboriginal groups, many of whose languages face extinction, struggle particularly about priorities between language efforts and political and economic recognition. A needs assessment of language resources in the new global order might recommend a reorganization of Canada's language emphases. Much sophisticated thinking in Canada about language policy (e.g. Fettes, 2003; Kymlicka and Patten, 2003) does not seem to be taken very seriously in Canadian language policy development overall, except in the territories.

See Also: Teresa L. McCarty: *Language Education Planning and Policies by and for Indigenous Peoples (Volume 1); Stephen May: Bilingual/Immersion Education: What the Research Tells Us (Volume 5)*

REFERENCES

Ashworth, M.: 1992, 'Views and visions', in B. Burnaby and A. Cumming (eds.), *Socio-Political Aspects of ESL in Canada*, OISE Press, Toronto, 35–49.
Assembly of First Nations: 1990, *Towards Linguistic Justice for First Nations*, Education Secretariat, Assembly of First Nations, Ottawa.
Beaty, S.: 1989, 'A new official languages Act for Canada—Its scope and implications', in P. Pupier and J. Woehrling (eds.), *Language and Law: Proceedings of*

the *First Conference of the International Institute of Comparative Linguistic Law*, Wilson and Lafleur, Montreal, 185–193.

Burnaby, B.: 1992, 'Official language training for adult immigrants in Canada: Features and issues', in B. Burnaby and A. Cumming (eds.), *Socio-Political Aspects of ESL in Canada*, OISE Press, Toronto, 3–34.

Burnaby, B.: 1996, 'Language policies in Canada: An overview', in M. Herriman and B. Burnaby (eds.), *Language Policy in English-Dominant Countries: Six Case Studies*, Multilingual Matters, Clevedon, England.

Burnaby, B.: 2002, *Provincial Governments' Initiatives in Aboriginal Language and Cultural Education*, Department of Indian and Northern Affairs, Ottawa.

Burnaby, B. and Beaujot, R.: 1986, *The Use of Aboriginal Languages in Canada: An Analysis of 1981 Census Data*, Social Trends Analysis Directorate and Native Citizens Directorate, Department of the Secretary of State, Ottawa.

Canadian Education Association: 1991, *Heritage Language Programs in Canadian School Boards*, Canadian Education Association, Toronto.

Canadian Education Association: 1992, *French Immersion Today* (CEA Information Note), Canadian Education Association, Toronto.

Canadian Parents for French: 2004, *The State of French Second Language Education in Canada, 2004*, Canadian Parents for French, Ottawa.

Centre for Canadian Language Benchmarks: Retrieved from www.language.ca, accessed on February 17, 2005, Centre for Canadian Language Benchmarks, Ottawa.

Churchill, S.: 1986, *The Education of Linguistic and Cultural Minorities in the OECD Countries*, Multilingual Matters, Clevedon, England.

Clarke, S. and MacKenzie, M.: 1980, 'Education in the mother tongue: Tokenism versus cultural autonomy in Canadian Indian schools', *Canadian Journal of Anthropology* 1(2), 205–217.

Commissioner of Official Languages: 1992, *Our Two Official Languages Over Time* (revised edition), Office of the Commissioner of Official Languages, Ottawa.

Commissioner of Official Languages: 2003, *Office of the Commissioner of Official Languages Performance Report for the Period Ending March 31, 2003*, Office of the Commissioner of Official Languages, Ottawa.

Cummins, J. and Danesi, M.: 1990, *Heritage Languages: The Development and Denial of Canada's Linguistic Resources*, Our Schools/Our Selves Education Foundation and Garamond Press, Toronto.

d'Anglejan, A. and De Koninck, Z.: 1992, 'Educational policy for a culturally plural Québec: An update', in B. Burnaby and A. Cumming (eds.), *Socio-Political Aspects of ESL in Canada*, OISE Press, Toronto, 97–109.

Duffy, A.: 2004, *Class Struggles: Public Education and the New Canadian*, www. atkinsonfoundation.ca/files/Duffy_web.pdf.

Fettes, M.: 2003, 'Critical realism, ecological psychology, and imagined communities', in J. Leather and J. van Dam (eds.), *Ecology of Language Acquisition*, Kluwer, Dordrecht, 31–47.

Fleras, A. and Elliott, J.L.: 1992, *The Challenge of Diversity: Multiculturalism in Canada*, Nelson Canada, Scarborough, Ontario.

Foucher, P.: 1985, *Constitutional Language Rights of Official-Language Minorities in Canada: A Study of the Legislation of the Provinces and Territories Respecting Education Rights of Official-Language Minorities and Compliance with Section 23 of the Canadian Charter of Rights and Freedoms*, Supply and Services Canada, Ottawa.

Government of Nunavut: Retrieved from www.gov.nu.ca/Nunavut/English/ departments/CLEY, accessed on February 20, 2005, Department of Culture, Language, Elders and Youth, Government of Nunavut, Iqaluit.

Kirkness, V. and Bowman, S.: 1992, *First Nations and Schools: Triumphs and Struggles*, Canadian Education Association/Association canadienne d'éducation, Toronto.

Kymlicka, W. and Patten, A. (eds.): 2003, *Language Rights and Political Theory*, Oxford University Press, Oxford, NY.

Labrie, N.: 1992, 'The role of pressure groups in the change of the status of French in Québec since 1960', in U. Ammon and M. Hellinger (eds.), *Status Change of Languages*, De Gruyter Verlag, Berlin and New York, 17–43.

Lambert, W.E. and Tucker, G.R.: 1972, *Bilingual Education of Children: The St. Lambert Experiment*, Newbury House, Rowley, Massachusetts.

Lapkin, S. (ed.): 1998, *French Second Language Education in Canada: Empirical Studies*, University of Toronto Press, Toronto and Buffalo.

Martel, A.: 1991, *Official Language Minority Education Rights in Canada: From Instruction to Management*, Office of the Commissioner of Official Languages, Ottawa.

National Indian Brotherhood: 1972, *Indian Control of Indian Education*, National Indian Brotherhood, Ottawa.

Office of the Auditor General of Canada: 2004, *Indian and Northern Affairs Canada: Education Program and Post-Secondary Student Support*. Online documents at URL: http://www.oag-bvg.gc.ca/domino.reports.nsf/html/20041105.ce.html, accessed on December 21, 2006.

Royal Commission on Aboriginal Peoples: 1996, *Report of the Royal Commission on Aboriginal Peoples*, www.ainc-inac.gc.ca/ch/rcap/sg/sgmm_e.html, Indian and Northern Affairs Canada, Ottawa.

Royal Commission on Bilingualism and Biculturalism: 1967, *Report of the Royal Commission on Bilingualism and Biculturalism: General Introduction and Book I, The Official Languages*, The Queen's Printer, Ottawa.

Saouab, A.: 1993, *Canadian Multiculturalism*, Library of Parliament, Research Branch, Supply and Services Canada, Ottawa.

Statistics Canada: *Language Composition of Canada* (catalogue number 97F0007XCB2001001). Retrieved from www12.statcan.ca, accessed on February 16, 2005, Statistics Canada, Ottawa.

Statistics Canada: *Selected Demographic and Cultural Characteristics (199), Aboriginal Origin (14), Age Groups (6), Sex (3) and Area of Residence, for Population, for Canada, Provinces and Territories, 2001 Census—20% Sample* (catalogue number 97F0011XCB2001048), Statistics Canada, Ottawa.

Task Force on Aboriginal Languages and Cultures: 2005, *Towards a New Beginning: A Foundational Report for a Strategy to Revitalize First Nation, Inuit and Métis Languages and Cultures*, Department of Canadian Heritage, Ottawa.

Toohey, K.: 1992, 'We teach English as a second language to Bilingual students', in B. Burnaby and A. Cumming (eds.), *Socio-Political Aspects of ESL in Canada*, OISE Press, Toronto, 87–96.

Wardhaugh, R.: 1983, *Language and Nationhood: The Canadian Experience*, New Star Books, Vancouver.

Western Canadian Protocol for Collaboration in Basic Education: 2000, *The Common Curriculum Framework for Aboriginal Language and Culture Programs, Kindergarten to Grade 12*. Retrieved from www.wcp.ca, accessed on February 20, 2005.

JOSEPH LO BIANCO

LANGUAGE POLICY AND EDUCATION IN AUSTRALIA

INTRODUCTION

As an immigrant, post-colonial and trading nation, Australia has inherited a complex linguistic demography with multiple language policy needs and interests and diverse language education challenges.

As a result, administrators, politicians and educators have needed to address a diverse range of language categories across several policy settings and in response to often conflicting language ideologies.

First, English, the national and de-facto official language that arises in Australian policy history under several guises. Originally conceptualised in its British norms and character as symbol and link to British Empire loyalty and civilisation, English was later challenged by evolving Australian variations and local ideologies of communication (Leitner, 2004, Volume I; Ramson, 2002; Turner, 1997). Today, English is increasingly discussed either as a key tool for integrating minorities or commercially as a commodity traded in the delivery and accreditation of internationally oriented higher education. In wider political discussions, English also arises sometimes as a feature of modern science, technology and commerce; i.e. a component and feature of economic globalisation.

Second, Australian indigenous communication, comprising essentially three groups: (i) the original 270 Australian languages (Dixon, 1980; Walsh, 1991), (ii) the remaining languages of today (Lo Bianco and Rhydwen, 2001) and (iii) the various creoles and varieties that have emerged through the dislocation and oppression of indigenous language speakers and the mixing of their language forms with English (Mühlhäusler, 1991). Indigenous speech forms, and how Australian communication has been influenced by them, feature in education and integration discussions of Aboriginal and Torres Strait Islander people (Nakata, 2000; Nicholls, 2001), but also, though less commonly, in consideration of national cultural directions.

Third, immigrant languages other than English that comprise a substantial demographic presence in both urban and rural settings (Clyne and Kipp, 2002). Known as "community languages," these are often intergenerationally vibrant though evolving local speech forms.

S. May and N. H. Hornberger (eds), Encyclopedia of Language and Education, 2nd Edition, Volume 1: Language Policy and Political Issues in Education, 343–353.
©2010 Springer Science+Business Media LLC.

The local settings and contexts of their use support networks of social, religious, educational, recreational and economic institutions. The visible presence that community languages forge within the wider society gives rise to complex relations between the linguistic norms that have evolved in Australia, the 'source' country authoritative norms and shifting language policies (Clyne 2005; Leitner, 2004, Volume II).

Fourth, foreign languages with dramatic shifts in language choices over time, originally reflecting British geography and a selection of the intellectual heritage of Western civilisation, more recently stressing Australia's proximity to Asian countries, economic regionalism and geopolitical interests (ASAA, 2002; COAG, 1994; Fitzgerald, 1997; Lo Bianco, 1987; Milner, 2002; Scarino and Papademetre, 2001).

Restricting the present discussion to education we can say that, broadly speaking, the aspirations of language policy can be divided into two.

First has been the goal of ensuring all Australian permanent residents gain access to the dominant language of the society, English in both its literate and spoken dimensions. Literacy extends to all children and among adults to disadvantaged sections of mainstream society, as well as to many immigrants, and as the critical medium for accessing employment, progressing through education and participating in the entitlements and duties of citizenship. Universal literacy (Lo Bianco and Freebody, 2001) is possibly the widest reaching language policy aim.

The second aspiration of language education policy refers not to state or public official action, but to the vigorous community-based efforts invested in the maintenance of minority languages, seeking essentially to secure their intergenerational transmission. Since this goal depends on establishing community-controlled institutions, and since these are by definition beyond the control of the dominant social structures, they have from time to time encountered opposition and hostility as well as encouragement and toleration.

Although it has only been in recent decades that these twin ambitions have been brought together in coherent policy statements emphasising complementarity, the divergent tendencies they represent have always been implicit policy. This is a consequence of Australia occupying a vast territory by a small population; of having European origins and but being located within an Asian geography, and of having a historically disputed process of settlement and national formation, particularly of relations between all newcomers with the indigenous inhabitants, the oldest continually surviving cultures in the world, which are strongly language based (Frawley, 2001; Leitner, 2004, Volume I).

For the bulk of the colonial (1788–1900) and national (post-1901) phases of Australian history, the language consequences of colonialism, settlement, development and modernisation, immigration, nation building, diplomacy, geography, education, trade, war and culture have been dealt with not as language planning but as matters resolved in the interplay of power, representative democracy, Federation and federalism, and mostly within the overarching control of social attitudes, themselves reflective of the relationships among the component parts of the population (indigenous, settler, immigrant). Language attitudes are most evident as ideologies of esteem or stigma attached to various kinds of speech or writing (see also Tollefson, Language Planning in Education, Volume 1).

Where formal policies have been promulgated, for the most part, these are found in rules and procedures that have regulated immigrant recruitment (such as the notorious 'dictation' test and country of origin biasing via subsidised transportation), the mostly assimilative biases of compulsory education and their literacy pedagogies (House of Representatives, 1992; Schmidt, 1993), foreign relations (such as diplomatic and strategic officer training) and the shifting curriculum status of foreign language teaching.

From 1987, however, Australia embarked on a process of explicit language planning, formulating sociolinguistically informed language decisions, making explicit declarations of aims and objectives, setting in place evaluation and research programmes. Often this has aimed to bring about deep change in the national language 'habitus', especially by fostering community-accepted multilingualism, unique among English-speaking nations (Romaine, 1991, p. 8). Initially very successful, then strongly contested, pluralistic language policy remains part of the policy framework of Australian language planning but with its immediate fortunes dictated by wider sociopolitical arrangements (Moore, 1996). The new national imaginary invoked by pluralism in language planning was wide-reaching and deep, shaping the notion of nation underlying wider policies (Macquarie Encyclopedia, 1997, p. 634), premised on intergenerationally stable multilingualism, in which divergent language interests would be accommodated in complementary relationship with an uncontested, society-unifying status for English.

Unlike the USA, where there has been a long and often bitter struggle over the official designation of English (Crawford, 2000; see also Ricento and Wright, Language Policy and Education in the United States, Volume 1), Australian multilingual and multicultural advocacy has always been premised on the secure status and shared use of English. The so-called mainstream has long had relatively permeable boundaries. Though social and ethnic barriers to inclusion are ever-present, over time an inbuilt dynamic of social mobility in a relatively new society often leads to boundary expansion (O'Farrell, 1986).

In such ways, English has undergone transformation responding to local communicative practices (Horvath, 1991), in turn changing language and national identification. This change within English has had an ambivalent relation with the social presence of a range of languages from diverse origins which have also claimed public recognition (Lo Bianco, 1997).

EARLY DEVELOPMENTS

Clyne (1997), citing his long-standing documentation of language policy, has argued that from earliest times Australian sociolinguistic history is marked by tension. The three nodes of tension are: 'English monolingualism as a symbol of the British tradition, English monolingualism as a marker of Australia's independent national identity, and multilingualism as both social reality and part of the ideology of a multicultural and outreaching Australian society' (p. 127).

This long-term tension of sociolinguistic relations has been punctuated by phases whose ideological underpinnings can be described (Lo Bianco, 2004) as follows:

1. *Britishism*: This is marked by preference for Australian national language norms to reflect prestige English models (with stigma attached to Australian forms of speech), mainly as a marker of identification with England (the local playing out of language-carried social distinctions), but also aspiring to broader Australian national monolingualism, permitting only a limited and elite enterprise of foreign language teaching, and bolstered by legal restrictions on community language institutions.

2. *Australianism*: This is marked by literary and even sociopolitical assertion for evolving Australian norms of English, as a marker of independent national identity; this Australianist language ideology had ambivalent relations with domestic multilingualism, sometimes interpreting language diversity as part of producing a distinctive Australian communicative culture, at other times seeing multilingualism as dangerous and divisive.

3. *Multiculturalism*: This contains two streams, indigenous and immigrant, marked by a common discourse of asserting language rights for community language speakers; invariably multiculturalism's effect on Australian language policy has involved advocacy for English as a second language (ESL) teaching, for multicultural policy and for public language services, and therefore for wide-ranging cultivation of language 'resources'.

4. *Asianism*: This is marked by an assertion of priority for the teaching of the key languages of select Asian countries, tied specifically to the North and South East regions of Asia, and accompanied by

economic, diplomatic and strategic justifications; sometimes Asianism invokes wider social and cultural changes for Australia itself, at other times it is a more restricted discourse embedded within short-term thinking about strategic and economic calculations of national interest; Asianism has had ambivalent relations with domestic multilingualism.

5. *Economism*: This is marked by an emphasis on English literacy tied to arguments about links between education, the labour market, a discourse of human capital, sometimes including arguments about English in globalisation, especially the competition for international full-fee paying students in higher education (Marginson, 1997).

Societies have distinctive national policy styles (Howlett, 1991) and in some ways Australian language education policy has evolved a distinctive 'language problem-solving' approach, characterised by low-ideology pragmatism (Ozolins, 1993).

Perhaps, the clearest example is the Adult Migrant English Program (AMEP; Martin, 1999) established in 1947, initially as ship-board English tuition for post-war displaced and refugee populations, and continually funded for almost 60 years. AMEP represents a pragmatic acceptance that intolerable communication and citizenship problems would result if immigrants were not assisted to acquire English, an apparently straightforward claim, widely held, but that in societies opposed to state intervention in social planning becomes untenable.

Of course, at one level, this is also an ideology, an ideology of social pragmatism and interventionism, one responding to community expectations that state measures are warranted so that minorities do not form ongoing, economically marginalised, linguistic enclaves. Policy making of this kind has received support from all political streams in Australia, and is therefore not sharply aligned politically, and represents low-ideology pragmatism, a shared project of 'problem amelioration'. AMEP has come to represent a major public investment, possibly the measure most responsible for facilitating the relatively high rate of economic, residential and social mobility characterising Australian immigration.

Other examples of language education pragmatism are 1970s schemes for interpreting and translating in community languages, alongside accreditation and certification procedures to encourage professionalism (Ozolins, 2001).

MAJOR CONTRIBUTIONS

At the Federal level, there have been five decisive policies for language education in Australia. These formally adopted policies, in chronological order, are:

1. Report on Post-Arrival Programs and Services for Migrants (Galbally, 1978)
2. National Policy on Languages (Lo Bianco, 1987)
3. Australian Language and Literacy Policy (Dawkins, 1992)
4. National Asian Languages Strategy (COAG, 1994)
5. Commonwealth Literacy Policy (embodied in various reports, media statements and funding programmes since 1997).

Although not identical in remit, scope or style, these five policies are the key formally adopted and implemented language education programmes of the past 25 years: receiving government endorsement, disbursing public finances, leading to implementation and monitoring processes. Each is a complex of discursive, textual and rhetorical components, an amalgam distinctive of the national policy style in societies lacking legalistic policy-making traditions (Howlett, 1991; Kagan, 1991; Lo Bianco, 2001).

It is important to recognise that many other reports and investigations have informed, guided or influenced policy; and to acknowledge the policy-influencing impact of lobbying and pressure from key interest groups; and occasionally from academic research (Lo Bianco, 2001); but these are materially different from actual policy. The five listed policies represent therefore the explicit and implemented language policy frameworks in the 25-year period between 1980 and 2005 in the near quarter century from 1980 (Lo Bianco, 2004).

The Galbally report was a government-commissioned review of services, not addressing indigenous, mainstream English, literacy or foreign relations issues. Nevertheless it represents a major language education policy, signalling the acceptance of multiculturalism by Australian conservative political forces. As a result, for the entire 1980s a broadly shared political programme among policy elites prevailed. Galbally led to public funding for part-time ethnic schools; and by extension to part-time indigenous language programmes; and large increases in funding for all multilingual services. Via the Galbally report, the previous association of multicultural policy with reformist social democratic Labour Party factions was extended to conservatives, who devised a distinctive political interpretation of pluralism.

Over time, the shared programme of support for a pluralist interpretation of Australian society was seen to comprise three principles: *social cohesion, economic benefits* and *cultural diversity.* Language education policy epitomised these principles.

The *National Policy on Languages* was the first comprehensive national language policy; also bi-partisan receiving public endorsement from all political parties. NPL operated four key strategies: '(i) the *conservation* of Australia's linguistic resources; (ii) the *development and expansion* of these resources; (iii) the *integration* of Australian language teaching and language use efforts with national economic, social and cultural policies; and (iv) the *provision* of information and services understood by clients' (Lo Bianco, 1987, p. 70, emphasis in original). The NPL was fully funded, and produced the first programmes in many areas: e.g. deafness and sign language, indigenous, community and Asian languages, cross-cultural and intercultural training in professions, extensions to translating and interpreting, funding for multilingual resources in public libraries, media, support for adult literacy, ESL, and co-ordinated research activity, e.g. the National Languages and Literacy Institute of Australia (NLLIA).

Although the 1992 ALLP positioned itself as a policy re-authorisation (claiming to 'build on' and 'maintain and develop' NPL), it was widely interpreted (Herriman, 1996; House of Representatives, 1992; Moore, 1996; Nicholls, 2001; Scarino and Papademetre, 2001; Singh, 2001) as restricting its scope and ambition, of directing policy emphasis away from pluralism and towards a more 'foreign' and less 'community' orientation and inaugurating a return to divisive prioritising of language needs. Still, the ALLP drew heavily on its predecessor, continued funding many of its programmes (often changing only titles and procedures), and was far more comprehensive than policies which followed it. Despite its shortcomings, ALLP was supportive of extensive language learning efforts and boosted adult literacy tied to workplace education.

The National Asian Languages scheme made available extensive funding; Federal outlays on its targeted languages, Chinese, Indonesian, Japanese and Korean, were over $220 million by the programme's termination in 2002. This vast investment in Asian language teaching was based on shared funding commitments with state, territory and independent education jurisdictions. The programme accelerated growth of a small number of Asian languages, surpassing school and university enrolments in European languages, but also distanced the focus of domestic community language contexts in language education.

From 1997 (see Lo Bianco, 1998a, b, 2001), however, a strong turn towards making English literacy a priority focus for educational intervention occurred. There is no single policy document in which this 'policy' was announced as a 'turn', its antecedents in the electoral platforms of the political parties lack specificity, essentially what took place was a dramatic elevation in political discourse of concern about English literacy standards, rhetorically a 'national crisis' (Freebody, 1998). Arising out of interpretation disputes of research data on children's assessed English literacy performance in 1996, all Ministers of education since have made solving the problem of literacy underperformance a prominent goal. The flow-on effects of elevating spelling and paragraph cohesion measures in primary school English literacy has been manifold: continuing media debates about categorical superiority of 'phonics' or 'whole language' literacy teaching, disputes about what counts as literacy, about the place of critical and technological literacy, with effects for adult sectors, non-English languages, indigenous education, teacher education, ESL, literacy pedagogy and teacher professionalism.

PROBLEMS AND DIFFICULTIES

Policies and practices have often had to compromise among competing demands, sometimes opting for wide coverage of languages producing difficulties of continuation between sectors and levels of schooling, issues of comparability, syllabus and programme design, evaluation and assessment. One consequence of this is the proliferation of ab initio language courses at higher education level.

The Australian Federal system can also be cumbersome and difficult for language planning, although there are only 6 states and 2 territories, these comprise 27 separate education jurisdictions.

A recurring difficulty is the 'third language' issue. Large numbers of immigrant children who are learning English as a second language are expected to study an additional language, the school's 'foreign' language offering, which in effect becomes a third language for them. Debate about the efficacy, and fairness, of this arises often as some teachers and parents request exemption from language study for these students.

A further difficulty has been the closing down of the NLLIA. Perhaps the boldest experiment of language education policy in Australia, in its heyday the Institute co-ordinated research in all areas of language and literacy, English and languages other than English, all linked to education, across 32 separate sites and other implementation domains. A change of political direction in 1996 led to a reduction and then complete removal of public funding for the NLLIA (later Language Australia), and ultimately its closure. Although formally independent of government NLLIA operated from 1990 to 2003 with both state and self-generated revenue, establishing an internationally recognised research, publications and consultancy profile. The loss of NLLA removes the key national and independent professional voice on language education policy.

The final difficulty, perhaps an amalgam of the others, relates to the loss of direction in language and literacy policy, the loss of the formerly collaborative nature of language policy. The sequence of policy changes discussed earlier highlights two key problems of language education policy 'Australian style'.

The first is the rapidity of change, the chopping and changing, of policy frameworks and ideologies. Although the effects of policies can be felt long after their termination, a consequence of distributed implementation arrangements, and of the power of positive discourses, the relatively short duration of formal policies produces problems of coherence, continuation and articulation across education sectors, and rapid changes are ultimately damaging to effective implementation.

The second problem is how policies undertaken in one area impact, whether by accident or design, on contiguous areas. Policy changes in English literacy, for example, impact on the teaching of indigenous languages, even if unintended; and policy measures for Asian languages impact on community language teaching, whether Asian or not, and other programmes, even if these are unintended.

The inability to quarantine the effects of policy suggests an interlinked language education ecology, and highlight the benefits of comprehensive and co-ordinated policy, but governments in Australia appear to have lost interest in this kind of policy making at present.

FUTURE DEVELOPMENTS

It has been widely recognised that Australia is unique among English dominant nations for its efforts to develop a comprehensive approach to language and literacy policy (e.g. Romaine, 1991). Despite the difficulties noted earlier, comprehensive policy making has proved very productive with many positive and lasting outcomes.

One result has been that, unlike many other societies, Australia, which used to be steadfastly monolingual in its educational orientation has near-universal coverage of schools teaching languages other than English, in some states, and possibly the largest number of languages other than English supported in formal and compulsory education than comparable countries.

Language education generally enjoys public esteem, even when related issues of immigration and multiculturalism are embroiled in often-bitter debate and contest.

See Also: *James W. Tollefson: Language Planning in Education (Volume 1); Thomas Ricento and Wayne Wright: Language Policy and Education in the United States (Volume 1)*

REFERENCES

ASAA: 2002, *Maximizing Australia's Asia Knowledge*, Asian Studies Association, La Trobe University Politics Department, Melbourne.
Clyne, M.: 1997, 'Language policy and education in Australia', in R. Wodak and D. Corson (eds.), *Encyclopedia of Language and Education*, Volume 1, Kluwer, The Netherlands, 127–135.
Clyne, M.: 2005, *Australia's Language Potential*, University of New South Wales Press, Sydney.

Clyne, M. and Kipp, S.: 2002, 'Australia's changing language demography', *People and Place* 10(3), 29–35.

COAG: 1994, *Asian Languages and Australia's Economic Future*, Council of Australian Governments, Queensland Government Printer, Brisbane.

Crawford, J.: 2000, *At War with Diversity. US Language Policy in an Age of Anxiety*, Multilingual Matters, Clevedon.

Dawkins, J.: 1992, *Australian Language and Literacy Policy*, Australian Government Publishing Service, Canberra.

Dixon, R.M.W.: 1980, *Australian Languages*, Department of Aboriginal Affairs, Canberra.

Fitzgerald, S.: 1997, *Is Australia an Asian Country?* Allen & Unwin, St. Leonards, New South Wales.

Frawley, J.: 2001, 'Sing out that song: Textual activities of social technologies in an Aboriginal community', in J. Lo Bianco and R. Wickert (eds.), *Australian Policy Activism in Language and Literacy*, Language Australia Publications, Melbourne.

Freebody, P.: 1998, 'Findings from the literacy scandal: Disconcert, tremulousness, and meditation', *English in Australia* 122, 10–14.

Galbally, F. (chair): 1978, *Review of Post-Arrival Programs and Services*, Australian Government Publishing Service, Canberra.

Horvath, B.: 1991, 'Finding a place in Sydney: Migrants and language change', in S. Romaine (ed.), *Language in Australia*, Cambridge University Press, Cambridge, 304–318.

House of Representatives: 1992, *Inquiry into Aboriginal and Torres Strait Islander Language Maintenance*, June, Parliament House, Canberra.

Howlett, M.: 1991, 'Policy instruments, policy styles and policy implementation', *Policy Studies* 19(2), 1–21.

Herriman, M.: 1996, 'Language policy in Australia', in M. Herriman and B. Burnaby (eds.), *Language Policy in English-Dominant Countries*, Multilingual Matters, Clevedon, 35–62.

Kagan, R.: 1991, 'Adversarial legalism and American Government', *Journal of Policy Analysis and Management* 10(3), 369–407.

Leitner, G.: 2004, *Australia's Many Voices: A Study in the Transformation of a Language Habitat*, Volumes I and II, Mouton de Gruyter, Amsterdam.

Lo Bianco, J.: 1987, *National Policy on Languages*, Australian Government Publishing Services, Canberra.

Lo Bianco, J.: 1997, 'English and pluralistic policies: The case of Australia', in W. Eggington and H. Wren (eds.), *Language Policy: Dominant English, Pluralistic Challenges*, John Benjamins, Amsterdam, 107–120.

Lo Bianco, J.: 1998a, 'Literacy, citizenship and multiculturalism', *Australian Language Matters* 6(1), 6–7.

Lo Bianco, J.: 1998b, 'ESL . . . is it migrant literacy? . . . Is it history?' *Australian Language Matters* 6(2), 1–3.

Lo Bianco, J.: 2001, 'Policy literacy', *Language and Education* 15(2–3), 212–227.

Lo Bianco, J.: 2004, *A Site for Debate, Negotiation and Contest of National Identity: Language Policy in Australia*, Council of Europe, Strasbourg.

Lo Bianco, J. and Freebody, P.: 2001, *Australian Literacies*, Language Australia Publications, Melbourne.

Lo Bianco, J. and Rhydwen, M.: 2001, 'Is the extinction of Australia's indigenous languages inevitable?' in J.A. Fishman (ed.), *Can Threatened Languages be Saved? Reversing Language Shift, Revisited: A 21st Century Perspective*, Multilingual Matters, Clevedon, UK, 391–423.

Macquarie Encyclopedia: 1997, *Events that Shaped the History of Australia* (revised edition), The Macquarie Library, Part XII, Social Issues and Policies, Macquarie University, Sydney.

Marginson, S.: 1997, *Markets in Education*, Allen & Unwin, Sydney.

Martin, S.: 1999, *New Life, New Language*, National Centre for English Language Teaching and Research, Macquarie University, Sydney.

Milner, A.: 2002, *Renewing our Asian Engagement*, Radio Australia, Asia Pacific Lecture series, November 11, Australian Broadcasting Corporation.

Moore, H.: 1996, 'Language policies as virtual realities: Two Australian examples', *TESOL Quarterly* 30(1), 473–497.

Mühlhäusler, P.: 1991, 'Overview of Pidgin and Creole languages of Australia', in S. Romaine (ed.), *Language in Australia*, Cambridge University Press, Cambridge, 159–174.

Nakata, M.: 2000, 'History, cultural diversity and English language teaching', in B. Cope and M. Kalantzis (eds.), *Multiliteracies*, Routledge, London, 106–121.

Nicholls, C.: 2001, 'Reconciled to what? Reconciliation and the Northern Territory's Bilingual Education Program', in J. Lo Bianco and R. Wickert (eds.), *Australian Policy Activism in Language and Literacy*, Language Australia Publications, Melbourne, 325–341.

O'Farrell, P.: 1986, *The Irish in Australia*, University of NSW Press, Sydney.

Ozolins, U.: 1993, *The Politics of Language in Australia*, Cambridge University Press, Cambridge.

Ozolins, U.: 2001, 'Inventiveness and regression: Interpreting/translating and the vicissitudes of Australian language policy', in J. Lo Bianco and R. Wickert (eds.), *Australian Policy Activism in Language and Literacy*, Language Australia Publications, Melbourne, 250–264.

Ramson, B.: 2002, *Lexical Images: The Story of the Australian National Dictionary*, Oxford University Press, Melbourne.

Romaine, S.: 1991, 'Introduction', in S. Romaine (ed.), *Language in Australia*, Cambridge University Press, Cambridge, 1–25.

Scarino, A. and Papademetre, L.: 2001, 'Ideologies, languages, policies: Australia's ambivalent relationship with learning to communicate in 'other' languages', in J. Lo Bianco and R. Wickert (eds.), *Australian Policy Activism in Language and Literacy*, Language Australia, Melbourne, 305–325.

Schmidt, A.: 1993, *The Loss of Australia's Aboriginal Language Heritage*, Aboriginal Studies Press, Canberra.

Singh, M.: 2001, Advocating the Sustainability of Linguistic Diversity, in J. Lo Bianco and R. Wickert (eds.), *Australian Policy Activism in Language and Literacy*, Language Australia, Melbourne, 123–148.

Turner, G.: 1997, 'Australian English as a national language', in E. Schneider (ed.), *Englishes Around the World (Volume 2). Caribbean, Africa, Asia, Australasia*, John Benjamin, Amsterdam, 345–348.

Walsh, M.: 1991, 'Overview of indigenous languages of Australia', in S. Romaine (ed.), *Language in Australia*, Cambridge University Press, Cambridge, 27–49.

KATHLEEN HEUGH

LANGUAGE POLICY AND EDUCATION IN SOUTHERN AFRICA

INTRODUCTION

Language policy and education in Southern Africa has evolved, as it has elsewhere in Africa, through several stages: pre-colonial, colonial, early independence and developments since UNESCO's 1990 Education for All Conference in Jomtien (see Alidou, 2004). The partition of Africa, accelerated after the Berlin Conference of 1884–1885, resulted in a division of linguistic communities, often exacerbated by a renaming of 'cross-border' languages in order to make further distinctions. While communities in Africa readily add to their informal multilingual repertoires, postcolonial language policies often reflect a tension between the use of indigenous languages and the language/s of colonial rule. The majority of countries in this region experienced British colonial rule for much of the first half of the twentieth century, if not longer, and hence English has come to occupy a significant position in: Tanzania, Zambia, Zimbabwe, Malawi, Botswana, Swaziland, Lesotho, South Africa, Mauritius, the Seychelles and even in Namibia which was never under British rule. Several countries experienced a succession of different (partial) occupations from the fifteenth century onwards and the region also includes more recent colonies of: Portugal (Angola and Mozambique), Belgium (Democratic Republic of Congo), France (Madagascar) and Germany (South West Africa/Namibia and Tanzania). Thus the influence of French, Portuguese and German is evident in education and language policy within the region.

The use of mother tongue (L1) education for primary education to the mid twentieth century in most countries was replaced by English only (Zambia) or early-transition to English after independence in several countries. Tanzania, South Africa and Namibia for different political reasons, retained and extended the use of the African languages, to the end of primary school. Malawi retained one local language as medium for 4 years. Political changes since the early 1990s, however, have resulted in a similarly diminished use of African languages, coupled with an accelerated transition to English medium in Namibia and South Africa. A convergence towards an early transition to a second language (L2) education system is not compatible with contemporary education research, which illustrates the interdependence of second

S. May and N. H. Hornberger (eds), Encyclopedia of Language and Education,
2nd Edition, Volume 1: Language Policy and Political Issues in Education, 355–367.
©2010 Springer Science+Business Media LLC.

language acquisition (SLA), cognitive development and academic achievement. Early transition does not, in African settings, facilitate the requisite competence in the L2 which is necessary for meaningful access to the curriculum. L2 education, therefore, does not offer equity with L1 education and it cannot deliver quality education. The focus of this chapter is on language education policy developments in the 'anglophone' countries of the region, paying particular attention to South Africa.

EARLY DEVELOPMENTS: (PRE-)COLONIAL PRACTICES

Discussions of language practices in Africa often neglect the historical use of local languages in education. The rediscovery of the Malian Timbuktu manuscripts has drawn recent attention to extensive and sophisticated pre-colonial literary use of African languages for mathematics, science, economics and religion at university mosques from the twelfth century onwards (e.g. Timbuktu Education Foundation, 2002). Various nineteenth century missionary groups which traveled through Southern Africa believed that their evangelical work would be advanced through the transcription of local languages, translation of the bible, the introduction of mother tongue literacy and primary education. Schools, established by missionaries for a small percentage of children in British colonies, used L1 medium for 4–6 years (e.g. Gorman, 1974). This practice suited the British colonial administration's general policy favouring segregation, thus education was left largely to the missionaries. Education in the French and Portuguese colonies, however, did not include the use of African languages. From the early twentieth century, various education commissions recommended the maintenance and use of indigenous languages alongside the addition of an international language (e.g. Gorman, 1974). Missionary education in 'anglophone' countries was compatible with these recommendations, particularly those of the influential Report on the Use of Vernacular Languages in Education (UNESCO, 1953).

The linguistic credentials of the missionaries and the consequences of their activities have, however, been criticized. Missionary groups favoured different orthographic conventions and their expertise in linguistics was uneven. They often mistakenly identified close varieties of one language as separate languages and this, coupled with different orthographic systems, contributed to what Msimang (cited in Cluver, 1996) has termed a 'linguistic balkanization' of Africa; or a 'misinvention' of African languages (Makoni, 2003). The net result has been to inflate, artificially, the number of languages, and establish different orthographies for the same or related language/s (e.g. for Sesotho as written in Lesotho vs. Sesotho as written in South Africa). Several arguments—including the apparent costs of such 'multiplicity', and, more recently, the 'artificiality' of languages—are advanced by post-colonial governments as reasons why African languages cannot be used in education. Schmied (1991), Obanya (1999), Bamgbose (2000) and Ouane (2003), nevertheless, offer detailed rebuttals to these arguments.

There are also positive aspects of early missionary transcriptions and production of texts in African languages. Together, with the rediscovery of the Timbuktu manuscripts, they demonstrate the feasibility of materials' production in, and education through, African languages. Language committees established in the late 1920s in South Africa built on earlier missionary linguistic work. The limitations of earlier divergent processes were recognized, and linguists sought even then to resolve orthographic differences and re-route developments along a convergent path (Cluver, 1996).

MAJOR CONTRIBUTIONS: POSTCOLONIAL PREOCCUPATION WITH INTERNATIONAL LANGUAGES

Postcolonial developments in the second half of the twentieth century in most African countries were accompanied by the identification of official languages for use in the political, economic and educational domains. Invariably, English came to be selected for high status functions in the former British colonies.

The end of the colonial period came rapidly. Tanzania, Malawi and Zambia gained independence in 1964, Botswana and Lesotho in 1966 and Swaziland in 1968. Under Julius Nyerere, Tanzania opted for a single African language, Kiswahili, as the official language and medium of instruction throughout primary school. Although Kiswahili was not a dominant L1 of any particular group it had been advanced under both German and British rule as a language of trade and lingua franca. In Malawi, President Banda's home language was declared an official language alongside English, and renamed Chichewa (although it continues to be known as Nyanja in Zambia and Mozambique), after independence in 1964. Chichewa was used until recently as the medium of instruction for the first 4 years of school with a switch to English medium thereafter. Zambia opted for English-only education after independence, ostensibly to avoid inter-ethnic rivalry (Tripathi, 1990). The educational development and use of Kiswahili in particular (see Blommaert, 1997; Brock-Utne, 2005; Rubagumya, 1994), and to a lesser extent Chichewa (Williams, 2001), illustrates that African languages can and do offer viable educational opportunities. Unfortunately, however, the advancement of only one African language in Tanzania, Malawi, and Botswana may result in the marginalization of linguistic minorities (e.g. Nyati-Ramahobo, 2000). This is particularly the case for the fragile San communities of Botswana which have effectively been 'invisibilized' (Skutnabb-Kangas, 2000) by the political dominance of Setswana. Zambia's English-only policy, adopted to avoid such ethnolinguistic inequities, has had other consequences. It has arrested further development and production of texts in African languages. It has resulted in neither high levels of English language proficiency nor educational success. It has also not arrested sociopolitical discontent, since those who are proficient in English and access higher education are resented as part of a political elite, impervious to the needs of those on the fringes of society (Tripathi, 1990).

In each case, the 'multiplicity' of African languages was seen as a threat to national unity in the postcolonial years (Bamgbose, 2000; Obanya, 1999; cf. May, Language Education Pluralism and Citizenship, Volume 1), and language policy reflected a tendency to marginalize most indigenous language communities. Missionary development of languages other than Kiswahili, Chichewa/Nyanja and Setswana, lost momentum or ceased altogether. Inevitably, this meant declining literacy activities and a gradual loss of literary resources in many languages.

Similar postcolonial developments were delayed by political events and sizable European settler communities in South Africa, Zimbabwe, Namibia and Mozambique (Schmied, 1991). South Africa occupied 'German' South West Africa (now Namibia) during World War 1 and retained control until independence in 1990. Language policy and practices changed, in both countries, with a new government in 1948. Policy was marked by a two-pronged approach: official Afrikaans-English bilingualism (with special consideration for German in Namibia) and development and use of African languages to reinforce separatism. An earlier British colonial ideology of separate development, infused with the European fascism of the 1930s, was refined into 'grand apartheid'. Convergent approaches to linguistic development amongst African languages were replaced by deliberate divergence. Apartheid logic included separate ethnolinguistic education systems. This meant 8 years of mother tongue/L1 education for African children, followed by a transition to an equal number of subjects in Afrikaans and English in secondary school. The use of mother tongue/L1 education under such circumstances tainted its educational legitimacy amongst African communities.

With the exception of apartheid's expanded use of African languages, and the development of Kiswahili and Chichewa, the range of mother tongue options in education shrank across most of the region during the first decade of independence. Initial mother-tongue/ L1 education was replaced either by a single African language followed by transition to English, or English-only. Political events were soon to alter the trajectory in South Africa and Namibia as well. Resistance to the compulsory use of Afrikaans medium for half of the subjects in secondary school for African students culminated in a student revolt in Soweto in 1976. Government was forced to make Afrikaans-medium optional and mother-tongue education was reduced from 8 to 4 years of primary. All the while, L1 speakers of Afrikaans and English continued to enjoy mother-tongue education, plus the other of these languages as a subject, to the end of secondary school. At no point were Afrikaans or English speakers compelled to learn an African language.

At the time, heated political debates deflected attention from the de facto achievements of mother-tongue education in South Africa. The secondary school leaving pass rate for African students rose to 83.7% by 1976. The English language pass rate improved to over 78%. Within a few years of the reduction of L1 education to 4 years, and earlier transition to English, the school leaving pass rates declined to 44% by 1992, with a parallel decline in English language proficiency (Heugh, 2002). Macdonald (1990) was to show that students could not become sufficiently proficient in English by the end of the fourth year to facilitate a successful transition to English medium in grade 5. Although African parents imagined that extended and earlier access to English in school would deliver higher level proficiency in English and education success, the educational gap between speakers of African languages and speakers of Afrikaans and English, who have L1 education throughout, has widened. The knock-on effect of this is that those leaving school and going into the teaching profession are now less well-equipped for teaching and there is a downward spiral of teaching competence across the entire system. The gap in educational achievement of African children vis à vis children of European descent is more noticeable in South Africa than in other countries because of the size of the 'settler' community and the analytical scrutiny which followed apartheid.

The implications of a significant longitudinal study, the Six Year Primary Project, in Nigeria in the 1970s, in a politically more neutral environment, were debated at length across the continent. This project demonstrated the educational and linguistic efficacy of extended use (6 years) of mother tongue medium in conjunction with expert teaching of English as a subject (e.g. Bamgbose, 2000). Other investigations into the use of African languages in education continued and were reported on through various education channels. In 1986 the OAU committed itself to the language plan of action for Africa (Mateene, 1999), which included the extended and expanded use of African languages in education. Subsequent and similar declarations regularly support this line of argument. Even though these debates were not tainted by the association of apartheid ideology with mother-tongue education, none of the declarations or statements of intent has materialized in practice. Postcolonial debates in Africa (e.g. Alexander, 1999; Bamgbose, 2000) and beyond (e.g. May 2001; Phillipson, 1992) demonstrate the resilience of ideological conditioning which reproduces earlier, inequitable government practices. International aid agencies have also been reluctant to support the development and use of African languages in education (e.g. Schmied, 1991). Alidou (2004) points out that since 1990 most African states have committed themselves to greater use of African languages, yet most continue to implement early transition models. In essence, the continued privileging of the international language, and sometimes one of many African languages, reproduces inequality and educational failure for those who receive education in an unfamiliar language (cf. May, Bilingual/Immersion Education: What the Research Tells Us, Volume 5).

Ironically, by accident rather than design, apartheid education offered optimal opportunity for first and second language development alongside cognitive and academic development from 1955–1976. Despite the intention of separate and unequal education, an unintended consequence was greater educational success than other education policy in the region. The feasibility of using several African languages to the end of primary school was demonstrated. Seven South African and several Namibian languages were elaborated for educational use and textbooks were translated from Afrikaans and English into these languages for the duration of primary school. Most significantly, this was accomplished with minimal costs: the expenditure per capita on African education was a fraction of that for other population groups at the time (cf. Grin, The Economics of Language Education, Volume 1; Heugh, 2002).

A common thread across Southern Africa, however, is that education is expected to deliver access to high-level competence in an international language, which is English in eleven of the fifteen countries of the region. Frequently this is presented as feasible in a predominantly second language education system. It is seldom advanced through a complementary process of extending the use of local languages with the systematic addition of (rather than replacement by) English (i.e. additive bilingual models of education; see May, Bilingual/Immersion Education: What the Research Tells Us, Volume 5).

WORK IN PROGRESS

During the 1990s, political changes across the region, especially in South Africa, brought renewed attention towards education and language policy. Apartheid rule gave way to a democratically inspired dispensation in 1994. The finalization of a new Constitution (RSA, 1996) introduced the principles which would guide new language policy developments. Two official languages, Afrikaans and English, were complemented by the bold addition of a further nine African languages. A new language education policy re-introduced the principle and right of L1 education within the context of 'additive bilingual and multilingual' models of education (DoE, 1997). Discriminatory linguistic practices of the past were to be jettisoned. The language education policy went further, to declare South African Sign Language a twelfth official language for educational purposes (cf. Branson and Miller, National Sign Languages and Language Policies Volume 1) and it made strong recommendations regarding the promotion of languages for trade and diplomacy in the school system. This promised to position South African language education policy as one of the most progressive in international contexts. The profiling of multilingualism in this framework was specifically supported during Nelson Mandela's presidency. After new elections in 1999, implementation of the new language policy was arrested. A default to apartheid-like ethnolinguistic parallel and separate development (e.g. Heugh, 2003), under the guise of 'language rights', scuppered an integrative approach to multilingualism. Parallel and equal development of eleven languages, including Afrikaans and English, separately, was not only a fruitless exercise; it facilitated a default to English, whenever in doubt, option.

Language education policy was kept separate from, rather than integrated into curriculum transformation. By 2002, it became clear that the language education policy had been subsumed by curriculum revision, and of the six aims of the original policy, only two had been partly included in the curriculum, viz. a tacit reference to the use of 'additive bilingualism' and a minimalist compulsory learning of an African language for 3 years. South African Sign Language and languages for trade and international communication were simply not mentioned in the curriculum. Language policy is either explicit and implemented through transparent means; or it is implicit, and implemented through default processes. In the case of the Revised National Curriculum Statements (e.g. DoE, 2002), opaque reference is made to the 1997 language policy, and additive bilingual education is misrepresented as premature transition to the 'first additional language' (i.e. to English for 75% of students). Preparation of education officials, in 2004, who were to train teachers for new curriculum implementation, included only one language education model for grades 4–6, viz. transition to English. A device, the repetition of a key clause referring to students 'who will learn in their first additional language', normalizes transition in the documentation. The curriculum reveals no understanding of the interdependence of (second) language acquisition, academic and cognitive development.

This example of a promising language education policy which undergoes systematic editing or revision to an unrecognizable form has also had its parallels in Mozambique, Zambia and Malawi since the mid-1990s. In each of these countries, concern regarding under-achievement in literacy and general education led to proposals for new language education policy supportive of extended use of African languages and additive bilingual principles. In each case, however, through a process of redrafting and revision of policy, there have been compromises in regard to the period of time afforded L1 education. Zambian language policy revision has finally accommodated literacy in the mother tongue for grade 1 (extended to grade 2) but the medium of instruction remains English from grade 1 (Muyeeba, 2004). In Malawi, the proposed expanded use of African language medium, in languages other than Chichewa, for 4 years has been whittled down to 2 years. Mozambique has begun implementation of 3 years of L1 education. Namibia has similarly opted for 3 years of L1 medium. Each example demonstrates early transition to English or Portuguese; not one is attempting an additive bilingual option.

PROBLEMS AND DIFFICULTIES

Attempts to transform education and achieve equitable provision and outcomes for students in South Africa are disappointing. Systemic assessments of literacy and numeracy in grades 3, 4 and 6 since 1998 are alarming. Since 1995, South Africa has been placed last in the Third (now Trends in) International Mathematics and Science Study (TIMSS) (Reddy, 2006; UNESCO, 2000). A common thread across these and other studies shows a correlation between students who are studying in their L2, English, and the lowest levels of achievement. Students studying through their L1, Afrikaans and English, have the highest levels of achievement. These findings are predictable when viewed through the prism of psycholinguistics and SLA theory, especially the interdependence of language, cognition and academic achievement (e.g. Doughty and Long, 2003; Macdonald, 1990; Thomas and Collier, 2002; see also May, Bilingual/Immersion Education: What the Research Tells Us, Volume 5).

The language model used in South Africa, early-exit from the L1 and transition to English for African children, is one which is used across most other countries in sub-Saharan Africa, and it is designed for educational failure. The question is: why since 1990 has there been an accelerated convergence towards this model when there is no evidence that it can offer success? Spolsky (2004) argues that blame cannot be directed at governments only, and that there needs to be an intro-spective examination of the role of advisors and experts. Postcolonial

literature and debates referred to earlier may explain macro-level constraints which impel developments away from democratic principles.
Less frequently documented are meso-level issues involving experts
and advisors. Some of these are presented below.

Terminological slippage, as shown in the South African example,
where an 'early-exit transitional bilingual' model is passed off as
'additive bilingual' education; or where the concept of cognitive 'transfer' as used by Cummins (e.g. since 1984) and others, is confused with
'transition to L2', has become commonplace. Documents and second
language programmes currently circulated in African countries increasingly contain terminological slippages and rhetorical devices similar
to those in the South African curriculum. The influence of early-exit
literacy/L2 programmes, designed in Europe and South Africa, and
accompanied by such textual inaccuracies are currently advanced in
Malawi, Zambia, Uganda and Ghana, for example. Independently,
similarly erroneous terminology has been found in recent advisory
documents supplied to the governments of Sierra Leone and Ethiopia.
The extent to which the slippage is intentional obfuscation or genuine
error is not always clear. An unfortunate consequence of information
technology is that theoretically flawed documentation is circulated
along with more academically rigorous material.

As Schmied (1991) and others point out, there are several donor
organizations concerned with L2 programme delivery in African countries. Evaluations for the donors of initial L1 literacy and early-exit transitional (L2) programmes, however, are often flawed. Firstly, control groups
are selected from a usually dysfunctional mainstream system, thus any
intervention will look promising in comparison. Secondly, as the
research of Thomas and Collier (2002) shows, evaluations of most
types of bilingual programmes show similarly positive results during
grades 1–3. The differences start emerging during grade 4 and are
increasingly obvious from grades 5 onwards, where it is clear that
students from early-exit programmes do not develop strong foundations in literacy and numeracy and their academic progress is on the
decline. Evaluations of programmes seldom reflect longitudinal effects
of the transition to L2, so claims of success prior to an analysis of grade
5 data are premature (Alidou et al., 2006).

In the meantime, participation in several cross-national studies: the
Southern Africa Consortium for Measuring Educational Quality
(SACMEQ), Monitoring Learning Achievement (MLA), and TIMSS
show disturbing signs of poor achievement in literacy, mathematics
and science, in the L2, across the region (UNESCO, 2000).

An adequate explanation for the reproduction of a flawed language
model, one based on a language unfamiliar to teacher and student alike,
includes both macro- and meso-level reasons. The long-term effect of

the wrong language model has been opaque or difficult to recognize in most countries where universal primary education has not yet been achieved and through rate to secondary education has been low. In South Africa, however, the evidence has been readily available, but obscured by the political-ideological aversion to apartheid and its education system.

FUTURE DIRECTIONS

Political developments since the early 1990s, coupled with new international frameworks, especially UNESCO's Education for All and the Millennium Development Goals, have brought about a reassessment and realignment of education priorities in the region. There is a greater awareness of the need for and possibilities of regional co-operation, and sharing of expertise. The Southern Africa Development Community specifically encourages regional educational cooperation. The Association for the Development of Education in Africa (ADEA) and the UNESCO Institute for Education recently commissioned a study of mother-tongue and bilingual education in sub-Saharan Africa (Alidou et al., 2006). Recommendations from studies like these are presented to the Education Ministers in Africa every 2 years, and are weightier than individual country studies. Cooperative agencies, such as the Association for the Development of African Languages in Education, Science and Technology (ADALEST), and ADEA emphasize that language education experts should not await new government decisions.

The need for strengthening research capacity has been identified in two areas: the economics of language education; and the relationship between language and cognition. Early-exit transitional models exacerbate repeater and drop-out rates and these are costly and wasteful. If the apartheid government could fund African language development and education on a minimal inequitable budget, then there is little reason why a post-apartheid government, intent on equal distribution of resources cannot afford this now. Contemporary advances in information technology and human language technology promise to render multilingual education far less costly than was the case during the apartheid period. They expedite cooperative (cross-border) language development activities (e.g. of the University of Malawi's Centre for Language Studies, or Department of Arts and Culture, South Africa).

There is growing recognition amongst the organizations mentioned above, that teacher education programmes are anachronistic and require fundamental reconceptualisation. Second language programmes, based on flimsy SLA theory, or from European-North American contexts, have little validity in Africa. Teacher education in Southern Africa requires: a strengthening of the teachers' own academic language development in relevant African languages; bilingual/multilingual methodology; SLA and enriched curriculum content training, for all teachers. Literacy theory and teaching methodology, responsive to the reality of 'print-poor' and large-class African settings is essential for early primary teachers. Those who continue to teach in the students' L2, cannot do this unless they have (near) native-like proficiency themselves.

The 2005 Education for All Global Monitoring Report identifies 'learners' cognitive development as the major explicit objective of all education systems' and the primary condition for quality education (UNESCO, 2004, p. 19). Education developments in Southern Africa which match language policy and implementation with this objective could turn around the socioeconomic development of the continent.

See Also: James W. Tollefson: Language Planning in Education (Volume 1); François Grin: The Economics of Language Education (Volume 1); Suresh Canagarajah: The Politics of English Language Teaching (Volume 1); Constant Leung: Second Language Academic Literacies: Converging Understandings (Volume 2); Nkonko M. Kamwangamalu: Second and Foreign Language Learning in South Africa (Volume 4); Do Coyle: CLIL—A Pedagogical Approach from the European Perspective (Volume 4); Joseph Lo Bianco: Bilingual Education and Socio-political Issues (Volume 5); Stephen May: Bilingual/ Immersion Education: What the Research Tells Us (Volume 5); Tove Skutnabb-Kangas and Teresa L. McCarty: Key Concepts in Bilingual Education: Ideological, Historical, Epistemological, and Empirical Foundations (Volume 5); Jim Cummins: Teaching for Transfer: Challenging the Two Solitudes Assumption in Bilingual Education (Volume 5); Marjolijn H. Verspoor: Cognitive Linguistics and its Applications to Second Language Teaching (Volume 6); Josep M. Cots: Knowledge about Language in the Mother Tongue and Foreign Language Curricula (Volume 6); Colin Baker: Knowledge about Bilingualism and Multilingualism (Volume 6); Ofelia Garcia: Multilingual Language Awareness and Teacher Education (Volume 6)

REFERENCES

Alidou, H., Boly, A., Brock-Utne, B., Diallo Y.S., Heugh, K., and Wolff, H.E.: 2006, *Optimizing Learning and Education in Africa—the Language Factor. A Stocktaking Research on Mother Tongue and Bilingual Education in Sub-Saharan Africa*, Association for the Development of Education in Africa (ADEA), Paris. http://www.adeanet.org/biennial-2006/doc/document/B3_1_MTBLE_en.pdf
Alexander, N.: 1999, 'An African Renaissance without African languages', *Social Dynamics* 25(1), 1–12.

Alidou, H.: 2004, 'Medium of instruction in post-colonial Africa', in J. Tollefson and A. Tsui (eds.), *Medium of Instruction Policies: Which Agenda? Whose Agenda?*, Lawrence Erlbaum, Mahwah & London, 195–214.

Bamgbose, A.: 2000, *Language and Exclusion: The Consequences of Language Policies in Africa*, Lit Verlag, Münster, Hamburg & London.

Blommaert, J.: 1997, 'Ideology and language in Tanzania: A brief survey', in R.K. Herbert (ed.), *African Linguists at the Crossroads* (Papers from the Kwaluseni 1st World Congress of African Linguistics, Swaziland, 18–22. VII. 1994). Köln: Rüdiger Köppe, 501–510.

Brock-Utne, B.: 2005, 'The continued battle over Kiswahili as the language of instruction in Tanzania', in B. Brock-Utne and R.K. Hopson (eds.), *Languages of Instruction for African Emancipation: Focus on Postcolonial Contexts and Considerations*, CASAS, Cape Town & Mkuki na Nyota, Dar es Salaam, 57–87.

Cluver, A.: 1996, 'Language Development in South Africa', *A Report written for the LANGTAG Report: Towards a National Language Plan for South Africa*, Department of Arts, Culture, Science and Technology, Pretoria.

Cummins, J.: 1984, *Bilingualism and Special Education: Issues in Assessment and Pedagogy*, Multilingual Matters, Clevedon.

DoE: 1997, *Language-in-Education Policy*, Department of Education, Pretoria.

DoE: 2002, *Revised National Curriculum Statement Grades R-9 (Schools) Policy. Languages English—First Additional Language*, Department of Education, Pretoria.

Doughty, C. and Long, M. (eds.): 2003, *The Handbook of Second Language Acquisition*, Blackwell, Maldin, Oxford, Melbourne & Berlin.

Gorman, T.: 1974, 'The development of language policy in Kenya with particular reference to the educational system', in W. Whiteley (ed.), *Language in Kenya*, OUP, Nairobi.

Heugh, K.: 2002, 'The case against bilingual and multilingual education in South Africa: Laying bare the myths', *Perspectives in Education* 20(1), 171–196.

Heugh, K.: 2003, 'Can authoritarian separatism give way to linguistic rights? A South African case study', *Current Issues in Language Planning* 4(2), 126–145.

Macdonald, C.: 1990, 'Crossing the Threshold into Standard Three', Main Report of the Threshold Project, Human Sciences Research Council, Pretoria.

Makoni, S.: 2003, 'From misinvention to disinvention of language: multilingualism and the South African Constitution', in S. Makoni, G. Smitherman, A. Ball, and A. Spears (eds.), *Black Linguistics. Language, society, and politics in Africa and the Americas*, Routledge, London and New York, 132–151.

Mateene, K.: 1999, 'OAU's strategy for linguistic unity and multilingual education', *Social Dynamics* 25(1), 164–178.

May, S.: 2001, *Language and Minority Rights*, Longman, London (Reprinted by Routledge, 2007).

Muyeeba, K.: 2004, 'Challenges of making and implementing policy in the multilingual state of Zambia', *Third International Conference of the Association for the Development of African Languages in Education, Science and Technology (ADALEST) and the Fifth Malawian National Language Symposium*, University of Malawi and GTZ, Malawi, 167–176. http://www.adalest.com/

Nyati-Ramahobo, L.: 2000, 'Language situation in Botswana', *Current Issues in Language Planning* 1(2), 243–300.

Obanya, P.: 1999, *The Dilemma of Education in Africa*, UNESCO Regional Office, Dakar.

Ouane, A.: 2003, 'Introduction: The view from inside the linguistic jail', in A. Ouane (ed.), *Towards a Multilingual Culture of Education*, UNESCO Institute for Education, Hamburg, 1–22.

Phillipson, R.: 1992, *Linguistic Imperialism*, Oxford University Press, Oxford.

Reddy, V.: 2006, *Mathematics and Science Achievement at South African Schools in TIMSS 2003*, Human Sciences Research Council, Pretoria.

RSA: 1996, *The Constitution of the Republic of South Africa, 1996, The Constitutional Assembly & the National Parliament*, Republic of South Africa, Cape Town.

Rubagumya, C.: 1994, *Teaching and Researching Language in African Classrooms*, Multilingual Matters, Clevedon.

Schmied, J.: 1991, *English in Africa: An Introduction*, Longman Linguistics Library, London and New York.

Skutnabb-Kangas, T.: 2000, *Linguistic Genocide in Education—or Worldwide Diversity and Human Rights*, Lawrence Erlbaum Associates, Mahwah.

Spolsky, B.: 2004, *Language Policy*, Cambridge University Press, Cambridge.

Thomas, W. and Collier, V.: 2002, *A National Study of School Effectiveness for Language Minority Students' Long-Term Academic Achievement*, Center for Research on Education, Diversity & Excellence, Santa Cruz, CA and Washington, DC. http://www.crede.org/research/llaa/1.les.html

Timbuktu Education Foundation: 2002, *Discovery of Timbuktu Manuscripts*, http://www.timbuktufoundation.org/manuscripts.html

Tripathi, P.: 1990, 'English in Zambia: the nature and prospects of one of Africa's 'new Englishes'', *English Today* 6(3), 34–38.

UNESCO: 1953, *The Use of Vernacular Languages in Education,* UNESCO, Paris.

UNESCO: 2000, *Education for All. Status and Trends 2000. Assessing learning achievement, International Consultative Forum on Education for All, for UNESCO*, Paris, 32. http://unesdoc.unesco.org/images/0011/001198/119823e.pdf

UNESCO: 2004, *Education For All. The Quality Imperative. EFA Global Monitoring Report 2005*, UNESCO, Paris. http://portal.unesco.org/education/en/ev.php-RL_ID= 35939&URL_DO=DO_TOPIC&URL_SECTION=201.html

Williams, E.: 2001, 'Testimony from testees: the case against current language policies in sub-Saharan Africa', in C. Elder, A. Brown, A. Hill, T. Lumley, T. McNamara, and K. O'Loughlin (eds.), *Studies in Language Testing: Experimenting with uncertainty: language testing essays in hounour of Alan Davies*, Cambridge University Press, Cambridge, 200–210.

LACHMAN KHUBCHANDANI

LANGUAGE POLICY AND EDUCATION IN THE INDIAN SUBCONTINENT

INTRODUCTION

The ideology of language in school is interwoven with the ideology of education in society. Education planners in the contemporary South Asian context have, by and large, committed themselves to *education for all,* but they have not yet been able to totally discard the elitist framework of *selective* education inherited from the colonial setup (prevailing till 1947).

In India, with a multilingual population and a federal polity, one finds a wide variation in different states as far as the medium, content, duration and nomenclature of educational stages are concerned. The decadal census enumerates 200 odd languages, spoken by the population exceeding 1 billion, spread in 30 states and 5 Union territories (Nanda, 1993). Over 80 languages are used as medium of instruction at different stages. About 18 of them are counted as principal medium languages, comprising 2 pan-Indian languages—Hindi and English; 2 languages without a specific region—Urdu and Sindhi; and 14 languages concentrated in different regions—Assamese, Bengali, Gujarati, Kannada, Kashmiri, Konkani, Malayalam, Manipuri, Marathi, Nepali, Oriya, Punjabi, Tamil and Telugu. Distinct scripts, based on Brahmi, Perso-Arabic and Roman systems of writing, are in vogue for these languages (for details, cf. Khubchandani, 2001).

The Constitution of India, passed in 1950, vests authority in its constituent states to choose a language or languages in a region as official language(s) (Article 345). It also allows linguistic minority groups to receive education in their mother tongue and to set up institutions of their choice for this purpose (Article 30). In the Indian federal setup, the Constitution originally listed the domain of education as a 'State' subject. However, since 1980, it has been shifted to the 'Concurrent List', allowing both the Union and state governments to initiate legislation on education policies.

Other countries in the South Asian region, known as SAARC—Bangladesh, Pakistan, Sri Lanka, Nepal, Bhutan and Maldives Islands—are also characterized by varied milieu where, apart from locally dominant languages, pan-regional languages such as Hindustani and English play a significant role in overall education structure. Bangladesh consists of a relatively homogeneous Bengali population. Pakistan is

S. May and N. H. Hornberger (eds), Encyclopedia of Language and Education,
2nd Edition, Volume 1: Language Policy and Political Issues in Education, 369–381.
©*2010 Springer Science+Business Media LLC.*

composed of nearly half of its population speaking Punjabi (48%): other prominent languages are Pashto (13%), Sindhi and Siraiki (12% each), Urdu (8%) and Baluchi (3%) (Rahman 1996, see also, Rahman, Language Policy and Education in Pakistan, Volume 1). Sri Lanka is going through the trauma of adjustments between two Sinhalese and Tamil-speaking populations.

EARLY DEVELOPMENTS

Before the consolidation of British rule on the Indian subcontinent at the turn of the nineteenth century, there were two competing systems of education: the *pathashala* (school) and *gurukul* (residential school) system of Brahmins; and the *maktab* (school) and *madraseh* (college) system of Muslims (see also, Rahman, Language Policy and Education in Pakistan, Volume 1). Two patterns, shaped by vocational relevance, were prominently recognized: *ordinary* tradition for providing practical education to administrators and merchants to cope with the day-to-day needs of society through locally dominant languages; and *advanced* tradition for providing education to the elites (sons of priests, the ruling class and high officials) by reading of scriptures and historical texts, through the classical languages—Sanskrit or Arabic-Persian.

The 'Great Debate' between Orientalists and Anglicists over the treatment of classical languages, contemporary indigenous languages (termed 'vernaculars') and the advent of 'imperial' English during 150 years of British rule has left a deep imprint on the role of language for plural societies in the region. The rival British education system known as *schools* soon eclipsed the traditional *pathashala* and *maktab* education systems in most parts of British India. The British administration could not resolve the three basic issues of education: the content, the spread and the medium (Dakin, 1968). Macaulay's hard line, recommending a policy of 'imparting Western knowledge through a Western tongue (English) and then only to a minority' (cf. the famous Minute of 1835, cited in Sharp, 1920), echoed in education programmes of the British throughout their stay in the subcontinent. During a later phase, the 1854 Wood Despatch suggested the use of vernacular medium 'to teach the far larger class who are ignorant of, or imperfectly acquainted with, English' (Naik, 1963; Richey, 1922). However, the introduction of vernacular education was extremely slow, and Macaulay's commandment 'of *first* developing Indian vernaculars to qualify them for use in education and administration' prevailed. This predicament has constrained the extension of Indian languages as medium of instruction beyond the secondary level to a great extent; thus, effectively postponing their introduction in formal domains (Khubchandani, 1981). This assumption is uncritically accepted as a cornerstone of language planning in India in post-colonial times as well (for further discussion, see Khubchandani, 1997, 2001; Pennycook, 1998).

During the long struggle for Indian Independence, the selective education structure was vehemently criticized by national leaders—Gohkale, Gandhi, Tagore and other intellectuals—who saw the need for universal elementary education and also put forward pleas for the use of mother tongue in administration (Saiyidain, Naik and Hussain, 1962). Mahatma Gandhi in 1938 proposed a scheme for *Basic Education*, which was practically the antithesis of the rulers' elitist moorings concerning the question of content, spread and medium (Zakir Hussain, 1950). It attempted to resolve the conflict between quality and quantity in education by laying stress on integrating education with *work experience* through 'down-to-earth' vernaculars (mother tongues/local lingua francas), and language acquisition with *communicability*.

In actual terms, three patterns of education emerged during the British rule:

1. the vernacular medium, in rural areas for primary education
2. the English medium, in urban centres for education of the elite, right from the primary stage
3. the two-tier medium, vernacular medium for primary education and English medium for the advanced stages, in towns.

The politicization of the language issue in India during the struggle for independence focussed on the *medium* controversy, pushing into the background the ideological issues concerning the *content* of education. The demand for vernacularization by the native elite was associated with the cultural and national resurgence, and eventually with the growth of democracy promoting equality of opportunity through education (Gandhi, 1916; Tagore, 1906). In post-independent India, regional languages have been getting a wider acceptance as far as the primary education is concerned (INDIA, 1993; Khubchandani, 2001, 2003a; Koul, 2001).

Today, educational infrastructure in South Asia, by and large, still shows the signs of bearing the distortions of colonial legacies, characterizing the struggles where the control is shifted from outside colonizers to the *creamy layer* of the society. In recent years Indian rulers, with opposing ideological orientations, have been taking proactive interest in modifying *content* of school curriculum and textbooks, contradicting one another. In public debates, such attempts of presenting Indian culture in school curriculum are labelled as:

1. Universalization, emphasizing global issues and modern patterns of life
2. Secularization, without partiality or prejudice against any one faith

3. Saffronization, idealizing the glory of ancient Indian heritage
4. Detoxification, removing distortions of colonization and other biases that have crept into Indian history.

MOTHER TONGUE EDUCATION

Many modern education experts during the twentieth century advanced several educational, psychological, sociopolitical and historical arguments in support of the axiom that the *best* medium for teaching a child is their mother tongue (UNESCO Report, 1953, p. 11). These pedagogical claims did not take into account the *plural* character of Indian society at large, which reveals apparent ambiguities in defining the concept of mother tongue itself. In linguistic and educational accounts, the terms "mother tongue" and "native speech" are often used indistinguishably. The term *native speech* can be distinguished as 'the first speech acquired in infancy, through which the child gets socialized: it claims some bearing on "intuitive" competence, and potentially it can be *individually* identifiable.' The term *mother tongue* is mainly 'categorized by one's allegiance to a particular *tradition*, and it is *societally* identifiable' (Khubchandani, 1983, p. 45).

During the initial years after gaining independence, different expert bodies on education such as the 1948 Central Advisory Board of Education, 1949 University Education Commission, and 1956 Official Language Commission put a greater weight on the *broad* interpretation of mother tongue—i.e. regarding all minority languages not having a written tradition as "dialects" of the dominant language in the region. This interpretation amounted to an implicit denial of equal rights to linguistic minorities on the ground of practicability, similar to the French view of treating minority languages (such as Provencal, Breton and Basque) as dialects of the dominant French. But ultimately the linguistic minorities succeeded in getting the authorities to accept the *narrow* interpretation of mother tongue, which is closer to the definition of native speech: 'the home language of child, the language spoken from the cradle' (1951 Census of India, 1954).

A recent UNESCO Report (2003) supports mother tongue medium as an 'essential component of inter-cultural education and linguistic diversity so as to ensure respect for fundamental rights', asserting self-esteem, identity, dignity and power by smaller groups through language (cf. Godenzzi, Language Policy and Education in the Andes, Volume 1). One sees an inevitable measure of fluidity in mother tongue claims in many plurilingual regions in India and Pakistan (see also, Rahman, Language Policy and Education in Pakistan, Volume 1). In such situations, one's total repertoire is influenced by more than one normative system. Many speech groups command native-like control over more than one language, with traits of diglossic complementation between languages for intra-group communication in the same space. Mother tongue *identity* and its *image* in this context do not necessarily claim congruity with *actual usage*, and these are again not rigidly identified with specific language *territories*, as is the experience of most European countries either in the past or in the present.

One notices a super-layered homogeneity in communication patterns on the "cline of urbanization" in the entire Hindi–Urdu–Punjabi region divided between north-central India and Pakistan. The highbrow registers of Hindi and Urdu are sharply marked by the polarization in the patterns of borrowing (Sanskritic or Perso-Arabic), whereas at the lowbrow level, distinction between the two is not regarded as so significant. In a communication paradigm, the split between Hindi, Urdu and Punjabi traditions is more ideological than linguistic (Khubchandani, 1983, 1997). In this context, the issues concerning the facility of expression in mother tongue get highlighted in somewhat simplistic terms— i.e. juxtaposing mother tongue against the colonial language English.

A child's earliest first-hand experiences in native speech do not necessarily show semblance with the formal "school version" of his/ her mother tongue. The elitist system of education does not account for the complexity of speech variation across dialects in flux (and in plurilingual societies, often across languages), at the grassroots level. The heterogeneity of communication patterns in many regions of the Subcontinent, the unequal cultivation of different languages for use as medium of instruction, the demands of elegant versions of mother tongue for formal purposes, the non-availability of personnel with adequate command over the *textbook* language, and the switching over to another medium in the multi-tier medium system without adequate preparation are some of the difficulties faced by the learners who are initiated into education through the mother tongue medium. These ground realities have led to the re-examination of the supremacy of the mother tongue medium stretched over the *entire* education career.

EDUCATION NETWORK

Education being a "concurrent" subject in federal multilingual India, there is inevitable flexibility in the weight assigned to different languages in educational programmes, in the framing of language curricula, in selecting textbooks, and so on. The National Council for Education Research and Training (NCERT) conducts a periodic survey to gather information about the spread of educational facilities, and various issues of content and medium of instruction at different levels. In addition, state councils of education, and many NGOs are also engaged in attending to the problems of designing and evaluating the position and functions of mother tongue and non-native language mediums as learning strategies.

The Sixth Survey (INDIA, 1993) records a total of 765,000 schools in the country at the Primary level (Classes I–V). On average, there is one primary school available for every 1,096 of the population. In the midst of a wide variation in different states, elementary education has acquired a distinct pattern in choosing the following as medium of instruction:

1. dominant regional languages
2. pan-Indian English/Hindi
3. neighbouring regional languages
4. newly cultivated languages (mostly tribal and other minority languages), as *preparatory* medium.

Dominant regional language schools account for 88% (672,000 in 1991) at the Primary level in the country. There are 17 such languages spread in respective states and Union territories, listed in order of the numerical strength of their speakers: Hindi, Telugu, Bengali, Marathi, Tamil, Urdu, Gujarati, Kannada, Malayalam, Oriya, Punjabi, Assamese, Kashmiri, Sindhi, Konkani, Nepali, and Manipuri. In addition, three tribal languages—Khasi and Garo in Meghalaya, Mizo in Mizoram— are also introduced as principal medium at Primary level. English is claimed as a dominant medium in northeastern states—Sikkim, Arunachal Pradesh and Nagaland (Khubchandani, 2003b).

Though many states prefer to promote the *exclusive* use of respective regional languages as the medium of instruction, in practice many students experience a *shift* in language medium at one or another stage, depending on context, domain and channel such as: students listen to one language and write answers in another; formal teaching in the classroom is conducted in one language but informal explanations are provided in another. This milieu promotes a good deal of code-switching and hybridization of two or more contact languages.

In a multi-tier medium system, a student initiates education through the mother tongue. But as they move upward on the education ladder, they shift to a more "cultivated" medium. The 1974 NCERT Survey enumerates 80 languages being used as medium of instruction at different stages of education (Chaturvedi, 1976). The emergence of cultural regionalism in recent years has led to more and more minority languages being utilized for literacy programmes in the rural hinterland. It has stimulated considerable creative literature in different tribal languages, and has helped in creating a vast body of textbooks and original writings in these languages. English, however, continues to dominate the scene as a *developed* medium, and Hindi and regional languages as *emerging* medium at the tertiary stage (Khubchandani, 1978; Sridhar, 1988).

BILINGUAL MEDIUM

Although many political and academic agencies lend their support to the claims of imparting education through a single *dominant* language in the region, in recent years there has been a growing demand for selective *bilingual* medium so as to keep pace with the socioeconomic demands of rapid modernization. As per the revised education policy, formulated in 1996, a flexible approach has been adopted for making differential provision when choosing medium of instruction in different types of schools such as: *state government* schools, *central* and *sainik* (military) schools, *navodaya* schools (as model schools for rural rich), *public* schools (managed by public registered bodies, usually catering to the needs of rich and urban areas—called "convent schools"), and *private* schools (run by NGOs—non-government organizations—with or without a grant from the State).

Apart from 17 prominent regional languages, listed earlier, and English, the Survey records 14 additional languages utilized as *partial* medium of instruction in bilingual schools: Maithili, Santali, Kurukh, Nicobarese, Tibetan, Limboo, Bhutia, Bodo, Kakborok, and five Naga languages (Ao, Sema, Angami, Lotha, Zeliang). A large number of schools in Bihar (approximately 21,000—i.e. 31%) have been experimenting with Sanskrit, a classical language, as *partial* medium. With the thrust for modernization, schools with major languages as medium of instruction have been increasing, and the number of ethnic schools has been decreasing.

There are three major contact languages—Hindi, Urdu, and English—spread with varied intensity, utilized as medium of instruction throughout the country (for a detailed review, see Khubchandani, 1978). The 1993 Survey records nearly 7% bilingual schools at Primary level (approximately 51,000 schools, out of the total 765,000). The proportion of bilingual schools is higher in urban cosmopolitan areas with their more heterogeneous populations.

The pan-Indian distribution of Hindi and Urdu schools, spread across 24 states out of 32, with a formidable total of nearly 324,000 schools (Ratio 424 schools out of 1,000), plays a prominent role in the Primary education network of the country. Hindi-medium facilities are provided in nearly 2,900 schools spread outside the north-central Hindi-Urdu belt. Urdu has a significant presence as a minority language medium in Hindi-dominant states, with nearly 7,200 schools; it is also spread in 10 states of the southern and western regions (over 8,000 schools).

A few multilingual states, mostly in eastern India, have introduced bilingual education as a state policy, in which a developing language is used as a *complementary* medium, together with English, Hindi, or the regional language as the principal medium. In this context, "composite" courses are developed by combining a tribal language and elementary Hindi as a single course (for details, see Khubchandani, 1983, pp. 127–128).

English-medium public schools, a dominant colonial legacy, also form a vital part of the Indian education system, starting from the Primary education itself. After Independence in 1947, English medium schools, numbering over 35,000 (Ratio 46/1000), continue to be identified with urbanity, status, power and career specialization. There are more English schools, more English teachers and learners, along with a flourishing English press, than when the British left the country. The base for English education has been expanding. English schools have become a regular feature of the education system available in almost all states (Koul, 2001). Until recently, the preference for English-medium education was confined to urban populations. Now this trend is extending to the countryside as well. Different types of schools, mentioned earlier, have been supportive of extending English as medium of instruction in rural areas.

It is essential that bilingual and bicultural education is introduced with a degree of planning, encouraging a proficiency in the language of the classroom and in the languages (vernaculars) of learners, and a high level of skill in teaching, apart from developing positive attitudes to speech variation in multilingual repertoires.

PROBLEMS AND DIFFICULTIES

At this juncture, the aspirations of the wider public and of educators are at a crossroads, and many diverse claims are being made for bringing radical transformation in the education structure. One of the serious handicaps in implementing language education policies by different education agencies at the central and state levels in India is the continuance of the inherited dichotomies of *Ordinary* and *Advanced* tradition, discussed earlier, and the urban-biased system of education as shaped during the colonial rule. Requirements of elegance in education (such as obsession with 'highbrow' standardized speech) have created a wide gap between the language(s) of home and that of school, leading to a large number of school dropouts in the country.

In multilingual societies, the *ideal* claim and the *real* function of a language might be at variance. One notices a wide gap between the language policies professed and actual practice in a classroom. It is not unusual to find in many institutions anomalous patterns of communication where the teacher and the taught interact in one language, classes are conducted in another, textbooks are written in a third and answers are given in a fourth language/style. In this process, one is not surprised to find that the public agenda of preserving language diversity and favouring mother tongue education serves the purpose of *justification*, but the hidden agenda of pressure groups pushing dominant languages motivates *implementation* when carrying out medium policies in schools (Tollefson and Tsui, 2004; see also Tollefson, Language Planning in Education, Volume 1). In the absence of political will, many proponents of the status quo try to walk on a tight rope. They adopt a *minimalist* approach to providing opportunities for mother tongue education with vague commitments and qualifying clauses which are, in turn, a result of negotiating with contradictory agendas of market forces, serving the interests of the elite, and succumbing to the demands of ethnic pressures.

Multilingual repertoires play a significant role in cultivating many Indian languages for their increasing use in higher education. Different educational subjects require a different type of preparation for a shift in the medium. Demonstration-oriented subjects of hard sciences and technology stress the autonomous, well-formulated and unambiguous use of language, utilizing language structures at the rudimentary level, accompanied by non-linguistic systems (such as mathematical formulae). In abstract subjects dealing with human phenomena (most of the arts, creative writing, religion and social sciences), language needs mature expression but the content tends to be less vigorously formulated, the likelihood of ambiguity is greater, and interpretations are relatively less precise than in hard science subjects. There is another category identified as meta-subjects, where the object of interpretation is language itself, such as law, logic, philosophy, semiotics, and linguistics. These subjects develop a kind of meta-language by exploiting subtleties of the language structure for sophisticated and well-formulated communication.

THREE LANGUAGE FORMULA

Amid sharp controversies concerning the role of different languages in Indian education, a broad consensus was arrived in the Three Language Formula around the 1960s, which provided a basis of policy for a minimum requirement of languages in school education. In 1966, the Education Commission recommended a liberalized version of the Formula; it expected a student to acquire sufficient control over *three* languages by the time he/she completes the Lower Secondary stage (Class X): mother tongue and two non-native modern languages, broadly, Hindi as an *official* medium and a link language for the majority of people for inter-state communication, and English as an *associate official* medium and an interface language for higher education and for "sophistic" and international communication.

In the course of time, the Formula has been differently interpreted by different states. The choice of determining the second or third place for Hindi or English was left to individual states. Hindi states, by and large, provide classical Sanskrit as the third language in place of a modern Indian language, whereas a few non-Hindi states (West Bengal and Orissa) favour Sanskrit at the cost of Hindi as the third language. For several linguistic minorities, it has become virtually a four-language formula, as many states insist on the compulsory teaching of the respective regional language.

ORALITY AND LITERACY

In the contemporary world, the uncritical pursuits of modernization promulgate our current perceptions of literacy as a universal truth. The government-sponsored Literacy Mission targeted universal literacy by the Millennium-end. The 2001 Census records nearly 74% literacy in India (compared with the 1991 literacy rate 52% and 1981 literacy rate 44%).

In the Oriental tradition, both oral and literate traditions have played a vital role. Indian heritage rejects the supremacy of one culture over the other. There is now a growing understanding of the assets of oral tradition among illiterate communities transmitted from generation to generation through varied forms of folklore, festivals, rituals and artefacts. In an oral milieu, both thought and expression tend to be aggregative and concrete—i.e. context-determined, whereas in a written tradition they aim at precision and abstraction—i.e. context-independent. As a backdrop to this, it is necessary to focus on the *continuum* between oral tradition and written culture, and to consider strategies of incorporating the characteristics of *mass* culture into the literate culture (Bright, 1988). Under the spell of contemporary radical thinking in education, there is a greater awareness of the need to make education *relevant* to the environment and learners' aspirations and needs, and to diversify it in regard to the medium, curriculum, teaching and learning methods and materials.

Formal education is initiated by literacy and streamlined through certain time-bound stages in a credential-based system; whereas non-formal education is enmeshed in the cultural milieu of the society, as a part of life-long education through literacy or *without it*. Traditional societies such as India, while relying heavily on the implicit mechanisms of oral tradition for the transmission of knowledge, assign literate groups (or individuals) certain essential liaison/intermediary functions; literacy in these societies, no doubt, forms an important asset and accomplishment for an individual, but *not a necessary condition* of his/her survival and dignity.

In this endeavour, diverse approaches of transmitting literacy skills on a universal basis have emerged on the Indian scene: (i) Conventional educators profess strict adherence to the *standard* language prevailing in the region; (ii) Liberal educators recommend a *bi-dialectal* approach of gradual phasing in time from home dialect to the standard speech; (iii) Some educators plead for a *dichotomous* approach by accommodating diversity of dialects/speech varieties at the spoken level, but at the same time insisting on the uniformity of standard language at the written level; (iv) Those supporting a grassroots approach endorse a *pluralistic* model of literacy, by which variation in speech is regarded as an asset to communication; thus cultivating *positive* values for the diversity in response to the demands of situation, identity and communication task. In this scheme, literacy in the standard variety is, no doubt, promoted for economic-oriented situations and communicative tasks; at the same time, learners are educated to question the pejorative attributes to other than standard varieties that still prevail in the society.

FUTURE DIRECTIONS

The grassroots approach emphasizes making education more meaningful, useful and productive to work-experience. Sensitivity to speech variation and a grasp over the communication ethos prevailing in Indian society is, no doubt, enhanced by 'doing' verbal events in natural settings. An elaboration of Gandhi's thinking concerning Basic Education could provide a sound basis for launching the schemes concerning education for all, as discussed earlier.

Various constraints in the spread of education are attributed to the multiplicity of languages, whereas the real issues to cope with are the confrontation between *tradition* and *modernity* concerning the role of language in education, and the dogmatic rigidity in claiming privileges and parity of different languages in the thrust for autonomy. It is necessary to adopt a pragmatic approach to linguistic usage in education and to take into account the mechanism of standardization of languages in plural societies. When dealing with plural societies, we would do well to realize the risks involved in *uniform* solutions.

See Also: *Tariq Rahman: Language Policy and Education in Pakistan (Volume 1); James W. Tollefson: Language Planning in Education (Volume 1)*

REFERENCES

Bright, W.: 1988, 'Written and spoken language in South Asia', in C. Duncan-Rose and T. Vennamann (eds.), *On Language: Rhetorica, Phonologica, Syntactica*, Routledge and Kegan Paul, London, 22–38.

388

380 LACHMAN KHUBCHANDANI

Chaturvedi, M.G.: 1976, *Position of Languages in School Curriculum in India*, National Council for Educational Research and Training, New Delhi.
Dakin, J.: 1968, 'Language and education in India', in J. Dakin, B. Tiffen, and H.G. Widdowson (eds.), *The Language in Education: The Problem in Commonwealth African and the Indo-Pakistan Subcontinent* (Language and Language Learning Series No. 20), Oxford University Press, London, 1–61.
Gandhi, M.K. (ed.): 1916, 'The present system of education', in *The Problem of Education* (Collected Works: 1962), Navajivan, Ahmedabad.
Government of India: 1948, *Report of the Committee on the Medium of Instruction at the University Level*, Pamphlet 57, Ministry of Education, New Delhi.
Government of India: 1949, *Report of the University Education Commission*, Ministry of Education, New Delhi.
Government of India: 1950, *The Constitution of India*, Ministry of Education, New Delhi.
Government of India: 1954, *Census of India—1951, Language Tables*, Registrar General of India, New Delhi.
Government of India: 1956, *Report of Official Language Commission*, Ministry of Education, New Delhi.
Government of India: 1966, *Report of the Education Commission*, Ministry of Education, New Delhi.
Government of India: 1993, *Sixth All-India Educational Survey*, National Council for Education, Research and Training, New Delhi.
Khubchandani, L.M.: 1978, 'Multilingual education in India', in B. Spolsky and R. Cooper (eds.), *Case Studies in Bilingual Education*, Volume II, Newbury house, Rowley, MA; Also 1981, In the Monograph Series; *Studies in Linguistics* 8, Centre for Communication Studies, Pune.
Khubchandani, L.M.: 1981, *Language, Education, Social Justice. Series: In Search of Tomorrow*, Volume II, Centre for Communication Studies, Pune.
Khubchandani, L.M.: 1983, *Plural Languages, Plural Cultures: Communication, Identity and Sociopolitical Change in Contemporary India*, University of Hawaii Press, East-West Center Book, Honolulu.
Khubchandani, L.M.: 1997, *Revisualizing Boundaries: A Plurilingual Ethos*, Sage Publications, New Delhi.
Khubchandani, L.M.: 2001, 'Language demography and language in education', in C.J Daswani (ed.), *Language Education in Multilingual India*, UNESCO, New Delhi, 3–47.
Khubchandani, L.M.: 2003a, 'Defining mother tongue education in plurilingual context', *Language Policy* 2(3), 239–254.
Khubchandani, L.M.: 2003, *Medium of instruction in Multilingual India*: *Mapping of Schools at the Primary Level*, UNESCO Report (forthcoming).
Koul, O.N.: 2001, 'Language preferences in education in India', in C.J. Daswani (ed.), *Language Education in Multilingual India*, UNESCO, New Delhi.
Naik, J.P.: 1963, *Selections from Educational Records of the Government of India*, Vol. 2, *Development of University Education 1860–1887*, National Archives of India, New Delhi.
Nanda, A.R.: 1993, *Census of India—1991. Population Totals, Paper I*, Registrar General of India, New Delhi.
Pennycook, A.: 1998, *English and the Discourses of Colonialism*, Routledge, London.
Rahman, T.: 1996, *Language and Politics in Pakistan*, Oxford University Press, Karachi (Review by Khubchandani, L.M.: 'Language loyalty in an Islamic state: Dilemmas of shifting identities', *International Journal of Sociology of Language* 140, 149–155).
Richey, J.A.: 1922, *Selections from Educational Records of the Government of India, 1840–1859*, Part II, Bureau of Education, London.

Saiyidain, K.G., Naik, J.P., and Husain, S.A.: 1962, *Compulsory Education in India: Studies on Compulsory Education*, Volume 11, UNESCO, Paris.

Sharp, H.: 1920, *Selections from Educational Records. 1781–1839*, Part I, Bureau of Education, London.

Sridhar, K.K.: 1988, *'Language policy for education in multilingual India: Issues and implementation'*, Roundtable of South Asian Linguistics Association, Hyderabad.

Tagore, R.B.: 1906, 'The problem of education', in R.B. Tagore (ed.), *Towards Universal Man* (Collected Works: 1961), Asia Publishing House, Bombay.

Tollefson, J.W. and Tsui, A.B.M.: 2004, *Medium of Instruction Policies: Which Agenda? Whose Agenda*, Lawrence Erlbaum, Mahwah, NJ.

UNESCO: 1953, *The Use of Vernacular Languages in Education. Series: Monographs on Fundamental Education,* The UNESCO Press, Paris.

UNESCO: 2003, *Education in a Multilingual World. An Education Position Paper.* The UNESCO Press, Paris.

Zakir Hussain: 1950, *Convention on the Cultural Unity of India*, T.A. Parekh Endowment, Bombay.

TARIQ RAHMAN

LANGUAGE POLICY AND EDUCATION IN PAKISTAN

INTRODUCTION

Pakistan is a multilingual state with six major languages—Punjabi (spoken by 44.15% out of a population of 153 million in 2003); Pashto (15.42); Sindhi (14.10); Siraiki (10.53); Urdu (7.57); Balochi (3.57)— and about 57 minor ones. Urdu is the national language and English the official one (Census, 2001). The 1973 constitution of the country, which was suspended in part both during the military rule of Generals Zia ul Haq (1977–1988) and Pervez Musharraf (1999-), is again in force. It provides the following guidelines on language policy:

1. The National language of Pakistan is Urdu, and arrangements shall be made for its being used for official and other purposes within 15 years from commencing day.
2. Subject to clause (1) the English language may be used for official purposes until arrangements for its replacement by Urdu.
3. Without prejudice to the state of the National language, a provincial Assembly may by law prescribe measures for the teaching, promotion and use of a provincial language in addition to the national language (Article 251).

This further relates to education policy and practice, as well as employment prospects of educated people, because the medium of instruction and the language of the domains of power—government, bureaucracy, military, judiciary, education, media, research, the corporate sector, commerce, etc.—are the languages desired by individuals to empower themselves and their children.

EARLY DEVELOPMENTS

Pakistan inherited certain policies relating to language and education from British India of which it was a part from 1846 till 1947. The language of the domains of power in this part of South Asia was Persian ever since the eleventh century (Alam, 2004, pp. 116–117). The Islamic seminaries (*madrassas*) taught in Persian though most of the texts were in Arabic. Very rarely, some texts were taught in the indigenous languages of the people. Some of these texts in Sindhi, Punjabi, and Pashto are referred to in Rahman (2004, p. 326, 384, 355). When the British conquered Sindh (in 1846) and the Punjab (in 1849), they allowed the

S. May and N. H. Hornberger (eds), Encyclopedia of Language and Education,
2nd Edition, Volume 1: Language Policy and Political Issues in Education, 383–392.
©*2010 Springer Science+Business Media LLC.*

madrassas to remain in the hands of the Muslim *ulema* (the equivalent of clergymen though Islam formally has no clergy). They were financed by local feudal lords or merchants. Public funds were used to create a chain of schools in which Urdu was the medium of instruction in the Punjab, the North West Frontier Province (NWFP), parts of British Baluchistan and some of the princely states now in the boundaries of Pakistan. In Sindh, however, they used Sindhi in schools as well as the lower domains of power, and this tradition continues to date.

In short, the British left behind a legacy of three streams of education roughly divided along socioeconomic class lines: the *madrassas* catered for rural and very poor children; the vernacular-medium schooling was for working and lower-middle class children; and the English-medium schools were for the middle and the upper classes. Those who overcame the obstacle of English joined their privileged counterparts in the college because that is where the vernacular-medium and the English-medium streams met. This system continues to date and the few changes in it are described in detail later.

MAJOR POLICIES

The Pakistani state has embarked upon a number of policies ever since the birth of the country. These were expansion of education and literacy (modernization); dissemination of Urdu (vernacularization); ideological socialization; and privatization. Let us take each of them in turn.

Modernization

All education policy documents of the state emphasize the link between modernization and an educated work force (Bengali, 1999). Thus, achieving 100% literacy was an avowed aim of all governments. This aim has not been achieved even now, though literacy increased from 16% in 1951 to 54% of the population in 2004 (GOP, 2004). School enrollment at the primary (classes 1 to 5) is 40%; secondary (6 to 12) is 19%; and tertiary (13 to 16—i.e. BA and MA which are both of 2 years duration each) is 5% of the population (Lahmeyer, 2004). In short, despite increases in all types of schools, the population growth of 2.5% per year, combined with an expenditure of about 2.7% of the GDP in 2004 (GOP, 2004) and an average of about 2% for many years, has prevented the achievement of the aim of full literacy.

Vernacularization

The Pakistani state embarked on a policy of disseminating Urdu as it was considered an identity symbol, next only in significance to Islam itself, of the Muslims of India during the movement for the creation of Pakistan. Official thinking was that Urdu would be an antidote for language-based ethnic movements, which could break up the new state. However, Urdu was opposed in this antiethnic role by ethnonationalists, seeking identity through their indigenous languages (Rahman, 1996). However, despite this opposition, people have learned Urdu for pragmatic reasons all over Pakistan, as it is the language of wider communication within the country. As all literate and many illiterate people (over 50% of the population) understand and speak it, it is much more widely known than the percentage of its native speakers (7.57) would suggest. It is disseminated through the government schools, the government colleges, and universities, which teach all except technical and scientific subjects in Urdu, the print media, radio, and the television. Even illiterates, who come in contact with urban people for providing services, as well as all city dwellers, know Urdu. As Indian films and songs are very popular and they are in a language which is very close to Urdu in its spoken form, Urdu is also spreading through the entertainment industry. The National Language Authority (*Muqtadra Qaumi Zaban*), the Urdu Science Board, and a number of institutions have created both bureaucratic and technical lexicons in Urdu and it is being used by certain provincial governments as well as the lower courts for all purposes. It is also available for use via the computer. Moreover, it is associated with Islam, being the language of examination for all the registered *madrassas* as well as the medium of instruction and of sermons for most of them. In short, Urdu is officially associated with the nationalist Pakistani identity and unofficially with urbanization and the Islamic identity in Pakistan (for both associations see Abdullah, 1976; Kamran, 1992).

"Urduization" is not only opposed by the language-based ethnonationalists. It is also resisted, though covertly and not through declared policy statements, by the Westernized English-using elite. Vernacularization has affected higher education more than school education, which was already in the vernaculars by the time Pakistan was established. Colleges taught the higher secondary classes (11 and 12) as well as the bachelor's level (13 and 14) in English, as did the universities at the master's level (15 and 16). This started changing as more and more of the nonscientific subjects came to be taught in the vernaculars (Urdu, except in parts of Sindh where Sindhi was used). Nowadays, all subjects except the sciences, engineering, and medicine are taught in the vernaculars.

Privatization

Though it is only recently that the Ministry of Education has officially recognized the trend toward the privatization of education at all levels, there have been private, expensive, elitist schools in the country ever since its inception. When controlled by the Christian missionaries they were said to be necessary in the name of religious tolerance (though they catered more for the Pakistani Muslim elite's children than for Christians), whereas those administered or controlled by the armed forces (public schools and cadet colleges) were said to be necessary for a modernizing country since they prepared leaders. The armed forces now control or influence—through senior military officers who are on their boards of governors or principals—most of the cadet colleges and elitist public schools in the country. Although the education policy documents declare that these institutions are financed by the fees paid by their pupils, the state subsidizes the elitist cadet colleges (public schools) (Rahman, 2004, pp. 147–148). The armed forces also control federal government educational institutions in cantonments and garrisons (GHQ, 2003), run their own schools and colleges (MOD, 2003) as well as a huge educational network through their philanthropic services, run mostly by retired military officers (Rahman, 2004, pp. 53–54).

Besides the armed forces, elite schools are run as business empires with campuses in most big cities of Pakistan. These schools charge exorbitant tuition fees and prepare their students for the British O' and A' level examinations. There are also a large number of nonelitist English-medium schools in all cities and even small towns of the country. They cater to those who cannot afford the elitist schools, but want to give their children better chances in life by teaching them English. Their fees, though far less than those of their elite counterparts, are still forbidding for their impecunious clientele. Ironically, they do not teach good English, as efficiency in that language is a product of exposure to it at home and in the peer group, which are available only to the Westernized, urban elite.

Privatization is now taking place in the field of higher education. There were 55 public and 51 recognized private sector universities in 2005 whereas there were only 7 public and no private ones in 1971 when Bangladesh became a separate country and the area now called Pakistan carried the name of the country (HEC, 2005). The first private university, the Aga Khan University in Karachi, was established in 1983. It taught only medicine and created two trends: first, that private entrepreneurs could establish a university; and second, that an institution of that name could teach only one subject. Soon universities teaching lucrative, market-oriented subjects like business studies, computers, and engineering proliferated. They charge very high fees, thus making them unaffordable for even the middle classes, which undergo much self-sacrifice to have their children in these institutions.

The armed forces, despite being organizations of the state, entered the business of higher education as entrepreneurs. There are at present five universities controlled directly or indirectly by the armed forces. While some cater primarily for the needs of the armed forces themselves, allowing civilian students to study only if there are places after their own students are accommodated, most function like private institutions catering primarily for civilian students who can afford their high fees.

All private sector universities attract students because they use English as a medium of instruction for all subjects and provide the kind of elitist infrastructure and facilities, which distinguish the elite from the masses (such as air conditioning).

Ideological Orientation

The state uses education to create a cohesive national identity, transcending ethnic identities in which Urdu and Islam are used as unifying symbols. Textbooks of social studies, history, and languages are informed by this theme. The other major theme informing them is that of creating support for the garrison state, which involves glorification of war and the military. Islam, the history of Muslim conquests and rulers, as well as the Pakistan movement, are pressed into legitimating these concerns. Although General Zia ul Haq's 11-year rule strengthened Islamization of the curricula, these trends were manifested in the early 1950s when the first educational policies were created. The text books of government schools, and especially the subject of Pakistan Studies, carry the major part of the ideological burden.

MAJOR CONTRIBUTORS AND WORK IN PROGRESS

There is not much scholarly work on language and education in Pakistan. Histories of education do, however, refer to language without problematizing the issue in terms of class, ideological polarization, ethnicity, and the divisive potential of these variables (Quddus, 1979; Zaman, 1981). For a Sindhi nationalist point of view see Kazi (1994). The only scholars who have dealt in detail with the relationship between language and education are Sabiha Mansoor and Tariq Rahman. Mansoor points out in her survey of students from Lahore how they rank English highest for efficiency, modernization, and prestige, with Urdu following and Punjabi at the bottom (Mansoor, 1993). In her doctoral thesis, she reviews the place of English in Pakistan, concluding that it is desired by students, parents, and teachers and has a significant role to play (Mansoor, 2002). Rahman (1996) examines the relationship between ethnicity and language and argues that language texts are used to support the hegemony of powerful elites, and change when the system of the distribution of power changes (Rahman, 2002, pp. 488–528). He specifically links the role of language as medium of instruction with socioeconomic class and the polarization in world view leading to different levels of religious tolerance and militancy in different educational institutions such as English-medium schools, Urdu-medium schools, colleges, and *madrassas* (Rahman, 2004, pp. 163–188; cf. Rampton et al., Language, Class and Education, Volume 1).

In the last few years, a number of liberal social activists and scholars have pointed out the anti-India bias and militancy inculcated in the textbooks of the social sciences and history and have recommended changes (Aziz, 1993; Nayyar and Salim, 2003; Saigol, 1995). Urdu, which is taught to all students, is the main ideology-carrying language (Rahman, 2002, pp. 520–522). An important contribution, which provides the model on which a number of studies are based, is that of the historian Aziz who pointed out that history books taught in schools were inaccurate, wrong, and biased (Aziz, 1993). Rubina Saigol (1995, 2000) a sociologist, pointed out the gender bias in favor of males and how the female identity was marginalized and suppressed, as were values of peace and tolerance, which inform feminist writings on education. In March 2004, the debate came to a crisis with the liberals arguing for a change in the textbooks in keeping with General Musharraf's recent policy of peace with India and controlling religious militancy whereas the conservatives, along with the militant nationalists, insisted on retaining nationalistic, pro-war, and pro-military lessons in the name of Islam and national identity or fear of India.

A trenchant critique of liberal, secular education comes from the revivalist Islamist leader Sayyid Abul Ala Maududi in his book *Taleemat* (1974). His work is carried on by the Institute of Policy Studies in Islamabad, as well as intellectuals of the Jamat-I-Islami such as S.A. Khalid, who has recently written a book defending the Islamic educational system, arguing that it is the only one resisting the intellectual hegemony of the West (Khalid, 2002).

Government reports are generally silent about both the *madrassas* and the English-medium schools. However, there are some reports on the *madrassas* (GOP, 1988) and at least one survey of private schools (GOP, 2001). The Higher Education Commission (HEC) also publishes figures about private and public sector universities, but none of these publications links language and educational policies to socioeconomic class, ideological polarization, intolerance of the religious "Other" and militancy in foreign policy. Similarly, there is no analysis of the effects of the policies on the weaker languages of the country, nor on language rights and social justice through education, or the maintenance of ethnic identity, or the rights and perceived injustice connected with such issues.

Recently some Non-Governmental Institutions (NGOs) have started taking an interest in educational matters and especially in creating gender-sensitive textbooks, but these efforts are concentrated in major cities and, being in English for the most part, do not affect the majority of students in the country.

PROBLEMS AND DIFFICULTIES

While discussing developments in the fields of education and language policy, the problems and difficulties have been touched upon already. It may, however, be useful to repeat that the policy of promoting Urdu at the cost of the indigenous languages of the people has increased the ethnic opposition to Urdu on the one hand whereas creating contempt for the indigenous identity on the other. This is most pronounced in the Punjab where Punjabi is regarded as a sign of rusticity, lack of sophistication, and lack of good breeding. The ethnic activists of the other languages—Sindhi, Pashto, Balochi and to some extent Siraiki— have managed to create a sense of pride in their identity and language, but they too acknowledge the pragmatic value of Urdu and remain impressed with English. This increases the pressure of English, which being the language of globalization, already threatens most of the world's languages (cf. Phillipson, Language Policy and Education in the European Union, Volume 1; Skutnabb-Kangas, Human Rights and Language Policy in Education, Volume 1). As the concept of language rights has not emerged in Pakistan and the demand for indigenous languages is seen only as part of ethnic resistance to the Center, the languages of the country do not have the chance of being written down, taught even at the elementary school level, or promoted in the media. This may make some of the minor languages obsolete and, though the major languages will probably survive as spoken mother-tongues because of their size, even the larger languages may become so intermingled with Urdu and English as to lose their present identity.

Another consequence of privatization and the elite's support of and investment in English is to increase the ideological polarization between the different socioeconomic classes. In two surveys of school students from the *madrassas*, the vernacular-medium schools and the elitist English-medium schools, one taken in 1999 and the other in 2003, it was found that the *madrassa* products were most intolerant of religious minorities in Pakistan and most supportive of a militant policy toward India in relation to Kashmir. The first survey is more detailed (Rahman, 2002, Annexure 14) but does not cover the views of teachers, whereas the second one is confined only to the urban parts of the Punjab and the NWFP but does reflect the opinions of the faculty which are close to, and sometimes less liberal than their students (Rahman, 2004, Annexures 1 and 2).

Other problems are linked with increasing computerization and globalization. As the language of both is predominantly English, with Urdu being in the experimental stages, most Pakistani students have yet to learn anything from computers, which, indeed, are not widely available to them either at home or in their schools, colleges, and even universities. Urban males do, however, encounter computers in internet cafes where they are seen as devices for playing games or gaining access to pornography. Students from English-medium institutions do, however, have access to computers both at home and in their educational institutions. They use them for gaining knowledge but even more so for integrating with the globalized (mostly American) culture, which distances them even more from their vernacular-educated and *madrassa*-educated counterparts than ever before. In short, the English-vernacular divide, which is also the class divide, is now also expressed as the digital divide (see Rampton et al., Language, Class and Education, Volume 1; Kalantzis and Cope, Language Education and Multiliteracies, Volume 1).

The pedagogic side of education is also divided according to socio-economic class and medium of instruction. The *madrassas* follow a modified form of the traditional, eighteenth century curriculum called the *Dars-I Nizami* (Robinson, 2002, p. 53.) in which the canonical Arabic texts, which are memorized, are symbolic of valorized cultural memory and continuity. They also have polemical texts in Urdu to refute what they see as heresy and Western ideas. The emphasis on *bellum justum* (*Jihad*), which is blamed for terrorism in the press, does not come from the traditional texts but from extra-curricular pamphlets in Urdu and, even more importantly, from warriors back from Afghanistan, Kashmir, or other battlefields in the Islamic world.

Both vernacular and English-medium schools emphasize rote learning because of the formal examinations after each course, but nowadays practical work and projects are given, especially in private institutions of higher learning, so that some move toward analysis and practical work is evident.

FUTURE DIRECTIONS

Language policy and education, as we have seen, are subordinated to the class interests of the urban, professional, English-using elite in Pakistan. For its political interests this elite has been using the name of Islam, and has strengthened the religious lobby, in the last few years.

This policy is said to have been reversed, but it may be revived by a future government. The rank and file needed to carry it on, especially if it takes the form of a low-intensity conflict with India over Kashmir, will come from the *madrassas* which will probably increasingly cater for more young males as the state shifts spending from the education sector to others. Given the state's encouragement of privatization in the recent past, this seems to be a future trend which can have negative consequences for peace in South Asia and the world.

Privatization, with its concomitant strengthening of English as an elitist preserve, may lead to "ghettoization" in Pakistan—i.e. the weak and the marginalized sections of society will remain underprivileged because the education system creates obstacles for them, which they may find difficult to transcend. This may have several consequences. First, the most educated people may lose faith in the country and give up on it. Second, the ideological polarization between the different socioeconomic classes might increase even further. And, above all, the incentive for reforming Pakistan's educational system and making it more conducive to creating a tolerant and peaceful society might also decrease.

Another trend may be to strengthen the power of the military in Pakistan. As more and more elitist schools and universities pass into the hands of the military, the number of teachers, administrators, and business concerns under the patronage of the military will increase. More students will also be influenced by them. This will probably privilege the military's views about national interest, the future of the country and economic priorities. This, in turn, may further dilute ideas of civilian supremacy, which underpin democracies, and jeopardize the chances of lasting peace in South Asia.

Most of these possibilities do not bode well for the future of the country, but it is only by recognizing them that potentially negative language and educational policies may be reversed.

See Also: *Lachman Khubchandani: Language Policy and Education in the Indian Subcontinent (Volume 1); Ben Rampton, et al.: Language, Class and Education (Volume 1); Mary Kalantzis and Bill Cope: Language Education and Multiliteracies (Volume 1)*

REFERENCES

Abdullah, S.: 1976, *Pakistan Mein Urdu Ka Masla* [Urdu: The Problem of Urdu in Pakistan], Maktaba Khayaban-e-Adab, Lahore.
Alam, M.: 2004, *The Languages of Political Islam*, Permanent Black, New Delhi and the University of Chicago Press.
Aziz, K.K.: 1993, *The Murder of History in Pakistan*, Vanguard Press, Lahore.

Bengali, K.: 1999, *History of Education Policy Making and Planning in Pakistan*, Sustainable Development Policy Institute, Islamabad.

Census: 2001, *1998 Census Report of Pakistan*, Population Census Organization, Statistics Division, Government of Pakistan, Islamabad.

GHQ: 2003, *Federal Government Institutions in Cantonments and Garrisons*, General Headquarters, Pakistan Army, IGT&E Branch (No. 04/77/94-GEI) dated November 21 2003. http://www.moe.gov.pk/mod3.htm (cited April 01 2005).

GOP: 1988, *Deeni madaris Ki Jame Report* [Urdu: The Comprehensive Report of the Religious Seminaries], Islamic Education Research Cell, Ministry of Education, Government of Pakistan, Islamabad.

GOP: 2001, *Census of Private Educational Institutions 1999–2000*, Federal Bureau of Statistics, Islamabad.

GOP: 2004, *Pakistan School statistics (2003–2004)*, Academy of Educational Planning and Development. http://www.aepam.gov.pk/edustat.htm (cited April 06 2005).

HEC: 2005, http://moe.gov.pk/enrollmentinPsUniversities.htm. (cited March 31 2005). Also see http://www.geocites.com/Athens/Parthenon/8107/univ.html (cited April 06 2005).

Kamran, J.: 1992, *Qaumiat Ki Tashkeel Aur Urdu Zaban* [Urdu: The formation of nationality and the Urdu language], Muqtadra Qaumi Zaban, Islamabad.

Kazi, A.A.: 1994, *Ethnicity and Education in Nation Building in Pakistan*, Vanguard, Lahore.

Khalid, S.M.: 2002, *Deeni Madaris Mein Taleem* [Urdu: Education in the Religious Seminaries], Institute of Policy Studies, Islamabad.

Lahmeyer: 2005, http://www.library.uu.nl/wesp/populstat/Asia/pakstag.htm (cited April 01 2005). Last modified by Lahmeyer on March 01 2004.

Mansoor, S.: 1993, *Punjabi, Urdu, English in Pakistan: A Sociolinguistic Study*, Vanguard, Lahore.

Mansoor, S.: 2002, *The Role of English in Higher Education in Higher Education in Pakistan*, Unpublished PhD thesis, University of Reading.

MOD: 2003, *Army Public Schools/College*, Ministry of Defence, Government of Pakistan, dated March 20 2003. http://www.moe.gov.pk/mod.htm (cited March 31 2005).

Nayyar, A.H. and Salim, A. (eds.): 2003, *The Subtle Subversion: The State of Curricula and Textbooks in Pakistan*, Sustainable development Policy Institute, Islamabad.

Quddus, N.J.: 1990, *Problems of Education in Pakistan*, Royal Book Company, Karachi.

Rahman, T.: 1996, *Language and Politics in Pakistan*, Oxford University Press, Karachi.

Rahman, T.: 2002, *Language, Ideology and Power: Language Learning Among the Muslims of Pakistan and North India*, Oxford University Press, Karachi.

Rahman, T.: 2004, *Denizens of Alien Worlds: A Study of Education, Inequality and Polarization in Pakistan*, Oxford University Press, Karachi.

Robinson, F.: 2002, *The Ulema of Farangi Mahal and Islamic Culture in South Asia*, Ferozsons, Lahore.

Saigol, R.: 1995, *Knowledge and Identity: Articulation of Gender in Educational Discourse in Pakistan*, ASR Publications, Lahore.

Saigol, R.: 2000, *Symbolic Violence: Curriculum. Pedagogy and Society*, Society for the Advancement of Education, Lahore.

Zaman, U.S.: 1981, *Banners Unfurled: A Critical Analysis of Developments in Education in Pakistan*, Royal Book Company, Karachi.

SACHIYO FUJITA-ROUND AND JOHN C. MAHER

LANGUAGE EDUCATION POLICY IN JAPAN

INTRODUCTION

The formulation of language education policy is normally guided by a combination of needs and needs-discourse: a new 'vision' of the state, economic shift, talk of 'crisis in education', residual loyalties to the past or, conversely, to what Raymond Williams (1977) termed 'emergent ideological assemblage'. Japan's educational governance is no less a tangled composite of needs than other nations. New social factors are emerging. A demographic 'big bang' (a declining population and the prospect of large-scale immigration) now hangs skyward over Japan. It threatens to shake old educational certainties, former ways of doing and talking. We always knew what to do about this and what to do with that but now we have 'the Other'.

In the imagined community in which language policy emerges in Japan, two geographical beacons are visible: Japanese (*Nihongo*) is the (sole) national language (*kokugo*) and English is pre-eminently the vehicle of internationalization. A straightforward ideological system underpins this stance which, mutatis mutandis, informs large tracts of policy-making at various educational levels. Its underpinning is the familiar modernist trope that Japan is remarkable as a 'monolingual' and 'monocultural' nation. The truth, of course, lies elsewhere. Japan has been, for many centuries, multilingual and multicultural (Maher and Yashiro, 1995, Maher and Macdonald, 1995, Yamamoto, 2000, Sugimoto, 2003) due to migration to and from Japan, cultural flows, geographical realignment (Okinawa, Hokkaido), the (Asian) colonial experience and so on. Likewise, the growth of non-Japanese nationalities is a real and emerging demographic tsunami given the decrease of the Japanese population and the need for a new (imported) labour force to maintain the present social and economical system.

The diversity of multilingualism in Japan entails geographical location. The northern border of the Japanese archipelago faces Sakhalin and the Russian Far East whilst the southern islands border the Korean peninsula, China and further Taiwan. Japan has roughly 3,000 islands and a population of 127 million in 2006. The largest number of native speakers are Japanese. There are 961,307 residents overseas with Japanese nationality (Ministry of Foreign Affairs, 2004) and thousands of older speakers of Japanese in the former imperial colonies of

S. May and N. H. Hornberger (eds), Encyclopedia of Language and Education,
2nd Edition, Volume 1: Language Policy and Political Issues in Education, 393–404.
©*2010 Springer Science+Business Media LLC.*

Taiwan and Korea. Apart from Japanese, there are minority languages: Japanese indigenous languages, such as Ainu (or Ainu Itak) and Ryukyuan (or Okinawan), old immigrant languages such as Korean and Chinese and newer immigrant languages such as Portuguese, Spanish and Filipino languages brought by foreign workers. All these speakers constitute the multilingual hybridity of twenty-first century Japan.

COMPULSORY EDUCATION IN JAPAN

In Japan, compulsory education (*gimu kyoiku*) is organized along public and private lines for children from elementary school to junior high school (aged 6 and 15); 6 years in elementary school (*shogakko*) and 3 years in junior high school (*chutogakko*) in which English is formally introduced as a school subject. Three-year senior high schools are classified as regular (*kotogakko*) or vocational (*koto senmon gakko*). In higher education, vocational schools (*senmon gakko*) provide a vocational or technical education, and junior colleges (*tanki daigaku*) are 2-year courses. Universities (*daigaku*) comprise an undergraduate level (4-year course) and postgraduate schools (*daigakuin*), 2 years for an MA degree and 3 years for a Doctoral degree. All schools follow a three-semester system starting in April.

Foreign nationals can send their children to public elementary school and junior high school during Japanese compulsory education, regardless of the child's level of Japanese proficiency. We repeat 'can send'. Under Japanese law, there is no obligation for such children to attend school. This has created serious 'leakage' in many *gastarbeiter* families who may or may not understand the educational system and whose children thereby fail to attend school or drop out. Language support for foreign children in Japanese varies considerably by locality. Alternatively, foreign nationals can choose international schools. The majority are English medium and/or ethnic schools: American, Brazilian, British, Canadian, Chinese, French, German, Indonesian, Korean, Peruvian schools. However, most of these schools are private and fees are very expensive. English-medium international schools are often assumed to be prestigious as they provide elite bilingual education.

EARLY DEVELOPMENTS

Early History

Drastic social change followed the Meiji Restoration (1868) and its nation-state enterprise. In national language policy a new Japanese government adopted a *hyojungo* (standard language) policy for the nation (Carroll, 2001, p. 52). For the implementation of this policy, a centralist approach to the issue of standardization was applied (Gottlieb, 2005, p. 8). The policy-makers and intelligentsia of Japan adopted the formula of language and nationalism employed by the empires of Europe and pressed this into service in the colonies of Taiwan and Korea (Lee, 1996, p. 117)

The Ministry of Education, Culture, Sports, Science and Technology (MEXT) was founded in 1871 and the Japanese school system started thereafter. In 1886, the first school education policy (*gakko-rei*) was published, setting the curricula for universities (education-for-the-elite) and for teacher education colleges, elementary and secondary schools. In this period, educational diglossia prevailed, whereby schoolchildren bound for the social elite were drilled in *kanji* (Chinese characters) and *kango* (Chinese literature). Meanwhile, the masses possessed only elementary school diplomas.

The backbone of the postwar education system was formulated in 1947, with an increasing number of students at senior high school; 59% in 1960, 82% in 1970, 90% in 1975 and 96.3% in 2004. This increase illuminates two basal changes in Japanese society: (i) the economic success of the 1970s and 1980s enabled families to spend more on education, (ii) the Japanese economy needed quality workers to lead its competitive economy in a globalizing world. These factors led to a call to 'internationalize the Japanese people'.

MAJOR ISSUES FOR LANGUAGE EDUCATION POLICY

'Internationalization' remains a pre-eminent, long-term goal of the Japanese Ministry of Education. This goal comprises the following policy strategies:

1. To improve teaching methods in foreign language classes, the goal of which is to provide children with a better understanding of the distinctive history and culture of other nations in the world;
2. To promote international exchange in the field of education, culture and sports;
3. To promote student exchange, with the aim of accepting 100,000+ students in Japan at any one time;
4. To improve programmes for the teaching of Japanese as a foreign language, thus responding to the growing enthusiasm for learning Japanese;
5. To improve educational programmes both for Japanese children living overseas and for 'returnees' (children who re-entered the educational system after prolonged stay overseas) to maintain the language and knowledge which they acquired abroad.

Returnees, with their various bilingualisms, were initially regarded as 'a problem' since they could not adjust themselves to the monolingual ethic of Japanese schools in the 1960s and 1970s. Social change in the 1980s, however, saw returnees re-classified under 'internationalization' (Goodman, 2003, p. 184); a convenient policy shift based not upon an awareness of emergent multiculturalism but rather political ideology and the need to avoid chaos in school.

On the surface, 'internationalization' seemed to stimulate foreign language education (cf. Wiley, Language Policy and Teacher Education, Volume 1). Regarding the fifth revised 'Foreign Language Policy' in 1989 (junior and senior high school), Otani et al. (2004, p. 163) noted the extension of communication-based activities to promote English oral expression in reading and writing. At the same time, the Ministry of Education promoted 'petit nationalism' by centralizing school management and enforcing the new patriotism of compulsory singing of the national anthem and 'honouring the flag'. The logic of internationalization in the Japanese context might mean educating Japanese people to 'be Japanese' and merely equipping them with the linguistic armour to compete outside Japan. At this point (2006), the current alarm in the language education community is that foreign language education is becoming subsumed under a quasi-nationalistic and ideologically encumbered policy of the central government called, ironically, 'internationalization'.

Diversity of Language and Education in Japan

The problematic of twenty-first century national language policy in Japan emerges subtly in the designation of actual language subjects in education. In the domain of compulsory education Japanese is termed 'Kokugo' ('nation-language'), and the Kokugo class is for Japanese native speakers whereas 'Nihongo', ('language of Japan'), is taught to non-Japanese native speakers.

Since the postwar period, foreign language policy for secondary education level has been revised six times and until the latest revision, foreign language education at secondary schools was elective and included French and German in addition to English. In 2002 for junior high school, and in 2003 for senior high school, foreign language education became compulsory. This altered the choice of foreign language subjects; at junior high schools, it was effectively limited to English. Some private schools and state schools specializing in foreign languages offer, electively, Chinese, French, German, Korean, Spanish, Russian, Italian, Portuguese (Otani, 2001, p. 166).

English. In the landmark 'Commission on Japan's Goals in the twenty-first Century' (2000), the Prime Minister's committee recommended the goal of 'global literacy:' to enable Japanese citizens to freely and efficiently exchange information with the world. The basic elements were: (i) mastery of information-technology tools (computer, internet) and (ii) mastery of English—the international lingua franca. The Commission also flew the kite that English might be designated an official second language of Japan. This latter proposal caused shockwaves and outrage, accusations that national identity was under attack and the Japanese language at risk.

From the standpoint of Japanese business, the notion of English as an official language makes sense since language policy as formulated in Japanese industry has made English the de facto language of business. In the mid-1980s many Japanese firms accelerated the transfer of production lines to other countries in Asia and elsewhere. Consider the following example. Matsushita Electrical Industrial Co., headquartered in Osaka, has about 230 overseas affiliates and routinely uses English test scores (TOEIC—Test of English for International Communication) for promotion in Japan. It employed 245,922 people in fiscal 2004–2005, only 28% of whom were Japanese, while 2,300 Japanese employees were working on assignments overseas lasting an average of 5 years (Matsushita Human Resources Development, 2005). As globalization and competition among multinationals intensifies, the operating system of Japanese commerce is English and English-speaking employees find themselves in demand.

There are two recent trends in bilingual education: English in the state elementary school curriculum from 2002, and partial-immersion schooling (i.e. schools in which 50% or more is conducted in Japanese and the rest in English). In principle, the latter partial-immersion education (English-Japanese) is circuited into the official education system by means of the so-called *tokku* programme, established by the Japanese government in 2003. These are special structural reform zones that are eligible for preferential deregulation. In such a programme, integrated bilingual education is offered in elementary, junior and senior high school: a full 12 years of education. In addition to regular subjects taught in Japanese, pupils receive several classes per week in English. Although the numbers of such schools are still limited, the first private bilingual school that applied for this *tokku* programme started in April 2005 (MEXT website). Prior to this government programme, one private immersion school had started a Japanese/English programme in 1992 (Bostwick, 2001).

The government's push to increase fluency in English for schools is spearheaded by such measures as the designation of Super English High Schools (SELHi) where English appears prominently in the curriculum and in the massive JET (The Japan Exchange and Teaching Programme) programme which annually provides native English teachers for state schools nationwide.

Korean. The immediate postwar period saw an explosion of Korean-medium schools. By 1946, there were 525 Korean schools in Japan (serving a population of 647,006 Koreans). However, Koreans were obliged to register as aliens and in 1948, the Ministry of Education ordered all Korean children to receive Japanese public education. The route to bicultural/bilingual education was thus effectively closed. Their children—*nisei, sansei* and *yonsei* (second, third and fourth generation) comprise a substantial minority in Japan, approximately 1 million (including those that have naturalized as Japanese). The large majority are now (monolingual) native Japanese speakers (Maher and Kawanishi, 1995).

The majority of ethnic Korean children attend local state Japanese schools, there these Korean children are 'invisible', ethnically unmarked, compared to the 'visible' Brazilian or Peruvian students. Okano (2006, p. 351) argues that Japan-born ethnic Koreans need no JSL (Japanese as second language), but that their ethnic language and culture does need support, as much as that of 'visible' newcomers.

In contrast, Korean as a foreign language is the fastest growing foreign language of study in Japan. Several factors contribute to this: the 1988 Seoul Olympics, 2002 World Cup in Korea and Japan, more print media in Korean, stabilization of trade-economic relations between Japan and Korea, leading to increased confidence among Korean-Japanese, and municipal interest in supporting Korean resident communities.

In an attempt to maintain the Korean language and culture and avoid the historical bias against minorities found in the school curriculum in Japanese schools, the General Association of (North) Korean Residents in Japan (*Sooren*), and to a lesser extent the Korean Residents Union (*Mindan*), run their own system with the provision of textbooks on Korean language or history. A mixed bilingual curriculum in Japanese and Korean is employed in 120 *Sooren* elementary and secondary schools throughout Japan, whereas the Union (*Mindan*) has far fewer (4) schools (Shin 2005).

Chinese. Chinese is found in the various Chinese communities with a total population of approximately 50,000 found in the urban centres of Tokyo-Yokohama, the Kansai region, and parts of southern Kyushu. There are five Chinese ethnic bilingual (Japanese-Chinese) schools in Tokyo, Yokohama, Osaka and Kobe. Kanno (2003) reported that at the ethnic Chinese school she observed there are fourth and fifth generations of 'old timer' students; the demographic of the school consists of 60% 'old timer', 30% 'new comer', and 10% 'mainstream' Japanese.

In Maher and Kawanishi's (1995) study of Korean students, discussed earlier, they noted the strong link between Korean ethnicity and language, as well as with the traditional refusal of (North) Korean residents to take Japanese nationality. In contrast, Chen (2005, p. 179) in a recent study of the Chinese community in Tokyo-Yokohama notes the more 'fluid and loose connection between language and Chinese identity'. The 'fluidity' in the language awareness of the overseas Chinese community seems to derive from some basic principles: (i) language learning (Japanese) is essential (ii) some language affiliation with Chinese is desirable, (iii) code-mixing is normal, (iv) learning English as an international language is essential for the community (see also Lam, Language Education Policy in Greater China, Volume 1).

Ainu. The United Nations' declaration on language rights in the Year of the Indigenous Peoples, 1993, was a landmark in the history of language maintenance among the peripheral language communities in Japan, particularly the indigenous Ainu. Supported by overseas language minorities, the Ainu have achieved significant progress in their struggle for language protection. In Hokkaido, where 23,767 identified themselves as Ainu in a Hokkaido Government Survey in 1999, there are now universities in the northern prefectures that offer Ainu language instruction. Local community groups also now operate *Ainugo Kyoshitsu* (Ainu language classes) in community centres in Hokkaido (DeChicchis, 1995; Komatsu, 2000).

Placing Ainu within Fishman's theory of 'reversing language shift' Maher (2001, p. 323) has pointed out that 'Ainu has a powerful symbolic resonance since it recalls the sociopolitical landscape of the past, the good old days and bad old days, colonialism, forced-removal from land, schooling in Japanese and prohibition of the Ainu language'. Language education for the historic community of the Ainu turned a further corner with the Ainu Culture Promotion Act of 1997. This removed older laws such as the 1901 Education Code, which aimed at the complete linguistic conformity of the Ainu and de facto elimination of the Ainu language. Whilst the provisions of the new law have not met all the demands of the Ainu people, the renewed language becomes a defining characteristic of Ainu culture (cf. Siddle, 1996 for a critique of the new legislation.)

Ryukyuan. The Ryukyuan group of languages—part of the typological system of Japanese—are spoken as a vernacular in the Okinawa prefecture. While these languages are also called 'Okinawan', Matsumori (1995, p. 20) argues that Ryukyuan is more appropriate as the group of dialects that also includes some islands which are part of Kagoshima-ken.

The return of the islands to Japan from United States' control in 1972 accelerated the decline of Ryukyuan. Standard Japanese is the medium of instruction throughout the Ryukyuan school system while Standard Japanese is employed in all media, magazines, books, official documents, public signs, etc. Ryukyuan plays no official role in public education in the Okinawan education system and its use has traditionally been discouraged in schools. Attitudes are changing though, owing to increased awareness of language endangerment and regional pride. There is increasing local interest in the language and its ethnolinguistic maintenance (reported by Ryukyuan speakers in Kotoba to Shakai Henshuuiin, 2004) although no policy proposal exists to reintegrate Ryukyuan into the school system.

The Deaf People and Japanese Sign Language. In no other language community are the prospects for policy change more real than in Japan's Deaf Community (cf. Branson and Miller, National Sign Languages and Language Policies, Volume 1). Japanese sign language (JSL) is a generic term for a cluster of deaf language varieties is used by a cross-section of an estimated 400,000 hearing-impaired people and is subject to dialectal and sociolectal variation. Major strides in sign language activity have been made in recent years. These include the guarantee of sign language interpreting in court, local-government initiated sign language services and television broadcasting in sign. The sticking point is school education. With the inauguration of the Kyoto Prefectural School for the Blind and Deaf in 1873, Japanese Sign Language was adopted as a means of instruction. However, when oralism was introduced in 1925, this resulted in the dissolution/prohibition of JSL in Japan's schools, where hearing teachers were required to teach 'signed Japanese' based upon Spoken Japanese word order and expression (Honna and Kato, 1995; see Branson and Miller, National Sign Languages and Language Policies, Volume 1). This has been the policy up to the recent past. In 1993, a memorandum on special education policy was issued by the Japanese Ministry of Education, acknowledging the use of sign language in deaf schools. Hailed in the popular press as the first statement in the history of educational policy to recognize language diversity in schools, the document was frankly invidious and immediately attacked by many language rights activists in the deaf community. The reason was obvious. The definition of sign language adopted by the government was Signed Japanese (based on the structure and lexis of standard Japanese) and not Japanese Sign Language, the indigenous language of the deaf community (Honna and Kato, 1995; Ichida, 2004).

Portuguese and Spanish. The economic upturn associated with the 1980s, the period of the so-called 'bubble economy', created a labour shortage, particularly in the construction and manufacturing industries. This drew in *gastarbeiter* to work in what was termed, ironically, the *san-K* (3-K) type of jobs: work that was considered *kitsui* (hard), *kitanai* (dirty) and *kiken* (dangerous). From the 1980s, the influx of Vietnamese-Chinese and Cambodian refugees, followed by foreign workers from Asia and South America (speakers of Portuguese and Spanish) in the 1990s, settled in Japan. Several commentators have pointed out the urgent need to deal with the problem of the children of recent immigrants who do not have Japanese language ability and who find it difficult to function in public schools (Ota, 2000). According to a survey by the Ministry of Education, the numbers of foreign national children with Japanese language support in Japanese state schools were 20,692 in 2005. Speakers of Portuguese (7,562), Chinese (4,460), and Spanish (3,156) as their mother tongue comprised more than 70% of the total (MEXT website).

In addition, 33 Brazilian language maintenance schools are approved by the Brazilian government, mostly in the industrial cities of central Japan between Tokyo and Nagoya. The rapid expansion in the number of immigrant language speakers both in urban and rural areas has focused serious attention on the dynamics of family bilingualism and language maintenance in the next generation of Japanese citizens.

Japanese as a Second Language. The steady increase in the number of foreign students enrolled in educational institutions impacts on the growing field of the teaching of Japanese as a foreign language. In 2004, the number of foreign students stood at 117,302. This compares with 45,000 in 1995 (Ministry of Education and Culture 2005). That two-thirds of the foreign student population come from mainland China, and the bulk of the rest from South Korea and Taiwan, points to the 'Asianization' of the foreign student body. The majority of students are enrolled in the social sciences, humanities or engineering. This population shift as well as its subject-specific orientation contrasts with the immediate post-war period, when a very small number of foreign students, mostly from North America and Europe, came to Japan for Japanese language-culture training.

Popular culture is crucial to the validity and pedagogical success of Japanese language teaching. This has long been recognized (Kishimoto, 1992) and will continue as twenty-first century students in Japan learn about Japanese society and practice TV drama, film, popular songs, *manga* (a generic term for comics and animation) and *anime* (animation) manga. However, recent social pressure, particularly 'frenzied' reports of criminal activity by foreigners (murder cases, various forms of crimes), have led to the Japanese government tightening the immigration laws. As a result, the number of foreign (especially Chinese) students is likely to decrease from 2007.

PROBLEMS AND DIFFICULTIES; FUTURE DIRECTIONS

The ethnic hybridity of Japan's towns and cities, the new 'imagining' of minority communities, cultural crossover in lifestyle, the arts and education, and the furious globalization of the Japanese economy and business, are among the many factors that impact upon language policy in twenty-first century Japan. However, these dynamic interfaces are an old story. We may recall that writing systems employed in Japan are mixed and diverse: two phonemic syllabaries arranged in Sanskrit phonetic order and adapted from *kanji*, Sino-Japanese *kanji* (Chinese characters), romaji (Romanized letters), European alphabet borrowing and Japanese Braille. A large percentage of spoken and written Japanese across most genres includes foreign words, loan words, now mostly English (Honna, 1995, p. 45). The fact that the Japanese language developed by internalizing such non-Japanese elements has caused tension between two contrastive viewpoints; progress towards the desired reforms and subsequent regression (Gottlieb, 1995, p. vii). Over the past century, language and language education policies have struggled at this interface, now hyper-accelerated by globalizing society.

The central government's push for 'internationalization' lacks an adequate framework based upon multilingualism and multiculturalism. However, at the local level, Japanese cities are increasingly multicultural and bring forth new expectations for educational change to meet the present increasing number of foreign national residents. At the national level, language education policy is predicated upon the concept 'internationalization', but nowhere does internationalization include support for regional and community or indigenous languages. The reality, the critically declining population of Japanese society, led the government to sign an agreement in 2004 to import Filipino nurses and care workers to look after the Japanese elderly. Such social changes will also change the demographics of foreign nationals and language policy (including the nature of Japanese as a foreign language education).

Whither Japan's minorities and language communities? Tracing the 'ethnic boom' of the 1980s–1990s, Maher (2006) has theorized that Korean and Ryukyuan, in particular, are now subject to 'metroethnicization:'

> a hybridized 'street' ethnicity deployed by a cross-section of people with ethnic or mainstream backgrounds who are oriented towards cultural hybridity, cultural/ethnic tolerance and multicultural lifestyle in friendships, music, the arts, eating and dress ... Metroethnicity is bored with sentimentalism about ethnic language.. involved cultural crossings, self-definition made up of borrowing and bricolage. Its desktop cultural expression is 'Cool'. The historic struggle of Japan's

language minorities may be giving way to a new metroethnic generation. Its performative style is based upon and derives simultaneously from the symbols of both disaffiliation and association. (Maher, 2006, p. 24)

Language education in Japan is in flux. It is neither revolutionary change nor planned incremental policy shift. Rather, flux occurs here and there: in schools, in companies and as the result of the government's now aging mantra of 'internationalization'. The prospect for a nation's language education policy is most influenced by the needs of its citizen-public: the younger generation will live with the emerging social realities. The absence of creative government responses to these realities is marked and the powerful question remains, turning itself over, repeatedly, in the public mind: in what manner will the next generation come to terms with Japan's new identity as a multilingual and multicultural society?

See Also: Agnes S. L. Lam: Language Education Policy in Greater China (Volume 1); David Block: Language Education and Globalization (Volume 1); Jan Branson and Don Miller: National Sign Languages and Language Policies (Volume 1)

REFERENCES

Bostwick, R.M.: 2001, 'Bilingual education of children in Japan: Year four of a partial immersion programme', in M. Noguchi and S. Fotos (eds.), *Studies in Japanese Bilingualism*, Multilingual Matters, Avon, 272–311.

Carroll, T.: 2001, *Language Planning and Language Change in Japan*, Curzon Press, Richmond, Surrey.

Chen, P.: 2005, *The Overseas Chinese in the Tokyo-Yokohama Region: Language Situation and Community*, PhD Dissertation, International Christian University, Tokyo, Mitaka.

DeChicchis, J.: 1995, 'The current state of the Ainu language', in J.C. Maher and K. Yashiro (eds.), *Multilingual Japan*, Multilingual Matters, Avon, 103–124.

Goodman, R.: 2003, 'The changing perception and status of Japan's returnee children (*kikokushijo*)', in R. Goodman, C. Peach, A. Takenaka, and P. White (eds.), *Global Japan*, Routledge, London,

Gottlieb, N.: 2005, *Language and Society in Japan*, Cambridge University Press, Cambridge.

Gottlieb, N.: 1995, *Kanji Politics: Language Policy and Japanese Script*, Kegan Paul International, London and Sydney.

Honna, N.: 1995, 'English in Japanese society: Language within language', in J.C. Maher and K. Yashiro (eds.), *Multilingual Japan*, Multilingual Matters, Avon, 45–62.

Honna, N. and Kato, M.: 1995, 'The deaf and their language: Progress toward equality', in J.C. Maher and G. Macdonald (eds.), *Diversity in zankoku Ronji womotsu Oya no kai (ed.) Japanese Culture and Language*, Kegan Paul International, London and Sydney, 270–284.

Ichida, Y.: 2004, 'Japanese sign language in the aspect of linguistics', in Zenkoku Rouji wo motsu Oya no Kai (ed.), Education for the Deaf People and the Language Right, Akashi Shoten, Tokyo, 10–46.

Kanno, Y.: 2003, 'Imagined communities, school visions, and the education of bilingual students in Japan', *Journal of Language, Identity, and Education*, 2(4), 285–300.
Kishimoto, T.: 1992, *Teaching Business Japanese and Culture Using Authentic Materials: A Popular Television Drama*, ED 348 867.
Komatsu, K.: 2000, 'Samani Ainu-go kyoshitsu no genjo to kadai', in M. Yamamoto (ed.), *Bilingual Education in Japan*, Akashi Shoten, Tokyo, 47–84.
Kotoba to Shakai Henshuuiin (ed.): 2004, *Language and Society*, Sangensha, Tokyo, 8.
Lee, Y.: 1996, *Ideology called 'National Language'*, Iwanami Shoten, Tokyo.
Maher, J. and Macdonald, G. (eds.): 1995, *Diversity in Japanese Culture and Language*, Kegan Paul International, London and Sydney.
Maher, J. and Yashiro, K. (eds.): 1995, *Multilingual Japan*, Multilingual Matters, Avon.
Maher, J.C.: 2001, 'Akor Itak—Our language, your language: Ainu in Japan', in J. Fishman (ed.), *Can Threatened Languages Be Saved? Reversing Language Shift Revisited: A 21st Century Perspective*, Multilingual Matters, Avon, 323–349.
Maher, J.C.: 2006, 'Metroethnicity, language and the principle of cool', *International Journal of the Sociology of Language* 25, 83–102.
Maher, J.C. and Kawanishi, Y.: 1995, 'Maintaining culture and language: Koreans in Osaka' in J.C. Maher and G. Macdonalds (eds.), *Diversity in Japanese Culture and Language* 160–177.
Matsumori, A.: 1995. 'Ryukyuan: Past, present and future' in J. Maher and K. Yashiro (eds.), *Multilingual Japan*, Multilingual Matters, Avon, 19–44.
Matsushita Human Resources Development: 2005, *Annual Report*, Matsushita Corporation Inc, Osaka.
Okano, K.: 2006, 'The impact of immigrants on long-lasting ethnic minorities in Japanese schools: Globalization from below', *Language and Education* 20(4), 338–354.
Ota, H.: 2000, *Newcomer Children in Japanese Public Schools*, Kokusaishoin, Tokyo.
Otani, Y. et al.: 2004, *Foreign Language Education Policy around the World*, Toshindo Publishing Co. Ltd, Tokyo.
Shin, C.: 2005, 'History of Korean ethnic school and Korean language education', in S. Sanada et al. (eds.), *Aspects in Language of Japanese Resident Korean People*, Izumishoin, Osaka, 271–297.
Siddle, R.: 1996, *Race, Resistance and the Ainu*, Routledge, London.
Sugimoto, Y.: 2003, *An Introduction to Japanese Society*, Cambridge University Press, Cambridge.
Williams, R.: 1977, *Marxism and Literature*, Oxford University Press, Oxford.
Yamamoto, M. (ed.): 2000, *Bilingual Education in Japan*, Akashi Shoten, Tokyo.

AGNES S. L. LAM

LANGUAGE EDUCATION POLICY IN GREATER CHINA

INTRODUCTION

The invasion of China by various nations in the nineteenth century exposed the ineptitude of the Qing Dynasty and precipitated the 1911 revolution to establish the Republic of China (ROC) in 1912. This was followed by rule by military factions and civil strife between the Guomindang (GMD, or the Kuomintang, KMT, or the Nationalist Party), created in 1911 and the Chinese Communist Party (CCP), founded in 1921. The two parties cooperated to withstand Japanese aggression (1937–1945) but resumed their conflict when the Japanese surrendered at the end of World War II in 1945. In 1949, the CCP established the People's Republic of China (PRC) in Beijing whereas the GMD retreated to Taiwan to establish its government there. Before this separation, in 1842, Hong Kong was ceded to Britain after China lost the Opium War, sparked off by China's attempt to halt opium trade under a British monopoly. In 1997, Hong Kong was returned to China. In 1557, the Portuguese were first permitted to settle in Macao, which reverted to Chinese rule in 1999 (see Dillon, 1998, p. 48, 130, 206, pp. 237–238, 305–307). The PRC currently consists of the China mainland, Hong Kong and Macao and wishes to achieve peaceful reunification with Taiwan. All four territories are included in the term 'Greater China'. This chapter introduces the language policies in each of these territories, relating their developments to their histories and identifying their major achievements, current circumstances and future directions.

THE CHINA MAINLAND

On the China mainland (area: 10 million square kilometres; population: 1,265,830,000; see Hook and Twitchett, 1991, p. 17; National Bureau of Statistics, PRC, 2001), many languages and dialects are spoken. The Han Chinese people, the majority population, speak several Chinese dialects falling into two main groups, the northern dialects and the southern dialects, but share the same writing script of about 3,500 years old. The national language, Chinese, is also known as Hanyu (Han language). The standard dialect for oral interaction is Putonghua (common language), a northern dialect mapping well onto Baihua, the written

S. May and N. H. Hornberger (eds), Encyclopedia of Language and Education,
2nd Edition, Volume 1: Language Policy and Political Issues in Education, 405–417.
©2010 Springer Science+Business Media LLC.

variety of Standard Chinese close to everyday spoken Chinese and promoted from around 1920. In addition, among the 55 officially recognized non-Han ethnic minorities making up 8.4% of the mainland
population, over 80 to 120 languages are used; they belong to language
families such as Sino-Tibetan, Altaic, Austronesian, Austroasiatic
and Indo-European (Zhou, 2003, pp. 23–26). Two minority groups,
the Huis and the Mans (Manchus), have largely acculturated to Chinese.
Another 29 groups now have officially recognized writing scripts; some
groups, such as the Chosen (Korean) group, use minority languages
which have speakers beyond China's borders; other groups such as
the Kazaks (using the Arabic alphabet) use a writing script also used
by speakers of other languages outside China; still others, such as
the Dongs, use a Roman alphabet newly designed or revised for them
after 1949.

Since the establishment of the PRC in 1949, to unify and strengthen
the country, China has implemented three language policies: the standardization of Chinese, the development of minority languages and
the propagation of foreign languages. The standardization of Chinese
was aimed at enhancing literacy and took a two-pronged approach from
the 1950s: the simplification of the writing script and the development
of a phonetic alphabet, Hanyu Pinyin, to aid pronunciation. From 1956,
all primary and secondary schools in Han Chinese regions were
required to begin to include the teaching of Putonghua in Chinese
classes. Putonghua was also propagated among the Han Chinese living
in minority regions. At the same time, from around 1951, linguistic
analysis of the minority languages was initiated with the aim of
enhancing literacy among the minorities. To this end, some minority
language writing scripts were affirmed, revised or created. In terms of
foreign language learning, in line with the PRC's early political affinity,
Russian was initially promoted as the most important foreign language.
When relations with the Soviet Union did not develop as expected in
the late 1950s, English regained importance.

By the early 1960s, China was ready to further ties with the West.
Unfortunately, events within China developed into the Cultural Revolution (1966–1976), cultural in the sense of enforcing a political culture
to continue the revolution. During that era, schooling was extremely
irregular and the promotion of Putonghua suffered a severe setback.
The local offices for promoting Putonghua were largely disbanded
but propagation work was not entirely halted. By comparison, the work
on minority languages suffered much more. In fact, even before the
Cultural Revolution, from around 1957 to 1965, the attitude towards
minority languages was vacillating between egalitarian respect and
Han chauvinistic disdain. During the Cultural Revolution, minority
languages were suppressed and some minority parents enrolled their

children in Han Chinese schools, resulting ironically in more bilingual-ism among minority learners. Likewise, foreign language learning was considered unpatriotic during the Cultural Revolution, particularly before the 1970s. In 1971, the PRC replaced Taiwan as a member of the United Nations and Richard Nixon's visit to China as President of the USA in 1972 paved the way for further exchange between China and the West.

After the Cultural Revolution, China began to implement the Policy of Four Modernizations (to modernize agriculture, industry, science and technology as well as defence) from 1978. In parallel, the work on all three language policies resumed. The 1982 revised Constitution of China reaffirmed that Putonghua should be promoted and 1986 saw the confirmation of the Character Simplification List originally publi-cized in 1964. Likewise, particularly important for the minorities, the 1982 Constitution reaffirmed that 'every ethnic group has the freedom to use and develop its own language and script' (National People's Congress, 1999, p. 6). Codification work on some minority languages was revived and some new scripts were officially recognized from 1977 to 1990. In the same period, policy directions concerning curricu-lum development in English Language Teaching (ELT), particularly at university level, attracted much support from ELT professionals in China and from overseas.

In 1991, the disintegration of the Soviet Union provided the political space for China to adopt an increasingly international stance. China joined the World Trade Organization in 2001 and will host the Olympics in 2008. The language education effects of this international orientation are twofold: more foreigners are interested to learn Chinese; the Chinese also need to develop greater competence in English. With more foreigners wishing to learn Chinese and the spread of Putonghua throughout the mainland, especially the urban areas, China's current concern is to aim for quality assurance in Chinese language compe-tence. Proficiency tests like the Putonghua Shuiping Ceshi (PSC or Putonghua Proficiency Test) for Han Chinese learners and the Hanyu Shuiping Kaoshi (HSK or Chinese Proficiency Test) for non-native learners of Chinese are accorded much importance. Currently, over 2,100 universities in 85 countries offer courses in Chinese as a Foreign Language (CFL) and the HSK is considered the standard test for CFL. Where ELT is concerned, in the new school syllabus publicized from 2001, the learning of English is conceived of as a continuous process from primary school to university. The current requirement is to start teaching English from Primary 3 but some schools in coastal areas may even do so from Primary 1. Han Chinese learners are increasingly encouraged to be bilingual in Chinese and English. International trends in content-based instruction (or learning a target language while acquiring new knowledge in other subjects through that language) have also been incorporated into bilingual education models or curricular goals such as the cultivation of foreign language majors who excel both in foreign language competence as well as knowledge of a profession such as foreign relations, trade, law, management, journalism, education, technology, culture or military affairs.

The Soviet Union's disintegration might also have prompted China to subtly adjust its policy towards its ethnic minorities, perhaps to prevent separatist tendencies. In the decades before 1991, the policy vacillated between non-assimilation and total suppression. From around 1991 onwards, the state has tried to promote a bilingual solution more overtly instead. Minorities are encouraged to learn Chinese and also to retain their own languages, which seems to be the linguistic ideal in line with the Constitution reaffirmed in 1982. At the local level of implementation, however, it has been observed that this central policy translates into several scenarios from promotion of minority languages to permission to learn minority languages or mere tolerance of minority languages (Zhou, 2005).

To summarize, for the Han Chinese, the majority population, the policy directions are now clear: competence in Putonghua and English are both educational goals while the use of their own Chinese dialects at home or in other informal situations is not forbidden and hence is often retained. Foreign language majors also learn a second foreign language such as Japanese, German, Russian or French. At the implementation level, ELT on the mainland has already attracted much scholarly attention and will continue to do so. It is CFL and the teaching and learning of other foreign languages by Chinese learners that will need to be further researched. Where minority learners are concerned, the policy is more ambivalent. The state encourages them to be bilingual in Chinese and their own minority language; however, 24 of the minority groups are still without an officially recognized writing script. Some of these groups (the Blangs, the Daurs, the Dongxiangs, the Nus and the Pumis) have had writing scripts designed (Zhou, 2003, pp. 126–127) or in use even before 1949 (the Uzbeks) (Zhou, 2003, p. 104), but the official status of their scripts is uncertain. In the absence of writing scripts and hence formal education in and through their own languages, the tendency for these minority groups to shift to Chinese is almost uncontested. Meanwhile, competence in English is also vital for all minority learners' educational and occupational advancement. Surmounting these circumstances is clearly a challenge for both the Chinese government and the minority learners. Research into the relative efficacy of different models of bilingual education for these learners as well as the intercultural effects that may result should prove particularly pertinent (this section is based on Lam, 2005. See also

Bolton, 2003; Bolton and Lam, 2006; Chen, 1999; Dai, Teng, Guan and Dong 1997; He, 1998; Wang, Chen, Cao and Chen, 1995; Zhou, 2003, 2005).

TAIWAN

The official language in Taiwan (area: 36,000 square kilometres; population: 22,610,000) is Mandarin, also known as Guoyu (national language) or Huayu (Chinese language). There are four main groups in Taiwan: the Fujianese (or Minnanren-speaking Minnanese, a Chinese dialect also known as Taiwanese), the Hakkas (speaking the Hakka dialect, another Chinese dialect), other Han Chinese from the mainland (or mainlanders, many of whom arrived with the GMD around 1949) and other Austronesian minorities falling into 12 major groups. The Fujianese and Hakkas together make up 85% of the population (with about three Fujianese to one Hakka person); the mainlanders make up another 13% and the minorities, less than 2% (Taiwan Government Information Office, 2004, p. 9, 21, 23; see also Kaplan and Baldauf, 2003, p. 51; Tsao, 2000, p. 61).

Taiwan's early inhabitants were Austronesian peoples. It first came under Chinese rule in 1662 when the Dutch who had occupied Taiwan from 1624 were defeated by Zheng Chenggong, a Ming loyalist escaping from the Manchus, who had overthrown the Ming Dynasty (1368–1644) to establish the Qing Dynasty (1644–1911). Zheng's family ruled Taiwan till they surrendered to the Manchus in 1683. Under Manchu rule, though Chinese emigration to Taiwan was forbidden till 1875, many mainland Chinese moved to Taiwan. The Manchus ruled Taiwan till 1895 when they ceded Taiwan to Japan after the Sino-Japanese War. Feeling betrayed by the Manchus, the Taiwanese established the Taiwan Republic on 16 May 1895 but were defeated by the Japanese after 148 days (Tsao, 2000, p. 96). During their 50-year rule, the Japanese made a sustained effort to develop Taiwan as their colony by building infrastructure, introducing modern financial institutions and forcing all schools to use Japanese. By the time they returned Taiwan to China, most Taiwanese elites spoke Japanese and Taiwanese fluently (see Taiwan Government Information Office, 2004, pp. 33–43; Zhang, 2003, pp. 20–38).

It was to GMD troops that the Japanese surrendered in 1945. So when the GMD lost its war with the CCP, it established its government in Taiwan. The GMD traced the legitimacy of its rule to the 1911 revolution and adopted the name: ROC (Taiwan). In language education as well, the GMD tracked the continuity of its policy to early developments on the mainland soon after the 1911 revolution when the need for a standard dialect to unify and strengthen the country came to the forefront. The main language policy of the 1912 ROC and of Taiwan from 1949 had been the propagation of the standard dialect, Mandarin (Guanhua or Court Officials' Language). In 1913, a Commission on the Unification of Pronunciation was established. By 1918, the Mandarin Phonetic System (MPS), consisting of symbols resembling parts of Chinese characters, was promulgated. In 1919, the Preparatory Committee for the Unification of the National Language (PCUNL) was established and Mandarin was made the medium of instruction in primary and secondary schools. The MPS was revised in 1932. Another system, Gwoyeu Romatzyh (or the National Phonetic Symbols II), a romanization system, was propagated in 1928 and its modified form was adopted in 1984. The latest system, Tongyong Pinyin, was recommended by the Educational Reform Council in 1996 and adopted in 2002 (Taiwan Government Information Office, 2004, pp. 27–28).

The use of Mandarin in Taiwan and Putonghua on the mainland could both be connected to the early codification work on Chinese on the mainland soon after the 1911 revolution; both dialects were codified using the Beijing dialect. Their current phonetic representation systems, Tongyong Pinyin in Taiwan and Hanyu Pinyin on the mainland, are both romanization systems, though some sounds are represented by different letters (Luo, 2003). For the writing script, while the PRC developed simplified Chinese characters, Taiwan has continued to use traditional complex characters (also retained by Hong Kong and Macao). Another measure facilitating the learning of Chinese in Taiwan and the PRC (including Hong Kong and Macao) also originated from language reform soon after 1911; it was the PCUNL's recommendation in 1920 that the subject, Chinese Literature, should be changed to Chinese language in primary school. This represented a radical departure from traditional Chinese studies, which compelled learners to memorize Classical Chinese texts, making it difficult for them to master Chinese. With the PCUNL's recommendation, the learning of Chinese in primary school would focus instead on Chinese texts written in Baihua, closer to everyday spoken Chinese (Tsao, 2000, p. 69). It should be mentioned though that literature written in this style in the 1930s and 1940s was banned from the school curriculum in Taiwan because of its empathy with Communist ideology; hence the Chinese curricula in secondary schools and universities in Taiwan were heavily based on Classical Chinese rather than Baihua. This imbalance was somewhat redressed in 1997 (Tsao, 2000, pp. 89–90).

The adoption of Mandarin in Taiwan was politically contentious. Unlike on the mainland, where there are several dialect groups and a genuine need for an interdialectal means of communication, in Taiwan, Minnanese is spoken by about 70% of the population (Taiwan Government Information Office, 2004, p. 28). It was the GMD immigrants to

Taiwan in 1949 who needed Mandarin as a lingua franca because they consisted of speakers from various dialect groups. The GMD made Mandarin the language of government and education and also banned the use of Japanese, by then the working language of many educated Taiwanese, thus depriving them of access to power. The first GMD troops sent to Taiwan were also undisciplined and their seizure of personal property and profiteering angered the original residents in Taiwan. In 1947, the tension between the original residents and the mainland newcomers erupted into the February 28 Incident with much loss of life (Tsao, 2000, p. 72). Martial law was imposed soon after and not lifted till 1987; under the rhetoric to withstand a Communist take-over, dissent was not tolerated and the use of native dialects or minority languages was considered unpatriotic.

After the end of martial law in 1987, the government has adopted a more pluralistic approach towards the learning of native languages and dialects (Taiwan Government Information Office, 2004, p. 27). A study conducted in the wake of this policy change reports that although shift to Mandarin has occurred to some extent, particularly among the Hakkas, some knowledge of the native dialects has been maintained and attitudes to native dialects are generally positive (Chang, 1996). Native languages and dialects are now more used in public domains (Mo, 2000). In 1997, they were first introduced in primary school as electives. From 2001, primary school students must be taught one of the three major native dialects or languages (Minnanese, the Hakka dialect and Yuanzhuminyu or original residents' language). Mandarin continues to be the medium of instruction at all educational levels (Kaplan and Baldauf, 2003, pp. 57–59) and remains the lingua franca of interethnic or interdialectal communication (Li and Lee, 2004, p. 759).

For several decades, English had been taught as a foreign language in Taiwan only from Secondary 1 but, from 2001, it has been a required subject from Primary 5. Japanese, banned earlier, was revived in the late 1970s for trade purposes. Recently, the Ministry of Education has also implemented a 5-year programme (1999–2004) to promote the learning of a second foreign language such as Japanese, French, German and Spanish in senior secondary school (Taiwan Government Information Office, 2004, p. 31).

In summary, Mandarin has been predominant in Taiwan for too long for it to lose its preeminence as a result of the current revitalization of the native languages and dialects. As on the mainland, English is also needed as a global language. It is the learning of the native languages and dialects that might prove unpredictable and needs to be more immediately researched. A study of the differential effects of the re-vival of the Chinese dialects and the Austronesian minority languages in Taiwan should prove particularly illuminating.

HONG KONG

The Hong Kong Special Administrative Region (HKSAR) (area: 1,100 square kilometres; population: 6,708,389; see Hong Kong Census and Statistics Department, 2003, 2005) consists of Hong Kong Island (ceded to Britain in 1842), the Kowloon Peninsula (ceded to Britain in 1860) and the New Territories and some outlying islands (leased to Britain in 1898 for 99 years). With the return of Hong Kong to China, the Basic Law of the HKSAR allows it autonomy in internal affairs such as education for 50 years from 1997. The population consists of: Chinese (95%), Filipinos (2%) and other ethnic groups (3%) (Hong Kong Census and Statistics Department, 2003). Cantonese is the native dialect spoken by the majority of the population. The official policy is to encourage competence in Cantonese, English and Putonghua.

From 1842 to 1974, although the British did not repress the use of Chinese overtly, English, as the language of government and the law courts, was the language of power. The Official Languages Ordinance passed in 1974 ushered in a period of equal legal status for both languages. From 1997, the Basic Law upholds Chinese as the official language in Hong Kong but also permits the use of English as an official language by the executive authorities, legislature and judiciary (People's Republic of China, 1992, p. 7). The Basic Law does not specify whether Chinese means Putonghua or Cantonese. In practice, Cantonese is usually used in spoken interaction whereas Baihua is the target variety in written expression. The official use of English is permitted even after 1997 because Hong Kong is an international city and many among the local elite, educated under the colonial regime, are professionally more competent in English than in Chinese (compare this to the banning of Japanese in the early decades of GMD rule in Taiwan).

Regardless of what the law specifies, a controversial issue in language education in Hong Kong has been what language to adopt as the medium of instruction, what effects this will have on the learning of Chinese and English, and whether teachers are competent enough to support educational plans. Though English is taught as a subject from Primary 1, most primary schools use Cantonese as a medium of instruction across the curriculum. The contention about the language of instruction is mainly in the secondary school sector. Of the two streams of education, English-medium and Chinese-medium, which have been carried over from colonial times, English-medium education is more favoured by parents, not only because English is an international language but also because it is often the language of higher

education in Hong Kong, particularly in the more competitive programmes. Generally speaking, the British government took a rather
laissez faire attitude to this issue and many schools were claiming they
were English-medium to attract more students, though instruction
might actually be conducted in a mixture of Chinese and English. In
1997, the HKSAR government took a firmer line and required public
secondary schools to show evidence that they were capable of teaching
in English before they were allowed to do so from 1998 (Sweeting,
2004, pp. 524–525). About a quarter of the schools met the requirements. Later, other schools were allowed to switch to using English
as a medium of instruction from Secondary 4 onwards if they could
recruit competent teachers. To ensure that teachers of both English
and Chinese (including Putonghua) have the competence needed, from
2004, new English and Putonghua teachers are required to pass language assessment before joining the profession while serving teachers
should do so by 2006 (Bray and Koo, 2004, pp. 146–147).

The teaching of and in Putonghua is a relatively recent phenomenon
in Hong Kong. In the years leading up to 1997, Putonghua was already
available as an additional lesson within the Chinese curriculum. In
1997, it was announced that Putonghua would become a core subject
from Primary 1 from 1998. Given the goal of acquiring competence
in Cantonese and Putonghua, an emerging issue is whether it is educationally more expedient to teach Chinese in Putonghua rather than
Cantonese since exposure to Cantonese is already readily available in
the community. Some schools have adopted this pedagogical approach
recently, even without being required to do so. A few schools have
gone even further by using Putonghua as a medium of instruction for
subjects other than Chinese (Bray, 2004, pp. 147–148). Pragmatic principals and parents may well decide on this matter in a market-driven
place like Hong Kong, even before a policy is formulated.

To summarize, the statuses and functions of Cantonese, Putonghua
and English in Hong Kong education are now fairly stable, at least
for the foreseeable future. But the Hong Kong post-primary educational
system is undergoing a major change from a 5+2+3 system (5 years of
secondary school, 2 years of pre-university and 3 years of university) to
a 3+3+4 system (3 years of junior secondary school, 3 years of senior
secondary school and 4 years of university), akin to that on the mainland. The first cohort under the new system was accepted in September
2006. These students are expected to compete for university admission
in September 2012. English curricula both at the senior secondary level
and the university level are undergoing revision to accommodate this
change. Related research is likely to be a major focus in language
education work in Hong Kong in the next decade.

MACAO

The Macao Special Administrative Region (area: 27.5 square kilo-metres; population: 465,300; see Macao Census and Statistics Department, 2005), formerly spelt as Macau, was a trading post of the Portuguese from 1557. In 1582, the Portuguese began to pay an annual rent to China for the lease of the Macao peninsula. In 1887, Portugal assumed sovereignty over Macao (Cheng, 1999, p. 3). The Basic Law of Macao allows it autonomy in internal matters such as education for 50 years from 1999. Around 96% of the population is Chinese (Berlie, 1999, p. 76). Cantonese is widely spoken but immigration from the mainland to Macao has resulted in a sizable population of Putonghua speakers. Both Chinese and Portuguese have been official languages since 1987. As in Hong Kong, even after Macao reverted to Chinese rule, Portuguese, the colonial language, can still be used as an official language. Competence in English is also an educational goal.

For centuries, the Portuguese government left education in Macao in the hands of the Catholic Church, apparently in line with their practice in Portugal. The Diocese of Macao was founded in 1576 (Cheng, 1999, p. 5) and led the development of education in Macao. The Chinese community also established some private Chinese schools. English-medium education developed from the second-half of the nineteenth century. By 1988/1989, Macao primary school students were studying in Chinese (84%), English (9%), Portuguese (5%) and both Chinese and Portuguese (2%). The educational gap was in the university sector. Only from the late 1980s did the government promote higher education in Macao. In 1988, it bought the University of East Asia, a private English-medium university founded in 1981 teaching some courses in Chinese, redeveloped it to offer programmes in all three languages: English, Chinese and Portuguese, and renamed it the University of Macau in 1991. Four other institutions using Portuguese as one of the teaching languages were also established in the 1990s (Bray and Koo, 2004, p. 151).

Although some form of higher education is now locally available in all three languages, the school sector has seen an increase of students in Chinese-medium education to about 93%, partly because of the immigration from the mainland in the last 20 years. New tertiary institutions, such as the Macao University of Science and Technology, established in 2000, are more likely to use Putonghua as the main medium of instruction (Bray and Koo, 2004, p. 153). While Putonghua and English (now usually taught from Primary 4 or 5 in non-English-medium schools) will continue to grow in educational prominence in Macao, competence in Portuguese, even if acquired only by a very small minority, is still considered valuable for Macao's positioning within the PRC and China's relations with the Latin world.

Compared to the other three territories, Macao has a very small population, which makes its language education problems relatively easier to manage. The fact that much of its educational development was historically led by the church has also given rise to a certain peaceable ethos in attempts to negotiate educational solutions. In terms of research, an interesting issue is whether the development of Portuguese competence, particularly within a trilingual educational model, can continue to be maintained.

CONCLUSION

In bilingual or multilingual settings, the choice of what language to teach or to use as a medium of instruction is always difficult (see also Tollefson, Language Planning in Education, Volume 1). On the China mainland, the propagation of Putonghua for Han Chinese is now widely accepted and requires only further quality assurance and materials development. However, the bilingual policy for minority learners needs to be carefully monitored and perhaps developed into a range of bilingual or multilingual education models to match a possible continuum of minority learner choices. It is fortunate that the language rights of minorities have been protected by the PRC constitution, even if insufficient educational opportunities or pragmatic choices by some minority learners may still result in greater competence in Putonghua and lesser competence in their own languages.

In Taiwan, the supremacy of Mandarin is now less controversial; as a medium of instruction for over half a century, it will probably remain the language of government and mainstream education while Minnanese, the Hakka dialect and the aboriginal languages continue to enjoy some revitalization as heritage languages and as alternative media of instruction perhaps in basic education. Bidialectalism and bilingualism (Mandarin and a native dialect or language) is a possible outcome. Total reverse language shift in Taiwan is unlikely as economic and educational benefits are now already attached to competence in Mandarin.

In Hong Kong and Macao, bidialectalism between Cantonese and Putonghua may be achieved by more and more learners. But it is unlikely that Putonghua will become the first dialect of the majority of the population in these two regions, unless there is massive immigration from the mainland, which the PRC will discourage, given the high population densities of the two territories. CFL around the world will grow in scope and this may, in turn, make competence in Putonghua even more valuable in Hong Kong and Macao. In market-driven Hong Kong, in particular, as Putonghua competence becomes desirable even to foreigners, more schools may convert to teaching Chinese in Putonghua, even in the absence of any specific government directive.

In all four territories, English will retain its pre-eminence as the language of international trade and educational advancement; hence, issues concerning enhancing competence in English will continue to be prominent in educational considerations, particularly in the transition to higher education, academic research and international interaction. Other foreign languages such as Japanese (especially in Taiwan), Russian (especially on the mainland), French, German, Spanish or Portuguese (in Macao) may also enjoy a revival as China opens up even more to the world. Given the complexities of the circumstances in each of the territories, Greater China offers tremendous opportunities for developing and testing new models of bilingual or multilingual education involving both domestic and international languages in a comparative context.

See Also: *James W. Tollefson: Language Planning in Education (Volume 1); Teresa L. McCarty: Language Education Planning and Policies by and for Indigenous Peoples (Volume 1); Suresh Canagarajah: The Politics of English Language Teaching (Volume 1); Stephen May: Language Education, Pluralism and Citizenship (Volume 1)*

REFERENCES

Berlie, J.A.: 1999, 'Macao's education: A question of language—Chinese, Portuguese, and English', in J.A. Berlie (ed.), *Macao 2000*, Oxford University Press (China), Hong Kong.
Bolton, K.: 2003, *Chinese Englishes: A Sociolinguistic History*, Cambridge University Press, Cambridge.
Bolton, K. and Lam, A.: 2006, 'Applied linguistics in China', in M. Berns (ed.), *Encyclopaedia of Language and Linguistics*, Volume 1 (second edition), Elsevier, Oxford.
Bray, M. and Koo, D.-Y.R.: 2004, 'Language and education', in M. Bray and R. Koo (eds.), *Education and Society in Hong Kong and Macao: Comparative Perspectives on Continuity and Change*, Comparative Education Research Centre, the University of Hong Kong and Kluwer Academic Publishers, Hong Kong.
Chang, M.-Y.: 1996, *Language Use and Language Attitudes among Taiwanese Elementary School Students in Native Language Instruction Programs: A Study on Language Maintenance, Language Shift, and Language Planning in Taiwan (China)*, Doctoral dissertation, Purdue University, West Lafayette, IN.
Chen, P.: 1999, *Modern Chinese: History and Sociolinguistics*, Cambridge University Press, Cambridge.
Cheng, C.M.-B.: 1999, 'A historical and cultural prelude', in J.A. Berlie (ed.), *Macao 2000*, Oxford University Press (China), Hong Kong.
Dai, Q.-X., Teng, X., Guan X.-Q., and Dong, Y.: 1997, *Zhongguo shaoshu minzu shuanyu jiaoyu gailun* [Introduction to Bilingual Education for China's Ethnic Minorities], Liaoning Nationalities Publishing House, Shenyang.

Dillon, M. (ed.): 1998, *China: A Cultural and Historical Dictionary*, Curzon Press, Richmond.
He, J.-F.: 1998, *Zhongguo shaoshu minzu shuangyu yanjiu: Lishi yu xianshi* [Research on Bilingualism among China's Ethnic Minorities: History and Reality], Central University of Nationalities, Beijing.
Hong Kong Census Statistics and Department: 2003, *2001 Population Census*, Retrieved August 13, 2005, from http://www.info.gov.hk/censtatd/eng/news/01c/01c.index.html
Hong Kong Census Statistics and Department: 2005, *Hong Kong in Figures*, Retrieved August 13, 2005, from http://www.info.gov.hk/censtatd/eng/hkstat/index2.html
Hook, B. and Twitchett, D. (eds.): 1991, *The Cambridge Encyclopedia of China* (second edition), Cambridge University Press, Cambridge.
Kaplan, R.B. and Baldauf, R.B.: 2003, *Language and Language-in-Education Planning in the Pacific Basin*, Kluwer Academic Publishers, Dordrecht.
Lam, A.S.L.: 2005, *Language Education in China: Policy and Experience from 1949*, Hong Kong University Press, Hong Kong.
Li, D.C.S. and Lee, S.: 2004, 'Bilingualism in East Asia', in T.K. Bhatia and W.C. Ritchie (eds.), *The Handbook of Bilingualism*, Blackwell, Malden, MA.
Luo, J.: 2003, 'A comparative study on "Tongyong Pinyin" and "Hanyu Pinyin"—A few considerations on Chinese romanization', in X.-B. Li and Z.-H. Pan (eds.), *Taiwan in the Twenty-First Century*, University Press of America, Lanham, MD.
Macao Census and Statistics Department: 2005, *Demography*, Retrieved August 13, 2005, from http://www.dsec.gov.mo/e_index.html
Mo, R.-P.J.: 2000, Taiwan on the Brink of Reversing Language Shift: Its Current Development and Contributory Factors, Doctoral dissertation, Purdue University, West Lafayette, IN.
National Bureau of Statistics of the People's Republic of China: 2001, *Communique on Major Figures of the 2000 Population Census (No. 1)*, Retrieved October 11, 2003, from http://www.stats.gov.cn/english/newrelease/statisticalreports/200204230084.htm
National People's Congress: 1999, *Zhongguo Renmin Gongheguo Xianfa* [The Constitution of the People's Republic of China], Falu Chubanshe, Beijing.
People's Republic of China: 1992, *The Basic Law of the Hong Kong Special Administrative Region of the People's Republic of China*, adopted by the Seventh National People's Congress at its Third Session on 4 April 1990.
Sweeting, T.: 2004, *Education in Hong Kong, 1941 to 2001: Visions and Revisions*, Hong Kong University Press, Hong Kong.
Taiwan Government Information Office: 2004, Taiwan Yearbook 2004, Government Information Office, Taipei.
Tsao, F.-F.: 2000, 'The language planning situation in Taiwan', in R.B. Baldauf and R.B. Kaplan (eds.), *Language Planning in Nepal, Taiwan and Sweden*, Multilingual Matters, Clevedon.
Wang, J., Chen, Z.-T., Cao, X.-Z., and Chen, N.-H.: (eds.), 1995, *Dangdai Zhongguo de Wenzi Gaige* [Contemporary Language and Script Reform in China], Dangdai Zhongguo Chubanshe, Beijing.
Zhang, W.-B.: 2003, *Taiwan's Modernization: Americanization and Modernizing Confucian Manifestations*, World Scientific, River Edge, NJ.
Zhou, M.-L.: 2003, *Multilingualism in China: The Politics of Writing Reforms for Minority Languages 1949–2002*, Mouton de Gruyter, Berlin.
Zhou, M.-L.: 2005, 'Legislating literacy for linguistic and ethnic minorities in contemporary China', *Current Issues in Language Planning* 6(2), 102–121.

SUBJECT INDEX

NAME INDEX

Abedi, J. 248, 291
Abercrombie, N. 71
Achebe, C. 34, 38
Addis, A. 26
Adger, C. 47
Ager, D. 244, 245
Aguirre Beltrán, G. 304
Ahlgren, I. 156, 158
Aikman, S. 139, 141, 321
Albó, X. 317, 318, 320–322, 325–327
Alexander, N. 360
Alidou, H. 11, 360, 363, 364
Alladina, S. 268
Allington, R. 77
Amanti, C. 48
Ames, P. 324
Ammon, U. 259, 261
Anaya, A. 317, 318, 321, 322, 325–327
Anderson, B. 154
Aneta P. 178, 224
Appadurai, A. 33, 222
Apple, M. 49
Arias, B. 292
Arnsperger, C. 89
Asato, J. 52
Ashworth, M. 336, 337
Atkinson, P. 78
Auerbach, E. 6, 49
August, D. 234

Baetens-Beardsmore, H. 234
Baker, C. 155, 185, 234, 293, 295, 365
Baldauf, R.B. 11, 140, 179, 409, 411
Bamgbose, A. 357–360
Banks, J. 48
Barkhuizen, G. 173
Barrera-Vázquez, A. 304
Barry, B. 22
Barton, D. 46
Bauman, Z. 32, 117
Bax, S. 40
Beaty, S. 332, 333
Beaujot, R. 338
Belcher, D. 217
Benesch, S. 214–216
Berdan, R. 237

Bergman, B. 158
Berlie, J.A. 414
Berliner, D. 293
Bernstein, B. 74
Bertely Busquets, M. 305, 309, 311
Bhatt, A. 46
Bishop, R. 53
Blackledge, A. 7, 179, 218
Block, D. 7, 11, 12, 58, 66, 92, 148, 172, 178, 197, 209, 224, 238, 239, 251, 264, 281, 282, 403
Blommaert, J. 5, 8, 26, 38, 41, 76, 267, 271, 357
Bloom, D. 87
Blot, R. 73
Bolton, K. 409
Bondebjerg, I. 257
Boostrom, R.E. 96
Borker, R. 58
Bostwick, R.M. 397
Bourdieu, P. 18, 22, 74, 79, 177, 217, 269
Bourne, J. 280
Bouvet, D. 158
Bowman, S. 338
Boxer, D. 62
Boyle, O. 293
Bradley, H. 72, 77
Branson, J. 112, 116, 153, 155–158, 160, 163, 293, 361, 400
Bray, M. 413, 414
Bright, W. 378
Brock-Utne, B. 138, 141, 357
Brown, Douglas H. 217
Brutt-Griffler, J. 9, 37, 38, 41
Bullen, E. 192
Bullivant, B. 15–17, 20
Burgess, T. 276
Burlingame, M. 248
Burnaby, B. 35, 59, 336, 338, 339
Burton, P. 57
Butler, J. 177
Buzzelli, C.A. 97, 99, 101, 103, 178

Cameron, D. 36, 41, 58, 177
Campbell, J.L. 271

NAME INDEX 429

Leitner, G. 343, 344
Leki, I. 215
Lemay, S. 158
Lemke, J. 171
Leung, C. 365
Lewis, E.G. 268, 275
Lewis, W. 158
Li, D.C.S. 411
Liddle, S. 158
Lillis, T. 187, 192
Lin, A. 53, 213, 218, 221
Lippi-G.R. 5, 6, 10
Lo Bianco, J. 7, 11, 19, 297, 343, 344,
    346, 348, 349
Locke, T. 53, 178
Long, M. 43, 362
López, L.E. 311, 318, 319, 321, 324,
    325, 327
Lourie, M. 285
Lucas, T. 220
Luke, A. 169, 171, 176, 185, 187,
    191, 196
Luke, C. 64, 185, 196
Luo, J. 410
Luykx, A. 146, 318
Lyons, J. 287

Mac P.A. 270
MacAonghuis, I. 270
Macdonald, C. 359, 362, 393
Macdonald, G. 393
Macias, R. 287
MacKenzie, M. 339
MacKinnon, K. 276
Macquarie Encyclopedia, 345
MacSwan, J. 233
Madrid-Fernandez, D. 247
Magga, O.H. 108, 115, 116, 139, 140,
    141, 143, 147
Mahar, D. 209
Maher, J.C. 230, 393, 398, 399, 402, 403
Mahshie, S.N. 158
Makoni, S. 53, 176, 177, 213, 356
Maltz, D. 58
Mandabach, F. 285
Mangiola, L. 49
Mannheim, B. 315
Marginson, S. 347
Marken, J. 98, 100
Marley, D. 248
Marsaja, G. 153, 163
Martel, A. 334
Martin, P. 220
Martin, S. 347
Martínez Buenabad, E. 310

Martínez, C. 233
Martin-Jones, M. 46, 184, 219
Martino, W. 187
Mateene, K. 359
Matsumori, A. 399
Matthews, J. 292, 293
May, S. 4, 7–9, 11, 17–20, 22, 24, 26,
    37–39, 41, 48–50, 52, 110, 116, 139,
    144, 146, 152, 154, 172, 174
Mazawi, A. 53
Mazrui, A. 34, 36, 75
McCarty, T. 7, 8, 11, 12, 27, 46, 114,
    116, 117, 125, 134, 146–148, 178,
    285, 288, 289, 297, 302, 305, 306,
    311, 318, 325, 327, 338, 339,
    365, 416
McClymer, J. 295
McConnell-Ginet, S. 58
McCoy, G. 279
McDonald, M. 58
McGrew, A. 31
McGroarty, M. 8, 18, 26, 27
McHoul, A. XIV
McKay, S. 40, 62, 223, 236, 238
McMahill, C. 60, 63
Mellor, B. 185, 190
Mercado, C. 293
Messerschmitt, D. S. 99
Mey, J. 172
Meyer, L. 247
Michaels, S. 196
Mignolo, W.D. 175, 229
Milk, R. 293
Miller, D. 112, 116, 153, 155–158, 160,
    163, 293, 297, 361, 400, 403
Miller, P. 87, 153, 155–158, 160
Milner, A. 344
Ministry of Education, 40, 244, 246,
    261, 274, 303–305, 317–320, 323,
    324, 332, 385, 395, 396, 398, 400,
    401, 411
Mirza, H. 79
Mitchell, C. 250
Mitchell, R. 40
Mitsikopoulou, B. 263
Mo, R.-P.J. 411
Modiano, M. 223, 224
Modiano, N. 223, 224, 305
Modood, T. 247, 273, 277, 281
Moll, L. 48
Monbiot, G. 256
Moore, H. 10, 345, 349
Morgan, B. 49, 171, 174, 185, 216
Morris, B. 250
Moya, R. 319

TABLE OF CONTENTS

VOLUME 2: LITERACY

TABLE OF CONTENTS

VOLUME 3: DISCOURSE AND EDUCATION

TABLE OF CONTENTS

VOLUME 4: SECOND AND FOREIGN LANGUAGE EDUCATION

TABLE OF CONTENTS

VOLUME 5: BILINGUAL EDUCATION

Section 1: 21st Century Bilingual Education: Advances in Understanding and Emerging Issues

TABLE OF CONTENTS

VOLUME 6: KNOWLEDGE ABOUT LANGUAGE

TABLE OF CONTENTS

VOLUME 7: LANGUAGE TESTING AND ASSESSMENT

TABLE OF CONTENTS

VOLUME 8: LANGUAGE SOCIALIZATION

TABLE OF CONTENTS

VOLUME 9: ECOLOGY OF LANGUAGE

TABLE OF CONTENTS

VOLUME 10: RESEARCH METHODS IN LANGUAGE AND
EDUCATION

CPSIA information can be obtained at www.ICGtesting.com
Printed in the USA
LVOW100527050512

280483LV00002B/24/P